SRA
READ-ALOUD
LIBRARY
Vocabulary and Listening
Comprehension

**Teacher
Edition**

**Terry Dodds
Fay Goodfellow
Rick Williams**

McGraw Hill **SRA**

Columbus, OH

SRAonline.com

 SRA

Send all inquiries to this address:
SRA/McGraw-Hill
4400 Easton Commons
Columbus, OH 43219

ISBN: 978-0-07-609441-7
MHID: 0-07-609441-3

5 LKV 21

Table of Contents

Appendix

Introduction

Rationale for the Program

Long before children are able to speak using higher level vocabulary, they are able to understand and respond to sophisticated words. An extensive vocabulary is vital to a child's success in all aspects of language arts. It is important for young children to develop higher level vocabulary on a verbal level long before they are able to read more difficult words. Higher level vocabulary is crucial to helping a young child develop reading comprehension skills.

In their book *Bringing Words to Life,* Beck, McKeown, and Kucan define three levels of vocabulary instruction by placing words into three tiers. Words in the first tier do not require direct instruction. They are basic words that young children learn in their everyday lives, such as house, tree, and car. The second tier of words requires explicit direct instruction. These words will allow children to expand their vocabulary into the world of mature speakers. Tier-two words enable children to become more precise and descriptive with their language. They are higher level words that are easy to explain in simple terms to young children. These are words like *curious, amazing,* and *starving.* Tier-three words are best taught within a content area such as science, social studies, or literature—*metamorphosis, community,* and *plot,* for example.

SRA Read-Aloud Library: Vocabulary and Listening Comprehension

SRA Read-Aloud Library: Vocabulary and Listening Comprehension combines two research-validated instructional approaches: Direct Instruction as designed by Siegfried Engelmann and robust vocabulary instruction as designed by Beck, McKeown, and Kucan. Vocabulary instruction in this program is explicit and developmental. It follows a tight instructional sequence that offers children an opportunity to interact with each word in a number of contexts both literature-based and expository. Simple, easy-to-understand definitions are offered to the children. The conceptual framework for parts of speech is provided to the children by categorizing words as naming, action, or describing. The focus of this program is to provide children with instruction in tier-two words and tier-three words as related to literary analysis.

SRA Read-Aloud Library Teacher Edition provides teachers and children a vocabulary development program that is trade book-based. An important goal of this program is to provide children lessons that will instill a joy and enthusiasm for learning new words.

Children are presented with six tier-two words each week. Four of the target words are taken directly from the story. Two words each week are concept words—words that are not in the story. These two words represent an abstract concept that can be applied to what is happening in the story. For example, children can understand the concept behind the word desperate as used in *The Ant and the Grasshopper* as wanting something very, very badly.

Program Components

A library of read-aloud trade books

A teacher edition that includes
- explicit direct instruction lessons
- blackline masters (BLMs) for children's activities
- a BLM master for the vocabulary tally sheet
- a BLM with the picture vocabulary cards for the week
- a BLM evaluation sheet for the Happy Face Game
- instructions for a weekly classroom center
- a BLM homework program
- a glossary of all of the words taught in this program

Teaching the Lessons

The lessons for each trade book should take five days to teach. Lessons will take 30 to 45 minutes each day depending on the length of the trade book. The preparation box provides you with an easy reference of the materials required to teach that day's lesson.

Lessons are designed to provide you with a thorough instructional sequence that uses the following conventions: What the teacher says is printed in blue. What the teacher does is in parentheses and printed in black. Responses that are expected from the children are printed in black italics.

See the following example:

Page 3. (Point to the inset of the ant and the grasshopper.) Who do you think these creatures are? (Idea: *The ant and the grasshopper.*)

A variety of formats for children's responses are offered:

- The question requires an answer that calls for the same response from all children. A hand or verbal signal can be used to get children to respond in unison. This provides them with an opportunity to become more actively involved in the lesson and to respond to more questions. See the following example: The name of a book or story is called the title. What's a title? *The name of a book or story.* What's another way of saying the name of a book or story? *Title.*
- If there are several possible responses to a question, the expected responses from the children will be preceded by the word Idea or Ideas. These open-ended responses will produce a variety of answers: What happens when Jack gets home? (Ideas: *His mother throws the beans out; she sends him to bed without any supper.*)
- Some questions require a response based on the personal experiences of the children. These questions are asked with no expected response listed: Tell about a time when you were considerate.

Lessons follow a consistent pattern throughout the program that provides explicit direct instruction as well as cumulative practice and review. Numerous encounters with the words over time enable children to incorporate them into their speaking vocabulary. Children participate in a number of activities that enable them to interact with the words in a variety of situations.

A typical week's sequence may be as follows:

Day 1: On the first day children are introduced to the book and learn the key elements of a book such as title, author, and illustrator. They participate in making predictions about what will happen in the story and share those predictions with their classmates. Children are invited to take a picture walk as they explore what might be happening in the story. Children are offered the opportunity to formulate questions they may have about the book. The teacher reads aloud the story to the children with minimal interruptions. The four target vocabulary words and their meanings are introduced for the first time within the context of the story. Words for the week are placed on the Vocabulary Tally Sheet. Finally, children receive a homework sheet with a simple weekly homework routine to take home.

Day 2: The second day's lesson begins with the story being read aloud by the teacher and discussed. The questioning sequence in the story encourages the children to become actively involved in responding to the story and to use higher level thinking skills. Children are encouraged throughout this discussion to use the target words in their discussion. Target vocabulary that was introduced in Day 1 is reviewed. One word each week is extended by teaching the children an alternate meaning for the word. The two-concept or expanded target vocabulary words and their meanings are also taught.

Day 3: The children participate in a number of activities that allow them to practice using the new vocabulary words, including retelling the story, playing word games, and completing an activity sheet.

Day 4: Literary analysis and cumulative review are provided on the fourth day of instruction. The children play a verbal game that uses all of the new words in addition to words that have been taught in earlier lessons. The children also learn songs that help them recall the literary elements and patterns.

Day 5: On the last day, children retell the story to a partner. An assessment is administered to measure mastery of the new vocabulary as well as to review items. Children are allowed to choose a book they would like the teacher to read to them as a reward. Each week children are taught the routine for the learning center that they will work in the following week. The Super Words Center provides children with an opportunity to practice using the new vocabulary and to review vocabulary from previous lessons. Words that are taught each week should be placed on a word wall and added to each week.

Using the Picture Vocabulary Cards

The picture vocabulary cards for the week can be found at the top of the BLM for the homework program. These word cards should be copied and used in each day's lesson as well as in the Super Words Center at the end of each week.

You may wish to enlarge and laminate the cards for classroom use. The smaller size cards work well in the Super Words Center and may also be laminated for greater durability. You may find it useful to have a small pocket chart for displaying the words during the lessons.

The children are not expected to read the words on the picture vocabulary cards. The words are for your information and for parents. However, as the children use the cards, some children will begin to read the words.

Using the Vocabulary Tally Sheet

The Vocabulary Tally Sheet (BLM A) provides you with a place to record the number of times each of the target words is used within a week. Each time you or the children use the word, place a tally mark on the Vocabulary Tally Sheet. It is important to model the use of the words in your everyday interactions with the children. This modeling is important for helping your children incorporate the higher level words into their speaking vocabulary.

Using the Homework Program

Homework helpers can provide valuable practice and reinforcement that are important to the success of this vocabulary program. Each lesson provides you with a blackline master homework sheet. The sheet gives the homework helper a simple weekly homework routine that can be used to reinforce the vocabulary words that are taught each week. The homework routine is consistent from week to week.

Copies of the picture vocabulary cards are on the sheet as well as the word game that was played in class with those words that week.

You may wish to send a letter at the beginning of the program to introduce the homework helper to the homework routine. Another option is to have an information session to explain and demonstrate the homework routine.

It is important to explain to the homework helper that when the expected answer is preceded by the word idea, the child may not use the exact wording given. The homework helper should encourage the child to give an answer that is as close as possible to the idea. If the child makes a mistake, the homework helper should tell the child the answer and repeat the item at the end of the game.

Encourage the homework helper to make the homework routine fun and interactive. Remind him or her that children are not expected to read the words on the picture vocabulary cards. The words are for homework helper information only. However, as children use the cards, some children will begin to read the words.

The homework program can also be used at school as an intervention component if homework cannot be completed outside of the school day.

Playing the Word Games

The word games in this program offer your children an opportunity to interact with the new vocabulary words and their meanings in a number of fun contexts. The games challenge them to use higher level thinking skills as they try to beat their teacher at "word play."

The correction procedure for most of the games is the same. If children make an error, you simply tell them or demonstrate the correct answer and then repeat the missed item at the end of the game.

The same game played in class that week is on the homework sheet. This provides further reinforcement of the vocabulary words and their meanings.

The Show Me, Tell Me Game

In the Show Me, Tell Me Game children are asked to show, through actions or facial expressions, what a vocabulary word means. They are then asked what the word is that they are "showing:"

Today, you will play the Show Me, Tell Me Game. I'll ask you to show me how to do something. If you can show me, you win one point. If you can't show me, I get the point.

Next, I'll ask you to tell me. If you can tell me, you win one point. If you can't tell me, I get the point.

The Choosing Games

The Choosing Game challenges children to make choices by choosing the correct word from two choices. In the easier version, children are shown the two picture vocabulary cards and must make the correct choice:

Today, you will play the Choosing Game. Let's think about the four words we have learned: **decided, shouted, squeaked,** and **muttered.** (Display the word cards.) I will say a sentence

that has two of our words in it. You will have to choose which word is the correct word for that sentence.

A second, more challenging version of the game, The Super Choosing Game, is played later in the program. In this game you ask children to choose the correct word without seeing the picture vocabulary word cards. Additionally, children are given the choice of three words, some of which they have learned.

Whoopsy!

In the game Whoopsy! children are asked to discriminate between sentences that use the vocabulary word correctly or incorrectly. When they catch you making an error, they must provide a corrected version of the sentence to earn a point:

Today, you will play Whoopsy! I'll say sentences using words we have learned. If the word doesn't fit in the sentence, you say, "Whoopsy!" Then I'll ask you to say a sentence where the word fits. If you can do it, you get a point. If you can't do it, I get the point. If the word I use fits the sentence, don't say anything.

The Opposites Game

The Opposites Game provides children with an opportunity to test their knowledge of opposites in a fun context.

Today you'll play the Opposites Game. I'll use a vocabulary word in a sentence. If you can tell me the opposite of that word, you win one point. If you can't tell me, I get the point.

Chew the Fat

Chew the Fat develops children's listening and discrimination skills as they try catch you using the vocabulary word incorrectly. They are then asked to finish the sentence starter with the correct usage of the word:

Today you will play Chew the Fat. Remember, a long time ago, when people wanted to just sit and talk about things that were happening in their lives, they would sit and chew the fat.

In this game, I will say some sentences with our vocabulary words in them. If I use the vocabulary word correctly, say, "Well done." If I use the word incorrectly, say, "Chew the fat." That means you want to talk about how I used the word. I'll say the beginning of the sentence again. If you can make the sentence end so that it makes sense, you'll get a point. If you can't, I get the point.

Tom Foolery

Tom Foolery develops children's listening and discrimination skills as they try catch you making up a false meaning for words that have more than one meaning. They are then asked to finish the sentence starter with the correct usage of the word:

Today I will teach you a new game called Tom Foolery. I will pretend to be Tom. Tom Foolery tries to trick children. Tom knows that some words have more than one meaning. He will tell you one meaning that will be correct. Then he will tell you another meaning that might be correct or incorrect.

If you think the meaning is correct, don't say anything. If you think the meaning is incorrect, say, "Tom Foolery." Then Tom will have to tell the truth and give the correct meaning. Tom is sly enough that he may include some words that do not have two meanings. Be careful! He's tricky!

Using the Activity Sheet

A blackline master activity sheet is provided each week. These sheets can be copied for individual children to use. Activity sheets give children practice with skills introduced in the program such as sequencing, matching, and beginning written expression.

Assessing Progress

Each week you should assess children's progress by playing the Happy Face Game. The Happy Face Game is a weekly assessment tool that tests children's understanding of that week's words and provides some cumulative review. A blackline master recording sheet can be found on page A–2 of this teacher edition.

A child needs to achieve a score of 9 out of 10 (occasionally 8 out of 10) to be at the mastery level. If a child does not achieve mastery, insert the missed words as additional items in the games in the next week's lessons. Retest those children individually on the missed items before they take the next mastery test.

Using the Super Words Classroom Center

At the end of each week, children should be introduced to the Super Words Center activity. Their participation in the Super Words Center will provide them with important hands-on practice as they interact conversationally with their peers using the new vocabulary.

Instructions for preparing each week's center are provided in the preparation box. The centers are designed to require a minimal amount of additional materials. Picture vocabulary cards for the games should be copied and placed in plastic bags or containers. You will need one set of materials for each pair of students who will be working at any given time in a center. For example, if up to four children will be working in a center, you will need two sets of cards.

A procedure for demonstrating the game is provided each week. It is important to demonstrate how to use the center before children are expected to use it independently.

Songs Found in the Program

Children delight in learning through music and songs. This program contains two cumulative songs that help children remember the literary elements and story patterns they are learning during the literary analysis portion of each week's lessons.

The Story Song
By Rick Williams

(Sung to the tune of "Barnyard Song,"
also known as "Bought Me a Cat.")

Read me a book, and the book pleased me.
I read my book under yonder tree.
Book says, "I'm a story."
Read me a book, and the book pleased me.
I read my book under yonder tree.
Title says what its name is.
Book says, "I'm a story."

Read me a book, and the book pleased me.
I read my book under yonder tree.
Author says, "I'm who wrote it."
Title says what its name is.
Book says, "I'm a story."

Read me a book, and the book pleased me.
I read my book under yonder tree.
Illustrator draws the pictures.
Author says, "I'm who wrote it."
Title says what its name is.
Book says, "I'm a story."

Read me a book, and the book pleased me.
I read my book under yonder tree.
Characters make it happen.
Illustrator draws the pictures.
Author says, "I'm who wrote it."
Title says what its name is.
Book says, "I'm a story."

Read me a book, and the book pleased me.
I read my book under yonder tree.
Illustrations are the pictures.
Characters make it happen.
Illustrator draws the pictures.
Author says, "I'm who wrote it."
Title says what its name is.
Book says, "I'm a story."

Read me a book, and the book pleased me.
I read my book under yonder tree.
Setting tells where it happens.
Illustrations are the pictures.
Characters make it happen.
Illustrator draws the pictures.
Author says, "I'm who wrote it."
Title says what its name is.
Book says, "I'm a story."

The Pattern Song
By Rick Williams

(Sung to the tune of "If You're Happy and
You Know It, Clap Your Hands.")

There are patterns all around us if we look.
There are patterns all around us if we look.
There are patterns all around,
If we look they can be found.
There are patterns all around us if we look.

If your Papa asks a question, answer back.
If your Papa asks a question, answer back.
If your Papa asks a question,
Please allow a small suggestion:
If your Papa asks a question, answer back.

(Chorus.)

There's a pattern in remembering your life.
There's a pattern in remembering your life.
If you think about the past,
Then your memories will last.
There's a pattern in remembering your life.

(Chorus.)

There's a pattern when you're trav'ling in a line.
There's a pattern when you're trav'ling in a line.
When you travel in a line,
Just say "linear"—that'll be fine!
There's a pattern when you're trav'ling in a line.

(Chorus.)

There's a pattern when you
There's a pattern when you
There's a pattern when you just repeat the words.
There's a pattern when you
There's a pattern when you
There's a pattern when you just repeat the words.
Though the humor here is fleeting,
Say it again, and you're repeating.
There's a pattern when you
There's a pattern when you
There's a pattern when you just repeat the words.

(Chorus.)

Did you know that there's a circle pattern, too?
Did you know that there's a circle pattern, too?
In a circle you will roam
But you'll always find your home.
Did you know that there's a circle pattern, too?

(Chorus.)

There's a pattern when you give the reasons why.
There's a pattern when you give the reasons why.
We agree, in the main,
But we like it when you explain.
There's a pattern when you give the reasons why.

(Chorus.)

There's a pattern when you count from one to twelve.
There's a pattern when you count from one to twelve.
Uno, dos, and tres, and cuatro,
Cinco, seis, siete, ocho,
Nueve, diez, once, doce, one to twelve!*

(Chorus.)

*A recording of "The Story Song" is available at SRAonline.com.

Word List

accident something bad that happens that no one expects, and someone gets hurt

active busy and full of energy

adopt get a child who doesn't have a family and make that child your own son or daughter

Africa the second largest continent in the world

allergic being near something gives you a rash or makes you cough or sneeze

amazed very, very surprised by something

angry feeling mad at someone or something

anxious really, really want to do something or want something to happen

appear can be seen

appetite an interest in food

aromas odors you like

attack try to hurt someone or something

attention 1. stand at attention—stand up straight and face the front, with feet together and arms at your sides; 2. pay attention—think really hard about only one thing

attractive nice to look at

awesome amazing and hard to believe

barber a person who cuts people's hair and trims or shaves men's beards

bare nothing is covering it

bloom 1. get good at doing things; 2. plants grow flowers on them

blossom 1. a flower that will turn into fruit; 2. grow or get better at things

bored tired and squirmy because you don't have anything interesting to do

brave not afraid to do something that was hard

burrow dig down in the ground and make a tunnel or a hole

business a company that makes or sells things to earn money

carpenter a person who builds things out of wood

cave a large hole in the side of a hill or mountain

celebrate do things that are fun on a special day

chatter make clicking sounds as your teeth knock together again and again

chattering making lots of quick, short sounds

cheat do the wrong thing; not honest

chore 1. a small job that has to be done nearly every day to keep everything running smoothly; 2. an unpleasant or difficult job

chores jobs you have to do nearly every day

chuckles laughs quietly

clever understands things quickly and is good at making plans

collect 1. find things in different places and put them together so you can use them; 2. people get a large number of things that are the same in some way because they really like those things and are interested in them

complaining saying you are unhappy with something

compromise agree to give up some of what you want, and agree to do some of what the other person wants

considerate pays attention to what someone else needs or wants or wishes for

construction 1. the job of building things like houses, factories, roads, and bridges; 2. an object that has been built or made

content satisfied with things just the way they are

cooperated worked together to do a job

cottage a small house in the country or near the beach

courage bravery; if you have courage, you will do something difficult or dangerous even though you may be afraid.

cowered made yourself as small as you could because you were afraid

crept moved quietly and slowly

cross mad because someone did something you didn't like

curious 1. interested in something and want to know more about it; 2. unusual, or hard to understand

customers the people who buy things in a store

damaged broken or ruined

dashed ran as fast as it could go

dawn the time of day when the sun is just starting to come up

decided carefully thought about something and chose to do it

decorations the things someone uses to make something else more beautiful

delicious tastes very, very good

den 1. a home for some kinds of wild animals, such as bears, foxes, skunks, and wolves; 2. a cozy, comfortable room in a house where people relax and do things they enjoy

desperate wanting something very, very badly

determined made up your mind about something and won't let anything stop you

devour eat quickly and hungrily

difficult 1. not easy to do, very hard to do; 2. not easy to get along with

dim not bright

disability can't do something because of a medical problem or an accident

disagreeable unfriendly and unhelpful

disappears can't be seen anymore

disappointment the sad feeling you have when you don't get something you want

disobedient when a person does not do what he or she is told to do

disruptive cause a lot of trouble

disturb 1. interrupt a person or an animal and upset them; 2. bother or worry

donate give something away in order to help other people

doorbell a button you push to let someone know you are at the door

dormant plants have lost their leaves and are not growing but are still alive

dreary dark and gloomy, sad and boring

drifted moved with the wind or water

drowsy sleepy and cannot think clearly

eager want very much to do something; can hardly wait

embrace 1. a really big hug; 2. put your arms around someone and hold that person tightly to show that you like or love him or her

emergency a serious situation that calls for fast action

emotions the different moods people feel

enormous very, very big

examine 1. look at something very carefully; 2. what a doctor does when he looks at your body and does tests to see if anything is wrong with you

excited so happy you can't be still because something good is going to happen to you

experience use one or more of the five senses to learn more about something

explained told more about something so someone could understand it

explore travel around so you can find out what places are like

familiar you remember it when you see it, and you know what it is right away

fascinated interested in something and you think about it a lot

favorite someone or something you like the most

feelings the emotions or moods that people feel

finally after a long, long time

fragrant has a sweet or pleasing smell

frost white, powdery ice that forms on things in freezing weather

frowned made a face that showed someone was unhappy, worried, or thinking really, really hard

frustrated upset and angry because no matter how hard you try, you can't do something

furious feeling very, very angry at someone or something

gale a wind so strong that it makes whole trees sway; it breaks twigs and branches off the trees

gasp take a short quick breath in through your mouth because you are shocked, surprised, or hurt

gathering picking things up and putting them together in a pile so you can use them later

generous happy to share what you have with others

gentle do things in a kind, careful way

gigantic enormous

glaring staring at someone in an angry way

glimpse see something for only a short time before it is gone

grains 1. wheat, oat, or rice seeds; 2. a hard, tiny piece of something

harvest gather in crops so you can use them for food

hibernate spend the winter in a deep sleep

honest people who tell the truth or do what is right are honest

hope a feeling you have when you believe and expect that things will get better

horrible really, really bad

howl, howled 1. a long, loud crying sound made by an animal like a wolf, dog, or monkey; 2. made a long, loud crying sound because you were hurt, unhappy, or angry

ignore pay no attention to

imaginary not real

imagination the part of your mind that lets you make pictures of imaginary things or of things that didn't really happen

impatient not patient

important valuable and powerful

impressions marks made by pressing down on something

ingredients the things you need to make something

injury damage done to a person's or an animal's body

insisted used a very firm voice to say what you were going to do, and you wouldn't change your mind

jagged has lots of sharp points

jealous want what someone else has

keen eager to do something

kind 1. friendly, helpful, and considerate; 2. sort or type

language sounds, words, and actions we use to tell others how we feel and what we want

lap 1. lick up food or drink with the tongue; 2. one time around something

legend 1. a story that explains how something came to be; 2. a list that explains what pictures or maps in a book mean

limbs 1. the branches of a tree; 2. arms and legs

load put things into or onto something

lonely unhappy because you have been left all alone

mailbox a place where cards and letters are left by a mail carrier

mail carrier a person who sorts and delivers mail to people

mail cart a wheeled wagon used to carry small loads of mail

meadow a field where grass and flowers grow

memories the things you remember that have happened to you before

memorize learn something so well you remember it exactly

migrate fly away to spend the winter somewhere else

mood how you feel; the expression "in the mood" means that when you are in the mood for something, you want to do it or have it

muttered spoke in a very quiet voice so no one could hear

naughty does things you know are wrong

nervous anxious and a little bit afraid

nuisance a person or an animal that is bothering you and causing you lots of problems

nursery 1. a place where plants are grown so they can be sold; 2. a room in a house where babies and young children sleep or play

nutritious food that has healthy things in it that help your body grow and be strong

obey do what you are told to do

occupations the jobs people do to earn money

odor a smell

opposites words that tell about the same kind of thing but are completely different in some way

parents your mother and your father

pasture a field where animals are kept so they can eat the grass

patience the emotion you show when you wait without feeling worried or upset

patiently how you act when you do a job without complaining or getting angry or upset by how long it is taking

perfect no mistakes

petals the outer parts of a flower

pleaded asked for something with all your heart, begged for something

politely how you speak when you use your best manners

post office a building where the mail is sorted and stamps are sold

practice do the same thing over and over so you get good at doing it

precious very special and important

prepare get ready for something to happen

present 1. a gift; 2. being somewhere; 3. (in the present) happening right now

pretended imagined you were doing something, even though you knew you weren't

prickly 1. has lots of small, sharp points that stick out from it; 2. tells about someone who loses his or her temper or gets upset very easily

promise 1. say you definitely will do something; 2. the words you say when you promise someone something

property 1. anything that is owned by someone; 2. land or the buildings that are on the land

protect keep safe from danger or injury

protective gear or clothing that will keep you safe

rascal 1. someone who would lie and trick to get his or her own way; 2. a young child who does things he or she knows is wrong

reasons the facts that explain why you think what you do

relieved happy because something bad doesn't happen or when something bad stops happening

rescue get someone or something away from danger and save them

responsible do your jobs properly and carefully without having anyone check up on you

restless always moving; can't sit still or be quiet

roared 1. shouted something in a very loud voice; 2. tells how people or things moved very fast and made a loud noise

root 1. dig and turn over dirt with paws or noses to find food; 2. the part of a plant that usually grows underground

rude do or say things that show bad manners; not polite

satisfied feeling happy because you have enough of what you want or need

scorched 1. dried out by the hot sun; 2. burned a little bit

scowled made an angry frown

scrawl 1. writing that is untidy and careless; 2. write in a messy or untidy way

seasons the different parts of the year; winter, spring, summer, and autumn

selfish you don't care about others, and you won't share what you have

senses the five ways we use our bodies to learn about the world: sight, hearing, touch, taste, and smell

sentence a group of words that tells who or what and what's happening

severely speak in a voice that is harsh, not gentle

shouted 1. spoke in a very loud voice; 2. said something very loudly because the person you were talking to was a long way away

shy worried and a little bit afraid around others

sighed let out a deep breath to show you were disappointed or tired

silly you want to do things or say things or wear funny clothes that will make everyone laugh

slithers moves by twisting and sliding along the ground

sloppy careless about how you do things; messy and untidy

sly very good at tricking others

snatched 1. grabbed something and quickly pulled it away; 2. stole something

snuggle cuddle in a warm and comfortable spot, close by someone or something

special 1. not ordinary; better than usual; 2. a sale of certain things for lower prices

sprawled sat or lay down with arms and legs spread out in a careless way

sprouted started to grow roots and leaves

squabbling arguing noisily or quarreling with someone about something that is not important

squeaked spoke in a very high voice

starving so very, very hungry that you think you might die

sturdy 1. something that is strong and well-built; 2. a person or animal that is strong and powerful

substitute 1. a person who takes the place of someone else; 2. replace one person or thing with another

successful doing well at something you want to do

talent a special skill or ability that you have even though you haven't practiced it

terrified very, very afraid

thirsty need to drink something

tradition something you always do or expect to always do

trembled shook because you were afraid or cold

triplets three babies all born on the same day to the same mother

unaware don't know something is happening

uncooperative won't do anything to help anyone else

unusual not usual or ordinary

upward moves in the direction up

whirled spun around very quickly

wild 1. not tame; not looked after by people; 2. badly behaved, out of control

wilderness a place where no people live

winding 1. twisting and turning as it goes along; 2. turning a key, a knob, or a handle to make something work

wonder think about something, either because you are interested in it and want to know more or because you are worried about it

worried unhappy because you can't stop thinking about all the bad things that could happen

Chart Graphics

Week 9, 10, 21, 33

Week 11, 30

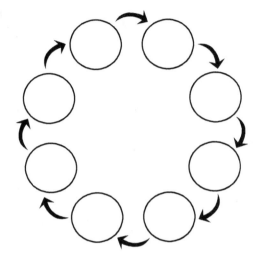

Week 14

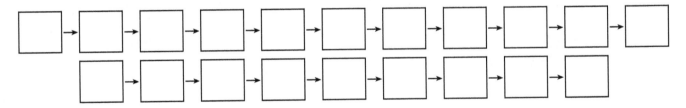

Week 15

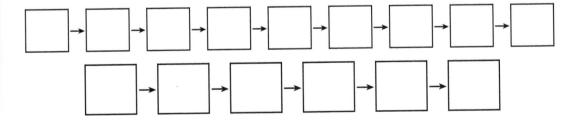

Week 16

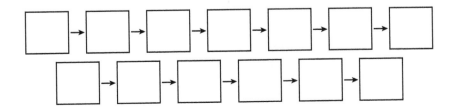

Chart Graphics

Week 18, 19, 34

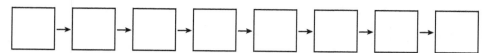

Week 20

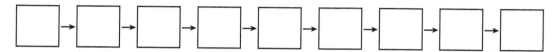

Week 22

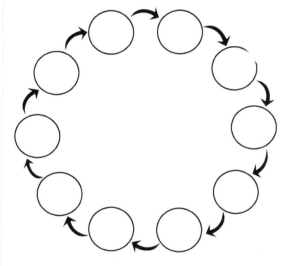

Week 25

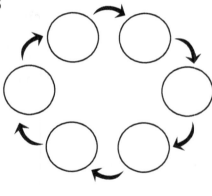

Week 23

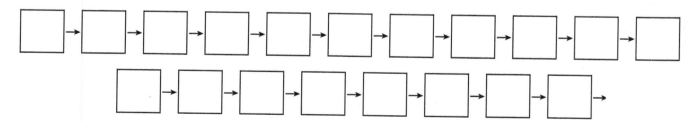

Week 35

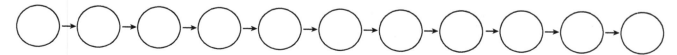

Week 1

Preparation: You will need *The Ant and the Grasshopper* for each day's lesson.

Post a copy of the Vocabulary Tally Sheet, BLM A, with this week's Picture Vocabulary Cards attached.

Each child will need the Homework Sheet, BLM 1a.

DAY 1

Introduce Program

Today we will begin to learn and use hard words. We will work together to learn about books and the things that make up a story. We will have lots of fun reading books, learning songs, and playing games together. Let's get started!

Introduce Book

The name of today's book is *The Ant and the Grasshopper.* The name of a book or a story is called the title. What is a title? *The name of a book or a story.* What's another word for the name of a book or a story? *Title.*

The title of this week's book is *The Ant and the Grasshopper.* What's the title of this week's book? *The Ant and the Grasshopper.*

The person who writes a book or a story is called the author. What's another word for a person who writes a book or a story? *Author.* What is an author? *The person who writes a book or a story.* This book was written by Amy Palmer. Who's the author of *The Ant and the Grasshopper*? *Amy Palmer.*

Pat Paris made the pictures for this book. Who made the pictures for *The Ant and the Grasshopper*? *Pat Paris.*

The cover of a book usually gives us some hints of what the book is about. Let's look at the front cover of *The Ant and the Grasshopper.* What do you see in the picture? (Ideas: *There are an ant and a grasshopper; the ant is on her bike; gardening tools are in her basket; the grasshopper looks like he is going to the beach.*)

Target Vocabulary

Tier II	Tier III
collect	title
pleaded	author
insisted	
prepare	
*desperate	
*considerate	

*Expanded Target Vocabulary Word

(Ask the following questions, allowing sufficient time for children to share their predictions with their partners.)

- Whom do you think this story is about?
- What do you think the grasshopper will do?
- Where do you think the story happens?
- When do you think this story happens?
- Why do you think the ant is holding a rake?
- How do you think the grasshopper is feeling?
- How do you think the ant is feeling?
- Do you think this story is about real animals?
- Tell why or why not.

(Call on several children to share their predictions with the class.)

Take a Picture Walk

We're going to take a picture walk through this book. When we take a picture walk, we look at the pictures and tell what we think will happen in the story.

(Show the illustrations on the following pages, and ask the specified questions.)

Page 3. (Point to the inset of the ant and the grasshopper.) Who do you think these creatures are? (Ideas: *The ant and the grasshopper.*)

(Point to the main illustration.) Where do you think this part of the story is happening? (Idea: *At the beach, at a lake.*) What are people doing in the illustration? (Ideas: *Swimming; buying food; sitting in the sun; walking; eating.*) When do you think this part of the story happens? (Ideas: *When it's nice; in the summer; when it's hot.*)

Page 4. What do you think is happening? (Ideas: *The grasshopper is going to play or sit in the sun; he is going to have a picnic; the ant is hauling some food; she is getting ready to work in her garden.*) Why do you think so? (Ideas: *The grasshopper has a mat, some toys, and a picnic basket; the ant has some gardening tools and food in the basket at the back of her bike.*)

Page 5. (Point to the thought balloon.) This is a thought balloon. It shows what the grasshopper is thinking about. What is the grasshopper thinking about? (Idea: *Eating popcorn.*)

(Point to the words "Beach Bug" on the grasshopper's shirt.) These words say Beach Bug. A beach bug is an insect who just likes to play and does not like to work. What do these words tell us about the grasshopper? (Ideas: *He just wants to play; he does not want to work.*) What is the ant doing? (Ideas: *Carrying food—a strawberry, a tomato; she's on her way to work in her garden.*)

Page 6. When do you think this part of the story happens? (Ideas: *On a cold day; in the fall.*) Where do you think all of the people have gone? (Ideas: *Home; back to school and work.*) How do you think the grasshopper is feeling? (Ideas: *Sad; unhappy; worried; cold; lonesome.*)

Page 7. When do you think this part of the story happens? (Ideas: *On a cold day; in the winter; on a snowy day.*) How do you think the grasshopper is feeling? (Ideas: *Sad; unhappy; worried.*)

What do you think is happening? (Ideas: *The grasshopper and the ant are talking; the grasshopper is at the ant's house; the grasshopper is asking for help.*)

Page 8. What do you think is happening here? (Ideas: *The grasshopper and the ant are getting food; the grasshopper and the ant are working together.*)

When do you think this part of the story happens? (Idea: *When it's nice; in the summer; when it's hot.*)

Now that we've finished our picture walk, it's your turn to ask me some questions. What would you like to know about the story? (Accept questions. If children tell about the pictures or the story instead of asking questions, prompt

them to ask a question.) Ask me a question about who is in the story. Ask me a why question.

Read Story
(Read story aloud to children with minimal interruptions.)

In the next lesson, we will read the story again, and I will ask you some questions.

(**Note:** If children have difficulty attending for an extended period of time, present the next part of this day's lesson at another time.)

Present Target Vocabulary

Now we will go over some vocabulary words that were used in the story.

◎— Collect.

In the story, the ant collected seeds, berries, beans, and corn. That means the ant found seeds, berries, beans, and corn in different places and put them together so she could use them. **Collect.** Say the word. *Collect.*

If you collect things, you find things in different places and put them together so you can use them. What word means to "find things in different places and put them together so you can use them"? *Collect.*

(Correct any incorrect responses, and repeat the item at the end of the sequence.)

Let's think about things you could collect. I'll name something. If you could collect that thing, say, "Collect." If not, don't say anything.

- Money dropped on the floor. *Collect.*
- Empty bottles for recycling. *Collect.*
- Houses on your street.
- A sunny day.
- Sidewalk.
- Wood for a fire. *Collect.*

What word means to "find things in different places and put them together so you can use them"? *Collect.*

◎— Pleaded.

In the story, when winter came, the grasshopper pleaded with the ant to help him. That means he really, really wanted the ant to help him, and he asked with all his heart. He begged the ant to help him. **Pleaded.** Say the word. *Pleaded.*

If you plead for something, you ask for it with all your heart. You beg for it. What word means "ask for something with all your heart; beg for something"? *Plead.*

(Correct any incorrect responses, and repeat the item at the end of the sequence.)

Let's think about some times when you might have pleaded for something. I'll name a time. If you might have pleaded at that time, say, "Pleaded." If not, don't say anything.

- It was bedtime, but you really, really wanted to stay up late to see a show on television. *Pleaded.*
- You were playing catch with your friend.
- Your mom packed your favorite lunch.
- You begged your mom to let your best friend sleep over. *Pleaded.*
- You rode your bike.
- You really, really wanted a puppy. *Pleaded.*

What word means "asked for something with all your heart; begged for something"? *Pleaded.*

◎⤙ Insisted.

In the story, when the grasshopper asked the ant to play, she insisted that she had to keep working. That means the ant used a very firm voice to say that she was going to keep working. She wouldn't change her mind. **Insisted.** Say the word. *Insisted.*

If you insisted, you used a very firm voice to say what you were going to do, and you wouldn't change your mind. What word means "used a very firm voice to say what you were going to do, and you wouldn't change your mind"? *Insisted.*

(Correct any incorrect responses, and repeat the item at the end of the sequence.)

Let's think about times when someone might insist on something. I'll tell about a time. If you might have heard someone insist, say, "Insisted." If not, don't say anything.

- It was raining, and your mom wanted you to wear your coat to school. *Insisted.*
- Your friend wanted to play ball, but you really wanted to play tag. *Insisted.*
- The children were listening to a story.
- The boy said he had to be first in line. *Insisted.*

- Everyone laughed at the joke.
- The girl had a pet gerbil.

What word means "used a very firm voice to say what you were going to do, and you wouldn't give in about it"? *Insisted.*

◎⤙ Prepare.

At the end of the story, both the grasshopper and the ant decide to prepare for winter. That means the ant and the grasshopper are getting ready for winter. **Prepare.** Say the word. *Prepare.*

If you prepare for something, you get ready for that thing to happen. What word means to "get ready for something to happen." *Prepare.*

(Correct any incorrect responses, and repeat the item at the end of the sequence.)

Let's think about when people might prepare for something. If I say a time when someone is preparing for something, say, "Prepare." If not, don't say anything.

- Your dad cuts up vegetables for a salad. *Prepare.*
- Your sister studies hard for her math test. *Prepare.*
- Everyone runs outside to play.
- You brush your teeth, wash your face, and put on your pajamas. *Prepare.*
- You get ready to swing the bat and hit the ball. *Prepare.*
- Your teacher says, "Good morning."

What word means to "get ready for something to happen"? *Prepare.*

Introduce Vocabulary Tally Sheet
(Display the Vocabulary Tally Sheet, BLM A. Explain to children that each time you or they use a new vocabulary word, you will put a mark by that word. Use the new vocabulary words throughout the week whenever an opportunity presents itself. Encourage children to do the same.)

Assign Homework
(Give each child a copy of the Homework Sheet, BLM 1a, with homework helper instructions. See the Introduction for homework instructions.)

Preparation: Picture Vocabulary Cards for *collect, pleaded, insisted,* and *prepare.*

Read and Discuss Story

(Read story aloud to children. Ask the following questions at the specified points in the story.)

Now I'm going to read *The Ant and the Grasshopper.* When I finish each part, I'll ask you some questions.

Page 3. How does the grasshopper spend his day? (Ideas: *Watching people; walking along the boardwalk; lying on the beach in the sunshine.*) How does the ant spend her day? (Ideas: *Working and preparing for winter; collecting food for the winter.*)

Page 4. Why does the ant spend all her time collecting food? (Idea: *So she would have enough food to eat in the wintertime.*)

Page 5. What is the grasshopper thinking about? (Idea: *The bag of popcorn that he ate.*) When you give someone advice, you tell that person what you think he or she should do. What advice does the ant give the grasshopper? (Idea: *That popcorn is good now but would not keep for winter.*) What do you think she wants the grasshopper to do? (Idea: *Help her work.*) Does the grasshopper follow the ant's advice? *No.* What does he do? *He goes to the beach.*

Page 6. How is the grasshopper feeling now? *Scared.* Why is he scared? (Ideas: *Everyone has left, and there is no food to eat.*) Whom do you think he will go to for help? (Idea: *The ant.*)

Page 7. (Read to the end of the sentence "Please give me something to eat.") Do you think the ant should share her food with the grasshopper? Tell why you think that. (Accept either response, as long as the child supports his or her answer with a reason.) (Ideas: *No, the grasshopper should have collected his own food when he had a chance; yes, the ant has enough, and she shouldn't let the grasshopper die.*)

Page 8. How does the story end? (Ideas: *The ant and the grasshopper both prepare for winter;*

the ant and the grasshopper both have time to play and have fun.)

Review Vocabulary

(Display the Picture Vocabulary Cards. Point to each card as you say the word. Ask children to repeat each word after you.) These pictures show **collect, insisted, pleaded,** and **prepare.**

- What word means "asked for something with all your heart; begged for something"? *Pleaded.*
- What word means to "find things in different places and put them together so you can use them"? *Collect.*
- What word means to "get ready for something to happen"? *Prepare.*
- What word means "used a very firm voice to say what you were going to do, and you wouldn't give in about it"? *Insisted.*

Extend Vocabulary

◎—← *Collect.*

In *The Ant and the Grasshopper,* we learned that **collect** means to "find things in different places and put them together."

Here's a new way to use the word **collect.**

- **Janice will collect stamps.** Say the sentence.
- **Ari and Rob collect rocks.** Say the sentence.
- **Let's collect spoons.** Say the sentence.

In these sentences, **collect** tells about how people collect things for a hobby. People get many things that are the same in some way because they really like those things and are interested in them. They collect things as a hobby.

What kinds of things do you collect? (Call on several children. Encourage them to start their answers with the words "I collect . . . .")

Present Expanded Target Vocabulary

◎—← *Desperate.*

In the story, the grasshopper pleads with the ant to share her food with him. He wants food very, very badly. He is afraid he is going to die. Another way of saying the grasshopper wants food very, very badly is to say he is desperate for food. When you are desperate, you want something very, very badly. **Desperate.** Say the word. *Desperate.*

If you are desperate, you want something very, very badly. What word means "wanting something very, very badly"? *Desperate.*

Let's think about when you or someone might feel desperate. If I say a time when you or someone would feel desperate, say, "Desperate." If not, don't say anything.

- How you would feel if you really, really needed to go to the bathroom. *Desperate.*
- How your friend would feel if you invited him or her over to play.
- How you would feel if you lost your new coat and couldn't find it anywhere. *Desperate.*
- How you would feel if you really, really wanted a little kitten, but your mom and dad kept saying no. *Desperate.*
- How your teacher would feel if you were really good listeners.
- How your family would feel if they got a new house.

What word means "wanting something very, very badly"? *Desperate.* (Repeat until firm.)

◎═ *Considerate.*

In the story, when the grasshopper comes to the ant's door asking for food, the ant pays attention to what the grasshopper needs and says she will help him.

Another way of saying the ant pays attention to what the grasshopper needs is to say the ant is considerate. When you pay attention to what someone else needs or wants or wishes for, you are being considerate. **Considerate.** Say the word. *Considerate.*

If you are considerate, you pay attention to what someone else needs, or wants, or wishes for. What word means "pays attention to what someone else needs or wants or wishes for"? *Considerate.*

Let's think about things someone might do that would be considerate. If I say something that would be considerate, say, "Considerate." If not, don't say anything.

- Does not push in line. *Considerate.*
- Uses a quiet voice in the library. *Considerate.*
- Grabs the crayons.
- Shares a book with a partner. *Considerate.*

- Colors on the table.
- Sets the table for dinner. *Considerate.*

What word means "pays attention to what someone else needs or wants or wishes for"? *Considerate.* (Repeat until firm.)

Tell about a time when you were considerate. (Call on several children. Encourage children to start their answers with the words "I was considerate when ....")

DAY 3

Preparation: Activity Sheet, BLM 1b.

Retell Story

(Show the pictures on the following pages from the story, and call on a child to tell what's happening. Call on a different child for each section.)

Today I'll show you the pictures Pat Paris made for *The Ant and the Grasshopper.* As I show you the pictures, I'll call on one of you to tell the class that part of the story.

Pages 3–4. Tell what happens at the **beginning** of the story.

Page 5. Tell what happens in the **middle** of the story. (Encourage children to include the target words *collect, pleaded, insisted,* and *prepare* when appropriate. If there is an opportunity on a page for a child to use one of the target words and he or she doesn't, model using the word.)

Page 8. Tell what happens at the **end** of the story.

How do you think the grasshopper feels now? (Ideas: *Happy; prepared.*) Tell why you think so. (Idea: *He has time to play, but he also has food for the winter.*)

How do you think the ant feels now? (Ideas: *Happy; prepared.*) Tell why you think so. (Idea: *She has food for the winter, but she also has some time to play and have fun.*)

Introduce Show Me, Tell Me Game

Today you will learn to play a new game called Show Me, Tell Me. I'll ask you to show me how to do something. If you show me, you win one point. If you can't show me, I get the point.

Next I'll ask you to tell me. If you tell me, you win one point. If you can't tell me, I get the point.

Let's practice: My turn to show you how I would look if I were pleading for a cookie. (Show a pleading face.) What was I doing? *Pleading.*

Let's do one together. Show me how you would collect spilled crayons from the floor. (Pretend to collect spilled crayons with children.) What did we do? *We collected the crayons.*

Now you're ready to play the game.

(Draw a T-chart on the board for keeping score. Children earn one point for each correct answer. If they make an error, demonstrate the action, and tell them the word. Record one point for yourself, and repeat missed words at the end of the game.)

- Show me how you would **collect** books after we have read together. (Pause.) Tell me what you did. *Collected books.*
- Show me how you would look if you were feeling **desperate** for a drink of water. (Pause.) Tell me how you felt. *Desperate for a drink at the fountain.*
- Show me how you would **prepare** to go outside in the rain. (Pause.) Tell me what you did. *Prepared to go outside in the rain.*
- Show me how you would be **considerate** to your teacher when he or she is speaking. (Pause.) Tell me what you did. *Was being considerate.*
- Show me how you would **insist** on having a turn at a game. (Pause.) Tell me what you did. *Insisted on having a turn at a game.*

(Count the points, and declare a winner.)
You did a great job of playing the Show Me, Tell Me Game!

Sequence: Beginning, Middle, End (Activity Sheet)

(Give each child a copy of the Activity Sheet, BLM 1b. Review the order of the story with children. Tell them to place the pictures in sequence to show beginning, middle, and end. Instruct children to color the pictures, cut them out, and paste or glue them in order of beginning, middle, and end.)

Learn "The Story Song" (Literary Analysis)

Let's think about what we already know about how books are made.

- What do we call the name of a book? *The title.*
- What do we call the person who writes the story? *The author.*

Today we will learn a song that will help us remember some important things about books.

Listen while I sing the first verse of "The Story Song." (Sing to the tune of "Barnyard Song," also known as "Bought Me a Cat." See www.kididdles.com.)

Read me a book, and the book pleased me.
I read my book under yonder tree.
Book says, "I'm a story."

Read me a book, and the book pleased me.
I read my book under yonder tree.
Title says what its name is.
Book says, "I'm a story."

Read me a book, and the book pleased me.
I read my book under yonder tree.
Author says, "I'm who wrote it."
Title says what its name is.
Book says, "I'm a story."

Play Show Me, Tell Me Game (Cumulative Review)

Let's play the Show Me, Tell Me Game you learned yesterday. I'll ask you to show me how to do something. If you show me, you win one point. If you can't show me, I get the point.

Next I'll ask you to tell me. If you tell me, you win one point. If you can't tell me, I get the point.

Now you're ready to play the game.

(Draw a T-chart on the board for keeping score. Children earn one point for each correct answer. If they make an error, correct them as you normally would, and record one point for yourself. Repeat missed words at the end of the game.)

- Show me what you would do if you **pleaded** with me to let you go to play time early. (Pause.) Tell me what you did. *Pleaded.*
- Show me how you would look if you were **desperate** to answer a question your teacher had asked you. (Pause.) Tell me how you are feeling. *Desperate.*
- Show me how you would **collect** pencils that had fallen on the floor. (Pause.) Tell me what you did. *Collected pencils.*
- Show me how you would **insist** that someone be quiet in the library. (Pause.) Tell me what you did. *Insisted someone be quiet.*
- Show me how you would **prepare** to listen to a story. (Pause.) Tell me what you did. *Prepared to listen to a story.*
- Show me how you would be **considerate** to a classmate who had lost all his pencils. (Pause.) Tell me what you did. *I was considerate.*
- Show me how you would look if you were **desperate** to watch your favorite television show. (Pause.) Tell me how you were feeling. *Desperate.*
- Show me what you would do if you **collected** seeds from the floor and put them in a cup. (Pause.) Tell me what you did. *Collected seeds.*
- Show me what you would do if you **collected** bottles to earn extra money. (Pause.) Tell me what you did. *Collected bottles.*
- Show me what you would do if you **prepared** your backpack for school. (Pause.) Tell what you did to your backpack. *Prepared it for school.*

(Count the points, and declare a winner.)
You did a great job of playing the Show Me, Tell Me Game!

DAY 5

Preparation: Happy Face Game Test Sheet, BLM B.

Retell the Story to a Partner
(Assign each child a partner, and ask the partners to take turns telling part of the story each time you turn to a new set of pages. Encourage use of target words when appropriate.)

Today I'll show you the pictures Pat Paris made for *The Ant and the Grasshopper.* As I show you the pictures, you and your partner will take turns telling part of the story.

Pages 3–4. Tell what happens at the **beginning** of the story.

Pages 5–7. Tell what happens in the **middle** of the story.

Page 8. Tell what happens at the **end** of the story.

How do you think the grasshopper feels at the end of the story? (Ideas: *Happy; prepared.*) Tell why you think so. (Idea: *He has had time to play, but he also has food for the winter.*)

How do you think the ant feels at the end of the story? (Ideas: *Happy; prepared.*) Tell why you think so. (Idea: *She has food for the winter, but she also has had some time to play and have fun.*)

Happy Face Game (Assess Vocabulary)
(Hold up a copy of the Happy Face Game Test Sheet, BLM B.)

Today you're going to play the Happy Face Game. When you play the Happy Face Game, it helps me know how well you know the hard words you are learning.

Before you can play the Happy Face Game, you must know about true and false.

If something is true, it's right or correct. What word means "right or correct"? *True.* What does **true** mean? *Right or correct.*

I'll say some things. If I say something true, say, "True." If not, don't say anything.

- You wear a shoe on your foot. *True.*
- You wear a hat on your hand.
- A dog has ears. *True.*
- A boy has ears. *True.*
- A table has ears.
- A table has legs. *True.*

What word means "right or correct"? *True.*

If something is false, it's wrong. What word means "wrong"? *False.* What does **false** mean? *Wrong.*

I'll say some things. If I say something false, say, "False." If not, don't say anything.

- You wear a shoe on your head. *False.*
- A dog can sit.
- A dog can fly. *False.*
- A fish can swim.
- An elephant can fly. *False.*
- Girls have wings. *False.*

What word means "wrong"? *False.*

(Distribute the Happy Face Game Test Sheet to children. Encourage them to do their own work and not to look at the work of others. Icons have been provided in front of numbers for children who do not yet recognize numerals. Instruct children to color the happy face if the statement you make is true. Instruct them to color the sad face if the statement you make is false.)

If I say something true, color the happy face. What will you do if I say something true? *Color the happy face.*

If I say something false, color the sad face. What will you do if I say something false? *Color the sad face.*

Let's do the first one together.
If you are **considerate,** you might help a friend. *True.*

Now it's your turn. Listen carefully to each sentence I say. Don't let me trick you!

Item 2: If your mom told you in a very firm voice that you had to wear your mittens to school and she wouldn't change her mind, she **insisted** you wear your mittens. *True.*

Item 3: If you are starving, you are **not** very hungry. *False.*

Item 4: If you put on your raincoat before coming to school on a rainy day, you are **prepared.** *True.*

Item 5: If you gather things that belong together, you are **not collecting** them. *False.*

Item 6: If you help a classmate with a problem, you are **considerate.** *True.*

Item 7: If you really, really wanted something very badly, you **pleaded.** *True.*

Item 8: **Desperate** is the same as **not** wanting something very much. *False.*

Item 9: A book has an **author** and a **title.** *True.*

Item 10: Dogs have four legs. *True.*

You did a great job of playing the Happy Face Game!

(Score children's work later. Scores of 8 out of 9 indicate mastery. If a child does not achieve mastery, insert the missed words in the next week's lessons. Retest those children individually on the missed items before they take the next mastery test.)

Extensions
Read a Story as a Reward
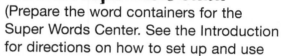 (Display *The Ant and the Grasshopper* or alternate versions of the story. Allow children to choose which book they would like you to read aloud to them as a reward for their hard work. Read the story for enjoyment with minimal interruptions.)

Introduce Super Words Center
(Prepare the word containers for the Super Words Center. See the Introduction for directions on how to set up and use the Super Words Center.)

(Place the new Picture Vocabulary Cards in the Super Words Center. Show children one of the word containers. If they need more guidance, role-play with two or three children as a demonstration.)

Let's think about how we work with our words in the Super Words Center.

You will work with a partner in the Super Words Center. Whom will you work with in the center? *A partner.*

First you'll choose a picture from the container. What do you do first? (Idea: *Choose a picture from the container.*)

Next you'll show your partner the picture and ask what word the picture shows. What do you do next? (Idea: *I show my partner the picture and ask what word the picture shows.*)

What do you do next? *Give my partner a turn.*

What do you do if your partner doesn't know the word? *Tell my partner the word.*

Preparation: You will need *Jack and the Bean Stalk* for each day's lesson.

Post a copy of the Vocabulary Tally Sheet, BLM A, with this week's Picture Vocabulary Cards attached.

Each child will need the Homework Sheet, BLM 2a.

DAY 1

Introduce Book

The name of today's book is *Jack and the Bean Stalk.* The name of a book or a story is called the title. What's a title? *The name of a book or a story.* What's another way of saying the name of a book or a story? *Title.*

The title of this week's book is *Jack and the Beanstalk.* What's the title of this week's book? *Jack and the Bean Stalk.*

The person who writes a book or a story is called the author. What's another word for the person who writes a book or a story? *An author.* What is an author? *The person who writes a book or a story.* This book was written by David Graham. Who's the author of *Jack and the Bean Stalk? David Graham.*

Pat Paris made the pictures for this book. Who made the pictures for *Jack and the Bean Stalk? Pat Paris.* The person who makes the pictures for a book or a story is called the illustrator. What's another word for the person who makes the pictures for a book or a story? *An illustrator.* What is an illustrator? *The person who makes the pictures for a book or a story.* Who's the illustrator of *Jack and the Bean Stalk? Pat Paris.*

The cover of a book usually gives us some hints of what the book is about. Let's look at the front cover of *Jack and the Bean Stalk.* What do you see in the picture? (Ideas: *There's a boy climbing up a big plant; he is up high; he's almost to the clouds; there's a house down below; there's a garden down below.*)

Jack and the Bean Stalk
author: David Graham • illustrator: Pat Paris

Target Vocabulary

Tier II	Tier III
cross	illustrator
crept	prediction
remember	
winding	
*brave	
*disobedient	

*Expanded Target Vocabulary Word

A stalk is the stem of a plant. What is a stalk? *The stem of a plant.* The plant in the picture is a bean plant. What kind of plant is in the picture? *A bean plant.* The stem the boy is climbing is a bean stalk. What do we call the stem the boy is climbing? *A bean stalk.* If you look carefully, you can see beans growing out from the bean stalk. (Call on a child to come and point to the beans on the bean stalk.)

We have looked carefully at the picture on the cover of *Jack and the Bean Stalk.* Now we can make guesses as to what the book is about. Our guesses are called predictions. What are our guesses called? *Predictions.*

(Assign each child a partner.) Get ready to tell your partner your predictions about the story *Jack and the Bean Stalk.* That means you tell your partner your guesses about what you think this story will be about. Use the information from the cover to help you.

(Ask the following questions, allowing sufficient time for children to share their predictions with their partners.)

- Whom do you think this story is about?
- What do you think the boy will find at the top of the bean stalk?
- Where do you think the story happens?
- When do you think this story happens?
- Why do you think the boy is climbing the bean stalk?
- How long do you think it will take him to get to the top?

- Do you think this story is a true story? Tell why or why not.

(Call on several children to share their predictions with the class.)

Take a Picture Walk

We're going to take a picture walk through this book. When we take a picture walk, we look at the pictures and tell what we think will happen in the story.

(Show the illustrations on the following pages, and ask the specified questions.)

Page 1. What do you think is happening? (Ideas: *The woman is talking to the boy; the boy is feeding the cow; the woman is going to milk the cow.*) Why do you think so? (Ideas: *The woman has a pail; the boy has hay on the pitchfork.*)

Page 2. Where do you think the boy is going with the cow? What do you think the man is saying to the boy?

Page 3. What do you think is happening? Why do you think so? What's different about those beans? (Idea: *They're all different colors.*)

Page 4. Why do you think the cow is going with the man? What do you think the boy is putting in his pocket?

Page 5. What do you think is happening? Why do you think so? How do you think the woman is feeling? How can you tell?

Pages 6–7. What do you think is happening? (Idea: *The boy climbed the bean stalk and found a castle.*)

Pages 8–9. Who do you think the woman is? (Idea: *The woman who lives in the castle.*)

Do you see how big she is next to the boy? In stories like *Jack and the Bean Stalk,* a very big and strong person like this woman is called a giant. What do we call this woman? *A giant.*

Pages 10–11. What do you think is happening? (Idea: *The man is eating.*) This man is also very big and strong. What do we call him? *A giant.*

Pages 16–17. Where is the boy now? (Idea: *Back at the giant's castle.*)

Pages 18–19. What is different about the eggs the hen lays? (Idea: *They're made of gold.*)

Pages 20–21. What do you think is happening? (Ideas: *The boy has stolen the hen and is climbing down the bean stalk; he is chopping down the bean stalk with his axe.*)

Page 22. How does the story end? (Ideas: *They are drinking tea; they are wearing very fancy clothes.*)

Now that we've finished our picture walk, it's your turn to ask me some questions. What would you like to know about the story? (Accept questions. If children tell about the pictures or the story instead of asking questions, prompt them to ask a question.) Ask me a question about who is in the story. Ask me a when question.

Read Story

(Read story aloud to children with minimal interruptions.)

In the next lesson, we will read the story again, and I will ask you some questions.

(**Note:** If children have difficulty attending for an extended period of time, present the next part of this day's lesson at another time.)

Present Target Vocabulary
Cross.

In the story, the giant's wife says the giant is very cross with her. That means the giant is mad at her because she has done something he doesn't like. She gives Jack breakfast, and then he steals the giant's gold. Now everything she does makes the giant mad. **Cross.** Say the word. *Cross.*

If you're cross with someone, you're mad because that person did something you didn't like. Now everything he or she does makes you mad. Say the word that means "mad because someone did something you didn't like." *Cross.*

(Correct any incorrect responses, and repeat the item at the end of the sequence.)

Let's think about things that might make you or someone else cross. I'll tell about something. If that thing could make someone cross, say, "Cross." If not, don't say anything.

- Someone stepping on your toe. *Cross.*
- Someone taking something that belongs to you. *Cross.*

- Eating lunch.
- Someone fixing your bike for you.
- Someone checking the book you wanted out of the library. *Cross.*
- Saying "Hello!"

What word means "mad because someone did something you didn't like"? *Cross.*

 Crept.

In the story, when the giant fell asleep, Jack crept out of the big pot. That means he moved as quietly and slowly as he could. He didn't want to wake up the giant. **Crept.** Say the word. *Crept.*

Crept comes from the word creep. It means "did creep." Crept is a way of moving. **When you creep, you move as quietly and slowly as you can.** Say the word that means "moved as quietly and slowly as you could." *Crept.*

(Call on a child.) Show me how you would creep to the door. (Pause.) Everyone, what did ___ do? *[He or she] crept to the door.* Everyone, show me how you would creep around the room. (Pause.) Good; you crept around the room. I hardly knew you were moving.

(Correct any incorrect responses, and repeat the item at the end of the sequence.)

Let's think about some times when a person or an animal might have crept. I'll tell about a time. If the person or the animal might have crept at that time, say, "Crept." If not, don't say anything.

- When the lion was sleeping, the mouse wanted to get away quietly. *Crept.*
- Todd wanted to get to the finish line first.
- Dad burned his hand and wanted to get to the doctor's office.
- You didn't want to wake up the sleeping baby. *Crept.*
- You want to surprise your teacher by coming into the classroom without her knowing. *Crept.*
- The cat wanted to get past the doghouse without the dog's hearing. *Crept.*

What word means "moved as quietly and slowly as you could?" *Crept.*

Remember.

In the story, the author asks you to remember that Jack is really hungry because he didn't have any supper the night before. **When you remember something, you still have that thing or idea in your mind. Remember.** Say the word. *Remember.*

If I had oatmeal for breakfast yesterday, I would remember that I had oatmeal for breakfast yesterday. Say the word that means "you still have a thing or an idea in your mind." *Remember.*

(Correct any incorrect responses, and repeat the item at the end of the sequence.)

Let's think about things that you could remember. If I say something that you could remember, say, "Remember." If not, don't say anything.

- What you had for supper last night. *Remember.*
- The name of your teacher. *Remember.*
- The title of every book in the library.
- The names of everyone in our school.
- Where you can find a pencil in our classroom. *Remember.*
- How tall our school is.

What word means "you still have a thing or an idea in your mind"? *Remember.*

Winding.

In the story, Jack climbs up the bean stalk and finds another land with a road that goes winding over the hills of the sky. That means the road is twisting and turning as it goes from the bean stalk to the giant's house. **Winding.** Say the word. *Winding.*

If a road, river, or line of people is winding its way somewhere, it is **twisting and turning as it goes along.** Say the word that means "twisting and turning as it goes along." *Winding.*

Watch me. I'll use my hand to show a winding road. (Move your hand from side to side in a winding motion.) Use your hand to show a winding river. (Pause.) Good; you used your hand to show a winding river.

(Correct any incorrect responses, and repeat the item at the end of the sequence.)

Let's think about some times when a road, river, or line of people might be winding somewhere. I'll tell about a time. If I tell about a time when someone or something might be winding, say, "Winding." If not, don't say anything.

- We play "Follow the Leader." *Winding.*
- The road to the airport twisted and turned. *Winding.*
- We went straight outside for a fire drill.
- You had to walk around the trees, rocks, and streams on your forest walk. *Winding.*
- The baseball player ran to first base.
- You walked home as fast as you could.

What word means "twisting and turning as it goes along"? *Winding.*

Present Vocabulary Tally Sheet
(See Week 1, page 3, for instructions.)

Assign Homework
(Homework Sheet, BLM 2a: See the Introduction for homework instructions.)

DAY 2

Preparation: Picture Vocabulary Cards for *cross, crept, remember,* and *winding.*

Read and Discuss Story

(Read story aloud to children. Ask the following questions at the specified points.)

Page 1. Why do Jack and his mother have to sell the cow? (Ideas: *The cow doesn't give milk; they have no money for food.*)

Page 4. Why does Jack sell the cow to the funny little old man? (Idea: *So he can get the magic beans.*) Does Jack believe the beans are magic? *No.* Then why does he sell the cow for the beans? (Idea: *The man said if the beans didn't grow up to the sky, he would give Jack his cow back.*) Do you think the funny little old man would really give the cow back? Tell why or why not.

Page 5. What happens when Jack gets home? (Ideas: *His mother throws the beans out; she sends him to bed without any supper.*)

Page 9. What good news does the giant woman give Jack? *She will give him some breakfast.* What bad news does she have? *Her husband likes to eat little boys.*

Page 10. Where does Jack hide? *In the oven.*

Page 11. (Read only to the end of the first sentence: "… I smell fresh meat.") What do you think he smells? (Idea: *Jack.*)

Page 11. (Read to the end of the page.) What does the giant say after he says he smells fresh meat? *"Fe, Fi, Fo, Fum, I smell fresh meat and I must have some."* (Have children repeat the rhyme until they all can say it.)

What does the giant's wife say he was smelling? *The sheep she cooked yesterday.*

After the giant finishes his breakfast, what does he ask for? *His gold.*

Page 14. Do you think Jack should have taken the giant's gold? Tell why or why not. (Accept either response as long as children give a reason they think so.)

Page 17. Where does Jack hide this time? *In a pot.*

Page 18. Everyone, say what the giant says when he smells fresh meat. *"Fe, Fi, Fo, Fum, I smell fresh meat and I must have some."*

Name some places the giant's wife looks for Jack. (Ideas: *In the oven; behind the door; in the cupboard; under the table.*)

After the giant finishes his breakfast, what does he ask for? *His hen.*

Page 21. What happens to the giant? (Ideas: *Jack kills him; he dies; he breaks his neck.*)

Page 22. How does the story end? (Ideas: *Jack's mother tells him that the giant stole the gold and magic hen from Jack's father; Jack and his mother and the magic hen live happily every after.*)

Review Vocabulary
(Display the Picture Vocabulary Cards. Point to each card as you say the word.) These pictures

show **cross, crept, remember,** and **winding.**
(Ask children to repeat each word after you.)

- What word means "you still have a thing or an idea in your mind"? *Remember.*
- What word means "moved as quietly and slowly as you could"? *Crept.*
- What word means "mad because someone did something you didn't like"? *Cross.*
- What word means "twisting and turning as it goes along"? *Winding.*

Extend Vocabulary

◎⤝ Winding.

In the story *Jack and the Bean Stalk*, we learned that **winding** means "twisting and turning as it goes along."

Here's a new way to use the word **winding.**

- **Petey was winding the watch.** Say the sentence.
- **Alice was winding up her mother's music box.** Say the sentence.
- **The little boy was winding up the toy rabbit and watching it hop.** Say the sentence.

In these sentences, **winding** means "turning a key, a knob, or a handle to make something work." What might you turn to wind a watch? (Idea: *A knob.*) What might you turn to wind up a music box? (Idea: *A key.*) What might you turn to wind up a toy rabbit? (Idea: *A key, a knob, or a handle.*)

Name something that needs winding up to make it work. (**Call on several children.**)

Present Expanded Target Vocabulary

◎⤝ Disobedient.

In the story, Jack's mother tells him to sell the cow. She wants him to sell the cow to get money so that they can buy some food. Jack doesn't do what his mother tells him to do. He trades the cow for some magic beans.

Another way of saying Jack doesn't do what his mother tells him to do is to say that Jack is disobedient. When Jack doesn't do what he is told to do, he is disobedient. **Disobedient.** Say the word. *Disobedient.*

When you do not do what you are told to do, you are disobedient. Say the word that means "not doing what you are told to do." *Disobedient.*

Let's think about things that would be disobedient. If I say something that would be disobedient, say, "Disobedient." If not, don't say anything.

- Not lining up when your teacher asks you to. *Disobedient.*
- Going to your friend's house when your aunt tells you to come home. *Disobedient.*
- Lining up quietly when your teacher asks you to.
- Staying up and watching television when the babysitter tells you to go to bed. *Disobedient.*
- Wearing a bicycle helmet when your dad tells you to.
- Cleaning your room when your grandma told you to.

What word means "not doing what you are told to do"? *Disobedient.*

Tell about a time when you were disobedient. (**Call on several children. Encourage them to start their answers with the words "I was disobedient when …"**)

◎⤝ Brave.

In the middle of the story *Jack and the Bean Stalk,* Jack is not afraid to climb back up the bean stalk, even though he knows it will be hard. He knows that the giant eats little boys, but he is not afraid. Jack is very brave because he is not afraid to do something that is hard. Another way of saying Jack is not afraid to do something that is hard is to say that Jack is brave. **Brave.** Say the word. *Brave.*

If you are brave, you are not afraid to do something even though you know it is hard. Say the word that means "not afraid to do something that is hard." *Brave.*

Let's think about some times when people might be brave. If I say a time when someone would be brave, say, "Brave." If not, don't say anything.

- Going downstairs in the dark. *Brave.*
- Playing with your favorite toy.
- Not crying or yelling when you get a bee sting. *Brave.*

- Telling your teacher the truth when you did something that you weren't supposed to do. *Brave.*
- Eating your lunch.
- Teaching your friend to play a game.

What word means "not afraid to do something that is hard"? *Brave.*

Preparation: Activity Sheet, BLM 2b.

Retell Story

(Show the pictures on the following pages from the story, and call on a child to tell what's happening. Call on a different child for each section.)

Today I'll show you the pictures Pat Paris made for *Jack and the Bean Stalk.* As I show you the pictures, I'll call on one of you to tell the class that part of the story.

Pages 1–3. Tell what happens at the **beginning** of the story.

Pages 4–19. Tell what happens in the **middle** of the story. (Encourage use of target words when appropriate. Model use as necessary.)

Pages 20–22. Tell what happens at the **end** of the story.

How do you think Jack and his mother feel now? (Ideas: *Happy; full [not hungry or starving]; rich.*) Tell why you think so. (Ideas: *They're having tea; they're wearing fancy clothes; they're smiling.*)

Review Show Me, Tell Me Game

Today you will play the Show Me, Tell Me Game. I'll ask you to show me how to do something. If you show me, you win one point. If you can't show me, I get the point.

Next I'll ask you to tell me. If you tell me, you win one point. If you can't tell me, I get the point.

Let's practice: My turn to show you how I would look if I felt cross because I had to stay very late after school. (Show a cross face.) How am I feeling? *Cross.*

Let's do one together. Show me how a dog would look if he crept past a mean person.

(Creep with children.) What did the dog do? *It crept.*

Now you're ready to play the game.

 (Draw a T-chart on the board for keeping score. Children earn one point for each correct answer. If they make an error, demonstrate the action and tell them the correct word. Record one point for yourself, and repeat missed words at the end of the game.)

- Show me what you would do if I told you to stand up and you were **disobedient.** (Pause.) Tell me how you were acting. *Disobedient.*
- Show me that you **remember** my name. (Pause.) Tell me what you did. *Remembered your name.*
- Show me how you would walk a **winding** path in "Follow the Leader." (Pause.) Tell me what kind of path you walked. *Winding.*
- Show me how you would look if you were being **brave.** (Pause.) Tell me how you looked. *As if I were brave.*
- Show me how you would **creep** to get safely past a sleeping giant. (Pause.) Tell me what you did. *Crept.*
- Show me how your teacher looks when you forget to wipe your feet before coming inside on a yucky, muddy day. (Pause.) Tell me how you looked. *Cross.*

(Count the points, and declare a winner.)
You did a great job of playing the Show Me, Tell Me Game!

Sequence: Beginning, Middle, End (Activity Sheet)

(Give each child a copy of the Activity Sheet, BLM 2b. Review the order of the story with children. They will place the pictures in sequence to show beginning, middle, and end. Instruct them to color the pictures, cut them out, and paste or glue them in sequential order.)

Title, Author, Illustrator (Literary Analysis)

Let's think about what we already know about how books are made.

- What do we call the name of the book? *The title.*
- What do we call the person who writes the story? *The author.*
- What do we call the person who draws the pictures? *The illustrator.*

Today we will sing a song that will help us remember some important things about books.

Listen while I sing the first verses of "The Story Song."

Read me a book, and the book pleased me.
I read my book under yonder tree.
Book says, "I'm a story."

Read me a book, and the book pleased me.
I read my book under yonder tree.
Title says what its name is.
Book says, "I'm a story."

Read me a book, and the book pleased me.
I read my book under yonder tree.
Author says, "I'm who wrote it."
Title says what its name is.
Book says, "I'm a story."

Now we'll add a new verse that tells about the illustrator. What does the illustrator of a story do? *The illustrator draws the pictures.* Let's add that to the song by singing "Illustrator draws the pictures." What are we going to add to our song? *Illustrator draws the pictures.*

Read me a book, and the book pleased me.
I read my book under yonder tree.
Illustrator draws the pictures.
Author says, "I'm who wrote it."
Title says what its name is.
Book says, "I'm a story."

Now we'll sing the whole song. (Repeat the song, adding the new verse.)

Play Show Me, Tell Me Game (Cumulative Review)

Let's play the Show Me, Tell Me Game that you learned last week. I'll ask you to show me how to do something. If you show me, you win one point. If you can't show me, I get the point.

Next, I'll ask you to tell me. If you tell me, you win one point. If you can't tell me, I get the point.

Now you're ready to play the game.

(Draw a T-chart on the board for keeping score. Children earn one point for each correct answer. If they make an error, correct them as you normally would, and record one point for yourself. Repeat missed words at the end of the game.)

- Show me how you would look if I told you that recess was cancelled for the rest of the week. (Pause.) Tell me how you are looking. *Cross.*
- Show me what you would do if you were a kitten trying to sneak past a ferocious dog. (Pause.) Tell me what you did. *Crept.*
- Show me that you **remember** the name of our school. (Pause.) Tell me what you are doing. *Remembering the name of our school.*
- Show me what you would do if I asked you to wave your hand and you were **disobedient.** (Pause.) Tell me how you are acting. *Disobedient.*
- Show me how you would walk a path around trees, rocks, and streams in the forest. (Pause.) Tell me what kind of path you are walking. *A winding path.*
- Show me how you would turn a key to make a music box work. (Pause.) Tell me what you are doing to the music box. *Winding it up.*
- Show me how you would look if you were not afraid to read a hard book aloud. (Pause.) Tell me how you are looking. *Brave.*
- Show me what you would do if you **collected** crayons from the floor and put them in a tub. (Pause.) Tell me what you are doing. *Collected crayons.*
- Show me how you would **prepare** to go out in the snow. (Pause.) Tell what you are doing. *I am preparing to go out in the snow.*

(Count the points, and declare a winner.)
You did a great job of playing the Show Me, Tell Me Game!

Retell Story to a Partner

(Assign each child a partner and ask the partners to take turns telling parts of the story each time you turn to a new set of pages. Encourage use of target words when appropriate.) Today I'll show you the pictures Pat Paris made for *Jack and the Bean Stalk.* As I show you the pictures, you and your partner will take turns telling part of the story.

Pages 1–3. Tell what happens at the **beginning** of the story.

Pages 4–19. Tell what happens in the **middle** of the story.

Pages 20–22. Tell what happens at the **end** of the story.

How do you think Jack and his mother feel at the end of the story? (Ideas: *Happy; full [not hungry or starving]; rich.*) Tell why you think so. (Ideas: *They're having tea; they're wearing fancy clothes; they're smiling.*)

Happy Face Game (Assess Vocabulary)

(Give each child a copy of the Happy Face Game Test Sheet, BLM B.)

Today you're going to play the Happy Face Game. When you play the Happy Face Game, it helps me know how well you know the hard words you are learning.

Before you can play the Happy Face Game, you have to remember about true and false.

If something is true, it's right or correct. What word means "right or correct"? *True.* What does **true** mean? *Right or correct.* I'll say some things. If I say something that is true, say "True." If not, don't say anything.

- You have hair on your head. *True.*
- Dogs say, "Meow!"
- Airplanes fly. *True.*
- A room has a door. *True.*
- You walk on the ceiling.
- You blow your nose and wipe your feet. *True.*

What word means "right or correct"? *True.*

If something is false, it's wrong. What word means "wrong"? *False.* What does **false** mean? *Wrong.*

I'll say some things. If I say something that is false, say, "False." If not, don't say anything.

- Books are good to eat. *False.*
- Chairs are for sitting on.
- Fish draw pictures. *False.*
- Vegetables are good for you.
- Cows can sing. *False.*
- You see with your stomach. *False.*

What word means "wrong"? *False.*

If I say something true, color the happy face. What will you do if I say something true? *Color the happy face.*

If I say something false, color the sad face. What will you do if I say something false? *Color the sad face.*

Listen carefully to each sentence I say. Don't let me trick you!

Item 1: If you are **brave,** you will run away screaming. *False.*

Item 2: If you don't do what your teacher asks you to do, you are being **disobedient.** *True.*

Item 3: If I ask you to say my name and you do, you **remember** my name. *True.*

Item 4: **Cross** means very happy. *False.*

Item 5: If you are turning the key on a music box, you are **winding** up the music box. *True.*

Item 6: If a road is very straight with no curves, it is a **winding** road. *False.*

Item 7: **Crept** means that someone moved while making a lot of noise. *False.*

Item 8: You are **disobedient** if you always do what you are asked to do. *False.*

Item 9: If you threw marbles all over the room, you **collected** them. *False.*

Item 10: If you wear your rubber boots and take an umbrella on a rainy day, you are **prepared.** *True.*

You did a great job of playing the Happy Face Game!

(Score children's work. Scores of 9 out of 10 indicate mastery. If a child does not achieve mastery, include the missed words in the games for next week's lessons. Retest those children individually for the missed items before they take the next mastery test.)

Extensions

Read a Story as a Reward

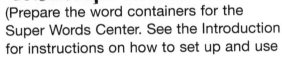 (Display *Jack and the Bean Stalk*, alternate versions of the story, or *The Ant and the Grasshopper*. Allow children to choose which book they would like you to read to them as a reward for their hard work.)

(Read story aloud to children for enjoyment with minimal interruptions.)

Present Super Words Center

(Prepare the word containers for the Super Words Center. See the Introduction for instructions on how to set up and use the Super Words Center.)

(Add the new Picture Vocabulary Cards to words from the previous week. Show children one of the word containers. If they need more guidance, role-play with two or three children as a demonstration.)

Let's think about how we work with our words in the Super Words Center.

You will work with a partner in the Super Words Center. Whom will you work with in the center? *A partner.*

First you will choose a picture from the container. What do you do first? (Idea: *Choose a picture from the container.*)

Next you will show your partner the picture and ask what word the picture shows. What do you do next? (Idea: *I show my partner the picture and ask what word the picture shows.*)

What do you do next? *Give my partner a turn.*

What do you do if your partner doesn't know the word? *Tell my partner the word.*

Week 3

The Three Little Pigs
Margot Zemach

The Three Little Pigs
author: Margot Zemach • illustrator: Margot Zemach

Preparation: You will need *The Three Little Pigs* for each day's lesson.

Number the pages of the story to assist you in asking questions at appropriate points.

Post a copy of the Vocabulary Tally Sheet, BLM A, with this week's Picture Vocabulary Cards attached.

Each child will need the Homework Sheet, BLM 3a.

🎯 Target Vocabulary

Tier II	Tier III
gathering	character
meadow	
roared	
angry	
*furious	
*delicious	

* Expanded Target Vocabulary Word

DAY 1

Introduce Book

Today's book is called *The Three Little Pigs*. Remember, the name of a book is called the title. What's the title of this week's book? *The Three Little Pigs.*

This book was written by Margot Zemach [Mar-go Zem-ack]. Remember, an author is the person who writes a book or a story. Who's the author of *The Three Little Pigs*? *Margot Zemach.*

Margot Zemach also made the pictures for this book. Remember, an illustrator is the person who makes the pictures for a book or a story. Who is the illustrator of *The Three Little Pigs*? *Margot Zemach.*

The cover of a book usually gives us some hints of what the book is about. Let's look at the front cover of *The Three Little Pigs*. What do you see in the illustration? (Ideas: *There are three pigs; one pig is looking at some flowers; one pig is smelling a turnip; one pig is sitting by a river; he is covered with mud; all the pigs are wearing clothes.*)

(Assign each child a partner.) Remember, when you make a prediction about something, you say what you think will happen. What do you do when you make a prediction? *You say what you think will happen.*

Now get ready to make some predictions to your partner about this book. Use the information from the cover to help you.

(Ask the following questions, allowing sufficient time for children to share their predictions with their partners.)

- Whom do you think this story is about?
- What do you think the pigs in the story will do?
- Where do you think the story happens?
- When do you think the story happens?
- Why do you think the pigs are doing what they are doing?
- How do you think the pigs are feeling?
- Do you think this story is about real pigs? Tell why or why not.

(Call on several children to share their predictions with the class.)

Take a Picture Walk

We are going to take a picture walk through this book. Remember, when we take a picture walk, we look at the pictures and tell what we think will happen in the story.

(Show the illustrations on the following pages, and ask the specified questions.)

Pages 1–2. What do you think is happening? (Idea: *The little pigs are leaving home.*) Why do you think so? (Ideas: *They are waving good-bye; they have a suitcase, a bag, and a box.*) How do you think the momma pig is feeling? *Sad.* Tell me why you think so. (Idea: *There's a tear on her cheek.*) Where do you think the little pigs are going? (Idea: *To build houses for themselves.*)

Week 3 • Day 1

Pages 3–4. What do you think is happening here? (Idea: *The little pig got some straw from the farmer, and he is building himself a house.*)

Pages 5–6. What is happening to the little pig's house? (Idea: *The wolf is blowing it down.*) What do you think will happen to the little pig? (Ideas: *He'll run away; the wolf will catch him; the wolf will eat him.*)

Pages 7–8. What do you think is happening here? (Ideas: *The little pig got some sticks from the man; he is building himself a house.*)

Pages 9–10. What is happening to the little pig's house? (Idea: *The wolf is blowing it down.*) What do you think will happen to the little pig? (Ideas: *He'll run away; the wolf will catch him; the wolf will eat him.*)

Pages 11–12. What do you think is happening here? (Ideas: *The little pig got some bricks from the man; he is building himself a house.*)

Pages 15–16. What is happening to the little pig's house? (Idea: *Nothing.*) How do you think the wolf is feeling? (Ideas: *Angry; frustrated; mad.*)

Pages 25–26. What do you think is happening here? (Idea: *The wolf is going down the chimney.*) How do you think the little pig is feeling? (Ideas: *Scared; frightened.*)

Page 27. What do you think the pig is eating? (Idea: *The wolf.*) Tell why you think so. (Ideas: *There are bones on the floor; the wolf's tail is coming out of the pot; we don't see the wolf anymore.*)

Now that we've finished our picture walk, it's your turn to ask me some questions. What would you like to know about the story? (Accept questions. If children tell about the story instead of asking questions, prompt them to ask a question.) Ask me a question about who is in the story. Ask me a why question.

Read Story Aloud
(Read story aloud to children with minimal interruptions.)

In the next lesson, we will read the story again, and I will ask you some questions.

(**Note:** If children have difficulty attending for an extended period of time, present the next part of this day's lesson at another time.)

Present Target Vocabulary
◎⊷ Gathering.

In the story, the first little pig meets a man who is gathering straw. That means the man is picking up bits of straw and putting them together in a pile so he can use them. **Gathering.** Say the word. *Gathering.*

If you are gathering things, you are picking them up and putting them together in a pile. Say the word that means "picking thing up and putting them together in a pile." *Gathering.*

(Correct any incorrect responses, and repeat the item at the end of the sequence.)

Let's think about things that you could be gathering. I'll name something. If you could be gathering that thing, say, "Gathering." If not, don't say anything.

- Wood for a fire. *Gathering.*
- Toys on the floor. *Gathering.*
- Tall trees in the park.
- Stars in the sky.
- Buildings.
- Crayons to make a picture. *Gathering.*

What word means "picking things up and putting them together in a pile"? *Gathering.*

◎⊷ Meadow.

In the story, the third little pig crosses the meadow to get to the apple tree. That means he crossed a field with grass and flowers growing in it. **Meadow.** Say the word. *Meadow.*

A meadow is a field where grass and flowers grow. Sometimes horses and cows are put in a meadow so they can eat the grass. Say the word that means "a field where grass and flowers grow." *Meadow.*

(Correct any incorrect responses, and repeat the item at the end of the sequence.)

Let's think about things that you might see in a meadow. I'll name something. If you might see it in a meadow, say, "Meadow." If not, don't say anything.

- Grass. *Meadow.*

- Lots of trees.
- Cows. *Meadow.*
- Flowers. *Meadow.*
- A city.
- Horses. *Meadow.*

What word means "a field where grass and flowers grow"? *Meadow.*

 Roared.

In the story, the wolf was so angry that he roared at the third little pig. That means the wolf shouted at the little pig using a very loud voice. **Roared.** Say the word. *Roared.*

If you roared, you shouted something in a very loud voice. Say the word that means "shouted something in a very loud voice." *Roared.*

(Correct any incorrect responses, and repeat the item at the end of the sequence.)

Let's think about times when someone or something might have roared. I'll tell about a time. If you might have heard someone or something roar, say, "Roared." If not, don't say anything.

- A lion was trapped under a net. *Roared.*
- A cat was being petted.
- The crowd saw the batter hit a home run. *Roared.*
- The tiger was mad. *Roared.*
- The children listened to the story.
- The man saw the car coming towards the little boy. *Roared.*

What word means "shouted something in a very loud voice"? *Roared.*

 Angry.

In the story, the wolf is angry when the little pig keeps tricking him. That means the wolf is mad at the little pig. **Angry.** Say the word. *Angry.*

If you are angry, you are feeling mad at someone or something. Say the word that means "feeling mad at someone or something." *Angry.*

(Correct any incorrect responses, and repeat the item at the end of the sequence.)

Let's think about when people might feel angry. If I say a time when someone would feel angry, say, "Angry." If not, don't say anything.

- Your mom fixed your favorite meal.
- Your sister got you into trouble. *Angry.*
- Someone took your new coat. *Angry.*
- Your little brother broke your game. *Angry.*
- You won a great prize.
- She hit her thumb with a hammer. *Angry.*

What word means "feeling mad at someone or something"? *Angry.*

Show me how your face would look if you felt angry when someone pushed you in line. (Pause.) Tell me how you are feeling. *Angry.*

Present Vocabulary Tally Sheet
(See Week 1, page 3, for instructions.)

Assign Homework
(Homework Sheet, BLM 3a: See the Introduction for homework instructions.)

DAY 2

Preparation: Picture Vocabulary Cards for *gathering, meadow, roared,* and *angry.*

Read and Discuss Story

 (Read story aloud to children. Ask the following questions at the specified points.)

Now I'm going to read *The Three Little Pigs.* When I finish each part, I'll ask you some questions.

Page 1. What does the momma pig tell her three little pigs? *"Build good, strong houses, and always watch out for the wolf. Now goodbye, my sons, goodbye."*

Why do you think she tells her little pigs that? (Ideas: *So they would be safe; so the wolf wouldn't catch them; they were leaving.*)

Page 3. What does the first little pig use to build his house? *Straw.* Do you think the straw house will be a good, strong house? *No.* Tell why not.

Page 5. What happens when the wolf comes along? (Idea: *He blows the straw house down and eats the pig.*)

Page 7. What does the second little pig use to build his house? *Sticks.* Do you think the house made of sticks will be a good, strong house? *No.* Tell why not.

Page 10. What happens when the wolf comes along? (Idea: *He blows down the house made of sticks and eats the pig.*)

Page 11. What does the third little pig use to build his house? *Bricks.* Do you think the brick house will be a good, strong house? *Yes.* Tell why you think so.

Pages 14–15. What happens when the wolf comes along? (Idea: *He can't blow the brick house down.*)

Page 18. (Point to a turnip.) The vegetable in this picture is called a turnip. What is this vegetable called? *A turnip.* Why do you think the wolf invites the pig to the turnip field? (Idea: *He is trying to trick him into coming out of his house.*)

Page 19. Does the wolf's trick work? *No.* Tell why not. (Idea: *The pig goes to the turnip field before the wolf comes.*) How do you think the wolf will feel? (Idea: If children do not suggest *angry,* say, *"If I were the wolf, I'd probably feel angry."*)

How does the wolf feel when he finds out that the pig has tricked him? *Very angry.*

How does the wolf try to trick the pig next? (Idea: *He says he knows where the pig can get apples.*)

Does the wolf's trick work? *No.* Tell why not. (Idea: *The pig goes to the apple tree before the wolf comes.*)

Page 21. How does the wolf try to trick the pig next? (Idea: *He says he will take the pig to the fair in town.*) Does the wolf's trick work? *No.* Tell why not.

Page 25. What happens to the wolf? (Idea: *He falls into the pot and is cooked.*)

Page 27. How does the story end? (Idea: *The pig has wolf soup for supper.*)

Review Vocabulary

(Display the Picture Vocabulary Cards. Point to each card as you say the word.) These pictures show **gathering, meadow, roared,** and **angry.** (Ask children to repeat each word after you.)

- What word means "a field where grass and flowers grow"? *Meadow.*
- What word means "picking things up and putting them together in a pile"? *Gathering.*
- What word means "shouted something in a very loud voice"? *Roared.*
- What word means "feeling mad at someone or something"? *Angry.*

Extend Vocabulary

◎ Roared.

In the story *The Three Little Pigs,* we learned that **roared** is a word that means "shouted something in a very loud voice."

Here's a new way to use the word **roared.**

- **The plane roared down the runway.** Say the sentence.
- **The race car roared around the track.** Say the sentence.
- **The children roared around the house.** Say the sentence.

In these sentences, **roared** tells how people or things moved and sounded. The people or things moved very fast and made a loud noise. They roared.

Present Expanded Target Vocabulary

◎ Furious.

In the story, the wolf isn't able to catch the third little pig, so he becomes very, very angry. Another way of saying he is very, very angry is that he is furious. When you are furious, you are very, very angry. **Furious.** Say the word. *Furious.*

If you are furious, you are feeling very, very angry at someone or something. Say the word that means "feeling very, very angry at someone or something." *Furious.*

Let's think about when people might feel furious. If I say a time when someone would feel furious, say, "Furious." If not, don't say anything.

- How my mother would feel if I spilled my juice on purpose. *Furious.*
- How you would feel if you got a new bicycle for your birthday.
- How your teacher would feel if nobody listened. *Furious.*

- How your friend would feel if you shared your toys.
- How you would feel if you always got blamed for things you didn't do. *Furious.*
- If you were the only one who had to clean up after everybody made a big mess. *Furious.*

What word means "feeling very, very angry at someone or something?" *Furious.*

◎━ *Delicious.*

In the story, when the wolf eats the first little pig, he says, "Yumm-yum!" When he eats the second little pig, he says, "Yumm-yum!" Do you think the wolf likes the way the little pigs taste? *Yes.* The wolf thinks the little pigs tasted very, very good.

Another way of saying the little pigs taste very, very good is to say they are delicious. **When something tastes delicious, it tastes very, very good. Delicious.** Say the word. *Delicious.*

If something tastes delicious, it tastes very, very good. Say the word that means "tastes very, very good." *Delicious.*

Let's think about things that might taste delicious. If I say something that would taste delicious, say, "Delicious." If not, don't say anything.

- Ripe strawberries. *Delicious.*
- A red, juicy apple. *Delicious.*
- Sour lemons.
- A cold glass of milk. *Delicious.*
- A crunchy carrot. *Delicious.*
- Rotten grapes.

What word means "tastes very, very good"? *Delicious.*

At the end of the story, the third little pig eats wolf soup. He says, "Yumm-yum!" He thinks the wolf soup is … *Delicious.*

DAY 3

Preparation: Activity Sheet, BLM 3b.

Retell Story

(Show the pictures on the following pages, and call on a child to tell what's happening. Call on a different child for each section.)

Today I'll show you the pictures Margot Zemach made for *The Three Little Pigs.* As I show you the pictures, I'll call on one of you to tell the class that part of the story.

Pages 1–2. Tell what happens at the **beginning** of the story.

Pages 3–24. Tell what happens in the **middle** of the story. (Encourage use of target words when appropriate. Model use as necessary.)

Pages 25–27. Tell what happens at the **end** of the story. How do you think the third little pig felt? (Ideas: *Happy; good; full; proud; safe.*)

Review Show Me, Tell Me Game

Today you will play the Show Me, Tell Me Game. I'll ask you to show me how to do something. If you show me, you win one point. If you can't show me, I get the point.

Next I'll ask you to tell me. If you tell me, you win one point. If you can't tell me, I get the point.

Let's practice: My turn to show you how I would look if I felt angry because I had to stay after school. (Show an angry face.) How am I feeling? *Angry.*

Let's do one together. Show me how a race car would sound if it roared. (Roar like a race car with children.) What did the race car do? *It roared.*

Now you're ready to play the game.

(Draw a T-chart on the board for keeping score. Children earn one point for each correct answer. If they make an error, demonstrate the correct action, and tell them the word. Record one point for yourself, and repeat missed words at the end of the game.)

- Show me how you would **gather** up your toys from the floor. (Pause.) Tell me what you did. *Gathered toys from the floor.*
- Show me how a lion would sound if it **roared.** (Pause.) Tell me what the lion did. *It roared.*
- Show me how your face would look if you felt **angry** when someone broke your favorite toy. (Pause.) Tell me how you felt. *Angry.*
- Show me how you would **gather** flowers in the meadow. (Pause.) Tell me where you gathered flowers. *In the meadow.*

- Show me how a vacuum cleaner would sound if it **roared.** (Pause.) Tell me what the vacuum cleaner did. *It roared.*

(Count the points, and declare a winner.)
You did a great job of playing the Show Me, Tell Me Game!

Sequence: Beginning, Middle, End (Activity Sheet)

 (Give each child a copy of the Activity Sheet, BLM 3b. Review the order of the story with children. Tell them to place the pictures in sequence to show beginning, middle, and end. Instruct children to color the pictures, cut them out, and paste or glue them in order of beginning, middle, and end.)

DAY 4

Preparation: Prepare two sheets of chart paper, each with a circle drawn in the middle. Fold the sheets of paper in half vertically to divide the circles in half. When you record children's responses, physical descriptors should be recorded on the left-hand side of each chart. Personality characteristics or actions should be recorded on the right-hand side of each chart.

Literary Analysis (Analyze Characters)

Let's think about what we already know about how books are made.

- What do we call the name of the book? *The title.*
- What do we call the person who writes the story? *The author.*
- What do we call the person who draws the pictures? *The illustrator.*

Let's sing the first verses of "The Story Song" to help us remember some important things about books.

(See the Introduction for the complete "Story Song.")

Today we will learn more about how stories are made.

The characters in a story are the people or animals the story is about. What do we call the people or animals a story is about? *The characters.* Who are the characters in a story? *The people or animals the story is about.*

In the story *The Three Little Pigs,* are the characters people or animals? *Animals.*

Who are the characters in the story? (Call on individual children.) (Ideas: *Momma pig; the first little pig; the second little pig; the third little pig; the wolf.*)

The most important characters in the story about the three little pigs are the third little pig and the wolf. Who are the most important characters in the story? *The third little pig and the wolf.* (Write the words *third little pig* in the middle of the circle on one of the sheets of chart paper; write *wolf* in the middle of the circle on the other sheet.)

Let's remember what we know about the third little pig. (Show children page 11 of the book.) What does the third little pig look like? (Call on individual children. Record each child's response on the left-hand side of the pig chart.) (Ideas: *Long nose; blue pants; black jacket; wears a cap; has two toes.*)

(Show children page 12 of the book. Ask the questions below. Call on individual children. Record each child's response on the right-hand side of the chart.)

Do you think the third little pig is happy or sad? (Idea: *Happy.*) Tell why you think so. (Idea: *It looks like he's smiling.*) Do you think he likes to work hard or is lazy? (Idea: *Likes to work hard.*) Tell why you so. (Idea: *Building a brick house by himself is a lot of work.*)

(Show children the picture on page 18.) What does the third little pig like to eat? *Turnips.*

(Show children the picture on page 20.) What else does the third little pig like to eat? *Apples.* What else can you tell us about the third little pig? (Ideas: *He's smart; he likes to play tricks; he likes wolf soup.*)

(Follow a similar process to describe the wolf. Record responses on the second piece of chart paper.)

Today you have learned about the wolf and the third little pig. They are the two most important characters in the story *The Three Little Pigs*.

Now we'll learn a new verse to "The Story Song." Our sentence about characters will be "Characters make it happen."

Let's add that to the song by singing, "Characters make it happen." What are we going to add to our song? *Characters make it happen.*

> Read me a book, and the book pleased me.
> I read my book under yonder tree.
> **Characters make it happen.**
> Illustrator draws the pictures.
> Author says, "I'm who wrote it."
> Title says what its name is.
> Book says, "I'm a story."

Now we'll sing together all that we've learned.

Play Show Me, Tell Me Game (Cumulative Review)

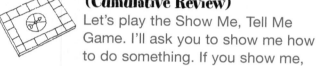

Let's play the Show Me, Tell Me Game. I'll ask you to show me how to do something. If you show me, you win one point. If you can't show me, I get the point.

Next I'll ask you to tell me. If you tell me, you will win one point. If you can't tell me, I get the point.

Now you're ready to play the game.

(Draw a T-chart on the board for keeping score. Children earn one point for each correct answer. If they make an error, correct them as you normally would, and record one point for yourself. Repeat missed words at the end of the game.)

- Show me what you would do if you **pleaded** with me to let you go to recess early. (Pause.) Tell me what you did. *Pleaded.*
- Show me how you would look if you were very, very **angry.** (Pause.) Tell me how you were feeling. *Furious.*
- Show me how you would look if I told you to wave and you didn't. (Pause.) Tell me how you acted. *Disobedient.*
- Show me how a crowd would sound if it **roared.** (Pause.) Tell me what the crowd did. *Roared.*

- Show me with your hand how a **winding** road would look. (Pause.) Tell me what kind of road you showed me. *A winding road.*
- Show me how you would gather flowers in the **meadow.** (Pause.) Tell me where you gathered flowers. *In the meadow.*
- Show me how you would look if you ate something that was very **delicious.** (Pause.) Tell me how what you ate tasted. *Delicious.*
- Show me what you would do if you **collected** seeds from the floor and put them in a cup. (Pause.) Tell me what you did. *Collected seeds.*
- Show me how you would look if you were **angry** with your friend for not playing with you. (Pause.) Tell me how you were feeling. *Angry.*
- Show me what you would do if you **prepared** your backpack for school. (Pause.) Tell me what you did to your backpack. *Prepared it for school.*

(Count the points, and declare a winner.)
You did a great job of playing the Show Me, Tell Me Game!

DAY 5

Preparation: Happy Face Game Test Sheet, BLM B.

Retell Story to a Partner

(Assign each child a partner, and ask the partners to take turns telling part of the story each time you turn to a new set of pages. Encourage use of target words when appropriate.)

Today I'll show you the pictures Margot Zemach made for her story *The Three Little Pigs*. As I show you the pictures, you and your partner will take turns telling part of the story.

Pages 1–2. Tell what happens at the **beginning** of the story. (Show the pictures from the story on pages 1 and 2.)

Pages 3–24. Tell what happens in the **middle** of the story. (Show the pictures from the story on pages 3 through 24.)

Pages 25–27. Tell what happens at the **end** of the story. (Show the pictures from the story on pages 25 through 27.)

How do you think the third little pig feels? (Ideas: *Happy; good; full; proud; safe.*)

Happy Face Game (Assess Vocabulary)

(Give each child a copy of the Happy Face Game Test Sheet, BLM B.)

Today you're going to play the Happy Face Game. When you play the Happy Face Game, it helps me know how well you know the hard words you are learning.

If I say something true, color the happy face. What will you do if I say something true? *Color the happy face.*

If I say something false, color the sad face. What will you do if I say something false? *Color the sad face.*

Listen carefully to each sentence I say. Don't let me trick you!

Item 1: If you are **furious,** you are very, very angry. *True.*

Item 2: If you are in a place with lots of tall trees, you are in a **meadow.** *False.*

Item 3: If you are **starving,** you are **not** very hungry. *False.*

Item 4: If you are **angry,** you are mad. *True.*

Item 5: If you are picking your toys up off the floor, you are **gathering** up your toys. *True.*

Item 6: If a lion **roared,** it made a very quiet sound. *False.*

Item 7: If you ate a meal that tasted good, you would say, "That was **delicious**!" *True.*

Item 8: A **winding** road goes in a straight line. *False.*

Item 9: **Pleaded** means "asked for something with all your heart; begged for something." *True.*

Item 10: If you are kind and helpful to others, you are a **considerate** person. *True.*

You did a great job of playing the Happy Face Game!

(Score children's work. Scores of 9 out of 10 indicate mastery. If a child does not achieve mastery, insert the missed words in the games in next week's lessons. Retest those children individually for the missed items before they take the next mastery test.)

Extensions
Read a Story as a Reward

(Display several books you have read since the beginning of the program or alternate versions of *The Three Little Pigs.* Allow children to choose which book they would like you to read aloud to them as a reward for their hard work.)

(Read story to children for enjoyment with minimal interruptions.)

Present Super Words Center

(Prepare the word containers for the Super Words Center. See the Introduction for instructions on how to set up and use the Super Words Center.)

(Add the new Picture Vocabulary Cards to words from the previous weeks. Show children one of the word containers. If they need more guidance, role-play with two or three children as a demonstration.)

Let's think about how we work with our words in the Super Words Center.

You will work with a partner in the Super Words Center. Whom will you work with in the center? *A partner.*

First you will draw a word out of the container. What do you do first? (Idea: *Draw a word out of the container.*)

Next you will show your partner the picture and ask what word the picture shows. What do you do next? (Idea: *I show my partner the picture and ask what word the picture shows.*)

What do you do next? *Give my partner a turn.*

What do you do if your partner doesn't know the word? *Tell my partner the word.*

Preparation: You will need *The Little Red Hen* for each day's lesson.

Number the pages of the story to assist you in asking questions at appropriate points.

Post a copy of the Vocabulary Tally Sheet, BLM A, with this week's Picture Vocabulary Cards attached.

Each child will need the Homework Sheet, BLM 4a.

DAY 1

Introduce Book

Today's book is called *The Little Red Hen.* What's the title of this week's book? *The Little Red Hen.*

This book was written by Margot Zemach [Mar-go Zem-ack]. Who's the author of *The Little Red Hen*? *Margot Zemach.*

Margot Zemach also made the pictures for this book. Remember, an illustrator is the person who makes the pictures for a book or a story. Who's the illustrator of *The Little Red Hen*? *Margot Zemach.*

The cover of a book usually gives us some hints of what the book is about. Let's look at the front cover of *The Little Red Hen.* What do you see in the illustration? (Ideas: *I see the little red hen; I see her three babies; the hen is wearing clothes; one baby has a hat.*)

(**Note:** If children do not use the word *chicks*, introduce it, saying:) Baby chickens are called chicks. What are baby chickens called? *Chicks.* What are chicks? *Baby chickens.*

(Assign each child a partner.) Remember, when you make a prediction about something, you say what you think will happen. What do you do when you make a prediction about something? *You say what you think will happen.*

Get ready to make some predictions to your partner about this book. Use the information from the cover to help you.

The Little Red Hen
author: Margot Zemach • illustrator: Margot Zemach

Target Vocabulary

Tier II	Tier III
cottage	character
harvest	
grains	
sprouted	
*determined	
*uncooperative	

* Expanded Target Vocabulary Word

(Ask the following questions, allowing sufficient time for children to share their predictions with their partners.)

- Whom do you think this story is about?
- What do you think the hen in the story will do?
- Where do you think the story happens?
- When do you think this story happens?
- Why do you think the birds are doing what they are doing?
- How do you think the birds are feeling?
- Do you think this story is about real birds? Tell why or why not.

(Call on several children to share their predictions with the class.)

Take a Picture Walk

We are going to take a picture walk through this book. Remember, when we take a picture walk, we look at the pictures and tell what we think will happen in the story.

(Show the illustrations on the following pages, and ask the specified questions.)

Page 1. Where do you think the chickens are? (Idea: *At home.*) Why do you think so? (Ideas: *I can see the lamp, the chairs, and the toys.*) What do you think is happening? (Ideas: *The chicks are playing; the hen is holding a towel.*) How do you think the hen is feeling? *Happy.* Tell me why you think so. (Idea: *It looks like she's smiling or talking or singing.*)

Pages 2–3. What do you think is happening here? (Ideas: *The hen is talking to the goose, the cat, and the pig; the goose, the cat, and the pig look like they are walking away.*)

Pages 4–5. What do you think is happening here? (Idea: *The hen is planting some seeds.*)

Pages 6–7. What do you think is happening here? (Ideas: *The seeds have come up; the plants are growing.*)

Pages 8–9. What do you think the hen is saying to the other animals?

Pages 10–11. What is the hen doing? (Idea: *Cutting down the plants.*) What are the other animals doing? (Idea: *Watching the hen work.*) How do you think the hen is feeling? Why do you think so? (Accept any reasonable responses as long as children give a reason why they think so.)

Pages 12–13. What are the goose, the cat, and the pig doing? (Idea: *Playing cards.*) How do you think the hen is feeling now? (Idea: *Tired.*) Why do you think so? (Ideas: *She is wiping her head; she is sitting down.*)

Pages 14–15. Who is the only one working? *The hen.*

Pages 16–17. What are the goose, the cat, and the pig doing now? (Idea: *Sitting on a bench.*) What do you think the hen is saying to the other animals?

Pages 18–19. What is the hen doing? (Idea: *Pushing the wagon.*)

Pages 20–21. What are the goose, the cat, and the pig doing now? (Idea: *Playing cards.*) What do you think the hen is saying to the other animals?

Pages 22–23. What do you think is happening here? (Idea: *The hen is baking bread.*)

Pages 26–27. What do you think the hen is saying to the other animals?

Page 28. What do you think is happening here? (Idea: *The hen and her chicks are eating the bread she made.*)

Now that we've finished our picture walk, it's your turn to ask me some questions. What would you like to know about the story? (Accept questions. If children tell about the pictures or

the story instead of asking questions, prompt them to ask a question.) Ask me a why question. Ask me a how question.

Read Story Aloud

(Read story aloud to children with minimal interruptions.)

In the next lesson we will read the story again, and I will ask you some questions.

(**Note:** If children have difficulty attending for an extended period of time, present the next part of this day's lesson at another time.)

Present Target Vocabulary

⊙← *Cottage.*

In the story, the little red hen lives with her chicks in a small cottage. That means they live in a small house. Cottages are often built in the country or near a beach. **Cottage.** Say the word. *Cottage.*

If you live in a cottage, you are living in a small house in the country or near a beach. Say the word that means "a small house in the country or near a beach." *Cottage.*

(Correct any incorrect responses, and repeat the item at the end of the sequence.)

Let's think about cottages. I'll tell you something. If what I say could be about a cottage, you say, "Cottage." If what I say would not be about a cottage, say, "Absolutely not."

- A small family could live there. *Cottage.*
- It would have 100 rooms. *Absolutely not.*
- It might be built near a beach. *Cottage.*
- It would have ten bathrooms. *Absolutely not.*
- Fifty families could live there. *Absolutely not.*
- Jack and his mother lived there before he climbed the bean stalk. *Cottage.*

What word means "a small house in the country or near a beach"? *Cottage.*

⊙← *Harvest.*

In the story, the little red hen asks the goose, the cat, and the pig to help her harvest the wheat. That means she asks them to help her gather the wheat from her garden. **Harvest.** Say the word. *Harvest.*

When you harvest something like wheat or potatoes, you gather these plants so you can

use them for food. **Plants that you gather for food are called crops.** Say the word that means to "gather crops so you can use them for food." *Harvest.*

(Correct any incorrect responses, and repeat the item at the end of the sequence.)

Let's think about things that you harvest. I'll name something. If you could harvest that thing, say, "Harvest." If not, don't say anything.

- Corn. *Harvest.*
- Pumpkins. *Harvest.*
- Jelly beans.
- Cars.
- Cows.
- Wheat. *Harvest.*

What word means to "gather crops so you can use them for food"? *Harvest.*

◉━ *Grains.*

In the story, the little red hen collects the golden grains from the wheat and pours them into a large sack. That means the hen collects the seeds from the wheat. **Grains.** Say the word. *Grains.*

Grains are seeds of plants such as wheat, oats, or rice. Say the word that means "the seeds of plants such as wheat, oat, or rice." *Grains.*

(Correct any incorrect responses, and repeat the item at the end of the sequence.)

Let's think about things that are grains. I'll name something. If the things I name are grains, say, "Grains." If not, don't say anything.

- Rice. *Grains.*
- Wheat. *Grains.*
- Oats. *Grains.*
- Potatoes.
- Oranges.
- Green beans.

What word means "the seeds of plants such as wheat, oats, or rice"? *Grains.*

◉━ *Sprouted.*

In the story, the little red hen planted grains of wheat and they sprouted. That means grains of wheat started to grow roots and leaves. **Sprouted.** Say the word. *Sprouted.*

If a seed sprouted, it started to grow roots and leaves. Say the word that means "started to grow roots and leaves." *Sprouted.*

(Correct any incorrect responses, and repeat the item at the end of the sequence.)

Let's think about things that might sprout. I'll name something. If that thing sprouted, say, "Sprouted." If not, don't say anything.

- The bean seed grew roots and leaves. *Sprouted.*
- The carrot seed grew roots and leaves. *Sprouted.*
- The apple tree grew flowers.
- Pears came on the pear tree.
- The baby lamb was born.
- The potato grew new roots and leaves. *Sprouted.*

What word means "started to grow roots and leaves"? *Sprouted.*

Present Vocabulary Tally Sheet
(See Week 1, page 3, for instructions.)

Assign Homework
(Homework Sheet, BLM 4a: See the Introduction for homework instructions.)

DAY 2

Preparation: Picture Vocabulary Cards for *cottage, harvest, grains,* and *sprouted.*

Read and Discuss Story
(Read story aloud to children. Ask the following questions at the specified points.)

Now I'm going to read *The Little Red Hen.* When I finish each part, I'll ask you some questions.

Page 1. Where does the little red hen live? *In a cottage.* Is she a good mother to her little chicks? *Yes.* Tell why you think so. (Idea: *She works hard to feed her chicks.*)

Page 2. What does the little red hen find? *A few grains of wheat.* What does she ask her friends? *"Who will plant this wheat?"* What do her friends say? *"Not I."*

Page 4. Who plants the seeds? *The little red hen.*

Pages 6–7. How do you think the hen and her chicks feel when they see the wheat has sprouted? (Ideas: *Happy; excited.*)

Page 9. What does she ask her friends? *"Who will harvest this wheat?"* What do her friends say? *"Not I."*

Page 11. Who harvests the wheat? *The little red hen.*

Page 12. (Read to the end of the first sentence: "At last the wheat was all cut down and it was time for it to be threshed.") When you thresh wheat, you separate the grains from the rest of the plant. What do you do when you separate the wheat grains from the rest of the plant? *You thresh the wheat.* What are you doing when you thresh wheat? *Separating the grains of wheat from the rest of the plant.*

Page 12. (Read to the end of the page.) What does she ask her friends? *"Who will thresh this wheat?"* What do her friends say? *"Not I."*

Page 15. Who threshes the wheat? *The little red hen.*

Page 17. What does she ask her friends? *"Who will take this wheat to the mill to be ground into flour?"* What do her friends say? *"Not I."*

Page 19. Who takes the wheat to the mill to be ground into flour? *The little red hen.*

Page 20. What does she ask her friends? *"Who will bake this flour into a lovely loaf of bread?"* What do her friends say? *"Not I."*

Page 23. Who bakes the flour into a lovely loaf of bread? *The little red hen.*

Page 25. What does she ask her friends? *"Who will eat this lovely loaf of bread?"* What do her friends say? *"I will!"*

Page 28. How does the story end? (Idea: *The little red hen and her chicks eat the bread.*)

We learned a word from the story *The Three Little Pigs* that might tell how the bread tasted. How do you think the bread tasted? *Delicious.*

Why doesn't the little red hen share her bread with the goose, the cat, and the pig? (Idea: *They don't help her when she asks them to.*) Do you think that is fair? *Yes.*

Predict what you think the goose, the cat, and the pig will do the next time the little red hen asks them for help.

Review Vocabulary

(Display the Picture Vocabulary Cards. Point to each card as you say the word.) These pictures show **cottage, harvest, grains,** and **sprouted.** (Ask children to repeat each word after you.)

- What word means means "the seeds of plants such as wheat, oats, or rice"? *Grains.*
- What word means "started to grow roots and leaves"? *Sprouted.*
- What word means to "gather crops so you can use them for food"? *Harvest.*
- What word means "a small house in the country or near a beach"? *Cottage.*

Extend Vocabulary

◎⊸ *Grains.*

In the story *The Little Red Hen,* we learned that grains are the seeds of plants such as rice, oats, or wheat.

Here's a new way to use the word **grain.**

- **He had a grain of sand in his shoe.** Say the sentence.
- **There was only one grain of salt left in the salt shaker.** Say the sentence.
- **The ant carried a grain of sugar back to its nest.** Say the sentence.

A grain of wheat, oats, and rice is a hard, tiny seed. In these sentences, grain means "a hard, tiny piece of something."

Present Expanded Target Vocabulary
◎⊸ *Determined.*

In the story, the little red hen never gives up when no one will help her. She just keeps working and working and working. She really wants to make her bread with wheat she has grown herself. She won't let anything stop her.

Another way of saying she has made up her mind and won't let anything stop her is to say she is determined. When you are determined, you know what you want to do, and you won't let anything stop you. **Determined.** Say the word. *Determined.*

If you are determined, you have made up your mind about something, and you won't let anything stop you. Say the word that means "you have made up your mind about something, and you won't let anything stop you." *Determined.*

Let's think about when people might feel determined. If I say a time when someone would feel determined, say, "Determined." If not, don't say anything.

- How you would feel if you wanted to finish all of your work before going home. *Determined.*
- How you would feel at the beach on a warm Saturday.
- How you would feel if you wanted to save enough money for a new bike. *Determined.*
- How you and your mom would feel watching a video together.
- How you would feel if you wanted to be first in a race. *Determined.*
- How you would feel if everyone said you couldn't do something but you knew you could. *Determined.*

What word means "you have made up your mind about something, and you won't let anything stop you"? *Determined.*

◎⚡ Uncooperative.

In the story, the goose, the cat, and the pig won't help the little red hen. Every time she asks them for help, they say no. They won't do anything to help the little red hen.

Another way of saying the goose, the cat, and the pig won't do anything to help the little red hen is to say they are uncooperative. When you are uncooperative, you won't do anything to help anyone else. **Uncooperative.** Say the word. *Uncooperative.*

If you are uncooperative, you won't do anything to help anyone else. Say the word that means "won't do anything to help anyone else." *Uncooperative.*

Let's think about times when someone might be uncooperative. If I tell about a time when someone is being uncooperative, say, "Uncooperative." If not, don't say anything.

- You drop all of your crayons on the floor, and no one listens when you ask for help. *Uncooperative.*
- It's clean-up time, but the only person who will clean up is you. *Uncooperative.*
- Your friend helps you fix your bike.
- You are trying to move a bench, but no one will pick up the other end. *Uncooperative.*
- No one listens to your instructions. *Uncooperative.*
- Everyone plays well together.

What word means "won't do anything to help anyone else"? *Uncooperative.*

Tell about a time when you were uncooperative. **(Call on several children. Encourage children to start their answers with the words "I was uncooperative when …")**

(After each response, ask the child:) What might you have done to be more cooperative?

Retell Story

(Show the pictures on the following pages from the story, and call on a child to tell what's happening. Call on a different child for each section.)

Today I'll show you the pictures Margot Zemach made for her story *The Little Red Hen.* As I show you the pictures, I'll call on one of you to tell the class that part of the story.

Pages 1–3. Tell what happens at the **beginning** of the story.

Pages 4–25. Tell what happens in the **middle** of the story. (Encourage use of target words when appropriate. Model use as necessary.)

Pages 26–28. Tell what happens at the **end** of the story.

How do you think the bread tasted? (Idea: *Delicious.*)

Review Show Me, Tell Me Game

Today you will play the Show Me, Tell Me Game. I'll ask you to show me how to do something. If you show me, you win one point. If you can't show me, I get the point.

Next I'll ask you to tell me. If you tell me, you win one point. If you can't tell me, I get the point.

Let's practice: My turn to show you how I would act if I were being **uncooperative.** (Act out refusing to put away your books.) How am I acting? *Uncooperative.*

Let's do one together. Show me how we would harvest a field of carrots. (Stoop and pick carrots with the children and put them in a pretend bag.) What did we do? (Respond with children.) *We harvested carrots.*

Now you're ready to play the game.

(Draw a T-chart on the board for keeping score. Children earn one point for each correct answer. If they make an error, demonstrate the action, and tell them the correct word. Record one point for yourself and repeat missed words at the end of the game.)

- Show me what you would do if you were picking up **grains** of rice on the table. (Pause.) Tell me what you were doing. *Picking up grains of rice.*
- Show me how you would **sprout** if you were a tiny seed. (Pause.) Tell me what you did. *Sprouted.*
- Show me how you would **harvest** a great crop of apples. (Pause.) Tell me what you were doing. *Harvesting apples.*
- Show me how you would look if you wanted to be the best at something. (Pause.) Tell me how you looked. *Determined.*
- Show me how you would act if I asked to you clean up and you did other things instead. (Pause.) Tell me how you were acting. *Uncooperative.*

(Count the points, and declare a winner.)
You did a great job of playing the Show Me, Tell Me Game!

Sequence: Beginning, Middle, End (Activity Sheet)

(Give each child a copy of the Activity Sheet, BLM 4b. Review the order of the story with children. Tell them to place the pictures in sequence to show beginning, middle, and end. Instruct children to color the pictures, cut them out, and paste or glue them in order of beginning, middle, and end.)

DAY 4

Preparation: Prepare two sheets of chart paper, each with a circle drawn in the middle. Fold the sheets of paper in half vertically to divide the circles in half. When you record children's responses, physical descriptors should be recorded on the left-hand side of each chart. Personality characteristics or actions should be recorded on the right-hand side of each chart.

Analyze Characters (Literary Analysis)

Let's think about what we already know about how books are made.

- What do we call the name of the book? *The title.*
- What do we call the person who writes the story? *The author.*
- What do we call the person who draws the pictures? *The illustrator.*
- What do we call the people or animals a story is about? *The characters.*

Let's sing the verses we've learned of "The Story Song" to help us remember these important things about books. (See the Introduction for the complete "Story Song.")

Today we will learn more about the characters in a story.

The characters in a story are the people or animals the story is about. What do we call the people or animals a story is about? *The characters.* Who are the characters in a story? *The people or animals the story is about.*

In the story *The Little Red Hen,* are the characters people or animals? *Animals.*

Who are the characters in the story? (Ideas: *The little red hen, her chicks, the goose, the cat, and the pig.*)

The most important characters in *The Little Red Hen* are the little red hen and her three friends. Who are the most important characters in the story? *The little red hen and her three friends.* (Write the words *little red hen* in the center of the circle on one of the sheets of chart paper; write *three friends* in the center of the circle on the other sheet.)

(Show children the pages from the story, and ask the specified questions. Call on individual children, recording each child's response on the left-hand side of the hen chart.)

Let's remember what we know about the little red hen.

Pages 18–19. What does the little red hen look like? (Ideas: *Red feathers; wears hat; wears a dress; sometimes wears an apron; has a beak; uses her wings for hands.*)

Pages 14–15. (Ask these questions. Call on individual children. Record each child's response on the right-hand side of the chart.) Do you think the little red hen works hard or is lazy? (Idea: *Works hard.*) Tell why you think that. (Idea: *She's threshing the wheat.*) What other things does she do that show you she works hard? (Ideas: *She plants the seeds; she harvests the wheat; she takes the flour to the mill; she makes the bread.*)

Pages 18–19. We learned a new word that means the little red hen really wants to make her bread with wheat she had grown herself. She won't let anything stop her. What word could we use to tell about the little red hen? She is … *Determined.*

Page 28. What does the little red hen like to eat? *Bread.* What else can you tell us about the little red hen? (Ideas: *She's a good mother; she likes to sing.*)

(Follow a similar process to describe the three friends. When describing the appearance of the three friends, write the words *goose, cat,* and *pig* as headings down the left-hand side of the chart paper. Record appropriate descriptive words under each heading.)

(When describing the personalities of the three friends, record words or phrases common to all the animals: lazy, like to play cards, uncooperative, like to sit in the sun, like homemade bread. Record responses on the right-hand side of the second piece of chart paper.)

Today you have learned about the little red hen and her three friends. They are the most important characters in the story *The Little Red Hen.*

Play Show Me, Tell Me Game (Cumulative Review)

Let's play the Show Me, Tell Me Game. I'll ask you to show me how to do something. If you show me, you win one point. If you can't show me, I get the point.

Next I'll ask you to tell me. If you tell me, you win one point. If you can't tell me, I get the point.

Now you're ready to play the game.

(Draw a T-chart on the board for keeping score. Children earn one point for each correct answer. If they make an error, correct them as you normally would, and record one point for yourself. Repeat missed words at the end of the game.)

- Show me how you would look if you just spent the weekend at a **cottage** at the beach. (Pause.) Tell me where you were, looking so happy. *At a cottage at the beach.*
- Show me what you would do if you were **harvesting** corn. (Pause.) Tell me what you were doing. *Harvesting corn.*
- Show me what you would do if you were **gathering** grains of salt on the table. (Pause.) Tell me what you were doing. *Gathering grains of salt.*
- Show me how a seed would look if it **sprouted.** (Pause.) Tell me what the seed did. *Sprouted.*
- Show me how you would look if you were **determined** to finish reading a book before recess. (Pause.) Tell me how you looked. *Determined.*

- Show me how it looks to be **uncooperative** when it's time to clean up. (Pause.) Tell me how you looked. *Uncooperative.*
- Show me how you would look if you were a farmer with a handful of **grains.** (Pause.) Tell me what you have in your hands. *Grains.*
- Show me what your face looks like when you eat something **delicious.** (Pause.) Tell me how it tastes. *Delicious.*
- Show me how you look when you are **gathering** workbooks and putting them away. (Pause.) Tell me what you were doing to the workbooks. *Gathering them.*
- Show me how you would look if you were a lion and you **roared.** (Pause.) Tell me what the lion did. *Roared.*

(Count the points, and declare a winner.)
You did a great job of playing the Show Me, Tell Me Game!

DAY 5

....
Preparation: Happy Face Game Test
Sheet, BLM B.
....

Retell Story to a Partner

(Assign each child a partner, and ask the partners to take turns telling part of the story each time you turn to a new set of pages. Encourage use of target words when appropriate.)

Today I'll show you the pictures Margot Zemach made for her story *The Little Red Hen.* As I show you the pictures, you and your partner will take turns telling part of the story.

Pages 1–3. Tell what happens at the **beginning** of the story.

Pages 4–25. Tell what happens in the **middle** of the story.

Pages 26–28. Tell what happens at the **end** of the story.

How do you think the hen feels at the end of the story? (Ideas: *Happy; good; full.*)

How do you think the friends feel at the end of the story? (Ideas: *Sad; hungry; starving; sorry; embarrassed.*)

Happy Face Game (Assess Vocabulary)

 (Give each child a copy of the Happy Face Game Test Sheet, BLM B.)

Today you're going to play the Happy Face Game. When you play the Happy Face Game, it helps me know how well you know the hard words you are learning.

If I say something true, color the happy face. What will you do if I say something true? *Color the happy face.*

If I say something false, color the sad face. What will you do if I say something false? *Color the sad face.*

Listen carefully to each sentence I say. Don't let me trick you!

Item 1: A **cottage** is a castle with one hundred rooms. *False.*

Item 2: When you **harvest** vegetables, you **gather** them so that you can eat them. *True.*

Item 3: If you are **cross** with someone, you are happy about something he or she has done. *False.*

Item 4: If you are **starving,** you are very, very hungry. *True.*

Item 5: When you are **determined,** you try hard. *True.*

Item 6: **Uncooperative** people always help. *False.*

Item 7: **Grains** of rice are the size of apples. *False.*

Item 8: You are **desperate** when you want something very, very badly. *True.*

Item 9: A **considerate** person pays attention to what someone else needs. *True.*

Item 10: When a seed starts to grow leaves and roots, we say that it **sprouted.** *True.*

You did a great job of playing the Happy Face Game!

(Score children's work. Scores of 9 out of 10 indicate mastery. If a child does not achieve mastery, include the missed words in the games in next week's lessons. Retest those children individually on the missed items before they take the next mastery test.)

Extensions
Read a Story as a Reward

 (Display the three books you have read since the beginning of the program or alternate versions of *The Little Red Hen.* Allow children to choose which book they would like you to read aloud to them as a reward for their hard work.)

(Read story to children for enjoyment with minimal interruptions.)

Present Super Words Center

(Prepare the word containers for the Super Words Center. See the Introduction for instructions on how to set up and use the Super Words Center.)

(Add the new Picture Vocabulary Cards to words from the previous weeks. Show children one of the word containers. If they need more guidance, role-play with two or three children as a demonstration.)

Let's think about how we work with our words in the Super Words Center.

You will work with a partner in the Super Words Center. Whom will you work with in the center? *A partner.*

First you will draw a word out of the container. What do you do first? (Idea: *Draw a word out of the container.*)

Next you will show your partner the picture and ask what word the picture shows. What do you do next? (Idea: *I show my partner the picture and ask what word the picture shows.*)

What do you do next? *Give my partner a turn.*

What do you do if your partner doesn't know the word? *Tell my partner the word.*

Preparation: You will need *The Three Billy Goats Gruff* for each day's lesson.

Post a copy of the Vocabulary Tally Sheet, BLM A, with this week's Picture Vocabulary Cards attached.

Each child will need the Homework Sheet, BLM 5a.

DAY 1

Introduce Book

Today's book is called *The Three Billy Goats Gruff.* What's the title of this week's book? *The Three Billy Goats Gruff.*

This book was written by Betty Jane Wagner. Who's the author of *The Three Billy Goats Gruff*? *Betty Jane Wagner.*

Shirley Cribb Breuel (Brew-al) made the pictures for this book. Who's the illustrator of *The Three Billy Goats Gruff*? *Shirley Cribb Breuel.*

The cover of a book usually gives us some hints of what the book is about. Let's look at the front cover of *The Three Billy Goats Gruff.* What do you see in the illustration on this cover? (Ideas: *Three goats; some mushrooms; a river; a frog; a bridge over the river.*)

(Assign each child a partner.) Remember, when you make a prediction about something, you say what you think will happen. Now get ready to make some predictions to your partner about this book. Use the information from the cover to help you.

(Ask the following questions, allowing sufficient time for children to share their predictions with their partners.)

- Whom do you think this story is about?
- What do you think the goats in the story will do?
- Where do you think the story happens?
- When do you think the story happens?
- Why do you think the sign on the bridge says "Keep Off"?
- How do you think the goats are feeling?
- Do you think this story is about real goats? Tell why or why not.

The Three Billy Goats Gruff
author: Betty Jane Wagner • illustrator: Shirley Cribb Breuel

Target Vocabulary

Tier II	Tier III
decided	character
shouted	
squeaked	
muttered	
*starving	
*disagreeable	

*Expanded Target Vocabulary Word

(Call on several children to share their predictions with the class.)

Take a Picture Walk

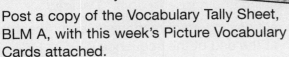
We are going to take a picture walk through this book. Remember, when we take a picture walk, we look at the pictures and tell what we think will happen in the story.

(Show the illustrations on the following pages, and ask the specified questions.)

Page 3. Where do you think the goats are? (Idea: *Where no green plants grow.*) Why do you think so? (Ideas: *I can't see any leaves; there is no grass; I can see only mushrooms growing.*)

Pages 4–5. What do you notice about the land on the other side of the river? (Ideas: *There are lots of bushes; the grass is green.*)

Pages 6–7. What do you see under the bridge? (Idea: *A person with big eyes and a long nose is sitting on a book; a frog with big eyes; a boat; a clock; a candle in a teacup; a lantern with a candle; a broken umbrella; a thing with N, S, E, and W.*) The thing with the N, S, E, and W is a weather vane. It turns with the wind to tell you which direction the wind is blowing. The letters stand for north, south, east, and west.

Pages 8–9. What do you think is happening here? (Idea: *The goats are standing at the edge of the river.*)

Pages 10–11. What do you think the man is saying to the goat on the bridge? How do you think the man is feeling? (Idea: *Angry.*)

Pages 14–15. Where is the goat now? (Idea: *On the green side of the river.*)

Pages 16–17. What do you think the man is saying to the goat on the bridge? How do you think the man is feeling? (Idea: *Angry.*)

Pages 20–21. Where is the goat now? (Idea: *On the green side of the river.*)

Pages 22–23. What do you think the man is saying to the goat? How do you think the man is feeling? (Idea: *Angry.*)

Pages 26–27. Where is the goat now? (Idea: *On the bridge.*)

What do you think the man is saying to the goat? How do you think the man is feeling? (Idea: *Angry.*)

Pages 28–29. How do you think the goat is feeling? How do you think the man is feeling? (Idea: *Angry.*)

Pages 30–31. What do you think is happening here? (Idea: *The man is falling into the river.*)

Now that we've finished our picture walk, it's your turn to ask me some questions. What would you like to know about the story? (Accept questions. If they tell about the pictures or the story instead of asking questions, prompt them to ask a question.) Ask me a what question. Ask me a how question.

Read Story Aloud
(Read story aloud to children with minimal interruptions.)

In the next lesson we will read the story again, and I will ask you some questions.

(**Note:** If children have difficulty attending for an extended period of time, present the next part of this day's lesson at another time.)

Present Target Vocabulary

◎—◁ Decided.

In the story, Big Billy Goat Gruff and Middle Billy Goat Gruff decided to send Little Billy Goat Gruff across the river. That means that, after they thought about it, they chose to send Little

Billy Goat Gruff across the river. They decided to send him across the river. **Decided.** Say the word. *Decided.*

If you decided to do something, you carefully thought about it and then chose to do it. Say the word that means "carefully thought about something and chose to do it." *Decided.*

(Correct any incorrect responses, and repeat the item at the end of the sequence.)

Let's think about things that you might decide to do. I'll name something. If you could decide to do that thing, say, "Decided." If not, don't say anything.

- The family thought about it and chose to move to Seattle. *Decided.*
- You thought about it and chose to buy flowers for Mother's Day. *Decided.*
- The sun is shining.
- It is hot outside.
- Dad thought about it and chose to buy a new lawn mower. *Decided.*
- You thought about it and chose to have fish for dinner. *Decided.*

What word means "carefully thought about something and chose to do it"? *Decided.*

◎—◁ Shouted.

In the story, the troll shouted at the billy goats when they tried to cross the bridge. That means he used a very loud voice to speak to the goats. He was angry at the goats for trying to cross his bridge. **Shouted.** Say the word. *Shouted.*

When you shout at someone, you use a very loud voice to speak to that person. You might use a very loud voice because you are angry. Say the word that means "used a very loud voice to speak to someone." *Shouted.*

(Correct any incorrect responses, and repeat the item at the end of the sequence.)

Let's think about some times when you would shout at someone. I'll name a time. If you would have shouted, say, "Shouted." If not, don't say anything.

- Your friend dropped a heavy book on your toe. *Shouted.*
- Your little brother broke your favorite toy. *Shouted.*

- Your mom said, "Hi!"
- A car drove by.
- Your dog ate your hot dog. *Shouted.*
- Your friend tripped you, and you scraped your knee. *Shouted.*

What word means "used a very loud voice to speak to someone"? *Shouted.*

In *The Three Little Pigs,* we learned another word that means "shouted something in a very loud voice." What was that word? *Roared.* That's right; **roared** and **shouted** mean the same thing. What two words mean the same thing? *Roared and shouted.*

◎–< Squeaked.

In the story, when the troll shouted at Little Billy Goat Gruff, saying, "Who is that trip-trapping across my river bridge?" Little Billy Goat squeaked, "It is only I, Little Billy Goat Gruff." That means he used a very high voice to answer the troll's question. He was afraid of the troll. He used a voice that was like the sound a mouse makes. **Squeaked.** Say the word. *Squeaked.*

When you squeak at someone, you use a very high voice to speak to him or her. You might use a very high voice because you are afraid. Say the word that means "used a very high voice to speak to someone." *Squeaked.*

(Correct any incorrect responses, and repeat the item at the end of the sequence.)

Let's think about some times when you would squeak to someone. I'll name a time. If you would have squeaked, say, "Squeaked." If not, don't say anything.

- You thought there was a creature under your bed. *Squeaked.*
- It was dark, and you heard a noise downstairs. *Squeaked.*
- You walked to school.
- You helped to clean the yard.
- You called for help when the water got too deep. *Squeaked.*
- You did your homework.

What word means "used a very high voice to speak to someone"? *Squeaked.*

◎–< Muttered.

In the story, the troll muttered that he would wait for Little Billy Goat's brother to come so he could eat him. That means the troll spoke in a quiet voice so the goats couldn't hear him. Usually when someone mutters, it means he or she is unhappy about something. **Muttered.** Say the word. *Muttered.*

When you mutter, you use a very quiet voice to speak, and you may be unhappy about something. Say the word that means "used a very quiet voice because you were unhappy about something." *Muttered.*

(Correct any incorrect responses, and repeat the item at the end of the sequence.)

Let's think about some times when you would mutter. I'll name a time. If you would have muttered, say, "Muttered." If not, don't say anything.

- Your mom told you that you had to clean your room before you could play. *Muttered.*
- Your dad said that you couldn't watch television. *Muttered.*
- You saw a big dog.
- The stars came out.
- You could see the mountains in the distance.
- The babysitter told you to go to bed before it was time. *Muttered.*

What word means "used a very quiet voice because you were unhappy about something"? *Muttered.*

Shouted, squeaked, and **muttered** are three words that tell how people said something. What three words tell how people said something? *Shouted, squeaked, and muttered.*

(Mutter "Oh, it's too early for me to go to bed. I don't want to go to bed right now.") Tell me if I shouted, squeaked, or muttered. *Muttered.*

(Shout "Owwww! Please be careful where you step!") Tell me if I shouted, squeaked, or muttered. *Shouted.*

(Squeak "Hello? Mom? Dad? Is somebody downstairs?") Tell me if I shouted, squeaked, or muttered. *Squeaked.*

Present Vocabulary Tally Sheet

(See Week 1, page 3, for instructions.)

Assign Homework

(Homework Sheet, BLM 5a: See the Introduction for homework instructions.)

DAY 2

Preparation: Picture Vocabulary Cards for *decided, shouted, squeaked,* and *muttered.*

 Read and Discuss Story

(Read story aloud to children. Ask the following questions at the specified points.)

Page 5. Where do the goats live? (Idea: *On a hillside.*) What is wrong with their home? (Idea: *There is no grass.*) What has happened to all the grass on their side of the river? (Idea: *The goats have eaten it.*)

Page 7. Who lives under the bridge? *A troll.* A troll is a pretend man. Trolls are mean and ugly. They live under bridges and in caves. Are trolls real? *No.* That's right; trolls are only in stories. Where do trolls live? *Under bridges and in caves.*

Page 9. Who has to cross the bridge first? *Little Billy Goat Gruff.* How do you think he is feeling? (Ideas: *Scared; nervous; afraid.*)

Page 13. Predict what you think the troll will do.

Page 15. How do you think Little Billy Goat Gruff is feeling now that he is on the other side of the river? (Ideas: *Happy; glad.*)

Page 17. Who has to cross the bridge next? *Middle Billy Goat Gruff.* How do you think he is feeling? (Ideas: *Scared; nervous; afraid.*)

Page 19. Predict what you think the troll will do.

Display page 21. How do you think Middle Billy Goat Gruff is feeling now that he is on the other side of the river? (Ideas: *Happy; glad.*)

Page 23. Who has to cross the bridge next? *Big Billy Goat Gruff.* How do you think he is feeling? How do you think the troll is feeling? (Ideas: *Angry; furious.*)

Page 25. Predict what you think will happen.

Page 31. What has happened to the troll? (Idea: *Big Billy Goat Gruff pushed him off the bridge, he pushed him into the water.*) How do you think Big Billy Goat Gruff is feeling now that he is on the other side of the river? (Ideas: *Happy; glad.*)

Page 32. How does the story end? (Idea: *The goats live happily ever after on the other side of the river; the troll is gone.*)

Stories often end with the words "The End." This story ends with a little poem. Listen while I read the poem to you. "Snip, snap, snout—This tale's told out!" This little poem means the same thing as "The End."

Let's say the poem together that means "The End." *Snip, snap, snout—This tale's told out!* (Repeat until you think children can say the poem on their own.)

Your turn. Say the poem that means "The End." *Snip, snap, snout—This tale's told out!*

Review Vocabulary

(Display the Picture Vocabulary Cards. Point to each card as you say the word.) These pictures show **decided, shouted, squeaked,** and **muttered.** (Ask children to repeat each word after you.)

- What word means "used a very loud voice to speak to someone"? *Shouted.*
- What word means "used a very high voice to speak to someone"? *Squeaked.*
- What word means "carefully thought about something and chose to do it"? *Decided.*
- What word means "used a very quiet voice because you were unhappy about something"? *Muttered.*

Extend Vocabulary

◎← *Shouted.*

In *The Three Billy Goats Gruff,* we learned that shouted means "used a very loud voice to speak to someone."

Here's a new way to use the word **shouted.**

- **Alisa shouted to her friend to come over.** Say the sentence.
- **The children shouted to the other team to come and play.** Say the sentence.

- **Her mom shouted, "Look both ways before you cross the street!"** Say the sentence.

In these sentences, **shouted** means "said something very loudly, because the person you were talking to was a long way away."

Tell about some other times when you might shout to someone because that person is a long way away. (Ideas: *You could call "Mommy!" if you hurt yourself and your mom was far away; you could yell, "Hey, Jacob, I'm over here!" if you wanted to tell your little brother where you were.*)

Present Expanded Target Vocabulary
◎← Starving.

At the beginning of the story, the three billy goats have no food on their side of the river. They are very, very hungry. Another way of saying they are very, very hungry is that they are starving. **Starving.** Say the word. *Starving.*

If you are starving, you are so very, very hungry that you think you might die. Say the word that means "so very, very hungry that you think you might die." *Starving.*

Let's think about when people might be starving. If I say a time when someone would be starving, say, "Starving." If not, don't say anything.

- You haven't had breakfast, lunch, or dinner. *Starving.*
- There is no food in the refrigerator. *Starving.*
- You have been lost in the desert for three days, and you can't find your way home. *Starving.*
- Your tummy is rumbling because you haven't had anything to eat for a long, long time. *Starving.*
- You just finished a big dinner, and you accidentally burp and say, "Excuse me!"
- You are walking to the store to buy more food for lunch.
- You have been sick for five days and couldn't eat. *Starving.*

What word means "so very, very hungry that you think you might die"? *Starving.*

◎← Disagreeable.

In the story the troll won't let the goats cross his bridge even though he knows they are starving. He is unfriendly and unhelpful.

Another way of saying the troll is unfriendly and unhelpful is to say he is disagreeable. He won't do anything to help the goats, and he shouts at them. **Disagreeable.** Say the word. *Disagreeable.*

If someone is disagreeable, he or she is unfriendly and unhelpful. Say the word that means "unfriendly and unhelpful." *Disagreeable.*

Let's think about times when someone might be disagreeable. If I tell about a time when someone is being disagreeable, say, "Disagreeable." If not, don't say anything.

- Your aunt isn't feeling well and has a bad headache. *Disagreeable.*
- You are unhappy because you had to do your schoolwork over again. *Disagreeable.*
- You got a new bike.
- You are enjoying playing with your friend.
- The class is acting up and won't be quiet, and your teacher is upset. *Disagreeable.*
- You find a quarter on your way home.

In Week 4, we learned a word that meant "won't do anything to help anyone else." Say the word that means "won't do anything to help anyone else." *Uncooperative.*

Disagreeable people are uncooperative and unfriendly. What word means "uncooperative and unfriendly?" *Disagreeable.*

Tell about a time when someone was disagreeable. (Call on several children. Encourage children to start their answers with the words "____ was disagreeable when …")

(After each response, ask the child:) What might _____ have done to be more cooperative and friendly? (Accept reasonable responses.)

DAY 3

Preparation: Activity Sheet, BLM 5b.

Retell Story
(Show the pictures on the following pages from the story, and call on a child to tell what's happening. Call on a different child for each section.)

Today I'll show you the pictures Shirley Cribb Breuel made for her story *The Three Billy Goats Gruff*. As I show you the pictures, I'll call on one of you to tell the class that part of the story.

Pages 3–7. Tell what happens at the **beginning** of the story.

Pages 8–29. Tell what happens in the **middle** of the story. (Encourage use of target words when appropriate. Model use as necessary.)

Pages 30–32. Tell what happens at the **end** of the story.

How do you think the grass tastes? (Idea: *Delicious.*)

Introduce Choosing Game

Today you will play the Choosing Game. Let's think about the four words we have learned: **decided, shouted, squeaked,** and **muttered.** (Display the Picture Vocabulary Cards.) I will say a sentence that has two of our words in it. You will choose the correct word for that sentence. Let's practice. (Display the cards for the two words in each sentence as you say the sentence.)

- If a person has made up his or her mind about something, has the person **squeaked** or **decided**? *Decided.*
- When you have called out very loudly, have you **muttered** or **shouted**? *Shouted.*
- If you say something in a high voice because you are frightened, have you **muttered** or **squeaked**? *Squeaked.*

If you tell me the correct answer, you win one point. If you can't tell me the correct answer, I get the point.

Now you're ready to play the game.

(Draw a T-chart on the board for keeping score. Display the cards for the two words in each sentence as you say the sentence. Children earn one point for each correct answer. If they make an error, tell them the word, and record one point for yourself. Repeat missed words at the end of the game.)

- If Haley chooses to go swimming instead of to the mall, has she **decided** or has she **muttered**? *Decided.*

- When the president calls out loudly to his friends, has he **muttered** or **shouted**? *Shouted.*
- When Allison speaks in a very high voice when she hears a noise in the dark, has she **squeaked** or **muttered**? *Squeaked.*
- When Antwon says something very quietly, hoping that his teacher won't hear, has he **muttered** or **shouted**? *Muttered.*
- When you call your friend who is very far away, have you **shouted** or **squeaked**? *Shouted.*

(Count the points, and declare a winner.) You did a great job of playing the Choosing Game!

Sequence: Beginning, Middle, End (Activity Sheet)

(Give each child a copy of the Activity Sheet, BLM 5b. Review the order of the story with children. Tell them to place the pictures in sequence to show beginning, middle, and end. Instruct children to color the pictures, cut them out, and paste or glue them in order of beginning, middle, and end.)

DAY 4

Preparation: Prepare two sheets of chart paper, each with a circle drawn in the middle. Fold the sheets of paper in half vertically to divide the circles in half. When you record children's responses, physical descriptors should be recorded on the left-hand side of each chart. Personality characteristics or actions should be recorded on the right-hand side of each chart.

Analyze Characters (Literary Analysis)

Let's think about what we already know about how books are made.

- What do we call the name of the book? *The title.*
- What do we call the person who writes the story? *The author.*

- What do we call the person who draws the pictures? *The illustrator.*
- What do we call the people or animals a story is about? *The characters.*

Let's sing the verses we've learned of "The Story Song" to help us remember these important things about books.

(See the Introduction for the complete "Story Song.")

Today we will learn more about the characters in a story.

The characters in a story are the people or animals the story is about. What do we call the people or animals a story is about? *The characters.* Who are the characters in a story? *The people or animals the story is about.*

In the story *The Three Billy Goats Gruff,* are the characters people or animals? *The goats are animal; the troll is a pretend man.*

Who are the characters in the story? (Call on several children.) (Ideas: *Little Billy Goat Gruff; Middle Billy Goat Gruff; Big Billy Goat Gruff; the troll.*)

The most important characters in the story *The Three Billy Goats Gruff* are the goats and the troll. Who are the most important characters in the story? *The goats and the troll.* (Write the word *goats* in the circle on one of the sheets of chart paper; write *troll* in the circle on the other sheet.)

(Show children the pages from the story, and ask the specified questions. Call on individual children, recording each child's response on the left-hand side of the goat chart.)

Let's remember what we know about the goats.

Cover page. What do the goats look like? (Ideas: *White; have horns; have collars; have gold rings on their horns.*)

Page 3. Do you think the goats are hungry or full? (Idea: *Hungry.*) Tell why you think so. (Ideas: *There's no grass to eat; their eyes are sad; they look skinny.*) We learned a new word that means the goats are so hungry they think they might die. What word could we use to tell about the goats? They are … *starving.*

Pages 18–19. In Week 1 we learned a new word that describes Middle Billy Goat Gruff. He wants food very, very badly. Say the word that describes Middle Billy Goat Gruff's wanting food very, very badly. He was … *desperate.*

Page 32. What do the Billy Goats Gruff like to eat? *Grass.*

(Follow a similar process to describe the troll. Record responses on the second piece of chart paper.)

Today you have learned about the goats and the troll. They are the most important characters in the story *The Three Billy Goats Gruff.*

Play Choosing Game (Cumulative Review)

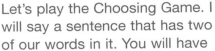

Let's play the Choosing Game. I will say a sentence that has two of our words in it. You will have to choose which word is the correct word for that sentence. (Display the Picture Vocabulary Cards for *decided, muttered, shouted, squeaked, disagreeable,* and *starving,* showing the cards for the two words in each sentence as you say the sentence.)

Now you're ready to play the Choosing Game.

(Draw a T-chart on the board for keeping score. Children earn one point for each correct answer. If they make an error, correct them as you normally would, and record one point for yourself. Repeat missed words at the end of the game.)

- If you were very hungry, would you have **squeaked** or be **starving?** *Starving.*
- When you say something very quietly after your mom yells at you, would you say that you **muttered** or that you **squeaked?** *Muttered.*
- Would you be **disagreeable** or **starving** if you get mad when you don't get your own way? *Disagreeable.*
- If your uncle calls you loudly from a long way away, has he **shouted,** or has he **muttered?** *Shouted.*
- When you are very scared and speak in a high voice, have you **squeaked** or **muttered?** *Squeaked.*

- When you drop a large rock on your foot, would you be **starving** or have **shouted?** *Shouted.*
- If you choose to stay at home and watch television instead of going for a walk, have you **decided,** or have you been **disagreeable?** *Decided.*
- If Josie speaks quietly so you can't hear her, would you say she **decided** or **muttered?** *Muttered.*

Now you will have to listen very carefully, because I'm not going to show you the word cards. (This part of the game includes the review word *collected* from Week 1.)

- If you picked things up from the floor after they fell, would you have **decided** or **collected?** *Collected.*
- If you speak quietly, hoping that no one else will hear, have you **shouted** or **muttered?** *Muttered.*
- If you are feeling a bit upset because you ate too much, would you be **starving** or **disagreeable?** *Disagreeable.*
- If you choose to have meat instead of fish for dinner, have you **decided** or **squeaked?** *Decided.*
- When you haven't eaten for two days and your tummy is rumbling, have you **collected** things, or are you **starving?** *Starving.*
- If your friend was in danger but he was a long way away, would you have **squeaked** or **shouted?** *Shouted.*
- Are you **disagreeable** or **starving** when you can't seem to get along with your friends? *Disagreeable.*
- If your voice gets very high because you are scared, would you say that you **muttered** or **squeaked?** *Squeaked.*

(Count the points, and declare a winner.)
You did a great job of playing the Choosing Game!

Preparation: Happy Face Game Test Sheet, BLM B.

Retell Story to a Partner

(Assign each child a partner, and ask the partners to take turns telling part of the story each time you turn to a new set of pages. Encourage use of target words when appropriate.)

Today I'll show you the pictures Shirley Cribb Breuel made for *The Three Billy Goats Gruff.* As I show you the pictures, you and your partner will take turns telling part of the story.

Pages 3–7. Tell what happens at the **beginning** of the story.

Pages 8–29. Tell what happens in the **middle** of the story.

Pages 30–32. Tell what happens at the **end** of the story.

How do you think the goats are feeling at the end of the story? (Ideas: *Happy; good; full.*)

Happy Face Game (Assess Vocabulary)

(Give each child a copy of the Happy Face Game Test Sheet, BLM B.)

Today you're going to play the Happy Face Game. When you play the Happy Face Game, it helps me know how well you know the hard words you are learning.

If I say something true, color the happy face. What will you do if I say something true? *Color the happy face.*

If I say something false, color the sad face. What will you do if I say something false? *Color the sad face.*

Listen carefully to each sentence I say. Don't let me trick you!

Item 1: If you **shouted,** you spoke in a very quiet voice. *False.*

Item 2: If you **squeaked,** you spoke in a very high voice. *True.*

Item 3: If you were **starving,** you wouldn't be very hungry. *False.*

Item 4: **Decided** means the same as chose. *True.*

Item 5: If you are picking your toys up off the floor, you are **collecting** your toys. *True.*

Item 6: **Muttered** means you spoke in a low voice that no one could hear. *True.*

Item 7: **Disagreeable** means happy and easy to get along with. *False.*

Item 8: When you **prepare,** you get ready to do something. *True.*

Item 9: **Pleaded** is the same as laughed. *False.*

Item 10: **Shouted** means you spoke in a loud, angry voice. *True.*

You did a great job of playing the Happy Face Game!

(Score children's work. Scores of 9 out of 10 indicate mastery. If a child does not achieve mastery, include the missed words in the games in the next week's lessons. Retest those children individually on the missed items before they take the next mastery test.)

Extensions
Read a Story as a Reward

(Display books you have read since the beginning of the program or alternate versions of *The Three Billy Goats Gruff.* Allow children to choose which book they would like you to read aloud to them as a reward for their hard work.)

(Read story aloud to children for enjoyment with minimal interruptions.)

Present Super Words Center

(Prepare the word containers for the Super Words Center. See the Introduction for instructions on how to set up and use the Super Words Center.)

(Add the new Picture Vocabulary Cards to words from earlier lessons. Show children one of the word containers. If they need more guidance, role-play with two or three children as a demonstration.)

Let's think about how we work with our words in the Super Words Center.

You will work with a partner in the Super Words Center. Whom will you work with in the center? *A partner.*

First you will draw a word out of the container. What do you do first? (Idea: *Draw a word out of the container.*)

Next you will show your partner the picture and ask him or her what word the picture shows. What do you do next? (Idea: *I show my partner the picture and ask him or her to tell me what word the picture shows.*)

What do you do next? *Give my partner a turn.*

What do you do if your partner doesn't know the word? *Tell my partner the word.*

Preparation: You will need *Flossie & the Fox* for each day's lesson.

Number the pages of the story to assist you in asking questions at appropriate points.

Post a copy of the Vocabulary Tally Sheet, BLM A, with this week's Picture Vocabulary Cards attached.

Each child will need the Homework Sheet, BLM 6a.

Flossie & the Fox
author: Patricia C. McKissack • illustrator: Rachel Isadora

Target Vocabulary

Tier II	Tier III
sly	character
rascal	
terrified	
horrible	
*clever	
*frustrated	

*Expanded Target Vocabulary Word

- When do you think the story happens?
- Why do you think the girl and the fox are smiling at each other?
- How do you think the girl and the fox met each other?
- Do you think this story is about a real fox and a real girl? Tell why or why not.

(Call on several children to share their predictions with the class.)

Take a Picture Walk

We are going to take a picture walk through this book. Remember, when we take a picture walk, we look at the pictures and tell what we think will happen in the story.

(Show the illustrations on the following pages, and ask the specified questions.)

Page 2. What do you think is happening here? (Ideas: *The little girl is putting her doll into the cut-off tree; she is taking her doll out of the cut-off tree.*)

Page 3. What do you think is in the big tubs? (Ideas: *Peaches; fruit; oranges.*) Who do you think the woman is with the little girl? (Idea: *Her grandmother.*)

Pages 5–6. When does this story happen? (Ideas: *A long time ago; on a sunny day.*) Why do you think so? (Ideas: *The woman is wearing a long dress; I can see the sun shining on the road; everything looks yellow.*) Where do you think the little girl is going?

DAY 1

Introduce Book

Today's book is called *Flossie & the Fox*. What's the title of this week's book? *Flossie & the Fox.*

This book was written by Patricia C. McKissack. Who's the author of *Flossie & the Fox*? *Patricia C. McKissack.*

Rachel Isadora made the pictures for this book. Who's the illustrator of *Flossie & the Fox*? *Rachel Isadora.*

The cover of a book usually gives us some hints of what the book is about. Let's look at the front cover of *Flossie & the Fox*. What do you see in the illustration? (Ideas: *A girl carrying a basket of eggs; a fox; they look like they are smiling at each other.*)

(Assign each child a partner.) Remember, when you make a prediction about something, you say what you think will happen. Get ready to make some predictions to your partner about this book. Use the information from the cover to help you.

(Ask the following questions, allowing sufficient time for children to share their predictions with their partners.)

- Whom do you think this story is about?
- What do you think the fox will do?
- What do you think the girl will do?
- Where do you think the story happens?

Page 7. What do you think is happening here? (Ideas: *The girl is looking at the fox; the fox is looking at the girl.*)

Page 10. Why do you think the fox is standing on his back legs like that?

Page 12. Why do you think the fox is watching the little girl?

Page 13. What do you think is happening here? (Ideas: *The girl is touching the fox's fur; the girl is petting the fox.*)

Pages 15–16. Where are they now? (Idea: *By a creek; near a pool; near some water.*) Why do you think the fox is following the girl?

Page 18. What is the girl looking at? *A cat.* Whom is the cat looking at? *The girl.* Why do you think the fox is hiding in the bushes?

Page 20. What is the fox doing? (Idea: *Howling.*) How do you think the fox is feeling? (Idea: *Angry.*) What do you think the cat is thinking?

Page 21. What do you think is happening here? (Idea: *The girl and the fox are watching the squirrel.*) Where is the squirrel? *Up in a tree.*

Pages 23–24. What is the girl looking at? (Idea: *The farm.*) How do you think the fox is feeling? (Ideas: *Very angry; furious.*)

Page 26. What is the girl looking at? (Idea: *The fox.*) What do you think the fox is looking at? (Ideas: *A dog; a wolf.*) Why do you think so? (Idea: *I can see the shadow on the road.*)

Pages 27–28. What do you think is happening here? (Ideas: *The fox is running away; the dog is chasing the fox.*)

Page 29. How do you think the girl is feeling? (Idea: *Happy.*) What is she carrying? *A basketful of eggs.*

Now that we've finished our picture walk, it's your turn to ask me some questions. What would you like to know about the story? (Accept questions. If children tell about the story instead of asking questions, prompt them to ask a question.) Ask me a who question. Ask me a why question.

Read Story Aloud
(Read story aloud to children with minimal interruptions.)

In the next lesson, we will read the story again, and I will ask you some questions.

(**Note:** If children have difficulty attending for an extended period of time, present the next part of this day's lesson at another time.)

Present Target Vocabulary

◎← Sly.

In the story, Big Mama says, "I tell you, that fox is one sly critter." She is using the word **sly** to tell about the fox. Big Mama means the fox is very good at tricking others. She is warning Flossie to be careful around the fox, because he might try to trick her. **Sly.** Say the word. *Sly.*

If you say someone is sly, you think that person is very good at tricking others. You have to be careful around sly people, because they might try to trick you. Say the word that means "very good at tricking others." *Sly.*

(Correct any incorrect responses, and repeat the item at the end of the sequence.)

Let's think of some things that people or animals might do. I'll tell about someone or something. If you think that person or thing is being sly, say, "Sly." If not, don't say anything.

- The magician is very good at turning a pair of gloves into a bunch of flowers. *Sly.*
- The mountain lion makes the squirrel think that she is sleeping. *Sly.*
- The dog barks.
- Bill's grandfather drives the car.
- Henry hides the candy behind his back so no one can see it. *Sly.*
- The sunset is bright yellow, orange, and red.

What word means "very good at tricking others"? *Sly.*

◎← Rascal.

In the story, Big Mama calls the fox a rascal. That means she thinks he isn't honest. He would lie and trick to get his own way. **Rascal.** Say the word. *Rascal.*

When you call someone a rascal, you think that person will lie and trick to get his or her own way. Say the word that means "someone who will lie and trick to get his or her own way." *Rascal.*

(Correct any incorrect responses, and repeat the item at the end of the sequence.)

Let's think about who would be a rascal. I'll tell about someone. If you think that person or animal is a rascal, say, "Rascal." If not, don't say anything.

- The wolf in *The Three Little Pigs. Rascal.*
- A little boy who lies and tricks people so he can win a game. *Rascal.*
- A girl with pigtails.
- A person who lies to you and tricks you. *Rascal.*
- A duck waddling down the street.
- Four puppies in a box.

What word means "someone who will lie and trick to get his or her own way"? *Rascal.*

Sometimes we put the words **sly** and **rascal** together to tell about someone. If I said the fox was a sly rascal, what would you know about the fox? (Idea: *The fox was very good at lying and tricking others.*)

 Terrified.

In the story, the fox tells Flossie, "A little girl like you should be simply terrified of me." That means he thinks Flossie should be very, very afraid of the fox. **Terrified.** Say the word. *Terrified.*

When you are terrified, you are very, very afraid. Say the word that means "very, very afraid." *Terrified.*

(Correct any incorrect responses, and repeat the item at the end of the sequence.)

Let's think about some things that might cause people to feel terrified. I'll name something. If you would be terrified, say, "Terrified." If not, don't say anything.

- The thunder and lightning are very loud. *Terrified.*
- The fire next door jumps onto your house. *Terrified.*
- Grandma comes to visit.
- The car is going very fast, and it has no brakes. *Terrified.*
- A bluebird flies across the sky.
- There is lots of tasty food on the table.

What word means "very, very afraid"? *Terrified.*

What kinds of things terrify you? (Call on several children. Encourage them to start their answers with the words "I am terrified of (by) _____.")

 Horrible.

In the story, when Flossie says she doesn't believe the fox is really a fox, he says it is a horrible situation. The fox is using the word **horrible** to tell how bad it is that Flossie doesn't believe him. **Horrible.** Say the word. *Horrible.*

When you say something is horrible, you mean it is really, really bad. Say the word that means "really, really bad." *Horrible.*

(Correct any incorrect responses, and repeat the item at the end of the sequence.)

Let's think about some horrible things. I'll name something or someone. If you think it is horrible, say, "Horrible." If not, don't say anything.

- The taste of cooked liver. *Horrible.*
- A friend who pushes you down in the mud. *Horrible.*
- From now on, you come to school on Saturday and Sunday too. *Horrible.*
- It rains so much that there is a flood. *Horrible.*
- Your best friend.
- The most beautiful place in the world to live.

What word means "really, really bad"? *Horrible.*

What are some things you think are horrible? (Call on several children. Encourage them to start their answers with the words "I think _____ is horrible.")

Present Vocabulary Tally Sheet
(See Week 1, page 3, for instructions.)

Assign Homework
(Homework Sheet, BLM 6a: See the Introduction for homework instructions.)

DAY 2

Preparation: Picture Vocabulary Cards for *sly, rascal, terrified,* and *horrible.*

Read and Discuss Story

(Read story aloud to children. Ask the following questions at the specified points.)

Now I'm going to read *Flossie & the Fox*. When I finish each part, I'll ask you some questions.

Page 1. A smokehouse is a small shack where people used to smoke meat like ham. A chicken coop is a small building where chickens are kept. A smokehouse and a chicken coop are found in a farmyard. Where are a smokehouse and a chicken coop found? *In a farmyard.* What is the little girl's name? *Flossie Finley.* Who is calling her? *Her grandmother.*

Page 4. What does Flossie call her grandmother? *Big Mama.* Where does this story happen? *In Tennessee.* When does this story happen? *In August.* What does Big Mama ask Flossie to do? *Take a basket of eggs to Miz Viola.*

Page 6. Big Mama tells Flossie, "Don't tarry now, and be particular 'bout those eggs." That means she wants Flossie to hurry to Miz Viola's and to be careful not to break the eggs. Why does Flossie go through the woods to get to Miz Viola's house? (Idea: *It is shorter and cooler than walking along the road.*) Has Flossie ever seen a fox? *No.* Do you think Flossie is worried about the fox? *No.* Why not?

Page 8. What do you think the fox wants? *The eggs.*

Page 9. How does the fox feel when Flossie says she doesn't believe he is a fox? (Idea: *At first he is angry.*)

Page 11. Why isn't Flossie afraid of the fox? (Idea: *She isn't sure he is a fox.*) What does the fox have to do to make Flossie afraid of him? (Idea: *He has to prove he is a fox.*)

Page 14. What does the fox do first to try to prove he is a fox? (Idea: *He lets her feel his fur.*) What does Flossie say after she has touched his fur? (Idea: *She thinks his fur feels like rabbit fur, so he must be a rabbit.*) How does the fox feel when Flossie says he is a rabbit? (Idea: *Angry.*) Is Flossie afraid of him? *No.* How do you know? (Ideas: *She taps her foot; she puts her hands on her hips; she tells the fox she won't accord him anything; she skips away.*)

Page 16. What does the fox do next to try to prove he is a fox? (Idea: *He tells her he has a long, pointed nose.*) What does Flossie say

about that? (Idea: *Rats have long, pointed noses, so he must be a rat.*) How does the fox feel when Flossie says he is a rat? (Idea: *Even more angry.*) Is Flossie afraid of him? *No.* How do you know? (Idea: *She skips on down the road.*)

Page 19. What does the fox do next to try to prove he is a fox? (Idea: *He tells the cat to tell Flossie he is a fox.*) What does the cat say? *"This is a fox because he has sharp claws and yellow eyes."* What does Flossie say about that? (Idea: *Cats have sharp claws and yellow eyes, so he must be a cat.*) How does the fox feel when Flossie says he is a cat? (Ideas: *Even more angry; furious.*) Is Flossie afraid of him? *No.* How do you know? (Ideas: *She tells him not to use that kind of language; she skips away.*)

Page 22. What does the fox do next to try to prove he is a fox? (Idea: *He tells her he has a bushy tail.*) What does Flossie say about that? (Idea: *Squirrels have bushy tails.*) What does the fox do? (Idea: *He starts to cry.*)

Page 24. What does the fox ask for? (Idea: *One last chance.*)

Page 25. What does the fox do next to try to prove he is a fox? (Idea: *He tells her he has sharp teeth and he can run fast.*) What does Flossie say about that? (Idea: *She says Mr. McCutchin's hounds have sharp teeth and can run fast.*)

Page 28. Why isn't the fox afraid of Mr. McCutchin's dogs? (Idea: *He can outsmart and outrun them because he is a fox.*)

Page 29. Do you think Flossie knows the fox is really a fox? *Yes.* Why do you think so? (Idea: *She says, "I know, I know."*)

Who is really the sly one in this story? (Idea: *Flossie.*)

Review Vocabulary

(Display the Picture Vocabulary Cards. Point to each card as you say the word.) These pictures show **sly, rascal, terrified,** and **horrible.** (Ask children to repeat each word after you.)

- What word means "very good at tricking others"? *Sly.*
- What word means "very, very afraid"? *Terrified.*

- What word means "really, really bad"? *Horrible.*
- What word means "someone who will lie and trick to get his or her own way"? *Rascal.*

Extend Vocabulary

 Rascal.

In the story *Flossie & the Fox,* we learned that **rascal** means "someone who will lie and trick to get his or her own way."

Here's a new way to use the word **rascal.**

- **My little brother is such a rascal.** Say the sentence.
- **The child who took the last of the grapes is a rascal.** Say the sentence.
- **That little rascal ate three cookies!** Say the sentence.

In these sentences, **rascal** means "a young child who is poorly behaved."

Present Expanded Target Vocabulary

 Clever.

I think Flossie knew the fox was after her eggs. She quickly figured out a plan to stop the fox from getting the eggs. Someone who can understand things quickly and is good at making plans is clever. **Clever.** Say the word. *Clever.*

If you are clever, you understand things quickly, and you are good at making plans. Say the word that means "understands things quickly and is good at making plans." *Clever.*

Let's think of times when people might be clever. If I say a time when someone would be clever, say, "Clever." If not, don't say anything.

- Harvey figures out how to fix the brakes on his bike with a piece of tape. *Clever.*
- Tanisha figures out how to stop the boys' fighting in just a second. *Clever.*
- The cat figures out how to get food from the cupboard before I can even turn around. *Clever.*
- The boys stand around while the water fountain overflows onto the floor.
- The cookie jar is right where we can reach it.
- It didn't take long before she thought of a way to get the kitten out of the tree. *Clever.*

What word means "understands things quickly and is good at making plans"? *Clever.*

Name someone you know who is clever. Explain why that person is clever.

 Frustrated.

In the story, each time the fox makes a new plan to prove he is a fox, his plan doesn't work. The fox becomes more and more upset and angry. The fox is frustrated. **Frustrated.** Say the word. *Frustrated.*

If you are frustrated, you become upset and angry because no matter how hard you try, you can't do something. Say the word that means "upset and angry because no matter how hard you try, you can't do something." *Frustrated.*

Let's think of times when someone might be frustrated. If I tell about a time when someone could be frustrated, say, "Frustrated." If not, don't say anything.

- I can't figure out how to do my homework no matter how hard I try. *Frustrated.*
- Tim can't find his snack even though he knows he brought it to school. *Frustrated.*
- Cody finishes all of his work and goes to play with the others.
- Cynthia puts her glasses down somewhere and is having trouble finding them. *Frustrated.*
- There isn't any cereal in the cupboard like Grandma said there was. Mindy looks and looks over and over again. *Frustrated.*
- Everything is going just perfectly.

Tell about a time when you were frustrated. (Call on several children. Encourage them to start their answers with the words "I was frustrated when …")

DAY 3

Preparation: Activity Sheet, BLM 6b.

Retell Story

(Show the pictures on the following pages from the story, and call on a child to tell what's happening. Call on a different child for each section.)

Today I'll show you the pictures Rachel Isadora made for her story *Flossie & the Fox*. As I show you the pictures, I'll call on one of you to tell the class that part of the story.

Pages 1–6. Tell what happens at the **beginning** of the story.

Pages 7–26. Tell what happens in the **middle** of the story. (Encourage use of target words when appropriate. Model use as necessary.)

Pages 27–29. Tell what happens at the **end** of the story.

Review Choosing Game

Today you'll play the Choosing Game. Let's think about the four words we have: **sly, rascal, terrified,** and **horrible.** (Display the Picture Vocabulary Cards.) I will say a sentence that has two of our words in it. You will have to choose which is the correct word for that sentence. Let's practice. (Display the cards for the two words in each sentence as you say the sentence.)

- Is a person who is very frightened **terrified** or **sly?** *Terrified.*
- When an animal tricks you into believing that it is asleep, is it **horrible** or **sly?** *Sly.*
- When something is really, really bad, is it **rascal** or **horrible?** *Horrible.*

Now you're ready to play the game. If you tell me the correct answer, you win one point. If you can't tell me the correct answer, I get the point.

(Draw a T-chart on the board for keeping score. Display the cards for the two words in each sentence as you say the sentence. Children earn one point for each correct answer. If they make an error, tell them the word, and record one point for yourself. Repeat missed words at the end of the game.)

- When Jack sees the gigantic monster, is he **sly** or **terrified?** *Terrified.*
- Bryan comes home and finds water on the floor and holes in all of the walls. Is the situation **horrible** or **clever?** *Horrible.*
- After the mouse wanders into the corner, the waiting cat pounces. Is the cat **horrible** or **clever?** *Clever.*

- The wolf tells the sheep that he just wants to talk for a while, but he really wants to eat the sheep. Is the wolf a **rascal** or **terrified?** *Rascal.*
- If you figure out how to solve a problem really quickly, are you **terrified** or **clever?** *Clever.*

(Count the points, and declare a winner.) You did a great job of playing the Choosing Game!

Sequence: Beginning, Middle, End (Activity Sheet)

(Give each child a copy of the Activity Sheet, BLM 6b. Review with children what the fox says or does to try to prove he is a fox.) What does the fox do first to try to prove he is a fox? (Idea: *He lets her feel his fur.*) What does Flossie say after she touches his fur? (Idea: *She thinks his fur feels like rabbit fur.*) Draw a line from the fur on the fox to the fur on the rabbit.

(Repeat procedure for remaining ideas: pointed nose, sharp claws and yellow eyes, bushy tail, sharp teeth. Have children color the pictures.)

DAY 4

Preparation: Prepare two sheets of chart paper, each with a circle drawn in the middle. Fold the sheets of paper in half vertically to divide the circles in half. When you record children's responses, record physical descriptors on the left-hand side of each chart and personality characteristics or actions on the right-hand side.

Analyze Characters (Literary Analysis)

Let's think about what we already know about how books are made.

- What do we call the name of the book? *The title.*
- What do we call the person who writes the story? *The author.*
- What do we call the person who draws the pictures? *The illustrator.*

- What do we call the people or animals a story is about? *The characters.*

Let's sing all that we've learned from "The Story Song" to help us remember these important things about books.

(See the Introduction for the complete "Story Song.")

Today we will learn more about the characters in a story.

Remember, the characters in a story are the people or animals the story is about. What do we call the people or animals a story is about? *The characters.* Who are the characters in a story? *The people or animals the story is about.*

In the story *Flossie & the Fox,* are the characters people or animals? (Ideas: *Flossie is a person; the fox is an animal.*)

Who are the characters in the story? (Ideas: *Flossie; the fox; Big Mama; the cat; the squirrel; the dog.*)

The most important characters in the story *Flossie & the Fox* are Flossie and the fox. Who are the most important characters in the story? *Flossie and the fox.* (Write the word *Flossie* in the circle on one of the sheets of chart paper; write *fox* in the circle on the other sheet.)

Let's remember what we know about Flossie. (Show picture on page 2.) What does Flossie look like? (Call on several children. Record each child's response on the left-hand side of the Flossie chart.) (Ideas: *Girl; dark skin; black hair; yellow dress; white apron; black stockings; black boots.*)

(Show picture on page 3. Ask the following questions, calling on several children. Record each child's response on the right-hand side of the chart.)

Do you think Flossie is happy or sad? (Idea: *Happy.*) Tell why you think so. (Idea: *She's smiling.*)

(Show pictures on pages 5 and 6.) Flossie pays attention to what her grandmother needs or wants. In Week 1 we learned a new word that means "pays attention to what someone needs or wants." Say the word that means Flossie pays attention to what her grandmother needs or wants. She was … *considerate.*

(Show the picture on page 29.) Flossie is able to make a plan to stop the fox from getting the eggs. We learned a new word that means someone understands things quickly and is good at making plans. What word could we use to tell about Flossie? Flossie is … *clever.*

(Follow a similar process to describe the fox. Record responses on the second piece of chart paper.)

Today you have learned about Flossie and the fox. They are the most important characters in the story *Flossie & the Fox.*

Play Choosing Game (Cumulative Review)

Let's play the Choosing Game. I will say a sentence that has two of our words in it. You will have to choose the correct word for that sentence. (Display the Picture Vocabulary Cards for *sly, rascal, terrified, horrible, clever,* and *frustrated,* showing the cards for the two words in each sentence as you say the sentence.)

Now you're ready to play the Choosing Game.

(Draw a T-chart on the board for keeping score. Children earn one point for each correct answer. If they make an error, correct them as you normally would, and record one point for yourself. Repeat missed words at the end of the game.)

- If you figured out how to fix the car very quickly, would you be **sly** or **clever? *Clever.***
- When you are good at tricking your little brother, are you **sly** or **terrified?** *Sly.*
- If a person told you he or she wanted to be your friend but really wanted to hurt you, would that person be a **rascal** or **frustrated?** *Rascal.*
- When you're having trouble tying your shoes even after you've tried and tried, are you **horrible** or **frustrated?** *Frustrated.*
- If a four-year-old keeps on running up and taking your sandwich away, is he **terrified** or a **rascal?** *A rascal.*
- When something happens that is really bad, do we say that it is **clever** or **horrible?** *Horrible.*

- When you just can't ride your bike and stay upright, are you **sly** or **frustrated**? *Frustrated.*
- If Freddie Fox figures out how to get into the henhouse past the locked door, is he **clever** or **horrible**? *Clever.*

Now you will have to listen very carefully, because I'm not going to show you the Picture Vocabulary Cards. (This part of the game includes the review word *pleaded* from Week 1.)

- When you tease your mom by hiding her mixing bowls, are you **horrible** or a **rascal**? *Rascal.*
- If you beg to have cookies for dessert, would you say that you are **terrified** or that you **pleaded**? *Pleaded.*
- The wolf from *The Three Little Pigs* spoke nicely to the pigs because he wanted to trick them. Was he **sly** or **frustrated**? *Sly.*
- When the little pigs wouldn't come out when the wolf spoke nicely, was the wolf **clever** or **frustrated**? *Frustrated.*
- If four cars crash on the street and people are hurt, is the situation **horrible** or **sly**? *Horrible.*
- If you were watching while those four cars crashed, would you be **clever** or **terrified**? *Terrified.*
- If someone says he or she wants to be your friend but really wants to hurt you, is that person a **rascal** or **frustrated**? *Rascal.*
- If your backpack tears open but you quickly figure out how to fix it with tape, are you **clever** or **horrible**? *Clever.*

(Count the points, and declare a winner.) You did a great job of playing the Choosing Game!

DAY 5

Preparation: Happy Face Game Test Sheet, BLM B.

Retell Story to a Partner

(Assign each child a partner, and ask the partners to take turns telling part of the story each time you turn to a new set of pages. Encourage use of target words when appropriate.)

Today I'll show you the pictures Rachel Isadora made for the story *Flossie & the Fox*. As I show you the pictures, you and your partner will take turns telling part of the story.

Pages 2–6. Tell what happens at the **beginning** of the story.

Pages 7–26. Tell what happens in the **middle** of the story.

Pages 27–29. Tell what happens at the **end** of the story.

How do you think Flossie feels at the end of the story?

How do you think the fox feels at the end of the story?

Happy Face Game (Assess Vocabulary)

(Give each child a copy of the Happy Face Game Test Sheet, BLM B.)

Today you're going to play the Happy Face Game. When you play the Happy Face Game, it helps me know how well you know the hard words you are learning.

If I say something true, color the happy face. What will you do if I say something true? *Color the happy face.*

If I say something false, color the sad face. What will you do if I say something false? *Color the sad face.*

Listen carefully to each sentence I say. Don't let me trick you!

Item 1: If Jonas gets up and reads the hard story to the class, he is being **brave**. *True.*

Item 2: A person who can solve problems quickly might be **clever**. *True.*

Item 3: The word **rascal** can mean that a young child is poorly behaved. *True.*

Item 4: Being **frustrated** is lots and lots of fun. *False.*

Item 5: If the fox **crept** across the meadow, he made a lot of noise. *False.*

Item 6: **Sly** people are good at tricking others. *True.*

Item 7: A **horrible** taste is a very, very bad taste. *True.*

Item 8: If you are very frightened, you are **terrified.** *True.*

Item 9: Someone who is very, very angry is **furious.** *True.*

Item 10: A **rascal** might tell a lie to trick you. *True.*

You did a great job of playing the Happy Face Game!

(Score children's work. Scores of 9 out of 10 indicate mastery. If a child does not achieve mastery, include the missed words in the games in the next week's lessons. Retest those children individually on the missed items before they take the next mastery test.)

Extensions
Read a Story as a Reward

(Display the books you have read since the beginning of the program. Allow children to choose which book they would like you to read to them as a reward for their hard work.)

(Read story aloud to children for enjoyment with minimal interruptions.)

Present Super Words Center

(Prepare the word containers for the Super Words Center.

Note: You will need to keep the cards that were removed from the center. They will be used again later in the program.

See the Introduction for instructions on how to set up and use the Super Words Center.)

(Put the Picture Vocabulary Cards from Weeks 5 and 6 into the word containers. Create a Concentration game by making as many duplicates of each card as you wish, depending on the size of your class. Show children one of the word containers. Demonstrate how the game is played by role-playing with a child. Repeat the demonstration until children can play with confidence.)

Let's think about how we work with our words in the Super Words Center.

You will work with a partner in the Super Words Center. Whom will you work with in the center? *A partner.*

There are two cards for each word in the Super Words Center. You will play a game called Concentration. When you play Concentration, you try to find two cards that match. **Match** means that both cards show the same picture and word. What does **match** mean? *Both cards show the same picture and word.*

First you will take all of the cards out of the container and place them facedown on the table. What do you do first? (Idea: *Take all of the cards out and place them facedown on the table.*)

Next you will pick one card, turn it faceup, show your partner the picture, and ask him or her what word the picture shows. What do you do next? (Idea: *I pick a card, turn it faceup, show it to my partner, and ask him or her what word the picture shows.*)

What do you do if your partner doesn't know the word? *Tell my partner the word.*

Next you will put the card faceup where you found it. What do you do next? (Idea: *Put the card faceup where I found it.*)

What do you do next? *Give my partner a turn.*

If your partner chooses another card that is the same as your first card, he or she can take those two cards. What can your partner do? (Idea: *My partner can take both cards if one of them is the same as my first card.*)

If your partner can't find one that is the same, he or she puts the card down faceup in the same place where it was picked up. Then it is your turn again. Whoever has the most pairs of cards when all of the cards have been taken is the winner.

(There are many ways to play Concentration. This one is fast to play. You may choose to modify the game depending on the children's skill level.)

Preparation: You will need *Stone Soup* for each day's lesson.

Number the pages of the story to assist you in asking questions at appropriate points.

Post a copy of the Vocabulary Tally Sheet, BLM A, with this week's Picture Vocabulary Cards attached.

Each child will need the Homework Sheet, BLM 7a.

Stone Soup
author: Heather Forest • illustrator: Susan Gaber

Target Vocabulary

Tier II	Tier III
curious	character
nutritious	
ingredients	
sighed	
*selfish	
*cooperated	

*Expanded Target Vocabulary Word

DAY 1

Introduce Book

Today's book is called *Stone Soup.* What's the title of this week's book? *Stone Soup.*

This book was written by Heather Forest. Who's the author of *Stone Soup*? *Heather Forest.*

Susan Gaber made the pictures for this book. Who's the illustrator of *Stone Soup*? *Susan Gaber.*

The cover of a book usually gives us some hints of what the book is about. Let's look at the front cover of *Stone Soup.* What do you see in the picture? (Ideas: *A man with a beard and a little girl; a stone dropping into a big pot.*)

(Assign each child a partner.) Remember, when you make a prediction about something, you say what you think will happen. Now get ready to make some predictions to your partner about this book. Use the information from the cover to help you.

(Ask the following questions, allowing sufficient time for children to share their predictions with their partners.)

- Whom do you think this story is about?
- What do you think they will do?
- Where do you think the story happens?
- When do you think the story happens?
- Why do you think they are looking into the pot?
- How are they going to make stone soup?
- Do you think this story is about real people? Tell why or why not.

(Call on several children to share their predictions with the class.)

Take a Picture Walk

We are going to take a picture walk through this book. Remember, when we take a picture walk, we look at the pictures and tell what we think will happen in the story.

(Show the illustrations on the following pages, and ask the specified questions.)

Pages 1–2. Where does the story happen? (Idea: *Up in the mountains.*) Where do you think the men are going? (Idea: *To one of the houses.*)

Pages 3–4. What do you think the men are saying to the woman? (Idea: *Hello, please help us.*) What makes you think so? (Ideas: *One man is lifting his hat; the other man has his hands together as if he were begging.*) What do you think the woman is saying to the men? (Ideas: *Stop; go away; no.*) What makes you think so? (Ideas: *She has her hand up; she looks angry.*)

Page 6. What do you think is happening here? (Ideas: *The men go to another house; a little boy opens the door.*) What do you think the little boy is saying?

Pages 7–8. What are the men doing? (Ideas: *Sitting on a stone wall; having a rest.*)

Pages 9–10. What do you think the men are shouting?

Pages 11–12. Why do you think the man is bringing the big pot? What do you think is in the pot? (Idea: *Nothing.*) If there's nothing in the pot, we say the pot is … *empty.*

Pages 13–14. What are the men putting in the pot? (Idea: *Water.*) Is the water hot or cold? *Hot.* Why do you think so? (Ideas: *There is fire underneath the pot; steam is coming out the top of the pot.*)

Pages 15–16. What are the men putting in the pot? *A stone.*

Page 17. (Point to the speech balloon.) This is a speech balloon. What is this called? *A speech balloon.* When you see it in a picture, it tells you someone is saying something. What does it tell you? *Someone is saying something.* What do you think the girl is saying? (Ideas: *I have a carrot; we should put a carrot in the soup; the soup would taste better if it had a carrot in it.*)

Page 20. (Point to the speech balloon.) What is this called? *A speech balloon.* What does it tell you? *Someone is saying something.* What do you think the man is saying?

Pages 21–22. (Point to each person in the row. Ask this question for each person:) What do you think this man (woman) is saying?

Pages 23–24. What are the people doing? (Idea: *Throwing things into the soup.*) The pot isn't empty anymore. Now the pot is … *Full.*

Pages 25–26. What do you think is happening here? (Ideas: *Everyone is coming for soup; they are eating the soup.*)

Pages 27–28. What time of the day is it in this picture? (Ideas: *Nighttime; sunset.*) What are the two men doing? *Waving goodbye.* What are the other people doing? *Waving goodbye.* Who is eating the last of the stone soup? (Ideas: *The animals; the dog; the cat; the bird.*)

Now that we've finished our picture walk, it's your turn to ask me some questions. What would you like to know about the story? (Accept questions. If children tell about the pictures or the story instead of asking questions, prompt them to ask a question.) Ask me a what question. Ask me a when question.

Read Story Aloud
(Read story aloud to children with minimal interruptions.)

In the next lesson we will read the story again, and I will ask you some questions.

(**Note:** If children have difficulty attending for an extended period of time, present the next part of this day's lesson at another time.)

Present Target Vocabulary

◎◀ **Curious.**

In the story when the travelers filled the pot with water and built a fire under it, "Curious people began to gather." That means the people all came to see what was happening. They were interested in what the men were doing, and they wanted to know more about it. **Curious.** Say the word. *Curious.*

If you are curious about something, you are interested in that thing, and you want to know more about it. Say the word that means "interested in something and want to know more about it." *Curious.*

(Correct any incorrect responses, and repeat the item at the end of the sequence.)

Let's think of some people. I'll tell about someone. If you think that person is curious, say, "Curious." If not, don't say anything.

- Jamie is interested in ants' nests, and he wants to know more about them. *Curious.*
- Jordan and his friends want to know more about space, so they watch a television show about space. *Curious.*
- Fern sees a tree standing beside a stream.
- Rex has a brown Cocker Spaniel puppy.
- Everyone runs to the window to see what has happened. *Curious.*
- All of us ask about the flying squirrel and where it lives. *Curious.*

What word means "interested in something and want to know more about it"? *Curious.*

◎◀ **Nutritious.**

The travelers say their stone soup will be nutritious. That means it has healthy things in it that will help your body grow and be strong. **Nutritious.** Say the word. *Nutritious.*

When food is nutritious, it has healthy things in it that help your body grow and be strong. Say the word that means "food that has healthy

54

things in it that help your body grow and be strong." *Nutritious.*

(Correct any incorrect responses, and repeat the item at the end of the sequence.)

Let's think about food that would be nutritious. I'll name a food. If you think that food is nutritious, say, "Nutritious." If the food I name is not nutritious, say, "Absolutely not."

- Corn. *Nutritious.*
- Pumpkin seeds. *Nutritious.*
- Jelly beans. *Absolutely not.*
- Potato chips. *Absolutely not.*
- Meat and potatoes. *Nutritious.*
- Bread and cheese. *Nutritious.*

What word means "food that has healthy things in it that help your body grow and be strong"? *Nutritious.*

 Ingredients.

In the story, one of the travelers tells the townspeople his soup needs "a special magical ingredient." That means he needs one more thing to make his soup. **Ingredients.** Say the word. *Ingredients.*

Ingredients are the things you need to make something. There is always a list of ingredients in a recipe when you are making a special food. What word means "the things you need to make something"? *Ingredients.*

(Correct any incorrect responses, and repeat the item at the end of the sequence.)

Let's think about some of the things you would need to make something. I'll name something. If what I name would be an ingredient in that thing, say, "Ingredient." If not, don't say anything.

- I'm making chicken soup—chicken. *Ingredient.*
- I'm making mud pies—oranges.
- I'm making a salad—lettuce. *Ingredient.*
- I'm making a peach pie—peaches. *Ingredient.*
- I'm making a sandwich—chocolate chips.
- I'm making beef stew—beef. *Ingredient.*

What word means "the things you need to make something"? *Ingredients.*

 Sighed.

In the story, one of the travelers sighed when he said the soup would taste better "if we only had a carrot." That means he let out a deep breath like this (model a sigh for children and repeat "if we only had a carrot"), to show he was disappointed he didn't have a carrot. **Sighed.** Say the word. *Sighed.*

When you sigh, you let out a deep breath to show you are very tired, or you are sad because something you wanted didn't happen. Say the word that means "let out a deep breath to show you were tired or sad." *Sighed.*

(Correct any incorrect responses, and repeat the item at the end of the sequence.)

Let's think about some times when someone might have sighed. I'll tell you about a time. If you think someone would have sighed, say, "Sigh." If not, don't say anything.

- Grandpa has been working hard in his garden all day. *Sighed.*
- Jordan wished he had a drink of water.
- Timothy felt like singing.
- When he got to the top of the hill, Dad put the big sack of potatoes down. *Sighed.*
- Terry thought that working hard was fun.
- Alvin missed his best friend since he'd moved away. *Sighed.*

What word means "let out a deep breath to show you were tired or sad"? *Sighed.*

Everybody, show me how you would sigh if I said we couldn't have recess today. (Pause.) Show me how you would sigh if you had worked all day to clean your room and you were very tired.

Present Vocabulary Tally Sheet
(See Week 1, page 3, for instructions.)

Assign Homework
(Homework Sheet, BLM 7a: See the Introduction for homework instructions.)

Preparation: Picture Vocabulary Cards for *curious, nutritious, ingredients,* and *sighed.*

 ### Read and Discuss Story

(Read story aloud to children. Ask the following questions at the specified points.)

Now I'm going to read *Stone Soup.* When I finish each part, I'll ask you some questions.

Page 1. Where does this story take place? (*In a village; in the mountains.*) A village is a very small town. What is a village? *A very small town.* Tell about the two travelers. (Ideas: *Their clothes are torn; their shoes have holes; they are tired and hungry.*)

Page 4. What three questions do the travelers ask the woman? *Do you care? Will you share? Do you have any food?* What does the woman say? *No.* What does the woman do? *She slams the door shut.*

Page 5. What three questions do the travelers ask the boy? *Do you care? Will you share? Do you have any food?* What does the boy say? *There is no food here.* What does the boy do? *He closes the door.* Do you think this is a friendly village or an unfriendly village? *An unfriendly village.* Why do you think so? (Ideas: *No one will give the travelers any food; everyone closes the door on them.*)

Page 8. Where do the travelers sit to rest? *Beside a well.* A well is a hole in the ground that collects fresh water. People can get water from a well. What is a well? *A hole in the ground that collects fresh water.* What can people get from a well? *Water.*

What do the travelers decide to make? *Their magical soup.*

Page 10. What do the travelers ask for? *A big black pot.* What do they tell the people they will make? *The most delicious soup anyone ever tasted.*

Page 12. Wow! That's the biggest pot I've ever seen. It's big enough for a giant. What kind of pot does the story say it is? *A gigantic black pot.*

Page 14. What do the travelers do first to make the soup? (Ideas: *They heat the water; they boil the water.*)

(**Note:** If children do not use the word *boil*, tell them:) When you heat water until it gets so hot it bubbles and steam comes out, we say you boil the water. What do the travelers do to the water? *They boil it.*

What do the travelers need for their soup? *A special magical ingredient.*

Page 16. What do the travelers put in the soup? *A stone.* Is it a magical stone? *No.* What kind of stone is it? *An ordinary stone.* That's right; the man picks up one of the stones that was just on the grass. What does he think will make the soup taste better? *A carrot.*

Page 18. When the travelers say they cannot make their Stone Soup, who speaks up? *A child.* What does the child say? *I might have a small carrot.*

Page 20. What does the man offer to put in the pot? *A potato.*

Page 22. What other ingredients are offered for the Stone Soup? (Ideas: *A green bean; a kernel of corn; an egg noodle; a slice of celery; a pinch of pepper; a sprig of parsley; a tiny turnip.*)

Page 24. Who puts something in the pot? (Idea: *Everyone in town.*) The author doesn't tell us what the people bring, but the illustrator drew pictures to show us. Just look at all the things that go into the Stone Soup!

Page 26. What other things do the people bring to have with their soup? (Ideas: *Bread; cheese; fruit.*) Is the stone the magic ingredient? *No.* What do the travelers say is the magic ingredient? *Sharing.*

Page 28. The travelers give the people the recipe for making Stone Soup. Listen while I read the recipe. (Read the poem at the end of the story.) What is different about this recipe? (Idea: *It's a poem.*) Let's say the poem together that ends the story *Stone Soup.*

(Repeat the poem with children two or three times.)

We read another story that ended with a poem. What story was that? *The Three Billy Goats Gruff.*

Review Vocabulary

(Display the Picture Vocabulary Cards. Point to each card as you say the word. Ask children to repeat each word after you.) These pictures show **curious, nutritious, ingredients,** and **sighed.**

- What word means "let out a deep breath to show you were tired or sad"? *Sighed.*
- What word means "food that has healthy things in it that help your body grow and be strong"? *Nutritious.*
- What word means "the things you need to make something"? *Ingredients.*
- What word means "interested in something and want to know more about it"? *Curious.*

Extend Vocabulary

◎⟞ Curious.

In the story *Stone Soup,* we learned that **curious** can be used to tell about people. When someone is curious about something, he or she is "interested in something and wants to know more about it."

Here's a new way to use the word **curious.**

- **What a curious thing to do!** Say the sentence.
- **It was curious that Hal wouldn't speak to anyone but his cat.** Say the sentence.
- **It was even more curious that Hal's cat talked back to him.** Say the sentence.

In these sentences, **curious** means "something unusual or hard to understand." Tell about some other things that you would find curious.

- It's curious that a platypus has a bill like a duck.
- It's curious to me that my nose runs and my feet smell.
- I think it's curious that you can draw a card, but you can also draw a picture.

Present Expanded Target Vocabulary

◎⟞ Selfish.

In the story, the people who live in the village don't care about the travelers. They don't want to share what they have with them. People who don't care about others or don't share what they have are selfish. **Selfish.** Say the word. *Selfish.*

If you are selfish, you don't care about others, and you won't share what you have. Say the word that means "you don't care about others, and you won't share what you have." *Selfish.*

Let's think about times when people are selfish. If I say a time when someone would be selfish, say, "Selfish." If not, don't say anything.

- You have enough cookies for everyone, but you keep them all for yourself. *Selfish.*
- You want to be first in line whether it's your turn or not. *Selfish.*
- You share all of your lunch with someone else who didn't bring any at all.
- You think that your feelings are more important than anyone else's. *Selfish.*
- You have lots of marbles, so you let each of your friends play with some of them.
- Bill keeps all of the building toys for himself. *Selfish.*

What word means "you don't care about others, and you won't share what you have"? *Selfish.*

◎⟞ Cooperated.

In the story, everyone in the village works together to make the soup. Later they work together to bring out bowls, spoons, chairs, and tables. They work together to add bread, cheese, and fruit for the feast. The people cooperated with each other. **Cooperated.** Say the word. *Cooperated.*

If people cooperate with each other, they work together to do a job. Say the word that means "worked together to do a job." *Cooperated.*

In Week 4 you learned a word that means "won't do anything to help anyone else." What word means "won't do anything to help anyone else"? *Uncooperative.*

Let's think about times when people might have cooperated. If I tell about a time when people cooperated, say, "Cooperated. If not, say, "Uncooperative."

- We all got together to push Al's car out of the ditch. *Cooperated.*
- Al drove away without offering us a ride even though we asked. *Uncooperative.*

- The kitten wouldn't stay off the couch no matter what we tried. *Uncooperative.*
- Together, we cleaned the yard and made it tidy. *Cooperated.*
- Colleen wouldn't join in when we were dancing the Chicken Dance. *Uncooperative.*
- The horses reared and neighed and wouldn't stand still. *Uncooperative.*

Tell about a time when you cooperated with others. (Call on several children. Encourage them to start their answers with the words "I cooperated with _____ when _____.")

DAY 3

Preparation: Prepare a sheet of chart paper with the title *Vegetables Are Nutritious.*

Each child will need the Activity Sheet, BLM 7b.

Retell Story

(Show the pictures on the following pages from the story, and call on a child to tell what's happening. Call on a different child for each section.)

Today I'll show you the pictures Susan Gaber made for the story *Stone Soup.* As I show you the pictures, I'll call on one of you to tell the class that part of the story.

Pages 1–8. Tell what happens at the **beginning** of the story.

Pages 9–26. Tell what happens in the **middle** of the story. (Encourage use of target words when appropriate. Model use as necessary.)

Pages 27–28. Tell what happens at the **end** of the story.

How do you think the people of the village feel at the end of the story? (Ideas: *Happy; friendly; not selfish.*) Predict what you think will happen when the next travelers come to the village.

Review Choosing Game

Today you will play the Choosing Game. (Display the Picture Vocabulary Cards.) Let's think about the four words we have:

curious, nutritious, ingredients, and sighed. I'll say a sentence that has two of our words in it. Your job is to choose which word is the correct word for that sentence. Let's practice. (Display the Picture Vocabulary Cards for the two words in each sentence as you say the sentence.)

- If food is full of things that are good for you, is it **nutritious** or **curious**? *Nutritious.*
- If you let out a deep breath to show that you are very tired, would you say that you **sighed** or that you are **curious**? *Sighed.*
- If you had a lot of things to use to make a meal, would you have **ingredients** or would it be **nutritious**? *Ingredients.*

Now you're ready to play the game. If you tell me the correct answer, you win one point. If you can't tell me the correct answer, I get the point.

(Draw a T-chart on the board for keeping score. Display the cards for the two words in each sentence as you say the sentence. Children earn one point for each correct answer. If they make an error, tell them the word, and record one point for yourself. Repeat missed words at the end of the game.)

- When Bob puts different vegetables in his stew, does he use **ingredients,** or is he **curious**? *Ingredients.*
- When Harry's father came home after a day of hard work, would you say that he was **curious** or that he **sighed**? *Sighed.*
- Your sandwich is full of meat, lettuce, and cheese. Has it **sighed,** or is it **nutritious**? *Nutritious.*
- Sofia is very interested in the game of basketball and wants to learn more. Is she **curious** or **angry**? *Curious.*
- When the puppy came and sniffed at me and walked all around me with his tail wagging, was he **curious,** or had he **sighed**? *Curious.*

(Count the points, and declare a winner.)
You did a great job of playing the Choosing Game!

Sequence: Beginning, Middle, End (Activity Sheet)

(Display pages 23 and 24 of the story.) The people of the village bring many different vegetables to put in the Stone Soup. Tell me the word that means "food that has healthy things in it to help your body grow and be strong"? *Nutritious.*

(Point to the title on the Activity Sheet.) This title says *Vegetables Are Nutritious.* Everybody, say the title. *Vegetables Are Nutritious.*

You tell me what vegetables went into the Stone Soup, and I'll write them down on this chart. (Point to each vegetable in the illustration, and ask:) What vegetable is this? (As the children identify the vegetables, print the names on the chart. If they cannot name the vegetable, tell them the name, and write it on the chart.) I can see why Stone Soup is so nutritious; it has so many good vegetables in it!

(Give each child a copy of the Activity Sheet, BLM 7b. Point to the words in the circle.) These words say *Vegetables Are Nutritious.* Everybody, say the words. *Vegetables are nutritious.*

(Beginning with the carrot, point to the drawing and ask children:) What is this? Is it nutritious?

(If the drawing shows a nutritious vegetable, have children draw a line from the picture to the words in the circle. If the drawing does not show a nutritious vegetable, have them cross out the picture. Have the children color the pictures that show nutritious vegetables.)

Preparation: Prepare two sheets of chart paper, each with a circle drawn in the middle. Fold the sheets of paper in half vertically to divide the circle in half. When you record children's responses, physical descriptors should be recorded on the left-hand side of each chart. Personality characteristics or actions should be recorded on the right-hand side of each chart.

Analyze Characters (Literary Analysis)

Let's think about what we already know about how books are made.

- What do we call the name of the book? *The title.*
- What do we call the person who writes the story? *The author.*
- What do we call the person who draws the pictures? *The illustrator.*
- What do we call the people or animals a story is about? *The characters.*

Let's sing "The Story Song" to help us remember these important things about books.

(See the Introduction for the complete "Story Song.")

Today we will learn more about the characters in a story.

Remember, the characters in a story are the people or animals the story is about. What do we call the people or animals a story is about? *The characters.* Who are the characters in a story? *The people or animals the story is about.*

In the story *Stone Soup,* are the characters people or animals? *People.*

Who are the characters in the story? (Ideas: *The two travelers; the woman at the door; the young boy; the girl; the other people from the village.*)

The most important characters in the story *Stone Soup* are the two travelers and the people in the village. Who are the most important characters in the story? *The two travelers and the people in the village.* (Write the words *two travelers* in the circle on one of the sheets of chart paper; write *people in the village* in the circle on the other sheet.)

Let's remember what we know about the two travelers. (Show children page 3 of the book.) What do the two travelers look like? (Call on several children. Record each child's response on the left-hand side of the two travelers chart.) (Ideas: *Men; torn clothes; have hats; have beards; are very thin.*)

(Show children page 3 of the book. Ask these questions. Call on several children. Record each child's response on the right-hand side of the chart.) Do you think the two travelers are poor or rich? (Idea: *Poor.*) Tell why you think so. (Idea: *They have holes in their clothes.*)

The travelers are very thin. They look so very, very hungry that I think they might die. In Week 5 we learned a new word that means "so very, very hungry you think you might die." Say the word that means the travelers are "so very, very hungry they think they might die." They were … *starving.*

(Show children the picture on pages 21 and 22.) The two travelers make a plan to get the people in the village to cooperate to make Stone Soup. In Week 6 we learned a word that means someone "understands things quickly and is good at making plans." What word could we use to tell about the two travelers? They were … *clever.*

(Follow a similar process to describe the people in the village. Record responses on the second piece of chart paper.)

Today you have learned about the two travelers and the people in the village. They are the most important characters in the story *Stone Soup.*

Play Choosing Game (Cumulative Review)

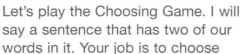

Let's play the Choosing Game. I will say a sentence that has two of our words in it. Your job is to choose the correct word for that sentence. (Display the Picture Vocabulary Cards for *curious, nutritious, ingredients, sighed, selfish,* and *cooperated.*)

Use the two Picture Vocabulary Cards that belong with each sentence as you say the sentence.)

Now you're ready to play the Choosing Game.

(Draw a T-chart on the board for keeping score. Children earn one point for each correct answer. If they make an error, correct them as you normally would, and record one point for yourself. Repeat missed words at the end of the game.)

- If you read ten books to learn more about baseball, would you be **curious,** or would you have **sighed?** *Curious.*
- When you make a meal, do you use **ingredients** or are you **curious?** *Ingredients.*
- If a kind of food is good for you, is it **ingredients,** or **nutritious?** *Nutritious.*
- If your friend said that he missed his mom, might he have **sighed** or **cooperated?** *Sighed.*
- When people keep all of the toys to themselves so no one else can play, is that person **sighed** or **selfish?** *Selfish.*
- What word means a little bit odd or strange— **sighed** or **curious?** *Curious.*
- If four friends got together to mow the lawn and tidy a yard, would they have **sighed** or **cooperated?** *Cooperated.*
- When Jenny's dad finished a long, hot job, would you say that he used **ingredients** or that he **sighed?** *Sighed.*

Now you will have to listen very carefully, because I'm not going to show you the Picture Vocabulary Cards. (This part of the game includes the review word *desperate* from Week 1.)

- Bob helped his sister to clean her room and put away her toys when she asked him to. Would you say that Bob was **desperate** or that he **cooperated?** *Cooperated.*
- When you want to know more about something, are you **nutritious** or **curious?** *Curious.*
- Beef stew needs beef, potatoes, carrots, and onions. Are those things **selfish** or **ingredients?** *Ingredients.*

- Do you eat healthy food because it is **nutritious** or because it **cooperated**? *Nutritious.*
- Would you say that strange bugs are **curious** or **selfish**? *Curious.*
- If Gordon let out a long breath when he heard the terrible news, would you say that he **sighed** or that he was **selfish**? *Sighed.*
- If you really, really want something, have you **cooperated** or are you **desperate**? *Desperate.*
- When Ben didn't share his snack, was he **curious** or **selfish**? *Selfish.*

(Count the points, and declare a winner.) You did a great job of playing the Choosing Game!

DAY 5

Preparation: Happy Face Game Test Sheet, BLM B.

Retell Story to a Partner

(Assign each child a partner, and ask the partners to take turns telling part of the story each time you turn to a new set of pages. Encourage use of target words when appropriate.)

Today I'll show you the pictures Susan Gaber made for the story *Stone Soup*. As I show you the pictures, you and your partner will take turns telling part of the story.

Pages 1–8. Tell what happens at the **beginning** of the story.

Pages 9–26. Tell what happens in the **middle** of the story.

Pages 27–28. Tell what happens at the **end** of the story.

How do you think the travelers feel at the end of the story?

How do you think the people in the village feel at the end of the story?

Assess Vocabulary

(Give each child a copy of the Happy Face Game Test Sheet, BLM B.)

Today you're going to play the Happy Face Game. When you play the Happy Face Game, it helps me know how well you know the hard words you are learning.

If I say something true, color the happy face. What will you do if I say something true? *Color the happy face.*

If I say something false, color the sad face. What will you do if I say something false? *Color the sad face.*

Listen carefully to each sentence I say. Don't let me trick you!

Item 1: If you are **selfish,** you care more about yourself than others. *True.*

Item 2: If you are **curious,** you want to find out more about something. *True.*

Item 3: **Ingredients** means the same as cleaning. *False.*

Item 4: **Curious** can mean odd or unusual. *True.*

Item 5: If food is **nutritious,** it is good for you. *True.*

Item 6: If you **cooperated,** you got along and helped others to do something. *True.*

Item 7: **Angry** means mad. *True.*

Item 8: If you have all the things you need to make a carrot cake, it means you have all the **ingredients.** *True.*

Item 9: A **cottage** is a very large house with lots of rooms. *False.*

Item 10: If you chose to go swimming, you **decided** to go swimming. *True.*

You did a great job of playing the Happy Face Game!

(Score children's work later. Scores of 9 out of 10 indicate mastery. If a child does not achieve mastery, insert missed words in the games in the next week's lessons. Retest those children individually for the missed items before they take the next mastery test.)

Extensions
Read a Story as a Reward

 (Display copies of the books you have read since the beginning of the program.

Allow children to choose which book they would like you to read to them as a reward for their hard work.)

(Read story aloud to children for enjoyment with minimal interruptions.)

Present Super Words Center

(Prepare the word containers for the Super Words Center.

Note: You will need to keep the Picture Vocabulary Cards that were removed from the center. They will be used again later in the program.

See the Introduction for instructions on how to set up and use the Super Words Center.)

(Put the Picture Vocabulary Cards from Weeks 4 and 7 into the word containers. Make duplicates of each card to create a Concentration game. You may make as many sets of duplicates as you wish to suit your class. Show children one of the word containers. If they need more guidance, role-play with two or three children as a demonstration.)

Let's think about how we work with our words in the Super Words Center.

You will work with a partner in the Super Words Center. Whom will you work with in the center? *A partner.*

There are two cards for each word in the Super Words Center. You will play a game called Concentration. When you play Concentration, you try to find two cards that match. **Match** means that both cards show the same picture

and word. What does **match** mean? *Both cards show the same picture and word.*

First you will take all of the cards out of the container and place them facedown on the table. What do you do first? (Idea: *Take all of the cards out and place them facedown on the table.*)

Next you will pick one card, turn it faceup, show your partner the picture, and ask what word the picture shows. What do you do next? (Idea: *I pick a card, turn it faceup, show it to my partner, and ask what word the picture shows.*)

What do you do if your partner doesn't know the word? *Tell my partner the word.*

Next you will put the card faceup where you found it. What do you do next? (Idea: *Put the card faceup where I found it.*)

What do you do next? *Give my partner a turn.*

If your partner chooses another card that is the same as your first card, he or she can take those two cards. What can your partner do? (Idea: *My partner can take both cards if he or she chooses one that is the same as my first card.*)

If your partner can't find one that is the same, your partner puts the card down faceup in the same place where he or she picked it up. Then it is your turn again. Whoever has the most pairs of cards when all of the cards have been taken is the winner.

(There are many ways to play Concentration. This one is fast to play. You may choose to modify the game depending on children's skill level.)

Week 8

The Wind Blew
author: Pat Hutchins • illustrator: Pat Hutchins

Preparation: You will need *The Wind Blew* for each day's lesson.

Number the pages of the story to assist you in asking questions at the appropriate points.

Post a copy of the Vocabulary Tally Sheet, BLM A, with this week's Picture Vocabulary Cards attached.

Each child will need the Homework Sheet, BLM 8b.

Target Vocabulary

Tier II	Tier III
snatched	illustrations
satisfied	add-on
whirled	
upward	
*gale	
*damaged	

*Expanded Target Vocabulary Word

DAY 1

Introduce Book

Today's book is called *The Wind Blew.* What's the title of this week's book? *The Wind Blew.*

This book was written by Pat Hutchins. Who's the author of *The Wind Blew*? *Pat Hutchins.*

Pat Hutchins also made the pictures for this book. Who is the illustrator of *The Wind Blew*? *Pat Hutchins.* The pictures an illustrator makes for a book are called the illustrations. What do you call the pictures an illustrator makes for a book? *Illustrations.* What are illustrations? *The pictures an illustrator makes for a book.*

The cover of a book usually gives us some hints of what the book is about. Let's look at the front cover of *The Wind Blew.* What do you see in the illustration? (Ideas: *Lots of people running; some things floating in the air; an umbrella; a hat; a balloon; a shirt; a kite; a white piece of cloth handkerchief.*)

(Assign each child a partner.) Remember, when you make a prediction about something, you say what you think will happen. Now get ready to make some predictions to your partner about this book. Use the information from the cover to help you.

(Ask the following questions, allowing sufficient time for children to share their predictions with their partners.)

- Who are the characters in this story? (Whom do you think this story is about?)

- What do you think they will do?
- Where do you think the story happens?
- When do you think the story happens?
- Why do you think the people are running?
- How are they going to get their things back?
- Do you think this story is about real people? Tell why or why not.

(Call on several children to share their predictions with the class.)

Take a Picture Walk

We are going to take a picture walk through this book. Remember, when we take a picture walk, we look at the pictures and tell what we think will happen in the story.

(Show the illustrations on the following pages, and ask the specified questions.)

Pages 1–2. When does the story happen? (Idea: *On a windy day.*) How do you know it's a windy day? (Ideas: *The branches on the trees are bent to one side; the rain isn't coming straight down.*) Who do you see in this first illustration? *A man.* What is he holding? *An umbrella.*

Pages 3–4. Whom do you see in this next illustration? *A girl.* What is she holding? *A balloon.* What's happening to the man's umbrella? (Ideas: *It's blowing away; it's turned inside out.*)

Pages 5–6. What's happening to the girl's balloon? (Idea: *It's blowing away.*) First we saw the illustration of the man; now we've added the illustration of the little girl. (Point to the wedding scene.) What do you think is happening here? (Ideas: *A wedding; the people have just gotten married.*) Why do you think so? The woman who is getting married is called the bride. What do we call a woman who is getting married? *A bride.* The man who is getting married is called the groom. What do we call a man who is getting married? *A groom.*

Pages 7–8. What's happening to the groom's hat? (Idea: *It's blowing away.*) (Point to each person in the illustration as you talk about them.) First we saw the illustration of the man; then we added the illustration of the little girl; now we've added the illustration of the groom. (Point to the boy with the kite.) Predict what will happen to the boy with the kite. (Idea: *The wind will blow the kite away.*)

Pages 9–10. What's happening to the woman's shirt? (Idea: *It's blowing away.*) (Repeat the procedure for talking about the people in the illustration, adding the boy with the kite. Point to the woman hanging the shirt on the line.) Predict what will happen to the woman with the shirt. (Idea: *The wind will blow the shirt away.*)

Pages 11–12. What's happening to the woman's shirt? (Idea: *It's blowing away.*) (Repeat the procedure for talking about the people in the illustration, adding the woman with the shirt. Point to the woman wiping her nose with the handkerchief.) Predict what will happen to the woman with the handkerchief. (Idea: *The wind will blow the handkerchief away.*)

Pages 13–14. What's happening to the woman's handkerchief? (Idea: *It's blowing away.*) (Repeat the procedure for talking about the people in the illustration, adding the woman with the handkerchief. Point to the judge.) This man is a judge. He is in charge of what happens in court. Predict what will happen to the judge.

Pages 15–16. What's happening to the judge's wig? (Idea: *It's blowing away.*) (Repeat the procedure for talking about the people in the illustration, adding the judge. Point to the postman.) Predict what will happen to the postman.

Pages 17–18. What's happening to the postman's letters? (Idea: *They're blowing away.*) (Repeat the procedure for talking about the people in the illustration, adding the postman. Point to the guard.) Predict what will happen to the guard.

Pages 19–20. What's happening to the guard's flag? (Idea: *It's blowing away.*) (Repeat the procedure for talking about the people in the illustration, adding the guard. Point to the two girls.) Predict what will happen to the two girls.

Pages 21–22. What's happening to the girls' scarves? (Idea: *They're blowing away.*) (Repeat the procedure for talking about the people in the illustration, adding the two girls. Point to the man with the newspaper.) Predict what will happen to the man with the newspaper.

Pages 23–24. What's happening to the man's newspaper? (Idea: *It's blowing away.*) (Repeat the procedure for talking about the people in the illustration, adding the man with the newspaper.)

Page 25. What do you think is happening here? (Idea: *Everyone's things are getting all mixed up.*)

Page 26. What do you think is happening here? (Idea: *Everyone's things are falling down from the sky.*) Where's the judge's wig now? *On one of the girls.* Who's wearing the girls' scarves? *The postman and the guard.* Who has the groom's hat? *The girl who had the balloon.*

Page 27. What happened to the wind? (Ideas: *It blew out to sea; it's on the ocean; it went away.*) Did all the people get their things back? *Yes.*

Pat Hutchins's illustrations have a pattern. She kept adding more and more people as she told her story. So the pattern for the illustrations is an add-on pattern. What kind of pattern did Pat Hutchins use to make her illustrations? *An add-on pattern.*

Now that we've finished our picture walk, it's your turn to ask me some questions. What would you like to know about the story? (Accept questions. If children tell about the pictures or the story instead of asking questions, prompt them to ask a question.) Ask me a where question. Ask me a how question.

Read Story Aloud
(Read story aloud to children with minimal interruptions.)

In the next lesson we will read the story again, and I will ask you some questions.

(If children have difficulty attending for an extended period of time, present the next part of this day's lesson at another time.)

Present Target Vocabulary

◎━ Snatched.

In the story, the wind snatched the balloon from little Priscilla. That means the wind grabbed the balloon and pulled it away from her quickly. **Snatched.** Say the word. *Snatched.*

Snatched is an action word. It tells what the wind was doing. What kind of word is **snatched**? *An action word.*

If you snatch something from someone, you grab it and quickly pull it away. Say the word that means "grabbed something and quickly pulled it away." *Snatched.*

(Correct any incorrect responses, and repeat the item at the end of the sequence.)

Let's think of some times when you might have snatched something. I'll name a time. If you might have snatched something at that time, say, "Snatched." If not, don't say anything.

- Your baby brother was coloring on the wall with a pen. *Snatched.*
- The cat was just about to eat a bone that could get caught in its throat. *Snatched.*
- A friend rode his bike at a safe speed.
- Your mom was holding a frying pan full of hot food.
- The girl beside you in school took your last pencil so you couldn't do your work. *Snatched.*
- Uncle Jim ate a hot dog at the table.

What action word means "grabbed something and quickly pulled it away"? *Snatched.*

◎━ Satisfied.

In the story, the wind is not satisfied with just taking the groom's hat, so it also takes the boy's kite. That means the wind is not happy because it doesn't have enough of what it wants or needs. **Satisfied.** Say the word. *Satisfied.*

Satisfied is a describing word. It tells about how someone is feeling. What kind of word is **satisfied**? *A describing word.*

When you are satisfied, you are happy because you have enough of what you want or need. Say the word that means "feeling happy because you have enough of what you want or need." *Satisfied.*

(Correct any incorrect responses, and repeat the item at the end of the sequence.)

Let's think about when people might feel satisfied. If I name a time when someone would feel satisfied, say, "Satisfied." If not, don't say anything.

- You've had enough to eat at dinner. *Satisfied.*
- You've had enough snack to fill your stomach and share a little with a friend. *Satisfied.*
- A tree is cut down in the park.
- We line up and go to the gym to play.
- The goldfish has enough water and enough food and a great view. *Satisfied.*
- Everyone is happy because everyone gets the same things. *Satisfied.*

What describing word means "feeling happy because you have enough of what you want or need"? *Satisfied.*

◎━ Whirled.

In the story, the wind whirled the postman's letters up into the sky. That means the wind spun the letters around very quickly. **Whirled.** Say the word. *Whirled.*

Whirled is an action word. It tells what the wind was doing to the postman's letters. What kind of word is **whirled?** *An action word.*

Watch me. I'll use my hand to show **whirled.** (Hold your hand so that it points toward the ceiling. Quickly spin your hand around, moving it upward as you spin it.) Use your hand to show **whirled.** (Pause.) Good; you used your hand to show **whirled.**

If something whirled, it spun around very quickly. Say the word that means "spun around very quickly." *Whirled.*

(Correct any incorrect responses, and repeat the item at the end of the sequence.)

Let's think about some times when someone or something might have whirled around. I'll tell about a time. If you might have seen someone or something that whirled, say, "Whirled." If not, don't say anything.

- The hurricane spun and spun. *Whirled.*
- Rex's toy top was spinning on the floor. *Whirled.*
- Jessica stood still.
- The dancers pretended they were falling leaves, spinning in the wind. *Whirled.*
- A brown snail crawled up the driveway.
- The airplane spun out of control. *Whirled.*

What action word means "spun around very quickly"? *Whirled.*

 Upward.

In the story, the wind "grabbed the shirt left out to dry and tossed it upward to the sky." That means the wind threw the shirt up toward the sky. **Upward.** Say the word. *Upward.*

Upward is a describing word. It tells about where something was tossed. What kind of word is **upward**? *A describing word.*

When something moves upward, it moves in the direction up. It doesn't go all the way up; it just moves in the direction up. Say the word that means "moves in the direction up." *Upward.*

Watch me. I'll use my hand to show **upward.** I'm going to move my hand upward toward my head. (Hold your hand near your waist. Slowly move your hand upward. Stop moving your hand when it reaches your shoulder.) Did my hand go all the way to my head? *No.* That's right; my hand didn't go all the way to my head; it went upward toward my head. (Use your hand to show *upward* toward the ceiling. Pause.) Good; you used your hand to show **upward.**

(Correct any incorrect responses, and repeat the item at the end of the sequence.)

Let's think about some times when someone or something might move upward. I'll tell you about a time. If you think someone or something would be moving upward, say, "Upward." If not, don't say anything.

- The cat climbs the tree. *Upward.*
- The rain drops down on the ground.
- The breeze picks up the leaves and carries them toward the sky. *Upward.*
- I raise my hands above my head to pretend that I am a seed that sprouted. *Upward.*
- The lamp falls with a crash.
- Everyone goes downstairs to see what made the sound in the basement.

What describing word means "moves in the direction up"? *Upward.*

Present Vocabulary Tally Sheet
(See Week 1, page 3, for instructions.)

Assign Homework
(Homework Sheet, BLM 8a: See the Introduction for homework instructions.)

DAY 2

Preparation: Picture Vocabulary Cards for *snatched, satisfied, whirled,* and *upward.*

Read and Discuss Story
(Read story aloud to children. Ask the following questions at the specified points in the story.)

Now I'm going to read *The Wind Blew.* When I finish each part, I'll ask you some questions. This is a fun story. The whole story is written as a poem. How is the story written? *As a poem.*

Page 4. Where does this story take place? (Ideas: *Outside; in a town.*)

Page 5. What happens to Mr. White's umbrella? *The wind blows it inside out.*

Page 6. What happens to Priscilla's balloon? *The wind blows it up in the air.* What new word did we learn that tells where the wind blows the balloon? *Upward.*

Page 8. What does the wind take next? *The groom's hat.*

Page 10. What does the wind take next? *The boy's kite.*

Page 12. What does the wind take next? *A shirt.*

Page 14. What does the wind take next? *A hanky.* **Hanky** is a short way of saying **handkerchief.** A handkerchief is like a tissue, except it's made of cloth instead of paper. How is a handkerchief different from a tissue? *It's made of cloth instead of paper.* People don't throw hankies away after they use them. They wash them and use them again and again. Do you know anyone who uses a hanky instead of a tissue?

Page 16. What does the wind take next? *The judge's wig.*

Page 18. What does the wind take next? *The postman's letters.* **Postman** is another name for a mail carrier. What do postmen and mail carriers do? (Idea: *They deliver the mail to your house or mailbox.*)

Page 20. What does the wind take next? *The striped flag.*

Page 22. What does the wind take next? *The twins' scarves.* Twins are two children who are born to the same mother on the same day. What do you call two children born to the same mother on the same day? *Twins.*

Page 24. What does the wind take next? *The man's newspaper.*

Page 26. What does the wind do after it has taken everyone's things? (Idea: *It mixes them together and throws them down.*)

Page 27. What does the wind do last? *It blows away to sea.*

We read two stories that ended with poems. What stories were they? *The Three Billy Goats Gruff* and *Stone Soup.*

How is this story different from *The Three Billy Goats Gruff* and *Stone Soup*? (Idea: *The whole story is a poem.*)

Review Vocabulary
(Display the Picture Vocabulary Cards. Point to each card as you say the word. Ask children to repeat each word after you.) These pictures show **snatched, satisfied, whirled,** and **upward.**

- What word means "moves in the direction up"? *Upward.*

- What word means "feeling happy because you have enough of what you want or need"? *Satisfied.*
- What word means "spun around very quickly"? *Whirled.*
- What word means "grabbed something and quickly pulled it away"? *Snatched.*

Extend Vocabulary
◎━ Snatched.

In the story *The Wind Blew,* we learned that **snatched** can be used to tell that someone grabbed something and quickly pulled it away.

Here's a new way to use the word **snatched.**

- **The robbers snatched the jewelry.** Say the sentence.
- **The burglar snatched the money.** Say the sentence.
- **The thief snatched the diamond ring off the counter.** Say the sentence.

Present Expanded Target Vocabulary
◎━ Gale.

In the story, the wind is a very strong wind. It is so strong that it makes whole trees sway. It breaks twigs and branches off the trees. A wind so strong that it makes whole trees sway and breaks twigs and branches off the trees is called a **gale. Gale.** Say the word. *Gale.*

Gale is a naming word. It names a thing. What kind of word is **gale?** *A naming word.*

A gale is a wind so strong that it makes whole trees sway and breaks twigs and branches off the trees. Say the word that means "a wind so strong that it makes whole trees sway and breaks twigs and branches off the trees." *Gale.*

I'll tell about some winds. If the wind I tell about is a gale, say, "Gale." If not, don't say anything.

- The wind breaks twigs and branches off the trees. *Gale.*
- The wind makes little ripples on the pond.
- The wind topples trees and pushes people down the street. *Gale.*
- The waves on the lake are huge when the wind blows. *Gale.*
- I could hardly feel the wind when I went outside yesterday.

- The large tree branch breaks off and falls on the car. *Gale.*

What naming word means "a wind so strong that it makes whole trees sway and breaks twigs and branches off the trees"? *Gale.*

◎—◁ Damaged.

In the story, the gale breaks twigs and branches off the trees. It turns the man's umbrella inside out. It scatters the newspaper and the mail. The wind breaks the umbrella. It ruins the newspaper and the mail so they can't be read. **Damaged.** Say the word. *Damaged.*

Damaged is an action word. It tells what happened to something. What kind of word is **damaged?** *An action word.*

When something is damaged, it is broken or ruined. Say the word that means "broken or ruined." *Damaged.*

I'll tell about some things. If the things I tell about could be damaged, say, "Damaged." If not, don't say anything.

- The hurricane takes the roof off the house. *Damaged.*
- The tornado picks up a car and smashes it. *Damaged.*
- Even though it rained hard, our vegetable garden wasn't hurt at all.
- The wind pushes the sailboat up on the shore and breaks it in half. *Damaged.*
- My bike falls over on the road, but it doesn't even get scratched.
- I couldn't use my rollerblades after my cousin ran over them with the car. *Damaged.*

What action word means "broken or ruined"? *Damaged.*

DAY 3

Preparation: Activity Sheet, BLM 8b.

Retell Story

(Show the pictures on the following pages from the story, and call on a child to tell what's happening. Call on a different child for each section.)

Today I'll show you the pictures Pat Hutchins made for the story *The Wind Blew*. As I show you the pictures, I'll call on one of you to tell the class that part of the story.

Pages 1–2. Tell what happens at the **beginning** of the story.

Pages 3–24. Tell what happens in the **middle** of the story. (Encourage use of target words when appropriate. Model use as necessary.)

Pages 25–27. Tell what happens at the **end** of the story.

How do you think the people in the town feel at the end of the story? (Ideas: *Happy; satisfied.*)

How do you think the people on the boat feel at the end of the story? (Ideas: *Happy; brave; excited.*)

Review Choosing Game

Today you will play the Choosing Game. Let's think about the four words we have learned: **snatched, satisfied, whirled,** and **upward.**
(Display the Picture Vocabulary Cards.) I will say a sentence that has two of our words in it. Your job is to choose the correct word for that sentence. Let's practice. (Display the cards for the two words in each sentence as you say the sentence.)

- If someone grabbed something away from you, was it **snatched** or **whirled**? *Snatched.*
- If you are very full after dinner, are you **whirled** or **satisfied?** *Satisfied.*
- When your balloon gets away from you, does it go **upward** or is it **satisfied?** *Upward.*

Now you're ready to play the game. If you tell me the correct answer, you win one point. If you can't tell me the correct answer, I get the point.

(Draw a T-chart on the board for keeping score. Display the cards for the two words in each sentence as you say the sentence. Children earn one point for each correct answer. If they make an error, tell them the word, and record one point for yourself. Repeat missed words at the end of the game.)

- If your sister grabbed your orange and pulled it away, was it **snatched** or **satisfied?** *Snatched.*

- When the plane leaves the runway, is it **whirled,** or does it go **upward?** *Upward.*
- When you spun your top on the floor, would you say it was **snatched** or **whirled?** *Whirled.*
- If you eat just enough at lunch to feel comfortable, are you **upward** or **satisfied?** *Satisfied.*
- When the bird grabbed the bread crust and pulled it away, was it **satisfied,** or had it **snatched?** *Snatched.*

(Count the points, and declare a winner.) You did a great job of playing the Choosing Game!

Match Item to Owner (Activity Sheet)

 (Give each child a copy of the Activity Sheet, BLM 8b. Review with children the item the wind took from each character in the story. If they have difficulty remembering the items, display pages 23 and 24 of the story.)

What does the wind blow away from the man with the glasses? *His umbrella.* Draw a line from the umbrella to the man with the glasses.

What does the wind blow away from the little boy? *His kite.* Draw a line from the little boy to the kite. (Repeat this process for the remaining items.)

DAY 4

Preparation: Prepare one sheet of chart paper with a circle drawn in the middle. Fold the sheet of paper in half vertically to divide the circle in half. When you record children's responses, physical descriptors should be recorded on the left-hand side of the chart. Personality characteristics or actions should be recorded on the right-hand side of the chart.

Analyze Characters (Literary Analysis)

Let's think about what we already know about how books are made.

- What do we call the name of the book? *The title.*
- What do we call the person who writes the story? *The author.*
- What do we call the person who draws the pictures? *The illustrator.*
- What do we call the people or animals a story is about? *The characters.*
- What do we call the pictures the illustrator makes? *Illustrations.*

Now we'll learn a new verse to "The Story Song." It goes like this:

Illustrations are the pictures. (Repeat the verse until children can sing it confidently.)

Let's sing "The Story Song" to help us remember these important things about books. We will add the new verse before we sing *Characters make it happen.*

(See the Introduction for the complete "Story Song.")

> *Read me a book, and the book pleased me.*
> *I read my book under yonder tree.*
> *Illustrations are the pictures.*
> *Characters make it happen.*
> *Illustrator draws the pictures.*
> *Author says, "I'm who wrote it."*
> *Title says what its name is.*
> *Book says, "I'm a story."*

Who are the characters in *The Wind Blew*? (Ideas: *The man with the umbrella; the girl with the balloon; the groom; the boy with the kite; the woman with the shirt; the woman with the handkerchief; the judge; the postman; the guard; the twins; the man with the newspaper.*)

The story *The Wind Blew* has one character that is not a person and or an animal. Who do you think that character is? *The wind.*

Use some words to tell what the wind looks like. (Ideas: *You can't see the wind; it's invisible.*)

Use some words to tell what the wind was like or what the wind can do. (Ideas: *Strong; takes things; breaks twigs and branches off the trees; sways whole trees.*)

Today you have learned about the most important character in the story *The Wind Blew.*

Play Choosing Game (Cumulative Review)

Let's play the Choosing Game. I will say a sentence that has two of our words in it. Your job is to choose which word is the correct word for that sentence. (Display the Picture Vocabulary Cards for *snatched, satisfied, whirled, upward, gale,* and *damaged,* showing the cards for the two words in each sentence as you say the sentence.)

Now you're ready to play the Choosing Game.

(Draw a T-chart on the board for keeping score. Children earn one point for each correct answer. If they make an error, correct them as you normally would, and record one point for yourself. Repeat missed words at the end of the game.)

- If the wind blows hard enough to break branches, would there be **damage** or is it a **gale?** *Gale.*
- When something is broken, is it **snatched** or **damaged?** *Damaged.*
- When your favorite toy was grabbed away from you, was it **snatched** or **satisfied?** *Snatched.*
- When the boat spun around on the water like a top, would you say that it was **satisfied** or **whirled?** *Whirled.*
- When a hot air balloon takes off, does it go **upward** or is it **snatched?** *Upward.*
- When the kitten has filled its tummy with food, is it **whirled** or **satisfied?** *Satisfied.*
- After the gale blew the boats onto the rocks, would you say that the boats were **satisfied** or **damaged?** *Damaged.*
- When a marble spins around and around, would you say that it is **damaged** or that it **whirled?** *Whirled.*

Now you will have to listen very carefully, because I'm not going to show you the Picture Vocabulary Cards. (This part of the game includes the review word *considerate* from Week 1.)

- Bob helps his sister clean her room and put away her toys when she asks him to. Would you say that Bob has been **snatched** or is **considerate?** *Considerate.*

- When the leaf twirled in circles as it fell, would you say that it **whirled** or that it **damaged?** *Whirled.*
- A big boulder smashes a car. Is the car **damaged** or **considerate?** *Damaged.*
- When the wind picks up a piece of paper and carries it toward the sky, is the paper a **gale,** or does it go **upward?** *Upward.*
- Everyone is picking up broken branches. Was there a **gale,** or was something **satisfied?** *A gale.*
- If I grabbed your toy and pulled it away from you, was I **considerate,** or was your toy **snatched?** *Snatched.*
- When you've had enough to eat, are you **snatched** or **satisfied?** *Satisfied.*
- After a hurricane blows through, are the houses **damaged** or **satisfied?** *Damaged.*

(Count the points, and declare a winner.)
You did a great job of playing the Choosing Game!

DAY 5

Preparation: Happy Face Game Test Sheet, BLM B.

Retell Story to a Partner

(Assign each child a partner, and ask the partners to take turns telling part of the story each time you turn to a new set of pages. Encourage use of target words when appropriate.)

Today I'll show you the pictures Pat Hutchins made for the story *The Wind Blew.* As I show you the pictures, you and your partner will take turns telling part of the story.

Page 1. Tell what happens at the **beginning** of the story.

Pages 2–24. Tell what happens in the **middle** of the story.

Pages 25–27. Tell what happens at the **end** of the story.

How do you think the people in the town feel at the end of the story? (Ideas: *Happy; satisfied.*)

How do you think the people on the boat feel at the end of the story? (Ideas: *Happy; brave; excited.*)

Assess Vocabulary

(Give each child a copy of the Happy Face Game Test Sheet, BLM B.)

Today you're going to play the Happy Face Game. When you play the Happy Face Game, it helps me know how well you know the hard words you are learning.

If I say something true, color the happy face. What will you do if I say something true? *Color the happy face.*

If I say something false, color the sad face. What will you do if I say something false? *Color the sad face.*

Listen carefully to each sentence I say. Don't let me trick you!

Item 1: If something is broken so that it can't be used, it is **satisfied.** *False.*

Item 2: If a robber took the jewelry, it was **snatched.** *True.*

Item 3: If the wind blew so hard that it **damaged** something, it was probably a **gale.** *True.*

Item 4: **Satisfied** means that you've had enough. *True.*

Item 5: If something spun and spun, you could say that it **whirled.** *True.*

Item 6: When an airplane leaves the airport, it is a **gale.** *False.*

Item 7: Airplanes and rockets go **upward.** *True.*

Item 8: If something is **damaged,** it means that you have had enough to eat. *False.*

Item 9: **Snatched** means the same as grabbing and pulling away. *True.*

Item 10: A **gale** is a very strong wind. *True.*

You did a great job of playing the Happy Face Game!

(Score children's work later. Scores of 9 out of 10 indicate mastery level. If a child does not achieve mastery, insert missed words in the games in next week's lessons. Retest those children individually on the missed items before they take the next mastery test.)

Extensions

Read a Story as a Reward

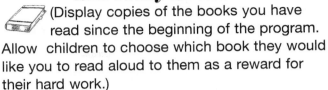

(Display copies of the books you have read since the beginning of the program. Allow children to choose which book they would like you to read aloud to them as a reward for their hard work.)

(Read story to children for enjoyment with minimal interruption.)

Present Super Words Center

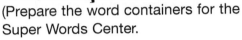

(Prepare the word containers for the Super Words Center.

Note: You will need to keep the cards that were removed from the center. They will be used again later in the program.

See the Introduction for instructions on how to set up and use the Super Words Center.)

(Put the Picture Vocabulary Cards from Weeks 3 and 8 into the word containers. Make duplicates of each card to create a Concentration game. Make as many sets of duplicates as you wish to suit your class. Show children one of the word containers. If they need more guidance, role-play with two or three children as a demonstration.)

Let's think about how we work with our words in the Super Words Center.

You will work with a partner in the Super Words Center. Whom will you work with in the center? *A partner.*

There are two cards for each word in the Super Words Center. You will play a game called Concentration. When you play Concentration, you try to find two cards that match. **Match** means that both cards show the same picture and word. What does **match** mean? *Both cards show the same picture and word.*

First you will take all of the cards out of the container and place them facedown on the table. What do you do first? (Idea: *Take all of the words out and place them facedown on the table.*)

Next you will pick one card, turn it faceup, show your partner the picture, and ask him or her what word the picture shows. What do you do next? (Idea: *I pick a card, turn it faceup, show it to my partner, and ask what word the picture shows.*)

What do you do if your partner doesn't know the word? *Tell my partner the word.*

Next you will put the card faceup where you found it. What do you do next? (Idea: *Put the card faceup where I found it.*)

What do you do next? *Give my partner a turn.*

If your partner chooses another card that is the same as your first card, he or she can take those two cards. What can your partner do? (Idea: *My partner can take both cards if he or she chooses one that is the same as my first card.*)

If your partner can't find one that is the same, he or she puts the card faceup in the same place where it was picked it up. Then it is your turn again. Whoever has the most pairs of cards when all of the cards have been taken is the winner.

(There are many ways to play Concentration. This one is fast to play. You may choose to modify the game depending on children's skill level.)

Preparation:
You will need *The Most Beautiful Kite in the World* for each day's lesson.

Number the pages of the story to assist you in asking questions at appropriate points.

Post a copy of the Vocabulary Tally Sheet with this week's Picture Vocabulary Cards attached.

Each child will need the Homework Sheet, BLM 9a.

The Most Beautiful Kite in the World
author: Andrea Spalding • illustrator: Leslie Watts

🎯 Target Vocabulary

Tier II	Tier III
disappointment	setting
frowned	
present	
enormous	
*excited	
*amazed	

*Expanded Target Vocabulary Word

DAY 1

Introduce Book

Today's book is called *The Most Beautiful Kite in the World*. What's the title of this week's book? *The Most Beautiful Kite in the World.*

This book was written by Andrea Spalding. Who's the author of *The Most Beautiful Kite in the World*? *Andrea Spalding.*

Leslie Watts made the pictures for this book. Who is the illustrator of *The Most Beautiful Kite in the World*? *Leslie Watts.*

The pictures an illustrator makes for a book are called the illustrations. What do you call the pictures an illustrator makes for a book? *Illustrations.* What are illustrations? *The pictures an illustrator makes for a book.* Who made the illustrations for this book? *Leslie Watts.*

The cover of a book usually gives us some hints of what the book is about. Let's look at the front cover of *The Most Beautiful Kite in the World*. What do you see in the illustration? (Ideas: *A girl outside; her hair is blowing around; it looks like she's pointing.*)

Let's look at the back cover of *The Most Beautiful Kite in the World*. (Hold the book open so the front and back covers are visible at the same time.) For this cover, Leslie Watts made one big picture. She put part of the picture on the front cover and part of the picture on the back cover. What do you see now that you can see the whole illustration? (Ideas: *The girl isn't pointing; she's holding on to a ball of string; the string goes to her kite; the kite is up in the air.*)

(Assign each child a partner.) Remember, when you make a prediction about something, you say what you think will happen.

Now get ready to make some predictions to your partner about this book. Use the information from the cover to help you.

(Ask the following questions, allowing sufficient time for children to share their predictions with their partners.)

- Who are the characters in this story? (Whom do you think this story is about?)
- What do you think she will do?
- Where do you think the story happens?
- When do you think the story happens?
- Why do you think the girl is flying the kite?
- How long do you think the kite will stay up?
- Do you think this story is about real people? Tell why or why not.

(Call on several children to share their predictions with the class.)

Take a Picture Walk

We are going to take a picture walk through this book. Remember, when we take a picture walk, we look at the pictures and tell what we think will happen in the story.

(Show the illustrations on the following pages, and ask the specified questions.)

Pages 1–2. Whom do you see in this first illustration? *A man and the girl.* Where do you think they are? (Idea: *In a store.*) What makes you think so? (Ideas: *I can see boxes and jars of candy; the man is on one side of the counter; the girl is on the other side of the counter.*) What is the girl pointing at? *The kite.* What do you think she is saying?

Pages 3–4. What is happening here? (Ideas: *The girl is running down the sidewalk; her dog is waiting for her to play ball.*) How do you think the girl is feeling? (Idea: *Happy.*)

Pages 5–6. What is the girl doing? (Idea: *Sleeping.*) What do you think she is dreaming about? (Ideas: *Kites; balloons; a pirate ship.*)

Pages 7–8. What is happening here? (Ideas: *The little girl is opening a present; her mom and dad are watching.*) Predict what you think will be in the present. (Idea: *A kite.*) What makes you think so? (Idea: *The present is shaped like a kite; the present is flat like a kite.*)

Pages 9–10. What's the little girl doing? (Idea: *Hugging her dad.*) Does she look happy? (Idea: *No.*) What makes you think so? (Ideas: *Her eyes look like they have tears in them; her mouth goes down like she's sad.*)

Pages 11–12. Where do you think they are going? (Idea: *To fly the kite.*) What makes you think so? (Ideas: *Her dad is carrying the kite; there's a big wind.*) What do you think is wrong? (Idea: *The kite isn't the kite she saw in the store.*)

Pages 13–14. What is happening here? (Idea: *The girl is trying to fly the kite.*)

Pages 15–16. What do you think the girl and the woman are talking about?

Pages 17–18. How is the kite different? (Idea: *It has things tied on the tail.*) Do you think the kite is flying any better?

Pages 19–20. What do you think the girl and the man are talking about?

Pages 21–22. Predict what you think the girl and her dad are going to do with the red paper.

Pages 23–24. What do you think the boy is watching?

Pages 25–26. What do you think is happening here? (Ideas: *The kite is way up in the sky; its tail is made up of butterflies; the kite is now yellow.*)

Pages 27–28. What is happening here? (Ideas: *The kite is lifting the little girl into the sky; everyone is watching her fly the kite.*) Do you think a kite could really lift someone off the ground?

Page 29. Where do you think the little girl is going? What do you think she has in her backpack?

Now that we've finished our picture walk, it's your turn to ask me some questions. What would you like to know about the story? (Accept questions. If children tell about the pictures or the story instead of asking questions, prompt them to ask a question.) Ask me a who question. Ask me a why question.

Read Story Aloud
(Read story aloud to children with minimal interruptions.)

In the next lesson we will read the story again, and I will ask you some questions.

(If children have difficulty attending for an extended period of time, present the next part of this day's lesson at another time.)

Present Target Vocabulary
◎← Disappointment.

In the story, when Jenny first tries to fly her kite, it keeps crashing to the ground. Jenny sighed with disappointment. You already know what **sighed** means. Show me what a sigh sounds like. (Pause.) That's right. When Jenny sighed, she let out a deep breath to show she was sad. She was feeling sad because she had wanted the kite from the store, and she didn't get it. **Disappointment.** Say the word. *Disappointment.*

Disappointment is a naming word. It names a feeling. What kind of word is **disappointment?** *A naming word.*

Disappointment is the sad feeling you have when you don't get something you want. Say the word that means "the sad feeling you

have when you don't get something you want."
Disappointment.

(Correct any incorrect responses, and repeat the item at the end of the sequence.)

Let's think about some things that could make you feel disappointment. I'll tell about a time. If you might have felt disappointment, say, "Disappointment." If not, don't say anything.

- Your mom says you can't have a friend over to play. *Disappointment.*
- You lose the money your grandpa gave you. *Disappointment.*
- You make a wish on your birthday, and it comes true.
- You drop your ice cream cone, and it is damaged. *Disappointment.*
- Your sister says, "I love you."
- Your dog eats your homework, and you have to do it over. *Disappointment.*

What naming word means "the sad feeling you have when you don't get something you want"?
Disappointment.

◎⚊ Frowned.

In the story, when the storekeeper told her how much the kite cost, Jenny frowned. That means she made a face that showed she was unhappy. The corners of her mouth went down, and she got wrinkles in her forehead. This is what it would look like if I frowned. (Model frowning.) It's your turn. Show me how you would look if you frowned. **Frowned.** Say the word. *Frowned.*

Frowned is an action word. It tells what someone's face was doing. What kind of word is **frowned?** *An action word.*

If you frowned, you made a face that showed you were unhappy. Say the word that means "made a face that showed you were unhappy."
Frowned.

People might also frown because they are worried or because they are thinking really, really hard. Show me how you would look if you were worried about something. (Pause.) Show me how you would look if you were thinking about something really, really hard. (Pause.) That's right; you can use a frown to show you are unhappy, worried, or thinking really, really hard.

(Correct any incorrect responses, and repeat the item at the end of the sequence.)

Let's think about some times when someone might have frowned. I'll describe a time. If you might have seen someone frowning, say, "Frowned." If not, don't say anything.

- It was a bright, sunny day, but you had to stay inside and help wash the dishes. *Frowned.*
- You fell and scraped your elbow. *Frowned.*
- You got a ride to school with a friend.
- Your pet parrot spoke a new word.
- Someone hurt your feelings. *Frowned.*
- You were enjoying your pizza, but then you bit your tongue. *Frowned.*

What action word means "made a face that shows someone was unhappy, worried, or thinking really, really hard"? *Frowned.*

◎⚊ Present.

In the story, Jenny thinks that maybe her father will buy her the kite as a birthday present. That means she thinks he will give her the kite for her birthday. Another word for a present is a gift. **Present.** Say the word. *Present.*

Present is a naming word. It names a thing. What kind of word is **present?** *A naming word.*

If someone gives you a present, they give you something. Another word for a **present** is a **gift.** Say the word that means "a gift." *Present.*

(Correct any incorrect responses, and repeat the item at the end of the sequence.)

Let's think about some things that could be presents. If I name something that could be a present, say, "Present." If not, don't say anything.

- A fantastic toy. *Present.*
- A cute little kitten. *Present.*
- A huge bowl of worms.
- An old stick.
- A computer game. *Present.*
- A great big box of building blocks. *Present.*

What naming word means "a gift"? *Present.*

◎⚊ Enormous.

In the story, when the kite finally flew, Jenny grinned an enormous grin. That means her grin was very, very big. Her grin was so big it was big enough for a giant. It was gigantic. **Enormous.** Say the word. *Enormous.*

Enormous is a describing word. It tells about how big something is. What kind of word is **enormous?** *A describing word.*

When something is enormous, it is really, really big. Say the word that means "really, really big." *Enormous.*

(Correct any incorrect responses, and repeat the item at the end of the sequence.)

Let's think about some things that could be enormous. I'll name something. If you think that thing could be enormous, say, "Enormous." If not, say, "Absolutely not."

- A mountain. *Enormous.*
- A giant. *Enormous.*
- A furry mouse.
- The biggest tree in the world. *Enormous.*
- A grain of sand.
- A jet airplane. *Enormous.*

What describing word means "very, very big"? *Enormous.*

Present Vocabulary Tally Sheet
(See Week 1, page 3, for instructions.)

Assign Homework
(Homework Sheet, BLM 9a: See the Introduction for homework instructions.)

DAY 2

Preparation: Picture Vocabulary Cards for *disappointment, frowned, present,* and *enormous.*

Read and Discuss Story

(Read story aloud to children. Ask the following questions at the specified points.)

Now I'm going to read *The Most Beautiful Kite in the World.* When I finish each part, I'll ask you some questions.

Page 2. Where was Jenny at the beginning of the story? (Idea: *In a store.*) Why did Jenny think her father would buy her the kite? (Idea: *Tomorrow was her birthday.*)

Page 4. Why do you think Jenny is so happy? (Ideas: *Tomorrow is her birthday; she thinks she'll get the kite.*)

Page 6. What kinds of things does Jenny dream about? *A kite, balloons, butterflies, seas, and pirate ships.* The story says she dreamed of "heaving seas." That means the waves were large, and they were moving up and down. Watch me. I'll use my hand and arm to show heaving seas. (Move your hand and arm in the air in large, swooping u-shapes, pausing at the top of each u.) Use your hand and arm to show heaving seas. (Pause.) Good; you used your hand and arm to show heaving seas.

Are the balloons, the kite, the sea, and the pirate ship real? *No.* That's right; they're just in Jenny's dream.

Page 8. Does Jenny get a kite for her birthday? *Yes.* Is it the kite she wanted? *No.* What kite does she get? (Idea: *One her father has made for her.*) Predict how Jenny will feel about the kite.

Page 10. Jenny's throat feels tight and dry. She has trouble swallowing her food. How is Jenny feeling? (Ideas: *Sad; as if she is going to cry.*) What new word did we learn that tells about Jenny's feelings? *Disappointment.* That's right; Jenny is disappointed that she didn't get the kite she wanted. Does she tell her father how she is feeling? *No.* Why not? (Ideas: *She doesn't want to hurt his feelings; she doesn't want him to know she is disappointed with her present.*)

Page 12. Jenny's father has a bounce in his step. How is he feeling? (Idea: *Happy; excited.*) Jenny's feet feel like lead. How is she feeling? (Ideas: *Sad; unhappy; disappointed.*)

Her eyes water. What does that mean? (Idea: *She is starting to cry.*) What does she say is making her eyes water? *The dust.*

Page 14. What happens when they try to fly the kite? (Ideas: *It doesn't go up; it crashes onto the ground.*) What does her father say it needs? *A tail.* How does he make the tail? *With a piece of string.* What does he send Jenny to find? *Bows for the tail.*

Page 16. What does Mrs. Omelchuck give Jenny? *Some yellow wool.* Does Jenny think that will work? *No.* How is she feeling now?

Page 17. What happens when they try to fly the kite this time? (Idea: *It is a little bit better, but it still crashes to the ground.*) We learned a word in Week 6 that describes how Jenny is feeling. She is becoming upset and angry because no matter how hard they try, they can't get the kite to fly. Say the word that tells how Jenny is feeling. *Frustrated.*

Page 18. What does Jenny's father send her to find? *Two or three more bows.* Is Jenny starting to feel better? *Yes.* Why do you think so? (Ideas: *The kite looks pretty with the yellow wool; it flies better the second time; she laughs.*)

Page 20. What does Mr. Braun give her? *The cover from his magazine.*

Page 22. What happens when they try to fly the kite this time? (Idea: *It stays up for a minute.*)

Page 24. What does Charlie give her? (Idea: *The purple paper from his sucker.*)

Page 26. How does Jenny feel when the kite finally flies? (Idea: *Very happy.*) How do you know? *She has an enormous grin.*

Now that the kite is flying, Jenny remembers her dream kite. What made the yellow, red, and purple butterflies on her real kite? (Ideas: *The yellow yarn; the red magazine cover; the purple sucker wrapper.*)

Page 28. Why is everyone looking up at the kite? (Ideas: *They think it is very beautiful; it is flying.*)

Page 29. At the end of the story is Jenny happy with her kite? *Yes.* What makes you think that? (Idea: *She can hardly wait to show it to her friends.*) What do you think Jenny has learned? (Ideas: *How to fly a kite; homemade presents are good; you don't always have to buy a present from a store.*)

Review Vocabulary

(Display the Picture Vocabulary Cards. Point to each card as you say the word.) These pictures show **disappointment, frowned, present,** and **enormous.** (Ask children to repeat each word after you.)

- What naming word means "the sad feeling you have when you don't get something you want"? *Disappointment.*
- What describing word means "very, very big"? *Enormous.*
- What naming word means "a gift"? *Present.*
- What action word means "made a face that showed someone was unhappy, worried, or thinking really, really hard"? *Frowned.*

Extend Vocabulary

◎◄ Present.

In the story *The Most Beautiful Kite in the World,* we learned that a present can be a gift, something someone gives to someone.

Here's a new way to use the word **present.**

- **The whole class is present today.** Say the sentence.
- **If I say your name, say, "Present."** Say the sentence.
- **Everyone here is present today.** Say the sentence.

In these sentences, **present** is a describing word that means being somewhere. Tell about some times when you have been present. (Encourage children to start their sentences with "I was present when …") (Ideas: *I was present when my cat had kittens; I was present when we went on a field trip; I was present when we had a fire drill.*)

Present Expanded Target Vocabulary

◎◄ Excited.

In the story, Jenny jumps out of bed, hurriedly dresses, and runs into the kitchen. She can hardly wait to take the wrapping paper off her present. She is so happy she can't be still, because she is thinking about the kite she is going to get for her birthday. The word that tells how Jenny is feeling is **excited. Excited.** Say the word. *Excited.*

Excited is a describing word. It tells how Jenny is feeling. What kind of word is **excited?** *A describing word.*

When you are excited, you are so happy you can't be still because you are thinking about something good that is going to happen to you. Say the word that means "so happy you can't be still because something good is going to happen to you." *Excited.*

I'll tell about some times. If you would feel excited, say, "Excited." If not, don't say anything.

- You are going away on a fun trip. *Excited.*
- Your dad came home with a shiny new car. *Excited.*
- Your mom said you would have a big birthday party with all of your friends. *Excited.*
- It was an ordinary day, and you had the same thing for breakfast again.
- Your family was chosen as the first family to fly to the moon. *Excited.*

What describing word means "so happy you can't be still because something good is going to happen to you"? *Excited.*

◎━◂ Amazed.

At the end of the story, everyone is amazed at how beautiful the kite is. That means they are very, very surprised by how beautiful the kite looked. **Amazed.** Say the word. *Amazed.*

Amazed is a describing word. It tells how someone is feeling. What kind of word is **amazed?** *A describing word.*

When you are amazed, you are very, very surprised by something. Say the word that means "very, very surprised by something." *Amazed.*

I'll tell about some times. If someone would feel amazed, say, "Amazed." If not, don't say anything.

- When the teacher came in the room, all the children were sitting still and being quiet. *Amazed.*
- The boy won the very first race he ever ran in. *Amazed.*
- You read a chapter book all by yourself. *Amazed.*
- A friend came over, and you played hide and seek.
- Mom made dinner.
- It snowed in the middle of the summer. *Amazed.*

What describing word means "very, very surprised by something"? *Amazed.*

Preparation: Activity Sheet, BLM 9b. Children will also need a yellow, red, and purple crayon.

Retell Story

(Show the pictures on the following pages from the story, and call on a child to tell what's happening. Call on a different child for each section.)

Today I'll show you the pictures Leslie Watts made for the story *The Most Beautiful Kite in the World.* As I show you the pictures, I'll call on one of you to tell the class that part of the story.

Pages 1–6. Tell what happens at the **beginning** of the story.

Pages 7–26. Tell what happens in the **middle** of the story. (Encourage use of target words when appropriate. Model use as necessary.)

Pages 27–29. Tell what happened at the **end** of the story.

How do you think Jenny feels at the end of the story? (Ideas: *Happy; excited.*)

What do you think Jenny's friends will say when she shows them her kite?

Review Whoopsy! Game

(Display the Picture Vocabulary Cards as you play this game.)

Today you will play the Whoopsy! Game. I'll say sentences using words we have learned. If the word doesn't fit in the sentence, you say, "Whoopsy!" Then I'll ask you to say a sentence where the word fits. If you can do it, you get a point. If you can't do it, I get the point. If the word I use fits the sentence, don't say anything.

Let's practice:

I had a disappointment when … I got a nice present from my friend. *Whoopsy!*

Listen to the beginning of the sentence again. I had a disappointment when … Say the beginning of the sentence. *I had a disappointment when.*

Can you finish the sentence so the word fits? (Idea: *I had a disappointment when I lost my bike.*)

Let's try another one. I frowned when ... I was very happy about seeing my friend. *Whoopsy!*

Listen to the beginning of the sentence again. I frowned when ... Say the beginning of the sentence. *I frowned when.*

Can you finish the sentence so the word fits? (Idea: *I frowned when I hurt my toe.*)

Now you're ready to play the game.

(Draw a T-chart on the board for keeping score. Children earn one point for each correct answer. If they make an error, help them to correct their sentence, and record one point for yourself. Repeat missed words at the end of the game.)

- I got a **present** when ... my dad didn't bring me anything after his business trip. *Whoopsy!* Say the beginning of the sentence again. *I got a present when.* Can you finish the sentence? (Idea: *I got a present when my dad brought me a toy after his business trip.*) (Continue to follow the pattern of recalling the beginning of the sentence before calling for ideas.)
- It was a **disappointment** when ... I had my favorite food for dinner. *Whoopsy!* [Say ... Can you?] (Idea: *It was a disappointment when we didn't have any dinner at all.*)
- I **frowned** when ... I hit my finger with a hammer.
- The **enormous** giant was ... no taller than my toe. *Whoopsy!* (Idea: *The enormous giant was taller than a skyscraper.*)
- I **frowned** when ... my brother took me to the zoo. *Whoopsy!* (Idea: *I frowned when my mom told me I couldn't go swimming.*)

(Count the points, and declare a winner.)
You did a great job of playing Whoopsy!

Match Item to Person (Activity Sheet)

(Give each child a copy of the Activity Sheet, BLM 9b. Review with children the items Jenny receives from each of the characters. If children have difficulty remembering the items, display the appropriate pages of the story.)

What does Jenny's father give Jenny? *The kite.* Draw a line from the kite to Jenny's father.

What does Mrs. Omelchuck give Jenny? *The yellow wool.* Draw a line from Mrs. Omelchuck to the yellow wool.

(Repeat this process for the remaining items. Ask children to color the items on the tail of the kite.)

Introduce Setting (Where) (Literary Analysis)

Let's think about what we already know about how books are made.

- What do we call the name of the book? *The title.*
- What do we call the person who writes the story? *The author.*
- What do we call the person who draws the pictures? *The illustrator.*
- What do we call the people or animals a story is about? *The characters.*
- What do we call the pictures the illustrator makes? *Illustrations.*

Let's sing "The Story Song" to help us remember these important things about books.

(See the Introduction for the complete "Story Song.")

Today we will learn more about how stories are made.

The setting of a story tells two things. One thing the setting tells is where the story happens. What is one thing the setting tells? *Where the story happens.*

Let's look at the pictures and talk about the story to figure out where *The Most Beautiful Kite in the World* happens.

(Show the following pages, and ask the specified questions.)

Pages 1–2. Where does the story begin? *In the store.*

Pages 3–4. Where does the next part of the story happen? *On the street.*

Pages 5–6. Where does the next part of the story happen? *In Jenny's bedroom.*

Pages 7–10. Where does the next part of the story happen? *In the kitchen.*

Pages 11–12. Where does the next part of the story happen? *Outside.*

Pages 13–14. Where does the next part of the story happen? *Outside.* You're right; they are outside. Do you think this place is hilly or flat? *Flat.* Do you think there is lots of grass or lots of trees? *Lots of grass.* A place that is big and flat and has lots of grass is called a prairie. **Prairie.** Say that word. *Prairie.* Where does the next part of the story happen? *On the prairie.*

Pages 15–16. Where does the next part of the story happen? *On Mrs. Omelchuck's porch.*

Pages 17–18. Where does the next part of the story happen? *On the prairie.*

Pages 19–20. Where does the next part of the story happen? *In Mr. Braun's yard.*

Pages 21–28. Where does the next part of the story happen? *On the prairie.*

Page 29. Where does the next part of the story happen? *On the street.*

The store, the street, Jenny's house, Mrs. Omelchuck's porch, and Mr. Braun's yard are all on the prairie. So if we could use only one word to tell the setting of the story, we would use the word **prairie.** Where is the setting of the story *The Most Beautiful Kite in the World*? *The prairie.*

Today you learned about the one of the parts of the setting of the story *The Most Beautiful Kite in the World.* You learned about where the story happens.

Now we'll learn a new verse to "The Story Song." We'll sing *setting tells where it happens.* (Repeat until children can say it with confidence.)

Read me a book, and the book pleased me.
I read my book under yonder tree.
Setting tells where it happens.
Illustrations are the pictures.
Characters make it happen.
Illustrator draws the pictures.
Author says, "I'm who wrote it."
Title says what its name is.
Book says, "I'm a story."

Play Whoopsy! (Cumulative Review)

 Let's play Whoopsy! I'll say sentences using words we have learned. If the word doesn't fit in the sentence, you say, "Whoopsy!" Then I'll ask you to say a sentence where the word fits. If you can do it, you get a point. If you can't do it, I get the point. If the word I use fits the sentence, don't say anything.

Now you're ready to play the game.

(Draw a T-chart on the board for keeping score. Children earn one point for each correct answer. If they make an error, correct them as you normally would, and record one point for yourself. Repeat missed words at the end of the game.)

- I was **excited** when … nothing new happened. *Whoopsy!* (Idea: *I was excited when a new boy came to our school.*)
- I was **amazed** when … my painting turned out to be so very beautiful.
- Jim had a **disappointment** when … he got a brand new bike. *Whoopsy!* (Idea: *Jim had a disappointment when he didn't get a brand new bike.*)
- The whole class was **present** … when no one came to school. *Whoopsy!* (Idea: *The whole class was present when everyone came to school.*)
- The **enormous** tree was … so tall that we couldn't see the top of it.
- Henry **frowned** when … he dropped his ice-cream cone on the ground.

- Tanisha got a **present** when … it wasn't her birthday. *Whoopsy!* (Idea: *Tanisha got a present when it was her birthday.*)
- The boy was **brave** when … he ran away from the tiny mouse. *Whoopsy!* (Idea: *The boy was brave when he stayed to fight the dragon.*)
- The teacher was **angry** when … her students did as they were told. *Whoopsy!* (Idea: *The teacher was angry when her students didn't do as they were told.*)
- I had a **disappointment** when … it was time to stop playing Whoopsy!

(Count the points, and declare a winner.)
You did a great job of playing Whoopsy!

DAY 5

Preparation: Happy Face Game Test Sheet, BLM B.

Retell Story to a Partner

(Assign each child a partner, and ask the partners to take turns telling part of the story each time you turn to a new set of pages. Encourage use of target words when appropriate.)

Today I'll show you the pictures Leslie Watts made for the story *The Most Beautiful Kite in the World.* As I show you the pictures, you and your partner will take turns telling part of the story.

Pages 1–6. Tell what happens at the **beginning** of the story.

Pages 7–26. Tell what happens in the **middle** of the story.

Pages 25–27. Tell what happens at the **end** of the story.

What do you think Jenny learned? (Ideas: *How to fly a kite; that homemade presents are good; you don't always have to buy a present from a store.*)

Assess Vocabulary

(Give each child a copy of the Happy Face Game Test Sheet, BLM B.)

Today you're going to play the Happy Face Game. When you play the Happy Face Game, it helps me know how well you know the hard words you are learning.

If I say something true, color the happy face. What will you do if I say something true? *Color the happy face.*

If I say something false, color the sad face. What will you do if I say something false? *Color the sad face.*

Listen carefully to each sentence I say. Don't let me trick you!

Item 1: If you have a **disappointment,** you are unhappy. *True.*

Item 2: If you **frowned,** your face showed others that you were unhappy. *True.*

Item 3: When you are **present,** it means you are here. *True.*

Item 4: Something that is **enormous** is very, very small. *False.*

Item 5: If you are **amazed,** you are very surprised by something. *True.*

Item 6: You don't get a **present** when it is your birthday. *False.*

Item 7: If something good is going to happen to you, you get **excited.** *True.*

Item 8: When you are **curious** about something, you are not interested in it. *False.*

Item 9: When you are **determined** about doing something, you have made up your mind about it and won't let anything stop you. *True.*

Item 10: A **disagreeable** person is fun to be with. *False.*

You did a great job of playing the Happy Face Game!

(Score children's work later. Scores of 9 out of 10 indicate mastery. If a child does not achieve mastery, insert the missed words in the games in the next week's lessons. Retest those children individually on the missed items before they take the next mastery test.)

Extensions
Read a Story as a Reward

(Display copies of the eight books that you have read since the beginning of the program. Allow children to choose which book they would like you to read aloud to them as a reward for their hard work.)

(Read story aloud to children for enjoyment with minimal interruptions.)

Present Super Words Center

(Prepare the word containers for the Super Words Center.

Note: You will need to keep the cards that were removed from the center. They will be used again later in the program.

See the Introduction for instructions on how to set up and use the Super Words Center.)

(Put the Picture Vocabulary Cards from Weeks 2 and 9 into the word containers. Make duplicates of each card to create a Concentration game. Make as many sets of duplicates as you wish to suit your class. Show children one of the word containers. If they need more guidance, role-play with two or three children as a demonstration.)

Let's think about how we work with our words in the Super Words Center.

You will work with a partner in the Super Words Center. Who will you work with in the center? *A partner.*

There are two cards for each word in the Super Words Center. You will play a game called Concentration. When you play Concentration you try to find two cards that match. **Match** means that both cards show the same picture and word. What does **match** mean? *Both cards show the same picture and word.*

First you will take all of the cards out of the container and place them facedown on the table. What do you do first? (Idea: *Take all of the words out and place them facedown on the table.*)

Next you will pick one card, turn it faceup, show your partner the picture, and ask him or her what word the picture shows. What do you do next? (Idea: *I pick a card, turn it faceup, show it to my partner, and ask what word the picture shows.*)

What do you do if your partner doesn't know the word? *Tell my partner the word.*

Next you will put the card faceup where you found it. What do you do next? (Idea: *Put the card faceup where I found it.*)

What do you do next? *Give my partner a turn.*

If your partner chooses another card that is the same as your first card, he or she can take those two cards. What can your partner do? (Idea: *My partner can take both cards if he or she chooses one that is the same as my first card.*)

If your partner can't find one that is the same, he or she puts the card down faceup in the same place where it was picked up. Then it is your turn again. Whoever has the most pairs of cards when all of the cards have been taken is the winner.

(There are many ways to play Concentration. This one is fast to play. You may choose to modify the game depending on children's skill level.)

Preparation: You will need *Welcome Back Sun* for each day's lesson.

Number the pages of the story to assist you in asking questions at appropriate points.

Post a copy of the Vocabulary Tally Sheet, BLM A, with this week's Picture Vocabulary Cards attached.

Each child will need the Homework Sheet, BLM 10a.

DAY 1

Introduce Book

Today's book is called *Welcome Back Sun.* What's the title of this week's book? *Welcome Back Sun.*

This book was written by Michael Emberley. Who's the author of *Welcome Back Sun*? *Michael Emberley.*

Michael Emberley also made the pictures for this book. Who's the illustrator of *Welcome Back Sun*? *Michael Emberley.* Remember, the pictures an illustrator makes for a book are called the illustrations. What do you call the pictures an illustrator makes for a book? *Illustrations.* What are illustrations? *The pictures an illustrator makes for a book.* Who made the illustrations for this book? *Michael Emberley.*

The cover of a book usually gives us some hints of what the book is about. Let's look at the front cover of *Welcome Back Sun.* What do you see in the illustration? (Ideas: *A man, a woman, a child; they're sitting near the top of a mountain.*)

(Assign each child a partner.) Remember, when you make a prediction about something, you say what you think will happen.

Now get ready to make some predictions to your partner about this book. Use the information from the cover to help you.

(Ask the following questions, allowing sufficient time for children to share their predictions with their partners.)

Welcome Back Sun
author: Michael Emberley • illustrator: Michael Emberley

◎← Target Vocabulary

Tier II	Tier III
memories	setting
examine	
complaining	
familiar	
*dreary	
*celebrate	

*Expanded Target Vocabulary Word

- Who are the characters in this story? (Whom do you think this story is about?)
- What is the man holding?
- Where do you think the story happens?
- When do you think the story happens?
- Why do you think they are up in the mountains?
- How did they get up so high?
- Do you think this story is about real people? Tell why or why not.

(Call on several children to share their predictions with the class.)

Take a Picture Walk

We are going to take a picture walk through this book. Remember, when we take a picture walk, we look at the pictures and tell what we think will happen in the story.

(Show the illustrations on the following pages, and ask the specified questions.)

Pages 1–2. What do you see in this first illustration? (Ideas: *Mountains; some houses; a village.*) (If children do not suggest the word *village*, remind them by saying:) When we read the story *Stone Soup*, we learned that a village is a very small town. What do you call a very small town? *A village.* Where is the village? (Ideas: *Down low; at the bottom of the mountains.*) The lowland between two mountains is called a valley. What do you call the lowland between two mountains? *A valley.* What is a valley? *The lowland between two mountains.* This village is in a valley. Where is the village? *In a valley.*

When do you think this story happens? (Idea: *In the winter; at night.*) What makes you think so? (Ideas: *I can see the snow; lights are on in the houses.*)

Pages 3–4. Who do you think the people are? (Idea: *A girl and her mother.*) How do you think they are feeling? (Idea: *Sad.*)

Page 6. What is happening here? (Idea: *Someone is watching the sun come up or go down behind the mountain.*)

Page 7. Do you think this girl lives in the United States? Tell why you think so.

Pages 9–10. Where are they now? (Ideas: *Outside; in the forest.*) What is the girl doing? *Skiing.* What is her mother doing? (Idea: *Cutting branches off the tree.*) What makes you think so? *She has scissors in her hands.*

Pages 11–12. What is happening here? (Idea: *Everyone is dancing.*)

Page 13. Whom is the girl hugging? (Ideas: *Her father; her grandfather.*)

Page 16. What is the little girl doing? *Sleeping.*

Page 18. What is happening here? (Idea: *People are climbing the hill.*) What are the people carrying? (Idea: *Lights.*)

Pages 19–20. What time do you think it is? (Ideas: *Early morning; sunrise.*) What makes you think so? (Idea: *Some of the mountaintops are turning pink.*) Do you think it's hot or cold out? *Cold.* What makes you think so? (Idea: *I can see the people's breath.*)

Page 22. Predict where you think the people are going.

Pages 23–24. What is happening here? (Ideas: *They are all looking at the sky; the sun has come up.*)

Pages 25–26. What do you think the people are watching? (Ideas: *The sunrise; the sun.*)

Page 28. Where is the little girl now? (Idea: *Back home.*) What is happening here? (Idea: *She's running down the stairs.*)

Page 29. What are the girl and her mother doing? (Idea: *Looking at the flowers.*) Where do you think the flowers came from? (Idea: *From the branches the mother cut in the woods.*) How

are the girl and her mother feeling now? (Ideas: *Happy; satisfied.*)

Now that we've finished our picture walk, it's your turn to ask me some questions. What would you like to know about the story? (Accept questions. If children tell about the pictures or story instead of asking questions, prompt them to ask a question.) Ask me a where question. Ask me a what question.

Read Story Aloud
(Read story aloud to children with minimal interruptions.)

In the next lesson, we will read the story again, and I will ask you some questions.

(If children have difficulty attending for an extended period of time, present the next part of this day's lesson at another time.)

Present Target Vocabulary

Memories.

In the story, when the people sit on the ridge watching the sun come back, they refresh their memories. That means they remember things that happened to them before. **Memories.** Say the word. *Memories.*

Memories is a naming word. It names a thing. What kind of word is **memories?** *A naming word.*

Memories are the things you remember that have happened to you before. Say the word that means "the things you remember that have happened to you before." *Memories.*

(Correct any incorrect responses, and repeat the item at the end of the sequence.)

Let's think about some things you might have memories of. I'll tell you about a time. If you remember that thing having happened to you, say, "Memories." If not, don't say anything.

- You came to school for the first time. *Memories.*
- You *will* go to the park *tomorrow.*
- You think about a time when you were sick. *Memories.*
- You remember something fun that you did with a friend. *Memories.*

- You think about the fun you *will* have when you are grown up.
- You think about your first day at this school and how you felt back then. *Memories.*

What naming word means "the things you remember that have happened to you before"? *Memories.*

◎–≺ Examine.

In the story, the little girl examines the branches each day. That means she looks at the branches very carefully. **Examine.** Say the word. *Examine.*

Examine is an action word. It tells what someone is doing. What kind of word is **examine?** *An action word.*

If you examine something, it means you look at it very carefully. Say the word that means to "look at something very carefully." *Examine.*

(Correct any incorrect responses, and repeat the item at the end of the sequence.)

Let's think about some things you might examine. I'll name something. If you could examine it, say, "Examine." If not, don't say anything.

- Some funny-looking eggs under a leaf. *Examine.*
- A butterfly's patterned wings. *Examine.*
- A memory.
- A song that your mom sings when she works.
- A deep crack in the sidewalk. *Examine.*
- A dog's bark.

What action word means to "look at something very carefully"? *Examine.*

◎–≺ Complaining.

In the story, when the little girl is climbing the mountain, she says her legs hurt, she is breathing hard, but she is not complaining. That means she is not telling anyone she is unhappy even though her legs and chest hurt. **Complaining.** Say the word. *Complaining.*

Complaining is an action word. It tells what someone is doing. What kind of word is **complaining?** *An action word.*

If you complain about something, you say you are unhappy with that thing. Say the word that means "saying you are unhappy with something." *Complaining.*

(Correct any incorrect responses, and repeat the item at the end of the sequence.)

Let's think about complaining. I'll say something. If what I say is complaining, say, "Complaining." If not, don't say anything.

- Oh, this soup is too hot. *Complaining.*
- Why can't we ever have what I like to eat for dinner? *Complaining.*
- This movie is good.
- I have four apples and two oranges.
- I don't like it when you shout. *Complaining.*
- Why is this room always a mess? *Complaining.*

What action word means "saying you are unhappy with something"? *Complaining.*

◎–≺ Familiar.

In the story the girl's mother told her, the small girl saw a familiar yellow glow coming from behind the mountaintop. That means she saw the yellow glow and remembered she had seen it before, and she knew what it was right away. **Familiar.** Say the word. *Familiar.*

Familiar is a describing word. It tells about how well you know something. What kind of word is **familiar?** *A describing word.*

When something is familiar, you remember it when you see it, and you know what it is right away. Say the word that means "you remember it when you see it, and you know what it is right away." *Familiar.*

(Correct any incorrect responses, and repeat the item at the end of the sequence.)

Let's think about some things that could be familiar to you. I'll name something. If you are familiar with that thing, say, "Familiar." If not, say nothing.

- Your house. *Familiar.*
- Your best friend. *Familiar.*
- A stranger at the store.
- Our classroom. *Familiar.*
- Someone you have never seen before.
- The children in our class. *Familiar.*

What describing word means "you remember it when you see it, and you know what it is right away"? *Familiar.*

Present Vocabulary Tally Sheet
(See Week 1, page 3, for instructions.)

Assign Homework
(Homework Sheet, BLM 10a: See the Introduction for homework instructions.)

DAY 2

Preparation: Picture Vocabulary Cards for *memories, examine, complaining,* and *familiar.*

Read and Discuss Story
(Read story aloud to children. Ask the following questions at the specified points.)

Now I'm going to read *Welcome Back Sun.* When I finish each part, I'll ask you some questions.

Page 2. What month is it in the story? *March.* When did they last see the sun? *In September.* I'll say the months; you count and tell me how many months it has been dark. October, November, December, January, February, March. How many months has it been dark? *Six.* No wonder they call this season the *murketiden!* [murk-e-ti-den] *Murketiden* means "the murky time." **Murky** means dark. And it's been dark for six whole months!

Where does the story happen? *In Norway.* The country Norway is much like the state of Alaska. Both places have mountains, and both have very long, dark winters. What place is Norway like? *Alaska.*

Page 4. How does the long, dark winter make the little girl feel? (Idea: *"Hungry for sunshine."*) How does it make her mama feel? (Ideas: *Unhappy; grouchy.*)

Page 6. The girl's mama tells her a story about another small girl. What happens in that story? (Ideas: *The sun gets lost, and the girl has to find it; she has to climb over mountains; she almost freezes to death; she finds the sun on the other side of a big mountain; she takes the sun home with her; people still do what the girl did.*)

Page 8. What does the little girl ask her father? *"Could we climb the Gausta, Papa?"* What does her father say? *"Soon."*

Page 10. Why do the girl and her mama go to collect the branches? (Idea: *When the buds open on the branches, they will know it is spring.*) There is a little bit of daylight now, but have they seen the sun? *No.*

Page 12. Why are these people dancing? (Idea: *The sun has come to their city.*) Has the sun come to the little village? (Ideas: *No; not yet.*)

Page 14. Why is the little girl hugging her papa? (Idea: *She is trying to make him feel better; she wants to ask him if they can climb the Gausta.*) Everyone very badly wants the sun to come back. We learned a word in Week 1 that means "wanting something very badly." What word was that? *Desperate.* Good. The family is desperate for the sun to come back. How are they feeling? *Desperate.*

Page 16. What food do they pack for the trip? *Cheese, flatbread, smoked salmon, water.* If your family was going to make this trip, what food would your family pack?

Page 20. How far up the mountain will some of the villagers go? *To the top.* How far up the mountain will the little girl's family go? *To the pass.* A pass is a narrow path that goes through the mountains.

Page 22. Is it hard work, climbing up the mountain? *Yes.* How do you know? (Ideas: *The little girl's hand is hot and sweaty; her legs hurt; she's breathing hard.*) She says her heart is thumping. Why is her heart thumping? (Ideas: *She is working hard to climb the mountain; she is excited because she will soon see the sun.*) (**Note:** If children don't use the word *excited,* say:) We learned a word in Week 9 that tells how the little girl is feeling. That word is **excited.** Sometimes when you are excited, your heart beats extra fast, and you can feel it thumping in your body.)

Page 24. When they reach the pass, what do they see? *The sun.* What is it like when they saw the sun? (Ideas: *There is a brilliant light; the light flashed off the snow and ice; it sparkles off* *the rocks and trees.*) A brilliant light is a very, very bright light. What kind of light is very, very bright? *A brilliant light.*

Page 26. How does the little girl feel when she sees the sun? (Idea: *Very, very happy.*) How do you know? *She can't stop smiling.*

Why doesn't she remember the trip home? (Idea: *She falls asleep.*)

Page 28. When she wakes up the next morning, what does she see? (Idea: *The sun.*)

Page 30. At the end of the story, the little girl knows spring has come. How does she know? (Ideas: *The sun shines in her village; flowers are on the branches they cut.*)

What words end the story? *Welcome back, Sun.* Where else did you see and hear those words? (Idea: *In the title.*)

Review Vocabulary

(Display the Picture Vocabulary Cards. Point to each card as you say the word. Ask children to repeat each word after you.) These pictures show **memories, examine, complaining,** and **familiar.**

- What action word means "saying you are unhappy with something"? *Complaining.*
- What describing word means "you remember it when you see it, and you know what it is right away"? *Familiar.*
- What action word means to "look at something very carefully"? *Examine.*
- What naming word means "the things you remember that have happened to you before"? *Memories.*

Extend Vocabulary

◎⟵ Examine.

In the story *Welcome Back Sun,* we learned that **examine** means to "look at something very carefully."

Here's a new way to use the word **examine.**

- **The doctor examined my new baby sister when she was born.** Say the sentence.
- **Doctor Lee examined my heart.** Say the sentence.
- **The eye doctor examined my eyes.** Say the sentence.

In these sentences, **examine** is an action word that tells what a doctor does when he looks at your body and does tests to see if anything is wrong with you. Tell about some times when you were examined by your doctor. (Ideas: *The doctor examined my back when I fell off the monkey bars; the dentist examined my teeth, and the nurse cleaned them; my doctor examined the cut on my knee.*)

Present Expanded Target Vocabulary

◎⟵ Dreary.

In the story, the winter days are all dark and murky. The sun never shines. The days are gloomy, sad, and boring. The word that describes the winter days is **dreary. Dreary.** Say the word. *Dreary.*

Dreary is a describing word. It tells about what the winter days were like. What kind of word is **dreary?** *A describing word.*

When something is dark and gloomy, sad and boring, it is dreary. Say the word that means "dark and gloomy, sad and boring." *Dreary.*

I'll tell about some things. If those things would be dreary, say, "Dreary." If not, don't say anything.

- The day is cloudy and rainy, and you have nothing interesting to do. *Dreary.*
- The illustrations in the story are dark and gloomy, sad and boring. *Dreary.*
- The sun comes up and makes it warm and light everywhere.
- Everything is interesting and exciting.
- The cold, gray clouds roll close to the ground and spit rain on us. *Dreary.*
- The bright yellow daffodils reach up to the bright, warm sun.

What describing word means "dark and gloomy, sad and boring"? *Dreary.*

◎⟵ Celebrate.

In the story, everyone goes up the mountain to find the sun. They laugh, dance, and eat good food. They are celebrating the return of the sun. That means they are doing things that are fun on the special day when the sun comes back to the mountains. **Celebrate.** Say the word. *Celebrate.*

Celebrate is an action word. It tells what people do. What kind of word is **celebrate?** *An action word.*

When people celebrate, they do things that are fun on a special day. Say the word that means to "do things that are fun on a special day." *Celebrate.*

I'll tell about some days. If people would celebrate that day, say, "Celebrate." If not, don't say anything.

- The fourth of July. *Celebrate.*
- Joan and Jack get married. *Celebrate.*
- You come home after school.
- The mail carrier leaves the mail.
- It's your birthday. *Celebrate.*
- Our class works so hard that it earns a party. *Celebrate.*

What action word means to "do things that are fun on a special day"? *Celebrate.*

DAY 3

Preparation: Activity Sheet, BLM 10b.

Retell Story

(Show the pictures on the following pages from the story, and call on a child to tell what's happening. Call on a different child for each section.)

Today I'll show you the pictures Michael Emberley made for the story *Welcome Back Sun.* As I show you each picture, I'll call on one of you to tell the class that part of the story.

Pages 1–4. Tell what happens at the **beginning** of the story.

Pages 5–26. Tell what happens in the **middle** of the story. (Encourage use of target words when appropriate. Model use as necessary.)

Pages 27–30. Tell what happens at the **end** of the story.

How are the little girl and her family feeling at the beginning of the story? (Ideas: *Hungry for sunshine; tired of the dark; desperate for the sun to come back.*)

How are the little girl and her family feeling at the end of the story? (Ideas: *Excited; satisfied that spring had come.*)

How do you feel during the winter?

How do you feel when spring comes?

Review Whoopsy!

(Display the Picture Vocabulary Cards as you play this game.)

Today you will play Whoopsy! I'll say sentences using words we have learned. If the word doesn't fit in the sentence, you say, "Whoopsy!" Then I'll ask you to say a sentence where the word fits. If you can do it, you get a point. If you can't do it, I get the point. If the word I use fits the sentence, don't say anything.

Let's practice:

I had **memories** when … I thought about what **will** happen next week. *Whoopsy!*

Listen to the beginning of the sentence again. I had **memories** when … Say the beginning of the sentence. *I had memories when.*

Can you finish the sentence so the word fits? (Idea: *I had memories when I remembered what happened last week.*)

Let's try another one. I **examine** a fish when … I don't look at it at all. *Whoopsy!*

Listen to the beginning of the sentence again. I **examine** a fish when … Say the beginning of the sentence. *I examine a fish when.*

Can you finish the sentence so the word fits? (Idea: *I examine a fish when I look at it very carefully.*)

Now you're ready to play the game.

(Draw a T-chart on the board for keeping score. Children earn one point for each correct answer. If they make an error, help them to correct their sentence, and record one point for yourself. Repeat missed words at the end of the game.)

- I was **complaining** when … there was nothing wrong and I was feeling fine. *Whoopsy!* Say the beginning of the sentence again. *I was complaining when.* Can you finish the sentence? (Idea: *I was complaining when*

everything went wrong and I was upset.)
(Continue to follow the pattern of recalling the beginning of the sentence before calling for ideas.)

- The boy was **familiar** because … he didn't look like anyone I knew. *Whoopsy!* (Idea: *The boy was familiar because he looked like someone I knew.*)
- Harvey had **memories** when … he thought about what happened yesterday.
- I **examine** the cool blue plant when … I look at something else instead. *Whoopsy!* (Idea: *I examine the cool blue plant when I look at it carefully.*)
- I was **complaining** when … my toe and my hand hurt.

(Count the points, and declare a winner.)
You did a great job of playing Whoopsy!

Making a List (Activity Sheet)

(Give each child a copy of the Activity Sheet, BLM 10b. Review with children the food the family packed for their trip. If children have difficulty remembering, reread page 15 of the story.)

Today we are going to make a list of the food the family packed for their trip. When we make a list, we write words or make pictures to help us remember. What do we do when we make a list? *We write words or make pictures to help us remember.*

(Show children the page with the pictures of food. Point to the food.) These are the foods the family packed for their trip. (Point to the cheese.) What is this? *Cheese.* (Point to the smoked salmon.) What is this? *Smoked salmon.* (Repeat for the remaining items.)

My turn to make a list. First I cut out each object. (Demonstrate.) What do I do first? *Cut out each object.* The title of this sheet is *Making a List.* What do these words say? *Making a list.* Next I glue the picture onto the list. What do I do next? *Glue the picture onto the list.* (Demonstrate process for two more items.)

Now it's your turn to make a list. (Children who are able to may copy each word beside the picture.)

Preparation: Prepare a sheet of chart paper, landscape direction, with the title *Welcome Back Sun.* Underneath the title, draw 11 boxes, connected by arrows. See the Introducton for an example.

Introduce Setting (Where) (Literary Analysis)

Let's think about what we already know about how books are made.

- What do we call the name of the book? *The title.*
- What do we call the person who writes the story? *The author.*
- What do we call the person who draws the pictures? *The illustrator.*
- What do we call the people or animals a story is about? *The characters.*
- What do we call the pictures the illustrator makes? *Illustrations.*
- What is one thing the setting of a story tells? *Where a story happens.*

Let's sing "The Story Song" to help us remember these important things about books.

(See the Introduction for "The Story Song.")

Today we will learn more about the setting of a story.

The setting of a story tells two things. One thing the setting tells is where the story happens. What is one thing the setting tells? *Where the story happens.*

Let's look at the pictures and talk about the story to figure out where *Welcome Back Sun* happens. (Record children's responses by writing the underlined words in the boxes on the chart paper you prepared.)

(Show the illustrations on the following pages, and ask the specified questions.)

Pages 1–2. Where does the story begin? (Ideas: *In a <u>village</u>; in a <u>valley</u>; in the <u>mountains</u> in <u>Norway</u>.*)

Pages 3–4. Where does the next part of the story happen? *In the girl's <u>house</u>.*

Pages 5–6. Where does the next part of the

story happen? *On the <u>mountain</u>.*

Pages 7–8. Where does the next part of the story happen? *In the <u>house</u>.*

Pages 9–10. Where does the next part of the story happen? *In the <u>woods</u>.*

Pages 11–12. Where does the next part of the story happen? *In <u>Oslo</u>.*

Pages 13–16. Where does the next part of the story happen? *In the <u>house</u>.*

Pages 17–18. Where does the next part of the story happen? *In the <u>village</u>.*

Pages 19–26. Where does the next part of the story happen? *On the <u>mountain</u>.*

Pages 27–30. Where does the next part of the story happen? *In the <u>house</u>.*

The village, the valley, the mountains, the house, and Oslo are all in Norway. So if we could use only one word to tell the setting of the story, we would use the word **Norway.** Where is the setting of the story *Welcome Back Sun*? *Norway.*

Today you learned about the one of the parts of the setting of the story *Welcome Back Sun.* You learned about where the story happens.

Play Whoopsy! (Cumulative Review)

Let's play Whoopsy! I'll say sentences using words we have learned. If the word doesn't fit in the sentence, you say "Whoopsy!" Then I'll ask you to say a sentence where the word fits. If you can do it, you get a point. If you can't do it, I get the point. If the word I use fits the sentence, don't say anything.

Now you're ready to play the game.

(Draw a T-chart on the board for keeping score. Children earn one point for each correct answer. If they make an error, correct them as you normally would, and record one point for yourself. Repeat missed words at the end of the game.)

- I had **memories** when … I thought about what I **will** do this **coming** weekend. *Whoopsy!* (Idea: *I had memories when I thought about what happened last weekend.*)
- I am **complaining** when … I say that my head

hurts.
- I **examine** a leaf when … I don't look at it carefully. *Whoopsy!* (Idea: *I examine a leaf when I look at it carefully.*)
- Philip thinks the girl looks **familiar** … because she looks like someone he knows.
- The **dreary** day is … bright, sunny, and fun. *Whoopsy!* (Idea: *The dreary day is dark, cloudy, and no fun at all.*)
- The girls **decided** to celebrate when … they won the dance contest.
- Dinner is **delicious** when … mom serves worm stew with dirt pudding. *Whoopsy!* (Idea: *Dinner is delicious when mom serves meatloaf and apple pie.*)
- The plant **sprouted** when … it poked up through the soil.
- The substitute teacher was **familiar** because … she had taught many times in our class.
- I was **complaining** when … I felt better than I had ever felt. *Whoopsy!* (Idea: *I was complaining when I felt worse than I had ever felt.*)

(Count the points, and declare a winner.)
You did a great job of playing Whoopsy!

<hr>

DAY 5

Preparation: Happy Face Game Test Sheet, BLM B.

Retell Story to a Partner

(Assign each child a partner, and ask the partners to take turns telling part of the story each time you turn to a new set of pages. Encourage use of target words when appropriate.)

Today I'll show you the pictures Michael Emberley made for *Welcome Back Sun.* As I show you the pictures, you and your partner will take turns telling part of the story.

Pages 1–4. Tell what happens at the **beginning** of the story.

Pages 5–26. Tell what happens in the **middle** of the story.

Pages 27–30. Tell what happens at the **end** of the story.

Assess Vocabulary

(Give each child a copy of the Happy Face Game Test Sheet, BLM B.)

Today you're going to play the Happy Face Game. When you play the Happy Face Game, it helps me know how well you know the hard words you are learning.

If I say something true, color the happy face. What will you do if I say something true? *Color the happy face.*

If I say something false, color the sad face. What will you do if I say something false? *Color the sad face.*

Listen carefully to each sentence I say. Don't let me trick you!

Item 1: If you have **memories,** you remember what happened before. *True.*

Item 2: You will feel **satisfied** if you do **not** have enough to eat. *False.*

Item 3: If a plant **sprouted,** it means that the plant died. *False.*

Item 4: When you **celebrate,** you have something to be happy about. *True.*

Item 5: If your dinner is **delicious,** it means that the dinner tastes terrible. *False.*

Item 6: When you **examine** a thing, you look at it very carefully. *True.*

Item 7: If someone is **familiar,** you are sure that you have **never** seen that person before. *False.*

Item 8: **Complaining** means saying good things about what is happening. *False.*

Item 9: A **sly** fox might try to trick you. *True.*

Item 10: **Dreary** can mean dark and gloomy. *True.*

You did a great job of playing the Happy Face Game!

(Score children's work later. Scores of 9 out of 10 indicate mastery. If a child does not achieve mastery, insert the missed words in the games in the next week's lessons. Retest those children individually on the missed items before they take the next mastery test.)

Extensions
Read a Story as a Reward

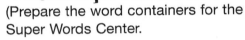

(Display copies of the books you have read since the beginning of the program. Allow children to choose which book they would like you to read aloud to them as a reward for their hard work.)

(Read the story aloud to children for enjoyment with minimal interruptions.)

Present Super Words Center

(Prepare the word containers for the Super Words Center.

Note: Keep the cards that were removed from the center. They will be used again later in the program.

See the Introduction for instructions on how to set up and use the Super Words Center.)

(Put the Picture Vocabulary Cards from Weeks 1 and 10 into the word containers. Make duplicates of each card to create a Concentration game. Make as many sets of duplicates as you wish. Show children one of the word containers. If they need more guidance, role-play with two or three children as a demonstration.)

Let's think about how we work with our words in the Super Words Center.

You will work with a partner in the Super Words Center. Whom will you work with in the center? *A partner.*

There are two cards for each word in the Super Words Center. You will play a game called Concentration. When you play Concentration, you try to find two cards that match. **Match** means that both cards show the same picture and word. What does **match** mean? *Both cards show the same picture and word.*

First you will take all of the cards out of the container and place them facedown on the table. What do you do first? (Idea: *Take all of the words out and place them facedown on the table.*)

Next you will pick one card, turn it faceup, show your partner the picture, and ask what word the picture shows. What do you do next? (Idea: *I pick a card, turn it faceup, show it to my partner, and ask what word the picture shows.*)

What do you do if your partner doesn't know the word? *Tell my partner the word.*

Next you will put the card faceup where you found it. What do you do next? (Idea: *Put the card faceup where I found it.*)

What do you do next? *Give my partner a turn.*

If your partner chooses another card that is the same as your first card, he or she can take those two cards. What can your partner do? (Idea: *My partner can take both cards if he or she chooses one that is the same as my first card.*)

If your partner can't find one that is the same, he or she puts the card down faceup in the same place where it was picked it up. Then it is your turn again. Whoever has the most pairs of cards when all of the cards have been taken is the winner.

(There are many ways to play Concentration. This one is fast to play. You may choose to modify the game depending on skill level.)

That's Good! That's Bad!
author: Margery Cuyler • illustrator: David Catrow

Preparation: You will need *That's Good! That's Bad!* for each day's lesson.

Number the pages of the story to assist you in asking questions at appropriate points.

Post a copy of the Vocabulary Tally Sheet, BLM A, with this week's Picture Vocabulary Cards attached.

Each child will need the Homework Sheet, BLM 11a.

🎯 Target Vocabulary

Tier II	Tier III
squabbling	setting
parents	
drifted	
prickly	
*relieved	
*opposite	

*Expanded Target Vocabulary Word

- Where do you think the story happens?
- When do you think the story happens?
- Why do you think the boy is smiling?
- How did he get up so high?
- Do you think this story is about real people and animals? Tell why or why not.

(Call on several children to share their predictions with the class.)

Take a Picture Walk

We are going to take a picture walk through this book. Remember, when we take a picture walk, we look at the pictures and tell what we think will happen in the story.

The title of this book is *That's Good! That's Bad!* If you say something is **good,** you mean it's pleasing or enjoyable. You like it. What do you know about something that's good? *I like it.* If you say something is **bad,** it's not pleasing or it could hurt you. You don't like it. What do you know about something that's bad? *I don't like it.* Another way of saying "That's good" is saying, "I like what's happening." What's another way of saying "That's good"? *I like what's happening.* Another way of saying "That's bad" is saying "I don't like what's happening." What's another way of saying "That's bad"? *I don't like what's happening.*

(Show the illustrations on the following pages and ask the specified questions.)

Page 1. Where do you think the people are? (Idea: *At the zoo.*)

DAY 1

Introduce Book

Today's book is called *That's Good! That's Bad!* What's the title of this week's book? *That's Good! That's Bad!*

This book was written by Margery Cuyler [Mar-jer-y Cuy-ler]. Who's the author of *That's Good! That's Bad!* *Margery Cuyler.*

David Catrow made the pictures for this book. Who's the illustrator of *That's Good! That's Bad!* *David Catrow.* Who made the illustrations for this book? *David Catrow.*

The cover of a book usually gives us some hints of what the book is about. Let's look at the front cover of *That's Good! That's Bad!* What do you see in the illustration? (Ideas: *A little boy holding a balloon; lots of animals—snake, baboon, hippopotamus, giraffe, elephant, bird.*)

Remember, when you make a prediction about something, you say what you think will happen. Now get ready to make some predictions to your partner about this book. Use the information from the cover to help you.

(Assign each child a partner. Ask the following questions, allowing sufficient time for children to share their predictions with their partners.)

- Who are the characters in this story? (Whom do you think this story is about?)
- What is the boy doing?

What makes you think so? (Ideas: *I can see the elephant; there is a big fence; it says z-o-o on the balloon man's hat.*)

Pages 2–3. What is happening here? (Idea: *The boy is floating away with the balloon.*) What do you think the boy would see if he looked down? (Ideas: *The animals in the zoo—elephant, rhinoceros, zebra, stork, swallow, snakes, giraffe, kangaroos, hippopotamus, lion, penguins, baboons; his mom and dad.*) Raise your hand if you think the boy thinks what's happening to him is good. Raise your hand if you think the boy thinks what's happening to him is bad.

Pages 4–5. Where do you think the boy is now? (Idea: *Over the jungle.*) What happens to his balloon? (Idea: *It breaks.*) Raise your hand if you think the boy thinks what's happening to him is good. Raise your hand if you think the boy thinks what's happening to him is bad.

Page 6. What is happening here? (Idea: *The boy is falling into the water.*) Raise your hand if you think the boy thinks what's happening to him is good. Raise your hand if you think the boy thinks what's happening to him is bad.

Page 7. How do you think he gets out of the water?

Pages 8–9. What is happening here? (Ideas: *The baboons are chasing the boy; they are trying to catch him.*) Raise your hand if you think the boy thinks what's happening to him is good. Raise your hand if you think the boy thinks what's happening to him is bad.

Pages 10–11. What is happening here? (Idea: *The baboon is grabbing his shirt.*) What do you think the boy is hanging on to? Raise your hand if you think the boy thinks what's happening to him is good. Raise your hand if you think the boy thinks what's happening to him is bad.

Pages 12–13. What do you think the snake is going to do? (Idea: *Bite him.*) How do you think the boy is feeling? (Idea: *Very afraid.*) What makes you think so? (Ideas: *His face is red; his eyes are big; his mouth is open as if he's screaming.*) Raise your hand if you think the boy thinks what's happening to him is good. Raise your hand if you think the boy thinks what's happening to him is bad.

Pages 14–15. Where do you think the little boy will land? (Idea: *On the giraffe's back.*) Raise your hand if you think the boy thinks what's happening to him is good. Raise your hand if you think the boy thinks what's happening to him is bad.

Pages 16–17. What is happening here? (Idea: *The boy is going to fall into the water.*) Raise your hand if you think the boy thinks what's happening to him is good. Raise your hand if you think the boy thinks what's happening to him is bad.

Pages 18–19. Who saves the little boy? *The elephant.* How does the elephant save him? (Idea: *With his trunk.*) Raise your hand if you think the boy thinks what's happening to him is good. Raise your hand if you think the boy thinks what's happening to him is bad.

Pages 20–21. Where is the little boy riding? (Idea: *On the elephant's trunk.*) What is the lion doing? Raise your hand if you think the boy thinks what's happening to him is good. Raise your hand if you think the boy thinks what's happening to him is bad.

Pages 22–23. What is the lion doing to the boy? (Idea: *Licking the boy.*) Raise your hand if you think the boy thinks what's happening to him is good. Raise your hand if you think the boy thinks what's happening to him is bad.

Pages 24–25. What is happening here? (Ideas: *The boy is in the water; he's crying.*) Raise your hand if you think the boy thinks what's happening to him is good. Raise your hand if you think the boy thinks what's happening to him is bad.

Pages 26–27. Who has the little boy now? (Idea: *The bird.*) What do you think the bird is going to do with the boy? Raise your hand if you think the boy thinks what's happening to him is good. Raise your hand if you think the boy thinks what's happening to him is bad.

Pages 28–29. What is happening here? (Idea: *The bird is flying away with the boy.*) Predict where the bird is taking the boy. Raise your hand if you think the boy thinks what's happening to him is good. Raise your hand if you think the boy thinks what's happening to him is bad.

Page 30. Where does the bird take the boy? (Idea: *Back to his mom and dad.*) How do you think the people are feeling now? (Ideas: *Happy; excited; amazed.*)

(**Note:** If children don't use the word *excited*, say:) We learned a word in Week 9 that might tell how the father is feeling. That word is **excited. Excited** means "so happy you can't be still because something good is happening to you." I'm sure the father is excited to get his son back. What word might tell how the father is feeling? *Excited.*

(**Note:** If children don't use the word *amazed*, say:) We learned another word in Week 9 that might tell how the little boy is feeling. That word is **amazed. Amazed** means "very, very surprised by something." I'm sure the little boy is amazed the bird brought him back to his parents.

Raise your hand if you think the boy thinks what's happening to him is good. Raise your hand if you think the boy thinks what's happening to him is bad.

Now that we've finished our picture walk, it's your turn to ask me some questions. What would you like to know about the story? (Accept questions. If children tell about the pictures or the story instead of asking questions, prompt them to ask a question.) Ask me a what question. Ask me a who question.

Read Story Aloud
(Read story aloud to children with minimal interruptions.)

In the next lesson, we will read the story again, and I will ask you some questions.

(If children have difficulty attending for an extended period of time, present the next part of this day's lesson at another time.)

Present Target Vocabulary

 Squabbling.

In the story, "Ten noisy baboons were squabbling in the grass by the river." That means they were arguing noisily about something that wasn't important. They were quarreling. **Squabbling.** Say the word. *Squabbling.*

Squabbling is an action word. It tells what someone is doing. What kind of word is **squabbling?** *An action word.*

If you are squabbling, you are noisily arguing with someone. You are quarreling about something that is not important. Say the word that means "arguing noisily or quarreling with someone about something that is not important." *Squabbling.*

(Correct any incorrect responses, and repeat the item at the end of the sequence.)

Let's think about some times when someone might squabble with someone else. I'll tell about a time. If you think the people are squabbling, say, "Squabbling." If not, don't say anything.

- Your friends are shouting at each other because they both want to be first down the slide. *Squabbling.*
- Three boys are arguing loudly over using the classroom computer. *Squabbling.*
- Everyone is getting along.
- There are three jump ropes, and eight girls are quarreling over them. *Squabbling.*
- It's dark in the hallway.
- There are enough marbles for everyone, so no one is arguing.

What action word means "arguing noisily or quarreling with someone about something that is not important"? *Squabbling.*

Parents.

In the story, the little boy thinks he will never see his parents again. That means he thinks he will never see his mother and father again. **Parents.** Say the word. *Parents.*

Parents is a naming word. It names people. What kind of word is **parents?** *A naming word.*

Your parents are your mother and your father. Say the word that means "your mother and your father." *Parents.*

(Correct any incorrect responses, and repeat the item at the end of the sequence.)

Let's think about some people who might be someone's parents. I'll name some people. If you think they could be the parents, say, "Parents." If not, don't say anything.

- Johnny's mother is Ann. Johnny's father is Peter. *Parents.*
- Johnny's grandmother is Annabelle. Johnny's grandfather is Paul.
- Harpo's mother is Roberta. His father is also named Harpo. *Parents.*

What naming word means "your mother and your father"? *Parents.*

⊙⤙ Drifted.

In the story, "The balloon drifted for miles and miles until it came to a hot, steamy jungle." That means the balloon moved with the wind. **Drifted.** Say the word. *Drifted.*

Drifted is an action word. It tells what someone or something did. What kind of word is **drifted?** *An action word.*

If someone or something drifted, it means it moved with the wind or with water. Say the word that means "moved with the wind or with water." *Drifted.*

(Correct any incorrect responses, and repeat the item at the end of the sequence.)

Let's think about **drifted.** I'll say something. If what I say drifted, say, "Drifted." If not, don't say anything.

- The stick in the stream. *Drifted.*
- The cloud in the sky. *Drifted.*
- The snow in the wind. *Drifted.*
- The house on the street.
- The cow in the field.
- The sailboat on the pond. *Drifted.*

What action word means "moved with the wind or with water"? *Drifted.*

⊙⤙ Prickly.

In the story the balloon "broke on the branch of a tall, prickly tree." That means the branch of the tree had lots of small, sharp points that stuck out from the leaves or stems of the tree. **Prickly.** Say the word. *Prickly.*

Prickly is a describing word. It tells about what a branch felt like. What kind of word is **prickly?** *A describing word.*

When something is prickly, it has lots of small, sharp points that stick out from it. Say the word that means "something that has lots of small, sharp points that stick out from it." *Prickly.*

(Correct any incorrect responses, and repeat the item at the end of the sequence.)

Let's think about some things that could be prickly. I'll name something. If you think that thing is prickly, say, "Prickly." If not, say, "Absolutely not."

- The stem of a rose. *Prickly.*
- A thistle plant. *Prickly.*
- A smooth piece of glass. *Absolutely not.*
- A board with lots of splinters sticking out. *Prickly.*
- A potato. *Absolutely not.*
- A cactus plant. *Prickly.*

What describing word means "something that has lots of small, sharp points that stick out from it"? *Prickly.*

Present Vocabulary Tally Sheet
(See Week 1, page 3, for instructions.)

Assign Homework
(Homework Sheet, BLM 11a: See the Introduction for homework instructions.)

DAY 2

Preparation: Picture Vocabulary Cards for *squabbling, parents, drifted,* and *prickly.*

Read and Discuss Story

(Read story aloud to children. Ask the following questions at the specified points.)

Now I'm going to read *That's Good! That's Bad!* When I finish each part, I'll ask you some questions.

Page 2. How do you think the little boy feels when the balloon first lifts him high up into the sky? (Idea: *Excited.*) What makes you think that? (Idea: *He says "Wow!"*)

(**Note:** If children don't use the word *excited* say:) We learned a word in Week 9 that tells how the little boy was feeling. That word is **excited.** Sometimes when you are excited, you say "Wow!"

Page 3. (Read only to the end of the sentence "Oh, that's good.") What could be good about flying over a zoo?

(Read to the end of the sentence "No, that's bad.") What could be bad about flying over a zoo?

Page 4. How do you think the little boy feels when the balloon pops? (Ideas: *Frightened; terrified.*)

(**Note:** If children don't use the word *terrified,* say:) We learned a word in Week 6 that tells how the little boy is feeling. That word is **terrified.** The little boy is feeling very, very afraid when the balloon pops. How is he feeling? *Terrified.* That's right; he is terrified he might fall.

Page 5. (Read only to the end of the sentence "Oh, that's bad.") What could be bad about the balloon popping?

(Read to the end of the sentence "No, that's good!") What could be good about the balloon popping?

Page 7. (Read only to the end of the word "giddyap.") How do you think the little boy feels when he rides the hippopotamus to shore? (Idea: *Clever.*)

(**Note:** If children don't use the word *clever,* say:) We learned a word in Week 6 that tells how the little boy is feeling. That word is **clever.** The little boy is thinking he is very good at understanding things quickly and making plans. He thinks he has been clever to climb up on the hippopotamus and ride to shore. How is he feeling? *Clever.*

(Read to the end of the sentence "Oh, that's good.") What could be good about riding on a hippopotamus?

(Read to the end of the sentence "No, that's bad!") What could be bad about riding on a hippopotamus?

Page 8. How do you think the little boy feels when the baboons chase him up the tree? (Idea: *Terrified.*) That's right; we can tell the little boy is very, very afraid by looking at his face. He is terrified.

Page 9. (Read only to the end of the sentence "Oh, that's bad.") What could be bad about being chased by baboons?

(Read to the end of the sentence "No, that's good.") What could be good about being chased by baboons?

Page 10. How do you think the little boy feels when the baboons want to play vine-swing with him? (Idea: *Excited.*) That's right; we can tell the little boy is excited because he says, "WHAT FUN! … WHEE!"

Page 11. (Read only to the end of the sentence "Oh, that's good.") What could be good about playing vine-swing with the baboons?

(Read to the end of the sentence "No, that's bad.") What could be bad about playing vine-swing with the baboons?

Page 12. How do you think the little boy feels when he sees the snake? (Idea: *Terrified.*) That's right; he is very, very afraid. He is terrified.

Page 13. (Read only to the end of the sentence "Oh, that's bad.) What could be bad about being so close to a snake?

(Read to the end of the sentence "No, that's good.") What could be good about being close to a snake?

Page 14. (Read only to the end of the word "Hooray!") How do you think the little boy feels when he loses his grip on the snake and lands on the back of the giraffe? (Ideas: *Happy; excited; amazed.*) That's right; he is very happy to get away from the snake. He is excited and amazed.

(Read to the end of the sentence "Oh, that's good.") What could be good about landing on the back of a giraffe?

(Read to the end of the sentence "No, that's bad!") What could be bad about landing on the back of a giraffe?

Page 16. How do you think the little boy feels when he slides off the giraffe's neck and lands in the quicksand? (Idea: *Terrified.*) He probably is very, very frightened to find himself in the quicksand. He probably is … *Terrified.*

Page 17. (Read only to the end of the sentence "Oh, that's bad.") What could be bad about landing in quicksand?

(Read to the end of the sentence "No, that's good!") What could be good about landing in quicksand?

Page 18. How do you think the little boy feels when the elephant lifts him up onto its shoulders? (Idea: *Happy.*) That's right; he is happy to get away from the quicksand.

Page 19. (Read only to the end of the sentence "Oh, that's good.") What could be good about being on the shoulders of an elephant?

(Read to the end of the sentence "No, that's bad!") What could be bad about being on the shoulders of an elephant?

Page 20. How do you think the little boy feels when he wakes up the lion? (Idea: *Terrified.*)

Page 21. (Read only to the end of the sentence "Oh, that's bad.") What could be bad about waking up a lion?

(Read to the end of the sentence "No, that's good!") What could be good about waking up a lion?

Page 22. How do you think the little boy feels when the lion purrs and licks his face? (Ideas: *Happy; safe.*) That's right; he thinks the lion isn't going to hurt him because the lion is purring.

Page 23. (Read only to the end of the sentence "Oh, that's good.") What could be good about being licked by a lion's tongue?

(Read to the end of the sentence "No, that's bad!") What could be bad about being licked by a lion's tongue?

Page 24. How do you think the little boy feels when he finds he is all alone deep in the dark jungle? (Idea: *Afraid; terrified.*) That's right, he is afraid. He is terrified. He sits down and starts to cry.

Page 25. (Read only to the end of the sentence "Oh, that's bad.") What could be bad about being all alone in the dark jungle?

(Read to the end of the sentence "No, that's good!") What could be good about being all alone in the dark jungle?

Page 26. How do you think the little boy feels when the stork picks him up with its beak? (Idea: *Happy.*)

Page 27. (Read only to the end of the sentence "Oh, that's good.") What could be good about being picked up by a stork?

(Read to the end of the sentence "No, that's bad!") What could be bad about being picked up by a stork?

Page 29. (Read only to the end of the word "sob.") How do you think the little boy feels when he is flying through the air with the stork? (Ideas: *Terrified; desperate.*) That's right; he is very, very afraid. He wants to be back with his parents, but he is afraid he is never going to see them again. He is terrified and desperate. How is he feeling? *Terrified and desperate.*

(**Note:** If children don't use the word *desperate,* say:) We learned a word in Week 1 that tells how the little boy is feeling. That word is **desperate.** The little boy wants to be back with his parents. He is afraid he is going to die. How is the little boy feeling? *Desperate.*

(Read to the end of the sentence "Oh, that's bad.") What could be bad about flying through the air with a stork?

(Read to the end of the sentence "No, that's good!") What could be good about flying through the air with a stork?

Page 30. At the end of the story, how do you think the little boy feels when he finally gets back to his parents? (Ideas*: Happy; satisfied; amazed.*)

(**Note:** If children don't use the word *satisfied,* say:) We learned a word in Week 8 that tells how the little boy id feeling. That word is **satisfied.** The little boy is satisfied because he has what he wants or needs. How is he feeling? *Satisfied.*

(**Note:** If children don't use the word *amazed,* say:) We learned a word in Week 9 that tells how the little boy is feeling. That word is **amazed.** The little boy is amazed because he is very, very surprised that he is safely back with his parents. How is he feeling? *Amazed.*

(Read to the end of the sentence "Oh, that's good.") What could be good about being back with his parents?

(Read to the end of the sentence "No, that's great!") How does he feel about being back with his parents? *Great; wonderful.*

Review Vocabulary

(Display the Picture Vocabulary Cards. Point to each card as you say the word.) These pictures show **squabbling, parents, drifted,** and **prickly.** (Ask children to repeat each word after you.)

- What action word means "moved with the wind or with the water"? *Drifted.*
- What describing word means "something that has lots of small, sharp points that stick out from it"? *Prickly.*
- What action word means "arguing noisily or quarreling with someone about something that is not important"? *Squabbling.*
- What naming word means "someone's mother and father"? *Parents.*

Extend Vocabulary

◎⟻ Prickly.

In the story *That's Good! That's Bad!* we learned that **prickly** means "something that has lots of small, sharp points that stick out from it."

Here's a new way to use the word **prickly.**

- **Dogs get prickly when you pull their tails.** Say the sentence.
- **My cat gets prickly when she really wants her supper.** Say the sentence.
- **My best friend gets prickly when I push him from behind.** Say the sentence.

In these sentences, **prickly** is describing word that tells about someone who loses his or her temper or gets upset very easily. Tell about some times when you were prickly. (Ideas: *I got prickly when Joshua kept messing up my hair; I was prickly when Colleen hurt my feelings; Henry was prickly after someone said he couldn't count.*)

Present Expanded Target Vocabulary

◎⟻ Relieved.

In the story, the little boy often has a happy feeling because he expects something bad to happen and then it doesn't. The word that describes the happy feeling you have when something bad doesn't happen or when something bad stops happening is **relieved.**

Relieved. Say the word. *Relieved.*

Relieved is a describing word. It tells about how a person feels. What kind of word is **relieved?** *A describing word.*

When you are relieved, you feel happy when something bad doesn't happen or when something bad stops happening. Say the word that means "happy when something bad doesn't happen or when something bad stops happening." *Relieved.*

I'll tell about some times. If you would feel relieved, say, "Relieved." If not, don't say anything.

- You thought you had lost your coat, but you found it in the car. *Relieved.*
- The shot I got from the nurse didn't hurt at all. *Relieved.*
- The mean dog bit my leg.
- How you would feel if your favorite ball didn't get stuck on the roof. *Relieved.*
- How your mom felt after she thought you were lost but then found you in your room. *Relieved.*
- The books fell and made a big mess on the living room floor.

What describing word means "happy because something bad doesn't happen or when something bad stops happening"? *Relieved.*

◎⟻ Opposites.

The words **good** and **bad** are in the title of the story. The words **good** and **bad** are **opposites.** That means they tell about the same kind of thing but they are completely different in some way. **Bad** means "not good." What does **bad** mean? *Not good.* **Good** means "not bad." What does **good** mean? *Not bad.* They are opposites. **Opposites.** Say the word. *Opposites.*

Opposites is a naming word. It names words. What kind of word is **opposites?** *A naming word.*

Opposites are words that tell about the same kind of thing but are completely different in some way. Say the word that means "the same kind of thing but completely different in some way." *Opposites.*

Let's think about some words that might be opposites. I'll name some words. If you think they are opposites, say, "Opposites." If not, don't say anything.

- Up, down. *Opposites.*
- Cry, laugh. *Opposites.*
- Ham, cheese.
- Hot, cold. *Opposites.*
- Eyes, nose.
- Straight, crooked. *Opposites.*

What naming word means "the same kind of thing but completely different in some way"? *Opposites.*

DAY 3

Preparation: Activity Sheet, BLM 11b.

Retell Story

(Show the pictures on the following pages, and call on a child to tell what's happening. Call on a different child for each section.)

Today I'll show you the pictures David Catrow made for the story *That's Good! That's Bad!* As I show you the pictures, I'll call on one of you to tell the class that part of the story.

Pages 1–3. Tell what happens at the **beginning** of the story.

Pages 4–29. Tell what happens in the **middle** of the story. (Encourage use of target words when appropriate. Model use as necessary.)

Page 30. Tell what happens at the **end** of the story.

How does the little boy feel when things are good? (Ideas: *Happy; relieved.*)

How does the little boy feel when things are bad? (Ideas: *Terrified; desperate.*)

Review Opposites Game

Today you will play the Opposites Game. I'll use a vocabulary word in a sentence. If you can tell me the opposite of that word, you win one point. If you can't tell me, I get the point.

Let's practice: The two boys were **squabbling.** Tell me the opposite of squabbling. (Idea: *Getting*

along.) "Getting along" could be the opposite of squabbling.

You may use **not** to help you say something that means the opposite. If I wanted to say the opposite of sunny, I could say, "not sunny."

Let's try another one. Jack and Diane **are John's parents.** Tell me the opposite of "are John's parents." (Idea: *Jack and Diane are not John's parents.*) "Are not John's parents" could be the opposite of "are John's parents."

Now you're ready to play the game.

(Draw a T-chart on the board for keeping score. Children earn one point for each correct answer. If they make an error, suggest an appropriate choice, and record one point for yourself. Repeat missed words at the end of the game.)

- The plant was **prickly.** Tell me the opposite of prickly. (Idea: *Smooth.*) Smooth could be the opposite of prickly.
- The boat on the lake **drifted.** Tell me the opposite of drifted. (Idea: *Did not drift.*) "Did not drift" could be the opposite of drifted.
- The girls were **squabbling.** Tell me the opposite of squabbling. (Idea: *Getting along.*) "Getting along" could be the opposite of squabbling.
- Ted and Alice **are Mia's parents.** Tell me the opposite of "are Mia's parents." (Idea: *Are not Mia's parents.*) "Are not Mia's parents" could be the opposite of "are Mia's parents."
- Manny was **relieved** to know that his dog had run away. Tell me the opposite of relieved. (Idea: *Upset.*) Upset could be the opposite of relieved.
- Mindy **shouted** at her friend. Tell me the opposite of shouted. (Idea: *Whispered.*) Whispered could be the opposite of shouted.

(Count the points, and declare a winner.)
You did a great job of playing the Opposites Game!

Making a List (Activity Sheet)

(Give each child a copy of the Activity Sheet, BLM 11b. Review with children the animals the boy sees in the zoo. If children have difficulty remembering, show them the picture on pages 2 and 3.)

Today we are going to make a list of the animals that are in the zoo in the story. When we make a list, we write words or make pictures to help us remember. What do we do when we make a list? *We write words or make pictures to help us remember.*

(Show children the page with the animals. Point to the animals.) These are the animals the boy sees at the zoo. (Point to the lion.) What is this? *A lion.* (Point to the elephant.) What is this? *An elephant.* (Repeat for the remaining items.)

My turn to make a list. First I cut out each object. (Demonstrate.) What do I do first? *Cut out each object.* The title of this sheet says *Animals in the Zoo.* What do these words say? *Animals in the Zoo.* Next I glue the picture onto the list. What do I do next? *Glue the picture onto the list.* (Demonstrate process for two more items.)

Now it's your turn to make a list. (Children who are able to may copy each word beside the picture.)

DAY 4

Preparation: Prepare a sheet of chart paper, portrait direction, with the title *That's Good! That's Bad!* Underneath the title, draw 8 circles, connected by arrows, making one larger circle. See the Introduction for an example.

Setting (Where)
(Literary Analysis)

Let's think about what we already know about how books are made.

- What do we call the name of the book? *The title.*
- What do we call the person who writes the story? *The author.*
- What do we call the person who draws the pictures? *The illustrator.*
- What do we call the people or animals a story is about? *The characters.*
- What do we call the pictures the illustrator makes? *Illustrations.*
- What is one thing the setting of a story tells? *Where a story happens.*

Let's sing "The Story Song" to help us remember these important things about books.

(See the Introduction for the complete "Story Song.")

Today we will learn more about the setting of a story.

The setting of a story tells two things. One thing the setting tells is where the story happens. What is one thing the setting tells? *Where the story happens.*

Let's look at the pictures and talk about the story to figure out where the story *That's Good! That's Bad!* happens.

(Record children's responses by writing the underlined words in the circles to make a circular pattern.)

(Show the illustrations on the following pages, and ask the specified questions.)

Pages 1–3. Where does the story begin? *At the zoo.*

Pages 4–5. Where does the next part of the story happen? *In the jungle.*

Pages 6–7. Where does the next part of the story happen? *At the river.*

Pages 8–13. Where does the next part of the story happen? *In the tree.*

Pages 14–19. Where does the next part of the story happen? *Near the swamp.*

Pages 20–23. Where does the next part of the story happen? *On the grassy plain.*

Pages 24–27. Where does the next part of the story happen? *In the jungle.*

Pages 28–30. Where does the last part of the story happen? *At the zoo.*

Where does this story begin and end? *At the zoo.* The middle of the story happens in the jungle, the river, the tree, the swamp, and the grassy plain. All these places are in Africa. So if we could use only one word to tell about the middle part of the setting, we would use the word **Africa.** What two words do we need to tell where this story happens? *Zoo and Africa.*

Today you learned about one of the parts of the setting of the story *That's Good! That's Bad!* You learned about where the story happens.

Play Opposites Game (Cumulative Review)

Let's play the Opposites Game. I'll use a vocabulary word in a sentence. If you can tell me the opposite of that word, you win one point. If you can't tell me, I get the point.

Let's practice: When Mom heard that we got home safely, she was **relieved.** Tell me the opposite of relieved. (Idea: *Upset.*) Upset could be the opposite of relieved.

Let's try another one. The tree trunk was **prickly.** Tell me the opposite of prickly. (Idea: *Smooth.*) Smooth could be the opposite of prickly.

Now you're ready to play the game.

(Draw a T-chart on the board for keeping score. Children earn one point for each correct answer. If they make an error, correct them as you normally would, and record one point for yourself. Repeat missed words at the end of the game.)

- When I'm late, my dad is **prickly.** Tell me the opposite of prickly. (Idea: *Happy.*) Happy could be the opposite of prickly.
- The leaf **did not drift** in the wind. (Idea: *Drifted.*) Drifted could be the opposite of "did not drift."
- Both boys wanted the same ball, and they were **getting along.** Tell me the opposite of "getting along." (Idea: *Squabbling.*) Squabbling could be the opposite of "getting along."
- Sam and Ella **were not** Tomaine's parents. Tell me the opposite of "were not." (Idea: *Were Tomaine's parents.*) "Were" could be the opposite of "were not."
- The cucumber was green and **prickly.** Tell me the opposite of prickly. (Idea: *Smooth.*) Smooth could be the opposite of prickly.
- Bill was **relieved** when we found his ruined shoe. Tell me the opposite of relieved. (Idea: *Upset.*) Upset could be the opposite of relieved.
- The track star **was determined** to win. Tell me the opposite of "was determined." (Idea: *Was not determined.*) "Was not determined" could be the opposite of "was determined."

- The sailors in the lifeboat **were starving.** Tell me the opposite of "were starving." (Idea: *Were not starving.*) "Were not starving" could be the opposite of "were starving."
- When we played, everyone was **cooperative.** Tell me the opposite of cooperative. (Ideas: *Uncooperative; not cooperative.*) Uncooperative could be the opposite of cooperative.
- That elephant is **enormous.** Tell me the opposite of enormous. (Ideas: *Tiny; little; small.*) Small could be the opposite of enormous.

(Count the points, and declare a winner.) You did a great job of playing the Opposites Game!

Preparation: Happy Face Game Test Sheet, BLM B.

Retell Story to a Partner

(Assign each child a partner, and ask the partners to take turns telling part of the story each time you turn to a new set of pages. Encourage use of target words when appropriate.)

Today I'll show you the pictures David Catrow made for the story *That's Good! That's Bad!* As I show you the pictures, you and your partner will take turns telling part of the story.

Pages 1–3. Tell what happens at the **beginning** of the story.

Pages 4–27. Tell what happens in the **middle** of the story.

Pages 28–30. Tell what happens at the **end** of the story.)

Assess Vocabulary

 (Give each child a copy of the Happy Face Game Test Sheet, BLM B.)

Today you're going to play the Happy Face Game. When you play the Happy Face Game, it helps me know how well you know the hard words you are learning.

If I say something true, color the happy face. What will you do if I say something true? *Color the happy face.*

If I say something false, color the sad face. What will you do if I say something false? *Color the sad face.*

Listen carefully to each sentence I say. Don't let me trick you!

Item 1: If you are **not** getting along, you may be **squabbling.** *True.*

Item 2: The two adults who take care of you are sometimes your **parents.** *True.*

Item 3: If a leaf **drifted** in the wind, it means that the leaf moved. *True.*

Item 4: Something that is **prickly** is smooth if you touch it. *False.*

Item 5: Food that is **nutritious** is **not** good for you. *False.*

Item 6: Your teacher may get **prickly** if you misbehave. *True.*

Item 7: If you get home safely in the dark, you are **relieved.** *True.*

Item 8: A word that tells about the same kind of things that are completely different is **opposite.** *True.*

Item 9: Being **disobedient** means that you're not doing what you're told to do. *True.*

Item 10: If you **collect** things, you find things in different places and put them together so you can use them. *True.*

You did a great job of playing the Happy Face Game!

(Score children's work later. Scores of 9 out of 10 indicate mastery. If a child does not achieve mastery, insert the missed words in the games in the next week's lessons. Retest those children individually on the missed items before they take the next mastery test.)

Extensions
Read a Story as a Reward

(Display copies of the books that you have read since the beginning of the program. Allow children to choose which book they would like you to read aloud to them as a reward for their hard work.)

(Read the story aloud to children for enjoyment with minimal interruptions.)

Present Super Words Center

(Prepare the word containers for the Super Words Center. Remove words that do not have an opposite from the containers. See the Introduction for instructions on how to set up and use the Super Words Center.)

(Add the new Picture Vocabulary Cards to the Super Words Center. Show children one of the word containers. If they need more guidance, role-play with two or three children as a demonstration.)

Let's think about how we work with our words in the Super Words Center.

You will work with a partner in the Super Words Center. Whom will you work with in the center? *A partner.*

First you will draw a word out of the container. What do you do first? (Idea: *Draw a word out of the container.*)

Next you will show your partner the picture and ask what word the picture shows. What do you do next? (Idea: *I show my partner the picture and ask what word the picture shows.*)

What do you do if your partner doesn't know the word? *Tell my partner the word.*

Next you will ask your partner to tell the opposite of that word. What do you do next? (Idea: *Ask my partner to tell the opposite of that word.*)

What will you do if your partner doesn't know the opposite? (Idea: *Tell my partner the opposite.*)

What will you do if neither of you knows the opposite? (Idea: *Put that card back and draw another.*)

What do you do next? *Give my partner a turn.*

(You may have children call on their teacher or a classroom "expert" if they do not know an opposite. You may also choose to prepare another word container for words children have difficulty with. These could be reviewed later at an appropriate time.)

The Way I Feel
author: Janan Cain • illustrator: Janan Cain

Preparation: You will need *The Way I Feel* for each day's lesson.

Number the pages of the story to assist you in asking questions at appropriate points.

Post a copy of the Vocabulary Tally Sheet, BLM A, with this week's Picture Vocabulary Cards attached.

Each child will need the Homework Sheet, BLM 12a.

Target Vocabulary

Tier II	Tier III
silly	explaining
shy	
bored	
mood	
*emotions	
*feelings	

*Expanded Target Vocabulary Word

- When do you think the story happens?
- Why do you think the child is making this face?
- How did she get upside down?
- Do you think this story is about real people? Tell why or why not.

(Call on several children to share their predictions with the class.)

Take a Picture Walk

We are going to take a picture walk through this book. Remember, when we take a picture walk, we look at the pictures and tell what we think will happen in the story.

(Show the illustrations on the following pages, and ask the specified questions.)

Pages 1–2. Why do you think this person is dressed like this? Where do you think this person is going? How would you be feeling if you were this person?

Pages 3–4. When does this part of the story happen? (Idea: *At night.*) How do you think the person is feeling?

Pages 5–6. What is happening here? How do you think the person is feeling?

Pages 7–8. Where does this part of the story happen? (Idea: *Outside.*) What is the girl doing? How do you think she's feeling?

Pages 9–10. Where does this part of the story happen? (Idea: *In a tree.*) What is the boy doing? *Crying.* How do you think he's feeling?

DAY 1

Introduce Book

Today's book is called *The Way I Feel*. What's the title of this week's book? *The Way I Feel.*

This book was written by Janan Cain [Ja-nan Cain]. Who's the author of *The Way I Feel*? *Janan Cain.*

Janan Cain also made the pictures for this book. Who's the illustrator of *The Way I Feel*? *Janan Cain.* Who made the illustrations for this book? *Janan Cain.*

The cover of a book usually gives us some hints of what the book is about. Let's look at the front cover of *The Way I Feel*. What do you see in the illustration? (Ideas: *A child; the child is upside down; the child is making a funny face.*) Do you think this child is a boy or a girl?

Remember, when you make a prediction about something, you say what you think will happen. Now get ready to make some predictions to your partner about this book. Use the information from the cover to help you.

(Assign each child a partner. Ask the following questions, allowing sufficient time for the children to share their predictions with their partners.)

- Who are the characters in this story? (Whom do you think this story is about?)
- What is the child doing?
- Where do you think the story happens?

Pages 11–12. How do you think this person is feeling? What makes you think so?

Pages 13–14. What is happening here? How do you think the boy is feeling?

Pages 15–16. What is the little girl doing? How do you think she's feeling?

Pages 17–18. What is happening here? Do you think the little girl knows the other child? Tell why you think so.

Pages 19–20. Where is the little boy? What do you think he wants to do? Why isn't he outside playing baseball? (Idea: *It's raining.*) How do you think he's feeling?

Pages 21–22. What is happening here? How do you think the child is feeling?

Pages 23–24. Where is the girl? (Ideas: *Outside; on the steps.*) What's happening inside the house? (Idea: *The father is playing with a little child.*) How do you think the girl is feeling?

Pages 25–26. Why do you think this girl is dressed like this? What do you think she is doing? How would you be feeling if you were this person?

Pages 27–28. What is happening here?

Now that we've finished our picture walk, it's your turn to ask me some questions. What would you like to know about this story? (Accept questions. If children tell about the pictures or the story instead of asking questions, prompt them to ask a question.) Ask me a why question. Ask me a how question.

Read Story Aloud
(Read story aloud to children with minimal interruptions.)

In the next lesson, we will read the story again, and I will ask you some questions.

(If children have difficulty attending for an extended period of time, present the next part of this day's lesson at another time.)

Present Target Vocabulary

◎⚞ Shy.

In the story, the little girl says, "If someone says 'hello' to me, I suddenly feel so **shy**." That means she is worried and a little bit afraid

around other people. She probably is very quiet when strangers are near. **Shy.** Say the word. *Shy.*

Shy is a describing word. It tells about a feeling. What kind of word is **shy**? *A describing word.*

If you are shy, you get worried and a little bit afraid around other people. You probably get very quiet when strangers are near. Say the word that means "worried and a little bit afraid around other people." *Shy.*

(Correct any incorrect responses, and repeat the item at the end of the sequence.)

Let's think about some times when someone might feel shy. I'll tell about a time. If you think the person I'm telling about is shy, say, "Shy." If not, don't say anything.

- When the boy goes into his new class at school, he is worried and a little bit afraid and doesn't want to talk to anyone. *Shy.*
- The baby smiles and laughs whenever anyone talks to him.
- The first time I go to my new babysitter I am worried and a bit afraid. *Shy.*
- Vonda is in a whole crowd of adults she has never met before. *Shy.*
- All the people at the party know each other and enjoy themselves.

What describing word means "worried and a little bit afraid around other people"? *Shy.*

◎⚞ Bored.

In the story, the boy says, "There's nothing I want to do. The day drags on and on." That means he is tired and squirmy because he doesn't have anything interesting to do. **Bored.** Say the word. *Bored.*

Bored is a describing word. It tells about a feeling. What kind of word is **bored**? *A describing word.*

If you are bored, you are tired and squirmy because you don't have anything interesting to do. Say the word that means "tired and squirmy because you don't have anything interesting to do." *Bored.*

(Correct any incorrect responses, and repeat the item at the end of the sequence.)

Let's think about some times when someone might feel bored. I'll tell about a time. If you think the person I'm telling about might be bored, say, "Bored." If not, don't say anything.

- I have to sit and listen to the adults talk and not do anything. Eew. *Bored.*
- I have to wait for a long time at the dentist's office, and there is nothing to do. *Bored.*
- I play with a truck, a doll, and some building toys.
- Mr. Williams makes me sit in a chair and do nothing because I keep interrupting him. *Bored.*
- The movie is really funny.
- I have to wait in the car while my dad fixes the tire. *Bored.*

What describing word means "tired and squirmy because you don't have anything interesting to do"? *Bored.*

 Silly.

In the story, the child feels silly when he makes a funny face and wears a goofy hat. That means he is doing things and wearing clothes that will make everyone laugh. **Silly.** Say the word. *Silly.*

Silly is a describing word. It tells about a feeling. What kind of word is **silly?** *A describing word.*

If you are feeling silly, you want to do things, or say things, or wear funny clothes that will make everyone laugh. Say the word that means "you want to do things or say things or wear funny clothes that will make everyone laugh." *Silly.*

(Correct any incorrect responses, and repeat the item at the end of the sequence.)

Let's think about some times when someone might feel silly. I'll tell about a time. If you think the person I'm telling about is being silly, say, "Silly." If not, don't say anything.

- Devonte makes faces and tries to make Damon look at him. *Silly.*
- Jocelyn barks like a dog and chases Caitlyn as if she were a cat. *Silly.*
- Everyone wears their best clothes to the concert.
- Kyle wears a purple wig and a big red foam nose. *Silly.*

- We pretend we are farm animals and make their sounds with our voices. *Silly.*
- We know it is serious when the principal tells us to sit quietly and listen.

What describing word means "you want to do things, or say things, or wear funny clothes that will make everyone laugh"? *Silly.*

 Mood.

In the story, the girl on the swing is feeling happy. She says her "mood is soaring high." That means at that time she is enjoying a good feeling. Your mood is the way you are feeling. If you are in a good mood, you are feeling good. If you are in a bad mood, you are feeling bad. **Mood.** Say the word. *Mood.*

Mood is a naming word. It is another word for how you feel. What kind of word is **mood?** *A naming word.*

When you are talking about your mood, you are talking about how you are feeling. Say the word that means "how you feel." *Mood.*

(Correct any incorrect responses, and repeat the item at the end of the sequence.)

Let's think about some words that could be moods. I'll name something. If it could tell about a mood, say, "Mood." If not, say nothing.

- Silly. *Mood.*
- Happy. *Mood.*
- Spaghetti.
- Sad. *Mood.*
- Ice cream.
- Angry. *Mood.*

What naming word means "how you feel"? *Mood.*

Present Vocabulary Tally Sheet
(See Week 1, page 3, for instructions.)

Assign Homework
(Homework Sheet, BLM 12a: See the Introduction for homework instructions.)

Preparation: Picture Vocabulary Cards for *shy, bored, silly,* and *mood.*

Read and Discuss Story

(Read story aloud to children. Ask the following questions at the specified points in the story.)

Now I'm going to read *The Way I Feel.* When I finish each part, I'll ask you some questions.

Page 1. This person is making a funny face and wearing a goofy hat. How does it make this person feel? *Silly.* What makes you feel silly?

Page 3. This person is all alone on a dark night. There's thunder and lightning. How does it make this person feel? *Scared.* What makes you feel scared?

Page 6. This girl made plans with her friend to come for a visit. Now her friend can't come. How does it make her feel? *Disappointed.* What makes you feel disappointed?

Page 8. This girl is enjoying a sunny day while she plays on her swing. How does it make her feel? *Happy.* How do you know she's happy? (Idea: *She's smiling.*) What makes you feel happy?

Page 10. This boy doesn't want to play or have fun. How does he feel? *Sad.* What makes you feel sad?

Page 12. How is this girl feeling? *Angry.* What does she feel like doing when she's angry? (Ideas: *Roaring; frowning; growling; stomping her feet.*) What makes you feel angry? What do you do when you're angry?

Page 13. What has happened to the boy's truck? (Idea: *The wheel has come off.*) Who fixed it for him? (Idea: *The man; his dad.*) How is this boy feeling? *Thankful.* What makes you feel thankful?

Page 16. What is the girl trying to do? (Idea: *Tie her shoelaces.*) Can she do it? *No.* Why not? *It's too hard.* How is this girl feeling? *Frustrated.* What makes you feel frustrated?

Page 17. Why is the little girl hiding behind her mother? (Idea: *She's shy.*) When do you feel shy?

Page 19. How is this boy feeling? (Idea: *Bored.*) Why is he feeling bored? (Ideas: *He can't decide what to do; it's raining.*) How else is this boy feeling? *Blue.* What word that we've already read about would be a blue mood? *Sad.*

Page 22. This girl is bouncing like a rubber ball. Does she want to sit still? *No.* What does she want to do? *Jump and play.* How is this person feeling? *Excited.* What makes you feel excited?

Page 23. What does this girl want to do? *Play with her father.* Why can't she play with him now? (Idea: *He's playing with her little sister.*) How is she feeling? *Jealous.* Why is she feeling jealous? (Idea: *She has to share her father with her little sister.*) What makes you feel jealous?

Page 26. This girl says, "I did it." What has she done? She got dressed by herself. How does that make her feel? *Proud.* What makes you feel proud?

Page 27. These people all have different feelings. (Starting at the top left and moving clockwise around the pages, point to each child in the illustration. Ask:) How do you think this child is feeling? What makes you think so? (Ideas: *Happy; angry; surprised; sleepy; scared.*)

Review Vocabulary

(Display the Picture Vocabulary Cards. Point to each card as you say the word. Ask children to repeat each word after you.) These pictures show **silly, shy, bored,** and **mood.**

- What describing word means "tired and squirmy because you don't have anything interesting to do"? *Bored.*
- What naming word means "how you feel"? *Mood.*
- What describing word means "you want to do things or say things or wear funny clothes that will make everyone laugh"? *Silly.*
- What describing word means "worried and a little bit afraid around others"? *Shy.*

Extend Vocabulary

 Mood.

In the story *The Way I Feel,* we learned that **mood** means "how you feel."

Here's a new way to use the word **mood.**

- **Ira was in the mood for ice cream.** Say the sentence.
- **Lorelei was in the mood for playing checkers.** Say the sentence.
- **April was in the mood for doing her schoolwork.** Say the sentence.

In these sentences, mood is part of the expression "in the mood." When you are in the mood for something, you want to do it or have it. Tell about something you might be "in the mood" for. (Ideas: *I was in the mood for pizza last night; I was in the mood for playing outside; I was in the mood for sitting and reading a good book.*)

Present Expanded Target Vocabulary

◎⟵ Emotions.

In the story, the children tell us about different moods they are feeling. Another word for the moods they are feeling is emotions. **Emotions.** Say the word. *Emotions.*

Emotions is a naming word. It is a name for all the different moods people feel. What kind of word is **emotions?** *A naming word.*

When people talk about their emotions, they are talking about the different moods they feel. Say the word that means "the different moods people feel." *Emotions.*

Let's think about some words that could be emotions. I'll name something. If it could tell about an emotion, say, "Emotion." If not, don't say anything.

- Scared. *Emotion.*
- Disappointed. *Emotion.*
- Asleep.
- Excited. *Emotion.*
- Eating.
- Frustrated. *Emotion.*

What naming word means "the different moods people feel"? *Emotions.*

◎⟵ Feelings.

In the story, we learned about lots of different feelings. Feelings are the emotions or moods that people feel. **Feelings.** Say the word. *Feelings.*

Feelings is a naming word. It is a name for all the different moods or emotions people feel. What kind of word is **feelings?** *A naming word.*

When people talk about their feelings, they are talking about the different moods or emotions they feel. Say the word that means "the different moods or emotions people feel." *Feelings.*

Let's think about some words that could be feelings. I'll name something. If it could tell about a feeling, say, "Feeling." If not, don't say anything.

- Thankful. *Feeling.*
- Angry. *Feeling.*
- Going for a walk.
- Shy. *Feeling.*
- Falling.
- Jealous. *Feeling.*

What naming word means "the different moods or emotions people feel"? *Feelings.*

(Display the Picture Vocabulary Cards for *mood, emotions,* and *feelings.*) This week we have learned three words that mean the same thing. All these words are naming words that tell how you feel. I'll tell you those three words: **mood, emotions, feelings.** Your turn. Tell me the three naming words that tell how you feel. *Mood, emotions, feelings.*

DAY 3

Preparation: Activity Sheet, BLM 12b.

Retell Story

Today I'll show you the pictures Janan Cain made for her explaining story *The Way I Feel.* As I show you the pictures, I'll call on one of you to explain the mood, feeling, or emotion shown in the picture.

Tell me what mood, feeling, or emotion the child is feeling. (Show the pictures from the story on pages 1 and 2. Call on a child to tell about the emotion. Repeat this procedure for the remaining feelings explained in the book. Encourage use of target words when appropriate. Model use as necessary.)

Listen while I read part of this story to you again. (Read any one verse.) This story is written as a poem. How is this story written? *As a poem.* What other story did we read that was a poem? *The Wind Blew.* Good remembering.

Review Show Me, Tell Me Game

Today you will play the Show Me, Tell Me Game. I'll ask you to show me how to do something. If you show me, you win one point. If you can't show me, I get the point.

Next I'll ask you to tell me. If you tell me, you win one point. If you can't tell me, I get the point.

Let's practice: My turn to show you how I would act if I were being **shy.** (Act out being shy.) How am I acting? *Shy.*

Let's do one together. Show me how you would look if you were feeling **bored.** (Look sullen and listless with the children.) How did we look? *Bored.*

Now you're ready to play the game.

(Draw a T-chart on the board for keeping score. Children earn one point for each correct answer. If they make an error, demonstrate the action, tell them the word, and record one point for yourself. Repeat missed words at the end of the game.)

- Show me how you would look if you were acting **silly.** (Pause.) Tell me how you are acting. *Acting silly.*
- Show me what you would do if you were feeling **shy.** (Pause.) Tell me what you're showing. *Feeling shy.*
- Show me the look you would have on your face if you were **bored.** (Pause.) Tell me how you are looking. *Bored.*
- Show me how you would look if you were in the **mood** for dancing. (Pause.) Tell me how you are looking. *In the mood for dancing.*
- Show me how you would look if you were in a **disagreeable** mood. (Pause.) Tell me how you are looking. *Disagreeable.*

(Count the points, and declare a winner.) You did a great job of playing the Show Me, Tell Me Game!

Making a List (Activity Sheet)

(Give each child a copy of the Activity Sheet, BLM 12b. Review with children the emotions presented in the story. If children have difficulty remembering any of them, turn to the appropriate page, and reread the verse.)

When we make a list, we write words or make pictures to help us remember. What do we do when we make a list? *We write words or make pictures to help us remember.*

Today we are going to make two lists of emotions. One list will be emotions that make us feel good, and one list will be emotions that make us feel bad.

(Show children the page with the emotions illustrations. Point to the emotions.) These are the emotions explained in the story. (Point to the picture showing *silly.*) What emotion does this picture show? *Silly.* (Point to the picture showing *scared.*) What emotion does this picture show? *Scared.* (Repeat for the remaining items.)

The title of this sheet says Emotions. What do these words say? *Emotions.* (Point to the happy face.) This part of the sheet has a happy face. This part is for the list of emotions that feel good. This part of the sheet has a sad face. This part is for the list of emotions that feel bad.

My turn to make a list. First I cut out each picture. (Demonstrate.) What do I do first? *Cut out each picture.* Next I sort the pictures into two groups. One group will be the emotions that make me feel good. The other group will be the emotions that make me feel bad.

(Pick up the *happy* picture.) This picture shows **thankful.** When I'm thankful, do I feel good or bad? *Good.* So I put **thankful** in my "feel good" group. Put **thankful** in your "feel good" group. (Repeat this procedure until all the pictures are sorted.

(Pick up the *thankful* picture from the "feel good" group.) Next I glue the picture onto the right list. What do I do next? *Glue the picture onto the right (correct) list.* Which list gets the thankful picture? (Idea: *The list with the happy face.*) Glue the thankful picture on the happy face list. (Demonstrate process for two more items.)

Now it's your turn to make lists. Finish your "feel good" and "feel bad" lists. (Children who are able to may copy each word beside the picture.)

Introduce Explaining Stories (Literary Analysis)

Let's think about what we already know about how books are made.

- What do we call the name of the book? *The title.*
- What do we call the person who writes the story? *The author.*
- What do we call the person who draws the pictures? *The illustrator.*
- What do we call the people or animals a story is about? *The characters.*
- What do we call the pictures the illustrator makes? *Illustrations.*
- What is one thing the setting of a story tells? *Where a story happens.*

Let's sing "The Story Song" to help us remember these important things about books.

(See the Introduction for the complete "Story Song.")

All the books we have read so far tell what happens to the characters. This book is not the same. It's different. Does this book tell what happens to the characters? *No.* This story is an explaining story. What kind of story is *The Way I Feel*? *An explaining story.*

An explaining story tells you more about things so you can understand them. What does an explaining story do? *It tells more about things so you can understand them.* What kind of story tells you more about things so you can understand them? *An explaining story.*

Today you learned about a new kind of story. You learned about an explaining story.

Play Show Me, Tell Me Game (Cumulative Review)

Let's play the Show Me, Tell Me Game. I'll ask you to show me how to do something. If you show me, you win one point. If you can't show me, I get the point.

Next I'll ask you to tell me. If you tell me, you win one point. If you can't tell me, I get the point.

Now you're ready to play the game.

(Draw a T-chart on the board for keeping score. Children earn one point for each correct answer. If they make an error, correct them as you normally would, and record one point for yourself. Repeat missed words at the end of the game.)

- Show me how you would look if you were feeling **bored.** (Pause.) Tell me how you looked. *Bored.*
- Show me how you would act if you were in a good **mood.** (Pause.) Tell me how you are feeling. *In a good mood.*
- Show me how you would look if you were in the **mood** for sleeping. (Pause.) Tell me how you looked. *In the mood for sleeping.*
- Show me how you would look if you were acting **silly.** (Pause.) Tell me how you were acting. *Silly.*
- Show me how you would look if you were feeling **shy.** (Pause.) Tell me how you are feeling. *Shy.*
- Show me how you would sound if you **sighed** because you were **disappointed.** (Pause.) Tell me what you did. *Sighed.*
- Show me how you would look if you were having all kinds of different **emotions.** (Pause.) Tell me what you were having. *All kinds of different emotions.*
- Show me how you would look if I hurt your **feelings.** (Pause.) Tell me how you looked. *As if my feelings were hurt.*
- Show me how you would look if you **muttered** after I asked you to stop talking. (Pause.) Tell me what you did. *Muttered.*
- Show me how you would look if you were feeling **cross** at someone. (Pause.) Tell me how you looked. *Cross.*

(Count the points, and declare a winner.)
You did a great job of playing the Show Me, Tell Me Game!

Retell Story to a Partner

(Assign each child a partner.) Today I'll show you the pictures Janan Cain made for her book *The Way I Feel.* As I show you the pictures, you and your partner will take turns explaining the feeling that is shown in that picture. (Partners should take turns explaining the feeling each time you turn to a new set of pages.)

What feeling is shown on this page? Explain to your partner what that feeling is like. (Show the pictures from the story on pages 1 and 2.)

(Repeat this procedure for the remaining feelings explained in the book.)

Assess Vocabulary

 (Give each child a copy of the Happy Face Game Test Sheet, BLM B.)

Today you're going to play the Happy Face Game. When you play the Happy Face Game, it helps me know how well you know the hard words you are learning.

If I say something true, color the happy face. What will you do if I say something true? *Color the happy face.*

If I say something false, color the sad face. What will you do if I say something false? *Color the sad face.*

Listen carefully to each sentence I say. Don't let me trick you!

Item 1: If you are in a good **mood,** you feel terrible. *False.*

Item 2: Your **feelings** are all of the moods or emotions you may feel. *True.*

Item 3: If you are feeling **shy,** you are happy about meeting strangers and feel good about it. *False.*

Item 4: If you act in a way that makes others laugh, you are acting **silly.** *True.*

Item 5: **Emotions** are the way that you might feel, such as sad, happy, disappointed, or scared. *True.*

Item 6: If someone **squeaked,** they spoke in a very high voice. *True.*

Item 7: If you are in the **mood** for pizza, it means that you do **not** want to have pizza to eat. *False.*

Item 8: If you are **bored,** it means that you feel squirmy and as if there is nothing that you want to do. *True.*

Item 9: If you are **amazed,** you are surprised. *True.*

Item 10: If you are **curious** about what is happening, you are **not** interested in what is happening. *False.*

You did a great job of playing the Happy Face Game!

(Score children's work later. Scores of 9 out of 10 indicate mastery. If a child does not achieve mastery, insert the missed words in the games in the next week's lessons. Retest those children individually on the missed items before they take the next mastery test.)

Extensions
Read a Story as a Reward

 (Display copies of several of the books that you have read since the beginning of the program. Allow children to choose which book they would like you to read aloud to them as a reward for their hard work.)

(Read story aloud to children for enjoyment with minimal interruptions.)

Present Super Words Center

(Prepare the word containers for the Super Words Center. Remove words that do not have an opposite from the containers. See the Introduction for instructions on how to set up and use the Super Words Center.)

(Add the new Picture Vocabulary Cards to the Super Words Center. Show children one of the word containers. If they need more guidance, role-play with two or three children as a demonstration.)

Let's think about how we work with our words in the Super Words Center.

You will work with a partner in the Super Words Center. Whom will you work with in the center? *A partner.*

First you will draw a word out of the container. What do you do first? (Idea: *Draw a word out of the container.*)

Next you will show your partner the picture and ask what word the picture shows. What do you do next? (Idea: *I show my partner the picture and ask what word the picture shows.*)

What do you do if your partner doesn't know the word? *Tell my partner the word.*

Next you will ask your partner to tell the opposite of that word. What do you do next? (Idea: *Ask my partner to tell the opposite of that word.*)

What will you do if your partner doesn't know the opposite? (Idea: *Tell my partner the opposite.*)

What will you do if neither of you knows the opposite? (Idea: *Put that card back and draw another.*)

What do you do next? *Give my partner a turn.*

(You may have children call on you or a classroom "expert" if they do not know an opposite. You may also choose to prepare another word container for words children have difficulty with. These could be reviewed later at an appropriate time.)

Dinosaur Days
author: Linda Manning • illustrator: Vlasta van Kampen

Preparation: You will need *Dinosaur Days* by Linda Manning for each day's lesson.

Number the pages of the story to assist you in asking questions at appropriate points.

Post a copy of the Vocabulary Tally Sheet, BLM A, with this week's Picture Vocabulary Cards attached.

Each child will need the Homework Sheet, BLM 13a.

Target Vocabulary

Tier II	Tier III
scrawl	fantasy
rude	
severely	
sprawled	
*imaginary	
*disruptive	

*Expanded Target Vocabulary Word

- When do you think the story happens?
- Why do you think the dinosaur is sliding down the post?
- How did it get its nails polished?
- Do you think the characters in this story are real? Tell why or why not.

(Call on several children to share their predictions with the class.)

Take a Picture Walk

We are going to take a picture walk through this book. Remember, when we take a picture walk, we look at the pictures and tell what we think will happen in the story.

(Show the illustrations on the following pages, and ask the specified questions.)

Pages 1–2. Where is the dinosaur? *In the kitchen.* What is it doing? (Ideas: *Drinking juice; sitting on the toast.*) How would you be feeling if you were the girl? What number do you see on the girl's shirt? *One.*

Pages 3–4. What is happening here? (Ideas: *The dinosaur is tied to the post; the little girl is touching its tongue.*)

Pages 5–6. Where is the dinosaur? *In the girl's bedroom.* What is it doing? *Coloring on her ceiling.* How would you be feeling if you were the girl? What number do you see on the girl's shirt? *Two.*

Pages 7–8. What is happening here? (Ideas: *The girl is sitting on the dinosaur's tail; she is*

DAY 1

Introduce Book

Today's book is called *Dinosaur Days.* What's the title of this week's book? *Dinosaur Days.*

This book was written by Linda Manning. Who's the author of *Dinosaur Days? Linda Manning.*

Vlasta van Kampen [Vlas-ta van Kamp-en] made the pictures for this book. Who's the illustrator of *Dinosaur Days? Vlasta van Kampen.* Who made the illustrations for this book? *Vlasta van Kampen.*

The cover of a book usually gives us some hints of what the book is about. Let's look at the front cover of *Dinosaur Days.* What do you see in the illustration? (Ideas: *A dinosaur sliding down a post; a little girl; the dinosaur has a flower in its mouth; it's wearing a necklace; it has purple nail polish on its claws.*)

Get ready to make some predictions to your partner about this book. Use the information from the cover to help you.

(Assign each child a partner. Ask the following questions, allowing sufficient time for children to share their predictions with their partners.)

- Who are the characters in this story? (Whom do you think this story is about?)
- What is the child doing?
- Where do you think the story happens?

touching the dinosaur's toes; the dinosaur is writing 2s on the floor.)

Pages 9–10. Where is the dinosaur? *In the living room*. What is it doing? (Ideas: *Sitting on the chair; making muddy footprints on everything.*) How would you be feeling if you were the girl? (Point to the calendar.) What number do you see on the calendar? *Three.*

Pages 11–12. What is happening here? (Ideas: *The girl is standing on the dinosaur's back; she is drying it off with a towel; there are 3s everywhere.*)

Pages 13–14. Where is the dinosaur? *Outside.* What is it doing? *Hanging on to a pole.* Where is the girl? *Up the tree.* What is she doing? (Idea: *Pulling numbers up into the tree.*) How would you be feeling if you were the girl? What number do you see hanging from the tree? *Four.*

Pages 15–16. What is happening here? (Idea: *The girl and the dinosaur are skipping.*)

Pages 17–18. Where is the dinosaur? *In the bathroom.* What is it doing? (Ideas: *Flying around; squeezing the toothpaste.*) What is the girl doing? (Idea: *Brushing her teeth.*) How would you be feeling if you were the girl? What number do you see? *Five.*

Pages 19–20. What is happening here? (Ideas: *The dinosaur is sitting on the sink; the girl is squeezing out the toothpaste.*)

Pages 21–22. Where is the dinosaur? (Ideas: *In the laundry room; near the washer.*) What is it doing? (Ideas: *Knocking over the soap; spilling the water.*) How do you think the girl is feeling? What number do you see? *Six.*

Pages 23–24. What is happening here? (Ideas: *The girl is telling the dinosaur to be good; she's pointing her finger at him; he's hiding his face.*)

Pages 25–26. Where are the dinosaurs? (Idea: *Outside.*) What are they doing? *Having a party.* (Point to the dinosaur with the chef's hat.) What is this dinosaur doing? (Ideas: *Barbecuing; cooking hamburgers and hot dogs.*) What is the girl doing? *Eating a hamburger.* How do you think the girl is feeling? What number do you see? *Seven.*

Pages 27–28. What is happening here? *Everyone is sleeping.*

Now that we've finished our picture walk, it's your turn to ask me some questions. What would you like to know about this story? (Accept questions. If children tell about the pictures or story instead of asking questions, prompt them to ask a question.) Ask me a why question. Ask me a how question.

Read Story Aloud
(Read story aloud to children with minimal interruptions.)

In the next lesson we will read the story again, and I will ask you some questions.

(If children have difficulty attending for an extended period of time, present the next part of this day's lesson at another time.)

Present Target Vocabulary

⊙◄ Scrawl.

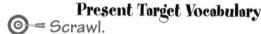

In the story the girl teaches the dinosaur how to write his name in dinosaur scrawl. That means writing that is careless and untidy. Another word for scrawl is **scribble. Scrawl.** Say the word. *Scrawl.*

Scrawl is a naming word. It names a kind of writing. What kind of word is **scrawl?** *A naming word.*

If someone's writing is a scrawl, it is careless and untidy. It doesn't look like writing; it looks like a scribble. Say the word that means "writing that is careless and untidy." *Scrawl.*

Watch me. I'll write my name in my best writing. (Write your name slowly, forming each letter carefully.) Now I'll write my name in a scrawl. (Scribble your name so it is not completely legible. Point to the first name.) This is my best writing. (Point to the second name.) This is a scrawl.

(Correct any incorrect responses, and repeat the item at the end of the sequence.)

Let's think about some writing that might be a scrawl. I'll tell about some writing. If you think the writing I'm telling about is a scrawl, say, "Scrawl." If not, don't say anything.

- Dr. Chen signs his name so fast that it is messy. *Scrawl.*
- The two-year-old boy uses a crayon to write all over the wall. *Scrawl.*
- She doesn't care how her printing looks. *Scrawl.*
- He takes the time to write his name neatly.
- You would almost say that Vonette scribbled her name. *Scrawl.*
- My teacher has the neatest writing I have ever seen.

What naming word means "writing that is careless and untidy"? *Scrawl.*

◎ = Rude.

In the story, the "rude rumbling dinosaur" spills the detergent and plugs up the drain. That means it does things that show bad manners. It does things that are not polite. **Rude.** Say the word. *Rude.*

Rude is a describing word. It tells about a way of acting or talking. What kind of word is **rude?** *A describing word.*

If you are rude, you do or say things that show bad manners. You do or say things that are not polite. Say the word that means "you do or say things that show bad manners; you are not polite." *Rude.*

(Correct any incorrect responses, and repeat the item at the end of the sequence.)

Let's think about some times when someone might be rude. I'll tell about a time. If you think the person I'm telling about is rude, say, "Rude." If not, don't say anything.

- Zach keeps interrupting the teacher when she is talking to the class. *Rude.*
- When it is Colleen's turn to listen, she talks instead. *Rude.*
- Vinnie sticks out his tongue and makes a raspberry noise. *Rude.*
- Fern walks quietly so she won't be heard.
- Faith forgets to say thank you when she gets a present. *Rude.*
- Greg and his brother wait until the speaker finishes his speech to ask a question.

What describing word means "you do or say things that show bad manners; you are not polite"? *Rude.*

◎ = Severely.

In the story, the girl quite severely says, "Don't do that again!" That means she speaks to him with a harsh voice. She does not say the words gently. **Severely.** Say the word. *Severely.*

Severely is a describing word. It tells about how someone says something. What kind of word is **severely?** *A describing word.*

If you speak severely, you speak in a voice that is harsh, not gentle. Say the word that means "you speak in a voice that is harsh, not gentle." *Severely.*

(Correct any incorrect responses, and repeat the item at the end of the sequence.)

Let's think about some times when someone might speak severely. I'll tell about a time. If you think the person I'm telling about would speak severely, say, "Severely." If not, don't say anything.

- The puppy will never listen. Its owner speaks to it. *Severely.*
- Your friend invites you to play at his house.
- The guard at the pool yells, "Do not run on the pool deck!" *Severely.*
- Ginnie whispers to her baby brother.
- Aunt Cary shouts at us to close the gate when we let the chickens out. *Severely.*
- Mom tells us, in a calm and quiet voice, how to behave.

What describing word means "you speak in a voice that is harsh, not gentle"? *Severely.*

◎ = Sprawled.

At the end of the story, all the dinosaurs sprawled in a heap under the tree. That means they were lying down with their legs spread out. **Sprawled.** Say the word. *Sprawled.*

Sprawled is an action word. It tells how someone did something. What kind of word is **sprawled?** *An action word.*

When you sprawl, you sit or lie down with your arms and legs spread out. Say the word that means "sat or lay down with arms and legs spread out." *Sprawled.*

(Correct any incorrect responses, and repeat the item at the end of the sequence.)

Watch me. I'll sit carefully on my chair. (Sit with your feet flat on the floor, hands folded on your lap. Then stand up.) What did I do? *You sat carefully on your chair.*

Now I'll sprawl on my chair. (Slide forward on your chair so only your upper back touches the back of the chair. Stretch your legs out, in different directions. Put one arm over the back of the chair, and hang your other arm over the side of your chair. Then stand up.) What did I do? *You sprawled on your chair.*

I'll quietly ask someone to do some actions in our classroom. Your job is to watch what that person does. If he or she sprawls, say, "Sprawled." If that person doesn't sprawl, don't say anything. (Whisper an instruction to a specific child to perform.)

- (Sprawl at a desk.) *Sprawled.*
- (Sit nicely in a chair.)
- (Sprawl on a table.) *Sprawled.*
- (Sprawl on the floor.) *Sprawled.*
- (Sit nicely at the Super Words Center.)
- (Sit nicely at your desk.)

What action word means "sat or lay down with arms and legs spread out"? *Sprawled.*

Present Vocabulary Tally Sheet
(See Week 1, page 3, for instructions.)

Assign Homework
(Homework Sheet, BLM 13a: See the Introduction for homework instructions.)

DAY 2

Preparation: Picture Vocabulary Cards for *scrawl, rude, severely,* and *sprawled.*

Read and Discuss Story
(Read story aloud to children. Ask the following questions at the specified points.)

Now I'm going to read *Dinosaur Days.* When I finish each part, I'll ask you some questions.

(**Note:** Before beginning the story, explain to children that in this book, the author talks to the reader; she asks what they would do if they found themselves face-to-face with some very unusual dinosaurs. The illustrator draws pictures to answer the question and shows what one girl does when faced with that problem.)

Page 2. When does the story begin? *On Monday.* This dinosaur is an apatosaurus. [a pat o **sore** us] What's the problem? (Idea: *The Apatosaurus slurps up the orange juice and squishes the toast.*)

Page 4. What does the girl do to solve the problem? *She tames him and teaches him to lie by a post.*

Page 6. When does this part of the story happen? *On Tuesday.* This dinosaur is a stegosaurus. [steg uh **sore** us] What's the problem? (Idea: *The stegosaurus draws on the ceiling and messes up the clothes.*)

Page 8. What does the girl do to solve the problem? *She catches her and holds her by two ticklish toes.*

(Repeat this process for pages 9 through 24, identifying the dinosaurs:

Wednesday - ankylosaurus [an keel o **sore** us]

Thursday - hadrosaurus [had ro **sore** us]

Friday - pteranodon [ter **an** o don]

Saturday - triceratops [try **sair** ah tops]

Sunday - tyrannosaurus Rex [tie ran uh **sore** us rex]

Page 28. How does the story end? (Idea: *All of the dinosaurs fall asleep.*)

Review Vocabulary
(Display the Picture Vocabulary Cards. Point to each card as you say the word. Ask children to repeat each word after you.) These pictures show **scrawl, rude, severely,** and **sprawled.**

- What describing word means "you do or say things that show bad manners; you are not polite"? *Rude.*
- What action word means "sat or lay down with arms and legs spread out"? *Sprawled.*
- What describing word means "you speak in a voice that is harsh, not gentle"? *Severely.*
- What naming word means "writing that is careless and untidy"? *Scrawl.*

Extend Vocabulary

⌖ Scrawl.

In the story *Dinosaur Days*, we learned that **scrawl** is a naming word that means "writing that is careless and untidy."

Here's a new way to use the word **scrawl.**

- **He scrawled his name at the end of the letter.** Say the sentence.
- **They scrawled on the paper with their markers.** Say the sentence.
- **He scrawled his name on the bag.** Say the sentence.

In these sentences, **scrawl** is an action word. When you scrawl on something, you write on it in a messy or untidy way. What do you do when you scrawl on something? *You write on it in a messy or untidy way.*

Present Expanded Target Vocabulary

⌖ Imaginary.

In the story, the dinosaurs live when real dinosaurs don't live. They go places real dinosaurs can't go. They do things real dinosaurs can't do. These dinosaurs are not real dinosaurs. They are imaginary dinosaurs. **Imaginary.** Say the word. *Imaginary.*

Imaginary is a describing word. It tells about how things are. What kind of word is **imaginary?** *A describing word.*

If something is imaginary, it is not real. What word means "something that is not real"? *Imaginary.*

Let's think about some things that could be imaginary. I'll name something. If it could tell about something that is imaginary, say, "Imaginary." If it tells about something that is real, say, "Real."

- Pigs that can build houses of brick. *Imaginary.*
- A girl who gets a kite for her birthday. *Real.*
- Goats that eat grass. *Real.*
- Trolls that live under bridges. *Imaginary.*
- A hen that makes bread. *Imaginary.*
- People who make Stone Soup. *Real.*

What describing word means "something that is not real"? *Imaginary.*

⌖ Disruptive.

In the story, the dinosaurs cause a lot of trouble in the girl's house. Nothing happens the way it should. The dinosaurs are very disruptive. **Disruptive.** Say the word. *Disruptive.*

Disruptive is a describing word. It tells about someone's actions. What kind of word is **disruptive?** *A describing word.*

When you are disruptive you cause a lot of trouble. The opposite of disruptive is well-behaved. Say the word that means "you cause a lot of trouble." *Disruptive.*

Let's think about some people who might do something disruptive. I'll tell about someone. If that person is being disruptive, say, "Disruptive." If that person is not being disruptive, say, "Well-behaved."

- Kyle doesn't yell when he gets upset. *Well-behaved.*
- The baby hits and kicks and screams when he or she doesn't get his or her way. *Disruptive.*
- The children won't be quiet when the substitute teacher comes. *Disruptive.*
- All of us sit quietly and read while we wait. *Well-behaved.*
- None of the children cry or shout when the lights go out. *Well-behaved.*
- The bullies scare the little kids. *Disruptive.*

What describing word means "you cause a lot of trouble"? *Disruptive.*

Tell about a time when you or someone you know was disruptive. (Call on several children. Encourage them to start their answers with the words "I was disruptive when _____" or "_____ was disruptive when _____" After each response, ask the child:) What might you have done to be well-behaved?

DAY 3

Preparation: Activity Sheet, BLM 13b.

Retell Story

Today I'll show you the pictures Vlasta Van Kampen made for the story *Dinosaur Days*. As

I show you the pictures, I'll call on one of you to tell the class about that part of the story.

(Show the pictures from the story on pages 1 through 4. Call on a child to tell what's happening. Encourage use of target words when appropriate. Model use as necessary. Repeat this procedure to the end of page 26.)

(Show the pictures from the story on pages 27 and 28. Chime-read the end of the story, with children chiming in with the days of the week.)

Listen while I read part of this story to you again. (Read any one verse.) This story is written as a poem. How is this story written? *As a poem.* What other stories have we read that were poems? *The Wind Blew; The Way I Feel.* Good remembering.

The Wind Blew and *Dinosaur Days* are the same in another way. They are both add-on stories. What kind of stories are *The Wind Blew* and *Dinosaur Days*? *Add-on stories.*

Review Opposites Game

 Today you'll play the Opposites Game. I'll use a vocabulary word in a sentence. If you can tell me the opposite of that word, you win one point. If you can't tell me, I get the point.

Let's practice: The boy wrote his name in a **scrawl.** Tell me the opposite of "in a scrawl." (Idea: *Neatly.*) Neatly could be the opposite of "in a scrawl."

Let's try another one. Natasha spoke to MacKenzie **severely.** Tell me the opposite of severely. (Idea: *Nicely.*) Nicely could be the opposite of severely.

Now you're ready to play the game.

(Draw a T-chart on the board for keeping score. Children earn one point for each correct answer. If they make an error, suggest an appropriate choice, tell them the word, and record one point for yourself. Repeat missed words at the end of the game.)

- The boys were very **rude.** Tell me the opposite of rude. (Idea: *Polite.*) Polite could be the opposite of rude.
- The student wrote her name **in a neat way.** Tell me the opposite of "in a neat way."

(Idea: *In a scrawl.*) "In a scrawl" could be the opposite of "in a neat way."

- The store owner spoke to the children **severely.** Tell me the opposite of severely. (Idea: *Nicely.*) Nicely could be the opposite of severely.
- The rag doll **sprawled** in the corner. Tell me the opposite of sprawled. (Idea: *Sat nicely.*) "Sat nicely" could be the opposite of sprawled.
- We all know that trolls are **imaginary.** Tell me the opposite of imaginary. (Idea: *Real.*) Real could be the opposite of imaginary.
- The children's shouting **was very disruptive.** Tell me the opposite of "was very disruptive." (Idea: *Was not disruptive.*) "Was not disruptive" could be the opposite of "was very disruptive."

(Count the points, and declare a winner.) You did a great job of playing the Opposites Game!

Sentence Frames (Activity Sheet)

In the story *Dinosaur Days,* things happen on each day of the week. Say the days of the week, starting with Monday. (Repeat until responses are firm.)

 (Give each child a copy of the Activity Sheet, BLM 13b.) My turn. I'll read the first item on the sheet. On Monday, "blank" comes. (Chime-read with children the first item on the sheet. Say "blank" when you get to the line. Have children decide which dinosaur comes that day. Have them cut out the picture of that dinosaur and glue it on the line. Children who are able to may copy each word beside the picture.)

(Repeat this process for the remaining items.)

Introduce Fantasy (Literary Analysis)

Let's think about what we already know about how books are made.

- What do we call the name of the book? *The title.*
- What do we call the person who writes the story? *The author.*

- What do we call the person who draws the pictures? *The illustrator.*
- What do we call the people or animals a story is about? *The characters.*
- What do we call the pictures the illustrator makes? *Illustrations.*
- What is one thing the setting of a story tells? *Where a story happens.*

Let's sing "The Story Song" to help us remember these important things about books.

(See the Introduction for the complete "Story Song.")

(Display all the books from Week 1 to Week 13.) Some of the books we have read tell about real characters. Some of the books we have read tell about imaginary characters. Let's sort the books into books with real characters and books with imaginary characters.

(Present the books one at a time, asking:) Are the characters in this book real or imaginary? (If children experience difficulty answering the question, ask a leading question. For example, when considering the book *Flossie and the Fox*, ask:) Could a real fox talk to a girl? *No.* So is *Flossie & the Fox* about real characters or imaginary characters? *Imaginary characters.*

(Children should identify these stories as imaginary: *The Ant and the Grasshopper, Jack and the Bean Stalk, The Three Little Pigs, The Little Red Hen, The Three Billy Goats Gruff, Flossie & the Fox,* and *Dinosaur Days.*)

Point to the books with imaginary characters. If a story has imaginary characters that do impossible things, the story is called **fantasy.** What do you call a story that has imaginary characters that do impossible things? *Fantasy.*

Today you learned about a new kind of story. You learned about stories that are fantasy.

Play Opposites Game (Cumulative Review)

Let's play the Opposites Game. I'll use a vocabulary word in a sentence. If you can tell me the opposite of that word, you win one point. If you can't tell me, I get the point.

Let's practice: Here's a trick about opposites. If a word has "un" at the beginning, you can make the opposite by taking "un" away.

My turn: The children were **unexcited** about going to the zoo. Tell me the opposite of unexcited. (Idea: *Excited.*) Excited is the opposite of unexcited.

Let's do one together. The campers were **unprepared** for the rain. Tell me the opposite of unprepared. (Idea: *Prepared.*) Prepared is the opposite of unprepared.

Now you're ready to play the game.

(Draw a T-chart on the board for keeping score. Children earn one point for each correct answer. If they make an error, correct them as you normally would, and record one point for yourself. Repeat missed words at the end of the game.)

- The house felt **unfamiliar** to Marco. Tell me the opposite of unfamiliar. (Idea: *Familiar.*) Familiar could be the opposite of unfamiliar.
- The animals in the story were **imaginary.** Tell me the opposite of imaginary. (Idea: *Real.*) Real could be the opposite of imaginary.
- Mr. Williams spoke **nicely** to Sabrina. Tell me the opposite of nicely. (Idea: *Severely.*) Severely could be the opposite of nicely.
- Mrs. DeJong was **sprawled** in her chair. Tell me the opposite of sprawled. (Idea: *Sitting nicely.*) "Sitting nicely" could be the opposite of sprawled.
- After lunch, everyone was **unsatisfied.** Tell me the opposite of unsatisfied. (Idea: *Satisfied.*) Satisfied could be the opposite of unsatisfied.
- The children **were not disruptive.** Tell me the opposite of "were not disruptive." (Idea: *Were disruptive.*) "Were disruptive" could be the opposite of "were not disruptive."
- Jordan **scrawled** his name on his worksheet. Tell me the opposite of scrawled. (Idea: *Printed neatly.*) "Printed neatly" could be the opposite of scrawled.
- The cat **was curious** when it saw the bird. Tell me the opposite of "was curious." (Idea: *Was not curious.*) "Was not curious" could be the opposite of "was curious."

- Nettie **frowned** when she got a new bike. Tell me the opposite of frowned. (Idea: *Smiled.*) Smiled could be the opposite of frowned.
- Lorraine was **unselfish** about sharing her chocolate. Tell me the opposite of unselfish. (Idea: *Selfish.*) Selfish could be the opposite of unselfish.

(Count the points, and declare a winner.)
You did a great job of playing the Opposites Game!

Preparation: Happy Face Game Test Sheet, BLM B.

Retell Story to a Partner

(Assign each child a partner.) Today I'll show you the pictures Vlasta van Kampen made for the story *Dinosaur Days.* As I show you the pictures, you and your partner will take turns telling part of the story. (Partners should take turns telling part of the story each time the day of the week changes.)

Pages 1–4. Tell what happens on **Monday.**

Pages 5–26. Tell what happens on **Tuesday.** (Encourage use of target words when appropriate. Repeat this procedure until you finish page 26.)

Pages 27–28. Tell what happens at the **end** of the story. (Chime-read the end of the story, with children chiming in with as much of the story as they can remember.)

Are the dinosaurs in this story real or imaginary? *Imaginary.* So what kind of story is *Dinosaur Days*? *Fantasy.* Good remembering a new kind of story.

Assess Vocabulary

(Give each child a copy of the Happy Face Game Test Sheet, BLM B.)

Today you're going to play the Happy Face Game. When you play the Happy Face Game, it helps me know how well you know the hard words you are learning.

If I say something true, color the happy face. What will you do if I say something true? *Color the happy face.*

If I say something false, color the sad face. What will you do if I say something false? *Color the sad face.*

Listen carefully to each sentence I say. Don't let me trick you!

Item 1: **Scrawl** means to print very neatly. *True.*

Item 2: If students are **disruptive,** they are making trouble in the classroom. *True.*

Item 3: A **rude** person speaks nicely to others. *False.*

Item 4: If you are **sprawled** on the floor, your arms and legs are everywhere, and it looks like you just fell where you were. *True.*

Item 5: If your teacher speaks **severely,** he or she is speaking quietly and nicely. *False.*

Item 6: **Imaginary** animals are not real. *True.*

Item 7: If Suzie **whirled,** she spun around very quickly. *True.*

Item 8: If a bird moves **upward,** it is moving toward the ground. *False.*

Item 9: If a fox was being a **rascal** in a story, it would tell the truth and not try to get its own way. *False.*

Item 10: If the name on the book was a **scrawl,** is would **not** be neat and easy to read. *True.*

You did a great job of playing the Happy Face Game!

(Score children's work later. Scores of 9 out of 10 indicate mastery. If a child does not achieve mastery, insert the missed words in the games in the next week's lessons. Retest those children individually on the missed items before they take the next mastery test.)

Extensions
Read a Story as a Reward

(Display copies of several of the books you have read since the beginning of the program. Allow children to choose which book they would like you to read aloud to them as a reward for their hard work.)

(Read the story aloud to children for enjoyment with minimal interruptions.)

Present Super Words Center

 (Prepare the word containers for the Super Words Center. See Introduction for instructions on how to set up and use the Super Words Center.)

(Add the new Picture Vocabulary Cards to the words from the previous weeks. Show children one of the word containers. If they need more guidance, role-play with two or three children as a demonstration as you introduce each part of the game.)

You will play a game called What's My Word? in the Super Words Center.

Let's think about how we work with our words in the Super Words Center.

You will work with a partner in the Super Words Center. Whom will you work with in the center? *A partner.*

First you will draw a word out of the container. What do you do first? (Idea: *Draw a word out of the container.*) Don't show your partner the word card. (Demonstrate.)

Next you will tell your partner three clues that tell about the word card. What do you do next? (Idea: *Tell my partner three clues that tell about the word card.*) (Demonstrate.)

After each clue, your partner can make a guess. If your partner is correct, say, "yes." If your partner is not correct, say, "no," and give another clue. (Demonstrate.)

Let your partner make three guesses. If any of your partner's guesses are correct, your partner gets a point. If your partner does not guess correctly, tell him or her your word, and show the word card. Give yourself a point. Then give your partner a turn. (Demonstrate.)

What do you do next? *Give my partner a turn.*

(This game does not need to be played for points.)

Preparation: You will need *Hooray, A Piñata!* for each day's lesson.

Number the pages of the story to assist you in asking questions at appropriate points.

Post a copy of the Vocabulary Tally Sheet, BLM A, with this week's Picture Vocabulary Cards attached.

Each child will need the Homework Sheet, BLM 14a.

DAY 1

Introduce Book

Today's book is called *Hooray, A Piñata!* What's the title of this week's book? *Hooray, A Piñata!*

A piñata is a container made out of paper. Piñatas are filled with candies and small toys. When you break the piñata, all the treats fall out and everyone scrambles to get some of them. Piñatas come in many different shapes.

This book was written by Elisa Kleven [E-li-sa Klev-en]. Who's the author of *Hooray, a Piñata! Elisa Kleven.*

Elisa Kleven also made the pictures for this book. Who is the illustrator of *Hooray, a Piñata! Elisa Kleven.* Who made the illustrations for this book? *Elisa Kleven.*

The cover of a book usually gives us some hints of what the book is about. Let's look at the front cover of *Hooray, a Piñata!* What do you see in the illustration? (Ideas: *A birthday party; someone playing a violin; a flute; a guitar; presents; a cake; a piñata.*)

(Assign each child a partner.) Get ready to make some predictions to your partner about this book. Use the information from the cover to help you.

(Ask the following questions, allowing sufficient time for children to share their predictions with their partners.)

Hooray, A Piñata!
author: Elisa Kleven • illustrator: Elisa Kleven

◎ Target Vocabulary

Tier II	Tier III
jagged	setting
pretended	
promise	
scowled	
*worried	
*allergic	

*Expanded Target Vocabulary Word

- Who are the characters in this story? (Whom do you think this story is about?)
- What do you think they will do?
- Where do you think the story happens?
- When do you think the story happens?
- Why do you think everyone has come?
- How many children are at the party?
- Do you think this story is about real or imaginary people? Tell why or why not.

(Call on several children to share their predictions with the class.)

Take a Picture Walk

We are going to take a picture walk through this book. Remember, when we take a picture walk, we look at the pictures and tell what we think will happen in the story.

(Show the illustrations on the following pages, and ask the specified questions.)

Page 1. Who do you see in this first illustration? *A boy and a girl.* Where do you think they are? (Idea: *In a sandbox.*) What makes you think so? (Ideas: *I can see the wood around the sandbox; I can see the sand and the sand toys.*) What is the girl doing? What is the boy doing?

Page 2. What is happening here? (Ideas: *The boy is talking to the girl; the girl is listening.*) What do you think they are talking about?

Pages 3–4. Where are they? (Ideas: *At the market; on the street.*) What things do you see?

Pages 5–6. Where are they now? (Idea: *In the toy store.*) What kinds of things could you buy in this store? What does the little girl buy? (Idea: *A piñata.*) What does her piñata look like? *A dog.*

Page 7. What's the little girl doing? (Idea: *Carrying the piñata.*) Do you think her feelings make her feel good or make her feel bad? *Good.* Think about all the words we know that tell about emotions that make you feel good. Which of those words could we use to tell about her feelings? (Ideas: *Proud; happy; satisfied.*)

(**Note:** If children don't use the word *satisfied,* say:) We learned a word in Week 8 that tells how the little girl is feeling. That word is **satisfied.** When you feel satisfied, you feel happy because you have enough of what you want or need. Say the word **satisfied.** *Satisfied.*

Page 8. What is the girl doing? (Idea: *Feeding the dog.*) What makes you think so? (Idea: *She has a dish and a box of food.*)

Page 9. What else is she doing with the dog? (Ideas: *Walking it on a leash; letting people pet it; letting it sniff other dogs; running with it outside.*)

Page 10. What are the girl and the dog doing? (Idea: *Playing in the sandbox.*) How do you think the little boy is feeling? (Ideas: *Left out; upset; worried.*)

Page 11. Where are the girl and the dog now? (Idea: *In the car.*) Where do you think they are going?

Page 12. Who do you think the woman is? (Idea: *Her grandmother.*) What do you think she's saying?

Page 13. Where are they now? (Idea: *On a merry-go-round.*)

Pages 14–15. What do you think is happening here?

Pages 16–17. What things are the girl and the dog doing together? (Ideas: *Swinging on a swing; eating lunch; listening to a story; riding her bike.*)

Page 19. What is the boy doing? (Idea: *Making party hats.*) What is the girl doing? *Putting a hat on her dog.* Do you think her feelings make her feel good or make her feel bad? *Bad.* Think about all the words we know that tell about

emotions that make you feel bad. Which of those words could we use to tell about her feelings? (Ideas: *Sad; disappointed.*) (**Note:** If children don't use the word *disappointed,* say:) We learned a naming word in Week 9 that tells how the little girl is feeling. That word is **disappointment.** Disappointment is the sad feeling you have when you don't get something you want. The describing word for this feeling is **disappointed.** Say the word **disappointed.** *Disappointed.*

Pages 20–21. What do you think is happening here? What does the piñata look like? (Ideas: *A monster; a thundercloud.*) How is the little girl feeling? *Excited.* (**Note:** If children don't use the word *excited,* say:) We learned a word in Week 9 that tells how the little girl is feeling. That word is **excited.** You are excited when you are so happy you can't be still because something good is going to happen to you. Say the word **excited.** *Excited.*

Page 22. What is everyone doing? (Idea: *Singing.*)

Page 23. Now what is everyone doing? (Idea: *Trying to break the piñata.*)

Pages 24–25. What do you think is happening here? (Ideas: *The piñata is broken; candies are everywhere; the children are gathering, or collecting, the candies.*) (**Note:** If children don't use the words *gathering,* or *collecting,* prompt them.)

Page 26. What is the girl doing? (Idea: *Making a hat out of part of the piñata.*) What is the boy doing? (Idea: *Making a mask out of part of the piñata.*) Did they break open the dog piñata? *No.* What is the dog piñata doing? (*Idea: Smelling the flowers.*)

Now that we've finished our picture walk, it's your turn to ask me some questions. What would you like to know about the story? (Accept questions. If children tell about the pictures or story instead of asking questions, prompt them to ask a question.) Ask me a why question. Ask me a who question.

Read Story Aloud
(Read the story aloud to children with minimal interruptions.)

In the next lesson, we will read the story again, and I will ask you some questions.

(If children have difficulty attending for an extended period of time, present the next part of this day's lesson at another time.)

Present Target Vocabulary

◎⚊ Jagged.

In the story, when the children go to the piñata store, Samson sees a big, jagged piñata that looks like a thundercloud. That means the piñata doesn't have smooth edges. It has edges that have lots of sharp points. **Jagged.** Say the word. *Jagged.*

Jagged is a describing word. It tells more about the edges of the piñata. What kind of word is **jagged?** *A describing word.*

If something is jagged, it has edges that have lots of sharp points. Say the word that means "it has edges that have lots of sharp points." *Jagged.*

Watch me. I'll use my hand to show a circle that has smooth edges. (Point your finger, and then move your arm in a smooth circle.) Use your hand to show a circle that has smooth edges. (Pause.) Good; you used your hand to show **smooth.**

Now watch me. I'll use my hand to show a circle that has jagged edges. (Point your finger, and then draw a jagged circle.) Use your hand to show a circle that has jagged edges. (Pause.) Good; you used your hand to show **jagged.**

Smooth and **jagged** are opposites. What kind of words are smooth and jagged? *Opposites.*

If something is jagged, it has edges that have lots of sharp points. Say the word that means "it has edges that have lots of sharp points." *Jagged.*

(Correct any incorrect responses, and repeat the item at the end of the sequence.)

Let's think about some things that could be jagged. I'll name some things. If these things might be jagged, say, "Jagged." If not, don't say anything.

- A rocky mountain. *Jagged.*
- A balloon filled with air.
- A broken rock. *Jagged.*
- Jelly on toast.
- A broken window. *Jagged.*
- A smashed mirror. *Jagged.*

What describing word means "it has edges that have lots of sharp points"? *Jagged.* What is the opposite of jagged? *Smooth.*

◎⚊ Pretended.

In the story, when Clara and Lucky are riding on the merry-go-round, she pretended they were flying. That means she imagined they were flying, even though she knew they weren't. She was playing make-believe. She knew she wasn't flying, but it was fun to pretend. **Pretended.** Say the word. *Pretended.*

Pretended is an action word. It tells what someone was doing. What kind of word is **pretended?** *An action word.*

If you pretended, it means you imagined you were doing something, even though you knew you weren't. You were playing make-believe. Say the word that means "you imagined you were doing something, even though you knew you weren't." *Pretended.*

Watch me. I'll pretend I'm the giant from *Jack and the Bean Stalk.* (Roar the rhyme *Fe, Fi, Fo, Fum, I smell fresh meat and I must have some.*) Pretend you're the giant from *Jack and the Bean Stalk.* (Pause.) Good; you pretended you were the giant from *Jack and the Bean Stalk.* You roared what he said in the story.

Did you think you were really the giant? *No.* That's right; it was just make-believe. You pretended to be the giant.

Now pretend to be the wolf from *The Three Little Pigs.* Pretend to huff and puff and blow the pig's house down. (Pause.) Good, you pretended you were the wolf from *The Three Little Pigs.*

Did you think you were really the wolf? *No.* That's right; it was just make-believe. You pretended to be the wolf.

(Correct any incorrect responses, and repeat the item at the end of the sequence.)

Let's think about some times when someone might have pretended. I'll tell about a time. If someone pretended, say, "Pretended." If not, don't say anything.

- The class walked like crabs in the gym. *Pretended.*
- Roland rode his bike.
- We acted liked gorillas. *Pretended.*
- We played airplanes and landed our plane in California. *Pretended.*
- We ate ice cream.
- Teddy washed his shirt in the sink.

What action word means "imagined you were doing something, even though you knew you weren't." *Pretended.*

 Promise.

In the story, Clara promises Samson she will take good care of her piñata. That means she tells Samson she will definitely take good care of her piñata. She gives her word. **Promise.** Say the word. *Promise.*

Promise is an action word. It tells what someone says. What kind of word is **promise?** *An action word.*

If you promise that you will do something, you give your word that you will do it. You definitely will do it. Say the word that means "you say you will definitely do something." *Promise.*

(Correct any incorrect responses, and repeat the item at the end of the sequence.)

Let's think about some times when someone might promise something. I'll tell about a time. If someone promises, say, "Promise." If not, don't say anything.

- I give you my word. I definitely will play with you after school. *Promise.*
- Maybe you can come to my house on Saturday.
- Dad says, "We will go to the movies next week for sure." *Promise.*
- "If you are very good, I will take you swimming," says Mom. *Promise.*
- It's time for bed.
- I promise that you will like this cake. *Promise.*

What action word means "you say you will definitely will do something"? *Promise.*

 Scowled.

In the story, the thundercloud piñata scowled at everyone. That means it had an angry frown on its face. **Scowled.** Say the word. *Scowled.*

Scowled is an action word. It tells what someone did. What kind of word is **scowled?** *An action word.*

When you scowl, you make an angry frown. Say the word that means "made an angry frown." *Scowled.*

Watch me. I'll scowl at you. (Make an angry frown.) I scowled at you. Now you scowl at me. (Pause.) You really know how to scowl, but I think I like it better when you smile at me.

(Correct any incorrect responses, and repeat the item at the end of the sequence.)

Let's think about some things that might have made you scowl. I'll name something. If you think that thing would have made you scowl, say, "Scowled." If not, don't say anything.

- The teacher said no one could play with our favorite class toys. *Scowled.*
- The man told us we had done a terrible thing. *Scowled.*
- We got a compliment on our neatness.
- Martin said that his friend had borrowed his tools so he couldn't finish his work. *Scowled.*
- We had breakfast in the gym.
- There were no more pancakes, so we had waffles instead.

What action word means "made an angry frown"? *Scowled.*

Present Vocabulary Tally Sheet
(See Week 1, page 3, for instructions.)

Assign Homework
(Homework Sheet, BLM 14a: See the Introduction for homework instructions.)

Preparation: Picture Vocabulary Cards for *jagged, pretended, promised,* and *scowled.*

Read and Discuss Story

(Read the story aloud to children. Ask the following questions at the specified points.)

Now I'm going to read *Hooray, A Piñata!* When I finish each part, I'll ask you some questions.

Page 2. Who is having the birthday? *Clara.* Tell about her plans for her birthday party. (Idea: *She will have cake, balloons, and a piñata.*) What is Samson excited about? (Idea: *He loves piñatas.*)

Page 4. What do the children like about piñatas? (Ideas: *To fill them with candy; to whack, smack and crack them; to mash and smash and break them; to watch the candy fall; eat the candy.*)

Page 6. Which piñata does Samson like? *The thundercloud.* Which piñata does Clara like? *The little dog.*

Page 7. Which piñata does she get? *The little dog.* Why doesn't Samson think the little dog is the best choice? (Idea: *It won't hold much candy.*)

Page 8. What does Clara name the little dog? *Lucky.* What is she going to do with the dog? *Take it to the park for a picnic.* Why doesn't Samson think she should do that? (Idea: *The piñata might get wrecked.*)

Page 9. What does Clara do with the little dog? (Ideas: *She feeds it and takes it for a walk.*)

Page 10. What does Clara do with the little dog? (Ideas: *She lets it greet people and other dogs; she lets it smell bushes, flowers, and trees.*) What does it mean when the story says, "They stopped to greet people and other dogs"? (Idea: *She lets it say hello to them.*) How is Clara treating her dog? (Idea: *As if it were real.*) Is Clara's dog real or imaginary? *Imaginary.* How do you know? *It is really a piñata.*

Page 12. Could Lucky really dig in the sand or shake himself clean or smell the air? *No.* Why not? (Ideas: *He isn't a real dog; he is imaginary.*)

Page 14. What does Clara's grandma give her? (Idea: *A blanket for Lucky and some money.*) What is Clara going to do with the money? (Idea: *Buy dog biscuits and a ride on the merry-go-round.*) What does Clara pretend? *They are flying.*

Page 16. What does Clara dream about? *Flying.* Are they really flying? *No.* That's right; they're just in Clara's dream. They are imaginary.

Page 18. What do Clara and the little dog do? (Ideas: *Ride the swing; eat cheese sandwiches; listen to stories; bicycle around the block with Samson.*)

What is Samson worried about? *The piñata.* Why do you think he is worried about it? (Idea: *If it breaks, they won't be able to have candy in it at Clara's birthday party.*)

Page 20. Why is Clara sad? (Idea: *She doesn't want to break the dog piñata on her birthday.*) How do you know Samson is disappointed when Clara says she doesn't want to break the piñata? (Idea: *He sighs.*) Show me what Samson does. That's right; when you sigh, you let out a deep breath to show you are disappointed. What does Samson say he might get Clara for her birthday? *A real puppy.* Why can't Clara have a real dog? *Dogs and cats make her mother sneeze.*

Page 22. What does Samson bring Clara for her birthday? *A rawhide bone for Lucky and the thundercloud piñata.* What do they put in the piñata? (Ideas: *Almond bars; cinnamon swirls; strawberry rolls; taffy; jelly beans; chocolate kisses.*)

Page 26. Who finally breaks open the piñata? *Clara.* How are most of the children feeling? *Excited.* (Prompt children if they don't use the word *excited.*) How do you know? *They can't be still because they know they are going to get lots of candy.* (Point to the little boy near the center of the illustration on page 26.) Why do you think this little boy is crying? (Ideas: *He's disappointed that he hasn't gotten any candy; maybe he's shy and doesn't like all the people around him.*)

Page 27. What do they do at the end of the story? (Idea: *They play with the pieces of the piñata.*)

Review Vocabulary

(Display the Picture Vocabulary Cards. Point to each card as you say the word. Ask children to repeat each word after you.) These pictures show **jagged, pretended, promise,** and **scowled.**

- What action word means "say you definitely will do something"? *Promise.*
- What action word means "imagined you were doing something, even though you knew you weren't"? *Pretended.*
- What action word means "made an angry frown"? *Scowled.*
- What describing word means "it has lots of sharp points"? *Jagged.*

Extend Vocabulary

◎━ Promise.

In the story *Hooray, A Pinata!* we learned that if you promise, you give your word that you will do something. You definitely will do it. Say the word that means "you say you will definitely do something." *Promise.*

Here's a new way to use the word **promise.**

- **I made a promise to my auntie that I would always tell the truth.** Say the sentence.
- **My uncle always keeps his promises.** Say the sentence.
- **She made a promise that she would be my best friend.** Say the sentence.

In these sentences, **promise** is a naming word that means "the words you say when you promise someone something." Tell about a promise you have made and whom you made the promise to. (Call on several children. Encourage children to start their answers with the words "I made a promise to ____ that ____.")

Present Expanded Target Vocabulary

◎━ Allergic.

In the story, Clara can't have a real dog because dogs and cats make her mother sneeze. The word that explains why Clara's mom sneezes around dogs and cats is **allergic.** Clara's mom is allergic to dogs and cats. **Allergic.** Say the word. *Allergic.*

Allergic is a describing word. It tells about a medical problem some people have. What kind of word is **allergic**? *A describing word.*

People may be allergic to dust, pollen, cat or dog hair, or to different kinds of foods. **If you are allergic to something, it gives you a rash, or it makes you sneeze or cough when you are near that thing.** Say the word that means "being near something gives you a rash or makes you cough or sneeze." *Allergic.*

I'll tell about some people. If those people are allergic to something, say, "Allergic." If not, don't say anything.

- Antonio sneezes when he plays on the grass. *Allergic.*
- Josie gets a rash when she eats peanut butter. *Allergic.*
- Tio has fun playing with his grandma's little dogs.
- Orlin sneezes, wheezes, and coughs after smelling the flower. *Allergic.*
- Sylvia rolls in the grass and pretends she is a crocodile.
- The children are itching and scratching after playing with the kittens. *Allergic.*

What describing word means "being near something gives you a rash or makes you cough or sneeze"? *Allergic.*

◎━ Worried.

At the end of the story, every time Samson sees Clara with Lucky, he says things like "What are you doing to that poor piñata?" or "You don't want it to get wrecked" or "Careful with that piñata!" Samson is unhappy because he keeps thinking about all the bad things that might happen to the piñata. That means he is worried about what might happen to the piñata. **Worried.** Say the word. *Worried.*

Worried is a describing word. It tells how someone is feeling. What kind of word is **worried**? *A describing word.* That's right; **worried** is a describing word that tells about a feeling or an emotion.

When you are worried, you are unhappy because you can't stop thinking about all the bad things that might happen. Say the word that means "unhappy because you can't stop thinking about all the bad things that might happen." *Worried.*

I'll tell about some times. If someone would feel worried, say, "Worried." If not, don't say anything.

- When Theo was late coming home from school, his mother couldn't stop thinking about the bad things that might have happened to him. *Worried.*
- Maria couldn't stop thinking about getting in trouble at school. *Worried.*
- Mom lost sight of Cindy at the beach and wondered if something bad had happened to her. *Worried.*
- How you feel when you know what to do and you just do it well.
- How you feel when you think that you are doing something wrong and you might get in trouble. *Worried.*
- Damon thought about the fun he had with his sister Crystal.
- What describing word means "unhappy because you can't stop thinking about all the bad things that might happen"? *Worried.*

DAY 3

Preparation: You will need a sheet of chart paper. Each child will need the Activity Sheet, BLM 14b. They will also need crayons.

Retell Story

(Show the pictures on the following pages from the story, and call on a child to tell what's happening. Call on a different child for each section.)

Today I'll show you the pictures Elisa Kleven made for the story *Hooray, A Piñata!* As I show you the pictures, I'll call on one of you to tell the class that part of the story.

Pages 1–2. Tell what happens at the **beginning** of the story.

Pages 3–26. Tell what happens in the **middle** of the story. (Encourage use of target words when appropriate. Model use as necessary.)

Page 26. Tell what happens at the **end** of the story.

How do you think Clara feels at the end of the story? (Ideas: *Happy; satisfied.*) (Prompt the children if they do not use *satisfied.*)

How do you think Samson feels at the end of the story? (Idea: *Happy; satisfied; proud.*)

How do you know that Clara and Samson are good friends?

Review Opposites Game

Today you'll play the Opposites Game. I'll use a vocabulary word in a sentence. If you can tell me the opposite of that word, you win one point. If you can't tell me, I get the point.

Let's practice: The broken window was **jagged.** Tell me the opposite of "was jagged." (Idea: *Smooth.*) Smooth could be the opposite of "was jagged."

Let's try another one. Amanda **pretended** that she was a flying horse. Tell me the opposite of pretended. (Idea: *Did not pretend.*) "Did not pretend" could be the opposite of pretended.

Now you're ready to play the game.

(Draw a T-chart on the board for keeping score. Children earn one point for each correct answer. If they make an error, suggest an appropriate choice, tell them the word, and record one point for yourself. Repeat missed words at the end of the game.)

- Clara **promised** to stop talking. Tell me the opposite of promised. (Idea: *Did not promise.*) "Did not promise" could be the opposite of promised.
- Brad looked at the children and **scowled.** Tell me the opposite of scowled. (Idea: *Smiled.*) Smiled could be the opposite of scowled.
- The broken window was **jagged.** Tell me the opposite of jagged. (Idea: *Smooth.*) Smooth could be the opposite of jagged.
- Manfred **pretended** that he was driving a truck just like his dad. Tell me the opposite of pretended. (Idea: *Did not pretend.*) "Did not pretend" could be the opposite of pretended.
- Sal **was worried** about the Happy Face Game. Tell me the opposite of "was worried." (Idea: *Was not worried.*) "Was not worried" could be the opposite of "was worried."

- Mark **was allergic** to dog hair. Tell me the opposite of "was allergic." (Idea: *Was not allergic.*) "Was not allergic" could be the opposite of "was allergic."

(Count the points, and declare a winner.) You did a great job of playing the Opposites Game!

Sentence Frames (Activity Sheet)

 (Review with children the items Clara's father put in the thundercloud piñata. If they have difficulty remembering the items, reread the last paragraph on page 22.) What other things might go in a piñata? (Record responses on a sheet of chart paper. Draw a quick sketch of each item as it is suggested.) (Ideas: *Top; toy car; pencil.*)

In last week's story we learned the days of the week. Say the days of the week, starting with Sunday. (Repeat until firm.)

(Give each child a copy of the Activity Sheet, BLM 14b.) My turn. I'll read the first item on the sheet. On Sunday I put a **blank** in the piñata. (Chime-read with children the first item on the sheet. Say "blank" when you get to the line. Have children decide which item they would put in the piñata. Have them draw a picture of that item on the line. Children who are able to may copy each word beside the picture.)

(Repeat this process for the remaining items. Ask children to color the piñata and the items they chose to put in it.)

DAY 4

Preparation: Prepare a sheet of chart paper, landscape direction, with the title *Hooray, A Piñata!* Underneath the title, draw 11 boxes, connected by arrows.

Underneath the 11 boxes, draw 9 boxes, connected by arrows. See the Introduction for an example.

Introduce Setting (Where) (Literary Analysis)

Let's think about what we already know about how books are made.

- What do we call the name of the book? *The title.*
- What do we call the person who writes the story? *The author.*
- What do we call the person who draws the pictures? *The illustrator.*
- What do we call the people or animals a story is about? *The characters.*
- What do we call the pictures the illustrator makes? *Illustrations.*
- What is one thing the setting of a story tells? *Where a story happens.*

Let's sing "The Story Song" to help us remember these important things about books.

(See the Introduction for the complete "Story Song.")

Today we will learn more about how stories are made.

The setting of a story tells two things. One thing the setting tells is where the story happens. What is one thing the setting tells? *Where the story happens.* The second thing the setting tells is when the story happens. What is the second thing the setting tells? *When the story happens.*

Let's look at the pictures and talk about the story to figure out where *Hooray, a Pinata!* happens.

(Follow the procedure established in Weeks 9, 10, and 11 to identify where the story happens. Record responses in the first row of boxes.) (Ideas: *In the sandbox; at the piñata store; at Clara's house; at the park; in the city; at grandma's house; at the merry-go-round; around Clara's block; in Clara's yard.*) (**Note:** You may wish to identify the city as San Francisco, as the hilly streets and the Golden Gate Bridge appear in the illustrations.)

(Record responses in the second row of boxes.) Now let's think about when this story happens.

(Show page 1. Read the sentence "Mama's taking me to pick one out this morning.") When in the day does the story begin? (Idea: *Early in the morning.*)

(Show page 7. Read the sentences "We could take him to the park for a picnic" and " 'Mom wants me home for lunch,' replied Samson.")

Turn page 10.) Samson is back, and he had to go home for lunch, so when does this part of the story happen? (Idea: *In the afternoon*.)

(Read the sentence "We're going to Grandma's for dinner.") When does the next part of the story happen? *Before dinner*.

(Show page 13. Read the sentence "After dinner they walked there together.") When does the next part of the story happen? *After dinner*.

(Show pages 14 and 15.) When does this part of the story happen? *At night*.

(Show page 16. Read the words "and on her swing the next morning.") When does the next part of the story happen? *The next morning*.

(Show page 18. Read the sentence "That afternoon, Clara and Samson made paper hats for everyone who was coming to her party the next day.") When does the next part of the story happen? *That afternoon*.

(Show page 20. Read the sentence "Early the next morning, Samson came by with two presents.") When does the next part of the story happen? *Early the next morning*.

(Show pages 21 through 26.) When does the rest of the story happen? (Ideas: *At Clara's birthday party; in the afternoon*.)

(Point to the words as you say each time of day.) Early morning, in the afternoon, before dinner, after dinner, and at night. All these things happen in one day. (Draw a line underneath these 5 boxes.)

This is really hard! Let's figure out how many days. (Point to the words as you say each time of day.) The next morning, that afternoon, early next morning, and in the afternoon. How many days are here? *Two*. (Draw a line underneath *the next morning* and *that afternoon*. Draw another line underneath *early next morning* and *in the afternoon*.

(Point to *in the afternoon*.) We know what day this is. What day is it? *Clara's birthday*. (Write *Clara's birthday* underneath the line.

(Point to the middle day.) So now we know what day this is. What day is it? (Idea: *The day before Clara's birthday*.) (Write *day before* underneath the middle line. Point to the first day.) And now

we can figure out what day this is. What day is it? (Idea: *Two days before Clara's birthday*.) (Write *two days before Clara's birthday* underneath the first line.)

When is the setting of the story *Hooray, a Piñata!* (Idea: *On Clara's birthday and on the two days before her birthday*.) You were great detectives! You used the clues and figured out when the story happened.

Today you learned about both of the parts of the setting of the story *Hooray, a Pinata!* You learned about where and when the story happened.

Now we'll learn a new verse to "The Story Song." This time, though, we'll just change the verse we already sing about setting so that it tells both when and where. Instead of singing *Setting tells when it happened*, we'll sing *Setting tells when and where*. We can use one verse to tell about both of the things that setting tells about.

(See the Introduction for the complete "Story Song.")

> *Read me a book, and the book pleased me.*
> *I read my book under yonder tree.*
> **Setting tells when and where.**
> *Illustrations are the pictures.*
> *Characters make it happen.*
> *Illustrator draws the pictures.*
> *Author says, "I'm who wrote it."*
> *Title says what its name is.*
> *Book says, "I'm a story."*

Play Opposites Game (Cumulative Review)

Let's play the Opposites Game. I'll use a vocabulary word in a sentence. If you can tell me the opposite of that word, you win one point. If you can't tell me, I get the point.

Let's practice: The broken rock was **jagged.** Tell me the opposite of jagged. (Idea: *Smooth*.) Smooth could be the opposite of jagged.

Let's try another one. Peter **was allergic** to dandelions. Tell me the opposite of "was allergic." (Idea: *Was not allergic*.) "Was not allergic" could be the opposite of "was allergic."

Now you're ready to play the game.

(Draw a T-chart on the board for keeping score. Children earn one point for each correct answer. If they make an error, correct them as you normally would, and record one point for yourself. Repeat missed words at the end of the game.)

- Teasha **pretended** that she could fly. Tell me the opposite of pretended. (**Idea:** *Did not pretend.*) "Did not pretend" could be the opposite of pretended.
- The robot **was not allergic** to cats. Tell me the opposite of "was not allergic." (**Idea:** *Was allergic.*) "Was allergic" could be the opposite of "was not allergic."
- Mr. Hamlin **was worried** about his dog Sacho. Tell me the opposite of "was worried." (**Idea:** *Was not worried*.) "Was not worried" could be the opposite of "was worried."
- Alisha **was not present** for the field trip. Tell me the opposite of "was not present." (**Idea:** *Was present.*) "Was present" could be the opposite of "was not present."
- Cameron **made a promise** that he would clean his room. Tell me the opposite of "made a promise." (**Idea:** *Did not make a promise.*) "Did not make a promise" could be the opposite of "made a promise."
- Mrs. Goodfellow **scowled** when she saw the huge pile of work. Tell me the opposite of scowled. (**Idea:** *Smiled.*) Smiled could be the opposite of scowled.
- Harper's dog was **enormous.** Tell me the opposite of enormous. (**Ideas:** *Small; little; tiny.*) Small could be the opposite of enormous.
- That storm **was not horrible.** Tell me the opposite of "was not horrible." (**Idea:** *Was horrible.)* "Was horrible" could be the opposite of "was not horrible."
- They **pretended** they were adults. Tell me the opposite of pretended. (**Idea:** *Did not pretend.*) "Did not pretend" could be the opposite of pretended.
- That clown is **acting silly.** Tell me the opposite of "acting silly." (**Idea:** *Not acting silly.*) "Not acting silly" could be the opposite of "acting silly."

(Count the points, and declare a winner.)
You did a great job of playing the Opposites Game!

DAY 5

Preparation: Happy Face Game Test Sheet, BLM B.

Retell Story to a Partner

(Assign each child a partner, and ask the partners to take turns telling part of the story each time you turn to a new set of pages. Encourage use of target words when appropriate.)

Today I'll show you the pictures Elisa Kleven made for the story *Hooray, a Piñata!* As I show you the pictures, you and your partner will take turns telling part of the story.

Page 1. Tell what happens at the **beginning** of the story.)

Pages 2–25. Tell what happens in the **middle** of the story.

Page 27. Tell what happens at the **end** of the story.)

How do you know Samson and Clara are good friends?

Assess Vocabulary

(Hold up a copy of the Happy Face Game Test Sheet, BLM B.)

Today you're going to play the Happy Face Game. When you play the Happy Face Game, it helps me know how well you know the hard words you are learning.

If I say something true, color the happy face. What will you do if I say something true? *Color the happy face.*

If I say something false, color the sad face. What will you do if I say something false? *Color the sad face.*

Listen carefully to each sentence I say. Don't let me trick you!

Item 1: If you are **allergic,** you might sneeze and cough. *True.*

Item 2: A **jagged** rock is one with lots of sharp points. *True.*

Item 3: If you **pretended,** you played an imagining game. *True.*

Item 4: **Worried** means thinking about the good things that could happen. *False.*

Item 5: If you **promised,** it means that you will definitely do something. *True.*

Item 6: Being **rude** is a good way to act. *False.*

Item 7: If you are **present,** you are here. *True.*

Item 8: If you are feeling **bored,** you have lots of **exciting** things to do. *False.*

Item 9: When you **scowled,** you made an angry face. *True.*

Item 10: If your feet hurt and your head ached and you did **not** tell anyone, you would be **complaining.** *False.*

You did a great job of playing the Happy Face Game!

(Score children's work later. Scores of 9 out of 10 indicate mastery. If a child does not achieve mastery, insert the missed words in the games in the next week's lessons. Retest those children individually on the missed items before they take the next mastery test.)

Extensions
Read a Story as a Reward

(Display copies of several of the books that you have read since the beginning of the program. Allow children to choose which book they would like you to read aloud to them as a reward for their hard work.)

(Read the story aloud to children for enjoyment with minimal interruptions.)

Present Super Words Center

(Prepare the word containers for the Super Words Center. See the Introduction for instructions on how to set up and use the Super Words Center.)

(Add the new Picture Vocabulary Cards to the words from the previous weeks. Show children one of the word containers. If they need more guidance, role-play with two or three children as a demonstration as you introduce each part of the game.)

You will play a game called What's My Word? in the Super Words Center.

Let's think about how we work with our words in the Super Words Center.

You will work with a partner in the Super Words Center. Whom will you work with in the center? *A partner.*

First you will draw a word out of the container. What do you do first? (Idea: *Draw a word out of the container.*) Don't show your partner the word card. (Demonstrate.)

Next you will tell your partner three clues that tell about the word card. What do you do next? (Idea: *I tell my partner three clues that tell about the word card.*) (Demonstrate.)

After each clue, your partner can make a guess. If your partner is correct, say, "yes." If your partner is not correct, say, "no," and give another clue. (Demonstrate.)

Let your partner make three guesses. If any of your partner's guesses are correct, your partner gets a point. If your partner does not guess correctly, tell your word, and show him or her the word card. Give yourself a point. Then give your partner a turn. (Demonstrate.)

What do you do next? *Give my partner a turn.*

(This game does not need to be played for points.)

Leo the Late Bloomer
author: Robert Kraus • illustrator: Jose Aruego

Preparation: You will need *Leo the Late Bloomer* for each day's lesson.

Number the pages of the story to assist you in asking questions at appropriate points.

Post a copy of the Vocabulary Tally Sheet, BLM A, with this week's Picture Vocabulary Cards attached.

Each child will need the Homework Sheet, BLM 15a.

🎯 Target Vocabulary

Tier II	Tier III
sloppy	setting
patience	
bloom	
sentence	
*content	
*anxious	

*Expanded Target Vocabulary Word

DAY 1

Introduce Book

Today's book is called *Leo the Late Bloomer.* What's the title of this week's book? *Leo the Late Bloomer.*

This book was written by Robert Kraus [Krouse as in house]. Who's the author of *Leo the Late Bloomer*? *Robert Kraus.*

Jose Aruego [Ar-**oo**-**ay**-go] made the pictures for this book. Who is the illustrator of *Leo the Late Bloomer*? *Jose Aruego.* Who made the illustrations for this book? *Jose Aruego.*

The cover of a book usually gives us some hints of what the book is about. Let's look at the front cover of *Leo the Late Bloomer.* What do you see in the illustration? (Ideas: *A little tiger; some flowers; some butterflies; the tiger looks like he's smelling one of the flowers.*)

(Assign each child a partner.) Get ready to make some predictions to your partner about this book. Use the information from the cover to help you.

(Ask the following questions, allowing sufficient time for children to share their predictions with their partners.)

- Who is the character in this story? (Whom do you think this story is about?)
- What do you think the tiger will do?
- Where do you think the story happens?
- When do you think the story happens?
- Why do you think the tiger is smelling the flower?

- How many butterflies do you see?
- Do you think this story is about a real or an imaginary tiger? Tell why or why not.

(Call on several children to share their predictions with the class.)

Take a Picture Walk

We are going to take a picture walk through this book. Remember, when we take a picture walk, we look at the pictures and tell what we think will happen in the story.

(Show the illustrations on the following pages, and ask the specified questions.)

Page 1. Whom do you see in this first illustration? *The tiger.* What is happening to the tiger? (Idea: *He's all tangled up in a vine.*) How do you think the tiger is feeling? (Ideas: *Worried; unhappy.*) What makes you think so? (**Note:** If children don't use the word *worried,* prompt them by saying:) You learned a word last week that tells how the little tiger is feeling. That word is **worried.** When you are worried, you feel unhappy because you can't stop thinking about all the bad things that could happen. Say the word **worried.** *Worried.*

Pages 2–3. What is the owl doing? (Idea: *Looking at a book.*) What is the snake doing? (Idea: *Looking at a book.*) What is the elephant doing? (Idea: *Looking at a book.*) What is the bird doing? (Idea: *Looking at a book.*) What is the crocodile doing? (Idea: *Looking at a book.*) What is the tiger doing? (Idea: *Looking at a* *book*.) Everyone looks happy except the tiger. How is he feeling? (**Idea:** *Unhappy*.) What do you think is wrong?

Page 4. What is the owl doing? (**Idea:** *Writing its name*.) What is the elephant doing? (**Idea:** *Writing its name*.) What is the snake doing? (**Idea:** *Writing its name*.) What is the bird doing? (**Idea:** *Writing its name*.) What is the crocodile doing? (**Idea:** *Writing its name*.) What is the tiger doing? (**Idea:** *Making a wiggly line*.) Everyone looks happy except the tiger. How is he feeling? (**Idea:** *Unhappy*.) What do you think is wrong?

(Repeat this procedure for the pictures on pages 5, 6, and 7.)

Pages 8–9. How do you think the father tiger is feeling? (**Ideas:** *Worried; sad; unhappy*.) What makes you think so? How do you think the little tiger is feeling? (**Ideas:** *Worried; sad; unhappy; frustrated*.) (Prompt children if they do not use *frustrated*.) What makes you think so? How do you think the mother tiger is feeling? (**Idea:** *Happy; satisfied*.) (Prompt children if they do not use *satisfied*.) What makes you think so?

Pages 10–11. What do you think is happening here? (**Ideas:** *The tigers are lying on a branch; the big tiger is hiding in the leaves*.)

Pages 12–13. What do you think is happening here? (**Ideas:** *The little tiger is smelling the flowers; the big tiger is watching the little tiger*.)

Page 14. How do you think the father tiger is feeling? (**Ideas:** *Worried; sad; unhappy*.) What makes you think so? How do you think the little tiger is feeling? (**Ideas:** *Happy; sleepy*.) What makes you think so? How do you think the mother tiger is feeling? (**Ideas:** *Happy; satisfied*.) What makes you think so?

Page 15. What is the father tiger doing? (**Idea:** *Watching television*.) What is the little tiger doing? (**Idea:** *Playing ball*.)

Pages 16–17. What is the tiger doing? (**Idea:** *Chasing the rabbit*.) What is the snake doing? (**Idea:** *Building a snow snake*.) What is the owl doing? (**Idea:** *Building a snow owl*.) What is the bird doing? (**Idea:** *Building a snow bird*.) What is the elephant doing? (**Idea:** *Building a snow elephant*.) What is the crocodile doing? (**Idea:** *Building a snow crocodile*.) Everyone looks

happy except the tiger. How is he feeling? (**Idea:** *Unhappy*.) What do you think is wrong?

Pages 18–19. (Repeat the procedure from pages 16 and 17.)

Pages 20–21. What do you think is happening here? What makes you think so?

Page 22. What is the tiger doing? *Reading*. How many books is he reading? *Five*. How is he feeling? (**Ideas:** *Proud; happy*.)

Page 23. What is the tiger doing? *Writing his name*. How many times does he write his name all at once? *Three*. How is he feeling? (**Ideas:** *Proud; happy*.)

(Repeat this procedure for pages 24 and 25.)

Pages 26–27. What do you think is happening here? (**Ideas:** *The father and mother tiger are looking at the little tiger; the little tiger is riding on the elephant; he is with the elephant, owl, bird, crocodile, and snake*.)

Page 28. How do you think the father tiger is feeling? (**Ideas:** *Happy; surprised; amazed*.) (Prompt children if they do not use *amazed*.) What makes you think so? How do you think the mother tiger is feeling? (**Ideas:** *Happy; satisfied*.) What makes you think so?

How do you think the little tiger is feeling? (**Idea:** *Happy*.) What makes you think so? The little tiger has his mouth open. What might he be saying?

Now that we've finished our picture walk, it's your turn to ask me some questions. What would you like to know about the story? (Accept questions. If children tell about the pictures or the story instead of asking questions, prompt them to ask a question.) Ask me a why question. Ask me a where question.

Read Story Aloud

(Read story aloud to children with minimal interruptions.)

   In the next lesson, we will read the story again, and I will ask you some questions.

(If children have difficulty attending for an extended period of time, present the next part of this day's lesson at another time.)

Present Target Vocabulary

 Sloppy.

In the story, Leo is a sloppy eater. That means he eats in a careless way. He is messy and untidy when he eats. **Sloppy.** Say the word. *Sloppy.*

Sloppy is a describing word. It tells more about how someone does something. What kind of word is **sloppy?** *A describing word.*

If you are sloppy, you are careless about how you do things. You are messy and untidy. Say the word that means "careless about what you do; messy and untidy." *Sloppy.*

(Correct any incorrect responses, and repeat the item at the end of the sequence.)

Let's think about some things that could be done in a sloppy way. I'll tell about some things. If these things were done in a sloppy way, say, "Sloppy." If not, don't say anything.

- The girl scribbled her answers on her paper. *Sloppy.*
- The twins put on their clothes in a careless and untidy way. *Sloppy.*
- Shirley spilled the juice when she poured it. *Sloppy.*
- He wasn't careless at all when he made breakfast.
- There was popcorn everywhere after he'd finished his snack. *Sloppy.*
- I didn't even know he'd made cookies—that's how clean the kitchen was.

What describing word means "careless about what you do; messy and untidy"? *Sloppy.*

 Patience.

In the story, Leo's mother tells Leo's father to have patience. That means she tells him to wait without feeling worried or upset. **Patience.** Say the word. *Patience.*

Patience is a naming word. It names an emotion. What kind of word is **patience?** *A naming word.*

If you have patience, you can wait without getting worried or upset. Say the word that means "you can wait without getting worried or upset." *Patience.*

(Correct any incorrect responses, and repeat the item at the end of the sequence.)

Let's think about some times when someone might have patience. I'll tell about a time. If someone had patience, say, "Patience." If not, don't say anything.

- The teacher waited quietly while the children found their crayons. *Patience.*
- Everyone waited while Colleen finished her drink. *Patience.*
- I couldn't wait to get my new bike, so I ran around in circles and yelled.
- Josea waited to have her turn to fly the kite. *Patience.*
- I sure wish Saturday would come faster!
- The cat waited for hours until the mouse came out of its hole. *Patience.*

What naming word means "you can wait without getting worried or upset"? *Patience.*

 Bloom.

In the story, Leo's father watches for signs that Leo is starting to bloom. That means Leo's father watches Leo to see if he is getting good at doing things. **Bloom.** Say the word. *Bloom.*

Bloom is an action word. It tells what someone does. What kind of word is **bloom?** *An action word.*

If you bloom, you get good at doing things. Say the word that means to "get good at doing things." *Bloom.*

(Correct any incorrect responses, and repeat the item at the end of the sequence.)

Let's think about some times when someone might bloom. I'll tell about a time. If someone blooms, say, "Bloom." If not, don't say anything.

- I practiced and practiced, and I got good at painting pictures. *Bloom.*
- Billy Joe practiced until he became a very good reader. *Bloom.*
- Elijah couldn't ride his bike for weeks, but he kept trying. Then, all of a sudden, he could do it. *Bloom.*
- I try to play the piano, but I never get any better.
- Quentin was always good at math.

- After she tried hard for a while, Caitlyn got to be good at counting to twenty. *Bloom.*

What action word means to "get good at doing things"? *Bloom.*

◎< *Sentence.*

In the story, when Leo first speaks, he doesn't say just a word; he says a sentence. That means he says a group of words that tells who or what and what's happening. **Sentence.** Say the word. *Sentence.*

Sentence is a naming word. **It names a group of words that tells who or what and what's happening.** What kind of word is **sentence?** *A naming word.*

Say the word that means "a group of words that tells who or what and what's happening." *Sentence.*

My turn. I'll say a sentence. Adam plays baseball. Whom or what is that sentence about? *Adam.* What's happening? *He's playing baseball.*

My turn. I'll say some words that are not a sentence. The girls. Whom or what is that sentence about? The girls. What's happening? It doesn't say. So these words are not a sentence.

Your turn. Tell me a sentence. **(Call on several children. For each child, repeat the sentence to ensure everyone heard it. If the child's sentence is not a complete sentence, add words to the answer to get a complete sentence.)** Whom or what is this sentence about? What's happening?

(Correct any incorrect responses, and repeat the item at the end of the sequence.)

Let's think about some words that might be a sentence. I'll say some words. If you think these words are a sentence, say, "Sentence." If not, don't say anything.

- The teacher played games with the children. *Sentence.*
- The teacher.
- Played games with the children.
- Henry and his friend.
- We all had fun singing. *Sentence.*
- The barn door closed with a crash. *Sentence.*

What naming word means "a group of words that tells who or what and what's happening"? *Sentence.*

Assign Homework
(Homework Sheet, BLM 15a: See the Introduction for homework instructions.)

DAY 2

Preparation: Picture Vocabulary Cards for *sloppy, patience, bloom,* and *sentence.*

Read and Discuss Story
(Read story aloud to children. Ask the following questions at the specified points.)

Now I'm going to read *Leo the Late Bloomer.* When I finish each part, I'll ask you some questions.

Page 1. Leo has a problem. A problem is something that makes you feel sad or worried. What's Leo's problem? *He can't do anything right.*

Page 2. What does Leo have a problem doing? (Idea: *Reading.*) How do you think Leo feels when he can't read like the other animals? (Ideas: *Unhappy; sad; frustrated.*)

(Note: If children don't use the word *frustrated,* prompt them by saying:) We learned a word in Week 6 that tells how Leo feels. That word is **frustrated.** When you are frustrated, you feel upset and angry because no matter how hard you try, you can't do something. Say the word **frustrated.** *Frustrated.*

Page 4. What does Leo have a problem doing? (Idea: *Writing.*) How do you think Leo feels when he can't write like the other animals? (Ideas: *Unhappy; sad; frustrated.*)

Page 5. What does Leo have a problem doing? (Idea: *Drawing.*) How do you think Leo feels when he can't draw like the other animals? (Ideas: *Unhappy; sad; frustrated.*)

Page 6. What does Leo have a problem doing? (Idea: *Eating without being messy.*) How do you think Leo feels when he can't eat without being messy like the other animals? (Ideas: *Unhappy; sad; frustrated.*)

Page 7. What does Leo have a problem doing? (Idea: *Talking.*) How do you think Leo feels when he can't talk like the other animals? (Ideas: *Unhappy; sad; frustrated.*)

Listen while I make the sound each animal makes. The owl says **Hoot**! What does the owl say? *Hoot!*

(Repeat this procedure for each animal.)

What do you think Leo would say if he could talk? (Idea: *Grrr.*)

Page 9. Is Leo's father worried? *Yes.* Why is Leo's father worried? (Idea: *He thinks something is wrong with Leo.*) Is Leo's mother worried? *No.* What does Leo's mother say Leo is? *A late bloomer.* A late bloomer is a person who takes a bit more time to learn new things. What do we call a person who takes a bit more time to learn new things? *A late bloomer.*

Page 14. Why does Leo's father keep worrying about Leo? (Idea: *Leo's still not blooming.*) Leo's mother tells Leo's father to have patience. What is she telling him to do? (Idea: *Wait without getting worried or upset.*)

Page 16. Does Leo bloom in the winter? *No.*

Page 18. Does Leo bloom in the spring? *No.*

Page 20. What finally happens to Leo? *He blooms in his own good time.* That's right. Leo blooms when he is ready. How do you think Leo's father feels? (Ideas: *Happy; satisfied; excited; amazed.*) (**Note:** If children don't use *satisfied, excited,* and *amazed,* prompt them to use these words.)

Page 22. What can Leo do now? *Read.*

Page 23. What can Leo do now? *Write.*

Page 24. What can Leo do now? *Draw.*

Page 25. What can Leo do now? *Eat neatly.*

Page 27. What can Leo do now? *Talk.* That's right; he can talk, and when he talks he says whole sentences. What sentence does Leo say? *I made it.* What do you think he means when he says that? (Ideas: *I bloomed; I learned to do things; I've grown up; I'm a boy tiger now, not a baby tiger.*) How do you think Leo's family feels about him now? (Ideas: *Proud; happy; excited.*)

Review Vocabulary

(Display the Picture Vocabulary Cards. Point to each card as you say the word. Ask children to repeat each word after you.) These pictures show **sloppy, patience, bloom,** and **sentence.**

- What word means to "get good at doing things"? *Bloom.*
- What word means "you can wait without feeling worried or upset"? *Patience.*
- What word means "careless about what you do; messy and untidy"? *Sloppy.*
- What word means "a group of words that tells who or what and what's happening"? *Sentence.*

Extend Vocabulary

◎ ◀ Bloom.

In the story *Leo the Late Bloomer* we learned that bloom means to "get good at doing things." Say the word that means to "get good at doing things." *Bloom.*

Here's a new way to use the word **bloom.**

- **The apple trees bloom in April.** Say the sentence.
- **Daffodils bloom in the spring.** Say the sentence.
- **The flowers in her garden bloomed all summer long.** Say the sentence.

In these sentences, **bloom** is an action word that means the plants grow flowers on them. Tell about some plants that you have seen bloom. (Call on several children. Encourage children to use this frame for their answers: "I have seen _____ bloom.")

Present Expanded Target Vocabulary

◎ ◀ Content.

In the story, Leo's mother is satisfied with Leo just the way he is. Leo's mother is content. **Content.** Say the word. *Content.*

Content is a describing word. It tells about an emotion Leo's mother is feeling. What kind of word is **content?** *A describing word.*

Content means you are satisfied with things just the way they are. Say the word that means "satisfied with things just the way they are." *Content.*

I'll tell about some people. If those people are content, say, "Content." If not, don't say anything.

- Grandma Alma likes her house just the way it is. *Content.*
- Grandpa Jim wished he had a bigger car.
- Nina wanted to have two more fish and an octopus in her aquarium.
- I had a baked potato, a steak, and some salad. It was just enough. *Content.*
- Gracie said she had everything that she needed. *Content*.
- I really want to get a new skateboard that goes faster than my old one.

What describing word means "satisfied with things just the way they are"? *Content.*

◎━◄ Anxious.

In the middle of the story Leo's father really, really wants Leo to do the things the other animals do. Leo's father is feeling anxious. **Anxious.** Say the word. *Anxious.*

Anxious is a describing word. It tells how someone is feeling. What kind of word is **anxious?** *A describing word.* That's right; **anxious** is a describing word that tells about a feeling or an emotion.

When you are anxious, you really, really want to do something or want something to happen. Say the word that means "really, really want to do something or want something to happen." *Anxious.*

I'll tell about some times. If someone would feel anxious, say, "Anxious." If not, don't say anything.

- Leo's father really, really wanted him to be able to read like the other animals. *Anxious.*
- Toby really, really wanted to be brave enough to go down the waterslide. *Anxious.*
- Luke didn't care if he got to ride the horse or not.
- Skylar really, really wanted to be able to read chapter books on her own. *Anxious.*
- Ryan really, really wanted his new teacher to like him. *Anxious.*
- Julie was happy with things the way they were.

What describing word means "really, really want to do something or want something to happen"? *Anxious.*

Preparation: Activity Sheet, BLM 15b. Children will need crayons.

Retell Story

(Show the pictures on the following pages from the story, and call on a child to tell what's happening. Call on a different child for each section.)

Today I'll show you the pictures Jose Aruego made for the story *Leo the Late Bloomer.* As I show you the pictures, I'll call on one of you to tell the class that part of the story.

Pages 1–7. Tell me what happens at the **beginning** of the story.

Pages 8–21. Tell me what happens in the **middle** of the story. (Encourage use of target words when appropriate. Model use as necessary.)

Pages 22–28. Tell me what happens at the **end** of the story.

How do you think Leo feels at the end of the story? (Idea: *Proud.*)

How do you think Leo's father feels at the end of the story? (Ideas: *Proud; content.*)

How do you think Leo's mother feels at the end of the story? (Ideas: *Proud; content.*)

Review Opposites Game

Today you'll play the Opposites Game. I'll use a vocabulary word in a sentence. If you can tell me the opposite of that word, you win one point. If you can't tell me, I get the point.

Let's practice: Brianne did a **sloppy** job on her scrapbook. Tell me the opposite of sloppy. (Idea: *Neat.*) Neat could be the opposite of sloppy.

Let's try another one. Michael showed **patience** when he waited for his grandma. Tell me the opposite of "showed patience." (Idea: *Did not show patience; impatience*). "Did not show patience" could be the opposite of "showed patience."

Now you're ready to play the game.

(Draw a T-chart on the board for keeping score. Children earn one point for each correct answer. If they make an error, suggest an appropriate choice and tell them. Record one point for yourself, and repeat missed words at the end of the game.)

- After weeks of practice, Joseph's printing **bloomed.** Tell me the opposite of bloomed. (Idea: *Did not bloom.*) "Did not bloom" could be the opposite of bloomed.
- Words that tell who and what happened **are a sentence.** Tell me the opposite of "are a sentence." (Idea: *Are not a sentence.*) "Are not a sentence" could be the opposite of "are a sentence."
- The flower **had a bloom.** Tell me the opposite of "had a bloom." (Idea: *Did not have a bloom.*) "Did not have a bloom" could be the opposite of "had a bloom."
- Marvin **was content** to read *The Lord of the Rings* over and over again. Tell me the opposite of "was content." (Idea: *Was not content.*) "Was not content" could be the opposite of "was content."
- Sal **was anxious** about jumping into the swimming pool. Tell me the opposite of "was anxious." (Idea: *Was not anxious.*) "Was not anxious" could be the opposite of "was anxious."
- Hayden **was sloppy** about doing his work. Tell me the opposite of "was sloppy." (Ideas: *Was not sloppy; was neat.*) "Was not sloppy" could be the opposite of "was sloppy."

(Count the points, and declare a winner.)
You did a great job of playing the Opposites Game!

Sentence Frames (Activity Sheet)
(Review with children the things Leo can do once he blooms. If children have difficulty remembering the items, reread pages 22 through 28.) What other things might Leo be able to do once he blooms? (Record responses on a sheet of chart paper. Draw a quick sketch of each item as it is suggested. (Ideas: *He could count to*

ten; he could write numbers; he could cut with scissors; he could catch a rabbit.*)

In the story from Week 13 we learned the days of the week. Say the days of the week, starting with Sunday. (Repeat until firm.)

(Give each child a copy of the Activity Sheet, BLM 15b.) My turn. I'll read the first item on the sheet. On Sunday Leo could "blank." (Chime-read with children the first item on the sheet. Say "blank" when you get to the line. Have children decide which item they think Leo could do. Have them draw a picture of that item on the line. Children who are able to may copy each word beside the picture.)

(Repeat this process for the remaining items. Ask children to color the pictures.)

DAY 4

Preparation: Prepare a sheet of chart paper, landscape direction, with the title *Leo the Late Bloomer.* Underneath the title, draw nine boxes, connected by arrows. Underneath the nine boxes, draw six boxes, connected by arrows.
See the Introduction for an example.

Develop Setting (Literary Analysis)
Let's think about what we already know about how books are made.

- What do we call the name of the book? *The title.*
- What do we call the person who writes the story? *The author.*
- What do we call the person who draws the pictures? *The illustrator.*
- What do we call the people or animals a story is about? *The characters.*
- What do we call the pictures the illustrator makes? *Illustrations.*
- What is one thing the setting of a story tells? *Where a story happens.*
- What is the second thing the setting of a story tells? *When a story happens.*

Let's sing the first (number) verses of "The Story Song" to help us remember these important things about books. (At this point it is unnecessary to sing the whole song. Choose which verses you would like children to sing. Include setting as it is a relatively new concept.)

Today we will learn more about the setting of a story.

The setting of a story tells two things. One thing the setting tells is where the story happens. What is one thing the setting tells? *Where the story happens.* The second thing the setting tells is when the story happens. What is the second thing the setting tells? *When the story happens.*

Let's look at the pictures and talk about the story to figure out where the story *Leo the Late Bloomer* happens.

(Follow the procedure established in Lessons 9, 10, and 11 to identify where the story happens. Record responses in the first row of boxes.

(Ideas: *In the jungle* (pages 2 and 3); *near a stump* (page 6); *on a branch* (pages 10 and 11); *in the flower garden* (pages 12 and 13); *in Leo's house* (page 15); *in the snow* (pages 16 and 17); *in the flower garden* (pages 18 and 19); *near a rock* (page 22); *near a stump* (page 25).)

Now let's think about when this story happens. (Record responses in the second row of boxes. The time concepts presented in this book are difficult. You may need to prompt children to give specific times for each box and for under the lines.)

(Show page 10. Read the sentence "Every day Leo's father watched him for signs of blooming." When does the story begin? (Idea: *In the day.*)

(Show page 12. Read the sentence "And every night Leo's father watched him for signs of blooming." (Turn to page 11.) When does this part of the story happen? (Idea: *At night.*)

(Show pages 16 and 17.) Look at the illustrations. When does the next part of the story happen? *In the winter*.

(Show pages 18 and 19.) Look at the illustrations. Lots of flowers are blooming. When does the next part of the story happen? *In the spring*.

(Show pages 20 and 21. Read the sentence "Then one day, in his own good time, Leo

bloomed." When does the next part of the story happen? (Idea: *One day*.)

(Show pages 22 through 28.) Look at the illustrations. When do these parts of the story happen? *Later*. (Record response in last box.)

In the day, at night, in the winter, and in the spring. All these things happened before Leo bloomed. (Draw a line underneath these four boxes. Write the words *Before Leo bloomed* under the line.)

One day. This is when Leo bloomed. (Draw a line underneath the middle box. Write the words *When Leo bloomed* underneath the middle line.)

The ending of the story happened later. (Draw a line underneath the last box. Write *After Leo bloomed* underneath the last line.)

When is the setting of the story *Leo the Late Bloomer*? (Idea: *Before and after Leo bloomed.*) You were great detectives! You used the clues and figured out when the story happened.

Today you learned about both parts of the setting of the story *Leo the Late Bloomer*. You learned about where and when the story happens.

Play Opposites Game (Cumulative Review)

Let's play the Opposites Game. I'll use a vocabulary word in a sentence. If you can tell me the opposite of that word, you win one point. If you can't tell me, I get the point.

Let's practice: Casio **was anxious** about the test. Tell me the opposite of "was anxious." (Idea: *Was not anxious*.) "Was not anxious" could be the opposite of "was anxious."

Let's try another one. Gillian **was content** to eat cereal every day. Tell me the opposite of "was content." (Idea: *Was not content*.) "Was not content" could be the opposite of "was content."

Now you're ready to play the game.

(Draw a T-chart on the board for keeping score. Children earn one point for each correct answer. If they make an error, correct them as you normally would, and record one point for yourself. Repeat missed words at the end of the game.)

- Brendan **could not bloom** without practice. Tell me the opposite of "could not bloom." (Idea: *Could bloom.*) "Could bloom" could be the opposite of "could not bloom."
- The robot **was not allergic** to cats. Tell me the opposite of "was not allergic." (Idea: *Was allergic.*) "Was allergic" could be the opposite of "was not allergic."
- The words "They fell when" **are not a sentence.** Tell me the opposite of "are not a sentence." (Idea: *Are a sentence.*) "Are a sentence" could be the opposite of "are not a sentence."
- Monica **had patience** when she waited for her little sister. Tell me the opposite of "had patience." (Idea: *Did not have patience.*) "Did not have patience" could be the opposite of "had patience."
- As usual, Nathan did a **sloppy** job. Tell me the opposite of sloppy. (Idea: *Neat.*) Neat could be the opposite of sloppy.
- The rose **had a bloom.** Tell me the opposite of "had a bloom." (Idea: *Did not have a bloom.*) "Did not have a bloom" could be the opposite of "had a bloom."
- Henrietta **had memories** of growing up in Georgia. Tell me the opposite of "had memories." (Idea: *Did not have memories.*) "Did not have memories" could be the opposite of "had memories."
- Nicole **was complaining** that her feet were sore. Tell me the opposite of "was complaining." (Idea: *Was not complaining.*) "Was not complaining" could be the opposite of "was complaining."
- The two boys looked **unfamiliar.** Tell me the opposite of unfamiliar. (Idea: *Familiar.*) Familiar could be the opposite of unfamiliar.
- Ian **was content** with a nutritious meal. Tell me the opposite of "was content." (Ideas: *Was not content; was unhappy.*) "Was not content" could be the opposite of "was content."

(Count the points, and declare a winner.)
You did a great job of playing the Opposites Game!

DAY 5

Preparation: Happy Face Game Test Sheet, BLM B.

Retell Story to a Partner

(Assign each child a partner, and ask the partners to take turns telling part of the story each time you turn to a new set of pages. Encourage children to use target words when appropriate.)

Today I'll show you the pictures Jose Aruego made for the story *Leo the Late Bloomer.* As I show you the pictures, you and your partner will take turns telling part of the story.

Pages 1–7. Tell what happens at the **beginning** of the story.

Pages 8–21. Tell what happens in the **middle** of the story.

Pages 22–28. Tell what happens at the **end** of the story.

Assess Vocabulary

 (Give each child a copy of the Happy Face Game Test Sheet, BLM B.)

Today you're going to play the Happy Face Game. When you play the Happy Face Game, it helps me know how well you know the hard words you are learning.

If I say something true, color the happy face. What will you do if I say something true? *Color the happy face.*

If I say something false, color the sad face. What will you do if I say something false? *Color the sad face.*

Listen carefully to each item I say. Don't let me trick you!

Item 1: If you are **content,** you are unhappy with what you have. *False.*

Item 2: If you show **patience,** you wait without **complaining.** *True.*

Item 3: If you get really good at something you have practiced, you **bloom.** *True.*

Item 4: If you are **sloppy,** you are very, very neat. *False.*

Item 5: A **sentence** is a few words that do **not** tell who or what and what's happening. *False.*

Item 6: When you are **anxious,** you are **excited** about something. *False.*

Item 7: If you are being **disruptive,** you are bothering other people. *True.*

Item 8: If you **examine** something, you do **not** look at it carefully. *False.*

Item 9: If you are in a very strong wind, you are in a **gale.** *True.*

Item 10: A blossom on a flower can be called a **bloom.** *True.*

You did a great job of playing the Happy Face Game!

(Score children's work later. Scores of 9 out of 10 indicate mastery. If a child does not achieve mastery, insert the missed words as additional items in the games in the next week's lessons. Retest those children individually on the missed items before they take the next mastery test.)

Extensions
Read a Story as a Reward

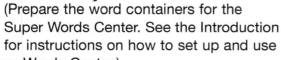(Display several of the books you have read since the beginning of the program. Allow children to choose which book they would like you to read aloud to them as a reward for their hard work.)

(Read the story to children for enjoyment with minimal interruptions.)

Present Super Words Center

(Prepare the word containers for the Super Words Center. See the Introduction for instructions on how to set up and use the Super Words Center.)

(Add the new Picture Vocabulary Cards to words from previous weeks. Show children one of the word containers. If they need more guidance, role-play with two or three children as a demonstration.)

You will play a game called What's My Word? in the Super Words Center.

Let's think about how we work with our words in the Super Words Center.

You will work with a partner in the Super Words Center. Whom will you work with in the center? *A partner.*

First, you will draw a word out of the container. What do you do first? (Idea: *Draw a word out of the container.*) Don't show your partner the word card.

Next, you will tell your partner three clues that tell about the word card. What do you do next? (Idea: *I tell my partner three clues that tell about the word card.*) After each clue, your partner can make a guess. If your partner is correct, say, "yes." If your partner is not correct, say, "no" and give another clue.

Let your partner make three guesses. If your partner guesses correctly on any of the guesses, your partner gets a point. If your partner does not guess correctly, tell your word, and show him or her the word card. Give yourself a point. Then give your partner a turn.

What do you do next? *Give my partner a turn.*

(This game need not be played for points.)

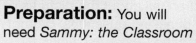

Sammy: the Classroom Guinea Pig
author: Alix Berenzy • illustrator: Alix Berenzy

Preparation: You will need *Sammy: the Classroom Guinea Pig* for each day's lesson.

Number the pages of the story to assist you in asking questions at appropriate points.

Post a copy of the Vocabulary Tally Sheet, BLM A, with this week's Picture Vocabulary Cards from BLM 16a attached.

Each child will need the Homework Sheet, BLM 16a.

🎯 Target Vocabulary

Tier II	Tier III
difficult	setting
appetite	
gentle	
explained	
*lonely	
*language	

*Expanded Target Vocabulary Word

- Where do you think the story happens?
- When do you think the story happens?
- Why do you think the guinea pig has its nose up in the air?
- How many colors are there on the guinea pig's fur?
- Do you think this story is about a real guinea pig? Tell why or why not.

(Call on several children to share their predictions with the class.)

Take a Picture Walk

We are going to take a picture walk through this book. Remember, when we take a picture walk, we look at the pictures and tell what we think will happen in the story.

(Show the illustrations on the following pages, and ask the specified questions.)

Page 1. What is Sammy doing? *Sleeping.* Where is Sammy sleeping? (Idea: *In a box.*) What is he holding onto? (Ideas: *Something blue; a piece of blue cloth.*)

Pages 2–3. What is Sammy doing now? (Idea: *Eating.*) How many doors on his box? (Idea: *Two.*) What else is in his cage? (Ideas: *A water bottle; a round thing; some straw or grass.*)

Page 4. What is Sammy doing? (Ideas: *Standing up on his back legs; looking at someone in the doorway.*) Who do you think the person in the doorway is?

DAY 1

Introduce Book

Today's book is called *Sammy: the Classroom Guinea Pig.* What's the title of this week's book? *Sammy: the Classroom Guinea Pig.*

This book was written by Alix Berenzy [bare-**en**-zee] Who's the author of *Sammy: the Classroom Guinea Pig*? *Alix Berenzy.*

Alix Berenzy also made the pictures for this book. Who is the illustrator of *Sammy: the Classroom Guinea Pig*? *Alix Berenzy.* Who made the illustrations for this book? *Alix Berenzy.*

The cover of a book usually gives us some hints of what the book is about. Let's look at the front cover of *Sammy: the Classroom Guinea Pig.* What do you see in the illustration? (Ideas: *A guinea pig; a bit of carrot.*)

(Assign each child a partner.) Remember, when you make a prediction about something, you say what you think will happen.

Get ready to make some predictions to your partner about this book. Use the information from the cover to help you.

(Ask the following questions, allowing sufficient time for children to share their predictions with their partners.)

- Who is the main character in this story? (Whom do you think this story is about?)
- What do you think the guinea pig will do?

Page 5. What is Sammy doing now? (Ideas: *Standing up on his back legs; sniffing a carrot.*)

Pages 6–7. What else does Sammy like to eat? (Ideas: *Cantaloupe; fruit; plants; dandelions.*)

Pages 8–9. What do you think is happening here? (Idea: *The children are coming into the classroom.*) What else are they doing? (Ideas: *Talking; laughing; showing each other things; playing.*) What is the teacher doing? (Idea: *Trying to get their attention.*) Do you think the children are being considerate? *No.* Is the teacher waiting without feeling upset? *No.* How do you think the teacher is feeling? (Idea: *Frustrated.*)

Pages 10–11. What do you think is happening here? (Idea: *Sammy is calling out, crying.*) What do you think is wrong?

Pages 12–13. What is Sammy doing now? (Idea: *Kicking things out of his cage.*) What are all the children doing? (Idea: *Looking at Sammy.*) How do you think the children are feeling? (Idea: *Worried.*) What makes you think so?

Page 15. Who is holding Sammy? (Idea: *The teacher.*) What is Sammy doing? (Idea: *Crying.*)

Pages 16–17. How do you think Sammy is feeling? (Ideas: *Sad; upset; disruptive.*) How is the girl feeling? (Ideas: *Worried; anxious.*) What do you think is wrong?

Page 19. What do you think is happening here? (Idea: *The teacher is checking Sammy's fur.*) How does Sammy look now? (Ideas: *Happy; content; satisfied.*)

Pages 20–21. Where is Sammy now? (Ideas: *On a desk; on a table.*) What makes you think so? What is Sammy looking at? *A crayon.*

Pages 22–23. What do you think is happening here? (Ideas: *Sammy is sniffing the girl; the girl is cuddling Sammy.*) How does Sammy look now? (Ideas: *Happy; content; satisfied.*)

Pages 24–25. What are the children doing? (Ideas: *Smiling; laughing; giggling.*) How are they feeling? *Happy.* How do you think the teacher is feeling? (Ideas: *Upset, angry.*) What makes you think so? (Ideas: *She is frowning; she has her hands on her hips.*)

Pages 26–27. How does the story end? (Idea: *Everyone is happy.*)

Now that we've finished our picture walk, it's your turn to ask me some questions. What would you like to know about the story? (Accept questions. If children tell about the pictures or the story instead of asking questions, prompt them to ask a question.) Ask me a what question. Ask me a how question.

Read Story Aloud
(Read story aloud to children with minimal interruptions.)

In the next lesson, we will read the story again, and I will ask you some questions.

Present Target Vocabulary

◎= Difficult.

In the story, it is a difficult trick for Sammy to stand on his hind legs to take a carrot. That means it is not an easy trick for Sammy. It is a very hard trick for him. **Difficult.** Say the word. *Difficult.*

Difficult is a describing word. It tells about how hard it is to do something. What kind of word is **difficult?** *A describing word.*

If something is difficult, it is not easy to do. It is very hard to do. Say the word that means "not easy to do; very hard to do." *Difficult.*

(Correct any incorrect responses, and repeat the item at the end of the sequence.)

Let's think about some things that could be difficult for children to do. I'll tell about some things. If these things are difficult for children to do, say, "Difficult." If these things are not difficult for children to do, say, "Easy."

- Climbing a very high mountain. *Difficult.*
- Working in a busy store. *Difficult.*
- Playing jump rope. *Easy.*
- Carrying heavy rocks to build a tall wall. *Difficult.*
- Repairing a computer. *Difficult.*
- Eating hot dogs and potato salad. *Easy.*

What describing word means "not easy to do; very hard to do"? *Difficult.*

◎= Appetite.

In the story Ms. B says Sammy's appetite is good. That means Sammy enjoys eating his food. **Appetite.** Say the word. *Appetite.*

Appetite is a naming word. It names **an interest in food.** What kind of word is **appetite?** *A naming word.*

If you have a good appetite, it means you enjoy eating your food. If you have a poor appetite, you aren't interested in eating at all. Say the word that tells about your interest in food. *Appetite.*

(Correct any incorrect responses, and repeat the item at the end of the sequence.)

Let's think about some times when someone might have an appetite. I'll tell about a time. If someone has an appetite, say, "Appetite." If not, don't say anything.

- The family was looking forward to eating their picnic lunch. *Appetite.*
- You have been sick for two days and couldn't eat a thing. Now you are starting to feel better and want something to eat. *Appetite.*
- Someone put food on your plate that you did **not** like to eat.
- You hear the ice-cream truck coming down your street. *Appetite.*
- The first bit of muffin that you ate was very good. Now you want to eat the rest of it. *Appetite.*
- Your sister offers you mud pie made with real mud from the garden.

What naming word means "an interest in food"? *Appetite.*

◎⟞ *Gentle.*

In the story, Ms. B has taught the children to be gentle with Sammy when they play with him. That means the children handle him carefully and make sure they don't hurt him. **Gentle.** Say the word. *Gentle.*

Gentle is a describing word. It tells how someone does something. What kind of word is **gentle?** *A describing word.*

If you are gentle, you do things in a kind, careful way. Say the word that means "do things in a kind, careful way." *Gentle.*

(Correct any incorrect responses, and repeat the item at the end of the sequence.)

Let's think about some times when someone might be gentle. I'll tell about a time. If someone

is being gentle, say, "Gentle." If not, don't say anything.

- I carefully held my new baby brother. *Gentle.*
- The tiny kitten was shivering as I petted her. *Gentle.*
- My friend was scared, so I spoke to him quietly and put my arm around him. *Gentle.*
- I hugged the new puppy so hard that it squealed.
- Mom pounded the nail into the floor.
- I shook my dad softly to wake him up. *Gentle.*

What describing word means "do things in a kind, careful way"? *Gentle.*

◎⟞ *Explained.*

In the story, Ms. B explained to the children how guinea pigs recognized and greeted each other. That means she told the children more about guinea pigs so they could understand them better. **Explained.** Say the word. *Explained.*

Explained is an action word. It tells about someone saying something. What kind of word is **explained?** *An action word.*

If you explained something, you told more about it so someone could understand it. Say the word that means "told more about something so someone could understand it." *Explained.*

(Correct any incorrect responses, and repeat the item at the end of the sequence.)

Let's think about some times when someone might want to explain something. I'll tell about a time. If you think the person explained something, say, "Explained." If not, don't say anything.

- The mechanic told my mother why the car wouldn't work. *Explained.*
- I played tag with my friends.
- Alvin taught us the rules of the game before we played. *Explained.*
- We didn't know what we had done wrong until the police officer told us. *Explained.*
- We thought we knew everything about camping until the ranger told us more. *Explained.*
- The train stopped.

What action word means "told more about something so someone could understand it"? *Explained.*

Present Vocabulary Tally Sheet

(See Week 1, page 3, for instructions.)

Assign Homework

(Homework Sheet, BLM 16a: See the Introduction for homework instructions.)

DAY 2

Preparation: Picture Vocabulary Cards for *difficult, appetite, gentle,* and *explained.*

Read and Discuss Story

(Read story aloud to children. Ask the following questions at the specified points.)

Pages 1–3. How do you know Sammy is content? (Ideas: *He is satisfied with things just they way they are; he has his house and his soft blue sock; he has fresh food, water to drink, and a block of salt.*) (Point to the salt next to the water bottle.) Now we know what this is. What is it? *A round block of salt.*

Pages 4–5. What is the teacher's name? *Ms. B.* What is Sammy waiting for? (Idea: *A treat from Ms. B.*) What treat does she give him? (Idea: *A piece of carrot.*)

Pages 6–7. What other things does Sammy like to eat? (Ideas: *Fruits; vegetables; cantaloupe rind; freshly cut grass; dandelions.*) Why don't the children bring him grass from the side of the road? (Idea: *It might be polluted by cars or other animals.*) If food is polluted, it has bad things in it or on it that could make it dangerous to eat. Why do the children have to be careful about where they get grass for Sammy to eat? (Idea: *Some lawns might have chemicals on them.*) If a lawn has chemicals on it to make the grass grow faster or to kill the weeds, the chemicals might make Sammy sick.

Pages 8–9. How do you know it is noisy when the children all come into the classroom? (Ideas:

They are all talking loudly; Ms. B says, "Settle down.")

Pages 10–13. How does Sammy let Ms. B and the children know he has a problem? (Ideas: *He calls "WHEEEP!"; he kicks wood shavings everywhere; he races around his cage.*) Does Sammy get everyone's attention? *Yes.*

Pages 14–15. What does Sammy say when Ms. B demands to know what is the matter? (Idea: *He shrieks "WHEEEP!"*)

Page 16. What do they check for first? (Idea: *Is he sick?*) Why does Ms. B think he is fine? (Ideas: *He isn't sitting quietly with his fur puffed up; his appetite is good; there is no wetness around his eyes or nose.*)

Page 17. What do they check for next? (Idea: *Is he afraid of something?*) Why does Ms. B think he isn't afraid? (Idea: *If he were afraid, he would run into his house and be very quiet.*)

Page 18. What do they check for next? (Idea: *Is something hurting him?*) Why doesn't Ms. B think something is hurting him? (Idea: *There are no red marks or bald spots on Sammy's skin.*) Now we know why Sammy has his chin up in the air. What does he want Ms. B to do? (Idea: *Scratch under his chin.*)

Page 20. How do they know Sammy doesn't want them to look at his fur anymore? (Idea: *He makes small squeals and squeaks.*)

Page 21. What does Sammy do when Ms. B lets him go? (Ideas: *He sniffs at things on the tabletop; he makes his exploring sound.*) Is Sammy feeling better? *Yes.*

Page 22. How does Sammy say hello to Maria? *He touches her nose with his nose.* How do they know Sammy is feeling happy? (Ideas: *He makes his happy sound; he says "DOOT! Dutt-dutt-DEET-doot!"*)

Page 23. Who is the first one to figure out what Sammy's problem is? *Maria.*

Pages 24–25. What is Sammy's problem? (Ideas: *He wants someone to pay attention to him; he has been left alone all weekend.*)

Pages 26–27. Why is Sammy content at the end of the story? (Ideas: *All his friends are back;*

someone scratches his chin; the children are playing with him.)

Review Vocabulary

(Display the Picture Vocabulary Cards. Point to each card as you say the word. Ask children to repeat each word after you.) These pictures show **difficult**, **appetite**, **gentle**, and **explained**.

- What word means "told more about something so someone could understand it"? *Explained.*
- What word means "an interest in food"? *Appetite.*
- What word means "do things in a kind, careful way"? *Gentle.*
- What word means "not easy to do; very hard to do"? *Difficult.*

Extend Vocabulary

 Difficult.

In the story *Sammy: the Classroom Guinea Pig* we learned that **difficult** means "not easy to do; very hard to do." Say the word that means "not easy to do; very hard to do." *Difficult.*

Raise your hand if you can tell us a sentence that uses **difficult** as a describing word that means "not easy to do; very hard to do." (Call on several children. If they don't use complete sentences, restate their examples as sentences. Have the class repeat the sentences.)

Here's a new way to use the word **difficult**.

When I said "I hate broccoli!" my aunt said I was being difficult. Say the sentence.

She was a difficult child during the long trip. Say the sentence.

I knew you were going to be difficult today. Say the sentence.

In these sentences, **difficult** is a describing word that means **not easy to get along with**. What word means "not easy to get along with"? *Difficult.*

Raise your hand if you can tell us a sentence that uses **difficult** as a describing word that means "not easy to get along with." (Call on several children. If they don't use complete sentences, restate their examples as sentences. Have the class repeat the sentences.)

Present Expanded Target Vocabulary

Lonely.

In the story, Sammy has been left at school by himself for the whole weekend. He is unhappy because he has been left all alone. He feels lonely. **Lonely.** Say the word. *Lonely.*

Lonely is a describing word. It tells about an emotion Sammy is feeling. What kind of word is **lonely**? *A describing word.*

Lonely means you are unhappy because you have been left all alone. Say the word that means "unhappy because you have been left all alone." *Lonely.*

I'll tell about some people or animals. If those people or animals are lonely, say, "Lonely." If not, don't say anything.

- Graham cried when he was left by himself in his bedroom. *Lonely.*
- Amy enjoyed being left alone so she could read her book.
- Frederick was sad when all of his friends left at the end of the summer. *Lonely.*
- Tom thought being alone was better than being with other people because he could get more work done.
- When the rest of the team went home, Norm was all by himself with no one to play with. *Lonely.*
- The puppy whined and yelped because he was left alone. *Lonely.*

What describing word means "unhappy because you have been left all alone"? *Lonely.*

Language.

In the story, Sammy can't speak in words but uses squeaks and squeals and whistles to talk. Sammy has his own language to let everyone know how he feels and what he wants. **Language.** Say the word. *Language.*

Language is a naming word. It names **the sounds, words, and actions we use to tell others how we feel and what we want.** What kind of word is **language**? *A naming word.*

People in different countries speak different languages. Most of the people who live in Spain or Mexico speak Spanish. Most of the people who live in France speak French. People who cannot make sounds use actions to tell what they want or feel or need. They use sign language to speak. What language are we speaking right now? *English.* Say the word that means "the sounds, words, and actions we use to tell others how we feel and what we want." *Language.*

I'll name some things. If the things I name are a language, say, "Language." If not, don't say anything.

- My friend Diego speaks Spanish. *Language.*
- Mary speaks French. *Language.*
- The guinea pig spoke in squeaks, squeals, and whistles to tell what he wanted. *Language.*
- Four heavy rocks crashed onto the highway.
- The visitors spoke English. *Language.*
- The rainstorm filled the stream.

What naming word means "the sounds, words, and actions we use to tell others how we feel and what we want"? *Language.*

What other languages do you know about? (You may wish to locate a book about American Sign Language and teach children how people who are speech-challenged or hearing impaired communicate with gestures.)

DAY 3

Preparation: Activity Sheet, BLM 16b. Children will need crayons.

Retell Story

(Show the pictures on the following pages from the story, and call on a child to tell what's happening. Call on a different child for each section.)

Today I'll show you the pictures Aliz Berenzy made for the story *Sammy: the Classroom Guinea Pig.* As I show you the pictures, I'll call on one of you to tell the class that part of the story.

Pages 1–11. Tell me what happens at the **beginning** of the story. (Encourage use of

target word when appropriate. Model use as necessary.)

Pages 12–23. Tell me what happens in the **middle** of the story.

Pages 24–27. Tell me what happens at the **end** of the story.

How do you think Sammy feels at the end of the story? (Ideas: *Happy; content; satisfied.*) How do you think the children feel at the end of the story? (Ideas: *Happy; thankful.*) How do you think Ms. B feels at the end of the story? (Ideas: *Happy; satisfied; thankful.*)

Introduce Chew the Fat

Today you will play a game called Chew the Fat. A long time ago, when people wanted to just sit and talk about things that were happening in their lives, they would sit and "chew the fat."

In this game, I will say some sentences with our vocabulary words in them. If I use the vocabulary word correctly, say, "Well done!" If I use the word incorrectly, say, "Chew the fat." That means you want to talk about how I used the word. I'll say the beginning of the sentence again. If you can make the sentence end so that it makes sense, you'll get a point. If you can't, I get the point.

Let's practice: It was **difficult** to ride the tractor because it was easy to drive. *Chew the fat.* Let's chew the fat. The first part of the sentence stays the same. I'll say the first part. It was difficult to ride the tractor because . . . How can we finish the sentence so it makes sense? (Idea: *It was hard to drive.*) Let's say the whole sentence together now. *It was difficult to ride the tractor because it was hard to drive.* Well done! I'm glad we chewed the fat!

Let's do another one together. Wally knew he had an **appetite** for apple pie because he didn't want to eat any. *Chew the fat.* The first part of the sentence stays the same. I'll say the first part. Wally knew he had an appetite because . . . How can we finish the sentence so that it makes sense? (Idea: *He wanted to eat all of the apple pie.*) Let's say the whole sentence now. *Wally knew he had an appetite because he wanted to* *eat all of the apple pie.* Well done! I'm glad we chewed the fat!

Let's try one more. Terry was being **difficult** because she was tired. *Well done!* I used the word **difficult** correctly, so you said, "Well done!"

Now you're ready to play the game.

(Draw a T-chart on the board for keeping score. Children earn one point for each correct answer. If they make an error, work with them to construct a correct sentence. Record one point for yourself, and repeat missed words at the end of the game.)

- Jillian was **gentle** when . . . she pounded the nail into the board. *Chew the fat.* I'll say the first part of the sentence again. Jillian was gentle when . . . (Idea: *She tapped the nail softly.*) Let's say the whole sentence together. *Jillian was gentle when she tapped the nail softly.* Well done! I'm glad we chewed the fat!
- Jim **explained** the rules because . . . we all knew how to play the game. *Chew the fat.* I'll say the first part of the sentence again. Jim explained the rules because . . . (Idea: *We didn't know how to play the game.*) Let's say the whole sentence together. *Jim explained the rules because we didn't know how to play the game.* Well done! I'm glad we chewed the fat!
- Bryan was **lonely** because everyone had gone home and left him with nothing to do. *Well done!*
- My best friend Evan didn't know what **language** I was speaking because . . . I spoke English. *Chew the fat.* I'll say the first part of the sentence again. My best friend Evan didn't know what language I was speaking because . . . (Idea: *I was speaking French.*) Let's say the whole sentence together. *My best friend Evan didn't know what language I was speaking because I was speaking French.* Well done!
- My homework was **difficult** because . . . I knew exactly what to do. *Chew the fat.* I'll say the first part of the sentence again. My homework was difficult because . . . (Idea: *I didn't know what to do.*) Let's say the whole sentence together. *My homework was difficult because I didn't know what to do.* Well done!

(Count the points, and declare a winner.)
You did a great job of playing Chew the Fat!

Sorting (Activity Sheet)

(Review with children the things Sammy likes to eat. If they have difficulty remembering, reread pages 5 through 7.)

(Give each child a copy of the Activity Sheet, BLM 16b.) Today we will play the Cross-Out Game. We'll name each picture. If Sammy likes to eat that item, we won't do anything. What will we do if Sammy likes to eat that item? *We won't do anything.* If Sammy does not like to eat that item, we'll cross it out. What will we do if Sammy does not like to eat that item? *Cross it out.*

Touch the first item. What is that? *Carrot.* Does Sammy like to eat carrots? *Yes.* So what will you do? *We won't do anything.* Touch the next item. What is that? *Eggs.* Does Sammy like to eat eggs? *No.* So what will we do? *Cross it out.*

(Repeat this process for the remaining items. Ask children to color the pictures they did **not** cross out.)

DAY 4

Preparation: Prepare a sheet of chart paper, landscape direction, with the title *Sammy: the Classroom Guinea Pig.* Underneath the title, draw seven boxes, connected by arrows.

Underneath the seven boxes, draw six boxes, connected by arrows.

See the Introduction for an example.

Record children's responses by writing the underlined words in the boxes.

Develop Setting (Where) (Literary Analysis)

Let's think about what we already know about how books are made.

- What do we call the name of the book? *The title.*
- What do we call the person who writes the story? *The author.*

- What do we call the person who draws the pictures? *The illustrator.*
- What do we call the people or animals a story is about? *The characters.*
- What do we call the pictures the illustrator makes? *Illustrations.*
- What is one thing the setting of a story tells? *Where a story happens.*
- What is the second thing the setting of a story tells? *When a story happens.*

Let's sing the first (number) verses of "The Story Song" to help us remember these important things about books. (At this point it is unnecessary to sing the whole song. Choose which verses you would like children to sing. Include setting as it is a relatively new concept. See the Introduction for the complete "Story Song.")

Today we will learn more about the setting of a story.

The setting of a story tells two things. One thing the setting tells is where the story happens. What is one thing the setting tells? *Where the story happens.* The second thing the setting tells is when the story happens. What is the second thing the setting tells? *When the story happens.*

Let's look at the pictures and talk about the story to figure out where *Sammy: the Classroom Guinea Pig* happens.

(Follow the procedure established in Lessons 9, 10, and 11 to identify where the story happens.) (Ideas: *In Sammy's house; in Sammy's cage; in the classroom; in Ms. B's hands; on the table; in Maria's arms; on the table.*)

Now let's think about when this story happens.

Page 4. (Read aloud the sentence ". . . today she was late.") When does the story begin? (Idea: <u>Today</u>.)

Page 8. (Point to the clock.) This clock says 8:30. What time does it say? <u>8:30</u>.

Page 24. (Read the sentence "I think it's because today is Monday.") What day of the week is it? <u>Monday</u>.

When is the setting of the story *Sammy: the Classroom Guinea Pig?* (Idea: *Monday morning.*) You were great detectives! You used the clues and figured out when the story happens.

Today you learned about both parts of the setting of *Sammy: the Classroom Guinea Pig.* You learned about where and when the story happens.

Play Chew the Fat (Cumulative Review)

Today you will play Chew the Fat. Remember, a long time ago, when people wanted to just sit and talk about things that were happening in their lives, they would sit and "chew the fat."

In this game, I will say some sentences with our vocabulary words in them. If I use the vocabulary word correctly, say, "Well done!"

If I use the word incorrectly, say, "Chew the fat." That means you want to talk about how I used the word. I'll say the beginning of the sentence again. If you can make the sentence end so that it makes sense, you'll get a point. If you can't, I get the point.

Let's practice: Audrey was **lonely** because . . . all of her friends came to visit her. *Chew the fat.* Let's chew the fat. The first part of the sentence stays the same. I'll say the first part. Audrey was lonely because . . . How can we finish the sentence so it makes sense? (Idea: *All of her friends went home.*) Let's say the whole sentence together now. *Audrey was lonely because all of her friends went home.* Well done! I'm glad we chewed the fat!

Let's do another one together. Piper spoke in a strange **language,** so we knew exactly what she was saying. *Chew the fat.* The first part of the sentence stays the same. I'll say the first part. Piper spoke in a strange language, so . . . How can we finish the sentence so that it makes sense? (Idea: *We couldn't understand her.*) Let's say the whole sentence now. *Piper spoke in a strange language, so we couldn't understand her.* Well done! I'm glad we chewed the fat!

Now you're ready to play the game.

(Draw a T-chart on the board for keeping score. Children earn one point for each correct answer. If they make an error, correct them as you normally would, and record one point for yourself. Repeat missed words at the end of the game.)

- Mark knew his **appetite** was back when he didn't feel hungry at all. *Chew the fat.* I'll say the first part of the sentence again. Mark knew his appetite was back when . . . (Idea: *He felt very hungry.*) Let's say the whole sentence together. *Mark knew his appetite was back when he felt very hungry.* Well done! I'm glad we chewed the fat!
- Mom **explained** what to do because . . . none of us knew. *Well done!*
- Ralph was being **difficult** because . . . he wouldn't do as we told him. *Well done!*
- Aaron was **gentle** when . . . he slammed the car door shut as hard as he could. *Chew the fat.* I'll say the first part of the sentence again. Aaron was gentle when . . . (Idea: *He closed the car door carefully.*) Let's say the whole sentence together. *Aaron was gentle when he closed the car door carefully.* Well done! I'm glad we chewed the fat!
- We decided to **celebrate** because . . . we all failed our test. *Chew the fat.* I'll say the first part of the sentence again. We decided to celebrate because . . . (Idea: *We all passed our test.*) Let's say the whole sentence together. *We decided to celebrate because we all passed our test.* Well done!
- The race was **difficult** because . . . it was short and easy. *Chew the fat.* I'll say the first part of the sentence again. The race was difficult because . . . (Idea: *It was long and hard.*) Let's say the whole sentence together. *The race was difficult because it was long and hard.* Well done! I'm glad we chewed the fat!
- Jody was **lonely** because . . . everyone left her party and her kitten wouldn't sit in her lap. *Well done!*
- The **shiny** stone was . . . dull and boring. *Chew the fat.* I'll say the first part of the sentence again. The shiny stone was . . . (Idea: *Bright and interesting.*) Let's say the whole sentence together. *The shiny stone was bright and interesting.* Well done! I'm glad we chewed the fat!
- Gina and Barry **explained** how a starship worked because . . . we all knew. *Chew the fat.* I'll say the first part of the sentence again. Gina and Barry explained how a starship worked because . . . (Idea: *None of us knew.*)

Let's say the whole sentence together. *Gina and Barry explained how a starship worked because none of us knew.* Well done!

(Count the points, and declare a winner.)
You did a great job of playing Chew the Fat!

DAY 5

Preparation: Happy Face Game Test Sheet, BLM B.

Retell Story to a Partner
(Assign each child a partner, and ask the partners to take turns telling part of the story each time you turn to a new set of pages. Encourage use of target words when appropriate.)

Today I'll show you the pictures Alix Berenzy made for the story *Sammy: the Classroom Guinea Pig.* As I show you the pictures, you and your partner will take turns telling part of the story.

Pages 1–11. Tell what happens at the **beginning** of the story.

Pages 12–23. Tell what happens in the **middle** of the story.

Pages 24–27. Tell what happens at the **end** of the story.

Assess Vocabulary
 (Hold up a copy of the Happy Face Game Test Sheet, BLM B.)

Today you're going to play the Happy Face Game. When you play the Happy Face Game it helps me know how well you know the hard words you are learning.

If I say something true, color the happy face. What will you do if I say something true? *Color the happy face.*

If I say something false, color the sad face. What will you do if I say something false? *Color the sad face.*

Listen carefully to each item I say. Don't let me trick you!

Item 1: If you are **difficult,** you won't do as you are told. *True.*

Item 2: If you have a good **appetite,** you aren't very hungry. *False.*

Item 3: If a job is **difficult,** it is very easy to do. *False.*

Item 4: Being **gentle** means being careful and touching softly. *True.*

Item 5: Something that is **shiny** is dull and boring. *False.*

Item 6: A game is easier if the rules are **explained** well. *True.*

Item 7: After you have done a good job, you want to **celebrate.** *True.*

Item 8: A **lonely** person might cry or feel sad. *True.*

Item 9: **Language** is the sounds, words, and actions we use to talk to each other. *True.*

Item 10: **Gentle** is the same as rough. *False.*

You did a great job of playing the Happy Face Game!

(Score children's work later. Scores of 9 out of 10 indicate mastery. If a child does not achieve mastery, insert the missed words in the games in the next week's lessons. Retest those children individually on the missed items before they take the next mastery test.)

Extensions
Read a Story as a Reward

(Display several of the books you have read since the beginning of the program. Allow children to choose which book they would like you to read aloud to them as a reward for their hard work.)

(Read the story to children for enjoyment with minimal interruptions.)

Present the Super Words Center

(Prepare the word containers for the Super Words Center. See the Introduction for instructions on how to set up and use the Super Words Center.)

(Add the new Picture Vocabulary Cards to the words from previous weeks. Show children one of the word containers. If they need more guidance, role-play with two or three children as a demonstration.)

You will play a game called What's My Word? in the Super Words Center.

Let's think about how we work with our words in the Super Words Center.

You will work with a partner in the Super Words Center. Whom will you work with in the center? *A partner.*

First you will draw a word out of the container. What do you do first? (Idea: *Draw a word out of the container.*) Don't show your partner the word card.

Next you will tell your partner three clues that tell about the word card. What do you do next? (Idea: *I tell my partner three clues that tell about the word card.*) After each clue, your partner can make a guess. If your partner is correct, say, "Yes." If your partner is not correct, say, "No" and give another clue.

Let your partner make three guesses. If your partner guesses correctly on any of the tries, your partner gets a point. If your partner does not guess correctly, say your word, and show him or her the word card. Give yourself a point. Then give your partner a turn.

What do you do next? *Give my partner a turn.*

(This game does not need to be played for points.)

Papa, Do You Love Me?
author: Barbara M. Joosse • illustrator: Barbara Lavallee

Preparation: You will need *Papa, Do You Love Me?* for each day's lesson.

Number the pages of the story to assist you in asking questions at appropriate points.

Familiarize yourself with the information in the glossary so that you can share it with the children as you read and discuss the story on Day 2.

Beginning on Day 2, display a map of the world.

Post a copy of the Vocabulary Tally Sheet, BLM A, with this week's Picture Vocabulary Cards attached.

Each child will need the Homework Sheet, BLM 17a.

Now get ready to make some predictions to your partner about this book. Use the information from the cover to help you.

Target Vocabulary

Tier II	Tier III
drowsy	pattern
scorched	(question/
trembled	answer)
cowered	
*protect	
*Africa	

*Expanded Target Vocabulary Word

(Ask the following questions, allowing sufficient time for children to share their predictions with their partners.)

- Who are the characters in this story? (Whom do you think this story is about?)
- What do you think the boy and the man are going to do?
- Where do you think the story happens?
- When do you think the story happens?
- Why do you think they are dressed the way they are?
- How many cows are under the tree?
- Do you think this story is about real people? Tell why or why not.

(Call on several children to share their predictions with the class.)

DAY 1

Introduce Book

Today's book is called *Papa, Do You Love Me?* What's the title of this week's book? *Papa, Do you Love Me?*

This book was written by Barbara M. Joosse [zhoos]. Who's the author of *Papa, Do You Love Me? Barbara M. Joosse.*

Barbara Lavallee [**la**-va-lay] made the pictures for this book. Who's the illustrator of *Papa, Do You Love Me? Barbara Lavallee.* Who made the illustrations for this book? *Barbara Lavallee.*

The cover of a book usually gives us some hints of what the book is about. Let's look at the front cover of *Papa, Do You Love Me?* What do you see in the illustration? (Ideas: *A boy and a man walking; they're holding sticks; they have bare feet; they're wearing clothes that look different from our clothes; a tree; some cows.*) Who do you think the boy and the man are? (Idea: *A father and his son.*) Why do you think that? (Idea: *The title is Papa, Do you Love Me?*)

(Assign each child a partner.) Remember, when you make a prediction about something, you say what you think will happen.

Take a Picture Walk

We are going to take a picture walk through this book. Remember, when we take a picture walk, we look at the pictures and tell what we think will happen in the story.

(Show the illustrations on the following pages, and ask the specified questions.)

Pages 1–2. What are the boy and his father doing? (Idea: *Talking.*) What is the woman doing? (Idea: *Milking the cow.*) Who do you think the woman is? (Idea: *The boy's mother.*) What other animals do you see? *Goats.* (Point to the round house under the tree.) What do you think this is? (Idea: *Their house.*)

Pages 3–4. Tell about the three things the boy's father is pointing to. (Ideas: *An animal in a tree; men with spears and shields; people sitting around a fire.*)

Pages 5–6. What do you think is happening here? (Ideas: *The animals on the shore are running; there are other animals in the water; the boy and his father are holding out their arms.*)

Pages 7–8. Why do you think the boy and his father and the animals are sitting under the tree? (Ideas: *They're in the shade; it's cooler there.*) What do you think has happened to the leaves on this side of the tree? (Ideas: *The sun has dried them up; they've fallen off; that side of the tree is dying.*) What do you think is wrapped around the trunk of the tree?

Pages 9–10. Why do you think the boy and his father are standing under the blanket? (Ideas: *They're in the shade; it's cooler there.*)

Pages 11–12. What are the boy and his father doing? (Ideas: *Getting water from the river; filling the bag with water.*)

Pages 13–14. What is the boy doing? (Idea: *Drinking water; getting a drink.*)

Page 15. What time is it in this illustration? (Idea: *Nighttime.*) (Point to the illustration of the boy near the left-hand side of the page.) What is the boy doing? (Ideas: *Standing on one foot; looking at the cattle under the tree.*) (Point to the other boy.) What is the boy doing now? (Idea: *Yawning.*) How do you think the boy is feeling? (Ideas: *Tired; sleepy.*)

Page 16. What do you think is happening now?

Pages 17–18. What is the boy doing now? (Idea: *Sleeping.*) (Point to the cow surrounded by the hyenas.) What do you think is happening here?

Page 19. What do you think the boy's father is saying to him? How do you think the boy is feeling? How do you think his father is feeling?

Page 20. What do you think the boy's father is saying to him? How do you think the boy is feeling? How do you think his father is feeling?

Pages 21–22. What do you think is happening here? (Ideas: *The boy and his father are wrapped in the blanket; they are singing; they are shouting.*)

Pages 23–24. What is the boy's father doing? (Idea: *Scaring away the lion.*)

Pages 25–26. When does this part of the story happen? (Ideas: *In the morning; when the sun is coming up.*) Where do you think they are going?

Now that we've finished our picture walk, it's your turn to ask me some questions. What would you like to know about the story? (Accept questions. If children tell about the pictures or the story instead of asking questions, prompt them to ask a question.) Ask me a where question. Ask me a why question.

Read Story Aloud
(Read story aloud to children with minimal interruptions.)

In the next lesson, we will read the story again, and I will ask you some questions.

Present Target Vocabulary
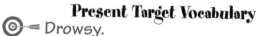
Drowsy.

In the story the boy asks his father, "What if I was the herd boy . . . but my eyelids got drowsy?" That means the boy wants to know what would happen if he started to feel sleepy and couldn't watch the animals. **Drowsy.** Say the word. *Drowsy.*

Drowsy is a describing word. It tells about how someone might feel. What kind of word is **drowsy?** *A describing word.*

If you are drowsy, you feel sleepy and cannot think clearly. Say the word that means "sleepy and cannot think clearly." *Drowsy.*

(Correct any incorrect responses, and repeat the item at the end of the sequence.)

Let's think about some times when someone might be drowsy. I'll tell about a time. If you think someone would feel drowsy, say, "Drowsy." If not, don't say anything.

- It is bedtime, and your father is reading you a story. *Drowsy.*
- It's a hot day, you've been playing hard, and you're lying in the sun. *Drowsy.*

- It's late, and you've been watching television in the dark. *Drowsy.*
- The alarm rings, and you jump out of bed all bright-eyed and bushy-tailed.
- You're playing goalie in a fast soccer game.
- Your eyelids feel very heavy, and you're having trouble thinking clearly. *Drowsy.*

What describing word means "sleepy and cannot think clearly"? *Drowsy.*

◎⚊ Scorched.

In the story the sun scorched the leaves, and they dropped off the branches. That means the hot sun dried out the leaves. **Scorched.** Say the word. *Scorched.*

Scorched is an action word. It tells what happened to something. What kind of word is **scorched?** *An action word.*

Scorched means dried out by the hot sun. What does **scorched** mean? *Dried out by the hot sun.* What word means "dried out by the hot sun"? *Scorched.*

(Correct any incorrect responses, and repeat the item at the end of the sequence.)

Let's think about some things that might be dried out by the hot sun. I'll tell about something. If you think that thing has been scorched, say, "Scorched." If not, don't say anything.

- By the end of the hot summer, the grass was brown and dry. *Scorched.*
- The plants in the garden were dry and crisp. *Scorched.*
- The seaweed waved slowly under the water.
- The grass in the shade was lush and green.
- The needles on the pine trees were reddish-brown and dry. *Scorched.*
- Near the waterfall, the plants were healthy and green.

What action word means "dried out by the hot sun"? *Scorched.*

◎⚊ Trembled.

In the story, the father says he'd shake his spear at the lion until "his great mane trembled." That means the lion's mane shook because the lion was afraid. **Trembled.** Say the word. *Trembled.*

Trembled is an action word. It tells what something did. What kind of word is **trembled?** *An action word.*

If you trembled, you shook because you were afraid or cold. Say the word that means "shook because you were afraid or cold." *Trembled.*

(Correct any incorrect responses, and repeat the item at the end of the sequence.)

Let's think about some times when someone might have trembled. I'll tell about a time. If someone might have trembled, say, "Trembled." If not, don't say anything.

- Judith was afraid during the lightning storm. *Trembled.*
- Shiloh walked quickly.
- Jimmy shook when he got out of the cold water. *Trembled.*
- Cameron was frightened by the booming thunder. *Trembled.*
- Zoe jumped happily off the high diving board.
- Gracie proudly showed her artwork.

What action word means "shook because you were afraid or cold"? *Trembled.*

◎⚊ Cowered.

In the story, the lion "cowered in his den." That means the lion made himself as small as he could because he was afraid. **Cowered.** Say the word. *Cowered.*

Cowered is an action word. It tells about what someone or something did. What kind of word is **cowered?** *An action word.*

If you cowered, you made yourself as small as you could because you were afraid. Say the word that means "made yourself as small as you could because you were afraid." *Cowered.*

(Call on a child.) Show me how you would cower. (Pause.) Everyone, what did _____ do? *He/she cowered.* Everyone, show me how you would cower. (Pause.) I could tell you were feeling very afraid. Now show me how you would look if you were feeling very brave. (Pause.) It was easy to see you were feeling brave. Excellent job using your bodies to show your emotions!

(Correct any incorrect responses, and repeat the item at the end of the sequence.)

Let's think about some times when someone or something might cower. I'll tell about a time. If you think the person or animal cowered, say, "Cowered." If not, don't say anything.

- The mouse was trapped by the cat in the corner of the room. *Cowered.*
- The kitten made itself as small as possible hoping that the dog wouldn't see it. *Cowered.*
- The raccoon made itself look as big as possible to frighten the big dog.
- The monkey made itself very small as the lion came near. *Cowered.*
- The man shouted and ran toward the cougar to scare it away.
- The children stayed together and stood up tall.

What action word means "made yourself as small as you could because you were afraid"? *Cowered.*

Present Vocabulary Tally Sheet
(See Week 1, page 3, for instructions.)

Assign Homework
(Homework Sheet, BLM 17a: See the Introduction for homework instructions.)

DAY 2

Preparation: Picture Vocabulary Cards for *drowsy, scorched, trembled,* and *cowered.*

Read and Discuss Story
(Read story aloud to children. Ask the following questions at the specified points in the story.)

Pages 1–2. What question does the boy ask? *Papa, do you love me?* Why does the father say he loves his son? (Idea: *His son came from his mama, his grandpapas and grandmamas, and from his father.*) What special name does the father call his son? *Tender Heart.* Some parents have special names they call their children to show them they love them. Raise your hand if you would like to share the special name your parents call you.

Pages 3–4. What question does the boy ask? *How much?* What answer does the father give? (Idea: *He loves him more than a warrior loves to leap, more than the bush baby loves the moon, and more than the elder loves his stories.*)

(Point to the bush baby.) A bush baby is an animal that sleeps all day and comes out only at night. Would a bush baby love the moon? *Yes.* How much? Tell why. (Idea: *A lot, because the moon would let it see things at night.*)

(Point to the warriors.) These men are warriors. Their job is to protect the people and animals of their village. Warriors often had jumping contests to see who could jump the highest. Would these warriors love to leap? *Yes.* How much? Tell why. (Idea: *A lot, because it would let them win the contest.*)

(Repeat this procedure with the illustration of the elders, sharing information from the glossary.)

Pages 5–6. What question does the boy ask? *How long?* What answer does the father give? (Idea: *He would love him as long as the wildebeest run on the mara, the hippopotamus wallows in mud, and the Serenget rolls to the sky.*)

(Follow the procedure established when you read pages 3 and 4 to explain the importance of the father's answer, sharing glossary information when appropriate.)

Page 7. What question does the boy ask? *Papa, what would you do if I was hot?* What answer does the father give? (Idea: *We'd rest under a Greenheart tree.*)

(Follow the procedure established when you read pages 3 and 4 to explain the importance of the father's answer, sharing glossary information about the Greenheart tree.)

Pages 8–10. What question does the boy ask? *What if the sun scorched the leaves and they dropped off the branches?* What answer does the father give? (Idea: *Then I'd stretch out my blanket till you were cool in my shade.*)

(Follow the procedure established when you read pages 3 and 4 to explain the importance of the father's answer, sharing glossary information about their robes.)

Pages 11–14. (Follow the procedure established to identify the boy's questions and his father's answers, sharing glossary information when appropriate.)

Pages 15–20. (Follow the procedure established to identify the boy's questions and his father's answers, sharing glossary information when appropriate.)

Pages 21–24. (Follow the procedure established to identify the boy's questions about his fears and his father's answers, sharing glossary information when appropriate.)

Pages 25–26. What three things does the father say he will do for his son? (Ideas: *Care for him, love him, teach him.*) How long will the father do these things for his son? *Always.*

Review Vocabulary

(Display the Picture Vocabulary Cards. Point to each card as you say the word. Ask children to repeat each word after you.) These pictures show **drowsy, scorched, trembled,** and **cowered.**

- What word means "dried out by the hot sun"? *Scorched.*
- What word means "made yourself as small as you could because you were afraid"? *Cowered.*
- What word means "shook because you were afraid or cold"? *Trembled.*
- What word means "sleepy and cannot think clearly"? *Drowsy.*

Extend Vocabulary

◎━ *Scorched.*

In *Papa, Do You Love Me?* we learned that **scorched** means "dried out by the hot sun." Say the word that means "dried out by the hot sun." *Scorched.*

Raise your hand if you can tell us a sentence that uses **scorched** as an action word that means "dried out by the hot sun." (Call on several children. If they don't use complete sentences, restate their examples as sentences. Have the class repeat the sentences.)

Here's a new way to use the word **scorched.**

- **Some of the trees were scorched by the forest fire.** Say the sentence.

- **The pot was scorched by the campfire.** Say the sentence.
- **He scorched his shirt with the iron.** Say the sentence.

In these sentences, **scorched** is an action word that means **burned a little bit.** What word means "burned a little bit"? *Scorched.*

Raise your hand if you can tell us a sentence that uses **scorched** as an action word that means "burned a little bit." (Call on several children. If they don't use complete sentences, restate their examples as sentences. Have the class repeat the sentences.)

Present Expanded Target Vocabulary
◎━ Protect.

In the story the boy is scared that a lion would eat him. His father says he would shelter him with his shield and shake his spear at the lion. The father is saying he would protect his son from the lion. **Protect.** Say the word. *Protect.*

Protect is an action word. It tells about what someone is doing. What kind of word is **protect?** *An action word.*

Protect means to keep safe from danger or injury. Say the word that means to "keep safe from danger or injury." *Protect.*

I'll tell about some people or animals. If those people or animals are being kept safe from danger or injury, say, "Protect." If not, don't say anything.

- I always wear my helmet when I ride my bicycle. *Protect.*
- Jackson went in the boat without a life jacket.
- Marcus wore knee pads and gloves when he was skateboarding. *Protect.*
- Damon wore a hat to keep the sun off his head. *Protect.*
- Dad forgot his safety glasses when he was working on the car.
- The painters didn't wear coveralls, and their clothes were covered in paint.

What action word means to "keep safe from harm or injury"? *Protect.*

◎━ Africa.

The characters in this story live in Africa. **Africa.** Say the word. *Africa.*

Africa is a naming word. It names a place. What kind of word is **Africa?** *A naming word.*

Africa is the second-largest continent in the world. (Point to the map of the world.) There are six continents in the world. They are the big land areas. We live in North America. (Point to North America.) This is Africa. (Point to Africa.) The people in the story are called Maasai [mä-sī]. They live in this part of Africa. (Point to the area that includes Kenya and Tanzania.) What continent do the Maasai people live on? *Africa.*

I'll point to places on the map. If those places are in Africa, say, "Africa." If those places are not in Africa, say ,"Absolutely not."

- (Point to Egypt.) *Africa.*
- (Point to the Pacific Ocean.) *Absolutely not.*
- (Point to the United States.) *Absolutely not.*
- (Point to the Sahara Desert.) *Africa.*
- (Point to the Democratic Republic of Congo.) *Africa.*
- (Point to the Antarctica.) *Absolutely not.*

What naming word is the second-largest continent in the world? *Africa.*

DAY 3

Preparation: Activity Sheet, BLM 17b. Children will need crayons.

Retell Story

Today I'll show you the pictures Barbara Lavallee made for the story *Papa, Do You Love Me?* As I show you the pictures, I'll call on one of you to tell the class that part of the story.

(Show the pictures on pages 1 and 2.) Tell me what question the boy asks. (Call on a child to say the question, either in the words of the author or in his or her own words.) What is the father's answer? (Call on a child to say the answer, either in the words of the author or in his or her own words.)

(Repeat this procedure for the rest of the story. Encourage use of target words when appropriate. Model use as necessary.)

How do you think the boy feels at the end of the story? (Ideas: *Loved; happy; content; safe.*)

How do you think the boy's father feels at the end of the story? (Ideas: *Loving; happy; content; proud.*)

Review Chew the Fat

Today you will play Chew the Fat. Remember, a long time ago, when people wanted to just sit and talk about things that were happening in their lives, they would sit and "chew the fat."

In this game, I will say some sentences with our vocabulary words in them. If I use the vocabulary word correctly, say, "Well done." If I use the word incorrectly, say, "Chew the fat." That means you want to talk about how I used the word. I'll say the beginning of the sentence again. If you can make the sentence end so that it makes sense, you'll get a point. If you can't, I get the point.

Let's practice: I knew I was **drowsy** because . . . I was feeling bright and alert and not sleepy at all. *Chew the fat.* Let's chew the fat. The first part of the sentence stays the same. I'll say the first part. I knew I was drowsy because . . . How can we finish the sentence so it makes sense? (Idea: *I was feeling sleepy and couldn't think straight.*) Let's say the whole sentence together now. *I knew I was drowsy because I was feeling sleepy and couldn't think straight.* Well done! I'm glad we chewed the fat!

Let's do another one together. The plants were **scorched** because . . . they were green and growing well. *Chew the fat.* The first part of the sentence stays the same. I'll say the first part. The plants were scorched because . . . How can we finish the sentence so that it makes sense? (Idea: *They were dry and brown.*) Let's say the whole sentence now. *The plants were scorched because they were dry and brown.* Well done! I'm glad we chewed the fat!

Now you're ready to play the game.

(Draw a T-chart on the board for keeping score. Children earn one point for each correct answer. If they make an error, work with them to construct a correct sentence. Record one point for yourself, and repeat missed words at the end of the game.)

- Rolf **trembled** when . . . he was warm and dry. *Chew the fat.* I'll say the first part of the sentence again. Rolf trembled when . . . (Idea: *He was wet and cold.*) Let's say the whole sentence together. *Rolf trembled when he was wet and cold.* Well done! I'm glad we chewed the fat!
- The mouse **cowered** in the corner when . . . the cat was outside for the day. *Chew the fat.* I'll say the first part of the sentence again. The mouse cowered in the corner when . . . (Idea: *The cat walked into the room.*) Let's say the whole sentence together. *The mouse cowered in the corner when the cat walked into the room.* Well done! I'm glad we chewed the fat!
- Billie felt **drowsy** when she was lying in the warm sun. *Well done.*
- I **protected** myself from the rain when . . . I held a banana over my head. *Chew the fat.* I'll say the first part of the sentence again. I protected myself from the rain when . . . (Idea: *I held an umbrella over my head.*) Let's say the whole sentence together. *I protected myself from the rain when I held an umbrella over my head.* Well done!
- **Africa** is the name of . . . a town in our state. *Chew the fat.* I'll say the first part of the sentence again. Africa is the name of . . . (Idea: *A continent.*) Let's say the whole sentence together. *Africa is the name of a continent.* Well done!

(Count the points, and declare a winner.)
You did a great job of playing Chew the Fat!

Sentence Frames (Activity Sheet)

(Review with children the animals shown or mentioned in the story *Papa, Do You Love Me?* If children have difficulty remembering, show them pages 2, 4, 5 through 6, and 18.)

(Give each child a copy of the Activity Sheet, BLM 17b.) Today we will play the Cross-Out Game. We'll name each picture. If that animal lives in Africa, we won't do anything. What will we do if that animal lives in Africa? *We won't do anything.* If that animal does not live in Africa, we'll cross it out. What will we do if that animal does not live in Africa? *Cross it out.*

Touch the first item. What is that? *Kangaroo.* Do kangaroos live in Africa? *No.* So what will you do? *Cross it out.* Touch the next item. What is that? *Bush baby.* Do bush babies live in Africa? *Yes.* So what will we do? *Don't do anything.* (Repeat this process for the remaining items. Ask children to color the pictures they did not cross out.)

Introduce Question/Answer Story Pattern (Literary Analysis)

Let's think about what we already know about how books are made.

- What do we call the name of the book? *The title.*
- What do we call the person who writes the story? *The author.*
- What do we call the person who draws the pictures? *The illustrator.*
- What do we call the people or animals a story is about? *The characters.*
- What do we call the pictures the illustrator makes? *Illustrations.*
- What is one thing the setting of a story tells? *Where a story happens.*
- What is the second thing the setting of a story tells? *When a story happens.*

Let's sing all the verses of "The Story Song" to help us remember these important things about books.

(See the Introduction for the complete "Story Song.")

A pattern is an action or something that repeats in a certain way.

Watch me. I'll clap a pattern. (Clap slow, slow, quick, quick, quick; repeat.) Clap the pattern with me. (Clap the pattern with children until all of them are clapping the pattern.) I'll clap the pattern once more. (Clap slow, slow, quick, quick, quick; repeat.) Now it's your turn to clap the pattern by yourself. (Pause.) You just repeated a clapping pattern.

Watch me. I'll draw a pattern. (Draw a circle, box, circle, box pattern on the board in a horizontal line.) Say the pattern with me. (Say "circle, box, circle, box" with children.) I'll add to my pattern. (Add a circle.) Now tell me what comes next in my pattern. *Box.* (Extend the pattern for two or three more repeats.) You just added on to a drawing pattern.

When authors write stories, they sometimes write in patterns.

Let's figure out the pattern for the story *Papa, Do You Love Me?*

Read the following pages aloud, and ask the questions.

Page 1. What happens first? (Idea: The boy asks a question.)

Page 2. Then what happens? (Idea: *The father answers the question.*)

Page 7. What happens first? (Idea: *The boy asks a question.*) Then what happens? (Idea: *The father answers the question.*)

Page 8. What happens first? (Idea: *The boy asks a question.*) Then what happens? (Idea: *The father answers the question.*)

Raise your hand if you think you know the pattern for the book *Papa, Do You Love Me?* (Do not call on a child to tell the pattern.)

I'll read two more pages from the book. See if you have figured out the pattern.

Page 11. What happens first? (Idea: *The boy asks a question.*) Then what happens? (Idea: *The father answers the question.*)

Page 21. What happens first? (Idea: *The boy asks a question.*) Then what happens? (Idea: *The father answers the question.*)

What do you think is the pattern for the story *Papa, Do You Love Me?* (Idea: *Question, answer, question, answer.*) You are right; the pattern for this story is question and answer. What's the pattern for this story? *Question and answer.*

You were great detectives! You used the clues and figured out what the pattern was.

Today we will learn a new song that will help us remember about story patterns. (**Note:** The tune of this song is "If You're Happy and You Know It, Clap Your Hands.")

Listen while I sing the chorus:

There are patterns all around us if we look.
There are patterns all around us if we look.
There are patterns all around;
If we look, they can be found.
There are patterns all around us if we look.

Now sing it with me.

Each time we sing the song, we start by singing the chorus. Every pattern that we learn will have a different verse about that pattern. I wonder if you will be able to find the pattern in our song as we add more verses.

Let's sing a verse about the question and answer pattern we just learned about in *Papa, Do You Love Me?* Listen while I sing the question and answer verse:

If your Papa asks a question, answer back.
If your Papa asks a question, answer back.
If your Papa asks a question,
Please allow a small suggestion:
If your Papa asks a question, answer back.

Let's sing it together now:

If your Papa asks a question, answer back.
If your Papa asks a question, answer back.
If your Papa asks a question,
Please allow a small suggestion:
If your Papa asks a question, answer back.

Now let's sing the chorus and then the first verse:

There are patterns all around us if we look.
There are patterns all around us if we look.
There are patterns all around;
If we look they can be found.
There are patterns all around us if we look.

If your Papa asks a question, answer back.
If your Papa asks a question, answer back.
If your Papa asks a question,
Please allow a small suggestion:
If your Papa asks a question, answer back.

Singing a song together is a very good way to remember the patterns we will learn!

Play Chew the Fat (Cumulative Review)

Today you will play Chew the Fat. In this game, I will say some sentences with our vocabulary words in them. If I use the vocabulary word correctly, say, "Well done!" If I use the word incorrectly, say, "Chew the fat." That means you want to talk about how I used the word. I'll say the beginning of the sentence again. If you can make the sentence end so that it makes sense, you'll get a point. If you can't, I get the point.

Let's do another one together. It's easy to **protect** your shoes . . . by using applesauce. *Chew the fat.* The first part of the sentence stays the same. I'll say the first part. It's easy to protect your shoes . . . How can we finish the sentence so that it makes sense? (Idea: *By using shoe polish.*) Let's say the whole sentence now. *It's easy to protect your shoes by using shoe polish.* Well done! I'm glad we chewed the fat!

Let's practice: **Africa** is the name of . . . the grocery store at the end of the street. *Chew the fat.* Let's chew the fat. The first part of the sentence stays the same. I'll say the first part. Africa is the name of . . . How can we finish the sentence so it makes sense? (Idea: *A continent.*) Let's say the whole sentence together now. *Africa is the name of a continent.* Well done! I'm glad we chewed the fat!

Now you're ready to play the game.

(Draw a T-chart on the board for keeping score. Children earn one point for each correct answer. If they make an error, correct them as you normally would, and record one point for yourself. Repeat missed words at the end of the game.)

- Sally **cowered** in her room when . . . there was **no** thunder and lightning. *Chew the fat.* I'll say the first part of the sentence again. Sally cowered in her room when . . . (Idea: *There was thunder and lightning.*) Let's say the whole sentence together. *Sally cowered in her room when there was thunder and lightning.* Well done! I'm glad we chewed the fat!
- Robert **trembled** when . . . the earthquake shook the house. *Well done!*
- All of the plants were **scorched** because . . . the sun was hot and there was no rain. *Well done!*
- Franklin knew he was **drowsy** when . . . his eyes were wide open and he didn't feel

tired. *Chew the fat.* I'll say the first part of the sentence again. Franklin knew he was drowsy when . . . (Idea: *His eyes were shutting and he felt very tired.*) Let's say the whole sentence together. *Franklin knew he was drowsy when his eyes were shutting and he felt very tired.* Well done! I'm glad we chewed the fat!
- We could see that the wood was just **scorched** because . . . it was all burned up. *Chew the fat.* I'll say the first part of the sentence again. We could see that the wood was just scorched because . . . (Idea: *It was burned only a little.*) Let's say the whole sentence together. *We could see that the wood was just scorched because it was burned only a little.* Well done!
- The kite **drifted** because . . . there was no wind. *Chew the fat.* I'll say the first part of the sentence again. The kite drifted because . . . (Idea: *There was wind.*) Let's say the whole sentence together. *The kite drifted because there was wind.* Well done! I'm glad we chewed the fat!
- Mother felt **relieved** when . . . she found out that everyone was healthy and well. *Well done!*
- The plant was **prickly** because . . . it had lots of thorns and rough bits that stuck out. *Well done!*
- Cindy **trembled** in the snow because . . . she was warm. *Chew the fat.* I'll say the first part of the sentence again. Cindy trembled in the snow because . . . (Idea: *She was cold.*) Let's say the whole sentence together. *Cindy trembled in the snow because she was cold.* Well done! I'm glad we chewed the fat!
- When you ride, you should **protect** your head with . . . a bicycle seat. *Chew the fat.* I'll say the first part of the sentence again. When you ride, you should protect your head with . . . (Idea: *A bicycle helmet.*) Let's say the whole sentence together. *When you ride, you should protect your head with a bicycle helmet.* Well done!

(Count the points, and declare a winner.)
You did a great job of playing Chew the Fat!

Preparation: Happy Face Game Test Sheet, BLM B.

Retell Story to a Partner

(Assign each child a partner, and ask the partners to take turns telling part of the story each time you turn to a new set of pages. Encourage use of target words when appropriate.)

Today I'll show you the pictures Barbara Lavallee made for the story *Papa, Do You Love Me?* As I show you the pictures, you and your partner will take turns telling part of the story.

Pages 1–11. Tell what happens at the **beginning** of the story.

Pages 12–23. Tell what happens in the **middle** of the story.

Pages 24–27. Tell what happens at the **end** of the story.

Assess Vocabulary

 (Hold up a copy of the Happy Face Game Test Sheet, BLM B.)

Today you're going to play the Happy Face Game. When you play the Happy Face Game, it helps me know how well you know the hard words you are learning.

If I say something true, color the happy face. What will you do if I say something true? *Color the happy face.*

If I say something false, color the sad face. What will you do if I say something false? *Color the sad face.*

Listen carefully to each item I say. Don't let me trick you!

Item 1: If you are **drowsy,** you are tired and ready to sleep. *True.*

Item 2: A person who is **uncooperative** likes to work with and help others. *False.*

Item 3: If you were in **Africa,** you would be on a faraway continent. *True.*

Item 4: If you had to **protect** your hands, you might wear gloves. *True.*

Item 5: If someone is very, very happy, he or she is **furious.** *False.*

Item 6: If you **trembled,** you might have been scared or cold. *True.*

Item 7: A log is **scorched** if it is burned just a little bit. *True.*

Item 8: If you **cowered,** you made yourself as small as you could. *True.*

Item 9: When you **shout,** you speak in a very quiet voice. *False.*

Item 10: A **clever** child is good at solving problems. *True.*

You did a great job of playing the Happy Face Game!

(Score children's work later. Scores of 9 out of 10 indicate mastery. If a child does not achieve mastery, insert the missed words in the games in the next week's lessons. Retest those children individually on the missed items before they take the next mastery test.)

Extensions

Read a Story as a Reward

 (Display copies of several of the books you have read since the beginning of the program. Allow children to choose which book they would like you to read aloud to them as a reward for their hard work.)

(Read story to children for enjoyment with minimal interruptions.)

Present the Super Words Center

(Prepare the word containers for the Super Words Center. See the Introduction for instructions on how to set up and use the Super Words Center.)

(Add the new Picture Vocabulary Cards to the words from the previous weeks. Show children one of the word containers. If they need more guidance, role-play with two or three children as a demonstration.)

Let's think about how we work with our words in the Super Words Center.

You will work with a partner in the Super Words Center. Whom will you work with in the center? *A partner.*

Today I will teach you how to play a game called What's New?

First, one partner will draw four word cards out of the container and put them on the table so both partners can see. What do you do first? (Idea: *Draw four cards out of the container and put them on the table so both partners can see.*)

Next you will take turns looking at the cards and saying the words the pictures show. What do you do next? (Idea: *We take turns looking at the cards and saying the words the pictures show.*)

Next, partner 2 looks away while partner 1 takes one of the four cards and places it back in the container. Then partner 1 draws a new card from the container and places it on the table with the other three. Watch while I show you what I mean. (Demonstrate this process with a child as your partner.) When you put down the new card, it's a good idea to mix the cards so they aren't in the same places anymore. (Demonstrate as you go.)

Now partner 1 says, "What's New?" Partner 2 has to use his or her eyes and brain and say what new word card has been put down. If partner 2 is correct, he or she gets a point. If partner 2 is not correct, partner 1 gets the point. (Demonstrate as you go.)

Next, partner 2 has a turn to choose four different cards, and the game starts again. What happens next? (Idea: *Partner 2 has a turn to choose four different cards, and the game starts again.*)

Have fun playing What's New!

Pablo's Tree
author: Pat Mora • illustrator: Cecily Lang

Preparation: You will need *Pablo's Tree* for each day's lesson.

Number the pages of the story to assist you in asking questions at appropriate points.

Familiarize yourself with the pronunciation of the Spanish words if you aren't fluent in Spanish.

Mamá — Mother
Lito — short for Grandfather
Abuelito — Grandfather
piñata — a decorative container
Cómo está mi nieto grande? How is my big grandson?
cuidado — care
Este árbol es para mi nieto. This tree is for my grandson.
Ay, Papá — Oh, Father

Post a copy of the Vocabulary Tally Sheet, BLM A, with this week's Picture Vocabulary Cards attached.

Each child will need the Homework Sheet, BLM 18a.

DAY 1

Introduce Book

Today's book is called *Pablo's Tree*. What's the title of this week's book? *Pablo's Tree.*

This book was written by Pat Mora [**mohr**-ah]. Who's the author of *Pablo's Tree*? *Pat Mora.*

Cecily Lang made the pictures for this book. Who's the illustrator of *Pablo's Tree*? *Cecily Lang.* Who made the illustrations for this book? *Cecily Lang.*

The cover of a book usually gives us some hints of what the book is about. Let's look at the front cover of *Pablo's Tree*. What do you see in the illustration? (Ideas: *A boy and a tree; the tree has bells on it; the tree has wind chimes on it; the boy is holding a wind chime.*)

Target Vocabulary

Tier II	Tier III
adopt	pattern
nursery	(remember)
wonder	
chuckles	
*tradition	
*decorations	

*Expanded Target Vocabulary Word

(**Note:** If children identify the wind chimes as something else, accept their answers as long as they are reasonable.) What do you think the boy's name is? (Idea: *Pablo.*) Why do you think that? (Idea: *The title is Pablo's Tree.*)

(Assign each child a partner.) Remember, when you make a prediction about something, you say what you think will happen.

Get ready to make some predictions to your partner about this book. Use the information from the cover to help you.

(Ask the following questions, allowing sufficient time for children to share their predictions with their partners.)

- Who is one of the characters in this story? (Whom do you think this story is about?)
- What is the boy holding?
- Where do you think the story happens?
- When do you think the story happens?
- Why do you think the boy's eyes are closed?
- How do you think the bells got on the tree?
- Do you think this story is about real people? Tell why or why not.

(Call on several children to share their predictions with the class.)

Take a Picture Walk

We are going to take a picture walk through this book. Remember, when we take a picture walk, we look at the pictures and tell what we think will happen in the story.

(Show the illustrations on the following pages, and ask the specified questions.)

Page 2. Who do you think the woman is? (Ideas: *Pablo's teacher; his mother; his aunt.*) What do you think Pablo is saying to her?

Page 3. What has the boy put in his suitcase? (Idea: *A book about whales.*) What is he holding? (Ideas: *A flute; a tambourine.*)

Page 4. What do you think is happening here? (Ideas: *They are going to the car; they are going on a trip; they are going somewhere.*)

(**Note:** If children have suggested the woman is a teacher, ask them to revise their choice, based on what is happening in the pictures on pages 3 and 4.)

Page 6. Who do you think the man is? (Idea: *Pablo's grandpa.*)

Why do you think so? (Ideas: *He is hugging Pablo's mother; he has gray hair; he looks older than Pablo's mother.*)

Page 7. What are they doing? (Idea: *Laughing.*)

Page 8. What are they doing? (Idea: *Hugging.*)

Pages 9–10. What is happening here? (Ideas: *Pablo is touching the tree; he's hugging his grandfather.*)

Pages 11–12. What is happening here? (Ideas: *Pablo is saying good-bye to his mother; his grandfather is playing a flute; Pablo is playing his tambourine.*)

Pages 13–14. What is Pablo's grandfather doing? (Ideas: *Carrying a tree; watering the tree.*) What is Pablo's mother carrying? (Ideas: *Blankets; baby bottles.*) When do you think this happened? (Idea: *Just before Pablo was born.*) Why do you think so? (Ideas: *The tree is smaller; Pablo isn't in the illustration; babies need blankets and baby bottles, so they are getting ready for Pablo to be born.*)

Pages 15–16. Where is Pablo's grandfather putting the tree? (Ideas: *On the sidewalk; near some flowers.*)

Page 17. What is Pablo's mother doing? (Idea: *Phoning someone.*) Whom do you think Pablo's mother is phoning?

Page 18. What is Pablo's grandfather doing? (Idea: *Waiting.*) Whom do you think he is waiting for?

Pages 19–20. What do you think is happening now? (Idea: *Pablo's grandfather is telling him something; he's telling him a story.*) Do you think Pablo is enjoying hearing what his grandfather is saying? Tell why you think so.

Page 21. Who do you think the baby is? (Idea: *Pablo.*) What makes you think so? (Idea: *The tree is small.*)

Page 22. What is Pablo's grandfather doing? (Idea: *Planting the tree.*)

Pages 23–24. Who do you think the little boy is? (Idea: *Pablo.*) What are they doing? (Idea: *Hanging things on the tree; putting streamers on the tree; putting balloons on the tree.*)

Pages 25–26. Who do you think the boy is? (Idea: *Pablo.*) What are they doing? (Idea: *Putting things on the tree.*)

Page 27. Who do you think the boy is? (Idea: *Pablo.*) What are they doing? (Idea: *Putting things on the tree.*)

Page 28. What are Pablo and his grandfather doing? (Idea: *Looking at the tree; eating apples.*) Do you think they are proud of the way the tree looks? *Yes.* Yes, they are looking at the tree and admiring how beautiful it looks.

Page 29. How are Pablo and his grandfather feeling? (Idea: *Happy.*) What makes you think so? (Idea: *They are both smiling.*)

(Reshow the illustrations on pages 22 through 27.) What do you notice about how Pablo has changed in these pictures? (Ideas: *He is getting bigger and bigger; he is getting older.*)

Now that we've finished our picture walk, it's your turn to ask me some questions. What would you like to know about the story? (Accept questions. If children tell about the pictures or the story instead of asking questions, prompt them to ask a question.) Ask me a when question. Ask me a how question.

Read Story Aloud
(Read story aloud to children with minimal interruptions.)

In the next lesson, we will read the story again, and I will ask you some questions.

Present Target Vocabulary

◎◄ Adopt.

In the story, Pablo's mother says one day, "I'm going to adopt a baby." That means she gets a baby who doesn't have a family and makes that baby her own son or daughter. **Adopt.** Say the word. *Adopt.*

Adopt is an action word. It tells what someone does. What kind of word is **adopt?** *An action word.*

When people adopt a child, they get a child who doesn't have a family and make that child their own son or daughter. Say the word that means "get a child who doesn't have a family and make that child your own son or daughter." *Adopt.*

(Correct any incorrect responses, and repeat the item at the end of the sequence.)

Let's think some times when someone might adopt a child. I'll tell about a time. If these times tell about someone adopting a child, say, "Adopt." If not, don't say anything.

- Teresa's mother and father died in a car accident. Teresa's aunt and uncle took Teresa and made her their daughter. *Adopt.*
- Neil and Amanda flew to Haiti to get a child who didn't have a family. *Adopt.*
- John liked to play with his friends.
- Georgia's family couldn't care for her and had to give her up. Georgia hoped that someone would come and get her to make her a part of their family. *Adopt.*
- Tracy's cousins invited her to their house for a short visit.
- Cecily was hoping that someone nice would get her and make her their daughter. *Adopt.*

What action word means "get a child who doesn't have a family and make that child your own son or daughter"? *Adopt.*

◎◄ Wonder.

In the story, Pablo wonders if his grandfather remembered to decorate his tree. That means Pablo thinks about whether or not his grandfather has decorated his tree. He is a little bit worried that maybe his grandfather hasn't remembered to do it. **Wonder.** Say the word. *Wonder.*

Wonder is an action word. It tells about what people do. What kind of word is **wonder?** *An action word.*

If you wonder about something, you think about it either because you are interested in it and want to know more, or because you are worried about it. Say the word that means to "think about something either because you are interested in it and want to know more, or because you are worried about it." *Wonder.*

(Correct any incorrect responses, and repeat the item at the end of the sequence.)

Let's think about some times when someone might wonder. I'll tell about a time. If someone might wonder, say, "Wonder." If not, don't say anything.

- Pietro thinks about the stars. He wants to know how far away they are. *Wonder.*
- Seth is worried that maybe his mother won't be home after school. *Wonder.*
- Nikolas doesn't think or worry about anything when he is riding his bike.
- Harper wants to know how rockets could fly so far. *Wonder.*
- Rick likes to make up funny words.
- Shannon worries that maybe her favorite program won't be on television. *Wonder.*

What action word means to "think about something either because you are interested in it and want to know more, or because you are worried about it"? *Wonder.*

◎◄ Nursery.

In the story, Pablo's grandfather goes to the nursery down the street to buy a small tree. That means he goes to a place where plants are grown so they can be sold. **Nursery.** Say the word. *Nursery.*

Nursery is a naming word. It names a place. What kind of word is **nursery?** *A naming word.*

If you go to a nursery, you go to a place where plants are grown so they can be sold. Say the word that means "a place where plants are grown so they can be sold." *Nursery.*

(Correct any incorrect responses, and repeat the item at the end of the sequence.)

Let's think about a nursery. I'll tell about some things you could buy. If you could buy them from a nursery, say, "Nursery." If not, don't say anything.

- A rose bush. *Nursery.*
- An apple.
- An apple tree. *Nursery.*
- Some lovely flowers for your garden. *Nursery.*
- A bag of popcorn.
- A new wheel for your skateboard.

What naming word means "a place where plants are grown so they can be sold"? *Nursery.*

◎← Chuckles.

At the end of the story, Lito chuckles and winks at Pablo. That means he laughs quietly. **Chuckles.** Say the word. *Chuckles.*

Chuckles is an action word. It tells about what happens. What kind of word is **chuckles?** *An action word.*

When you chuckle you laugh quietly. Say the word that means "laughs quietly." *Chuckles.*

(Correct any incorrect responses, and repeat the item at the end of the sequence.)

Let's think about some times when someone might chuckle. I'll tell about a time. If you think the person would chuckle, say, "Chuckles." If not, don't say anything.

- Frederico thinks it's funny to watch his dog chase his tail. *Chuckles.*
- Mama hears the baby crying.
- Morrie thinks about a funny thing that happened yesterday. *Chuckles.*
- The flower vase falls and breaks.
- A tree falls in the forest and makes a loud sound.
- Tomás tells Lito a funny story. *Chuckles.*

What action word means "laughs quietly"? *Chuckles.*

Present Vocabulary Tally Sheet
(See Week 1, page 3, for instructions.)

Assign Homework
(Homework Sheet, BLM 18a: See the Introduction for homework instructions.)

Preparation: Picture Vocabulary Cards for *adopt, nursery, wonder,* and *chuckles.*

Have available a tambourine, a flute, a small wind chime, and a small bell.

Read and Discuss Story
(Read story aloud to children. Ask the following questions at the specified points in the story.)

Page 1. What is Pablo worried about? (Idea: *That his grandfather might not have remembered to decorate his tree.*)

Pages 3–4. What two questions does Pablo's mama ask him? *Do you have your suitcase? What new birthday toys are you taking to Abuelito's?* What answer does Pablo give? (Idea: *He is bringing his purple car, his book about whales, his tambourine, and his flute.*)

(If children are unfamiliar with musical instruments, show them the tambourine and the flute. You will play them later.)

When does this part of the story happen? *The day after Pablo's birthday.* What does Pablo's grandfather do to get ready for Pablo's birthday visit? (Idea: *He decorates Pablo's tree.*) What do Pablo and his grandfather do together on this special birthday visit? (Ideas: *Sit under Pablo's tree; play with Pablo's new toys.*)

Page 5. Pablo tries to guess what his grandfather will use to decorate his tree. What are his guesses? (Idea: *Lights, little piñatas, little animals, and candy.*) How does Pablo's mother answer his questions? (Idea: *She just smiles and winks.*)

Watch me; I'll wink. (Wink.) People sometimes wink when they know a secret, but they aren't going to share it. Show me how you would wink if the class were planning a surprise for me but I didn't know what it was. (Pause.)

Do you think Pablo's mother knows what Grandfather has put on Pablo's tree? *Yes.* How do you know? (Idea: *She just smiles and winks.*)

Page 6–8. How is Pablo feeling? (Idea: *Excited.*) That's right; he can hardly wait to see his tree.

Pages 9–10. What has Pablo's grandfather used to decorate Pablo's tree? *Colored bells and wind chimes.* What will happen when the wind blows? (Ideas: *The tree will make sounds; the wind chimes and bells will make sounds; Pablo will hear music.*)

(Ring the bell, and gently shake the wind chime.) Imagine you can hear lots of bells and wind chimes making music. Do you think you would like to hear Pablo's tree making music?

Page 11. Is Pablo's mother staying? *No.* Just Pablo and his grandfather are going to spend time together.

Page 12. What would you be hearing if you were Pablo? (Ideas: *Grandfather playing the flute; Pablo's tambourine; the bells and the wind chimes.*)

(Choose children to play the bell, the wind chimes, and the tambourine. Softly play the flute while children gently play the other instruments.) Now imagine what it would sound like if lots of bells and wind chimes were playing with the flute and the tambourine.

What question does Grandfather ask? *"Pablo, do you remember the story of your tree?"*

The next part of the story tells about Pablo and Grandfather remembering the story of Pablo's tree.

Pages 13–14. When did Grandfather buy the tree? (Idea: *When Pablo's mother said she was going to adopt a baby.*) Why did Grandfather buy the tree? (Idea: *For his grandson.*) That's right; he bought the tree to celebrate his grandson coming into their family. Why didn't Grandfather plant the tree? (Idea: *He was waiting for the baby to come.*)

Pages 15–16. Why wouldn't Grandfather leave the tree in the front yard near the sidewalk? (Idea: *It was too noisy.*) Why wouldn't Grandfather leave the tree in the rose garden? (Idea: *There were too many thorns.*)

Pages 17–18. What did Grandfather do to get ready to welcome Pablo into their family? (Idea: *He washed his face; he combed his hair; he put the tree by the front door.*)

Pages 19–20. (Point to the illustration of Pablo on page 20.) Why does Pablo have his eyes closed and his arms around himself? (Idea: *He is imagining his mother lifting him out of the car.*)

Pages 21–22. What did Grandfather do after he held Pablo? (Idea: *He planted his tree in the sun.*)

Page 23. What did Grandfather hang on the tree on Pablo's first birthday, the year he turned one? *Yellow, orange, and red streamers.* What did Pablo do when he saw the streamers? (Idea: *He grabbed them in his fist.*)

Page 24. What did Grandfather hang on the tree on Pablo's second birthday, the year he turned two? *Different-colored balloons.* What did Pablo do when he saw the balloons? (Ideas: *He ran around and around the tree; he touched the balloons when Grandfather lifted him up.*)

Page 25. What did Grandfather hang on the tree on Pablo's third birthday, the year he turned three? *Paper lanterns.*

Page 26. What did Lito hang on the tree on Pablo's fourth birthday, the year he turned four? *Tiny birdcages.* What does Lito hang on the tree on Pablo's tree this year? *Bells and wind chimes.* So how old is Pablo this year? *Five.* That's right; this is Pablo's fifth birthday.

Page 27. What does Pablo do when he sees the bells and chimes? (Ideas: *He races around and around the tree; he touches the branches and makes them ring.*)

Page 28–29. What question does Pablo ask? *"What will you put on my tree next year, Lito?"* What is Grandfather's answer? (Idea: *He chuckles and winks and says, "Pablo, that's a surprise."*) Do you think Grandfather has already decided what to put on Pablo's tree on his sixth birthday, the year he turns six?

Why do you think Pablo's grandfather chose to plant a tree when Pablo was born? (Idea: *Pablo and the tree would grow bigger and stronger together.*)

(**Note:** If children have difficulty identifying the connection between Pablo and the tree, ask these leading questions:)

What size was the tree when Pablo was adopted? (Idea: *It was small.*)

What happened to Pablo each year as he grew older? (Ideas: *He grew bigger and stronger; he could do more things.*)

What happened to Pablo's tree each year as it grew older? (Ideas: *The tree grew bigger and stronger; the branches could hold heavier things.*)

Review Vocabulary

(Display the Picture Vocabulary Cards. Point to each card as you say the word. Ask children to repeat each word after you.) These pictures show **adopt, wonder, nursery,** and **chuckles.**

- What word means "laughs quietly"? *Chuckles.*
- What word means to "think about something, either because you are interested in it and want to know more or because you are worried about it"? *Wonder.*
- What word means "a place where plants are grown so they can be sold"? *Nursery.*
- What word means "get a child who doesn't have a family and make that child your own son or daughter"? *Adopt.*

Extend Vocabulary

◎ ◄ Nursery.

In the story *Pablo's Tree,* we learned that a nursery is a place where plants are grown so they can be sold. Say the word that means "a place where plants are grown so they can be sold." *Nursery.*

Raise your hand if you can tell us a sentence that uses **nursery** as a naming word that means "a place where plants are grown so they can be sold." (Call on several children. If they do not use complete sentences, restate their examples as sentences. Have the class repeat the sentences.)

Here's a new way to use the word **nursery.**

- **The baby slept in the nursery.** Say the sentence.
- **All the children's toys were kept in the nursery.** Say the sentence.
- **He painted pictures of animals on the walls of the nursery.** Say the sentence.

In these sentences, **nursery** is a naming word that means **a room in your house where babies and young children sleep or play.** What word means "a room in your house where babies and young children sleep or play"? *Nursery.*

Raise your hand if you can tell us a sentence that uses **nursery** as naming word that means "a room in your house where babies and young children sleep or play." (Call on several children. If they do not use complete sentences, restate their examples as sentences. Have the class repeat the sentences.)

Present Expanded Target Vocabulary
◎ ◄ Tradition.

In the story, Pablo's grandfather always decorates Pablo's tree for his birthday. Pablo always spends the night after his birthday at his grandfather's house. They always sit under Pablo's tree. They always play with Pablo's new toys. These are things they do every year. Pablo expects that he and his grandfather will do these things. Something you always do, or expect to always do, is a tradition. **Tradition.** Say the word. *Tradition.*

Tradition is a naming word. It names a thing. What kind of word is **tradition?** *A naming word.*

A tradition is something you always do or expect to always do. Say the word that means "something you always do or expect to always do." *Tradition.*

I'll tell about some things people do. If those things are traditions, say, "Tradition." If not, don't say anything.

- Every year the whole family had a picnic at the lake on the Fourth of July. *Tradition.*
- Father always read to the family on Sunday evening. *Tradition.*
- Once in a while, Elmo would eat a cheese sandwich for lunch.
- Every time she visits, my grandmother tells us the same story she told my mother when she was a child. *Tradition.*
- At our house, we go camping for vacation every year. *Tradition.*

We never do the same thing twice.

What naming word means "something you always do or expect to always do"? *Tradition.*

(Share one of your family's traditions with children. Suggestions: Special foods you always serve on certain occasions; times when everyone gets together; a family picnic; special activities when your family gets together; a birthday tradition.) Raise your hand if you would like to share one of your family's traditions.

◎◄ Decorations.

Let's think about the story. On Pablo's birthday, his grandfather always puts special things on Pablo's tree to make it more beautiful. The things he puts on the tree are called decorations. **Decorations.** Say the word. *Decorations.*

Decorations is a naming word. It names things. What kind of word is **decorations?** *A naming word.*

Decorations are the things someone uses to make something else more beautiful. What word means "the things someone uses to make something else more beautiful"? *Decorations.*

I'll name some things. If the things I name are decorations, say, "Decorations." If not, don't say anything.

- Jonah put up balloons for his birthday party. *Decorations.*
- Mom put a colorful cloth and flowers on the table. *Decorations.*
- The children hung sun catchers in the windows to make them beautiful. *Decorations.*
- The party room was completely bare.
- The teacher hung up our artwork to make our classroom look prettier. *Decorations.*
- There were no candles or icing on Flora's cake.

What naming word means "the things someone uses to make something else more beautiful"? *Decorations.*

If we were going to have a class party, what decorations would you like to put up? (Encourage children to start their answers with the words "For our class party, the decorations I would like to put up would be _____.")

DAY 3

Preparation: Activity Sheet, BLM 17b. Children will need crayons.

Retell Story

(Show the pictures on the following pages from the story, and call on a child to tell what's happening. Call on a different child for each section.)

Today I'll show you the pictures Cecily Lang made for the story *Pablo's Tree.* As I show you the pictures, I'll call on one of you to tell the class that part of the story.

Pages 1–5. Tell what happens at the **beginning** of the story.

Pages 6–27. Tell what happens in the **middle** of the story. (Encourage use of target words when appropriate. Model use as necessary.)

Pages 28–29. Tell what happens at the **end** of the story.

How do you know that Grandfather loves Pablo? (Ideas: *He decorates the tree for Pablo every year; he invites Pablo to come to spend the day and night after his birthday; he plays with Pablo.*)

How do you know Pablo loves his grandfather? (Ideas: *He likes to spend time playing with him; he is excited when he sees him; he can hardly wait until next year for his birthday tradition.*)

Review Chew the Fat

Today you will play Chew the Fat. Remember, a long time ago, when people wanted to just sit and talk about things that were happening in their lives, they would sit and "chew the fat."

In this game, I will say some sentences with our vocabulary words in them. If I use the vocabulary word correctly, say, "Well done." If I use the word incorrectly, say, "Chew the fat." That means that you want to talk about how I used the word. I'll say the beginning of the sentence again. If you can make the sentence end so that it makes sense, you'll get a point. If you can't, I get the point.

Let's practice: Ted and Alice wanted to **adopt** a child because . . . the child had parents already. *Chew the fat.* Let's chew the fat. The first part of the sentence stays the same. I'll say the first part. Ted and Alice wanted to adopt a child because . . . How can we finish the sentence so it makes sense? (Idea: *The child had no parents.*) Let's say the whole sentence together now. *Ted and Alice wanted to adopt a child because the child had no parents.* Well done! I'm glad we chewed the fat!

Let's do another one together. Bob and Carol went to the **nursery** because . . . they wanted to buy a new car. *Chew the fat.* The first part of the sentence stays the same. I'll say the first part. Bob and Carol went to the nursery because . . . How can we finish the sentence so that it makes sense? (Idea: *They wanted to buy a new plant.*) Let's say the whole sentence now. *Bob and Carol went to the nursery because they wanted to buy a new plant.* Well done! I'm glad we chewed the fat!

Now you're ready to play the game.

(Draw a T-chart on the board for keeping score. Children earn one point for each correct answer. If they make an error, work with them to construct a correct sentence. Record one point for yourself, and repeat missed words at the end of the game.)

- Harvey heard Larry's **chuckles** when . . . Harvey told a sad story. *Chew the fat.* I'll say the first part of the sentence again. Harvey heard Larry's chuckles when . . . (Idea: *Harvey told a funny story.*) Let's say the whole sentence together. *Harvey heard Larry's chuckles when Harvey told a funny story.* Well done! I'm glad we chewed the fat!
- Sassi **wondered** how computers work because . . . she wasn't interested in them. *Chew the fat.* I'll say the first part of the sentence again. Sassi wondered how computers work because . . . (Idea: *She was interested in them.*) Let's say the whole sentence together. *Sassi wondered how computers work because she was interested in them.* Well done! I'm glad we chewed the fat!
- It was a big outdoor store that sold plants, so . . . I knew it was a **nursery.** *Well done!*
- Harry and Maude wanted to **adopt** a child because . . . they already had too many children of their own. *Chew the fat.* I'll say the first part of the sentence again. Harry and Maude wanted to adopt a child because . . . (Idea: *They didn't have any children of their own.*) Let's say the whole sentence together. *Harry and Maude wanted to adopt a child because they didn't have any children of their own.* Well done!

- The babies all slept in the **nursery** because . . . it was a room for grown-ups. *Chew the fat.* I'll say the first part of the sentence again. The babies all slept in the nursery because . . . (Idea: *It was a room for babies.*) Let's say the whole sentence together. *The babies all slept in the nursery because it was a room for babies.* Well done!

(Count the points, and declare a winner.) You did a great job of playing Chew the Fat!

Adding Details (Activity Sheet)

(Review with children the decorations that are on Pablo's tree for each of his birthdays in the story. If they have difficulty remembering the decorations, show them pages 23 through 27.)

(Give each child a copy of the Activity Sheet, BLM 18b.) Today you will decorate Pablo's tree for all of his five birthdays. Then you can decide what decoration you think Grandfather will put on Pablo's tree for his sixth birthday and draw that decoration on his tree.

Touch the first tree. What decoration does Grandfather put on Pablo's tree on his first birthday? *Streamers.* Draw streamers on the tree that says *1.* (Pause.) (Repeat this process for the remaining trees. Ask children to color the pictures.)

DAY 4

Preparation: Prepare a sheet of chart paper, landscape direction, titled *Pablo's Tree.*

Underneath the title draw eight boxes connected by arrows.

See the Introduction for an example.

Record children's responses by writing the underlined words in the boxes.

Introduce Remember Story Patterns (Literary Analysis)

A pattern is an action or something that repeats in a certain way.

Watch me. I'll show you a touching pattern. (Touch your head twice, then your shoulders twice. Repeat the pattern once more.) Do the pattern with me. (Touch your head twice, then your shoulders twice, with children. Keep repeating the pattern until all children are following it.) I'll do the pattern once more. (Head, head, shoulders, shoulders, repeat once more.) Now it's your turn to do the pattern by yourself. (Pause.) You just repeated a touching pattern.

Watch me. I'll draw a pattern. (Draw a line, circle, circle, line, circle, circle pattern on the board in a horizontal line.) Say the pattern with me. (Say "line, circle, circle, line, circle, circle" with children.) I'll add to my pattern. (Add a line.) Now tell me what comes next in my pattern. *Circle.* Now tell me what comes next in my pattern. *Circle.* (Extend the pattern for two or three more repeats.) You just repeated a drawing pattern.

When authors write stories, they sometimes write in patterns.

The story *Papa, Do You Love Me?* has a pattern. What is that pattern? *Question, answer.*

Let's figure out the pattern for the story *Pablo's Tree.*

(Read aloud page 1, and quickly show the illustrations on pages 2 through 10. Read aloud page 12 and show the illustration.) When is this part of the story happening? (Ideas: *Now; right now; today; the day after Pablo's fifth birthday.*) What question does Grandfather ask? *"Pablo, do you remember the story of your tree?"* (Write on the chart *Today.*)

(Quickly show the illustrations on pages 13 through 16.) When is this part of the story happening? (Idea: *While the family was waiting for Pablo to come to their family.*) (Write on the chart *before Pablo came.*)

(Read pages 19 and 20. Quickly show the illustrations on pages 21 and 22.) When is this part of the story happening? (Ideas: *After Pablo came.*) (Write on the chart *after Pablo came.*)

(Quickly show the illustration on page 23.) When is this part of the story happening? (Idea: *On Pablo's first birthday.*) (Write on the chart *1.*)

(Quickly show the illustration on page 24.) When is this part of the story happening? (Idea: *On Pablo's second birthday.*) (Write on the chart *2.*)

(Quickly show the illustration on page 25.) When is this part of the story happening? (Idea: *On Pablo's third birthday.*) (Write on the chart *3.*)

(Quickly show the illustration on page 26.) When is this part of the story happening? (Idea: *On Pablo's fourth birthday.*) (Write on the chart *4.*)

(Quickly show the illustrations on pages 26 and 27.) When is this part of the story happening? (Idea: *Today; right now; on Pablo's fifth birthday.*) (Write on the chart *today.*)

Let's read the pattern. (Chime read the pattern with children.) Today, before Pablo came, after Pablo came, 1, 2, 3, 4, today.

This pattern starts today. Then Pablo remembers about before he came; after he came; when he was one, two, three, and four; and then the pattern ends at today. This pattern is called a remembering pattern. What kind of pattern does *Pablo's Tree* have? *A remembering pattern.*

Let's sing our new song that will help us remember about story patterns. (**Note:** The tune of this song is *If You're Happy and You Know It, Clap Your Hands.*)

(See the Introduction for the complete "Pattern Song.")

Listen while I sing the chorus:

There are patterns all around us if we look.
There are patterns all around us if we look.
There are patterns all around,
if we look they can be found.
There are patterns all around us if we look.

Now sing it with me.

Each time we sing the song, we start by singing the chorus. Every pattern that we learn will have a different verse about that pattern. I wonder if you will be able to detect the pattern in our song as we add more verses.

Let's sing a verse about the question-and-answer pattern we learned about in *Papa, Do You Love Me?* Listen while I sing the question-and-answer verse:

If your Papa asks a question, answer back.
If your Papa asks a question, answer back.
If your Papa asks a question,
Please allow a small suggestion:
If your Papa asks a question, answer back.

Let's sing it together now.

Now let's sing the chorus and then the first verse.

Now let's add a new verse to remember the remembering pattern we learned about in *Pablo's Tree.* Listen while I sing the verse:

> There's a pattern in remembering your life.
> There's a pattern in remembering your life.
> If you think about the past,
> Then your memories will last.
> There's a pattern in remembering your life.

Now sing it with me.

Now let's sing the verses we know. Remember, we start with the chorus. After each verse, we sing the chorus again. I wonder if you will detect the pattern we make as we sing the song.

Singing a song together is a very good way to remember the patterns we will learn!

Play Chew the Fat (Cumulative Review)

Today you will play Chew the Fat. Remember, a long time ago, when people wanted to just sit and talk about things that were happening in their lives, they would sit and "chew the fat."

In this game, I will say some sentences with our vocabulary words in them. If I use the vocabulary word correctly, say, "Well done." If I use the word incorrectly, say, "Chew the fat." That means you want to talk about how I used the word. I'll say the beginning of the sentence again. If you can make the sentence end so that it makes sense, you'll get a point. If you can't, I get the point.

Let's practice: Harry and Sally wanted to **adopt** a child because . . . they had four boys and two girls already. *Chew the fat.* Let's chew the fat. The first part of the sentence stays the same. I'll say the first part. Harry and Sally wanted to adopt a child because . . . How can we finish the sentence so it makes sense? (Idea: *They had no children of their own.*) Let's say the whole sentence together now. *Harry and Sally wanted to adopt a child because they had no children of their own.* Well done! I'm glad we chewed the fat!

Let's do another one together. Aunt Dorthea's visit is a **tradition** in our house because . . . she comes to visit once in a while. *Chew the fat.* The first part of the sentence stays the same. I'll say the first part. Aunt Dorthea's visit is a tradition in our house because . . . How can we finish the sentence so that it makes sense? (Idea: *She comes to visit every year.*) Let's say the whole sentence now. *Aunt Dorthea's visit is a tradition in our house because she comes to visit every year.* Well done! I'm glad we chewed the fat!

Now you're ready to play the game.

[T] (Draw a T-chart on the board for keeping score. Children earn one point for each correct answer. If they make an error, correct them as you normally would, and record one point for yourself. Repeat missed words at the end of the game.)

- The children wanted to have a surprise party for their teacher, so . . . they didn't put up any **decorations**. *Chew the fat.* I'll say the first part of the sentence again. The children wanted to have a surprise party for their teacher, so . . . (Idea: *They put up lots of decorations.*) Let's say the whole sentence together. *The children wanted to have a surprise party for their teacher, so they put up lots of decorations.* Well done! I'm glad we chewed the fat!

- We went to the **nursery** because . . . we needed a new rosebush for the front yard. *Well done!*

- Leslie **wondered** how machines worked because . . . he was interested in them. *Well done!*

- Mari **chuckled** when . . . Luke told her how he had made Dawn mad. *Chew the fat.* I'll say the first part of the sentence again. Mari chuckled when . . . (Idea: *Luke told her how he had made Dawn laugh.*) Let's say the whole sentence together. *Mari chuckled when Luke told her how he had made Dawn laugh.* Well done! I'm glad we chewed the fat!

- The babies play together in the **nursery** because . . . it is the place where police officers work. *Chew the fat.* I'll say the first part of the sentence again. The babies play together in the nursery because . . . (Idea: *It is the place where babies play.*) Let's say the whole sentence together. *The babies play together in the nursery because it is the place where babies play.* Well done!

- Bob was **bored** because . . . he had so many exciting things to do. *Chew the fat.* I'll say the first part of the sentence again. Bob was bored because . . . (Idea: *He had nothing to do.*) Let's say the whole sentence together. *Bob was bored because he had nothing to do.* Well done! I'm glad we chewed the fat!
- Lorne was acting **silly** when . . . he put on a funny hat and told funny jokes. *Well done!*
- Presidents' Day is a **tradition** because . . . we celebrate it every year. *Well done!*
- People want to **adopt** a child so . . . they can get a child who already has parents. *Chew the fat.* I'll say the first part of the sentence again. People want to adopt a child so . . . (Idea: *They can get a child who has no parents.*) Let's say the whole sentence together. *People want to adopt a child so they can get a child who has no parents.* Well done! I'm glad we chewed the fat!
- When farmers **harvest** their crops, they . . . plant the seeds. *Chew the fat.* I'll say the first part of the sentence again. When farmers harvest their crops, they . . . (Idea: *Gather the crops for food.*) Let's say the whole sentence together. *When farmers harvest their crops, they gather the crops for food.* Well done!

(Count the points, and declare a winner.)
You did a great job of playing Chew the Fat!

DAY 5

Preparation: Happy Face Game Test Sheet, BLM B.

Retell Story to a Partner

(Assign each child a partner, and ask the partners to take turns telling part of the story each time you turn to a new set of pages. Encourage use of target words when appropriate.)

Today I'll show you the pictures Cecily Lang made for the story *Pablo's Tree.* As I show you the pictures, you and your partner will take turns telling part of the story.

Pages 1–5. Tell what happens at the **beginning** of the story.

Pages 6–27. Tell what happens in the **middle** of the story.

Pages 28–29. Tell what happens at the **end** of the story.

Assess Vocabulary

 (Hold up a copy of the Happy Face Game Test Sheet, BLM B.)

Today you're going to play the Happy Face Game. When you play the Happy Face Game, it helps me know how well you know the hard words you are learning.

If I say something true, color the happy face. What will you do if I say something true? *Color the happy face.*

If I say something false, color the sad face. What will you do if I say something false? *Color the sad face.*

Listen carefully to each item I say. Don't let me trick you!

Item 1: **Decorations** are used to make something look prettier than it usually looks. *True.*

Item 2: If you adopt a baby, you get him or her because the baby has no **parents.** *True.*

Item 3: A **tradition** is something you do every year. *True.*

Item 4: In a **nursery,** you will find plants of many different kinds. *True.*

Item 5: **Ingredients** are the things you need to make something. *True.*

Item 6: You will find lots of trees in a **meadow.** *False.*

Item 7: Babies sleep in a **nursery.** *True.*

Item 8: If you **wonder** about something, it means you are interested in it. *True.*

Item 9: **Chuckles** can mean that you are upset or angry. *False.*

Item 10: If a mouse **squeaked,** it used a very high voice. *True.*

You did a great job of playing the Happy Face Game!

(Score children's work later. Scores of 9 out of 10 indicate mastery. If a child does not achieve mastery, insert the missed words in the games in the next week's lessons. Retest those children individually on the missed items before they take the next mastery test.)

Extensions

Read a Story as a Reward

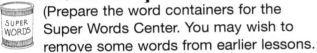(Display several of the books you have read since the beginning of the program. Allow children to choose which book they would like you to read aloud to them as a reward for their hard work.)

(Read story to children for enjoyment with minimal interruptions.)

Present the Super Words Center

(Prepare the word containers for the Super Words Center. You may wish to remove some words from earlier lessons. Choose words children have mastered.) (See the Introduction for instructions on how to set up and use the Super Words Center.)

(Add the new Picture Vocabulary Cards to words from the previous weeks. Show children one of the word containers. If they need more guidance, role-play with two or three children as a demonstration.)

Today I will remind you about how to play a game called What's New.

Let's think about how we work with our words in the Super Words Center.

You will work with a partner in the Super Words Center. Whom will you work with in the center? *A partner.*

First, one partner will draw four word cards out of the container and put them on the table so both partners can see. What do you do first? (Idea: *Draw four cards out of the container and put them on the table so both partners can see.*)

Next you will take turns looking at the cards and saying the words the pictures show. What do you do next? (Idea: *We take turns looking at the cards and saying the words the pictures show.*)

Next, partner 2 looks away while partner 1 takes one of the four cards and places it back in the container. Then partner 1 draws a new card from the container and places it on the table with the other three. Watch while I show you what I mean. (Demonstrate this process with a child as your partner.) When you put down the new card, it's a good idea to mix the cards so they aren't in the same places anymore. (Demonstrate as you go.)

Now partner 1 says, "What's new?" Partner 2 has to use his or her eyes and brain and say what new word card has been put down. If partner 2 is correct, he or she gets a point. If partner 2 is not correct, partner 1 gets the point. (Demonstrate as you go.)

Next, partner 2 has a turn to choose four different cards, and the game starts again. What happens next? (Idea: *Partner 2 has a turn to choose four different cards, and the game starts again.*)

Have fun playing What's New!

Preparation: You will need *Dreams* for each day's lesson.

Number the pages of the story to assist you in asking questions at appropriate points.

Post a copy of the Vocabulary Tally Sheet, BLM A, with this week's Picture Vocabulary Cards attached.

Each child will need the Homework Sheet, BLM 19a.

DAY 1

Introduce Book

Today's book is called *Dreams*. What's the title of this week's book? *Dreams.*

This book was written by Ezra Jack Keats. Who's the author of *Dreams*? *Ezra Jack Keats.*

Ezra Jack Keats also made the pictures for this book. Who's the illustrator of *Dreams*? *Ezra Jack Keats.* Who made the illustrations for this book? *Ezra Jack Keats.*

The cover of a book usually gives us some hints of what the book is about. Let's look at the front cover of *Dreams*. What do you see in the illustration? (Ideas: *A boy sitting in a window; he is holding a mouse in his hand; he's watching the mouse; he's smiling.*)

(Assign each child a partner.) Remember, when you make a prediction about something, you say what you think will happen.

Get ready to make some predictions to your partner about this book. Use the information from the cover to help you.

(Ask the following questions, allowing sufficient time for children to share their predictions with their partners.)

• Who are the characters in this story? (Whom do you think this story is about?)

Dreams

author: Ezra Jack Keats • illustrator: Ezra Jack Keats

Target Vocabulary

Tier II	Tier III
gasp	pattern
finally	(linear)
howled	
dashed	
*attack	
*rescue	

*Expanded Target Vocabulary Word

• What is the boy holding?
• Where do you think the story happens?
• When do you think the story happens?
• Why do you think the boy is smiling?
• How do you think he got the mouse? Do you think this story is about a real person and a real mouse? Tell why or why not.

(Call on several children to share their predictions with the class.)

Take a Picture Walk

We are going to take a picture walk through this book. Remember, when we take a picture walk, we look at the pictures and tell what we think will happen in the story.

(Show the illustrations on the following pages, and ask the specified questions.)

Pages 1–2. What kind of a building do the children live in? (Idea: *An apartment.*) Who do you think the girl is? (Ideas: *A friend; a neighbor.*) What do you think the boy is saying to her? (Idea: *Look at my mouse.*) When does this part of the story happen? (Ideas: *At sunset; in the evening; late afternoon.*) How do you know? (Idea: *The sky is orange and yellow.*)

Pages 3–4. When does this part of the story happen? (Idea: *At night.*) How do you know? (Idea: *The sky is darker.*) What things are happening in the different apartments? (Ideas: *A mother is kissing her baby; a girl is waving; a parrot is in its cage; someone is watering a* *flower; a dog is looking out a window; a little girl is pointing to the dog.*)

Pages 5–6. What do you think the people are doing? (Idea: *Sleeping.*) (Point to the window that is yellow and orange.) What do you think is happening in this apartment? Why do you think the mouse is sitting on the window ledge?

Pages 7–8. What do you think is happening in all of the apartments except the one with the mouse? Why do you think so? (Point to the window that is dark.) What do you think is happening in this apartment?

Pages 9–10. When do you think this part of the story happens? (Idea: *At night.*) Why do you think so? (Idea: *The sky is dark.*) (Point to the window that is dark.) What do you think is happening in this apartment? (Ideas: *The people are asleep; the people aren't home.*)

Pages 11–12. What is the boy doing? (Idea: *Looking out the window.*)

Pages 13–14. What does the boy see? (Ideas: *A dog is chasing a cat; a cat is in a box.*) How do you think the boy is feeling? (Ideas: *Worried; anxious.*)

Pages 15–16. What is happening here? (Ideas: *The mouse is falling; the boy is watching.*)

Pages 17–18. What is happening to the mouse? (Idea: *It's falling.*) (Point to the shadow on the wall.) What is this? (Idea: *The mouse's shadow.*) Wow, that shadow is way bigger than the mouse!

Pages 19–20. What is happening to the mouse? (Idea: *It's still falling.*) (Point to the shadow on the wall.) What is happening to the mouse's shadow? (Idea: *It's getting bigger and bigger.*) Wow, that shadow is enormous!

Pages 21–22. What's happening here? (Idea: *The dog is running away.*) Why do you think the dog is running away? (Ideas: *It's scared; it's terrified.*) What do you think scared the dog? (Ideas: *The huge shadow; the enormous shadow.*) I think the dog was terrified by that enormous shadow.

Pages 23–24. Why do you think the boy is rubbing his head? (Ideas: *He's surprised by what he saw; he's amazed the mouse could scare away a big dog.*)

Pages 25–26. When does this part of the story happen? (Ideas: *In the morning; at dawn; at sunrise.*) How do you know? (Idea: *The sky is getting lighter.*) What is happening in the different apartments? (Ideas: *A parrot is in its cage; a girl is brushing her hair; someone is getting up; someone is peeking out the window; a girl is playing with a dog; a woman is wearing an apron; maybe she is making breakfast.*) (Point to the window that is yellow and pink.) What do you think is happening in this apartment? Why do you think so?

Pages 27–28. What is happening here? *Roberto is sleeping.*

Now that we've finished our picture walk, it's your turn to ask me some questions. What would you like to know about the story? (Accept questions. If children tell about the pictures or the story instead of asking questions, prompt them to ask a question.) Ask me a why question. Ask me a how question.

Read Story Aloud
(Read story aloud to children with minimal interruptions.)

In the next lesson, we will read the story again, and I will ask you some questions.

Present Target Vocabulary
🎯 *Gasp.*

In the story, when Roberto looks out his window, what he sees down in the street makes him gasp. That means he takes a short, quick breath in through his mouth because he is shocked by what he sees. **Gasp.** Say the word. *Gasp.*

Gasp is an action word. It tells what someone does. What kind of word is **gasp**? *An action word.*

When you gasp, you take a short, quick breath in through your mouth because you are shocked, surprised, or hurt. Say the word that means to "take a short, quick breath in through your mouth because you are shocked, surprised, or hurt." *Gasp.*

I'll pretend my best friend who lives in India just walked into our classroom. I'll gasp because I'm surprised. Watch me. (Take a short, quick breath in through your mouth. Have a surprised expression on your face.)

I'll pretend I stubbed my toe on the leg of my desk. I'll gasp because I'm hurt. Watch me. (Take a short, quick breath in through your mouth. Have a hurt expression on your face.)

I'll pretend I just saw a car crash. I'll gasp because I'm shocked. Watch me. (Take a short, quick breath in through your mouth. Have a shocked expression on your face.)

It's your turn. Gasp because you have just heard something bad that shocked you. (Pause.) Gasp because you have just seen something that surprised you. (Pause.) Gasp because you have hurt yourself. (Pause.)

(Correct any incorrect responses, and repeat the item at the end of the sequence.)

Let's think about some times when someone might gasp. I'll tell about a time. If you think someone would gasp, say, "Gasp." If not, don't say anything.

- Antonio saw an elephant walking down his street. *Gasp.*
- John saw Rita slip and hurt her back badly. *Gasp.*
- Brenna relaxed in the bathtub.
- The policeman saw a man parking his car on the sidewalk. *Gasp.*
- This is a noisy bell.
- Jack couldn't believe how big the giant was. *Gasp.*

What action word means to "take a short, quick breath in through your mouth because you are shocked, surprised, or hurt"? *Gasp.*

◎—< Finally.

In the story Roberto can't sleep. Finally he gets up and goes to the window. That means after a long, long time, Roberto gets up and goes to the window. **Finally.** Say the word. *Finally.*

Finally is a describing word. It tells about when something happened. What kind of word is **finally?** *A describing word.*

If you finally do something, you do it after waiting for a long, long time. Say the word that means "after a long, long time." *Finally.*

(Correct any incorrect responses, and repeat the item at the end of the sequence.)

Let's think about some times when someone finally might do something. I'll tell about a time. If someone finally might do something, say, "Finally." If not, don't say anything.

- Jan waited a long, long time before she told her mother she had lost her new shoes. *Finally.*
- Kimberly waited and waited at the hospital before someone checked her sore foot. *Finally.*
- Josie waited for five weeks for her present to come by mail. *Finally.*
- The pizza came before we knew it.
- The delivery man was the fastest we had ever seen.
- The train was so long that we had to wait almost forever for it to pass. *Finally.*

What describing word means "after a long, long time"? *Finally.*

◎—< Howled.

In the story, the dog howled and ran away. That means the dog made a long, loud crying sound. Animals such as wolves, dogs, and monkeys howl. **Howled.** Say the word. *Howled.*

Howled is an action word. It tells what animals like a wolf, dog, or monkey did. What kind of word is **howled?** *An action word.*

It's my turn. I'll howl like a wolf. (Make a howling sound.) Your turn; howl like a wolf. (Pause.)

It's my turn. I'll howl like a dog. (Make a howling sound.) Your turn; howl like a dog. (Pause.)

If an animal like a wolf, dog, or monkey howled, it made a long, loud crying sound. Say the word that means "made a long, loud crying sound an animal like a wolf, dog, or monkey would make." *Howled.*

(Correct any incorrect responses, and repeat the item at the end of the sequence.)

Let's think about some times when an animal might have howled. I'll tell about a time. If you might have heard an animal howl, say, "Howled." If not, don't say anything.

- The wolf made a long, loud crying sound when it saw the moon. *Howled.*
- The lonely dog was tied up in the back yard. *Howled.*

- The coyotes in the forest made long, loud crying sounds when the sun rose. *Howled.*
- The frog said, "Ribbit!"
- The monkeys were very noisy. *Howled.*
- The mother bear and her cubs were eating blueberries.

What action word means "made a long, loud crying sound an animal like a wolf, dog, or monkey would make"? *Howled.*

 Dashed.

In the story, the cat dashed across the street and jumped through Archie's open window. That means the cat ran across the street as fast as it could go. **Dashed.** Say the word. *Dashed.*

Dashed is an action word. It tells about how someone or something moved. What kind of word is **dashed?** *An action word.*

If you dashed, you ran as fast as you could go. Say the word that means "ran as fast as you could go." *Dashed.*

(Correct any incorrect responses, and repeat the item at the end of the sequence.)

Let's think about some times when someone or something might dash. I'll tell about a time. If you think the person or animal would have dashed, say, "Dashed." If not, don't say anything.

- When his mother called him, he hurried into the house right away. *Dashed.*
- When Elton heard the announcer, he ran on stage as fast as he could. *Dashed.*
- Eric took his time walking to the music store.
- I learned to walk slowly at the pool so I wouldn't slip and fall.
- The squirrel ran up the tree to get away from the cat. *Dashed.*
- Why hurry? We have lots of time!

What action word means "ran as fast as you could go"? *Dashed.*

Present Vocabulary Tally Sheet
(See Week 1, page 3, for instructions.)

Assign Homework
(Homework Sheet, BLM 19a: See the Introduction for homework instructions.)

Preparation: Picture Vocabulary Cards for *gasp, finally, howled,* and *dashed.*

Read and Discuss Story

(Read story aloud to children. Ask the following questions at the specified points in the story.)

Page 2. When does this part of the story happen? (Idea: *After supper.*) Who is the boy holding the mouse? *Roberto.* Who is the girl he is talking to? *Amy.* Is the mouse real? *No.* What is the mouse made of? *Paper.* What question does Amy ask? *Does it do anything?* What is Roberto's answer? *I don't know.*

Page 4. Where does this story take place? (Idea: *In the city.*) Where does everyone go? (Idea: *To bed.*)

Page 6. What apartment do you think the one person who is dreaming lives in? (Idea: *The one with the window painted orange and yellow.*)

Page 8. Who do you think is the one person who isn't dreaming? (Idea: *Roberto.*) All the other people are dreaming. How does Ezra Jack Keats show that the people are dreaming? (Idea: *He painted bright colors in their windows.*) Sometimes artists paint pictures that don't look like real things; they use colors to make you think about things. (Point to the window in the top row that is blue, green, and white.) This picture makes me think of waves and seaweed, so I think this person might be dreaming about the ocean. What does this picture make you think of? (Ideas: *A storm; a waterfall.*) So what might this person be dreaming about? (Repeat this process for the other two windows in the top row and the four windows in the middle row. There are no right or wrong answers to these questions. Children are giving their personal impressions of the paintings.)

Page 10. What is Roberto's problem? (Idea: *He can't fall asleep.*) How do we know it is getting later and later? (Idea: *Ezra Jack Keats painted the sky darker and darker.*)

Page 12. What does Roberto do when he looks down in the street? (Idea: *He gasps.*) Everybody gasp like Roberto did. (Pause.) That's right; he is really shocked by what he sees!

Page 14. What does Roberto see? (Idea: *A dog has trapped Archie's cat in a box.*)

Page 16. Does Roberto push the paper mouse off the window on purpose? *No.* That's right; it's an accident.

Pages 18–22. What scares away the dog? (Idea: *The paper mouse's shadow.*) The mouse's shadow gets bigger and bigger because the mouse gets closer and closer to the light. (You may wish to use a flashlight to show children how shadows get bigger the closer they are to the light.) Where do you think the light is coming from? (Idea: *A streetlight.*)

Page 24. Where does the cat go? (Idea: *Into Archie's apartment; through Archie's open window.*) What does Roberto mean when he says, "That was some mouse!" (Ideas: *That was an amazing mouse; that little paper mouse scared away that big dog.*)

Pages 26–28. Who is the only person who doesn't get up in the morning? *Roberto.* Look at the illustration. What do you think Roberto is doing? (Idea: *Dreaming.*) What do you think Roberto is dreaming about?

At the beginning of the story, what question does Amy ask? *Does the paper mouse do anything?* What is Roberto's answer? *I don't know.* What do you think Roberto would tell Amy now? (Idea: *It can save a cat from a dog.*)

Review Vocabulary

(Display the Picture Vocabulary Cards. Point to each card as you say the word. Ask children to repeat each word after you.) These pictures show **gasp, finally, howled,** and **dashed.**

- What word means "made a long, loud crying sound an animal like a wolf, dog, or monkey would make"? *Howled.*
- What word means "ran as fast as it could go"? *Dashed.*
- What word means "after a long, long time"? *Finally.*

- What word means "take a short, quick breath in through your mouth because you are shocked, surprised, or hurt"? *Gasp.*

Extend Vocabulary
◎― Howled.

In the story *Dreams,* we learned that **howled** tells about making a long, loud crying sound an animal like a wolf, dog, or monkey would make. Say the word that means "made a long, loud crying sound an animal like a wolf, dog, or monkey would make." *Howled.*

Raise your hand if you can tell us a sentence that uses **howled** as an action word that means "made a long, loud crying sound an animal like a wolf, dog, or monkey would make." (Call on several children. If they don't use complete sentences, restate their examples as sentences. Have the class repeat the sentences.)

Here's a new way to use the word **howled.**

- **The little girl howled when she skinned her knee.** Say the sentence.
- **The boys howled when their mother sent them to their rooms.** Say the sentence.
- **The baby howled when his brother took away his rattle.** Say the sentence.

In these sentences, **howled** is an action word that means **you made a long, loud cry because you were hurt, unhappy, or angry.** What word means "made a long, loud crying sound because you were hurt, unhappy, or angry"? *Howled.*

Raise your hand if you can tell us a sentence that uses **howled** as an action word that means "made a long, loud cry because you were hurt, unhappy, or angry." (Call on several children. If they don't use complete sentences, restate their examples as sentences. Have the class repeat the sentences.)

Present Expanded Target Vocabulary
◎― Attack.

In the story *Dreams,* Roberto sees that the big dog has chased Archie's cat into a box. The big dog is snarling. Roberto is worried that the big dog will hurt the cat. Roberto is worried that the big dog will attack the cat. **Attack.** Say the word. *Attack.*

Attack is an action word. It tells what someone or something does. What kind of word is **attack?** *An action word.*

When people or animals attack, they try to hurt someone or something. Say the word that means "try to hurt someone or something." *Attack.*

I'll tell about some people or animals. If someone or something is trying to hurt those people or animals, say, "Attack." If not, don't say anything.

- The lion chases the antelope and drags it to the ground. *Attack.*
- The cat jumps and tries to hurt the dog. *Attack.*
- The mother bear tries to protect her baby cubs. *Attack.*
- Rod ignores the alligator as he walks by.
- Sarah howls as the mean dog tries to hurt her. *Attack.*
- The tiger turns and walks away.

What action word means "try to hurt someone or something"? *Attack.*

⊚⇐ *Rescue.*

In the story, when Roberto sees the dog snarling at Archie's cat, Roberto wants to do something to get the cat away from the dog and save it. He wants to rescue the cat. **Rescue.** Say the word. *Rescue.*

Rescue is an action word. It tells what someone does. What kind of word is **rescue?** *An action word.*

When you rescue people or animals, you get them away from danger and save them. Say the word that means "get people or animals away from danger and save them." *Rescue.*

I'll tell about some people or animals. If those people or animals are in danger and you would want to save them, say, "Rescue." If not, don't say anything.

- Nadia's kitten was stuck up in a tree. *Rescue.*
- Mick and Keith got the little girl out of the sinking boat. *Rescue.*
- Joel watched the baseball game.
- First the paramedics got the old man off the roof. *Rescue.*

- Landon sat quietly in his chair and didn't say much.
- It was time to make supper.

What action word means "get people or animals away from danger and save them"? *Rescue.*

DAY 3

Preparation: Activity Sheet, BLM 19b. Children will need crayons.

Retell Story

(Show the pictures on the following pages from the story, and call on a child to tell what's happening. Call on a different child for each section.)

Today I'll show you the pictures Ezra Jack Keats made for the story *Dreams.* As I show you the pictures, I'll call on one of you to tell the class that part of the story.

Pages 1–2. Tell what happens at the **beginning** of the story.

Pages 3–24. Tell what happens in the **middle** of the story. (Encourage use of target words when appropriate. Model use as necessary.)

Pages 25–28. Tell what happens at the **end** of the story.

If you were going to use just colors to paint one of your dreams, what colors would you use? (Call on several children. Encourage the children to start their answers with the words "I would use _____ to paint my dream because my dream is _____.")

Review Chew the Fat

Today you will play Chew the Fat. Remember, a long time ago, when people wanted to just sit and talk about things that were happening in their lives, they would sit and "chew the fat."

In this game, I will say some sentences with our vocabulary words in them. If I use the vocabulary word correctly, say, "Well done." If I use the word incorrectly, say, "Chew the fat." That means that you want to talk about how I used the word. I'll say the beginning of the sentence again. If you can make the sentence end so that it makes sense, you'll get a point. If you can't, I get the point.

Let's practice: Jethro let out a **gasp** when . . . he saw a plant in the garden. *Chew the fat.* Let's chew the fat. The first part of the sentence stays the same. I'll say the first part. Jethro let out a gasp when . . . How can we finish the sentence so it makes sense? (Idea: *He saw a skyscraper in the garden.*) Let's say the whole sentence together now. *Jethro let out a gasp when he saw a skyscraper in the garden.* Well done! I'm glad we chewed the fat!

Let's do another one together. The poodle **dashed** into the street . . . very slowly. *Chew the fat.* The first part of the sentence stays the same. I'll say the first part. The poodle dashed into the street . . . How can we finish the sentence so that it makes sense? (Idea: *Very quickly.*) Let's say the whole sentence now. *The poodle dashed into the street very quickly.* Well done! I'm glad we chewed the fat!

Now you're ready to play the game.

(Draw a T-chart on the board for keeping score. Children earn one point for each correct answer. If they make an error, work with them to construct a correct sentence. Record one point for yourself, and repeat missed words at the end of the game.)

- Rick **howled** when . . . he saw the piano on the back of the truck. *Chew the fat.* I'll say the first part of the sentence again. Rick howled when . . . (Idea: *He saw the piano fall off the truck.*) Let's say the whole sentence together. *Rick howled when he saw the piano fall off the truck.*) Well done! I'm glad we chewed the fat!
- **"Finally,"** Cherisse said, . . . after she hadn't waited long at all for her ice cream. *Chew the fat.* I'll say the first part of the sentence again. "Finally," Cherisse said, . . . (Idea: *After she had waited a long time for her ice cream.*) Let's say the whole sentence together. *"Finally," Cherisse said after she had waited a long time for her ice cream.* Well done! I'm glad we chewed the fat!
- The coyote made a long, loud cry because . . . that's how they sound when they **howl.** *Well done!*
- The wolf decided to **attack** the sheep because . . . he was **not** hungry. *Chew the fat.*

I'll say the first part of the sentence again. The wolf decided to attack the sheep because . . . (Idea: *He was hungry.*) Let's say the whole sentence together. *The wolf decided to attack the sheep because he was hungry.* Well done!
- We didn't **rescue** the boaters because . . . their boat was sinking. *Chew the fat.* I'll say the first part of the sentence again. We didn't rescue the boaters because . . . (Idea: *Their boat wasn't sinking.*) Let's say the whole sentence together. *We didn't rescue the boaters because their boat wasn't sinking.* Well done!

(Count the points, and declare a winner.)
You did a great job of playing Chew the Fat!

Adding Details (Activity Sheet)

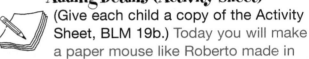
(Give each child a copy of the Activity Sheet, BLM 19b.) Today you will make a paper mouse like Roberto made in school. (Have children color the ears, tail, hands, and feet pink. Then have them cut out the pieces and glue or paste them together. These paper mice may be glued or pasted onto a sheet of marbleized paper.)

(You may wish to have children experiment with marbling, which is the technique Ezra Jack Keats used in creating the background for his illustrations as well as the dream windows. This is done by swirling oil-based printing ink on top of water, then laying paper on the ink and lifting the paper off. Search the web using the search words *making marbleized paper* and *Nancy Hands Kraus* for complete instructions.)

Introduce Linear Pattern (Literary Analysis)

A pattern is an action or something that repeats in a certain way.

Watch me. I'll show you a touching pattern. (Touch your head once, your shoulders twice, your knees once, and your shoulders once. Repeat the pattern once more.) Do the pattern with me. (Touch your head once, your shoulders twice, your knees once, and your shoulders once with children. Keep repeating the pattern until all children are following the pattern.) I'll do the pattern once more. (Head, shoulders, shoulders, knees, shoulders, repeat once more.) Now it's your turn to do the pattern by yourself. (Pause.) You just repeated a touching pattern.

Watch me. I'll draw a pattern. (Draw a triangle, triangle, circle, square, triangle, triangle, circle, square pattern on the board in a horizontal line.) Say the pattern with me. *Triangle, triangle, circle, square, triangle, triangle, circle, square.* I'll add to my pattern. (Add a triangle.) Now tell me what comes next in my pattern. *Triangle.* Now tell me what comes next in my pattern. *Circle.* Now tell me what comes next in my pattern. *Square.* (Extend the pattern for two or three more repeats.) You just repeated a drawing pattern.

When authors write stories, they sometimes write in patterns.

The story *Papa, Do You Love Me* has a pattern. What is that pattern? *Question, answer.*

The story *Pablo's Tree* has a pattern. What is that pattern? *Remembering.*

Let's see if we can figure out the pattern for this story. You tell me what happens in the story, and I'll write it down.

(Show the illustrations on the following pages and ask the specified questions.)

Pages 1–2. What two important things happen at the beginning of the story? (Ideas: _Roberto_ and _Amy_ are _talking; mouse_ is on _windowsill_.)

Pages 3–4. Then what happens? (Idea: _Everyone_ goes to _bed_.)

Pages 7–8. Then what happens? (Idea: _Nearly everyone_ is _dreaming_.)

Pages 11–14. Then what happens? (Idea: _Roberto_ sees the _dog_ chasing the _cat_.)

Pages 15–16. Then what happens? (Idea: _The mouse falls._)

Pages 17–22. Then what happens? (Idea: _The shadow scares_ the _dog_.)

Pages 25–28. Then what happens? (Idea: _Roberto_ is _dreaming_.)

(Point to the story map on the chart paper. Draw a line under the story map.) Look at the shape of this story. It's a line. This story starts and ends at a different place, so this story has a linear pattern. What kind of a pattern starts and ends at a different place? *A linear pattern.*

Let's sing our new song that will help us remember about story patterns. (**Note:** The tune of this song is *If You're Happy and You Know It, Clap Your Hands.*)

Each time we sing the song, we start by singing the chorus. Every pattern that we learn will have a different verse about that pattern. I wonder if you will be able to figure out the pattern in our song as we add more verses.

Let's sing everything we've learned so far.

(See the Introduction for the complete "Pattern Song.")

Now let's add a new verse to remember the linear pattern we learned about in *Dreams.* Listen while I sing the verse:

> There's a pattern when you're trav'ling in a line.
> There's a pattern when you're trav'ling in a line.
> When you travel in a line,
> Just say "linear"—that'll be fine!
> There's a pattern when you're trav'ling in a line.

Now sing it with me.

Now let's sing the verses we know. Remember, we start with the chorus. After each verse, we sing the chorus again. I wonder if you will figure out the pattern we make as we sing the song.

Singing a song together is a very good way to remember the patterns we will learn!

Play Chew the Fat (Cumulative Review)

Today you will play Chew the Fat. Remember, a long time ago, when people wanted to just sit and talk about things that were happening in their lives, they would sit and "chew the fat."

In this game, I will say some sentences with our vocabulary words in them. If I use the vocabulary word correctly, say, "Well done." If I use the word incorrectly, say, "Chew the fat." That means you want to talk about how I used the word. I'll say the beginning of the sentence again. If you can make the sentence end so that it makes sense, you'll get a point. If you can't, I get the point.

Let's practice: Mr. Stuart **finally** got his new car after . . . he did not wait at all. *Chew the fat.* Let's chew the fat. The first part of the sentence stays the same. I'll say the first part. Mr. Stuart finally got his new car after . . . How can we finish the sentence so it makes sense? (Idea: *He waited for a long time.*) Let's say the whole sentence together now. *Mr. Stuart finally got his new car after he waited for a long time.* Well done! I'm glad we chewed the fat!

Let's do another one together. The dog **howled** because . . . he wasn't hurt. *Chew the fat.* The first part of the sentence stays the same. I'll say the first part. The dog howled because . . . How can we finish the sentence so that it makes sense? (Idea: *He was hurt.*) Let's say the whole sentence now. *The dog howled because he was hurt.* Well done! I'm glad we chewed the fat!

Now you're ready to play the game.

(Draw a T-chart on the board for keeping score. Children earn one point for each correct answer. If they make an error, correct them as you normally would, and record one point for yourself. Repeat missed words at the end of the game.)

- I heard my teacher **gasp** when . . . I did not drop the big container of paint. *Chew the fat.* I'll say the first part of the sentence again. I heard my teacher gasp when . . . (Idea: *I dropped the big container of paint.*) Let's say the whole sentence together. *I heard my teacher gasp when I dropped the big*

container of paint. Well done! I'm glad we chewed the fat!

- The squirrel **dashed** across the road because . . . a car was coming. *Well done!*
- When the wolf **howled** . . . , he made a loud, long cry. *Well done!*
- The shark wanted to **attack** the school of fish because . . . it was not hungry. *Chew the fat.* I'll say the first part of the sentence again. The shark wanted to attack the school of fish because . . . (Idea: *It was hungry.*) Let's say the whole sentence together. *The shark wanted to attack the school of fish because it was hungry.* Well done! I'm glad we chewed the fat!
- The rock was **jagged,** and that means . . . it was smooth. *Chew the fat.* I'll say the first part of the sentence again. The rock was jagged, and that means . . . (Idea: *It had lots of sharp points.*) Let's say the whole sentence together. *The rock was jagged and that means it had lots of sharp points.* Well done!
- The kitten was purring because . . . it was **content.** *Well done!*
- If you **rescue** someone, . . . you save that person from danger. *Well done!*
- If the sky is **dreary,** that means . . . it is sunny with no clouds. *Chew the fat.* I'll say the first part of the sentence again. If the sky is dreary, that means . . . (Idea: *It is dark and cloudy.*) Let's say the whole sentence together. *If the sky is dreary, that means it is dark and cloudy.* Well done!
- If you say you **finally** got your lunch, it means that . . . you got it right away. *Chew the fat.* I'll say the first part of the sentence again. If you say you finally got your lunch, it means that . . . (Idea: *You had to wait a long time for it.*) Let's say the whole sentence together. *If you say you finally got your lunch, it means that you had to wait a long time for it.* Well done! I'm glad we chewed the fat!
- If Brad **howled** in pain when he stubbed his toe, he . . . spoke quietly. *Chew the fat.* I'll say the first part of the sentence again. If Brad howled in pain when he stubbed his toe, he . . . (Idea: *Made a long, loud cry.*) Let's say the whole sentence together. *If Brad howled in pain when he stubbed his toe, he made a long, loud cry.* Well done!

(Count the points, and declare a winner.)
You did a great job of playing Chew the Fat!

DAY 5

Preparation: Happy Face Game Test Sheet, BLM B.

Retell Story to a Partner

(Assign each child a partner, and ask the partners to take turns telling part of the story each time you turn to a new set of pages. Encourage use of target words when appropriate.)

Today I'll show you the pictures Ezra Jack Keats made for the story *Dreams.* As I show you the pictures, you and your partner will take turns telling part of the story.

Pages 1–2. Tell what happens at the **beginning** of the story.

Pages 3–24. Tell what happens in the **middle** of the story.

Pages 25–28. Tell what happens at the **end** of the story.

Assess Vocabulary

 (Hold up a copy of the Happy Face Game Test Sheet, BLM B.)

Today you're going to play the Happy Face Game. When you play the Happy Face Game, it helps me know how well you know the hard words you are learning.

If I say something true, color the happy face. What will you do if I say something true? *Color the happy face.*

If I say something false, color the sad face. What will you do if I say something false? *Color the sad face.*

Listen carefully to each item I say. Don't let me trick you!

Item 1: If you **gasp,** you might be surprised or shocked. *True.*

Item 2: If you **finally** got a bandage on your cut, it means you did **not** have to wait. *False.*

Item 3: If a dog **howled,** it might be because it was hurt. *True.*

Item 4: If I say that a plant **sprouted** from a seed, I mean that the plant grew from the seed. *True.*

Item 5: If a shark **attacks** a school of fish, it does **not** want to hurt them. *False.*

Item 6: A **rescue** boat saves people who are in danger on the water. *True.*

Item 7: When you are in a **bad mood,** you feel happy. *False.*

Item 8: A person's mom and dad are his or her **parents.** *True.*

Item 9: Coyotes **howled** at dawn because that's what coyotes do. *True.*

Item 10: When Archer **dashed** across the road, he ran very slowly. *False.*

You did a great job of playing the Happy Face Game!

(Score children's work later. Scores of 9 out of 10 indicate mastery. If a child does not achieve mastery, insert the missed words in the games in the next week's lessons. Retest those children individually on the missed items before they take the next mastery test.)

Extensions
Read a Story as a Reward

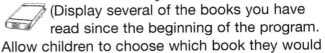 (Display several of the books you have read since the beginning of the program. Allow children to choose which book they would like you to read aloud to them as a reward for their hard work.)

(Read story to children for enjoyment with minimal interruptions.)

Present the Super Words Center

 (Prepare the word containers for the Super Words Center. You may wish to remove some words from earlier lessons. Choose words the children have mastered.

See the Introduction for instructions on how to set up and use the Super Words Center.)

(Add the new Picture Vocabulary Cards to the words from the previous weeks. Show children one of the word containers. If they need more guidance, role-play with two or three children as a demonstration.)

Today I will remind you how to play a game called What's New?

Let's think about how we work with our words in the Super Words Center.

You will work with a partner in the Super Words Center. Whom will you work with in the center? *A partner.*

First, one partner will draw four word cards out of the container and put them on the table so both partners can see. What do you do first? (Idea: *Draw four cards out of the container and put them on the table so both partners can see.*)

Next you will take turns looking at the cards and saying the words the pictures show. What do you do next? (Idea: *We take turns looking at the cards and saying the words the pictures show.*)

Next, partner 2 looks away while partner 1 takes one of the four cards and places it back in the container. Then partner 1 draws a new card from the container and places it on the table with the other three. Watch while I show you what I mean. (Demonstrate this process with a child as your partner.) When you put down the new card, it's a good idea to mix the cards so they aren't in the same places anymore. (Demonstrate as you go.)

Now partner 1 says, "What's new?" Partner 2 has to use his or her eyes and brain and say what new word card has been put down. If partner 2 is correct, he or she gets a point. If partner 2 is not correct, partner 1 gets the point. (Demonstrate as you go.)

Next, partner 2 has a turn to choose four different cards, and the game starts again. What happens next? (Idea: *Partner 2 has a turn to choose four different cards, and the game starts again.*)

Have fun playing What's New!

Wake Up, Farm!
author: Alvin Tresselt • illustrator: Carolyn Ewing

Preparation: You will need *Wake Up, Farm!* for each day's lesson.

You may wish to obtain recordings of farm animal sounds for this story. Use the search words *farm animal sounds* if you are using the Internet. CDs and cassette tapes are also available.

Number the pages of the story to assist you in asking questions at appropriate points.

Post a copy of the Vocabulary Tally Sheet, BLM A, with this week's Picture Vocabulary Cards attached.

Each child will need the Homework Sheet, BLM 20a.

Target Vocabulary

Tier II	Tier III
dim	pattern
root	(remember)
chattering	
impatient	
*dawn	
*active	

*Expanded Target Vocabulary Word

(Ask the following questions, allowing sufficient time for children to share their predictions with their partners.)

- Who is the main character in this story? (Whom do you think this story is about?)
- What do you think the boy is looking at?
- Where do you think the story happens?
- When do you think the story happens?
- Why do you think the boy is looking out the window?
- How many birds do you see in the barn window?
- Do you think this story is about a real person? Tell why or why not.

(Call on several children to share their predictions with the class.)

DAY 1

Introduce Book

This week's book is called *Wake Up, Farm!* What's the title of this week's book? *Wake Up, Farm!*

This book was written by Alvin Tresselt. Who's the author of *Wake Up, Farm! Alvin Tresselt.*

Carolyn Ewing made the pictures for this book. Who's the illustrator of *Wake Up, Farm! Carolyn Ewing.* Who made the illustrations for this book? *Carolyn Ewing.*

The cover of a book usually gives us some hints of what the book is about. Let's look at the front cover of *Wake Up, Farm!* What do you see in the illustration? (Ideas: *A boy is looking out a window; the sky looks like it's morning; there's a barn and a tractor.*)

(Assign each child a partner.) Remember, when you make a prediction about something, you say what you think will happen. Get ready to make some predictions to your partner about this book. Use the information from the cover to help you.

Take a Picture Walk

We are going to take a picture walk through this book. Remember, when we take a picture walk, we look at the pictures and tell what we think will happen in the story.

(Show the illustrations on the following pages, and ask the specified questions.)

Pages 1–2. When do you think the story begins? (Idea: *At night*.) What makes you think so? (Ideas: *The boy is sleeping; there are stars in the sky.*)

Pages 3–4. When does this part of the story happen? (Idea: *In the morning.*) What makes you think so? (Idea: *The sky is getting lighter*.) What is the rooster doing? (Ideas: *Crowing; saying "Cock-a-doodle-doo."*) What are the hens doing? (Ideas: *Sitting on their nests; standing in the doorway; standing on the ground.*)

Pages 5–6. What is the horse doing? (Ideas: *Licking her baby; nudging her baby; feeding her baby.*)

Pages 7–8. What are the ducks doing? (Ideas: *Waving their wings; standing on the edge of the pond; getting ready to go for a swim.*) What are the pigs doing? (Ideas: *Looking for food; snuffling; grunting.*)

Pages 9–10. What is the goose doing? (Idea: *Walking through the tall grass.*) What is the turkey doing? (Ideas: *Walking around; showing its tail feathers.*)

Pages 11–12. What is the donkey doing? (Ideas: *Standing by the fence; crying.*)

Pages 13–14. What are the sheep doing? (Idea: *Going into the field.*) What is the dog doing? (Ideas: *Watching the sheep; herding the sheep.*)

Pages 15–16. What are the pigeons doing? (Idea: *Flying.*)

Pages 17–18. (Point to the kitten on page 17.) What is this kitten doing? (Idea: *Jumping.*) What are the other cats doing? (Idea: *The mother cat is licking her baby; the babies are curled up with their mother.*)

Pages 19–20. What's happening here? (Ideas: *The dog is growling at the chipmunk; the chipmunk is looking at the dog.*)

Pages 21–22. What is the rabbit doing? (Idea: *Eating its carrots.*) What are the bees doing? (Ideas: *Buzzing around their hives; flying; making honey.*)

Pages 23–24. Why do you think the farmer has come into the cow barn? What are the cows doing? (Ideas: *The farmer will milk the cows; the cows are waiting to be fed.*)

Pages 25–26. What is the boy doing? (Ideas: *Waking up; calling out; yawning.*)

Pages 27–28. When do you think this part of the story is happening? (Idea: *In the morning.*) Where do you think the boy is going? (Idea: *To*

school.) What makes you think so? (Idea: *I see the school bus.*)

Now that we've finished our picture walk, it's your turn to ask me some questions. What would you like to know about the story? (Accept questions. If children tell about the pictures or the story instead of asking questions, prompt them to ask a question.) Ask me a who question. Ask me a why question.

Read Story Aloud
(Read story aloud to children with minimal interruptions.)

In the next lesson, we will read the story again, and I will ask you some questions.

Present Target Vocabulary

(**Note:** At this point in the program, children will be introduced to the concept of defining words using opposites. If they do not yet know the concept of opposites, you may wish to practice more concrete and familiar examples with them, such as hot/cold, up/down, big/little, empty/full, and so on.)

◎ Dim.

In the story, everything slept until "the stars grew dim and the moon sank in the west." That means everything slept until the stars were not bright. **Dim.** Say the word. *Dim.*

Dim is a describing word. It tells about what the stars looked like. What kind of word is **dim?** *A describing word.*

If something is dim, it is not bright. Dim and **bright** are opposites. That means they tell about the same kind of thing, but they are completely different in some way. Say the word that means "not bright." *Dim.* **Dim** and **bright** are opposites. **Dim** and **bright** are . . . *opposites.*

(Correct any incorrect responses, and repeat the item at the end of the sequence.)

Let's think about some things that might be **dim.** I'll tell about something. If you think that thing is dim, say, "Dim." If you think that thing is not dim, say, "Bright."

* There was only a little night-light on in the hallway. *Dim.*
* The sun shone on a hot summer day. *Bright.*

- We could not see much when we went into the cave. *Dim.*
- The flash on the camera hurt my eyes. *Bright.*
- Never look straight at the sun. *Bright.*
- It's hard to see when there is no moon. *Dim.*

What describing word means "not bright"? *Dim.*

◎◄ Root.

In the story, "The roly-poly pigs root about in their pen, looking for their breakfast." That means the pigs dig in their pen and turn over the dirt, looking for some food. Sometimes pigs even use their noses to help them root about looking for food. **Root.** Say the word. *Root.*

Root is an action word. It tells what something does. What kind of word is **root?** *An action word.*

When animals root, they dig and turn over dirt with paws or noses to find food. Say the word that means to "dig and turn over dirt with paws or noses to find food." *Root.*

Pretend you are a pig. Show me how you would root about. Don't forget to use your nose sometimes. (Pause.)

(Correct any incorrect responses, and repeat the item at the end of the sequence.)

Let's think about some times when an animal might root. I'll tell about an animal. If that animal is digging and turning over the dirt with paws or noses looking for food, say, "Root." If not, don't say anything.

- The anteater digs in the anthill looking for ants. *Root.*
- The bear digs under the rotten log looking for bugs. *Root.*
- We pick the cherries from Farmer Tresselt's trees.
- Mr. Keats drives to the market.
- "Pretend you're a pig digging with his nose!" cried the teacher. *Root.*
- The dog digs and turns over the dirt looking for her bone. *Root.*

What action word means to "dig and turn over dirt with paws or noses to find food"? *Root.*

◎◄ Chattering.

In the story, the dog "barks at a chattering chipmunk who is looking for a leftover tidbit in the feeding dish." That means the chipmunk is making lots of quick, short sounds. **Chattering.** Say the word. *Chattering.*

Chattering is a describing word. It tells about someone or something. What kind of word is **chattering?** *A describing word.*

If an animal or a bird is making lots of quick, short sounds, it is chattering. Say the word that tells about an animal that is making lots of quick, short sounds. *Chattering.*

(Correct any incorrect responses, and repeat the item at the end of the sequence.)

Let's think about some times when an animal might have been chattering. I'll tell about an animal. If you might have heard that animal making lots of quick, short sounds, say, "Chattering." If not, don't say anything.

- The birds in the garden were making lots of quick, short sounds. *Chattering.*
- The squirrel made lots of short sounds when Mr. Williams disturbed his food-gathering. *Chattering.*
- The dog howled at the moon.
- The owl made a long wailing sound.
- The cat made lots of quick, short sounds when she saw the bird outside the window. *Chattering.*
- The fish moved its mouth, but no sound came out.

What describing word tells about an animal that is making lots of quick, short sounds? *Chattering.*

◎◄ Impatient.

In the story, "The impatient cows are awake and waiting." That means the cows are restless and upset because they are waiting to be milked. They do not wait without worrying or being upset. They are not patient. **Impatient.** Say the word. *Impatient.*

Impatient is a describing word. It tells about people or animals. What kind of word is **impatient?** *A describing word.*

If you are impatient, you are not patient. You do not wait without worrying or being upset. Patient and impatient are opposites. That means they tell about the same kind of thing, but they are completely different in some way. Say the word that means "not patient." *Impatient.* **Patient** and **impatient** are . . . *Opposites.*

(Correct any incorrect responses, and repeat the item at the end of the sequence.)

Let's think about **patient** and **impatient.** I'll tell about a time. If you think the person or animal is being patient, say, "Patient." If you think the person or animal is not being patient, say, "Impatient."

- The dog sits quietly outside the store. *Patient.*
- The dog barks and pulls at his leash while he waits for his owner to come. *Impatient.*
- The kitten cries and cries for her breakfast. *Impatient.*
- Supper is late, but the people don't get upset. *Patient.*
- Mrs. Berenzy was upset when she was asked to wait in line. *Impatient.*
- The boys and girls waited while their teacher talked quietly to Clifford. *Patient.*

What describing word means "not patient"? *Impatient.* What word is the opposite of **impatient?** *Patient.*

Present Vocabulary Tally Sheet
(See Week 1, page 3, for instructions.)

Assign Homework
(Homework Sheet, BLM 20a: See the Introduction for homework instructions.)

DAY 2

Preparation: Picture Vocabulary Cards for *dim, root, chattering,* and *impatient.*

Read and Discuss Story

(Read story aloud to children. Ask the following questions at the specified points in the story. Have children repeat in unison the onomatopoeic sounds of the animals as they are identified.)

Page 1. (First paragraph.) When does this part of the story happen? (Idea: *At night*.) If you were at this farm, what would you see? (Ideas:

Stars; everyone sleeping.) What would you hear? (Ideas: *Nothing; quiet; silence*.)

Page 2. (Second paragraph.) When does this part of the story happen? (Ideas: *In the morning; when the sun comes up*.) If you were at this farm, what would you see? (Ideas: *The sky growing bright; two birds*.) What would you hear? (Idea: *Birds singing*.) Let's say the last sentence on this page together. *Wake up, farm!*

Page 4. (First paragraph.) If you were at this farm, what would you see? (Idea: *The rooster standing on the fence*.) What would you hear? *Cock-a-doodle-doo!* Let's say the last two sentences of this part of the story together. *Wake up, chickens! Wake up, farm!*

Page 4. (Last paragraph.) If you were at this farm, what would you see? (Ideas: *Hens leaving their nests; hens coming out of the henhouse*.) What would you hear? *Cluck, cluck, cluck.*

Page 5. If you were at this farm, what would you see? (Idea: *The mother horse licking her baby*.) What do you think you would hear? (Ideas: *Neighing; neh-heh-heh-heh*.) Let's say the last sentence on this page together. *Wake up to a new day!*

Page 7. If you were at this farm, what would you see? (Ideas: *The ducks waddling out of the bushes; ducks jumping in the water; ducks swimming*.) What would you hear? (Idea: *Quack, quack, quack*.) Everyone, when the ducks say "quack, quack, quack," what does the author say they are saying? *It's time to wake up!*

Page 8. If you were at this farm, what would you see? (Idea: *Pigs rooting around in their pen*.) What would you hear? (Idea: *Oink! Grunt!*)

Page 9. If you were at this farm, what would you see? (Idea: *A goose in the grass; the goose's head above the grass*.) What would you hear? (Idea: *Honk! Honk! Honk!*) Let's say the last sentence on this page together. *Wake up, farm!*

Page 10. If you were at this farm, what would you see? (Idea: *The turkey with its feathers spread out; the turkey walking around the yard*.) What do you think you would you hear? (Idea: *Gobble! Gobble! Gobble!*)

Page 11. If you were at this farm, what would you see? (Idea: *The donkey wiggling his ears.*) What would you hear? (Idea: *Hee-haw.*)

Page 13. (Explain to children that a sheepfold is a pen where sheep are kept at night so they are safe.) If you were at this farm, what would you see? (Idea: *The sheep coming out of their pen.*) What would you hear? (Idea: *Ba-a-a-a.*)

Page 16. (Explain to children that a dovecote is a building where birds such as pigeons or doves are kept.) If you were at this farm, what would you see? (Idea: *Pigeons flying around over the big red barn.*) What would you hear? (Idea: *Cooo, cooo, cooo!*) Let's say the last sentence on this page together. *Wake up, farm!*

Page 17. If you were at this farm, what would you see? (Idea: *The mother cat licking her kittens.*) What would you hear? (Ideas: *Purrr; mew; meow.*)

Page 20. If you were at this farm, what would you see? (Ideas: *The chipmunk; the dog.*) What would you hear? (Ideas: *The chattering of the chipmunk; cht, cht, cht; the barking of the dog; bow, wow, wow; woof, woof, woof.*) Let's say the last sentence on this page together. *Everybody wake up!*

Page 21. If you were at this farm, what would you see? (Ideas: *The rabbit twitching its nose; a carrot.*) What would you hear? (Ideas: *The crunching sound the rabbit makes when it eats carrots; crunch, crunch, crunch.*)

Page 22. If you were at this farm, what would you see? (Ideas: *Beehives; bees; pink clover.*) What would you hear? (Idea: *Buzz-z-z-z-z!*)

(Read aloud the first paragraph on page 23.) If you were at this farm, what would you see? (Idea: *The cows.*) What would you hear? (Idea: *Moo, moo, moo!*) Let's say the last sentence of this part of the story. *Wake up, farm!*

Page 23. If you were at this farm, what would you see? (Idea: *The farmer coming into the barn.*) What would you hear? (Ideas: *The farmer's boots, squish-squish-squish; the door opening, cr-e-e-a-k; the light switch being turned on, click.*)

Page 26. If you were at this farm, what would you see? (Idea: *The little boy waking up; his bedroom.*) What would you hear? *"Breakfast! Come and get it!"*

Page 28. If you were at this farm, what would you see? (Idea: *The boy going down the driveway; the school bus; the horses; the cows; the barn; the house.*) What would you hear? (Ideas: *The sound of the bus, putt-putt-putt; the children talking and laughing, hah-hah, hah.*) Everyone say the last sentence of the story. *Good morning, farm!*

Review Vocabulary

(Display the Picture Vocabulary Cards. Point to each card as you say the word. Ask children to repeat each word after you.) These pictures show **dim, root, chattering,** and **impatient.**

- What word means "not patient"? *Impatient.*
- What word tells about an animal that is making lots of quick, short sounds? *Chattering.*
- What word means "to dig and turn over dirt with paws or noses to find food"? *Root.*
- What word means "not bright"? *Dim.*

Extend Vocabulary

 Root.

In the story *Wake Up, Farm!* we learned that **root** means "to dig and turn over dirt with paws and noses to find food." Say the word that means "to dig and turn over dirt with paws and noses to find food." *Root.*

Raise your hand if you can tell us a sentence that uses **root** as an action word that means "to dig and turn over the dirt, looking for food." (Call on several children. If they don't use complete sentences, restate their examples as sentences. Have the class repeat the sentences.)

Here's a new way to use the word **root.**

- **A carrot has a long root.** Say the sentence.
- **The root helps the plant get water and food.** Say the sentence.
- **Peanuts grow on the root of the peanut plant.** Say the sentence.

In these sentences, **root** is a naming word that means **the part of a plant that usually grows underground.** Roots bring water and food to a plant and hold the plant in the ground. What word means "the part of a plant that usually grows underground"? *Root.*

Raise your hand if you can tell us a sentence that uses **root** as a naming word that means "the part of a plant that usually grows underground." (Call on several children. If they don't use complete sentences, restate their examples as sentences. Have the class repeat the sentences.)

Present Expanded Target Vocabulary
◎━ Dawn.

In the story *Wake Up, Farm!* the "where" part of the setting is on the farm. The "when" part of the setting is when the sun is just starting to come up. Dawn is the time of day when the sun is just starting to come up. **Dawn.** Say the word. *Dawn.*

Dawn is a naming word. It names a part of the day. What kind of word is **dawn?** *A naming word.*

Dawn is the time of day when the sun is just starting to come up. Say the word that means "the time of day when the sun is just starting to come up." *Dawn.*

Another word for the time of day when the sun is just starting to come up is **sunrise. Sunrise** and **dawn** mean the same thing. What two words mean "the time of day when the sun is just starting to come up"? *Sunrise and dawn.*

I'll tell about some different times of day. If the time of day I tell about is when the sun is just starting to come up, say, "Dawn." If not, don't say anything.

- The rooster crowed just as the sun was coming up. *Dawn.*
- The clouds were orange, yellow, and pink, and it was starting to get dark.
- The clouds were pink, orange, and yellow, and it was getting lighter and lighter. *Dawn.*
- The sun was high overhead, and Mom said to get the sunscreen.
- It was cool and fresh at the very beginning of a new day. *Dawn.*
- In the afternoon it is often hot.

What naming word means "the time of day when the sun is just starting to come up"? *Dawn.* What other word means the same thing as **dawn?** *Sunrise.*

 Active.

In the story *Wake Up, Farm!,* when it is dawn, all the animals start moving around. The rooster hops onto a fence post; the hens scratch for yesterday's leftover corn. The pigs root around looking for food. They are busy and full of energy. They are active. **Active.** Say the word. *Active.*

Active is a describing word. It tells about people or animals. What kind of word is **active?** *A describing word.*

When people or animals are active, they are busy and full of energy. Say the word that means "busy and full of energy." *Active.*

I'll tell about some people or animals. If these people or animals are active, say, "Active." If not, don't say anything.

- The ducks jump in the pond for a swim. *Active.*
- The children play soccer. *Active.*
- Everyone ran outside to play in the sprinkler. *Active.*
- Mr. Kraus fixed the fence, swept the porch, and then made breakfast for his family. *Active.*
- Bears sleep for most of the winter.
- I slept in until noon and lazed around for the rest of the day.

What describing word means "busy and full of energy"? *Active.*

DAY 3

Preparation: Activity Sheet, BLM 20b. Children will need crayons.

Retell Story
(Show the pictures on the following pages from the story, and call on a child to tell what's happening. Call on a different child for each section.)

Today I'll show you the pictures Carolyn Ewing made for *Wake Up, Farm!* As I show you the pictures, I'll call on one of you to tell the class that part of the story.

Pages 1–2. Tell me what happens at the **beginning** of the story. (Encourage children to include the target words *dim* and *dawn*. Model use as necessary.)

Pages 3–26. Tell me what happens in the **middle** of the story. (Encourage use of target words when appropriate. Model use as necessary.)

Pages 27–28. Tell me what happens at the **end** of the story.

Introduce Tom Foolery

Preparation: Prepare Picture Vocabulary Cards for all words with dual meanings. Display them prominently in a pocket chart, on a chalkboard ledge, or another obvious location. These words are *bloom, collect, curious, difficult, examine, howled, mood, nursery, present, prickly, promise, roared, scorched, scrawl, shouted, snatched, root,* and *winding.*

Today I will teach you a new game called Tom Foolery. I will pretend to be Tom. Tom Foolery tries to trick children. Tom knows that some words have more than one meaning. He will tell you one meaning that will be correct. Then he will tell you another meaning that might be correct or incorrect.

If you think the meaning is correct, don't say anything. If you think the meaning is incorrect, say, "Tom Foolery." Then Tom will have to tell the truth and give the correct meaning. Tom is sly enough that he may include some words that do **not** have two meanings. Be careful! He's tricky!

Let's practice: **Root** means "to dig and turn over dirt with paws or noses to find food." Root also means . . . a piece of rock that is buried deep in the earth. *Tom Foolery!* Oh, you're right. Root also means "the part of a plant that usually grows underground."

Let's do another one together. **Shouted** means that you yelled when you were mad. Shouted also means that you sang a song using your best singing voice. *Tom Foolery!* Oh, you're right. Shouted also means that you called to someone in a loud voice to get his or her attention.

When we play Tom Foolery, Tom will keep score. If you catch him being tricky, you will get one point. If you don't catch him, Tom gets the point. Watch out! Tom just might try to give himself extra points while you're not looking!

Now you're ready to play the game.

(Draw a T-chart on the board for keeping score. Children earn one point for each correct answer. If they make an error, continue through the process as you normally would to give the correct meaning. Record one point for yourself, and repeat missed words at the end of the game.)

- **Collect** means to "find things in different places and put them together so you can use them." Collected also means to get a red pencil and mark homework. *Tom Foolery!* Oh, you're right. Collect means "get a large number of things that are the same in some way because you really like those things."
- **Dim** means that there is not much light. Dim also means a coin that is worth ten cents. *Tom Foolery!* Oh, you're right. A coin that is worth ten cents is a *dime.* We've learned only one meaning for dim.
- **Impatient** means you are angry and worried when you have to wait. Impatient also means a person who goes to the hospital but only for the day. *Tom Foolery!* Oh, you're right. A person who goes to the hospital is a *patient.* We've learned only one meaning for impatient.
- **Roared** means that someone "shouted something in a very loud voice." Roared also means that you have nothing to do and you don't like to feel that way. *Tom Foolery!* Oh, you're right. Roared also "tells how people or things moved very fast and made a loud noise."

(Count the points, and declare a winner.) You did a great job of playing Tom Foolery!

Adding Details (Activity Sheet)

(Give each child a copy of the Activity Sheet, BLM 20b.) Today I will say (or play) some animal sounds for you. You decide which animal is making that sound. (Say or play the first animal sound. Have children write *1* underneath the picture of the animal that makes that sound. Repeat the process for each animal.)

(**Note:** You may find the animal sounds on the Internet, on a CD, or on a tape. If you do not have access to actual animal sounds, use the onomatopoeic sounds found in the book or in the text of this lesson.)

Preparation: Prepare a sheet of chart paper, landscape direction, titled *Wake Up, Farm!*

Underneath the title, draw nine boxes connected by arrows.

See the Introduction for an example.

Record children's responses by writing the underlined words in the boxes.

Introduce Repeating Patterns (Literary Analysis)

When authors write stories, they sometimes write in patterns.

The story *Papa, Do You Love Me?* has a pattern. What is that pattern? *Question, answer.*

The story *Pablo's Tree* has a pattern. What is that pattern? *Remembering.*

The story *Dreams* has a pattern. What is that pattern? *A linear pattern.*

Let's see if we can figure out the pattern for this story. I'll ask you some questions. You tell me what the author, Alvin Tresselt, said, and I'll write it down.

(Read aloud the following pages, and ask the specified questions.)

Page 1. (Second paragraph.) What words does Alvin Tresselt use to end this part of the story? *Wake up, farm!*

Page 4. (First paragraph.) What words does Alvin Tresselt use to end this part of the story? *Wake up, chickens! Wake up, farm!*

Page 5. What words does Alvin Tresselt use to end this part of the story? *Wake up to a new day!*

Page 7. What words does Alvin Tresselt use to end this part of the story? *It's time to wake up!*

Page 9. What words does Alvin Tresselt use to end this part of the story? *Wake up, farm!*

Page 16. What words does Alvin Tresselt use to end this part of the story? *Wake up, farm!*

Page 20. What words does Alvin Tresselt use to end this part of the story? *Everybody wake up!*

Page 23. (First paragraph.) What words does Alvin Tresselt use to end this part of the story? *Wake up, farm!*

Page 28. What words does Alvin Tresselt use to end the story? *Good morning, farm!*

(Read the words written in all the boxes except the last one, emphasizing the words "wake up.") What pattern did Alvin Tresselt make for his story *Wake Up, Farm*? (Idea: *He used the words "wake up" over and over.*) That's right. He repeated the words "wake up", so this story has a repeating pattern. What kind of pattern repeats the same words over and over? *A repeating pattern.*

(Point to the words "Good morning, farm!" on page 28.) Alvin Tresselt ended his story with the words "Good morning, farm!" When Alvin Tresselt changed the pattern, it was his way of saying "The End." What words did Alvin Tresselt use to say "The End"? *Good morning, farm!*

Let's remember our new song that will help us remember about story patterns. (**Note:** The tune of this song is "If You're Happy and You Know It, Clap Your Hands.")

Each time we sing the song, we start by singing the chorus. Every pattern that we learn will have a different verse about that pattern. I wonder if you will be able to hear the pattern in our song as we add more verses.

Let's sing everything that we know so far.

(See the Introduction for the complete "Pattern Song".)

Now let's add a new verse to remember the remembering pattern we learned about in *Wake Up, Farm!* Listen while I sing the verse: (**Note:** this is easier than it might look. Just sing the first part of each sentence that you would *normally* sing, but repeat it twice before you finish the sentence. It's a repeating joke. Get it? The children will love it!)

> There's a pattern when you
> There's a pattern when you
> There's a pattern when you just repeat the words.
> There's a pattern when you
> There's a pattern when you
> There's a pattern when you just repeat the words.
> Though the humor here is fleeting,
> Say it again, and you're repeating.
> There's a pattern when you
> There's a pattern when you
> There's a pattern when you just repeat the words.

Did you hear me repeating some words? Now sing it with me, and we'll repeat together.

Now let's sing all of what we've learned so far. Don't forget to put a chorus before and after each verse!

Singing a song together is a very good way to remember the patterns we will learn!

Play Tom Foolery (Cumulative Review)

Today I will help you remember how to play our new game called Tom Foolery. I will pretend to be Tom. Tom Foolery has a reputation for trying to trick children.

Tom knows that some words have more than one meaning. He will tell you one meaning that will be correct. Then he will tell you another meaning that might be correct or incorrect.

If you think the meaning is correct, don't say anything. If you think the meaning is incorrect, say, "Tom Foolery." Then Tom will have to tell the truth and give the correct meaning. Tom is sly enough that he may include some words that do not have two meanings. Be careful! He's tricky!

Let's practice: **Dawn** means "the time of day when the sun is just starting to come up." Dawn is also what you might do when you're tired. *Tom Foolery!* Oh, you're right. A yawn is what you might do if you are tired. We learned only one meaning for dawn.

Let's do another one together. **Chattered** means "lots of quick short sounds an animal or bird might make." But a mirror can be chattered if you drop it on the floor. *Tom Foolery!* Oh, you're right. A mirror can be shattered if you drop it on the floor. We've learned only one meaning for chattered.

When we play Tom Foolery, Tom will keep score. If you catch him being tricky, you will get one point. If you don't catch him, Tom gets the point. Watch out! Tom just might try to give himself extra points while you're not looking!

Now you're ready to play the game.

(Draw a T-chart on the board for keeping score. Children earn one point for each correct answer. If they make an error, correct them as you normally would, and record one point for yourself. Repeat missed words at the end of the game.)

- When you **root,** you turn over dirt looking for food. Root also means what you wear on your feet when it is cold or rainy. *Tom Foolery!* Oh, you're right. It's a boot that you wear on your foot when it's cold and rainy. Another meaning for root is the underground part of a plant.
- **Collected** means getting a large group of things that are the same in some way. Collected also means to scatter things around the room and not put them away. *Tom Foolery!* Oh, you're right. Collected also means to "find things in different places and put them together so you can use them." It's what we do in class every day.
- **Grains** are seeds like wheat and barley that we can eat. Grains are also hard tiny pieces of something like salt or sand.
- **Dim** means that there is not very much light. Dim also means an arm or a leg. *Tom Foolery!* Oh, you're right. Another word for an arm or a leg is limb. We've learned only one meaning for dim.
- **Roared** means that someone "shouted something in a very loud voice." Roared also means that you made a snorting and snuffling sound while you were sleeping. *Tom Foolery!* Oh, you're right. Snorting and snuffling when you sleep is snored. The other meaning for

roared is "moved very fast and made a loud noise."

- **Shouted** means that you yelled at someone when you were mad. Shouted also means that you didn't believe what someone told you. *Tom Foolery!* Oh, you're right. Shouted also means "spoke in a very loud voice." I think I was thinking about doubted.
- **Sloppy** means that your things are not very neat. Sloppy can also mean that your printing is perfect. *Tom Foolery!* Oh, you're right. We learned only one meaning for sloppy.
- If you are **active,** you are full of energy and busy. Active also means that you can't keep your shoes on. *Tom Foolery!* Oh, you're right. Active means only the first thing. I made up the other one.
- If you are **impatient,** you get upset and worried when you have to wait. Impatient is also how you might feel when someone else is taking a very long turn and you think it should be your turn.

(Count the points, and declare a winner.)
You did a great job of playing Tom Foolery!

DAY 5

Preparation: Happy Face Game Test Sheet, BLM B.

Retell Story to a Partner

(Assign each child a partner, and ask the partners to take turns telling part of the story each time you turn to a new set of pages. Encourage use of target words when appropriate.)

Today I'll show you the pictures Carolyn Ewing made for *Wake Up, Farm!* As I show you the pictures, you and your partner will take turns telling part of the story.

Pages 1–2. Tell what happens at the **beginning** of the story.

Pages 3–24. Tell what happens in the **middle** of the story.

Pages 25–28. Tell what happens at the **end** of the story.

Assess Vocabulary

 (Hold up a copy of the Happy Face Game Test Sheet, BLM B.)

Today you're going to play the Happy Face Game. When you play the Happy Face Game, it helps me know how well you know the hard words you are learning.

If I say something true, color the happy face. What will you do if I say something true? *Color the happy face.*

If I say something false, color the sad face. What will you do if I say something false? *Color the sad face.*

Listen carefully to each item I say. Don't let me trick you!

Item 1: If you are **impatient,** you are having lots of trouble waiting. *True.*

Item 2: If the light is **dim,** you can't see very well because there isn't much light. *True.*

Item 3: **Dawn** is the time of day when the sun goes down. *False.*

Item 4: **Chattering** is a lot of quick, short sounds an animal might make. *True.*

Item 5: **Root** means to look in the closet without moving things around. *False.*

Item 6: An **active** person sits in a chair all day long without moving. *False.*

Item 7: A **root** is the underground part of a plant. *True.*

Item 8: If your printing is neat and tidy, it is a **scrawl.** *False.*

Item 9: When someone speaks to you **severely,** he or she is using a harsh voice. *True.*

Item 10: If the children were **sprawled** out on the floor, they were lying down with their legs and arms spread out. *True.*

You did a great job of playing the Happy Face Game!

(Score children's work later. Scores of 9 out of 10 indicate mastery. If a child does not achieve mastery, insert the missed words in the games in the next week's lessons. Retest those children individually on the missed items before they take the next mastery test.)

Extensions
Read a Story as a Reward

(Display several of the books you have read since the beginning of the program. Allow children to choose which book they would like you to read aloud to them as a reward for their hard work.)

(Read story to children for enjoyment with minimal interruptions.)

Present the Super Words Center

(Prepare the word containers for the Super Words Center. You may wish to remove some of the words from earlier lessons. Choose words children have mastered.

See the Introduction for instructions on how to set up and use the Super Words Center.)

(Add the new Picture Vocabulary Cards to words from the previous weeks. Show children one of the word containers. If they need more guidance, role-play with two or three children as a demonstration.)

Today I will help you remember how to play the game called What's New?

Let's think about how we work with our words in the Super Words Center.

You will work with a partner in the Super Words Center. Whom will you work with in the center? *A partner.*

First, one partner will draw four word cards out of the container and put them on the table so both partners can see. What do you do first? (Idea: *Draw four cards out of the container and put them on the table so both partners can see.*)

Next you will take turns looking at the cards and saying the words the pictures show. What do you do next? (Idea: *We take turns looking at the cards and saying the words the pictures show.*)

Next, partner 2 looks away while partner 1 takes one of the four cards and places it back in the container. Then partner 1 draws a new card from the container and places it on the table with the other three. Watch while I show you what I mean. (Demonstrate this process with a child as your partner.) When you put down the new card, it's a good idea to mix the cards so they aren't in the same places anymore. (Demonstrate.)

Now partner 1 says, "What's new?" Partner 2 has to use his or her eyes and brain and say what new word card has been put down. If partner 2 is correct, he or she gets a point. If partner 2 is not correct, partner 1 gets the point. (Demonstrate.)

Next, partner 2 has a turn to choose four different cards, and the game starts again. What happens next? (Idea: *Partner 2 has a turn to choose four different cards, and the game starts again.*) Have fun playing What's New!

Preparation: You will need *Jamaica and the Substitute Teacher* for each day's lesson.

Number the pages of the story to assist you in asking questions at appropriate points.

Post a copy of the Vocabulary Tally Sheet, BLM A, with this week's Picture Vocabulary Cards attached.

Each child will need the Homework Sheet, BLM 21a.

Jamaica and the Substitute Teacher
author: Juanita Havill • illustrator: Anne Sibley O'Brien

Target Vocabulary

Tier II	Tier III
substitute	pattern
favorite	(linear)
memorize	
perfect	
*honest	
*cheat	

*Expanded Target Vocabulary Word

DAY 1

Introduce Book

Today's book is called *Jamaica and the Substitute Teacher.* What's the title of this week's book? *Jamaica and the Substitute Teacher.*

This book was written by Juanita Havill [**ha**-vill]. Who's the author of *Jamaica and the Substitute Teacher*? *Juanita Havill.*

Anne Sibley O'Brien made the pictures for this book. Who's the illustrator of *Jamaica and the Substitute Teacher*? *Anne Sibley O'Brien.* Who made the illustrations for this book? *Anne Sibley O'Brien.*

The cover of a book usually gives us some hints of what the book is about. Let's look at the front cover of *Jamaica and the Substitute Teacher.* What do you see in the illustration? (Ideas: *Two girls sitting at their desks; they are both writing something; a woman is holding a paper; she's wearing glasses.*)

(Assign each child a partner.) Remember, when you make a prediction about something, you say what you think will happen. Get ready to make some predictions to your partner about this book. Use the information from the cover to help you.

(Ask the following questions, allowing sufficient time for children to share their predictions with their partners.)

- Who are the characters in this story? (Whom do you think this story is about?)
- What do you think the girls are writing?
- Where do you think the story happens?
- Why do you think one of the girls is looking up?
- How did the girl get all those ponytail holders in her hair?
- Do you think this story is about real people? Tell why or why not.

(Call on several children to share their predictions with the class.)

Take a Picture Walk

We are going to take a picture walk through this book. Remember, when we take a picture walk, we look at the pictures and tell what we think will happen in the story.

(Show the illustrations on the following pages, and ask the specified questions. Encourage children to use previously taught target words in their answers.)

Page 1. Where do you think the girls are going? (Idea: *Into their classroom.*)

Pages 2–3. Who do you think the woman is? (Ideas: *The teacher; the substitute teacher.*) Which girl do you think is Jamaica? Why do you think so? (**Note:** Accept either answer. You will ask this question again later.)

Pages 4–5. (Note: If children previously chose Brianna as Jamaica, repeat the question:) Which girl do you think is Jamaica? (Ideas: *The girl wearing the pink T-shirt; the girl with the pink ponytail holders in her hair.*) Why do you think so? (Ideas: *The girl wearing the blue T-shirt is wearing a name tag that starts with B; "Jamaica" starts with J.*) What do you think Jamaica is doing? (Idea: *Thinking.*)

Page 7. What is Jamaica doing? (Ideas: *Holding up a toy bird; holding a toy penguin.*) What are most of the other children doing? (Idea: *Looking at Jamaica.*) How do you think Jamaica is feeling? (Ideas: *Happy; proud.*) Why do you think so?

Page 9. What is happening here? (Idea: *The children and the teacher are reading.*)

Page 10. What is happening here? (Ideas: *The teacher is showing a paper to Jamaica; Jamaica is pulling something off the paper.*) How do you think Jamaica is feeling? (Ideas: *Pleased; proud.*) Why do you think so? How do you think the other girl is feeling? (Ideas: *Shocked; surprised; amazed.*) Why do you think so?

Page 13. What is Jamaica doing? (Idea: *Thinking about something.*) How do you know?

Pages 14–15. What is happening here? (Ideas: *All the children except Jamaica are writing something on their papers; the children are writing a list of words.*) How do you think Jamaica is feeling? (Ideas: *Worried; nervous; anxious.*) Why do you think so?

Page 17. What is the teacher doing? (Ideas: *Holding a paper; looking at Jamaica.*) How do you think the teacher is feeling? (Idea: *Upset.*) What makes you think so?

Page 18. What is Jamaica doing? (Ideas: *Sitting on her chair; Looking at the paper she wrote the list of words on.*)

Pages 20–21. What is happening here? (Ideas: *Jamaica is standing next to the teacher's desk; the teacher is talking to Jamaica.*) How do you think Jamaica is feeling? (Ideas: *Nervous; anxious; sad.*) What makes you think so?

Page 22. What is Jamaica doing? (Idea: *Talking to the teacher.*) What is the teacher holding? (Idea: *Jamaica's paper.*)

Page 25. How do you think Jamaica is feeling now? (Ideas: *Content; satisfied.*) How do you think the teacher is feeling now? (Idea: *Calm.*)

Page 26. What is Jamaica doing? (Idea: *Drawing a picture.*) Who do you think she is drawing? (Idea: *The teacher.*) What makes you think so? (Ideas: *Jamaica is coloring the dress the same as the one the teacher is wearing; the person in her picture is wearing a blue scarf like the teacher's.*)

Page 28. These words say "for Mrs. Duval from Jamaica." What has Jamaica done? (Idea: *She has made a card for her teacher.*) Have you ever made a card for someone? Tell the class about the card you made. (Call on several children. Encourage them to start their answers with the words "I made a card for _____. It had _____ on it.")

Now that we've finished our picture walk, it's your turn to ask me some questions. What would you like to know about the story? (Accept questions. If children tell about the pictures or the story instead of asking questions, prompt them to ask a question.) Ask me a what question. Ask me a how question.

Read Story Aloud
(Read story aloud to children with minimal interruptions.)

In the next lesson, we will read the story again, and I will ask you some questions.

Present Target Vocabulary

◎← Substitute.

In the story, Jamaica's teacher is away, so her class has a substitute. That means another teacher comes to take the place of their teacher while she is away. **Substitute.** Say the word. *Substitute.*

Substitute is a describing word. It tells what kind of teacher the children had. What kind of word is **substitute?** *A describing word.*

If you are a substitute, you take the place of someone else. Sometimes in team sports such as football and basketball, a substitute player might take the place of one of his or her teammates who got tired or hurt. Say the word that means "a person who takes the place of someone else." *Substitute.*

(Correct any incorrect responses, and repeat the item at the end of the sequence.)

Let's think about some people that might be substitutes. I'll tell about someone. If you think that person is a substitute, say, "Substitute." If not, don't say anything.

- The music teacher has a sore throat, so another teacher takes his place. *Substitute.*
- Susan needs a rest from playing soccer. *Substitute.*
- Peter plays the entire game without a rest.
- Our teacher is ill, so another teacher comes. *Substitute.*
- The batter hurts his arm, so the coach calls the next player on the bench. *Substitute.*
- The principal of our school never misses a day of work!

What describing word means "a person who takes the place of someone else"? *Substitute.*

◎⊷ Favorite.

In the story, Jamaica tells Mrs. Duval, "Cats are my favorite animals." That means that of all the animals, she likes cats the most. **Favorite.** Say the word. *Favorite.*

Favorite is a describing word. It tells about what kind of animals. What kind of word is **favorite?** *A describing word.*

If something is your favorite, you like it the most. Say the word that means "someone or something you like the most." *Favorite.*

(Correct any incorrect responses, and repeat the item at the end of the sequence.)

Let's think about some things that might be someone's favorite. I'll tell about something. If that thing is someone's favorite, say, "Favorite." If not, don't say anything.

- Of all her books, Shelley likes *Tikki Tikki Tembo* the most. *Favorite.*
- Of all the soccer teams, Gustavo likes the American team the most. *Favorite.*
- Carlos likes all the players on the Mexican team.
- Dad likes lots of cars, but he likes the red one the most. *Favorite.*
- Tommy says that his mom likes pumpkin pie the most. *Favorite.*

- Every flavor of cookie is fantastic.

What describing word means "someone or something you like the most"? *Favorite.*

(Assign each child a partner, or call on several children to answer these questions:) What is your favorite animal? What is your favorite number? What is your favorite color? What is your favorite game?

◎⊷ Memorize.

In the story, Jamaica looked at the words on her spelling list "and tried to memorize every word." That means she tried to learn each word so she could remember it exactly. **Memorize.** Say the word. *Memorize.*

Memorize is an action word. It tells what someone is doing. What kind of word is **memorize?** *An action word.*

If you memorize something, you learn it so well you can remember it exactly. Say the word that means "learn something so well you remember it exactly." *Memorize.*

(Correct any incorrect responses, and repeat the item at the end of the sequence.)

Let's think about some things that someone might want to learn so well that he or she could remember it exactly. I'll tell about something. If you might want to memorize that thing, say, "Memorize." If not, don't say anything.

- The words you say in a play. *Memorize.*
- All the phone numbers in the phone book.
- Your best friend's phone number. *Memorize.*
- Your own address and phone number. *Memorize.*
- The number of grains of sand on the beach.
- How many times you blink in a day.

What action word means "learn something so well you remember it exactly"? *Memorize.*

You've already memorized the days of the week. Everyone, say the days of the week, starting with Sunday.

◎⊷ Perfect.

In the story, Jamaica wants to have a perfect paper in spelling. That means she wants a spelling paper that has no mistakes. She wants to spell all the words the right way. **Perfect.** Say the word. *Perfect.*

Perfect is a describing word. It tells about a naming word. What kind of word is **perfect?** *A describing word.*

If something is perfect, it has no mistakes. Say the word that means "has no mistakes." *Perfect.*

(Correct any incorrect responses, and repeat the item at the end of the sequence.)

Let's think about some things that could be perfect. I'll tell about something. If you think that thing is perfect, say, "Perfect." If not, don't say anything.

- The horse makes no mistakes when it jumps all the jumps in the contest. *Perfect.*
- We do our best, but not all of the answers are correct.
- All the children in the class make no mistakes on their math sheets. *Perfect.*
- The children sing the words to "The Story Song" with no mistakes. *Perfect.*
- Mr. Carlin remembers all of his jokes and stories. *Perfect.*
- It's okay if there are some little mistakes in your painting.

What describing word means "has no mistakes"? *Perfect.*

Present the Vocabulary Tally Sheet
(See Week 1, page 3, for instructions.)

Assign Homework
(Homework Sheet, BLM 21a: See the Introduction for homework instructions.)

DAY 2

Preparation: Picture Vocabulary Cards for *substitute, favorite, memorize,* and *perfect.*

Read and Discuss Story
(Read story aloud to children. Ask the following questions at the specified points in the story.

Encourage them to use previously taught target words in their answers.)

Now I am going to read *Jamaica and the Substitute Teacher.* When I finish each part, I'll ask you some questions.

Page 1. Where does this part of the story happen? (Idea: *At school.*) Why are Jamaica and Brianna hurrying? (Idea: *They want to see who their substitute is.*)

(Point to the date written on the chalkboard on page 2.) These words say "Tuesday, May third." When does this part of the story happen? *On Tuesday, May third.*

(Point to the name written on the chalkboard on page 2.) These words say "Mrs. Duval." Who do you think Mrs. Duval is? (Idea: *The substitute teacher.*)

Page 3. What plans does Mrs. Duval have for the class? (Ideas: *They will work hard; they will have fun.*) Why does Jamaica give a thumbs-up to Brianna? (Ideas: *Mrs. Duvall seems like a nice substitute; Jamaica thinks everything will be good.*)

Page 5. Mrs. Duval starts the day with a game: hunt for a hidden object. What is the first clue she gives? (Idea: *It lives in Antarctica.*) What is the second clue she gives? (Idea: *Its name starts with the same letter as the object it is hidden in.*) Wow, that's a hard game. No wonder Jamaica is thinking so hard!

Page 6. Who finds the hidden object? *Jamaica.* What is the object? *A plastic penguin.* Where is it hidden? *In a pot.*

P (say the sound) Penguin, **p** (say the sound) pot. Those words begin with the same letter; they begin with the letter **p.** What does Jamaica get to do because she has won the game? (Idea: *She gets to hide an object tomorrow.*)

Page 8. Why does Mrs. Duval say Jamaica reads very well? (Ideas: *She reads loudly and clearly; she knows all the words.*) How does Jamaica feel when Mrs. Duval praises her reading? (Ideas: *Like singing; happy; proud.*)

Page 11. What happens after reading groups? (Idea: *It's math time.*) What does the class do during math time? *Puzzles.* Who has all the right answers? *Jamaica, Cynthia, and Thomas.* What reward does Mrs. Duval give them? (Idea: *They can choose a sticker.*) What sticker does Jamaica choose? *A gray kitten with yellow eyes.* What does Jamaica find out about Mrs. Duval? (Idea: *She likes cats.*)

Page 12. What happens right after lunch? (Idea: *Mrs. Duval reads the class a story.*) Then what does the class do? *Spelling.* Why does this worry Jamaica? (Idea: *She hasn't studied her words for the test.*) Do you think Jamaica will have enough time to memorize all the words?

Page 14. What word is Jamaica having trouble with? *Calf.* How does Jamaica get the right spelling for **calf?** (Idea: *She looks at Brianna's paper.*) Do you think Mrs. Duval sees Jamaica copy the word from Brianna's paper?

Page 16. What does Jamaica write on Brianna's paper? *100% (one hundred percent).* What does that mean? (Idea: *Brianna spelled all the words the right way.*) What does Brianna write on Jamaica's paper? *A happy face and A++++.* What does that mean? (Idea: *Jamaica spelled all the words the right way.*) Does Jamaica really know all the words? (Idea: *No; she copied "calf" from Brianna's paper.*)

Page 19. What does Jamaica do when she gets her test back? (Idea: *She crosses out the happy face.*) What does Jamaica do when Mrs. Duval asks the class to pass their spelling papers to the front? (Idea: *She put hers in her desk.*) Why do you think Jamaica can't think of anything to draw? (Idea: *She is upset because she copied from Brianna's paper.*)

Page 20. Why does Mrs. Duval ask Jamaica to come see her? (Idea: *Jamaica hasn't handed in her spelling paper.*)

Page 23. Does Jamaica tell Mrs. Duval she has copied? *Yes.*

Page 24. What does Mrs. Duval say to Jamaica after Jamaica says she is sorry? (Ideas: *You don't have to be perfect to be special; all my students are special; I'm glad you're one of my students.*)

Page 27. Do you think Jamaica is looking forward to coming to school tomorrow? *Yes.* Tell why you think so.

Review Vocabulary

(Display the Picture Vocabulary Cards. Point to each card as you say the word. Ask children to repeat each word after you.) These pictures show **substitute, favorite, memorize, and perfect.**

- What word means "learn something so well you remember it exactly"? *Memorize.*
- What word means "someone or something you like the most"? *Favorite.*
- What word means "has no mistakes"? *Perfect.*
- What word means "a person who takes the place of someone else"? *Substitute.*

Extend Vocabulary

 Substitute.

In the story *Jamaica and the Substitute Teacher,* we learn that **substitute** is a describing word that means "a person who takes the place of someone else." Say the word that means "a person who takes the place of someone else." *Substitute.*

Raise your hand if you can tell us a sentence that uses **substitute** as a describing word that means "a person who takes the place of someone else." (Call on several children. If they do not use complete sentences, restate their examples as sentences. Have the class repeat the sentences.)

Here's a new way to use the word **substitute.**

- **She substitutes blackberries for raspberries in her muffins.** Say the sentence.
- **The coach substitutes goalkeepers after each half of the game.** Say the sentence.
- **He substitutes honey for sugar when he bakes cookies.** Say the sentence.

In these sentences, **substitute** is an action word that means to **replace one person or thing with another.** What action word means to "replace one person or thing with another"? *Substitute.*

Present Expanded Target Vocabulary
Honest.

In *Jamaica and the Substitute Teacher,* Jamaica is being honest when she tells Mrs. Duval her score on the spelling test should be minus one. **Honest.** Say the word. *Honest.*

Honest is a describing word. It tells about people. What kind of word is **honest**? *A describing word.*

When people are honest, they tell the truth or do what is right. Say the word that tells about people who tell the truth or do what is right. *Honest.*

I'll tell about some people. If these people are being honest, say, "Honest." If not, don't say anything.

- When Miranda finds some money on the playground, she takes it to the office. *Honest.*
- When Johnson breaks the cup, he tells his teacher he has done it. *Honest.*
- The man tells a lie.
- Mariah tells her neighbor that she has broken the window. *Honest.*
- Harvey says he is late for school because an alien from space came to visit.
- When the clerk gives us too much change, we give back the extra. *Honest.*

What describing word tells about people who tell the truth or do what is right? *Honest.*

◎— *Cheat.*

In *Jamaica and the Substitute Teacher,* Jamaica copies the spelling of the word **calf** from Brianna's paper. When Jamaica does that, she is cheating. **Cheat.** Say the word. *Cheat.*

Cheat is an action word. It tells what someone does. What kind of word is **cheat?** *An action word.*

When you cheat, you do what is wrong; you are not honest. Say the word that means "do what is wrong; not honest." *Cheat.* What word means "do what is wrong; not honest"? *Cheat.*

I'll tell about some people. If these people cheat, say, "Cheat." If these people are being honest, say, "Honest."

- He moves his marker six places on the game board when the die shows a three. *Cheat.*
- Matalee trips Nigel so he can't win the race. *Cheat.*
- The clerk tries to give us less change than we should really have gotten. *Cheat.*
- Everybody plays fair and square. *Honest.*

- Mr. Smith says that all the jokes are his own but, really, someone else wrote them. *Cheat.*
- Mal makes a mistake when he teaches me the rules. *Honest.*

What action word means "do what is wrong; not honest"? *Cheat.*

DAY 3

Preparation: Activity Sheet, BLM 21b. Children will need crayons.

Retell Story

(Show pictures on the following pages from the story, and call on a child to tell what's happening. Call on a different child for each section.)

Today I'll show you the pictures Anne Sibley O'Brien made for the story *Jamaica and the Substitute Teacher.* As I show you the pictures, I'll call on one of you to tell the class that part of the story.

Pages 1–3. Tell me what happens at the **beginning** of the story. (Encourage children to include the target word *substitute.* Model use as necessary.)

Pages 4–25. Tell me what happens in the **middle** of the story. (Encourage use of target words when appropriate. Model use as necessary.)

Pages 26–28. Tell me what happens at the **end** of the story.

Review Tom Foolery

Collect or prepare Picture Vocabulary Cards for all words with dual meanings. Display them prominently in a pocket chart, on a chalkboard ledge, or another obvious location. These words are *bloom, collect, curious, difficult, examine, howled, mood, nursery, present, prickly, promise, roared, root, scorched, scrawl, shouted, snatched, root,* and *winding.*

Today I will help you remember how to play the game called Tom Foolery. I will pretend to be Tom. Tom Foolery has a reputation of trying to trick children. Tom knows that some words have more than one meaning. He will tell you one meaning that will be correct. Then he will tell you another meaning that might be correct or incorrect. If you think the meaning is correct, don't say anything. If you think the meaning is incorrect, sing out "Tom Foolery!"

Then Tom will have to tell the truth and give the correct meaning. Tom is sly enough that he may include some words that do **not** have two meanings. Be careful! He's tricky!

Let's practice: **Substitute** means "a person who takes the place of someone else." Substitute also means . . . a ship that can go underwater. *Tom Foolery!* Oh, you're right. Substitute also means to "replace one person or thing with another."

Let's do another one together. **Favorite** means "someone or something you like the most." Favorite also means . . . to use one hand less when it is sore. *Tom Foolery!* Oh, you're right. Favorite just means "someone or something you like the most."

When we play Tom Foolery, Tom will keep score. If you catch him being tricky, you will get one point. If you don't catch him, Tom gets the point. Watch out! Tom just might try to give himself extra points while you're not looking!

Now you're ready to play the game.

[T] (Draw a T-chart on the board for keeping score. Children earn one point for each correct answer. If they make an error, continue through the process as you normally would to give the correct meaning. Record one point for yourself, and repeat missed words at the end of the game.)

- A **rascal** is someone who would lie and cheat to get his or her own way. Rascal also means . . . a fight in which you try to hold the other person and pin him or her down. *Tom Foolery!* Oh, you're right. A rascal is a young child who is poorly behaved. I must have been thinking of wrestle.

- When you **memorize,** you remember something perfectly. Memorize also means . . . to write a note. *Tom Foolery!* Oh, you're right.

Memorize means only to remember something exactly. I'll have to memorize that!

- When your work is **perfect,** there are no mistakes. If your spelling paper has no mistakes, it is perfect.

- **Curious** means you wonder about things, and want to know more. Curious also means . . . to heal a sore or an illness. *Tom Foolery!* Oh, you're right. Curious also means "unusual, or hard to understand."

- If you are **honest,** you tell the truth. Honest also means . . . the one who is on a swing the most. "Of all the people on the swings today, George was the on-est." *Tom Foolery!* Oh, you're right. Honest just means you tell the truth or do what is right.

(Count the points, and declare a winner.)
You did a great job of playing Tom Foolery!

Matching Words with Same Initial Sound (Activity Sheet)

(Review with children the guessing game Mrs. Duval played with the class.)

(Give each child a copy of the Activity Sheet, BLM 21b.) Today it will be your turn to hide some objects. Remember, the object you hide and the place you hide it have to start with the same sound. (Children will draw a line from the object to the place where it would be hidden. You may wish to complete this activity sheet as a guided activity, working with children to identify the initial sounds of the objects and the hiding places.)

DAY 4

Preparation: Prepare a sheet of chart paper, landscape direction, with the title *Jamaica and the Substitute Teacher.* Underneath the title, draw eleven boxes connected by arrows.

See the Introduction for an example.

Record children's responses by writing the underlined words in the boxes.

Review Linear Pattern (Literary Analysis)

When authors write stories, they sometimes write in patterns. Let's see if we can figure out the pattern for this story. You tell me what happens in the story, and I'll write it down.

Pages 1–3. What important thing happens at the beginning of the story? (Ideas: *Mrs. Duval is their substitute teacher.*)

Pages 4, 5, and 7. Then what happens? (Idea: *They play the game Hunt for a Hidden Object. Jamaica wins the game.*)

Page 9. Then what happens? (Idea: *It is reading group time. Jamaica is a good reader.*)

Page 10. Then what happens? (Idea: *It is math time. Jamaica earns a sticker.*)

Page 12. (Read first two sentences.) Then what happens? (Idea: *It is story time.*) Then what happens? (Idea: *It is spelling time.*)

Pages 14–15. Then what happens? (Idea: *Jamaica copies from Brianna's paper.*)

Pages 17–19. Then what happens? (Idea: *Jamaica puts her paper in her desk.*)

Pages 20–23. Then what happens? (Idea: *Jamaica tells Mrs. Duval she copied.*)

Page 25. Then what happens? (Idea: *Mrs. Duval says she is glad Jamaica is one of her students.*)

Pages 26–27. Then what happens? (Idea: *Jamaica makes a card for Mrs. Duval.*)

(Point to the story map on the chart paper. Draw a line under the story map.) Look at the shape of this story. It's a line. This story starts and ends at different times, so it has a **linear** pattern. What kind of pattern does a story have when it starts and ends at different times? *A linear pattern.*

What other story that we read had a linear pattern? *Dreams.*

Let's sing "The Pattern Song" to help us remember about story patterns.

(See the Introduction for the complete "Pattern Song.")

Singing a song together is a very good way to remember the patterns we will learn!

Play Tom Foolery (Cumulative Review)

Today I will help you remember how to play our new game called Tom Foolery. I will pretend to be Tom. Tom Foolery has a reputation for trying to trick students.

Tom knows that some words have more than one meaning. He will tell you one meaning that will be correct. Then he will tell you another meaning that might be correct or incorrect. If you think the meaning is correct, don't say anything. If you think the meaning is incorrect, sing out "Tom Foolery!"

Then Tom will have to tell the truth and give the correct meaning. Tom is sly enough that he may include some words that do *not* have two meanings. Be careful! He's tricky!

Let's practice: If you tell the truth or do what is right, you are **honest.** Honest also means . . . a mother bird that is hatching her eggs. *Tom Foolery!* Oh, you're right. We learned only one meaning for honest.

Let's do another one together. **Favorite** means "someone or something you like the most." Favorite also means . . . helping someone who asks you to do something special. *Tom Foolery!* Oh, you're right. I must be thinking of doing a favor, not being a favorite.

When we play Tom Foolery, Tom will keep score. If you catch him being tricky, you will get one point. If you don't catch him, Tom gets the point. Watch out! Tom just might try to give himself extra points while you're not looking!

Now you're ready to play the game.

(Draw a T-chart on the board for keeping score. Children earn one point for each correct answer. If they make an error, correct them as you normally would, and record one point for yourself. Repeat missed words at the end of the game.)

- Everyone knows that a gift is also a **present.** We also have a present of our country who lives in Washington, D.C. *Tom Foolery!* Oh, you're right. It's a president we have in Washington, D.C. Another meaning for present is "being somewhere." I could say you are present when you are here.

- **Memorize** means to "learn something so well you remember it." Memorize also means . . . to write a short note to someone. *Tom Foolery!* Oh, you're right. We know only one meaning for memorize. I must have been thinking of a memo.

- When something is **perfect,** it has no mistakes. Perfect also means a good grade on a flawless assignment.
- **Cheat** means to "do what is wrong; not honest." Cheat is also a large wild cat. *Tom Foolery!* Oh, you're right. A large wild cat is a cheetah.
- **Substitute** means "a person who takes the place of someone else." Substitute also means something that you learn about. *Tom Foolery!* Oh, you're right. When you learn about something such as math or reading, it is called a subject.
- We call a linear pattern **linear** because it goes in a line. It also means that story characters end up in a different place from where they started.
- **Blooming** means that a plant is growing flowers. Blooming also means that an adult is turning back into a child. *Tom Foolery!* Oh, you're right. Blooming also means that a child is growing and getting better at doing things.
- **Sloppy** means "careless about how you do things; messy and untidy." Sloppy can also mean that your printing or writing is perfect. *Tom Foolery!* Oh, you're right. We learned only one meaning for sloppy.
- If you have an **appetite,** you are hungry. Appetite also means that the lid on the jar of vegetables won't come off. *Tom Foolery!* Oh, you're right. I made that second meaning up. If you have an appetite, you are hungry.
- **Gentle** means that "you touch things or people very softly." Gentle also means the opposite of lady. *Tom Foolery!* Oh, you're right. I was thinking of gentleman. The opposite of gentleman is lady.

(Count the points, and declare a winner.)
You did a great job of playing Tom Foolery!

DAY 5

Preparation: Happy Face Game Test Sheet, BLM B.

Retell a Story to a Partner
(Assign each child a partner, and ask the partners to take turns telling part of the story each time you turn to a new set of pages. Encourage use of target words when appropriate.)

Today I'll show you the pictures Anne Sibley O'Brien made for the story *Jamaica and the Substitute Teacher.* As I show you the pictures, you and your partner will take turns telling part of the story.

Pages 1–3. Tell what happens at the **beginning** of the story.

Pages 4–25. Tell what happens in the **middle** of the story.

Pages 26–28. Tell what happens at the **end** of the story.

Assess Vocabulary
 (Hold up a copy of the Happy Face Game Test Sheet, BLM B.)

Today you're going to play the Happy Face Game. When you play the Happy Face Game, it helps me know how well you know the hard words you are learning.

If I say something true, color the happy face. What will you do if I say something true? *Color the happy face.*

If I say something false, color the sad face. What will you do if I say something false? *Color the sad face.*

Listen carefully to each item I say. Don't let me trick you!

Item 1: A **substitute** takes the place of someone or something else. *True.*

Item 2: If you **cheat,** you do the right thing. *False.*

Item 3: When you remember something perfectly, you **memorize** it. *True.*

Item 4: **Perfect** means full of mistakes. *False.*

Item 5: When brothers and sisters are **squabbling** with each other, they are sharing their toys and getting along with each other. *False.*

Item 6: Your **favorite** toy is the one you like the most. *True.*

Item 7: When you are **honest,** you tell the truth and do the right thing. *True.*

Item 8: If your friend **snatched** your hat, he or she grabbed it and quickly pulled it away. *True.*

Item 9: If you make a **promise** to work hard, that means that you will not work hard. *False.*

Item 10: A **sentence** *never* tells who or what happened. *False.*

You did a great job of playing the Happy Face Game!

(Score children's work later. Scores of 9 out of 10 indicate mastery. If a child does not achieve mastery, insert the missed words in the games in the next week's lessons. Retest those children individually on the missed words before they take the next mastery test.)

Extensions
Read a Story as a Reward

(Display several of the books you have read since the beginning of the program. Allow children to choose which book they would like you to read aloud to them as a reward for their hard work.)

(Read story aloud to children for enjoyment with minimal interruptions.)

Present the Super Words Center

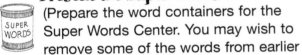

(Prepare the word containers for the Super Words Center. You may wish to remove some of the words from earlier lessons. Choose words the children have mastered.

See the Introduction for instructions on how to set up and use the Super Words Center.)

(Add the new Picture Vocabulary Cards to the words from the previous weeks. Show children one of the word containers. If they need more guidance, role-play with two or three children as a demonstration.)

Today I will help you remember how to play the game called What's New?

Let's think about how we work with our words in the Super Words Center.

You will work with a partner in the Super Words Center. Whom will you work with in the center? *A partner.*

First, one partner will draw four word cards out of the container and put them on the table so both partners can see. What do you do first? (Idea: *Draw four cards out of the container, and put them on the table so both partners can see.*)

Next you will take turns looking at the cards and saying the words the pictures show. What will you do next? (Idea: *We will take turns looking at the cards and saying the words the pictures show.*)

Next, partner 2 looks away while partner 1 takes one of the four cards and places it back in the container. Then partner 1 draws a new card from the container and places it on the table with the other three. Watch while I show you what I mean. (Demonstrate this process with one child as your partner.) When you put down the new card, it's a good idea to mix the cards so they aren't in the same places any more. (Demonstrate as you go.)

Now partner 1 says, "What's New?" Partner 2 has to use his or her eyes and brain and say what new word card has been put down. If partner 2 is correct, he or she gets a point. If partner 2 is not correct, partner 1 gets the point. (Demonstrate as you go.)

Next, partner 2 has a turn to choose four different cards, and the game starts again. What happens next? (Idea: *Partner 2 has a turn to choose four different cards, and the game starts again.*)

Have fun playing What's New!

Week 22

Loon Lake
author: Jonathan London • illustrator:
Susan Ford

Preparation: You will need *Loon Lake* for each day's lesson.

Number the pages of the story to assist you in asking questions at appropriate points.

Post a copy of the Vocabulary Tally Sheet with this week's Picture Vocabulary Cards attached.

Each child will need the Homework Sheet, BLM 22a.

Loon Lake
author: Jonathan London • illustrator: Susan Ford

🎯 **Target Vocabulary**

Tier II	Tier III
precious	pattern (circle)
glimpse	afterword
wild	realistic
slithers	fact
*legend	
*disappears	

*Expanded Target Vocabulary Word

- Who are the characters in this story? (Whom do you think this story is about?)
- What do you think made the waves on the water?
- Where do you think the story happens?
- When do you think the story happens?
- Why do you think the people are wearing those red vests?
- How far out on the lake do you think the people are?
- Do you think this story is about real people? Tell why or why not.

(Call on several children to share their predictions with the class.)

Take a Picture Walk

We are going to take a picture walk through this book. Remember, when we take a picture walk, we look at the pictures and tell what we think will happen in the story.

(Show the illustrations on the following pages, and ask the specified questions. Encourage children to use previously taught target words in their answers.)

Pages 1–2. Where do you think the illustrator was sitting when she painted this picture? (Ideas: *High in the sky; in an airplane; in a helicopter.*) When an artist makes a picture look as if she were looking down from the sky, we call it a bird's-eye view. What kind of painting is this first illustration? *A bird's eye view.* What do you

DAY 1

Introduce Book

Today's book is called *Loon Lake*. What's the title of this week's book? *Loon Lake.*

This book was written by Jonathan London. Who's the author of *Loon Lake*? *Jonathan London.*

Susan Ford made the pictures for this book. Who's the illustrator of *Loon Lake*? *Susan Ford.* Who made the illustrations for this book? *Susan Ford.*

The cover of a book usually gives us some hints of what the book is about. Let's look at the front cover of *Loon Lake*. What do you see in the illustration? (Ideas: *a man and a girl in a boat (canoe); two birds; a lake; some mountains; a sunrise or sunset.*)

(Assign each child a partner.) Remember, when you make a prediction about something, you say what you think will happen. Get ready to make some predictions to your partner about this book. Use the information from the cover to help you.

(Ask the following questions, allowing sufficient time for children to share their predictions with their partners.)

see in the sky? (Ideas: *A bird; a loon; clouds.*) What do you see on the ground? (Ideas: *A tent; a canoe; a lake; lots of trees.*)

Pages 3–4. What do you think the man is pointing at? (Idea: *The loon.*) What do you think the girl is doing? (Ideas: *Shouting; calling out.*) When do you think this part of the story happens? (Ideas: *At sunrise; at sunset.*) Why do you think so?

Pages 5–6. When do you think this part of the story happens? (Idea: *At night.*) Why do you think so? (Ideas: *The sky is dark; I see the moon.*)

(Turn back to pages 3 and 4, and show the illustration.) Now we know for sure when this part of the story happens. When does this part of the story happen? (Idea: *At sunset.*)

Pages 7–8. What is happening here? (Ideas: *A man is throwing beads into the water; the beads are landing on the loon.*) What is painted on the side of the canoe? (Ideas: *A bird; a loon.*)

Pages 9–10. What do the people see? (Ideas: *An animal; an otter.*) Why do you think the man has his finger in front of his mouth? (Ideas: *He is saying "sh-sh-sh"; he's telling the girl to be quiet.*)

Pages 11–12. What is this animal doing? *Swimming.* What is the name of this animal? *A beaver.* (**Note:** If children don't correctly name the beaver, say, "We'll learn the name of this animal when we read the story.") Do you think this animal is swimming close to the edge of the water or out in the middle of the lake? *Close to the edge of the water.* Why do you think so? (Ideas: *I can see water reeds and lily pads; I can see plants growing.*)

Pages 13–14. What is happening here? (Ideas: *The bird is going under the water; the bird is catching a fish.*)

Pages 15–16. What is different about this painting? (Idea: *We see on top of the water and under the water at the same time.*) Sometimes an artist makes a picture look as if he or she has sliced open the scene and put a window in so you can see above and below. We call that a cutaway view. What kind of painting is this

illustration? *A cutaway view.* What do you see above the water? (Ideas: *The man and the girl; the canoe; the top of the lake; the splash; the trees; the mountains; the stars and the moon.*) What do you see below? (Ideas: *The bottom of the lake; sand or mud; the lower stems of the reeds; small plants; the loon swimming under the water.*)

Pages 17–18. What is the happening here? (Ideas: *The mother loon and her two babies are hiding in the reeds; the father loon is flapping his wings.*) Why do you think the father loon is flapping his wings? (Ideas: *Trying to scare away the people; protecting his family.*)

Page 19–20. What are the birds doing now? (Idea: *Swimming out of the reeds.*)

Pages 21–22. What are the birds doing? *Flying away.*

Pages 23–24. What are the girl and her father doing? (Ideas: *Toasting marshmallows; enjoying a bonfire.*) What do you think she is telling her father?

Pages 25–26. What is happening here? (Ideas: *The father is sleeping in the tent; it is raining; the girl is watching the rain.*) What do you think the girl is thinking about? (Ideas: *The loons; the rain; the canoe ride on the lake.*)

Now that we've finished our picture walk, let's talk about how Susan Ford made the illustrations for *Loon Lake*. There are lots of different ways to make illustrations for a book: painting; drawing with a pen or a pencil; using markers, crayons, pastels, or chalk; or cutting out different pieces of paper and gluing them together. How do you think Susan Ford made her illustrations? (Idea: *She used both pastels and paint to make her illustrations.*)

Pages 21–22. Which part of this illustration do you think was made with pastels? (Ideas: *The trees; the shore.*) Which part of this illustration do you think was made with paint? (Ideas: *The birds; the splashes.*) Susan Ford tried to make her pictures look as real as she could, so we say her illustrations are realistic. What kind of illustrations did Susan Ford make for *Loon Lake*? *Realistic illustrations.*

It's your turn to ask me some questions. What would you like to know about the story? (Accept questions. If children tell about the pictures or the story instead of asking questions, prompt them to ask a question.) Ask me a why question. Ask me a how question.

Read Story Aloud
(Read story aloud to children with minimal interruptions.)

In the next lesson, we will read the story again, and I will ask you some questions.

Present Target Vocabulary
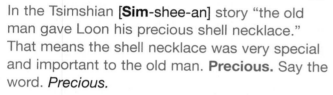
◎─◄ Precious.

In the Tsimshian [**Sim**-shee-an] story "the old man gave Loon his precious shell necklace." That means the shell necklace was very special and important to the old man. **Precious.** Say the word. *Precious.*

Precious is a describing word. It tells about the necklace. What kind of word is **precious?** *A describing word.*

If something is precious, it is very special and important to the person who owns it. Say the word that means "very special and important." *Precious.*

(Correct any incorrect responses, and repeat the item at the end of the sequence.)

Let's think about some things that might be precious to different people. I'll tell about something. If you think that thing is precious to the person, say, "Precious." If not, don't say anything.

- His violin is the most special thing he owns. *Precious.*
- Mom's wedding ring is very special to her. *Precious.*
- It is just an old piece of wood.
- That book isn't special—I have seven others just like it.
- The picture of her very first car is special to her. *Precious.*
- He knows he can have fresh vegetables again tomorrow if he wants them.

What describing word means "very special and important"? *Precious.*

What is most precious to you? Why is it precious? (Call on several children. Encourage them to start their answers with the words: "_____ is most precious to me because _____.")

◎─◄ Glimpse.

The girl telling the story says, "Now I glimpse him floating behind a screen of reeds." That means she sees the loon for only a short time as he floats behind the reeds. **Glimpse.** Say the word. *Glimpse.*

Glimpse is an action word. It tells what's happening. What kind of word is **glimpse?** *An action word.*

If you glimpse something, you see it for only a short time before it is gone. Say the word that means "see something for only a short time before it is gone." *Glimpse.*

(Correct any incorrect responses, and repeat the item at the end of the sequence.)

Let's think about some times when you might glimpse something. I'll tell about a time. If you think you would glimpse something, say, "Glimpse." If not, don't say anything.

- As their car goes down the highway, she sees a deer for only a short time before it jumps into the woods. *Glimpse.*
- The fish darts out from behind the reeds and then is quickly gone again. *Glimpse.*
- The moon can be seen for hours.
- He sees his friend in the busy airport terminal but only for a short time. *Glimpse.*
- Marietta stays for a week so she and her friend can talk a lot.
- The raccoon peeks out from behind the tree for a short time and then runs quickly out of sight. *Glimpse.*

What action word means "see something for only a short time before it is gone"? *Glimpse.*

◎─◄ Wild.

In the story, the girl hears Loon's wild wail. That means the girl hears a sound made by a wild bird, not a tame bird. **Wild.** Say the word. *Wild.*

Wild is a describing word. It tells what kind of bird. What kind of word is **wild?** *A describing word.*

If an animal is wild, it is not tame. A tame animal is looked after by people. A wild animal is not looked after by people. Say the word that means "not tame; not looked after by people." *Wild.*

(Correct any incorrect responses, and repeat the item at the end of the sequence.)

Let's think about some animals. Some of these animals are usually wild. Some of these animals are usually tame. If the animal I name is usually wild, say, "Wild." If the animal I name is usually tame, say, "Tame."

- Tiger. *Wild.*
- Dog. *Tame.*
- Hummingbird. *Wild.*
- Salmon. *Wild.*
- House cat. *Tame.*
- Moose. *Wild.*

What describing word means "not tame; not looked after by people"? *Wild.*

⊙━ Slithers.

In the story, "Otter slithers out of the water and into low brush." That means Otter moves by twisting and sliding along the ground at the edge of the lake. **Slithers.** Say the word. *Slithers.*

Slithers is an action word. It tells how things move. What kind of word is **slithers**? *An action word.*

If something slithers, it moves by twisting and sliding along the ground. Say the word that means "moves by twisting and sliding along the ground." *Slithers.*

Watch me. I'll use my hands to show how something slithers. (Hold out one hand flat, palm down. Place your other hand on top of the first, and move the top hand from side to side in a twisting, sliding motion.) Use your hands to show how something slithers. (Pause.) Good; you used your hands to show how something slithers.

(Correct any incorrect responses, and repeat the item at the end of the sequence.)

Let's think about some animals that could slither. I'll name an animal. If you think that animal slithers when it moves, say, "Slithers." If not, don't say anything.

- Snake. *Slithers.*
- Horse.
- Lizard. *Slithers.*
- Cat.
- Eagle.
- Crocodile. *Slithers.*

What action word means "moves by twisting and sliding along the ground"? *Slithers.*

Present Vocabulary Tally Sheet
(See Week 1, page 3, for instructions.)

Assign Homework
(Homework Sheet, BLM 22a: See the Introduction for homework instructions.)

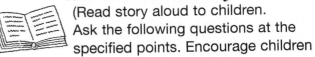

DAY 2

Preparation: Picture Vocabulary Cards for *precious, glimpse, wild,* and *slithers.*

(You may wish to play a recording of a loon's call for children. Using the search words *sound of a loon,* you will find many Internet sites that have sound recordings you can play.)

Read and Discuss Story
(Read story aloud to children. Ask the following questions at the specified points. Encourage children to use previously taught target words in their answers.)

Page 1. What three names do the native people give to the loon? *Rain Bird; Rain Goose; Call-up-a-Storm.*) All these names have something to do with rain or a storm. Long ago, the native people probably thought the loon brought . . . (Idea: *Rain.*)

Page 4. When do they hear the loon's call? (Idea: *At sunset.*) What does the loon's call sound like? (Idea: *A crazy yodeling laugh.*) (**Note:** You may wish to play a recording of a loon's call for children.) What happens when the girl tries to make the loon's laughing call? (Idea: *The loon laughs back.*)

Page 6. Why do they go out in their canoe? (Idea: *They want to see a loon up close.*)

Page 7. What is Papa doing? (Idea: *He's telling the girl a story about how the Loon got his white necklace.*) Tell me the story that tells how the loon got his white necklace. (Ideas: *An old blind man asked the loon for help; the loon used his magic to help him see again; the old man gave the loon his shell necklace.*)

Page 10. What animal do they see? *An otter.*

Page 12. What animal do they see next? *A beaver.*

Page 14. What animal do they see next? *A loon.* Do they get a good look at the loon? *No.* Why not? (Idea: *It dives under the water before they get close.*)

Page 16. The story says, "He rests in a nest of stars on the still water." Is the loon really resting in a nest of stars? *No.* What does the author mean? (Idea: *The reflection of the stars on the water is all around the loon.*)

Page 18. What three things does the loon do to show that the people in the canoe are making him anxious? (Ideas: *Rears up; shakes his head; flaps his wings.*) When a bird rears up, it lifts itself up to try to look bigger. (Point to the female bird in the reeds.) This loon is swimming calmly. (Point to the male loon.) This bird rears up to try to look bigger. How close to the loon do they paddle? *Thirty feet.* (**Note:** Identify a distance of thirty feet for children; e.g. the length of your classroom, the length of their house, the height of a telephone pole, or the distance from one side to the other on a two-lane road.)

Page 19. Why doesn't the girl shout out? (Idea: *She doesn't want to frighten the birds back into the reeds.*)

Page 22. How do loons get up in the air? (Idea: *They run on the water until they are going fast enough for their wings to lift them up into the air.*) What are the splashes on the water from? (Idea: *Their feet.*)

Page 23. How does Papa know there will be rain tonight? (Idea: *He sees the dark cloud passing across the moon.*)

Page 26. Do you think the loons bring the rain? Tell why you think the way you do.

Review Vocabulary

(Display the Picture Vocabulary Cards. Point to each card as you say the word. Ask children to repeat each word after you.) These pictures show **precious, glimpse, wild,** and **slithers.**

- What word means "very special and important"? *Precious.*
- What word means "see something for only a short time before it is gone"? *Glimpse.*
- What word means "not tame; not looked after by people"? *Wild.*
- What word means "moves by twisting and sliding along the ground"? *Slithers.*

Extend Vocabulary

 Wild.

In the story *Loon Lake,* we learned that **wild** is a describing word that means "not tame, not looked after by people." Say the word that means "not tame, not looked after by people." *Wild.*

Raise your hand if you can tell us a sentence that uses **wild** as a describing word that means "not tame, not looked after by people." (Call on several children. If they don't use complete sentences, restate their examples as sentences. Have the class repeat the sentences.)

Here's a new way to use the word **wild.**

- **The children ran wild, throwing paper airplanes everywhere.** Say the sentence.
- **The babysitter cannot control the wild children.** Say the sentence.
- **When the teacher leaves the room, the children go wild.** Say the sentence.

In these sentences, **wild** is a describing word that means **badly behaved or out of control.** What action word means "badly behaved or out of control"? *Wild.*

Present Expanded Target Vocabulary
Legend.

Loons have white feathers that go around their necks like a necklace. In the story *Loon Lake,* Papa tells the native story of how the loon got its white necklace. This kind of story that explains how something came to be is called a legend. **Legend.** Say the word. *Legend.*

Legend is a naming word. It names a kind of story. What kind of word is **legend?** *A naming word.*

A legend is a story that explains how something came to be. Say the word that means "a story that explains how something came to be." *Legend.*

I'll name some stories. If the story explains how something came to be, say, "Legend." If not, don't say anything.

- How the Leopard Got Its Spots. *Legend.*
- *Frog and Toad Are Friends.*
- Why Mosquitoes Buzz in People's Ears. *Legend.*
- How Music Came to Be. *Legend.*
- *The Wind Blew.*
- *Cloudy, with a Chance of Meatballs.*

What naming word means "a story that explains how something came to be"? *Legend.*

◎◀ Disappears.

In the story, "Loon quick-dives quietly." He can't be seen anymore. He disappears. **Disappears.** Say the word. *Disappears.*

Disappears is an action word. It tells what happens. What kind of word is **disappears?** *An action word.*

When you disappear, you can't be seen anymore. Say the word that means "you can't be seen anymore." *Disappears.* What word means "you can't be seen anymore"? *Disappears.*

I'll tell about someone or something. If what I tell about disappears, say, "Disappears." If not, don't say anything.

- Melodie hides behind the tree. *Disappears.*
- Father comes around the corner of the barn.
- The seal slips below the surface of the ocean. *Disappears.*
- Thomson and his sister come up the driveway.
- The huge cloud leaves the sky. *Disappears.*
- Zoe, Billie, and Gracie come inside for supper.

What action word means "can't be seen anymore"? *Disappears.*

Preparation: Activity Sheet, BLM 21b. Children will need crayons.

Retell Story

(Show pictures on the following pages from the story, and call on a child to tell what's happening. Call on a different child for each section.)

Today I'll show you the pictures Susan Ford made for the story *Loon Lake.* As I show you the pictures, I'll call on one of you to tell the class that part of the story.

Pages 1–4. Tell me what happens at the **beginning** of the story.

Pages 5–24. Tell me what happens in the **middle** of the story. (Encourage use of target words when appropriate. Model use as necessary.)

Pages 25–26. Tell me what happens at the **end** of the story.

Review Tom Foolery

Preparation: Prepare Picture Vocabulary Cards for all words with dual meanings. Display them prominently in a pocket chart, on a chalkboard ledge, or another obvious location. These words are *bloom, collect, curious, difficult, examine, howled, mood, nursery, present, prickly, promise, roared, root, scorched, scrawl, shouted, snatched, wild,* and *winding.*

Today we will play Tom Foolery. I will pretend to be Tom. Tom Foolery has a reputation for trying to trick children. Tom knows that some words have more than one meaning. He will tell you one meaning that will be correct. Then he will tell you another meaning that might be correct or incorrect. If you think the meaning is correct, don't say anything. If you think the meaning is incorrect, sing out "Tom Foolery."

Then Tom will have to tell the truth and give the correct meaning. Tom is sly enough that he may include some words that do *not* have two meanings. Be careful! He's tricky!

Let's practice: **Glimpse** means "see something for only a second before it is gone." Glimpse also means a huge balloon that flies around and carries people. *Tom Foolery!* Oh, you're right. I must have been thinking of a blimp that is like a huge balloon.

Let's do another one together. **Wild** means "not tame; not looked after by people." Wild also means that it is quite warm and pleasant outdoors. *Tom Foolery!* Oh, you're right. I must have been thinking of mild. All of you know that another meaning for wild is "badly behaved."

When we play Tom Foolery, Tom will keep score. If you catch him being tricky, you will get one point. If you don't catch him, Tom gets the point. Watch out! Tom just might try to give himself extra points while you're not looking!

Now you're ready to play the game.

(Draw a T-chart on the board for keeping score. Children earn one point for each correct answer. If they make an error, continue through the process as you normally would to give the correct meaning. Record one point for yourself, and repeat missed words at the end of the game.)

- **Disappears** means that something or someone "can't be seen anymore." Disappears also means a certain kind of ears that you can show or not show, depending on how you feel. *Tom Foolery!* Oh, you're right. We know only the first meaning. I would sure like to have a pair of "disapp ears," though.
- A **legend** is "a story that explains how something came to be." Legend also means to be stuck on a ledge that you can't get down from. *Tom Foolery!* Oh, you're right. We know only the first meaning for legend. Legend has nothing to do with ledges.
- Something that is **precious** is important or special to you.
- When something is **difficult,** it is hard to do. Difficult also means easy to get along with. *Tom Foolery!* Oh, you're right. Difficult means "not easy to get along with," doesn't it?

- Something that **slithers** moves by twisting and sliding along the ground. Slithers are also what you get in your fingers when you handle rough wood without gloves on. *Tom Foolery!* Oh, you're right. I must have been thinking about slivers, not slithers. I hate it when I get a slither. I mean sliver.

(Count the points, and declare a winner.)
You did a great job of playing Tom Foolery!

Coloring a Picture Realistically (Activity Sheet)

(Discuss with children the illustration on pages 19 and 20. Explain that the pictures Susan Ford made look real. Explain that the colors in the pictures help them to look real. Have two copies of the BLM for yourself to demonstrate "real" versus "not real.")

(Give each child a copy of the Activity Sheet, BLM 22b.) Today you'll use your crayons to color this picture of Loon Lake so it looks real. (Read the coloring instructions to the students. Display pages 19 and 20 or a photograph of a loon while children color.)

I'll start by coloring the water pink. (Demonstrate.) Do you think that's what I should do? *No.* Why shouldn't the water be pink? (Ideas: *Because water is blue, not pink; there is no such thing as pink water; pink water doesn't look real.*) That's right. We're going to use the colors that we would really see, not just colors we like.

Now I'll color the reeds and lilies black. (Demonstrate.) Don't the reeds and lilies look wonderful? *No.* What's wrong? (Ideas: *Reeds and lilies should be green; living plants are green, not black; we're trying to make this picture look real.*) I guess you're right. Black reeds and lilies just don't look real.

Would it be realistic if I used my black crayon to color part of the loon? *Yes.* Why would that be the right thing to do? (Ideas: *Because the loon is really black and white; the color black will make the loon look real.*) Now it's your turn to make the picture look real. Be careful when you color. Make sure your picture looks realistic.

Introduce Circle Pattern (Literary Analysis)

When authors write stories, they sometimes write in patterns. Let's see if we can figure out the pattern for this story. You tell me what happens in the story, and I'll write it down.

(Show the illustrations on the following pages, and ask the specified questions.)

Pages 1–2. Where are the girl and her papa when the story begins? (Idea: <u>In the tent</u>.)

Pages 3–4. Then what happens? (Idea: *They <u>hear</u> the <u>loon</u>.*)

Pages 5–6. Then what happens? (Idea: *They <u>go</u> out on the <u>lake</u> in their <u>canoe</u>.*)

Pages 7–8. Then what happens? (Idea: *Papa <u>tells</u> the <u>legend</u> of the <u>loon</u>.*)

Pages 9–10. Then what happens? (Idea: *They <u>see</u> the <u>otter</u>.*)

Pages 11–12. Then what happens? (Idea: *They <u>see</u> the <u>beaver</u>.*)

Pages 13–18. (Show the illustrations.) Then what happens? (Idea: *They <u>follow</u> the <u>loon</u>.*)

Pages 19–20. Then what happens? (Idea: *They <u>see</u> the <u>loon family</u>.*)

Pages 21–22. Then what happens? (Idea: *The <u>loons fly away</u>.*)

Pages 23–24. Then what happens? (Idea: *They have a <u>campfire</u>.*)

Pages 25–26. Where are the girl and her papa when the story ends? (Idea: <u>In the tent</u>.)

(Point to the story map on the chart paper.) Look at the shape of this story. It's a circle. This story starts and ends at the same place, so this story

has a **circle** pattern. What kind of a pattern does a story have that starts and ends at the same place? *A circle pattern.*

Today we will learn a new verse for "The Pattern Song" that will help us remember about circle story patterns.

Listen while I sing the verse for you:

> *Did you know that there's a circle pattern too?*
> *Did you know that there's a circle pattern too?*
> *In a circle you will roam*
> *But you'll always find your home.*
> *Did you know that there's a circle pattern too?*

Get ready to sing the new verse with me.

Now let's sing all that we've learned together.

(See the Introduction for the complete "The Pattern Song.")

Singing a song together is a very good way to remember the patterns that we're learning!

Play Tom Foolery (Cumulative Review)

Today we will play Tom Foolery. I will pretend to be Tom. You know that Tom has a reputation for trying to trick you. Tom knows that some words have more than one meaning. He will tell you one meaning that will be correct. Then he will tell you another meaning that might be correct or incorrect.

If you think the meaning is correct, don't say anything. If you think the meaning is incorrect, sing out "Tom Foolery." Then Tom will have to tell the truth and give the correct meaning. Tom is sly enough that he may include some words that do *not* have two meanings. Be careful! He's tricky!

Let's practice: A road that twists and turns is a **winding** road. Another meaning for winding is complaining in a babyish voice. *Tom Foolery!* Oh, you're right. I was thinking of whining. Another meaning for winding is turning a key or a knob to make something like a music box work.

Let's do another one together. Something **precious** is anything that is very important to you. Also, people can put precious on you when they try hard to make you do something. *Tom Foolery!* Oh, you're right. I guess I was thinking of pressure. Precious is something that is special or important to you.

When we play Tom Foolery, Tom will keep score. If you catch him being tricky, you will get one point. If you don't catch him, Tom gets the point. Watch out! Tom just might try to give himself extra points while you're not looking!

Now you're ready to play the game.

[T] (Draw a T-chart on the board for keeping score. Children earn one point for each correct answer. If they make an error, correct them as you normally would, and record one point for yourself. Repeat missed words at the end of the game.)

- A **nursery** is a place for babies. A nursery is also a place where people learn to be nurses. *Tom Foolery!* Oh, you're right. Another meaning for nursery is a place where you buy plants.
- A **wild** duck is a duck that is not tame. A wild party is a party where everyone is well-behaved. *Tom Foolery!* Oh, you're right. A wild party is a party where people wouldn't be well-behaved, isn't it?
- If something **disappears,** it goes out of sight. If a seal slips under the surface of the ocean, it disappears.
- A **legend** is a story that explains how something came to be. When you climb a mountain, a legend is a place where you can stop and rest your feet. *Tom Foolery!* Oh, you're right. I'm still thinking about ledge, not legend. They aren't the same at all!
- If you **explained** something to someone, you told more about it so that person could understand it. Explained also means shouted something in a loud voice. *Tom Foolery!* Oh, you're right. I was thinking of exclaimed.
- A circle pattern starts in one place, goes away from there, and then goes back again. A circle pattern is like a circle.
- If you **slither,** you move by twisting and sliding on the ground. Some people like to wear slithers when their feet are cold. *Tom Foolery!* Oh, you're right. I suppose I was thinking of slippers, not slithers. My feet must be cold.

- When a wolf **howled,** it made a long, loud crying sound. Howled can also mean the sound Lou made when he got hurt.
- **Glimpse** means to "see something for only a second before it is gone." Glimpse also means "more than one glimp." *Tom Foolery!* Oh, you're right. I made that second meaning up. That's why my name is Tom Foolery!
- When you are **lonely,** you are "unhappy because you have been left all alone." Lonely also means that you want to let someone borrow some money. *Tom Foolery!* Oh, you're right. I made that second meaning up. I must have been thinking of a loan.

(Count the points, and declare a winner.) You did a great job of playing Tom Foolery!

DAY 5

Preparation: Happy Face Game Test Sheet, BLM B.

Introduce Afterword

(Assign each child a partner.) Sometimes after people finish writing a story about something real, they want to tell you more facts about that real thing. This information is put in the book after the last word of the story, so it is called an **afterword.** Today I'll read the afterword that Jonathan London wrote for *Loon Lake* so you can learn more about loons.

The story *Loon Lake* is make-believe. It was made from the author's imagination. When a story is made up from the author's imagination we say the story is fiction. What do we call a story that is made up from the author's imagination? *Fiction.*

The afterword tells us true facts about loons. Facts are true and can be proved. For example, it is a fact that there are _____ children in our class. We can prove that fact is true by counting the children in our class.

When part of a book tells true facts about something, that part of the book is called nonfiction. What do we call the parts of books that tell true facts about something? *Nonfiction.*

(Read the afterword aloud a paragraph at a time.)

Paragraph 1. Expressions are the way that people say things. What expressions do we have because of the loon's cry? *Crazy as a loon, loony.*

Paragraph 2. What are loons best at? *Diving and swimming.* What are loons worst at? *Walking on land.*

Paragraph 3. How many loon families usually live on a lake? *One.*

Paragraph 4. How many eggs does a loon lay? *Two or three.* How soon can the babies dive for their own fish? *One week.*

Paragraph 5. How long do the parents look after their babies? *Six weeks.* How do the parents help their babies when they get tired? (Idea: *They let them ride on their backs.*)

Paragraph 6. What do loons eat? (Ideas: *Fish; frogs; crayfish; water plants; insects; leeches.*) What is unusual about how loons catch their food? (Idea: *They fly underwater, using their wings.*)

Paragraph 7. Where do loons go in the winter? (Idea: *To ocean coasts where there is no ice.*) You already know a word that means "fly away to spend the winter somewhere else." What do the loons do in winter? *Migrate.* How fast can loons fly? *Sixty miles an hour.* (**Note:** Give a concrete example children can understand. For example, say "That's a mile in one minute. If we started watching the clock now, by the time the second hand has gone around one time, the loon could fly from our school to _____.") Wow! That's fast!

(Read the last paragraph of the afterword.)

Where do the loon parents go the next spring? (Idea: *Back to the same lake they came from.*)

Where do the loon babies go the next spring? (Idea: *To a different lake.*)

We have learned many facts about loons from this afterword. Think about the one fact that you thought was most interesting. (**Pause.**) Share that fact with your partner. (**Pause.**) Tonight you will share that fact with someone at your home.

Assess Vocabulary

 (Hold up a copy of the Happy Face Game Test Sheet, BLM B.)

Today you're going to play the Happy Face Game. When you play the Happy Face Game, it helps me know how well you know the hard words you are learning.

If I say something true, color the happy face. What will you do if I say something true? *Color the happy face.*

If I say something false, color the sad face. What will you do if I say something false? *Color the sad face.*

Listen carefully to each item I say. Don't let me trick you!

Item 1: A **precious** thing is important to you. *True.*

Item 2: Something that **disappears** goes out of sight. *True.*

Item 3: **Wild** can mean not tame *or* it can mean badly-behaved. *True.*

Item 4: A **legend** is a story that tells you how to make soup. *False.*

Item 5: A creature that **slithers** moves by hopping and bouncing. *False.*

Item 6: A **glimpse** is a quick look. *True.*

Item 7: English and Spanish are both **languages.** *True.*

Item 8: A person who has **patience** does *not* worry or feel upset when he or she has to wait. *False.*

Item 9: When someone **scowls,** he or she makes an angry face. *True.*

Item 10: When the kitten **trembled,** it was afraid or cold. *True.*

You did a great job of playing the Happy Face Game!

(Score children's work later. Scores of 9 out of 10 indicate mastery. If a child does not achieve mastery, insert the missed words in the games in the next week's lessons. Retest those children individually on the missed words before they take the next mastery test.)

Extensions
Read a Story as a Reward

(Display copies of several of the books you have read since the beginning of the program. Allow children to choose which book they would like you to read aloud to them as a reward for their hard work.)

(Read story aloud to children for enjoyment with minimal interruptions.)

Present the Super Words Center

(Prepare the word containers for the Super Words Center. You may wish to remove some words from earlier lessons. Choose words the children have mastered.

See the Introduction for instructions on how to set up and use the Super Words Center.)

(Add the new Picture Vocabulary Cards to the words from previous weeks. Show children one of the word containers. If they need more guidance, role-play with two or three children as a demonstration.)

Today I will teach you about how to play a new game called What's Missing?

Let's think about how we work with our words in the Super Words Center.

You will work with a partner in the Super Words Center. Whom will you work with in the center? *A partner.*

First, one partner will draw four word cards out of the container and put them on the table so both partners can see. What do you do first? (Idea: *Draw four cards out of the container and put them on the table so both partners can see.*)

Next you will take turns looking at the cards and saying the words the pictures show. What do you do next? **Idea:** *We take turns looking at the cards and saying the words the pictures show.*

Next, partner 2 looks away while partner 1 takes one of the four cards and places it facedown on the table away from the other cards. Then partner 1 draws a new card from the container and places it on the table with the other three. Watch while I show you what I mean. (Demonstrate with one child as your partner.) When you put down the new card, it's a good idea to mix the cards so they aren't in the same places anymore. (Demonstrate as you go.)

Now partner 1 says, "What's Missing?" Partner 2 has to use his or her eyes and brain and say which old card has been taken away. After partner 2 has guessed, turn over the facedown card. If partner 2 is correct, he or she gets a point. If partner 2 is not correct, partner 1 gets the point. (Demonstrate as you go.)

Next, partner 2 has a turn to choose four different cards, and the game starts again. What happens next? (Idea: *Partner 2 has a turn to choose four different cards, and the game starts again.*)

Have fun playing What's Missing!

The Apple Pie Tree
author: Zoe Hall • illustrator: Shari Halpern

Target Vocabulary

Tier II	Tier III
bare	pattern
appear	(linear)
blossom	collage
petals	facts
*seasons	
*present	

*Expanded Target Vocabulary Word

- Who are the characters in this story? (Whom do you think this story is about?)
- What do you think the story is about?
- Where do you think the story happens?
- When do you think the story happens?
- Why do you think the robins built the nest?
- How many apples are on the tree?
- Do you think this story is about real things? Tell why or why not.

(Call on several children to share their predictions with the class.)

DAY 1

Introduce Book

Today's book is called *The Apple Pie Tree*. What's the title of this week's book? *The Apple Pie Tree.*

This book was written by Zoe [**zoh**-ee] Hall. Who's the author of *The Apple Pie Tree*? *Zoe Hall.*

Shari Halpern made the pictures for this book. Who's the illustrator of *The Apple Pie Tree*? *Shari Halpern.* Who made the illustrations for this book? *Shari Halpern.*

The cover of a book usually gives us some hints of what the book is about. (Open up the book so the children can see the front and back covers at the same time.) Let's look at the cover of *The Apple Pie Tree.* What do you see in the illustration? (Ideas: *A tree; branches; leaves; apples; two robins; a nest; a butterfly; a bee.*)

(Assign each child a partner.) Remember, when you make a prediction about something, you say what you think will happen. Get ready to make some predictions to your partner about this book. Use the information from the cover to help you.

(Ask the following questions, allowing sufficient time for children to share their predictions with their partners.)

Take a Picture Walk

We are going to take a picture walk through this book. Remember, when we take a picture walk, we look at the pictures and tell what we think will happen in the story.

(Show the illustrations on the following pages, and ask the specified questions. Encourage children to use previously taught target words in their answers.)

Page 1. What do you see in this illustration? (Ideas: *An apple; a big container with something white in it (flour); a small container with something white in it (sugar); a rectangle of something yellow (butter); two brown sticks.*)

(**Note:** It isn't necessary at this time for children to identify the ingredients, although some may do so based on the title of the book.)

Pages 2–3. What do you think is happening here? (Ideas: *The children are looking out the window at the tree; the tree has no leaves.*)

Pages 4–5. Where are the children? (Idea: *Outside.*) How is the tree different? (Idea: *It has leaves.*) What else do you see in the tree? (Ideas: *Two robins; a nest.*) What are the birds doing? (Idea: *Building the nest.*) Why do you think so? (Idea: *One robin has a twig in its mouth.*)

Pages 6–7. How is the tree different? (Idea: *It has flowers.*) How is the robin's nest different? (Ideas: *It's bigger; it has three eggs in it.*)

Pages 8–9. How is the tree different? (Ideas: *The flowers are bigger; the flowers have opened.*) How is the robin's nest different? (Idea: *It has three baby birds in it.*) What is the big robin doing? (Ideas: *Feeding its babies; giving worms to the babies.*)

Pages 10–11. How is the tree different? (Idea: *The flowers are even bigger.*) How are the baby birds different? (Ideas: *They have brown feathers on their heads; they have red breasts.*) What do you see on two of the flowers? *Bees.*

Pages 12–13. What is happening here? (Ideas: *The flowers are floating to the ground; the robins are flying; the cat is chasing the flowers.*)

Pages 14–15. What is happening here? (Ideas: *It's raining; the wind is blowing; the birds are all in the nest.*) How is the tree different? (Idea: *There are no flowers.*)

Pages 16–17. How is the tree different? (Ideas: *There are little green and brown round things on it; there are tiny apples on it.*) What are the robins doing? *Flying around.*

Pages 18–19. What are the children doing? (Ideas: *Playing in the sprinkler; playing in the water.*) How is the tree different? (Idea: *The apples are bigger.*) How are the baby birds different? (Idea: *They are bigger.*)

Pages 20–21. How is the tree different? (Ideas: *It's full of leaves; the apples are bigger; some of the apples are red.*) Where are the baby birds? (Ideas: *Gone; they're not there.*) What are the deer doing? *Eating the apples.*

Pages 22–23. What is happening here? (Ideas: *Someone is picking an apple; the person is on a ladder.*)

Pages 24–25. What is happening here? (Ideas: *They are making a pie; the girl is sprinkling something on the apples; the little boy is holding a piece of apple peel.*)

Pages 26–27. What do you see in this illustration? (Ideas: *An apple pie; a whole apple; an apple core; some pieces of apple peel.*)

Pages 28–29. What is happening here? (Ideas: *The children are eating the pie.*)

Now that we've finished our picture walk, let's talk about how Shari Halpern made the illustrations for *The Apple Pie Tree.*

There are lots of different ways to make illustrations for a book: painting; drawing with a pen or a pencil; using markers, crayons, pastels, or chalk; or cutting out different pieces of paper and gluing them together. How do you think Shari Halpern made her illustrations? (Idea: *She cut out different pieces of paper and glued them together.*)

Pages 2–3. Sometimes Shari Halpern used just plain paper in her illustrations. Which part of the illustration do you think was made from plain paper? (Ideas: *The blue walls; the faces; the green part of the eyes.*)

Sometimes Shari Halpern used paper that already had a pattern on it. Which part of the illustration do you think was made from paper that already had a pattern on it? (Idea: *The curtain.*)

Sometimes Shari Halpern painted paper to get the exact colors she wanted. Which part of the illustration do you think was made from painted paper? (Ideas: *The tree; the ground; the children's hair.*)

When an artist makes an illustration by cutting out different pieces of paper and gluing them together, we say the artist made a collage. What do you call an illustration that is made by cutting out different pieces of paper and gluing them together? *A collage.*

Shari Halpern made her illustrations by cutting out different pieces of paper and gluing them together, so we say her illustrations are collages. What kind of illustrations did Shari Halpern make for *The Apple Pie Tree*? *Collages.*

It's your turn to ask me some questions. What would you like to know about the story? (Accept questions. If children tell about the pictures or the story instead of asking questions, prompt them to ask a question.) Ask me a why question. Ask me a when question.

Read Story Aloud
(Read story aloud to children with minimal interruptions.)

In the next lesson, we will read the story again, and I will ask you some questions.

Present Target Vocabulary

◎— Bare.

In the story, the girl says that the apple tree is bare during the winter months. That means the branches are not covered with leaves. **Bare.** Say the word. *Bare.*

Bare is a describing word. It tells about the tree. What kind of word is **bare?** *A describing word.*

If something is bare, nothing is covering it. Say the word that means "nothing is covering it." *Bare.*

(Correct any incorrect responses, and repeat the item at the end of the sequence.)

Let's think about some things that might be bare. I'll tell about something. If you think that thing is bare, say, "Bare." If not, don't say anything.

- She has no shoes or socks on her feet. *Bare.*
- John is wearing overalls and a heavy coat.
- There are no pictures on the walls. *Bare.*
- The rock is covered with moss.
- When the family moves, their house is empty. *Bare.*
- All of the leaves are falling off the tree. *Bare.*

What describing word means "nothing is covering it"? *Bare.*

◎— Appear.

In the story, buds appear on the branches of the apple tree. That means buds can be seen on the branches. **Appear.** Say the word. *Appear.*

Appear is an action word. It tells what happens. What kind of word is **appear?** *An action word.*

When things appear, they can be seen. Say the word that means "can be seen." *Appear.* What word means "can be seen"? *Appear.*

We learned a word in Week 22 that means "can't be seen anymore." That word is **disappear.** Say the word **disappear.** *Disappear.*

Appear and **disappear** are opposites. What kind of words are **appear** and **disappear?** *Opposites.*

What word is the opposite of **appear?** *Disappear.* What word is the opposite of **disappear?** *Appear.*

(Correct any incorrect responses, and repeat the item at the end of the sequence.)

I'll tell about someone or something. If what I tell about appears, say, "Appear." If what I tell about disappears, say, "Disappear."

- The sun goes down. *Disappear.*
- Uncle Josh drives up in his new car. *Appear.*
- The otter swims past us and then, "Sploot!" —he is gone! *Disappear.*
- When my mom makes spaghetti, I eat my plateful really fast. *Disappear.*
- My puppy, Dexter, runs up and jumps on me. *Appear.*
- Joe and Amy suddenly fall into a deep hole. *Disappear.*

What action word means "can be seen"? *Appear.* What action word means "can't be seen anymore"? *Disappear.*

◎— Blossom.

In the story, the tree has blossoms all over. That means the tree is covered with flowers that will turn into fruit. **Blossom.** Say the word. *Blossom.*

Blossom is a naming word. It names the things covering the tree. What kind of word is **blossom?** *A naming word.*

A blossom is a flower that will turn into fruit. Say the word that means "a flower that will turn into fruit." *Blossom.*

(Correct any incorrect responses, and repeat the item at the end of the sequence.)

Let's think about some things that might blossom. If the thing I name might blossom, say, "Blossom." If not, don't say anything.

- Cherry tree. *Blossom.*
- Broom.
- Pear tree. *Blossom.*

- Blackberry bush. *Blossom.*
- Apple tree. *Blossom.*
- Car.

What naming word means "a flower that will turn into fruit"? *Blossom.*

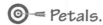 Petals.

In the story, the girl says that the flower petals fall when a gentle wind blows.

(Draw a simple plant on the board. Point to the petals.) That means these outer parts of the flower fall to the ground. **Petals.** Say the word. *Petals.*

Petals is a naming word. It names a part of a flower. What kind of word is **petals?** *A naming word.*

Petals are the outer parts of a flower. Say the word that means "the outer parts of a flower." *Petals.*

(Correct any incorrect responses, and repeat the item at the end of the sequence.)

Let's think about petals. I'll name something. If what I say could have petals, say, "Petals." If what I say would not have petals, say, "Absolutely not."

- Cherry blossom. *Petals.*
- A clock. *Absolutely not.*
- Rose. *Petals.*
- A table. *Absolutely not.*
- Your uncle Jim. *Absolutely not.*
- Water lily. *Petals.*

What naming word means "the outer parts of a flower"? *Petals.*

Present Vocabulary Tally Sheet
(See Week 1, page 3, for instructions.)

Assign Homework
(Homework Sheet, BLM 23a: See the Introduction for homework instructions.)

Preparation: Picture Vocabulary Cards for *bare, appear, blossom,* and *petals.* You may want to have a cinnamon stick available.

Read and Discuss Story
(Read story aloud to children. Ask the following questions at the specified points. Encourage them to use previously taught target words in their answers.)

Page 1. What do you think the answer to the question is? *Apples.* (Point to the illustration.) These are the things you need to make something. You already know the word that means "the things you need to make something." What word means "the things you need to make something"? *Ingredients.* That's right; all these things are the ingredients you need to make apple pie. Let's name these ingredients. (Ideas: *Apples; flour; sugar; butter; cinnamon.*)

(**Note:** You may wish to show children a cinnamon stick and let them smell it.)

Page 2. When does this part of the story happen? *In winter.* What does the tree look like in winter? (Ideas: *Bare; brown; it has no leaves.*)

Page 4. When does this part of the story happen? *In spring.* What does the tree look like in spring? (Idea: *It is getting leaves.*) What else happens to this tree in spring? (Idea: *Robins build a nest in it.*)

Page 7. What else happens to the tree in spring? *Buds appear.* What do the robins do? (Ideas: *Lay eggs in their nest; guard the eggs.*)

Pages 8–9. What else happens in the spring? (Ideas: *The flower buds open; the baby robins hatch.*)

Page 11. What else happens in spring? (Ideas: *The tree is covered with blossoms; the baby robins start to get their feathers.*)

Page 12. What else happens in spring? (Ideas: *The breezes blow; the petals fall; the little birds learn to fly.*)

Page 14. What protects the birds on stormy, rainy days? (Idea: *The tree.*)

Page 17. What happens to the blossoms? (Idea: *They turn into small green apples.*)

Pages 18–19. When does this part of the story happen? *In summer.* What happens to the apples in summer? (Idea: *They get bigger.*) What happens to the baby robins in summer? (Idea: *They grow up.*)

Page 21. What else happens in summer? (Ideas: *The apples grow bigger; the branches bend down.*)

Page 22. When does this part of the story happen? *In autumn.* What happens to the apples in autumn? (Idea: *Someone picks them.*)

Pages 24–26. What do the children make from the apples? *Apple pie.*

Pages 27–28. What do the children like about the apple pie? (Ideas: *It smells so good; it tastes delicious.*)

At the end of the story the children say, "There's nothing as good as an apple pie you grew yourself." Raise your hand if you think that is true. (Pause.) Raise your hand if you think that is false. (Pause.)

Review Vocabulary

(Display the Picture Vocabulary Cards. Point to each card as you say the word. Ask children to repeat each word after you.) These pictures show **bare, appear, blossom,** and **petals.**

- What word means "the outer parts of a flower"? *Petals.*
- What word means "nothing is covering it"? *Bare.*
- What word means "a flower that will turn into fruit"? *Blossom.*
- What word means "can be seen"? *Appear.*

Extend Vocabulary
◎◄ Blossom.

In *The Apple Pie Tree,* we learned that **blossom** is a naming word that means "a flower that will turn into fruit." Say the word that means "a flower that will turn into fruit." *Blossom.*

Raise your hand if you can tell us a sentence that uses **blossom** as a naming word that means "a flower that will turn into fruit." (Call on several children. If they don't use complete sentences, restate their examples as sentences. Have the class repeat the sentences.)

Here's a new way to use the word **blossom.**

- **Teresa blossoms into a wonderful singer.** Say the sentence.
- **Leo the Late Bloomer takes a long time to blossom.** Say the sentence.
- **The class blossoms as excellent readers.** Say the sentence.

In these sentences, **blossom** is an action word that means **grow or get better at things.** What action word means "grow or get better at things"? *Blossom.*

Raise your hand if you can tell us a sentence that uses **blossom** as an action word that means "grow or get better at things." (Call on several children. If they don't use complete sentences, restate their examples as sentences. Have the class repeat the sentences.)

Present Expanded Target Vocabulary
◎◄ *Seasons.*

In *The Apple Pie Tree,* we learn what happens to the tree in winter, spring, summer, and autumn. Winter, spring, summer, and autumn are the four parts of the year. We call these parts the seasons. **Seasons.** Say the word. *Seasons.*

Seasons is a naming word. It names the parts of the year. What kind of word is **seasons?** *A naming word.*

The seasons are the four parts of the year: winter, spring, summer, and autumn. Say the word that means "the four parts of the year: winter, spring, summer, and autumn." *Seasons.*

I'll name some activities. If that activity happens in winter, say, "Winter." If that activity happens in spring, say, "Spring." If that activity happens in summer, say, "Summer." If that activity happens in autumn, say, "Autumn." (**Note:** If these activities happen in other seasons in your area, accept those responses.)

- Throwing snowballs. *Winter.*
- Leaves change color and fall off the trees. *Autumn.*
- Snow melts, and water runs down the street. *Spring.*
- Bears sleep for a long, long time, or hibernate. *Winter.*
- You wear shorts, T-shirts, and sunscreen. *Summer.*
- People rake big piles of dead leaves and enjoy pumpkins and other squashes. *Autumn.*

What naming word means "the four parts of the year: winter, spring, summer, and autumn"? *Seasons.*

◎⚬ *Present.*

The Apple Pie Tree is written as if it were happening right now. When a story is written as if it were happening right now, the story is written in the present. **Present.** Say the word. *Present.*

Present is a naming word. It names a time. What kind of word is **present?** *A naming word.*

When things happen in the present, they are happening right now. Say the words that mean "happening right now." *In the present.*

I'll tell about something. If what I tell about is happening right now, say, "In the present." If not, don't say anything.

- (Clap your hands, and keep clapping them.) I am clapping right now. *In the present.* (Stop clapping.)
- I was clapping.
- I am teaching you a lesson right now. *In the present.*
- Your hearts are beating, and you are paying attention to me with your eyes, ears, and brains. *In the present.*
- The dog is barking right now. *In the present.*

What words mean "happening right now"? *In the present.*

We know two other ways to use the word **present.** In Week 9, we learned the word **present** is a naming word that means "a gift." What word means "a gift"? *Present.* Raise your hand if you can tell us a sentence that

uses **present** as a naming word that means "a gift." (Call on several children. If they don't use complete sentences, restate their examples as sentences. Have the class repeat the sentences.)

We also learned the word **present** is a describing word that means "being somewhere." What word means "being somewhere"? *Present.* Raise your hand if you can tell us a sentence that uses **present** as a describing word that means "being somewhere." (Call on several children. If they don't use complete sentences, restate their examples as sentences. Have the class repeat the sentences.)

Now we've learned that the words "in the present" mean "happening right now." Raise your hand if you can tell us a sentence that is in the present or happening right now. (Call on several children. If they don't use complete sentences, restate their examples as sentences. Have the class repeat the sentences.)

DAY 3

Preparation: Activity Sheet, BLM 23b. Children will need crayons.

Retell Story

(Show the pictures on the following pages from the story, and call on a child to tell what's happening. Call on a different child for each section.)

Today I'll show you the pictures Shari Halpern made for the story *The Apple Pie Tree.* As I show you the pictures, I'll call on one of you to tell the class that part of the story.

Pages 2–3. Tell me what happens in the **winter.** (Encourage children to include the target word *bare.* Model use as necessary.)

Pages 4–17. Tell me what happens in the **spring.** (Encourage children to include the target words *appear, blossom,* and *petals* when appropriate. Model use as necessary.)

Pages 18–21. Tell me what happens in the **summer.** (Encourage children to include target words when appropriate. Model use as necessary.)

Pages 22–29. Tell me what happens in the **autumn.**

Review Tom Foolery

Preparation: Prepare Picture Vocabulary Cards for all words with dual meanings. Display them prominently in a pocket chart, on a chalkboard ledge, or another obvious location. These words are *bloom, blossom, collect, curious, difficult, examine, howled, mood, nursery, present, prickly, promise, roared, root, scorched, scrawl, shouted, snatched, wild,* and *winding.*

Today we will play Tom Foolery. I will pretend to be Tom. Tom Foolery has a reputation for trying to trick children. Tom knows that some words have more than one meaning. He will tell you one meaning that will be correct. Then he will tell you another meaning that might be correct or incorrect.

If you think the meaning is correct, don't say anything. If you think the meaning is incorrect, sing out "Tom Foolery." Then Tom will have to tell the truth and give the correct meaning. Tom is sly enough that he may include some words that do *not* have two meanings. Be careful! He's tricky!

Let's practice: If something is **bare,** nothing is covering it. Bare also means a big container made with wood or metal. *Tom Foolery!* Oh, you're right. I was thinking of barrel, not bare.

Let's do another one together. **Present** can mean that you are here. "In the present" means that something happened yesterday. *Tom Foolery!* Oh, you're right. If something is happening in the present, it's happening right now.

When we play Tom Foolery, Tom will keep score. If you catch him being tricky, you will get one point. If you don't catch him, Tom gets the point. Watch out! Tom just might try to give himself extra points while you're not looking!

Now you're ready to play the game.

(Draw a T-chart on the board for keeping score. Children earn one point for each correct answer. If they make an error, continue through the process as you normally would to give the correct meaning. Record one point for yourself, and repeat missed words at the end of the game.)

- If you **gasp,** you breathe in really quickly. You also use gasp to make your car go. *Tom Foolery!* Oh, you're right. I must have been thinking of gas instead of gasp.
- **Seasons** are the four different times of the year. You also call "Season!" (sea's in), when the tide comes in at the beach. *Tom Foolery!* Oh, you're right. We know only the first meaning for seasons.
- When you **finally** get something, it means that you waited a while to get it.
- Someone who **dashed** ran very quickly. You can also dash potatoes (I *love* dashed potatoes!). *Tom Foolery!* Oh, you're right. We know only one meaning for dashed. And it's mashed potatoes, isn't it?
- **Petals** are "the outer parts of a flower." Petals are also what you put your feet on to make your bike move. *Tom Foolery!* Oh, you're right. I'm thinking of pedals, not petals.

(Count the points, and declare a winner.)
You did a great job of playing Tom Foolery!

Seasons (Activity Sheet)

(Review with students the names of the seasons, starting with winter.)

(Give each child a copy of the Activity Sheet, BLM 23b. Children will place the pictures in the sequence of the seasons, starting with winter. Instruct children to color the pictures, cut them out, and paste or glue them in sequential order. Children who are able to may copy the words *winter, spring, summer,* and *autumn* under the appropriate picture.)

Preparation: Prepare a sheet of chart paper, landscape direction, with the title *The Apple Pie Tree*. Underneath the title, draw a row of ten boxes connected by arrows. Underneath the first row of boxes, draw a second row of seven boxes connected by arrows. The first box in the second row is underneath the second box in the first row.

See the Introduction for an example.

Record children's responses by writing the underlined words in the boxes.

Review Linear Pattern (Literary Analysis)

When authors write stories, they sometimes write in patterns.

Let's see if we can figure out the pattern for this story. First let's think about only the apple tree, not the robins. You tell me what happens in the story, and I'll write it down.

(Show the illustrations on the following pages, and ask the specified questions.)

Pages 2–3. What does the apple tree look like in winter? (Ideas: *It is <u>bare</u>; it has <u>no leaves</u>*.)

Pages 4–5. Then what happens? (Idea: *It gets <u>leaves</u>*.)

Pages 6–7. Then what happens? (Idea: *It gets <u>buds</u>*.)

Pages 8–9. Then what happens? (Idea: *The <u>buds open</u>*.)

Pages 10–11. Then what happens? (Idea: *The <u>bees</u> come to the <u>blossoms</u>*.)

Pages 12–13. Then what happens? (Idea: *The <u>petals fall</u>*.)

Pages 14–15. Then what happens? (Idea: *It <u>rains</u>*.)

Pages 16–21. Then what happens? (Idea: *Small green <u>apples grow</u>*.)

Pages 22–23. Then what happens? (Idea: *They <u>pick</u> the <u>apples</u>*.)

Pages 24–29. Then what happens? (Idea: *They <u>make</u> the <u>pie</u>*.)

(Point to the story map on the chart paper. Draw a line under the story map.) Look at the shape of the story of the apple tree. It's a line. This story starts and ends at different times, so this story has a **linear** pattern. What kind of pattern does a story have when it starts and ends at different times? *A linear pattern.*

Now let's think about only the robins, not the apple tree. You tell me what happens in the story, and I'll write it down.

Pages 4–5. What do the robins do first? (Idea: *<u>Build a nest</u>*.)

Pages 6–7. Then what happens? (Idea: *They <u>guard</u> their <u>eggs</u>*.)

Pages 8–9. Then what happens? (Idea: *The <u>baby robins hatch</u>*.)

Page 11. Then what happens? (Idea: *The baby robins <u>grow feathers</u>*.)

Pages 12–13. Then what happens? (Idea: *The baby robins <u>learn to fly</u>*.)

Pages 14–15. Then what happens? (Idea: *The robins are <u>safe in their nest</u>*.)

Page 19. Then what happens? (Idea: *The little robins have <u>grown up</u>*.)

(Point to the story map on the chart paper. Draw a line under the story map.) Look at the shape of the story of the robins. It's a line. This story starts and ends at different times, so this story has a **linear** pattern. What kind of pattern does a story have when it starts and ends at different times? *A linear pattern.*

So this story has a two linear patterns: one for the apple tree, and one for the robins.

What other stories have we read that had linear patterns? (Ideas: *Wake Up, Farm!, Jamaica and the Substitute Teacher.*)

Let's sing "The Pattern Song" to help us remember about story patterns.

(See the Introduction for the complete "Pattern Song.")

Singing a song together is a very good way to remember the patterns we will learn!

Play Tom Foolery (Cumulative Review)

Today we will play Tom Foolery. I will pretend to be Tom. You know that Tom has a reputation for trying to trick children. Tom knows that some words have more than one meaning. He will tell you one meaning that will be correct. Then he will tell you another meaning that might be correct or incorrect.

If you think the meaning is correct, don't say anything. If you think the meaning is incorrect, sing out "Tom Foolery." Then Tom will have to tell the truth and give the correct meaning. Tom is sly enough that he may include some words that do *not* have two meanings. Be careful! He's tricky!

Let's practice: A **present** is a gift that you give or receive. "In the present" can also mean something that will happen tomorrow. *Tom Foolery!* Oh, you're right. You all know that "in the present" means something that is "happening right now."

Let's do another one together. **Seasons** tells about times of the year. If I give you a season, I am explaining why I did something. *Tom Foolery!* Oh, you're right. I suppose I must have been thinking of reason, not season. We know only the first meaning.

When we play Tom Foolery, Tom will keep score. If you catch him being tricky, you will get one point. If you don't catch him, Tom gets the point. Watch out! Tom just might try to give himself extra points while you're not looking!

Now you're ready to play the game.

(Draw a T-chart on the board for keeping score. Children earn one point for each correct answer. If they make an error, correct them as you normally would, and record one point for yourself. Repeat missed words at the end of the game.)

- **Africa** is "the second-largest continent in the world." Africa is also the name of the place where we live. *Tom Foolery!* Oh, you are very hard to fool. The place where we live is called _____.

- If a mouse **cowered** when it saw the cat, it made itself as small as it could because it was afraid.

- When you **appear,** you come into sight. Appear is also a wooden sidewalk that juts out into a lake. *Tom Foolery!* Oh, you're right. I was thinking of something called "a pier." (Print the two homonyms *appear* and *a pier* on the board to demonstrate the difference.) Those words sound the same, but they mean different things.

- **Present** can mean that you are here. Present also means nice or pleasing. *Tom Foolery!* Oh, you're right. I must be thinking of pleasant, not present. Another meaning for present is "a gift."

- If a table is **bare,** nothing is covering it. If a tree has no leaves left on it, the tree is bare.

- **Blossom** means "a flower that will turn into fruit." Blossom is also a person who is in charge of something. *Tom Foolery!* Oh, you're right. I guess I was thinking of boss. Another meaning for blossom is to "grow and get better at things."

- **Disappointment** means that things didn't turn out the way you had hoped. A disappointment can make you sad or upset.

- A **sly** person might try to trick you. Sly can also mean that you move on your bottom or back or tummy. *Tom Foolery!* Oh, you're right. I was thinking of slide. I know someone who is sly, though.

- If you are **clever,** you are good at figuring out how to do things. Clever also tells about whether it is rainy or sunny or cloudy. *Tom Foolery!* Oh, you're right. It's not clever, is it? I was thinking of weather.

(Count the points, and declare a winner.)
You did a great job of playing Tom Foolery!

DAY 5

Preparation: Happy Face Game Test Sheet, BLM B.

Review Afterword

Sometimes after people write a story about something that is real, they want to tell you more facts about that real thing. This information is put in the book **after** the last **word** of the story, so it is called an **afterword.**

The story *The Apple Pie Tree* is make-believe. It was made from the author's imagination. When a story is made up from the author's imagination we say the story is fiction. What do we call a story that is made up from the author's imagination? *Fiction.*

The afterword tells us true facts about how bees help our apple trees grow. Facts are things that are true and that can be proved. For example, it is a fact that I am your teacher. We can prove that fact because we are all in this class together and we know that I'm the teacher.

When part of a book tells true facts about something, that part of the book is called nonfiction. What do we call the parts of books that tell true facts about something? *Nonfiction.*

Today I'll read one of the afterwords that Zoe Hall wrote for *The Apple Pie Tree,* so you can learn more about how bees help apples grow.

Learn from an Afterword
(**Note:** If you find the illustrations too small to show to the whole class, make an overhead transparency of the page, or draw similar illustrations on chart paper or on the board.)

This book has two afterwords. The first one tells how bees help apples grow.

(Read the afterword aloud one part at a time, and show the illustrations.)

Part 1. What color is apple blossom pollen? *Yellow.* Where do you find pollen? (Idea: *On the tiny stems inside each apple blossom.*)

Part 2. Why do the bees come to the blossoms? (Ideas: *They like the bright petals; they want the sweet nectar.*) Where does the pollen collect? (Idea: *On the bees' bodies.*)

Part 3. How does the pollen get to another flower? (Idea: *When the bee goes to a new flower to get nectar, the pollen sticks to the sticky tops of the tiny stems inside the blossom.*)

Part 4. What happens after a blossom is pollinated? (Ideas: *The flower petals fall off; the base of the blossom starts to grow into an apple.*)

We have learned many facts about how bees help apples grow in this afterword. Think about the one fact you thought was most interesting. (Pause.) Share that fact with your partner. (Pause.) Tonight you will share that fact with someone at your home.

(**Note:** You may wish to make apple pie with your class. If you do, follow a similar procedure to read the second afterword before making the apple pie.)

Assess Vocabulary
 (Hold up a copy of the Happy Face Game Test Sheet, BLM B.)

Today you're going to play the Happy Face Game. When you play the Happy Face Game, it helps me know how well you know the hard words you are learning.

If I say something true, color the happy face. What will you do if I say something true? *Color the happy face.*

If I say something false, color the sad face. What will you do if I say something false? *Color the sad face.*

Listen carefully to each item I say. Don't let me trick you!

Item 1: A **bare** tree has no leaves. *True.*

Item 2: A **blossom** is a flower that turns into fruit. *True.*

Item 3: There are seven **seasons:** Monday, Tuesday, Wednesday, Thursday, Friday, Saturday, and Sunday. *False.*

Item 4: "In the **present**" means that something is "happening right now." *True.*

Item 5: When you **appear,** people can't see you. *False.*

Item 6: **Blossom** means to "get better at doing things." *True.*

Item 7: If a plant is **scorched,** it has been dried out by the hot sun. *True.*

Item 8: A police officer can **protect** you from danger. *True.*

Item 9: If you **wonder** about something, you do not think about it because you are not interested in it and do not want to know more. *False.*

Item 10: If a family has no children, they may want to **adopt** a child who does not have a family. *True.*

You did a great job of playing the Happy Face Game!

(Score children's work later. Scores of 9 out of 10 indicate mastery. If a child does not achieve mastery, insert the missed words in the games in the next week's lessons. Retest those children individually on missed words before they take the next mastery test.)

Extensions
Read a Story as a Reward

(Display copies of several of the books that you have read since the beginning of the program. Allow children to choose which book they would like you to read aloud to them as a reward for their hard work.)

(Read the story aloud to children for enjoyment with minimal interruptions.)

Present the Super Words Center

(Prepare the word containers for the Super Words Center. You may wish to remove words from earlier lessons. Choose words that children have mastered.

See the Introduction for instructions on how to set up and use the Super Words Center.)

(Add the new Picture Vocabulary Cards to the words from the previous weeks. Show children one of the word containers. If they need more guidance, role-play with two or three children as a demonstration.)

Today I will help you remember how to play the game called What's Missing?

Let's think about how we work with our words in the Super Words Center.

You will work with a partner in the Super Words Center. Whom will you work with in the center? *A partner.*

First, one partner will draw four word cards out of the container and put them on the table so both partners can see. What do you do first? (Idea: *Draw four cards out of the container and put them on the table so both partners can see.*)

Next you will take turns looking at the cards and saying the words the pictures show. What do you do next? (Idea: *We take turns looking at the cards and saying the words the pictures show.*)

Next, partner 2 looks away while partner 1 takes one of the four cards and places it facedown on the table away from the other cards. Then partner 1 draws a new card from the container and places it on the table with the other three.

Watch while I show you what I mean. (Demonstrate with a child as your partner.) When you put down the new card, it's a good idea to mix the cards so they aren't in the same places anymore. (Demonstrate as you go.)

Now partner 1 says, "What's Missing?" Partner 2 has to use his or her eyes and brain and say which old card has been taken away. After partner 2 has guessed, turn over the facedown card. If partner 2 is correct, he or she gets a point. If partner 2 is not correct, partner 1 gets the point. (Demonstrate as you go.)

Next, partner 2 has a turn to choose four different cards, and the game starts again. What happens next? (Idea: *Partner 2 has a turn to choose four different cards, and the game starts again.*)

Have fun playing What's Missing!

WHEN WE GO CAMPING

When We Go Camping
author: Margriet Ruurs • illustrator: Andrew Kiss

Preparation: You will need *When We Go Camping* for each day's lesson.

Number the pages of the story to assist you in asking questions at appropriate points.

Post a copy of the Vocabulary Tally Sheet, BLM A, with this week's Picture Vocabulary Cards attached.

Each child will need the Homework Sheet, BLM 24a.

Target Vocabulary

Tier II	Tier III
snuggle	realistic
explore	pattern
disturb	(explaining)
odor	foreword
*wilderness	
*reasons	

*Expanded Target Vocabulary Word

DAY 1

Introduce Book

This week's book is called *When We Go Camping.* What's the title of this week's book? *When We Go Camping.*

This book was written by Margriet Ruurs [mar-**greet** rew-urss]. Who's the author of *When We Go Camping*? *Margriet Ruurs.*

Andrew Kiss made the pictures for this book. Who's the illustrator of *When We Go Camping*? *Andrew Kiss.* Who made the illustrations for this book? *Andrew Kiss.*

The cover of a book usually gives us some hints of what the book is about. Let's look at the front cover of *When We Go Camping.* What do you see in the illustration? (Ideas: *Two people in a tent; a boy and a girl in a tent; two children in a tent; a canoe; a campfire; some food cooking; a moose; a squirrel; trees; birds flying; a mountain.*)

(Assign each child a partner.) Remember, when you make a prediction about something, you say what you think will happen. Get ready to make some predictions to your partner about this book. Use the information from the cover to help you.

(Ask the following questions, allowing sufficient time for children to share their predictions with their partners.)

- Who are the characters in this story? (Whom do you think this story is about?)
- What kind of birds do you think are flying in the sky?
- Where do you think the story happens?
- When do you think the story happens?
- Why do you think the children are being so still?
- How far away from the children do you think the moose is?
- Do you think this story is about real people and animals? Tell why or why not.

(Call on several children to share their predictions with the class.)

Take a Picture Walk

(**Note:** There are many different wild animals in the illustrations. Do not expect children to find all the animals during this picture walk. If children locate an animal but do not know what it is, briefly respond with the name of the animal. Children will have an opportunity on Day 5 to locate all the animals and learn more about them with the help of the legend. Encourage children to use previously taught target words in their answers.)

We are going to take a picture walk through this book. Remember, when we take a picture walk, we look at the pictures and tell what we think will happen in the story.

(Show the illustrations on the following pages, and ask the specified questions.)

(Title page.) What other story have we read that has a setting nearly the same as the setting for *When We Go Camping*? *Loon Lake.* I wonder if there will be a loon in this story.

Page 1. Where else did you see this illustration? *On the cover of the book.* What are the children watching? (Ideas: *An animal; a moose.*) When do you think this part of the story happens? Why do you think so?

Pages 3–4. What are the children doing? (Idea: *Pulling the canoe into the water.*) What do you think they are going to do? (Ideas: *Go canoeing; go fishing.*) What makes you think so? (Ideas: *They're pulling the canoe into the water; there's a fishing rod beside the boat; there's a box of hooks.*) What animals do you see? (Ideas: *Loons; a blue heron; a rabbit; a squirrel.*)

Pages 5–6. What other people do you see? (Ideas: *A father; a man; a mother; a woman.*) Who is fishing? *The man.* What is the woman doing? (Ideas: *Sitting on a log; drinking coffee; watching the children; enjoying the view.*) What animals do you see? (Ideas: *Ducks; a blue heron; a loon; a deer; a crow; a squirrel.*)

Pages 7–8. What is happening here? (Ideas: *The boy is pulling on a rope; he is lifting a cooler off the ground; the woman is cooking something over the fire; the girl is washing; the man is chopping wood.*) What animals do you see? (Ideas: *A bear; a marmot; a rabbit; a woodpecker; a squirrel.*)

Pages 9–10. What are the children looking at? (Idea: *A tree stump; a tree that has been cut down; a tree.*) What animal do you think cut down the tree? *A beaver.* What animals do you see? (Ideas: *A skunk; a deer; a woodpecker; a raccoon; a porcupine; a frog; a squirrel.*)

Pages 11–12. What do you think is happening? (Ideas: *They're going on a hike; they're going for a walk in the woods.*) (Point to the meadow.) What do you call a field where grass and flowers grow? *A meadow.* What animals do you see in the meadow? (Ideas: *Elk; a hawk; a squirrel; deer.*)

Pages 13–14. What is happening here? (Ideas: *The girl is looking at a frog; the boy is watching a robin pull a worm out of the ground.*) What

other animals do you see? (Ideas: *A blue jay; a butterfly; a squirrel.*)

Pages 15–16. Where does this part of the story happen? (Idea: *At the lake.*) What are the children doing? (Idea: *Playing in the water with sticks.*) What do you think they are looking for? (Ideas: *Fish; water bugs; frogs, tadpoles.*) What animals do you see? (Ideas: *A deer; a red-winged blackbird; a loon; a squirrel.*)

Pages 17–18. What are the children doing? (Idea: *Swimming.*) How do you think the water feels? (Ideas: *Cold; refreshing.*) What is the father doing? (Ideas: *Looking across the lake; holding a camera.*) What do you think he is trying to get a picture of? What animals do you see? (Ideas: *A bird—a killdeer; a squirrel.*)

Pages 19–20. What are the people doing? (Idea: *Picking berries.*) What animals do you see? (Ideas: *A beaver; a crow; a squirrel.*)

Pages 21–22. What is happening here? (Ideas: *They are cooking dinner; the mom is putting a fish in a pan; the children are adding sticks to the fire.*) What animals do you see? (Ideas: *A fish; a squirrel.*)

Pages 23–24. When do you think this part of the story happens? (Ideas: *At sunset; in the evening.*) What animals do you see? (Ideas: *An otter; a bald eagle; an owl; a squirrel.*)

Pages 25–26. What is happening here? (Ideas: *They're having a campfire; they're toasting marshmallows.*) What animals do you see? (Ideas: *Raccoons; a wolf; an owl; a squirrel.*) In what season do you think this story happens? (Idea: *Summer.*) Why do you think so? (Ideas: *The family is on vacation; the children are swimming in the lake; the grass is green, and the flowers are blooming; many people go camping in the summer.*)

Now that we've finished our picture walk, let's talk about how Andrew Kiss made the illustrations for *When We Go Camping*. There are lots of different ways to make illustrations for a book: painting; drawing with a pen or a pencil; using markers, crayons, pastels, or chalk; or cutting out different pieces of paper and gluing them together.

How do you think Andrew Kiss made his illustrations? (**Idea:** *He painted them.*) That's right; Andrew Kiss used oil paints to paint the pictures for the book *When We Go Camping*. (**Note:** If you have tubes of oil paint, you may wish to show them to children and model how different pigments are mixed to get different colors.)

Andrew Kiss tried to make his pictures look as real as he could, so we say his illustrations are realistic. What kind of illustrations did Andrew Kiss make for *When We Go Camping*? *Realistic illustrations.*

Pages 17–18. Andrew Kiss also did something special for children who like to look especially carefully at his illustrations. Raise your hand if you found something special in his paintings that we haven't talked about. (**Call on individual children. If no one has noticed the hidden pictures, point to the fish in the lake.**) What do you think this is? (**Ideas:** *A fish; a trout.*) Does it look like a real fish? *No.* That's right; the shape of the fish is hidden in the ripples on the lake. There are hidden animals in each of Andrew Kiss's illustrations. We'll try to find more of them later this week.

It's your turn to ask me some questions. What would you like to know about the story? (**Accept questions. If children tell about the pictures or the story instead of asking questions, prompt them to ask a question.**) Ask me a what question. Ask me a where question.

Read Story Aloud
(Read story aloud to children with minimal interruptions.)

In the next lesson, we will read the story again, and I will ask you some questions.

Present Target Vocabulary

◎⊷ *Snuggle.*

In the story the child says, "I snuggle into my sleeping bag, then roll over and quietly peek outside." That means the child cuddles in a warm and comfortable spot, close by someone or something. **Snuggle.** Say the word. *Snuggle.*

Snuggle is an action word. It tells what someone is doing. What kind of word is **snuggle?** *An action word.*

If you snuggle somewhere, you cuddle in a warm and comfortable spot, close by someone or something. Say the word that means to "cuddle in a warm and comfortable spot, close by someone or something." *Snuggle.*

(Correct any incorrect responses, and repeat the item at the end of the sequence.)

Let's think about some times when you might snuggle. I'll tell about a time. If you think that someone is snuggling, say, "Snuggle." If not, don't say anything.

- The boy and his dog are cuddling close to each other in front of the fireplace. *Snuggle.*
- Tamsin cuddled up close to her mom in the cold room. *Snuggle.*
- It is so hot that Jack and Jill stay well apart.
- Marfa says, "Please move away—you're too close!"
- Belinda curls up in her dad's lap and listens to music. *Snuggle.*
- Nasser cuddles his kitten, and they fall asleep together. *Snuggle.*

What action word means to "cuddle in a warm and comfortable spot, close by someone or something"? *Snuggle.*

◎⊷ Explore.

In the story the children go out in their canoe to explore the lake. That means they travel around the lake so they can find out what the lake is like. **Explore.** Say the word. *Explore.*

Explore is an action word. It tells what is happening. What kind of word is **explore?** *An action word.*

When you go exploring, you travel around so you can find out what places are like. Say the word that means to "travel around so you can find out what places are like." *Explore.*

(Correct any incorrect responses, and repeat the item at the end of the sequence.)

I'll tell about someone. If that person is exploring, say, "Explore." If not, don't say anything.

- Julie and Justin travel though the jungles of Africa to see what is there. *Explore.*
- Mr. Pfister is so scared of the cave that he stands still and won't move.
- When the kids get under the porch, they travel around to see what it is like down there. *Explore.*
- Christopher Columbus wanted to find out what places were like, so he sailed his ships. *Explore.*
- Binford knows that the river is dangerous, so he doesn't go canoeing with the others.
- Lewis and Clark were curious about where they could go if they traveled down the rivers. *Explore.*

What action word means to "travel around so you can see what places are like"? *Explore.*

What places would you like to explore? Why? (Call on several children. Encourage them to start their answers with the words "I would like to explore _____ because _____.")

◎═ Disturb.

In the story the sound of a twig snapping disturbs the elk, and they disappear. That means the sound interrupts the elk and upsets them. **Disturb.** Say the word. *Disturb.*

Disturb is an action word. It tells what is happening. What kind of word is **disturb?** *An action word.*

If you disturb people or animals, you interrupt what they are doing and upset them. What word means to "interrupt what people or animals are doing and upset them"? *Disturb.*

(Correct any incorrect responses, and repeat the item at the end of the sequence.)

Let's think about some times someone might disturb a person or an animal. If someone interrupts or upsets a person or animal, say, "Disturb." If not, don't say anything.

- Lorenzo tries to speak to his brother when his brother is on the telephone. *Disturb.*
- Marco shakes Polo's shoulder to get his attention. *Disturb.*
- Sara leaves her mom alone when she is concentrating on sewing.

- Lewis keeps interrupting Clark while he is searching for the trail. *Disturb.*
- I keep quiet when my dad is fixing the window I broke.
- The mama bear stands up and grunts and growls when we wake her up. *Disturb.*

What action word means to "interrupt what people or animals are doing and upset them"? *Disturb.*

◎═ Odor.

In the story, the child says, "Sometimes I can smell the musky odor that tells me that a bear has been here to eat berries, too." That means the child recognizes the bear's smell. **Odor.** Say the word. *Odor.*

Odor is a naming word. It names a thing. What kind of word is **odor?** *A naming word.*

An odor is a smell. Say the word that means "a smell." *Odor.*

(Correct any incorrect responses, and repeat the item at the end of the sequence.)

Let's think about when you might smell an odor. I'll tell about something. If you think you might smell an odor, say, "Odor." If not, don't say anything.

- Mom is making popcorn. *Odor.*
- The skunk is frightened. *Odor.*
- The peach pie is cooling on the windowsill. *Odor.*
- When I broke my nose, I couldn't smell a thing!
- The ice has no smell at all.
- Wow! That turkey smells delicious! *Odor.*

What naming word means "a smell"? *Odor.*

Present Vocabulary Tally Sheet
(See Week 1, page 3, for instructions.)

Assign Homework
(Homework Sheet, BLM 24a: See the Introduction for homework instructions.)

Read and Discuss Story

(Read story aloud to children. Ask the following questions at the specified points in the story. Encourage children to use previously taught target words in their answers.)

Page 2. What does the person who is telling the story love to do? *Go camping.*

When does the story begin? (Idea: *Early in the morning.*) What words from the story let you know it is cold early in the morning? (Ideas: *My nose is cold; my breath forms a little cloud.*) What do the children do when they first wake up? (Ideas: *Snuggle into their sleeping bags; peek outside.*)

Page 4. What do the children hear as they push their canoe into the water? (Ideas: *The sound of chickadees; chickadees singing.*) What are they going to do? (Idea: *Explore; travel around the lake so they can see what it is like.*)

Pages 5–6. We experience the world around us using our five senses. Those senses are sight, hearing, touch, taste, and smell. What are the five senses? *Sight, hearing, touch, taste, and smell.* (Repeat the senses with children until they can say them confidently without assistance.) What three senses does this part of the story tell about? (Ideas: *Sight—mountaintops on the far shore; circles in the lake from their paddles; sound—the loon's laugh; touch—the feel of the water against the paddles.*)

Page 7. What are three of the things they do when they go camping? (Ideas: *Catch trout; chop wood; make a fire.*)

Page 8. Why does the boy hoist their food high up in a tree? (Idea: *To keep the bears away.*)

Page 9. Who cut down the tree? *A beaver.* Why do the beavers cut down trees? *For their lodge.* A lodge is a home for a beaver. (Point to the lodge in the lake.) This is a beaver lodge. What is this? *A beaver lodge.*

Page 10. Why do you think the woodpecker will soon have to find a new place to hammer for insects? (Idea: *The beaver is cutting down the tree; the beaver will soon take the tree out to its lodge.*)

Pages 11–12. What do they think the sound is at first? *A cougar.* What is the sound? *Elk, eating grass.* What scares the elk away? (Idea: *A twig snapping; a twig breaking; someone stepped on a twig.*)

Page 13. What things does the person wonder about? (Ideas: *Does a butterfly like butter; why is a dragonfly called a dragonfly.*) What things in nature do you wonder about?

Page 14. Where do you think the robin's babies are? (Idea: *In their nest; in a nest in a tree.*) We had to read this far in the story before we knew for sure who is telling the story. Who is looking at the robin? *The boy.* So who would say, "Come look! The robin wants a worm to feed her babies." *The boy.* So who is telling the story? *The boy.*

Pages 15–16. Remember, we experience the world around us using our five senses. What are those senses? *Sight, hearing, touch, taste, and smell.* What three senses does this part of the story tell about? (Ideas: *Sight—water bugs gliding across the top of the water; sound—frogs croaking; touch—mud squishing between their toes.*)

Pages 17–18. Are the children enjoying the water in the lake? *Yes.* Why isn't the father swimming? (Idea: *He thinks the water is freezing cold.*)

Pages 19–20. What kinds of berries are the children picking? (Ideas: *Raspberries; saskatoons; blackberries.*) What four senses does this part of the story tell about? (Ideas: *Sight—red raspberries, purple saskatoons; touch—soft raspberries, warm saskatoons; taste—sweet blackberries; smell—musky odor of the bear.*) What do you think the musky odor of a bear is like? (Ideas: *A wet dog; wet sheep; sweaty horse.*)

Pages 21–22. Why do you think cooking when you're camping is more fun that cooking at home? (Ideas: *You cook over a campfire; you cook different kinds of foods.*)

Pages 23–24. What two senses does this part of the story tell about? (Ideas: *Sight—shadows on the lake, an eagle gliding in the sky; sound—an howl hooting.*) Why do you think an eagle gliding is like a kite without a string? (Ideas: *An eagle gliding doesn't move its wings; it just floats in the wind like a kite.*)

Page 26. What kinds of things does the story say the family does around the campfire? (Ideas: *Snuggle close to each other; tell scary tales.*) What sounds do they hear as they fall asleep? (Ideas: *Crickets; frogs; the waves on the shore.*)

Where are the children at the beginning of the story? (Idea: *In their tent.*) Where are the children at the end of the story? (Idea: *In their tent.*) The children start and end the story in the same place. So what is the pattern of the story *When We Go Camping*? *A circle pattern.*

Review Vocabulary

(Display the Picture Vocabulary Cards. Point to each card as you say the word. Ask children to repeat each word after you.) These pictures show **snuggle, explore, disturb,** and **odor.**

- What word means "a smell"? *Odor.*
- What word means to "cuddle in a warm and comfortable spot, close by someone or something"? *Snuggle.*
- What word means to "interrupt what people or animals are doing and upset them"? *Disturb.*
- What word means to "travel around so you can find out what places are like"? *Explore.*

Extend Vocabulary
◎◄ Disturb.

In *When We Go Camping,* we learned that **disturb** means to "interrupt what people or animals are doing and upset them." Say the word that means to "interrupt what people or animals are doing and upset them." *Disturb.*

Raise your hand if you can tell us a sentence that uses **disturb** as an action word that means to "interrupt what people or animals are doing and upset them." (Call on several children. If

they don't use complete sentences, restate their examples as sentences. Have the class repeat the sentences.)

Here's a new way to use the word **disturb.**

- **It disturbs me when I see someone who is homeless and hungry.** Say the sentence.
- **It disturbs me when I see a dog left in a car on a hot day.** Say the sentence.
- **It disturbs me when I see people driving too fast.** Say the sentence.

In these sentences, **disturb** is an action word that means **bother or worry.** What action word means "bother or worry"? *Disturbs.*

Raise your hand if you can tell us a sentence that uses **disturb** as an action word that means "bother or worry." (Call on several children. Encourage them to start their answers with the words "It disturbs me when _____." If they don't use complete sentences, restate their examples as sentences. Have the class repeat the sentences.)

Present Expanded Target Vocabulary
◎◄ Wilderness.

In *When We Go Camping,* the family goes to a place where no people live. We call this place a wilderness. A wilderness can be a desert, where there is a lot of sand or rocks, or a forest, where there are many trees and many different kinds of animals. **Wilderness.** Say the word. *Wilderness.*

Wilderness is a naming word. It names a place. What kind of word is **wilderness?** *A naming word.*

A wilderness is a place where no people live. Say the word that means "a place where no people live." *Wilderness.*

I'll tell about some places. If that place is a wilderness, say, "Wilderness." If not, don't say anything.

- High in the mountains. *Wilderness.*
- At the North Pole. *Wilderness.*
- At a busy beach in the middle of the summer.
- In the middle of a crater on the moon. *Wilderness.*
- In the desert. *Wilderness.*
- At your house.

What naming word means "a place where no people live"? *Wilderness.*

⊙― Reasons.

The story starts with the sentence "I love to go camping!" Then the person telling the story explains why he loves to go camping. He tells about the chickadees, the squirrels, and the loons. He tells about seeing an elk and watching a robin hunt for worms. He tells about splashing in the lake and picking wild berries. All these things are the reasons he loves to go camping. **Reasons.** Say the word. *Reasons.*

Reasons is a naming word. It names things. What kind of word is **reasons?** *A naming word.*

Reasons are the facts that explain why you think what you do. Say the word that means "the facts that explain why you think what you do." *Reasons.*

I'm going to tell you something I think. Here's what I think: I think the children in this class are getting smarter every day. Now I'll tell you something more. If what I tell about is a reason I think that children in this class are getting smarter every day, say, "Reason." If not, don't say anything.

- You learn how to sit quietly and listen to a story. *Reason.*
- You can't count to a million.
- You can count forward and backward to ten. *Reason.*
- You haven't fixed the computer so that it works faster.
- You say kind things to each other when you do smart things. *Reason.*
- You remember to say "Good morning!" when you come to class. *Reason.*

What word means "the facts that explain why you think what you do"? *Reasons.*

Raise your hand if you can tell us another reason why I might think the children in this class are getting smarter every day. (Call on several children. Encourage them to start their answers with the words "The reason I think the children in this class are getting smarter is _____." If they don't use complete sentences, restate their examples as sentences. Have the class repeat the sentences.)

Preparation: Activity Sheet, BLM 24b. Children will need one crayon.

Retell Story

(Show pictures on the following pages from the story, and call on a child to tell what's happening. Call on a different child for each section.)

Today I'll show you the pictures Andrew Kiss made for the story *When We Go Camping.* As I show you the pictures, I'll call on one of you to tell the class that part of the story.

Page 1. Tell me what happens at the **beginning** of the story. (Encourage children to include the target word *snuggle.* Model use as necessary.)

Pages 3–24. Tell me what happens in the **middle** of the story. (Encourage use of target words when appropriate. Model use as necessary.)

Page 25. Tell me what happens at the **end** of the story.

Introduce Super Choosing Game

 Today you will play the Super Choosing Game. We've played a game like this before, but this one is a little bit different. Let's think about the six words we have: **snuggle, explore, disturb, odor, wilderness,** and **reasons.** (Display the Picture Vocabulary Cards.)

I will say a sentence that has two or three of the words we have learned in it. You will have to choose which one is the best word for that sentence. Not all of the words will be from this lesson, though. That's why it's the *Super Choosing* Game. Let's practice. (You should not show cards for the words outside of this lesson.)

- If you get close to people in a comfortable place, do you disturb them, snuggle with them, or cross them? *Snuggle.*
- When you go out to find out about new places, do you take a glimpse, give a reason, or explore? *Explore.*
- If you are in a place where there are no people, are you in the park, in a gale, or in the wilderness? *Wilderness.*

Now you're ready to play the game. If you tell me the correct answer, you win one point. If you can't tell me the correct answer, I get the point.

(Draw a T-chart on the board for keeping score. Children earn one point for each correct answer. If they make an error, tell them the correct answer. Record one point for yourself, and repeat missed words at the end of the game.)

- If you interrupt and upset people, do you disturb them, smell an odor, or do you give them a reason? *Disturb.*
- Does a bear have an emotion, is he brave, or does he have an odor? *Odor.*
- If your friend laughed quietly, would you say that she shouted, chuckled, or answered? *Chuckled.*
- If Mr. Galiano went out looking for some islands, would you say that he frowned, dashed, or explored? *Explored.*
- When I told you why I did something, would you say that I promised, was amazed, or explained? *Explained.*
- When a problem bothers me, does it disturb me, explain to me, or promise me? *Disturb.*

(Count the points, and declare a winner.) You did a great job of playing the Super Choosing Game!

Complete Activity Sheet

 (Discuss with children the idea of going camping. Use these questions to help get the discussion started.) Have you ever been camping? Did you enjoy it? Would you like to go camping? What do you think would be the best thing about going camping? What do you think you would not like about going camping?

(Give each child a copy of the Activity Sheet, BLM 24b.) Today our class will use our crayons to make a graph to show whether or not we would like to go camping.

Touch under the words in front of the first line of boxes. Those words say, "I would like to go camping." What do those words say? *I would like to go camping.*

Touch under the words in front of the second line of boxes. Those words say, "I would not like to go camping." What do those words say? *I would not like to go camping.*

(Call on children one at a time. Ask each child the question "Would you like to go camping?" The child should respond with either of the two sentences. If the child responds, "I would like to go camping," the class colors one box on the line after that sentence. If the child responds, "I would not like to go camping," the class colors one box on the line after that sentence. After each child has had a turn to respond, help the class draw some conclusions from the graphs. For example, most of the children would like/ would not like to go camping, nearly all the children would like/would not like to go camping, (number of children) would like/would not like to go camping.)

Story Patterns
(Literary Analysis)

When authors write stories, they sometimes write in patterns. Let's see if we can figure out the pattern for this story. You tell me what happens in the story, and I'll write it down.

(Read story aloud to children. Ask the following questions at the specified points.)

Page 2. (First sentence.) What is the first sentence of the story? *I love to go camping!* The first sentence of this story tells what the boy thinks. What does the first sentence of the story tell? *What the boy thinks.*

(Read the rest of page 2.) What reasons does the boy give to explain why he likes to go camping? (Number the responses as a list. Ideas:

1. *Wakes up early;*
2. is *in a tent;*
3. can *snuggle* in his *sleeping bag;*
4. can *peek outside*.)

Pages 3–4. What new reason does the boy give to explain why he likes to go camping? (Continue to number the responses as you add them to the list. Idea: 5. *We can* explore.)

Pages 5–6. What new reasons does the boy give to explain why he likes to go camping? (Ideas: 6. *We can* paddle *our* canoe; 7. see *the* mountains; 8. hear *the* loons.)

(Continue this procedure until you have reread all of the story except the last paragraph and compiled a list of all the reasons the boy likes to go camping. Your list will be similar to this one:

9. catch trout
10. chop wood
11. make a fire
12. hoist food
13. see beavers cut down trees
14. see elk
15. wonder about butterfly, dragonfly
16. see robin catch worms
17. watch water bugs
18. hear frogs croak
19. squish mud between his toes
20. splash; swim in the lake
21. pick and eat berries
22. cook on a campfire
23. catch a trout
24. hear the owls
25. see the eagle
26. sit around the campfire
27. tell scary tales)

The last paragraph uses different words to tell how much the boy likes to go camping. (Read the last paragraph of the story. Show the illustrations on pages 25 and 26.) What words does the boy use to tell us how much he likes to go camping? *I dream of camping.*

(Point to the chart.) What does the boy do first? (Idea: *He tells what he thinks.*) What does the boy do next? (Idea: *He tells all the reasons why he thinks that.*) What does the boy do last? (Idea: *He tells what he thinks using different words from his first words.*)

When the boy tells his story, his reasons tell why he likes to go camping so we can understand better. We already know a word that means "told more about something so someone could

understand it." What word means "told more about something so someone could understand it"? *Explained.* That's right; the boy explained why he liked to go camping, so this story is an explaining story. What kind of story is *When We Go Camping*? *An explaining story.*

This story starts by telling what the boy thinks. Then it gives the reasons he thinks so. It ends by using different words that tell what the boy thinks. This pattern is an explaining pattern. What kind of pattern does a story have when it starts by telling what you think, gives reasons why you think so, and ends by using different words to tell what you think? *An explaining pattern.*

Today we will learn a new verse for "The Pattern Song" that will help us remember about story patterns.

Listen while I sing the verse for you:

> There's a pattern when you give the reasons why.
> There's a pattern when you give the reasons why.
> We agree, in the main,
> But we like it when you explain.
> There's a pattern when you give the reasons why.

Now sing it with me. Don't forget that the phrase "but we like it when you explain" has a fancy rhythm!

Now let's sing the whole song together.

(See the Introduction for the complete "Pattern Song.")

Singing a song together is a very good way to remember the patterns we will learn!

Play Super Choosing Game (Cumulative Review)

Let's play the Super Choosing Game. I will say a sentence that has three of our vocabulary words in it. You will have to choose which one is the correct word for that sentence. Remember, this game is *Super* Choosing because I will use some words from other lessons. You will have to be sharp! (Display the Picture Vocabulary Cards for *snuggle, explore, disturb, odor, wilderness,* and *reason*. Do not display the word cards from earlier lessons.)

Now you're ready to play the Super Choosing Game.

⊤ (Draw a T-chart on the board for keeping score. Children earn one point for each correct answer. If they make an error, correct them as you normally would, and record one point for yourself. Repeat missed words at the end of the game.)

- When you cuddle up to people do you disturb them, snuggle with them, or gasp at them? *Snuggle.*
- If you are interrupted when you are thinking very hard, have you explored, did you smell an odor, or are you disturbed? *Disturbed.*
- Is a place where no people live the wilderness, a cottage, or a reason? *The wilderness.*
- If you can smell something, is it considerate, a blossom, or an odor? *Odor.*
- If you can give facts about why you think something, are you complaining, giving reasons, or squabbling? *Giving reasons.*
- When you go off to find new places and things, do you explore, imagine, or slither? *Explore.*
- If you are bothered by a noisy television show, do you have patience, are you gentle, or are you disturbed? *Disturbed.*
- If you like to keep everything for yourself, are you terrified, excited, or selfish? *Selfish.*
- If you are very surprised and excited about something, do you sigh, are you amazed, or are you rescued? *Amazed.*

Now you will have to listen very carefully, because I'm not going to show you the word cards.

- Henry Hudson didn't shower for ten weeks. Did he have a mood, damage, or an odor? *Odor.*
- If I interrupt you while you are listening to a story, do I disturb you, rescue you, or mutter at you? *Disturb.*
- Healthful stew needs meat, potatoes, carrots, and onions. Are those things enormous, angry, or ingredients? *Ingredients.*

- When you look at something carefully, do you celebrate it, examine it, or howl at it? *Examine.*
- You try and try to do a job, but you can't. Are you frustrated, clever, or horrible? *Frustrated.*
- If Norman is hard to get along with, is he starving, is he in the wilderness, or is he disagreeable? *Disagreeable.*
- If you make dinner, do you root it, attack it, or prepare it? *Prepare.*
- When you are cross or sad or impatient, do you have grains, do you harvest, or do you have feelings? *Feelings.*

(Tally the points, and declare a winner.)
You did a great job of playing the Super Choosing Game!

DAY 5

Preparation: Happy Face Game Test Sheet, BLM B.

Introduce Foreword

Sometimes when an author writes a story, he or she want to tell readers something about the story before they read it. This information is put in the book **before** the first **word** of the story, so it is called a **foreword**. Today I'll read the foreword that Margriet Ruurs wrote for *When We Go Camping.*

The story *When We Go Camping* is make-believe. It was made from the author's imagination. When a story is made up from the author's imagination we say the story is fiction. What do we call a story that is made up from the author's imagination? *Fiction.*

The foreword tells us true facts about camping. Facts are things that are true and that can be proved. For example, it is a fact that I have read the book *When We Go Camping* to you. We can prove that fact because you were all here when I read the book to you.

When part of a book tells true facts about something, that part of the book is called nonfiction. What do we call the parts of books that tell true facts about something? *Nonfiction.*

(Read the foreword to children.) What did Margriet Ruurs want us to know about the book before we read it? (Ideas: *She wanted us to know that when we go camping we can learn about the environment and the animals; she wanted us to know we should take care of the environment; she wanted us to enjoy the story; she wanted to give us some clues to help us find all the animals.*)

Review Afterword, Introduce Legend

Sometimes after authors finish writing a story about things that are real, they want to tell you more facts about those real things. This information is put in the book **after** the last **word** of the story, so it is called an **afterword.** What do you call information put in a book after the last word of the story? *An afterword.*

The afterword for *When We Go Camping* is a special kind of afterword called a **legend.** You already know that one meaning of **legend** is "a story that explains how something came to be."

Another meaning of legend is **a list that explains what pictures or maps in a book mean.** What is another meaning of legend? *A list that explains what pictures or maps in a book mean.*

(Read the part of the legend about the moose. Turn back to the illustration on page 1, and help children locate and identify all the animals mentioned in this part of the legend.)

(Repeat this procedure for the remaining illustrations.)

We have learned about many different animals from this special afterword called a legend.

Think about one animal that lives in the wilderness you thought was most interesting. Now think of a fact you learned about that animal. (Pause.) Share the name of the animal and that fact with your partner. (Pause.) Tonight you will share what you have learned about that animal with someone at your home.

Assess Vocabulary

(Hold up a copy of the Happy Face Game Test Sheet, BLM B.)

Today you're going to play the Happy Face Game. When you play the Happy Face Game,

it helps me know how well you know the hard words you are learning.

If I say something true, color the happy face. What will you do if I say something true? *Color the happy face.*

If I say something false, color the sad face. What will you do if I say something false? *Color the sad face.*

Listen carefully to each item I say. Don't let me trick you!

Item 1: **Wilderness** is a place where lots of people live. *False.*

Item 2: An **odor** is something you can smell. *True.*

Item 3: A **tradition** is something you do only one time. *False.*

Item 4: If bees are busy and full of energy, they are **active**. *True.*

Item 5: **Reasons** are facts that explain why you think what you do. *True.*

Item 6: When squirrels are **chattering** in the trees, they are making lots of quick, short sounds. *True.*

Item 7: When you **cuddle** up to someone, you snuggle. *True.*

Item 8: If you are **disturbed,** it can mean that something is bothering you. *True.*

Item 9: An **honest** person would cheat on a test. *False.*

Item 10: The sky changes from dim to light at **dawn.** *True.*

You did a great job of playing the Happy Face Game!

(Score children's work later. Scores of 9 out of 10 indicate mastery. If a child does not achieve mastery, insert the missed words in the games in the next week's lessons. Retest those children individually on the missed words before they take the next mastery test.)

Extensions
Read a Story as a Reward

(Display several books you have read since the beginning of the program. Allow children to choose which book they would like you to read aloud to them as a reward for their hard work.)

(Read story aloud to children for enjoyment with minimal interruptions.)

Present Super Words Center

(Prepare the word containers for the Super Words Center. You may wish to remove words from earlier lessons. Choose words that children have mastered. See the Introduction for instructions on how to set up and use the Super Words Center.)

(Add the new Picture Vocabulary Cards to the words from the previous weeks. Show children one of the word containers. If they need more guidance, role-play with two or three children as a demonstration.)

Today I will help you remember how to play What's Missing?

Let's think about how we work with our words in the Super Words Center.

You will work with a partner in the Super Words Center. Whom will you work with in the center? *A partner.*

First, one partner will draw four word cards out of the container and put them on the table so both partners can see. What do you do first? (Idea: *Draw four cards out of the container and put them on the table so both partners can see.*)

Next you will take turns looking at the cards and saying the words the pictures show. What do you do next? (Idea: *We take turns looking at the cards and saying the words the pictures show.*)

Next, partner 2 looks away while partner 1 takes one of the four cards and places it facedown on the table away from the other cards. Then partner 1 draws a new card from the container and places it on the table with the other three.

Watch while I show you what I mean. (Demonstrate with a child as your partner.) When you put down the new card, it's a good idea to mix the cards so they aren't in the same places anymore. (Demonstrate as you go.)

Now partner 1 says, "What's Missing?" Partner 2 has to use his or her eyes and brain and say what old card has been taken away. After partner 2 has guessed, turn over the facedown card. If partner 2 is correct, he or she gets a point. If partner 2 is not correct, partner 1 gets the point. (Demonstrate as you go.)

Next, partner 2 has a turn to choose four different cards, and the game starts again. What happens next? (Idea: *Partner 2 has a turn to choose four different cards, and the game starts again.*)

Have fun playing What's Missing!

Week 25

Preparation: You will need *Time to Sleep* for each day's lesson.

Number the pages of the story to assist you in asking questions at appropriate points.

Post a copy of the Vocabulary Tally Sheet, BLM A, with this week's Picture Vocabulary Cards attached.

Each child will need the Homework Sheet, BLM 25a.

Time to Sleep
author: Denise Fleming • illustrator: Denise Fleming

🎯 Target Vocabulary

Tier II	Tier III
cave	pattern (circle)
den	
burrow	
frost	
*hibernate	
*migrate	

*Expanded Target Vocabulary Word

DAY 1

Introduce Book

This week's book is called *Time to Sleep.* What's the title of this week's book? *Time to Sleep.*

This book was written by Denise Fleming. Who's the author of *Time to Sleep*? *Denise Fleming.*

Denise Fleming also made the pictures for this book. Who's the illustrator of *Time to Sleep*? *Denise Fleming.* Who made the illustrations for this book? *Denise Fleming.*

The cover of a book usually gives us some hints of what the book is about. Let's look at the front cover of *Time to Sleep.* What do you see in the illustration on this cover? (Ideas: *A bear sleeping; the head and front paws of a bear; leaves that are orange and red.*)

(Assign each child a partner.) Remember, when you make a prediction about something, you say what you think will happen. Get ready to make some predictions to your partner about this book. Use the information from the cover to help you.

(Ask the following questions, allowing sufficient time for children to share their predictions with their partners.)

- Who is the main character in this story? (Whom do you think this story is about?)
- What is the bear doing?
- Where do you think the story happens?
- When do you think the story happens?

- Why do you think the bear is sleeping?
- How many leaves do you see?
- Do you think this story is about real animals? Tell why or why not.

(Call on several children to share their predictions with the class.)

Take a Picture Walk

We are going to take a picture walk through this book. Remember, when we take a picture walk, we look at the pictures and tell what we think will happen in the story.

(Show the illustrations on the following pages, and ask the specified questions. Encourage children to use previously taught target words in their answers.)

Pages 1–2. What season do you think it is when the story begins? (Idea: *Autumn; fall.*) Why do you think so? (Ideas: *There is a lot of orange, red, brown, and yellow in the illustration; I see the autumn colors.*) What is the bear doing? (Idea: *Sniffing.*)

Pages 3–6. What is the bear doing? (Ideas: *Sniffing something on the ground; looking at something on the ground; looking at a snail; talking to a snail.*)

Pages 7–8. What do you see? (Ideas: *The snail and the skunk.*) What is the skunk doing? (Ideas: *Digging in the ground; looking at the snail; talking to the snail.*)

Pages 9–10. What do you see? *The skunk.* What is the skunk doing? (Ideas: *Looking up in the tree; sniffing the air.*)

Pages 11–12. What do you see? (Ideas: *The skunk; the turtle.*) What is the skunk doing? (Idea: *Looking at the turtle.*) What is the turtle doing? (Idea: *Walking away from the skunk.*)

Pages 13–14. What do you see? (Ideas: *The skunk; the turtle.*) What is the skunk doing? (Idea: *Talking to the turtle.*) What is the turtle doing? (Idea: *Talking to the skunk.*)

Pages 15–16. What is happening here? (Idea: *The turtle is climbing up a hill.*)

Pages 17–18. What do you see? (Idea: *An animal; a woodchuck.*) What is the animal doing? (Idea: *Looking down the hill.* **Note:** If children do not identify the animal as a woodchuck, it is not necessary to name the animal.)

Pages 19–20. What is the animal doing? (Idea: *Standing up on its back legs.*) What else do you see? (Idea: *A ladybug.*)

Pages 21–22. What is the animal doing? (Ideas: *Looking at the ladybug; talking to the ladybug.*)

Pages 23–24. Where is the ladybug going? (Idea: *To a cave.*) What other animals do you see? (Idea: *Geese.*)

Pages 25–26. What do you see? (Idea: *The bear.*) What is sitting on the bear's nose? (Idea: *The ladybug.*) What do you think the bear and the ladybug are doing? (Idea: *Talking.*)

Pages 27–28. What do you see? (Idea: *The bear.*) What is the bear doing? (Idea: *Sleeping.*)

Page 29. What do you see? (Ideas: *Nighttime; snow falling; a tree; lots of words.*) Where do you think all the animals are?

Now that we've finished our picture walk, let's talk about how Denise Fleming made the illustrations for *Time to Sleep.* There are lots of different ways to make illustrations for a book: painting; drawing with a pen or a pencil; using markers, crayons, pastels, or chalk; or cutting out different pieces of paper and gluing them together.

How do you think Denise Fleming made her illustrations? (Idea: *She cut out different pieces of paper and glued them together to make a picture.*) You are almost right. Denise Fleming used stencils and made her own paper to fill in those stencils to make these pictures. She calls her illustrations "pulp paintings."

(**Note:** You may wish to make a stencil of a leaf and use it to explain how Denise Fleming made rag pulp, colored it, and used it to fill in the stencils. As this is a very complicated process, we suggest that you use only one stencil and one color to explain the process. If you wish children to experiment with paper making, look at the information on the World Wide Web that explains Denise Fleming's process of forcing cotton pulp through hand-cut stencils to make the distinctive art that accompanies her picture books. Use the search words *Denise Fleming paper making* to find out more about her technique.)

It's your turn to ask me some questions. What would you like to know about the story? (Accept questions. If children tell about the pictures or the story instead of asking questions, prompt them to ask a question.) Ask me a how question. Ask me a why question.

Read Story Aloud
(Read story aloud to children with minimal interruptions.)

In the next lesson, we will read the story again, and I will ask you some questions.

Present Target Vocabulary
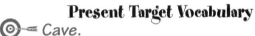
◎◐ *Cave.*

In the story, Bear says, "It is time to crawl into my cave and sleep." That means it is time for the bear to crawl into a large hole and sleep. **Cave.** Say the word. *Cave.*

Cave is a naming word. It names a place. What kind of word is **cave?** *A naming word.*

A cave is a large hole in the side of a hill or mountain. Say the word that means "a large hole in the side of a hill or mountain." *Cave.*

(Correct any incorrect responses, and repeat the item at the end of the sequence.)

Let's think about some places that might be caves. I'll tell about some places. If you think the place I'm telling about is a cave, say, "Cave." If not, don't say anything.

- The explorers squeeze past the rocks and go into the large hole in the side of the mountain. *Cave.*
- The hikers put on their safety equipment and carefully climb into the big hole. *Cave.*
- The girls walk down the street and past the school.
- As the boys peer into the large hole in the side of the hill, they catch a glimpse of two shining eyes. *Cave.*
- There are no holes in the hills or mountains.
- The bears live in a hole in the mountain. *Cave.*

What naming word means "a large hole in the side of a hill or mountain"? *Cave.*

 Den.

In the story, Snail tells Skunk, "It is time for you to curl up in your den and sleep." That means it is time for the skunk to go into its home and sleep. **Den.** Say the word. *Den.*

Den is a naming word. It names a place. What kind of word is **den?** *A naming word.*

A den is a home for some kinds of wild animals, such as bears, foxes, skunks, and wolves. Say the word that means "a home for some kinds of wild animals, such as bears, foxes, skunks, and wolves." *Den.*

(Correct any incorrect responses, and repeat the item at the end of the sequence.)

Let's think about some places that might be dens. I'll tell about some places. If you think the place I'm telling about is a den, say, "Den." If not, don't say anything.

- The fox digs a hole in the ground so she will have a place to have her babies. *Den.*
- The eagle builds a nest high in a tree.
- The bear finds a cave in the side of a hill where it can live for the winter. *Den.*
- The wolf lives in its home most of the time. *Den.*
- Henry lives in an apartment on Fifty-fourth Street.
- The skunk goes into its home for a nice nap. *Den.*

What naming word means "a home for some kinds of wild animals, such as bears, foxes, skunks, and wolves"? *Den.*

 **Burrow.**

In the story, Turtle tells Woodchuck, "It is time for you to burrow down and sleep." That means it is time for the woodchuck to dig down, make a tunnel or a hole, and sleep. **Burrow.** Say the word. *Burrow.*

Burrow is an action word. It tells about what an animal is doing. What kind of word is **burrow?** *An action word.*

When animals burrow down into the ground, they dig down in the ground and make a tunnel or a hole. Say the word that means "dig down in the ground and make a tunnel or a hole." *Burrow.*

(Correct any incorrect responses, and repeat the item at the end of the sequence.)

Let's think about some animals that might burrow. I'll tell about what an animal is doing. If you think the animal is burrowing, say, "Burrow." If not, don't say anything.

- The gopher digs a hole in the farmer's field. *Burrow.*
- The fish swims upstream.
- A chipmunk digs a hole in the park. *Burrow.*
- A mole is living in a tunnel under my mom's front lawn. *Burrow.*
- The frog lives in a pond.
- The ground is so rocky that gophers and chipmunks can't build homes there.

What action word means "dig down in the ground and make a tunnel or a hole"? *Burrow.*

Frost.

In the story Snail says, "This morning there was frost on the grass." That means the grass was white because it had been very cold the night before. **Frost.** Say the word. *Frost.*

Frost is a naming word. It names a thing. What kind of word is **frost?** *A naming word.*

Frost is white, powdery ice that forms on things in freezing weather. What word means "white, powdery ice that forms on things in freezing weather"? *Frost.*

Let's think about some times when there might be frost. I'll tell you about a time. If you think you would see frost, say, "Frost." If not, don't say anything.

- After the winter storm, white, powdery ice covers the outside of the windows. *Frost.*
- It rains in the night.
- It is so hot that everyone is sweating.
- I slip on the white powdery ice that is on the sidewalk. *Frost.*
- The trees are covered with thick layers of white, powdery ice. They look like they are made of sugar icing. *Frost.*
- The white powder on my face is flour because I have been baking.

What naming word means "white, powdery ice that forms on things in freezing weather"? *Frost.*

Present Vocabulary Tally Sheet
(See Week 1, page 3, for instructions.)

Assign Homework
(Homework Sheet, BLM 25a: See the Introduction for homework instructions.)

DAY 2

Preparation: Picture Vocabulary Cards for *cave, den, burrow,* and *frost.*

Read and Discuss Story

(Read story aloud to children. Ask the following questions at the specified points in the story. Encourage children to use previously taught target words in their answers.)

Page 2. What does Bear smell? *Winter.* What does Bear want to do? (Idea: *Crawl into her cave and sleep.*) What must Bear do before she goes to sleep? (Idea: *Tell Snail winter is in the air.*)

Page 4. What does Bear tell Snail? (Ideas: *Winter is in the air; it is time to seal your shell and sleep.*)

Page 6. What does Snail say? (Ideas: *You are right; it is time to sleep; this morning there was frost on the grass; I must tell Skunk.*)

Page 7. What does Snail tell Skunk? (Ideas: *Winter is on its way; it is time for you to curl up in your den and sleep.*)

Page 9. What does Skunk say? (Ideas: *I will sleep; I must tell Turtle.*)

Page 12. What does Skunk tell Turtle? (Ideas: *I have news; winter is on its way.*)

Page 14. What does Turtle say? (Ideas: *The days have been growing shorter; it is time to sleep; I must tell Woodchuck.*)

Page 15. What does Turtle tell Woodchuck? (Ideas: *Winter is on its way; it is time for you to burrow down and sleep.*)

Page 17. What does Woodchuck say? (Ideas: *My skin is so tight I could not eat another bite; I am ready to sleep; I must tell Ladybug.*)

Pages 19–22. What does Woodchuck tell Ladybug? (Ideas: *Winter is on its way; the leaves are falling from the trees; it is time for you to slip under a log and sleep.*) What does Ladybug say? (Idea: *I must tell Bear.*)

Page 23. What does Ladybug tell Bear? (Ideas: *Wake up; the sky is full of geese honking good-bye; winter is on its way.*)

Page 25. What else does Ladybug tell Bear? (Idea: *It is time to crawl into your cave and sleep.*) What does Bear tell Ladybug? (Ideas: *I am in my cave; I was asleep.*) What does Ladybug say? (Ideas: *I am so sorry; please go back to sleep.*) It looks like the ladybug disturbed the bear's sleep.

Page 29. What is everyone saying? (Idea: *Good night.*) What do you think everyone is doing at the end of the story? (Idea: *Going to sleep.*)

Review Vocabulary
(Display the Picture Vocabulary Cards. Point to each card as you say the word. Ask children to repeat each word after you.) These pictures show **cave, den, burrow,** and **frost.**

- What word means "a home for some kinds of wild animals, such as bears, foxes, skunks, and wolves"? *Den.*
- What word means "a large hole in the side of a hill or mountain"? *Cave.*

- What word means "white, powdery ice that forms on things in freezing weather"? *Frost.*
- What word means "dig down in the ground and make a tunnel or a hole"? *Burrow.*

Extend Vocabulary

 Den.

In the story *Time to Sleep,* we learn that **den** means "a home for some kinds of wild animals, such as bears, foxes, skunks, and wolves." Say the word that means "a home for some kinds of wild animals, such as bears, foxes, skunks, and wolves." *Den.*

Raise your hand if you can tell us a sentence that uses **den** as a naming word that means "a home for some kinds of wild animals, such as bears, foxes, skunks, and wolves." (Call on several children. If they don't use complete sentences, restate their examples as sentences. Have the class repeat the sentences.)

Here's a new way to use the word **den.**

- **Some people have their television in their den.** Say the sentence.
- **The Johnson family keeps their board games in the den.** Say the sentence.
- **Leroy's dad likes to read in the den.** Say the sentence.

In these sentences, **den** is a naming word that means **a cozy, comfortable room in a house where people relax and do things they enjoy.** What naming word means "a cozy, comfortable room in a house where people relax and do things they enjoy"? *Den.*

Raise your hand if you can tell us a sentence that uses **den** as a naming word that means "a cozy, comfortable room in a house where people relax and do things they enjoy." (Call on several children. If they don't use complete sentences, restate their examples as sentences. Have the class repeat the sentences.)

Present Expanded Target Vocabulary

Hibernate.

In the story *Time to Sleep,* the bear, the snail, the skunk, the turtle, the woodchuck, and the ladybug are all getting ready to sleep because winter is coming. Another way of saying the animals are going to sleep for the winter is that the animals are going to hibernate for the winter. **Hibernate.** Say the word. *Hibernate.*

Hibernate is an action word. It tells what animals do. What kind of word is **hibernate?** *An action word.*

When animals hibernate, they spend the winter in a deep sleep. Say the word that means "spend the winter in a deep sleep." *Hibernate.*

I'll tell about some animals. If that animal is hibernating, say, "Hibernate." If not, don't say anything.

- The bear sleeps all winter. *Hibernate.*
- The mouse races across the snow looking for seeds.
- The squirrel sleeps in the hollow tree all winter. *Hibernate.*
- In the winter, the raccoon sleeps for a long, long time. *Hibernate.*
- The brown bat sleeps in a cave all winter. *Hibernate.*
- Your dog runs and plays in the snow.

What action word means "spend the winter in a deep sleep"? *Hibernate.*

Migrate.

In the story *Time to Sleep,* Ladybug says, "The sky is full of geese honking good-bye." The geese are flying away to spend the winter somewhere else. Another way of saying the geese are flying away to spend the winter somewhere else is that the geese are migrating. **Migrate.** Say the word. *Migrate.*

Migrate is an action word. It tells what some animals do. What kind of word is **migrate?** *An action word.*

When birds and insects migrate, they fly away to spend the winter somewhere else. Say the word that means "fly away to spend the winter somewhere else." *Migrate.*

I'll tell about some animals. If that animal is migrating, say, "Migrate." If that animal is hibernating, say, "Hibernate."

- The ducks fly south for the winter. *Migrate.*
- The turtle sleeps all winter at the bottom of the pond. *Hibernate.*

- The monarch butterflies fly from Michigan to Mexico. *Migrate.*
- As they always do, the swallows come back to Capistrano. *Migrate.*
- The frog sleeps at the bottom of the pond all winter. *Hibernate.*
- The Canada geese fly south for the winter with their loud, honking call. *Migrate.*

What action word means "fly away to spend the winter somewhere else"? *Migrate.*

DAY 3

Preparation: Activity Sheet, BLM 25b. Children will each need one crayon.

Retell Story

(Show the pictures on the following pages from the story, and call on a child to tell what's happening. Call on a different child for each section.)

Today I'll show you the pictures Denise Fleming made for the story *Time To Sleep.* As I show you the pictures, I'll call on one of you to tell the class that part of the story.

Pages 1–2. Tell me what happens at the **beginning** of the story.

Pages 3–28. Tell me what happens in the **middle** of the story. (Encourage use of target words when appropriate. Model use as necessary.)

Page 29. Tell me what happens at the **end** of the story.

Review Super Choosing Game

Today you will play the Super Choosing Game. Let's think about the six words we have: **cave, den, burrow, frost, hibernate,** and **migrate.** (Display the Picture Vocabulary Cards.)

I will say a sentence that has two or three of the words we have learned in it. You will have to choose which one is the correct word for that sentence. Not all of the words will be from this lesson, though. That's why it's the *Super Choosing Game.* Let's practice. (You should not show cards for words from previous lessons.) Let's practice.

- When an animal sleeps for weeks and weeks at a time in the winter, does it migrate, burrow, or hibernate? *Hibernate.*
- If you have a comfortable room in your house, do you have a burrow, a den, or a roost? *A den.*
- When it is cold and white, powdery ice is on the windows, do you have moss, frost, or are you cross? *Frost.*

Now you're ready to play the game. If you tell me the correct answer, you win one point. If you can't tell me the correct answer, I get the point.

(Draw a T-chart on the board for keeping score. Children earn one point for each correct answer. If they make an error, tell them the correct answer. Record one point for yourself, and repeat missed words at the end of the game.)

- Some animals tunnel or dig to make their homes. Do they live in a burrow, a nest, or a tree house? *A burrow.*
- Some birds live in a different place in the winter. Do those birds cooperate, migrate, or whirl? *Migrate.*
- A hole in the side of a hill or mountain is called a cave, a brave, or a wave? *A cave.*
- Another name for an animal home is a when, a fen, or a den? *A den.*
- If an animal lives in a burrow, does it live in a mole, a hole, or a pole? *A hole.*
- The powdery, white ice that forms on things in freezing weather is lost, cost, or frost? *Frost.*

(Count the points, and declare a winner.)
You did a great job of playing the Super Choosing Game!

Complete Activity Sheet

(Work together with children to make a list of the animals mentioned in *Time to Sleep.* List the animals on a piece of chart paper or on the board.)

(Give each child a copy of the Activity Sheet, BLM 25b.) Today we will use our crayons to make a graph to show which of the animals in the story were our favorites. Touch under the words above the first line of boxes. Those words say "The animal I liked best in this story is . . ."

What do those words say? *The animal I liked best in this story is . . .*

Touch under the words in front of the first line of boxes. That word says "Bear." What does that word say? *Bear.* (Repeat for each of the animals. Call on children one at a time. Ask each child the question "Which animal in the story is your favorite?" The child should respond using the frame "My favorite animal is _____ because _____." Have the class color a box on the appropriate row. After each child has had a turn, help the class draw some conclusions from the graphs. For example, most children liked the _____ best; the _____ was our least favorite animal; (number of children) The children's favorite animal was _____.)

DAY 4

Preparation: Prepare a sheet of chart paper, portrait direction, with the title *Time to Sleep.* Underneath the title make a circle of six circles connected by arrows. Leave enough room at the bottom of the page to write two sentences. (These will be added on Day 5.)

See the Introduction for an example.

Record children's responses by writing the underlined words in the circles.

Literary Analysis (Story Patterns)

When authors write stories, they sometimes write in patterns. Let's see if we can figure out the pattern for this story. You tell me what happens in the story, and I'll write it down.

(Show the illustrations on the following pages, and ask the specified questions.)

Pages 1–2. What animal starts the story? <u>Bear</u>. What does Bear want to do? (Idea: *Sleep.*) Whom is Bear going to talk to before she goes to sleep? *Snail.*

Pages 3–6. Whom is Bear talking to? <u>Snail</u>. What does Snail want to do? (Idea: *Sleep.*) Whom is Snail going to talk to before Snail goes to sleep? *Skunk.*

Pages 7–10. Whom is Snail talking to? <u>Skunk</u>. What does Skunk want to do? (Idea: *Sleep.*) Whom is Skunk going to talk to before Skunk goes to sleep? *Turtle.*

Pages 11–14. Whom is Skunk talking to? <u>Turtle</u>. What does Turtle want to do? (Idea: *Sleep.*) Whom is Turtle going to talk to before Turtle goes to sleep? *Woodchuck.*

Pages 15–18. Whom is Turtle talking to? <u>Woodchuck</u>. What does Woodchuck want to do? (Idea: *Sleep.*) Whom is Woodchuck going to talk to before Woodchuck goes to sleep? *Ladybug.*

Pages 19–22. Whom is Woodchuck talking to? <u>Ladybug</u>. What does Ladybug want to do? (Idea: *Sleep.*) Whom is Ladybug going to talk to before Ladybug goes to sleep? *Bear.*

Pages 23–28. Whom is Ladybug talking to? <u>Bear</u>. (Point to the first circle with *Bear* written in it.) What does Bear want to do? (Idea: *Sleep.*)

(Point to the story map on the chart paper.) Look at the shape of this story. It's a circle. This story starts and ends with the same animal at the same place, so this story has a **circle** pattern. What kind of pattern does a story have that starts and ends at the same place? *A circle pattern.*

Let's sing The "Pattern Song" to help us remember about story patterns.

(See the Introduction for the complete song.)

Singing a song together is a very good way to remember the patterns we will learn!

Play Super Choosing Game (Cumulative Review)

Let's play the Super Choosing Game. I will say a sentence that has some of our vocabulary words in it. You will have to choose which one is the correct word for that sentence. Remember, this game is *Super* Choosing because I will use some words from other lessons. You will have to be sharp! (Display the Picture Vocabulary Cards for *cave, den, hibernate, burrow, frost,* and *migrate.* Do not display the cards from earlier lessons.)

Now you're ready to play the Super Choosing Game.

(Draw a T-chart on the board for keeping score. Children earn one point for each correct answer. If they make an error, correct them as you normally would, and record one point for yourself. Repeat missed words at the end of the game.)

- When you move into a hole in a hill or a mountain, are you moving into a save, a cave, or a pave? *A cave.*
- When you spend time in a comfortable room in your house, are you in your pen, ten, or den? *Den.*
- When an animal flies south every winter, is it favorite, does it memorize, or does it migrate? *Migrate.*
- When an animal curls up in its home and sleeps there for most of the winter, does the animal blossom, migrate, or hibernate? *Hibernate.*
- If white, powdery ice is on your windows in the wintertime, is it cost, frost, or bare? *Frost.*
- Does an animal that digs a hole or tunnel live in a burrow, a cottage, or a decoration? *A burrow.*
- What can an animal home be called: a den, a gale, or jagged? *A den.*
- If you touch something softly, are you lonely, gentle, or prickly? *Gentle.*
- If you pick things up and put them in groups, are you gathering, appearing, or drifting? *Gathering.*

Now you will have to listen very carefully because I'm not going to show you the word cards.

- Simon made up his mind to go exploring. He would not let anything stop him. Was he examined, determined, or enormous? *Determined.*
- When your food tastes very good, is it delicious, anxious, or furious? *Delicious.*
- If something is very important to you, is it perfect, dreary, or precious? *Precious.*
- When someone or something made a short, high-pitched sound, would you say that it peeked, squeaked, or leaked? *Squeaked.*
- If you thought about what to do and then made a choice, would you say that you decided, snatched, or trembled? *Decided.*

- When you remember things that happened to you in the past, do you have memories, seasons, or petals? *Memories.*
- When you are happy with the way things are, are you silly, shy, or satisfied? *Satisfied.*
- If a balloon moves toward the sky, is it going dim, severely, or upward? *Upward.*

(Count the points, and declare a winner.)
You did a great job of playing the Super Choosing Game!

DAY 5

Preparation: Happy Face Game Test Sheet, BLM B. Display the story map chart from Day 4.

Retell Story as a "Chime-In"

Today we'll retell the story *Time to Sleep* as a chime-in story. When we tell a story as a chime-in story, you join in and say parts of the story with me.

Let's decide what words we will use for the chime-in parts. What important words do the animals say when they realize winter is coming? *It's time to sleep.* (Print the words *It's time to sleep* underneath the story map on the chart.)

Before each animal goes to find a place to hibernate, what does the animal say? *But first I must tell . . .* (Print the words *But first I must tell _____* under *It's time to sleep.*)

I'll start to tell the story. When the animals are ready to say these words (point to the sentences at the bottom of the story map chart), you all chime in.

(Show the illustrations on the following pages.)

Pages 1–2. Paraphrase the story in a manner similar to this:) Bear sniffs and smells winter in the air. Bear says . . . *It's time to sleep. But first I must tell Snail.*

Pages 5–6. Snail has seen frost on the grass. Snail says . . . *It's time to sleep. But first I must tell Skunk.*

Pages 9–10. Skunk has seen yellow and red leaves on the trees. Skunk says . . . *It's time to sleep. But first I must tell Turtle.*

Pages 13–14. Turtle has noticed the days have been growing shorter. Turtle says . . . *It's time to sleep. But first I must tell Woodchuck.*

Pages 17–18. Woodchuck has eaten so much his skin is getting tight. Woodchuck says . . . *It's time to sleep. But first I must tell Ladybug.*

Pages 23–24. Ladybug has seen the geese migrating south. Ladybug says . . . *It's time to sleep. But first I must tell Bear.*

Pages 25–26. Ladybug wakes up Bear to tell him it is time to sleep. Bear says, "I *was* asleep!" and goes back to sleep.

(Point to the story map, starting with Bear, and going counterclockwise around the circle, have children say goodnight to each animal in turn, finishing with *"Goodnight, everyone. See you in the spring."*)

Assess Vocabulary

 (Hold up a copy of the Happy Face Game Test Sheet, BLM B.)

Today you're going to play the Happy Face Game. When you play the Happy Face Game, it helps me know how well you know the hard words you are learning.

If I say something true, color the happy face. What will you do if I say something true? *Color the happy face.*

If I say something false, color the sad face. What will you do if I say something false? *Color the sad face.*

Listen carefully to each item I say. Don't let me trick you!

Item 1: A **cave** is a small hole that even an ant couldn't fit into. *False.*

Item 2: **Migrate** means to go to another place for part of the year. *True.*

Item 3: **Frost** is a white, powdery cake that you cook for dinner. *False.*

Item 4: A gopher or chipmunk might **burrow** into a hole. *True.*

Item 5: **Den** is another word for a comfortable room in your house. *True.*

Item 6: When animals **hibernate,** they sleep for weeks and weeks. *True.*

Item 7: If you have a good **appetite,** you have an interest in food. *True.*

Item 8: If you **crept** across the classroom, you moved as quietly and as slowly as you could. *True.*

Item 9: **Pleaded** means "begged." *True.*

Item 10: Something that is **difficult** is easy to do. *False.*

You did a great job of playing the Happy Face Game!

(Score children's work later. Scores of 9 out of 10 indicate mastery. If a child does not achieve mastery, insert the missed words in the games in the next week's lessons. Retest those children individually on the missed words before they take the next mastery test.)

Extensions
Read a Story as a Reward

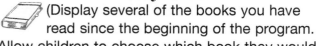 (Display several of the books you have read since the beginning of the program. Allow children to choose which book they would like you to read aloud to them as a reward for their hard work.)

(Read story aloud to children for enjoyment with minimal interruptions.)

Present Super Words Center

 (Prepare the word containers for the Super Words Center. You may wish to remove some words from earlier lessons. Choose words that children have mastered. See the Introduction for instructions on how to set up and use the Super Words Center.)

(Add the new Picture Vocabulary Cards to the words from previous weeks. Show children one of the word containers. If they need more guidance, role-play with two or three children as a demonstration.)

Today I will help you remember how to play What's Missing?

Let's think about how we work with our words in the Super Words Center.

You will work with a partner in the Super Words Center. Whom will you work with in the center? *A partner.*

First, one partner will draw four word cards out of the container and put them on the table so both partners can see. What do you do first? (Idea: *Draw four cards out of the container and put them on the table so both partners can see.*)

Next you will take turns looking at the cards and saying the words the pictures show. What do you do next? (Idea: *We take turns looking at the cards and saying the words the pictures show.*)

Next, partner 2 looks away while partner 1 takes one of the four cards and places it facedown on the table away from the other cards. Then partner 1 draws a new card from the container and places it on the table with the other three. Watch while I show you what I mean.

(Demonstrate this process with a child as your partner.) When you put down the new card, it's a good idea to mix the cards so they aren't in the same places any more. (Demonstrate as you go.)

Now partner 1 says, "What's missing?" Partner 2 has to use his or her eyes and brain and say which old card has been taken away. After partner 2 has guessed, turn over the facedown card. If partner 2 is correct, he or she gets a point. If partner 2 is not correct, partner 1 gets the point. (Demonstrate as you go.)

Next, partner 2 has a turn to choose four different cards, and the game starts again. What happens next? (Idea: *Partner 2 has a turn to choose four different cards, and the game starts again.*)

Have fun playing What's Missing!

Preparation: You will need *The First Day of Winter* for each day's lesson.

Number the pages of the book to assist you in asking questions at appropriate points.

Post a copy of the Vocabulary Tally Sheet, BLM A, with this week's Picture Vocabulary Cards attached.

Each child will need the Homework Sheet, BLM 26a.

The First Day of Winter
author: Consie Powell • illustrator: Consie Powell

⊙ Target Vocabulary

Tier II	Tier III
limbs	pattern
chores	(counting)
awesome	illustrations
devour	(mixed media)
*impressions	
*dormant	

* Expanded Target Vocabulary Word

DAY 1

Introduce Book

We have been reading some books that had both fiction and nonfiction parts. What parts of the books were nonfiction? (Ideas: *The foreword, and the afterword.*) What part of the books was fiction? (Idea: *The part made up from the author's imagination.*)

We will be reading some books that are true.

When an author writes books about things that are true, those books are called nonfiction books. What kind of books are about true things? *Nonfiction books.*

This week's book is called *The First Day of Winter.* What's the title of this week's book? *The First Day of Winter.*

This book was written by Consie Powell. Who's the author of *The First Day of Winter*? *Consie Powell.*

Consie Powell also made the pictures for this book. Who's the illustrator of *The First Day of Winter*? *Consie Powell.* Who made the illustrations for this book? *Consie Powell.*

The cover of a book usually gives us some hints of what the book is about. Let's look at the front cover of *The First Day of Winter.* What do you see in the illustration? (Ideas: *Three children playing in the snow; one has a snowball; one is catching snowflakes on his tongue; one is catching snowflakes on her mittens; a white rabbit is hiding in a bush; two birds are sitting on branches; there are snowflakes; there's a tree.*)

(Assign each child a partner.) Remember, when you make a prediction about something, you say what you think will happen. Get ready to make some predictions to your partner about this book. Use the information from the cover to help you.

(Ask the following questions, allowing sufficient time for children to share their predictions with their partners.)

- Who are the main characters in this story? (Whom do you think this story is about?)
- What are the children doing?
- Where do you think this story happens?
- When do you think this story happens?
- Why do you think the rabbit is hiding?
- How far do you think it is to the house?
- Do you think this story is about real people? Tell why or why not.

(Call on several children to share their predictions with the class.)

Take a Picture Walk

We are going to take a picture walk through this book. Remember, when we take a picture walk, we look at the pictures and tell what we think will happen in the book.

(Show the illustrations on the following pages, and ask the specified questions. Encourage children to use previously taught target words in their answers.)

Page 1. What season is it when the book begins? (Idea: *Winter.*) Why do you think so? (Ideas: *There's snow on the ground; I see snowshoes, a toboggan, a snow shovel; some of the trees have no leaves; the people are putting on warm coats, boots, hats, and mittens.*) Where do you think the family is going? (Idea: *Outside to play in the snow.*)

Pages 2–3. This illustration has two parts: a background that shows an outdoor scene and an oval that shows a close-up. First tell me about the background scene. What do you see? (Ideas: *A green tree covered with snow; a bird on a branch; some trees with no leaves; snow; a fence.*) Now tell me about the close-up in the oval. What is happening in this part of the illustration? (Idea: *A child is hiding under a branch of the green tree.*)

Pages 4–5. This illustration has two parts: a background that shows an outdoor scene and an oval that shows a close-up. First tell me about the background scene. What do you see? (Ideas: *Lots of snow; a bird; a crow; an animal sliding down into the water.*) Now tell me about the close-up in the oval. What is happening in this part of the illustration? (Idea: *Two children are sliding down the snowy hill on big inner tubes.*)

Pages 6–7. This illustration has two parts: a background that shows an outdoor scene and an oval that shows a close-up. First tell me about the background scene. What do you see? (Ideas: *Snow; trees; bushes; grasses; funny marks in the snow.*) What do you think made the funny marks in the snow? (Pause.) Now tell me about the close-up in the oval. What is happening in this part of the illustration? (Idea: *Children are making snow angels; children are making marks in the snow.*)

Pages 8–9. First tell me about the background scene. What is different about this illustration? (Idea: *We can see on top of the water and under the water at the same time.*) Sometimes an artist makes an illustration look as if he or she has sliced open the scene and put a window in so

you can see above and below. We call that a cutaway view. What kind of illustration is this? *A cutaway view.*

What do you see above the water? (Ideas: *Snow; the tops of some water plants.*) What do you see below? (Ideas: *A turtle; some bugs; a beaver; some fish; some sticks; some rocks; some dirt or sand.*) What other book did we read that had a cutaway view? (Idea: *Loon Lake.*) Now tell me about the close-up in the oval. What is happening in this part of the illustration? (Idea: *Four children are skating; one boy has a hockey stick.*) Where do you think the children are skating? (Idea: *On the frozen pond.*)

Pages 10–11. First tell me about the background scene. What is different about this illustration? (Idea: *We can see on top of the snow and under the snow at the same time.*) What kind of illustration is this? *A cutaway view.* What do you see above the snow? (Ideas: *Bare branches; birds.*) What do you see below? (Ideas: *A chipmunk; some voles; some other animals; some snakes, a frog.* **Note:** If children don't correctly name the animals, tell them that they will learn the names of the animals when you read the book aloud to them.) Now tell me about the close-up in the oval. What is happening in this part of the illustration? (Idea: *Five people are inside their house; two children are doing a jigsaw puzzle; a boy is playing with his dog; a boy is reading the paper; a girl is toasting marshmallows; the cat is sleeping on the back of the chair.*)

Pages 12–13. First tell me about the background scene. What do you see? (Ideas: *Snow; houses; trees; branches; snowflakes.*) Now tell me about the close-up in the oval. Where have we seen this illustration before? (Idea: *On the front cover.*) What are the children doing? (Idea: *Playing in the snow.*)

Pages 14–15. First tell me about the background scene. What do you see? (Ideas: *Snow; lots of trees and bushes; the leaves on the trees look dead; some trees have seeds.*) Now tell me about the close-up in the oval. What is happening in this part of the illustration? (Idea: *The people are carrying wood; the dog is playing with a stick.*) Why do you suppose they have so much wood stacked in the shed? (Idea: *They need it to keep their house warm in the winter.*)

Pages 16–17. First tell me about the background scene. What do you see? (Ideas: *Snow; lots of trees and bushes; animals walking on the snow; animals sitting on the snow; a squirrel coming down a tree.*) Now tell me about the close-up in the oval. What is happening in this part of the illustration? (Ideas: *Everyone is wearing snowshoes; they are going for a walk in the snow.*) Where do you think they might be going?

Pages 18–19. First tell me about the background scene. What is different about this illustration? (Idea: *We can see on top of the snow and under the snow at the same time; we can see inside the trees.*) What kind of illustration is this? *A cutaway view.* What do you see above the snow? (Ideas: *Trees; bushes; plants.*) What do you see below? (Ideas: *Ants; insects; bugs.*)

What do you see in the cutaway view of the trees? (Ideas: *Butterflies; ladybugs; insects; bugs.* **Note:** If children don't correctly name the animals, tell them that they will learn the names when you read the book aloud to them.) Now tell me about the close-up in the oval. What is happening in this part of the illustration? (Idea: *They are building a snow fort; they are making snowballs.*)

Pages 20–21. First tell me about the background scene. What do you see? (Ideas: *Snow; trees; the pond; lots of footprints.*) Now tell me about the close-up in the oval. What is happening in this part of the illustration? (Ideas: *The boy is shoveling snow; one girl is playing with the dog; the other girl is looking at the footprints in the snow.*)

Pages 22–23. First tell me about the background scene. What do you see? (Ideas: *A birdfeeder; some bread in a bag; lots of birds.*) Now tell me about the close-up in the oval. What is happening in this part of the illustration? (Ideas: *The girl is watching the birds eating seeds at the bird feeder.*)

Pages 24–25. First tell me about the background scene. What do you see? (Ideas: *Snow; trees; lots of birds and animals; some*

of them eating something.*) Now tell me about the close-up in the oval. What is happening in this part of the illustration? (Ideas: *Two people are making cookies; some people are eating cookies.*)

There are lots of different ways to make illustrations for a book: painting; drawing with a pen or a pencil; using markers, crayons, pastels, or chalk; or cutting out different pieces of paper and gluing them together.

Let's see if we can figure out how Consie Powell made the illustrations for *The First Day of Winter*.

(Show the illustration on page 9.) What do you think Consie Powell used to draw the people? (Ideas: *Ink; a pen.*) How do you know she didn't use a pencil? (Idea: *The lines are dark, not light like a pencil.*) Consie Powell didn't use a pen to draw the lines; she likes to dip a small brush in the ink. That way her lines can change from narrow to wide and back again if she wants.

(Point to the lines used to draw the snow.) Here she wanted a thick line. (Point to the lines used to draw the children.) And here she wanted a thin line. (Point to the line in the mud beneath the beaver.) Here she wanted a line that started thin, got thicker, and then got thin again. She could do that with a brush but not with a pen.

What do you think Consie Powell used to color the water and the mud? (Idea: *Watercolors.*) That's right; she mixed lots of water and a little color and painted these big areas, being careful to stay inside the lines. When an artist uses a lot of water and a little paint to cover a large area on an illustration, we say she put a wash on the painting.

(Point to the crosshatching on the mud at the bottom of the pond and the lines on the beaver.) What do you think Consie Powell used to add shading and details to her drawings? (Idea: *Pencil crayons.*)

(Point to the bushes at the top of the oval.) If you look carefully here, you can see many different colors of pencil lines she used to draw the bushes.

On this page, Consie Powell used three different things to make her illustrations: ink, watercolors, and pencil crayons. When an artist uses different things to make an illustration, we say he or she used mixed media. What did Consie Powell use in *The First Day of Winter* to make her illustrations? *Mixed media.*

It's your turn to ask me some questions. What would you like to know about the book? (Accept questions. If children tell about the pictures or the book instead of asking questions, prompt them to ask a question.) Ask me a how question. Ask me a why question.

Read Story Aloud
(Read story aloud to children with minimal interruptions.)

In the next lesson, we will read the book again, and I will ask you some questions.

Present Target Vocabulary
 Limbs.

The person telling the story says, "We'll hide and seek beneath the limbs of one big old fir tree." That means we'll play hide and seek under the branches of the tree. **Limbs.** Say the word. *Limbs.*

Limbs is a naming word. It names things. What kind of word is **limbs?** *A naming word.*

Limbs are the branches of a tree. Say the word that means "the branches of a tree." *Limbs.*

(Correct any incorrect responses, and repeat the item at the end of the sequence.)

Let's think about some things that might be limbs. I'll name some things. If you think the things I'm naming are limbs, say, "Limbs." If not, don't say anything.

- There are robins' nests in the branches of the tree. *Limbs.*
- The branches of the tree are bent low by the heavy snow on them. *Limbs.*
- The part of the tree that grows underground is strong and healthy.
- The branches of the trees are hidden by the leaves. *Limbs.*
- The leaves of the trees need water.
- The man has a sore back so he has trouble sleeping.

What naming word means "the branches of a tree"? *Limbs.*

 Chores.

In the book, on the seventh day of winter the family completed their chores. That means they finished all the jobs they had to do. **Chores.** Say the word. *Chores.*

Chores is a naming word. It names things. What kind of word is **chores?** *A naming word.*

Chores are jobs you have to do nearly every day. Say the word that means "jobs you have to do nearly every day." *Chores.*

(Correct any incorrect responses, and repeat the item at the end of the sequence.)

Let's think some things that might be chores. I'll tell about something. If you think I'm telling about a chore, say, "Chore." If not, don't say anything.

- Setting the table for dinner. *Chore.*
- Playing with your best friend.
- Putting dirty clothes into the clothes hamper. *Chore.*
- Getting presents on your birthday.
- Picking up toys. *Chore.*
- Feeding the cat. *Chore.*

What naming word means "jobs you have to do nearly every day"? *Chores.*

Awesome.

In the book the evening grosbeaks devour all the seed "with awesome speed." That means people were amazed by how fast the birds could eat the seeds. They could hardly believe their eyes. **Awesome.** Say the word. *Awesome.*

Awesome is a describing word. It tells about a naming word. What kind of word is **awesome?** *A describing word.*

If something is awesome, it is amazing and hard to believe. Say the word that means "amazing and hard to believe." *Awesome.*

(Correct any incorrect responses, and repeat the item at the end of the sequence.)

Let's think some things that might be awesome. I'll tell about something. If you think I am telling about something awesome, say, "Awesome." If not, don't say anything.

- The mountain is so high I can hardly believe my eyes. *Awesome.*
- The sight of a hundred elephants charging across the plains in Africa is amazing. *Awesome.*
- It is just another ordinary day as I walk to school.
- The sound of Niagara Falls pouring over the cliff is amazing! *Awesome.*
- My bedroom is painted pale blue.
- I like to eat yogurt and fruit for lunch.

What describing word means "amazing and hard to believe"? *Awesome.*

 Devour.

In the story, "eleven evening grosbeaks devour all our seed." That means they eat all the seeds quickly and hungrily. **Devour.** Say the word. *Devour.*

Devour is an action word. It tells what happens. What kind of word is **devour?** *An action word.*

When you devour something, you eat quickly and hungrily. What word means "eat quickly and hungrily"? *Devour.*

(Correct any incorrect responses, and repeat the item at the end of the sequence.)

Let's think about some times when someone might devour something. I'll tell you about a time. If you think you would see someone devouring something, say, "Devour." If not, don't say anything.

- The children eat the ice cream quickly and hungrily. *Devour.*
- Jojuan doesn't have much appetite for the food on his plate.
- The lion hungrily eats the gazelle as soon as it has killed it. *Devour.*
- The cat refuses to eat the food in its dish.
- The monkeys gobble down the whole bunch of bananas. *Devour.*
- The rescued boys quickly eat everything they are given. *Devour.*

What action word means "eat quickly and hungrily"? *Devour.*

Present Vocabulary Tally Sheet
(See Week 1, page 3, for instructions.)

Assign Homework
(Homework Sheet, BLM 26a: See the Introduction for homework instructions.)

Preparation: Picture Vocabulary Cards for *limbs, chores, awesome,* and *devour.*

Read and Discuss Book
(**Note:** This book is long and complex. You may wish to read parts of it throughout the day rather than in one sitting. Read the book aloud to children. Ask the following questions at the specified points. Encourage children to use previously taught target words in their answers.)

Page 1. What two things are special about the twenty-first of December? (Ideas: *It's the shortest day of the year; it's the first day of winter.*) What are we invited to do? (Idea: *Go outside and have fun.*) What do we need to remember to do? (Idea: *Look around.*) Why should we look around? (Idea: *Lots of things are happening that we might not notice.*)

Page 2. What will we do on the first day of winter? (Idea: *Play hide and seek underneath the big old fir tree.*) How many children do you see? *One.*

Page 3. (Call on a child to come forward and touch the tree. Read aloud the words on the oval.) What two important facts have we learned about the fir tree? (Idea: *It has waxy needles and a cone shape.*) The leaves on a fir tree are called needles. What do we call the leaves on a fir tree? *Needles.* How many fir trees are nearby? *One.*

Page 4. What will we do on the second day of winter? (Idea: *Go sliding on tubes.*) How many children do you see? *Two.*

Page 5. (Call on a child to come forward and touch the slider with fur. Call on a student to come forward and touch the slider with feathers. Read aloud the words on the oval.) What animal is the slider with fur? *An otter.* What animal is the slider with feathers? *A raven.* How many animal sliders do you see? *Two.*

Let's try to figure out the main idea on pages 4 and 5. The main idea is the reason this part was written. What is the main idea? *The reason this part was written.* When Consie Powell wrote these words and made these illustrations, what do you think she wanted us to know? (Idea: *Both animals and people slide on the snow.*) That's right; so the main idea on pages 4 and 5 is that both animals and people slide on the snow. What is the main idea on pages 4 and 5? *Both animals and people slide on the snow.*

Page 6. What will we do on the third day of winter? (Idea: *Make snow angels.*) How many children have left their marks on the snow? *Three.*

Page 7. (Call on a child to come forward and touch the three sets of marks in the snow. Read aloud the words written on the oval.) Which marks show where an owl caught a mouse? (Call on a child to touch the marks.) Why do you think this shows where an owl caught a mouse? (Ideas: *I can see the mouse footprints leading up to the marks, and then they disappear; I can see where the wings of the owl hit the snow.*) Which marks show where a ruffed grouse left a snow burrow? (Call on a child to touch the marks.) Why do you think this shows where a ruffed grouse left a snow burrow? (Ideas: *I can see inside the burrow; I can see the footprints and wing marks.*) Which marks show where pine siskins searched for seeds? (Call on a child to touch the marks.) Why do you think this shows where pine siskins searched for seeds? (Ideas: *I can see some seeds; I can see the footprints and wing marks.*) How many places do you see where animals have left their marks in the snow? *Three.*

Let's try to figure out the main idea on pages 6 and 7. Remember, the main idea is the reason this part was written. What is the main idea? *The reason this part was written.* When Consie Powell wrote these words and made these illustrations, what do you think she wanted us to know? (Idea: *Both animals and people leave their marks on the snow; both people and animals*

can make marks in the snow.*) That's right; so the main idea on pages 6 and 7 is that both animals and people leave their marks on the snow. What is the main idea on pages 6 and 7? *Both animals and people leave their marks on the snow.*

Page 8. What will we do on the fourth day of winter? (Idea: *Go skating on the ice.*) How many children are skating? *Four.*

Page 9. (Call on individual children to come forward and touch the four kinds of animals under the ice. Read aloud the words on the oval.) Where are the prowling dragonfly nymphs? (Call on a child to touch the two nymphs.) Where is the snapping turtle? (Call on a child to touch the snapping turtle.) Where is the beaver? (Call on a child to touch the beaver.) Where are the bluegills? (Call on a child to touch the bluegills.)

Let's try to figure out the main idea on pages 8 and 9. Remember, the main idea is the reason this part was written. What is the main idea? *The reason this part was written.* When Consie Powell wrote these words and made these illustrations, what do you think she wanted us to know? (Idea: *In winter, people play on the ice, but animals live underneath the ice.*) That's right; the main idea on pages 8 and 9 is that people play on the ice, but animals live under the ice. What is the main idea on pages 8 and 9? *People play on the ice, but animals live under the ice.*

(Continue this procedure as you read each of the remaining days of winter, counting the items and identifying the main ideas.

Fifth day: Both people and animals stay inside when it is really cold.

Sixth day: Children are different, and snowflakes are different.

Seventh day: Both people and trees are all ready for winter.

Eighth day: Both people and animals can walk on top of the snow.

Ninth day: Both people and animals find protection from the cold.

Tenth day: Both animals and people make footprints in the snow.

Eleventh day: We can help feed the birds that stay all winter.

Twelfth day: Both people and animals need food.)

(Do not read the afterword titled "What Happens on Winter Days?" It will be read on Day 5 of the lesson.)

Let's remember what Consie Powell told us to do when we started to read the book. What did we need to remember to do? (Idea: *Look around.*) Why did she want us to look around? (Idea: *Lots of things are happening that we might not notice.*) When Consie Powell wrote the words and made the illustrations for *The First Day of Winter,* what do you think she wanted us to know? (Idea: *If we look carefully, we'll notice people and animals doing lots of things in the winter.*) That's right; so the main idea of *The First Day of Winter* is that if we look carefully, we'll notice people and animals doing lots of things in the winter. What is the main idea of the book *The First Day of Winter*? *If we look carefully, we'll notice people and animals doing lots of things in the winter.*

Review Vocabulary

(Display the Picture Vocabulary Cards. Point to each card as you say the word. Ask children to repeat each word after you.) These pictures show **chores, devour, awesome,** and **limbs.**

What word means "jobs you have to do nearly every day"? *Chores.*

What word means "eat quickly and hungrily"? *Devour.*

What word means "amazing and hard to believe"? *Awesome.*

What word means "the branches of a tree"? *Limbs.*

Extend Vocabulary

 Limbs.

In *The First Day of Winter,* we learned that **limbs** mean "the branches of a tree." Say the word that means "the branches of a tree." *Limbs.*

Raise your hand if you can tell us a sentence that uses **limbs** as a naming word that means "the branches of a tree." (Call on several

children. If they don't use complete sentences, restate their examples as sentences. Have the class repeat the sentences.)

Here's a new way to use the word **limbs.**

- **His limbs are stiff and sore after he finishes his exercises.** Say the sentence.
- **The baby's limbs grow longer and stronger.** Say the sentence.
- **If we didn't have limbs, we couldn't move or pick up things.** Say the sentence.

In these sentences, **limbs** is a naming word that means **arms and legs.** What naming word means "arms and legs"? *Limbs.*

Raise your hand if you can tell us a sentence that uses **limbs** as a naming word that means "arms and legs." (Call on several children. If they don't use complete sentences, restate their examples as sentences. Have the class repeat the sentences.)

Present Expanded Target Vocabulary
Impressions.

In *The First Day of Winter,* the people and the animals leave marks in the snow. Another way of saying the people and animals leave marks in the snow is to say they leave impressions in the snow. **Impressions.** Say the word. *Impressions.*

Impressions is a naming word. It names things. What kind of word is **impressions?** *A naming word.*

Impressions are marks made by pressing down on something. Say the word that means "marks made by pressing down on something." *Impressions.*

I'll tell about a person or an animal. If that person or animal made marks by pressing down on something say, "Impressions." If not don't say anything.

- Our feet make marks in the wet sand. *Impressions.*
- You cannot see any marks on the smooth wood floor.
- We know a deer has been in our garden because we can see its footprints in the dirt. *Impressions.*

- In the winter, the hooves of the moose leave marks in the snow. *Impressions.*
- There are marks on the sofa where people have been sitting. *Impressions.*
- She makes her bed carefully so all the blankets are smooth.

What naming word means "marks made by pressing down on something"? *Impressions.*

◎⟨ **Dormant.**

In *The First Day of Winter,* there are no leaves on many of the trees. The trees are not growing, but they are still alive. Another way of saying the trees are not growing but they are still alive is to say the trees are dormant. **Dormant.** Say the word. *Dormant.*

Dormant is a describing word. It tells about something. What kind of word is **dormant?** *A describing word.*

Dormant means plants have lost their leaves and are not growing but are still alive. Say the word that means "plants have lost their leaves and are not growing but are still alive." *Dormant.*

I'll tell about some plants. If that plant is dormant, say, "Dormant." If not, don't say anything.

- In the winter the birch tree loses its leaves and stops growing. *Dormant.*
- In the summer the lawns turn brown and stop growing, but the grass is still alive. *Dormant.*
- The lawns are lush and green.
- If there is no rain, some trees will lose their leaves and stop growing. *Dormant.*
- The jungle is thick with huge trees and long green vines.

What describing word means "plants have lost their leaves and are not growing but are still alive"? *Dormant.*

DAY 3

Preparation: Prepare a sheet of chart paper with the title *Winter Activities.*
Activity Sheet, BLM 26b. Children will need their crayons.

Summarize Book

Today we are going to summarize what we learned in the story *The First Day of Winter.*

When we summarize, we use our own words to tell about the most important things in the story. What do we do when we summarize? *We use our own words to tell about the most important things in the story.*

(Show the pictures on the following pages from the story, and call on a child to tell what's happening. Call on a different child for each section.)

I'll show you the pictures Consie Powell made for the story *The First Day of Winter.* As I show you the pictures, I'll call on one of you to tell the class the important thing that is happening in that part of the book.

Page 1. Tell me what important thing happens at the **beginning** of the book.

Pages 2–23. Tell me what important things happen in the **middle** of the book. (Encourage use of target words when appropriate. Model use as necessary.)

Pages 24–25. Tell me what important thing happens at the **end** of the book.

Review Super Choosing Game

Today you will play the Super Choosing Game. Let's think about the six words we have: **limbs, chores, awesome, devour, impressions,** and **dormant.** (Display the Picture Vocabulary Cards.)

I will say a sentence that has some of the words we have learned in it. You will have to choose which one is the correct word for that sentence. Not all of the words will be from this lesson, though. That's why it's the *Super* Choosing Game. Let's practice. **(You should not show cards for words from previous lessons.)**

- Are the branches of a tree legends, limps, or limbs? *Limbs.*
- When you eat something quickly and hungrily, do you disrupt it, devour it, or disturb it? *Devour.*

- When something is amazing and hard to believe, is it a favorite, boring, or awesome? *Awesome.*

Now you're ready to play the game. If you tell me the correct answer, you get one point. If you can't tell me the correct answer, I get the point.

(Draw a T-chart on the board for keeping score. Children earn one point for each correct answer. If they make an error, tell them the correct answer. Record one point for yourself, and repeat missed words at the end of the game.)

- Is another name for your arms and legs limbs, frost, or gasp? *Limbs.*
- Are those jobs that you have to do every day at home called bores, floors, or chores? *Chores.*
- When the leaves have fallen off the tree but it is still alive, is it blooming, dormant, or wild? *Dormant.*
- When you leave footprints in the sand or the snow, are they called traditions, rascals, or impressions? *Impressions.*
- If your printing looks more like scribbling, would you call it relieved, a mall, or a scrawl? *Scrawl.*
- If you call out in class or say inappropriate things, are you rude, mood, or root? *Rude.*

(Count the points, and declare a winner.) You did a great job of playing the Super Choosing Game!

Complete Activity Sheet

(Review with children the different winter activities mentioned in the text. Record the activities on the chart paper as they are identified. Ideas: *Snow tubing; making snow angels; skating; playing in the snow; stacking wood; snowshoeing; building a fort; having a snowball fight.* Have children suggest other winter activities. Record them on the chart paper. **Note:** You need to record at least one more activity than the number of children in your class.)

(Give each child a copy of the Activity Sheet, BLM 26b. Children will select and initial a winter activity from the chart, print the activity, and then draw an illustration to accompany the activity. If children are not yet able to copy the sentence, scribe it for them while they are working on their illustrations. Make a cover with the title *Winter Fun,* and staple the pages together.)

DAY 4

Preparation: Prepare a sheet of chart paper, portrait direction, with the title *The First Day of Winter.* Underneath the title, make twelve boxes connected by arrows. Leave room to write underneath the boxes.

See the Introduction for an example.

Record children's responses by writing the ordinal words in the boxes and the examples underneath.

Patterns (Literary Analysis)

When authors write books, they sometimes write in patterns. Let's see if we can figure out the pattern for this book. You tell me what happens in the story, and I'll write it down.

(Read the first verse of the rhyme from page 2, and show the illustrations on pages 2 and 3.) When does the book begin? *On the <u>first</u> day of winter.* What important things come in ones? (Ideas: *<u>1 child</u>, <u>1 nearby fir tree</u>.*)

(Read the second verse of the rhyme from page 4, and show the illustrations on pages 4 and 5.) When does this part of the book happen? *On the <u>second</u> day of winter.* What important things come in twos? (Ideas: *<u>2 sliding children</u>; <u>2 sliding animals</u>; <u>2 snow tubes</u>.*)

(Read the third verse of the rhyme from page 6 and show the illustrations on pages 6 and 7.) When does this part of the book happen? *On the <u>third</u> day of winter.* What important things come in threes? (Ideas: *<u>3 children playing</u>; <u>3 snow angels</u>; <u>3 impressions in the snow</u>.*)

(Follow the established procedure, recording the ordinals to twelfth and examples found on the corresponding pages.)

(Point to the book map on the chart paper.)
Listen while I read from our book map. First, second, third, fourth . . . twelfth. One child, one nearby fir tree, two sliding children, two sliding animals, two snow tubes, three children playing, three snow angels, three impressions in the snow. Raise your hand if you know what the pattern is for *The First Day of Winter*. (Ideas: *A number pattern; a counting pattern*.)

This book has a **counting** pattern. What kind of pattern does a story have that has numbers that go up in order? *A counting pattern.*

Today we will learn a new verse for "The Pattern Song" that will help us remember about story and book patterns.

Listen while I sing the verse for you:

There's a pattern when you count from one to twelve.
There's a pattern when you count from one to twelve.
Uno, dos and tres and cuatro,
Cinco, seis, siete, ocho,
Nueve, diez, once, doce, one to twelve!*

Now sing it with me.

Now let's sing the whole song together.

(See the Introduction for the complete "Pattern Song.")

Singing a song together is a very good way to remember the patterns we are learning!

Play Super Choosing Game (Cumulative Review)

Let's play the Super Choosing Game. I will say a sentence that has some of our vocabulary words in it. You will have to choose which one is the correct word for that sentence. Remember, this game is *Super* Choosing because I will use some words from other lessons. You will have to be sharp! (Display the Picture Vocabulary Cards for *limbs, chores, awesome, devour, impressions,* and *dormant*. Do not display the word cards from earlier lessons.)

Now you're ready to play the Super Choosing Game.

(Draw a T-chart on the board for keeping score. Children earn one point for each correct answer. If they make an error, correct them as you normally would, and record one point for yourself. Repeat missed words at the end of the game.)

- If your tree has lost its leaves but is still alive, is the tree a door mat, a floor mat, or dormant? *Dormant.*
- If you ate your vegetables hungrily and quickly, did you snuggle with them, cold shower them, or devour them? *Devour.*
- The jobs that you do every day are scores, blossoms, or chores? *Chores.*
- What is another name for the branches of a tree: caves, limbs, or dens? *Limbs.*
- When you make prints with your feet in dirt or sand, are they odors, the wilderness, or impressions? *Impressions.*
- Are your arms and legs also called roots, limbs, or seasons? *Limbs.*
- When something is really amazing and hard to believe, is it perfect, awesome, or awful? *Awesome.*
- When birds fly away to spend the winter somewhere else, do they insist, hibernate, or migrate? *Migrate.*
- If Alan tells the truth and does what is right, is he allergic, cowering, or being honest? *Being honest.*

Now you will have to listen very carefully, because I'm not going to show you the word cards.

- In the wintertime, are trees dormant, impatient, or parents? *Dormant.*
- If you push on a marshmallow with your finger and you leave a small hole behind, is it a nursery, an impression, or a promise? *An impression.*
- When your day was the most amazing day ever, would you call it bare, drowsy, or awesome? *Awesome.*
- Is the time of the day when the sun is just starting to come up called a cottage, harvest, dawn? *Dawn.*
- If you saw a bird for a very short time before it was gone, did you examine, glimpse, or explore the bird? *Glimpse.*

- Are tree branches also called dims, limbs, or moods? *Limbs.*
- When I go home, I feed the cats, water the plants, and check the mail. Am I moving upward, scowling, or doing chores? *Doing chores.*
- What would a dinosaur do with his lunch? Would he scorch, devour, or collect it? *Devour.*

(Count the points, and declare a winner.) You did a great job of playing the Super Choosing Game!

DAY 5

Preparation: You may wish to photocopy the afterword "What Happens on Winter Days?" so you can show the illustrations on the appropriate pages while reading the text from the afterword. Happy Face Game Test Sheet, BLM B.

Review Afterword

(Assign each child a partner.) Sometimes after people write a book about something real, they want to tell you more facts about that real thing. This information is put in the book **after** the last **word** of the main part of the book, so it is called an **afterword.** Today I'll read the afterword that Consie Powell wrote for *The First Day of Winter,* so you can learn more about winter.

(**Note:** Main idea is a complex skill for young children. If children have difficulty telling you the main idea, use the format found in Day 2.)

(Read the afterword aloud a paragraph at a time.)

Paragraph 1. Remember, the main idea is the reason this part was written. What is the main idea? *The reason this part was written.* In this part of the book, Consie Powell wanted you to know evergreen trees have changed so they can live in the cold and the snow. What is the main idea of this part of the afterword? (Idea: *Evergreen trees have changed so they can live in the cold and snow.*)

Paragraph 2. In this part of the afterword, Consie Powell wanted you to know that people aren't the only ones who like to slide on snow. What is the main idea of this part of the afterword? (Idea: *People aren't the only ones who like to slide on snow.*)

Paragraph 3. In this part of the afterword, Consie Powell wanted you to know that wing prints tell what birds have been doing. What is the main idea of this part of the afterword? (Idea: *Wing prints tell what birds have been doing.*)

Paragraph 4. In this part of the book, Consie Powell wanted you to know the pond is frozen, but there's a lot of life under the ice. What is the main idea of this part of the afterword? (Idea: *The pond is frozen, but there's a lot of life under the ice.*)

Paragraph 5. In this part of the book, Consie Powell wanted you to know that people and wild animals deal with cold in different ways. What is the main idea of this part of the afterword? (Idea: *People and wild animals deal with cold in different ways.*)

Paragraph 6. In this part of the book, Consie Powell wanted you to know there are many different sizes and shapes of snowflakes. What is the main idea of this part of the afterword? (Idea: *There are many different sizes and shapes of snowflakes.*)

Paragraph 7. In this part of the book, Consie Powell wanted you to know you have to look closely to tell the different trees apart in winter. What is the main idea of this part of the afterword? (Idea: *You have to look closely to tell the different trees apart in winter.*)

Paragraph 8. Critters is another word for animals. What is another word for animals? *Critters.* In this part of the book, Consie Powell wanted you to know animals walk on snow by spreading their weight over a large area. What is the main idea of this part of the afterword? (Idea: *Animals walk on snow by spreading their weight over a large area.*)

Paragraph 9. In this part of the book, Consie Powell wanted you to know that bugs must protect themselves during the winter so they don't get eaten. What is the main idea of this part of the afterword? (Idea: *Bugs must protect* themselves during the winter so they don't get eaten.)

Paragraph 10. In this part of the book, Consie Powell wanted you to know that different animals make different kinds of tracks. What is the main idea of this part of the afterword? (Idea: *Different animals make different kinds of tracks.*)

Paragraph 11. In this part of the book, Consie Powell wanted you to know we can help animals that stay for the winter by putting out food for them. What is the main idea of this part of the afterword? (Idea: *We can help animals that stay for the winter by putting out food for them.*)

Paragraph 12. In this part of the book, Consie Powell wanted you to know animals must find food in order to survive through the winter. What is the main idea of this part of the afterword? (Idea: *Animals must find food in order to survive through the winter.*)

We have learned many facts about winter from this afterword. Think about one fact you thought was most interesting. (Pause.) Share that fact with your partner. (Pause.) Tonight you will share that fact with someone at your home.

Assess Vocabulary

(Hold up a copy of the Happy Face Game Test Sheet, BLM B.)

Today you're going to play the Happy Face Game. When you play the Happy Face Game, it helps me know how well you know the hard words you are learning.

If I say something true, color the happy face. What will you do if I say something true? *Color the happy face.*

If I say something false, color the sad face. What will you do if I say something false? *Color the sad face.*

Listen carefully to each item I say. Don't let me trick you!

Item 1: **Limbs** is another word for arms and legs. *True.*

Item 2: **Devour** means to eat hungrily and quickly. *True.*

Item 3: **Impressions** in the sand at the beach could be footprints or handprints. *True.*

Item 4: A **dormant** plant is one that still has all of its leaves but is dead. *False.*

Item 5: The most amazing thing that you have ever done could be called **awesome.** *True.*

Item 6: **Chores** are usually made of wood, and you walk on them. *False.*

Item 7: Branches of a tree are also called **limbs.** *True.*

Item 8: If you are **active,** you are *not* busy and *not* full of energy. *False.*

Item 9: If you **dashed** into the school building, you ran as slowly as you could go. *False.*

Item 10: The outside parts of a flower are called metals. *False.*

You did a great job of playing the Happy Face Game!

(Score children's work later. Scores of 9 out of 10 indicate mastery. If a child does not achieve mastery, insert the missed words in the games in the next week's lessons. Retest those children individually on the missed words before they take the next mastery test.)

Extensions
Read a Book as a Reward
(Display copies of several books you have read since the beginning of the program. Allow children to choose which book they would like you to read aloud to them as a reward for their hard work.)

(Read the story aloud to children for enjoyment with minimal interruptions.)

Present Super Words Center
(Prepare the word containers for the Super Words Center (see notation below).

See the Introduction for instructions on how to set up and use the Super Words Center.)

(This new game is a Concentration-style game, but it uses all the opposite words from earlier lessons. You may choose to prepare the containers with *only* opposites or you may wish to mix the opposites with current vocabulary or vocabulary for children to review. Supply at least two copies of each of the opposites cards. Use your discretion to determine the number of cards to be placed in the container. Eighteen cards, for example, will generate a Concentration grid of 3 x 6. Twenty-four cards will create a grid of 4 x 6. You will know best what children are able to deal with.)

Today I will teach you a new game called Hot and Cold to play in the Super Words Center. What do you know about the words **hot** and **cold?** (Idea: *They are opposites.*) This game is called Hot and Cold because your job is to find as many opposites as you can.

Let's remember how we work with our words in the Super Words Center.

You will work with a partner in the Super Words Center. Whom will you work with in the center? *A partner.*

First you will draw all of the cards out of the container and lay them facedown. There are enough cards to make (X) rows of (Y) cards. (Demonstrate for children.) What do you do first? (Idea: *Draw all of the cards out and lay them facedown.*)

Next, the first player will turn over one card and place it faceup so that both players can see (demonstrate). What will you do next? (Idea: *The first player turns over a card and places it faceup so that both can see.*)

Next, the first player turns over another card and places it faceup so both can see (demonstrate).

What will you do next? (Idea: *The first player turns over another card and places it faceup so that both can see.*)

This is the important part. If the cards are opposites, the first player takes both cards and sets them aside in his or her game pile. If they are not opposites, the first player places both cards facedown. Either way, it is now the second player's turn. (Demonstrate for children. They will be familiar with the process for playing Concentration, however.)

What will the first player do if the two cards are opposites? (Idea: *Keep those cards and put them in his or her game pile.*) What will the first player do if the two cards are not opposites? (Idea: *Turn them over.*) Either way, whose turn is it next? (Idea: *The second player's.*)

I think you are almost ready to play Hot and Cold. Can you think of some words that are opposites? (Call on several children. List the opposites they suggest to prepare them for playing the game.) Have fun playing Hot and Cold!

(**Note:** If you wish, you may teach children to say "I'm hot!" in a happy voice when they find opposites and "I'm cold!" in a sad voice when they do not.)

Officer Buckle and Gloria
author: Peggy Rathmann • illustrator: Peggy Rathmann

Preparation: You will need *Officer Buckle and Gloria* for each day's lesson.

Number the pages of the story to assist you in asking questions at appropriate points.

Post a copy of the Vocabulary Tally Sheet, BLM A, with this week's Picture Vocabulary Cards attached.

Each child will need the Homework Sheet, BLM 27a.

🎯 Target Vocabulary

Tier II	Tier III
obey	fiction
accident	cartoon-style
imagination	illustration
attention	
*unaware	
*jealous	

* Expanded Target Vocabulary Word

- Who are the main characters in this story? (Whom do you think this story is about?)
- What do you think the man in the uniform is doing?
- Where do you think the story happens?
- When do you think the story happens?
- Why do you think the children are watching the dog?
- How did the dog get upside down?
- Do you think this story is about real people? Tell why or why not.

(Call on several children to share their predictions with the class.)

Take a Picture Walk

(Show the illustrations on the following pages, and ask the specified questions. Encourage children to use previously taught target words in their answers.)

We are going to take a picture walk through this book. Remember, when we take a picture walk, we look at the pictures and tell what we think will happen in the story.

Page 1. What do you think the man in uniform is doing? (Idea: *Falling off his chair.*) What kind of job do you think this man has? (Idea: *He's a police officer.*) Why do you think that that is his job? (Ideas: *He's wearing a blue hat and uniform; he has a star on his shirt; he has a cell phone and clips on his belt.*) (Point to the bulletin board.) What do you think is on these notes?

DAY 1

Introduce Book

This week's book is called *Officer Buckle and Gloria.* What's the title of this week's book? *Officer Buckle and Gloria.*

This book was written by Peggy Rathmann. Who's the author of *Officer Buckle and Gloria? Peggy Rathmann.*

Peggy Rathmann also made the pictures for this book. Who's the illustrator of *Officer Buckle and Gloria? Peggy Rathmann.* Who made the illustrations for this book? *Peggy Rathmann.*

The cover of a book usually gives us some hints of what the book is about. Let's look at the front cover of *Officer Buckle and Gloria.* What do you see in the illustration? (Ideas: *A dog doing a back flip; a police officer; a crowd of children pointing to the dog; stars around the edge of the cover with words and pictures in them.*)

(Assign each child a partner.) Remember, when you make a prediction about something, you say what you think will happen. Get ready to make some predictions to your partner about this book. Use the information from the cover to help you.

(Ask the following questions, allowing sufficient time for children to share their predictions with their partners.)

Page 2. Where do you think the officer is? (Idea: *On a stage.*) How do you think the children are feeling? (Idea: *Bored.*) Why do you think so? (Idea: *They are drowsy; they are not paying attention.*) The children certainly look like they are tired and squirmy because they don't have anything interesting to do.

Page 3. Where is the officer now? (Idea: *At a school.*) What is the girl on the stairs doing? (Ideas: *Carrying a big pile of books.*) What has happened to the boy on the stairs? (Idea: *A book has fallen on his head.*) What is the boy behind the officer doing? (Idea: *Tripping over his shoelace.*) What has happened to the person beside the water fountain? (Idea: *He or she has slipped in the puddle of water and fallen down.*) What is the woman standing on? (Idea: *A swivel chair; a chair with wheels.*) How do you think the officer is feeling? (Idea: *Worried.*) Why do you think the officer might be feeling that way? (Idea: *The people in the school are doing unsafe things.*)

Pages 4–5. What is riding along with the police officer? (Idea: *A dog.*) What do you think the officer is telling the dog to do? (Idea: *Sit.*)

Page 6. What is happening here? (Idea: *The officer is talking to the children; the dog is standing on its two hind legs; it's holding up its paw like the policeman is holding up his hand.*) What are the children doing? (Idea: *Watching the dog and the policeman.*)

Page 7. What is happening here? (Ideas: *The officer is looking at the dog; the dog is listening to the officer and smiling.*) Is the dog still copying the policeman? *No.* Do you think the officer knows the dog has been copying him? (Ideas: *No.*)

Page 8. What is the dog doing? (Ideas: *Doing tricks; dancing; standing on its head.*) What is the officer doing? (Idea: *Talking to the children.*) What are the children doing? (Ideas: *Watching the dog; paying attention to the dog.*)

Page 9. What is happening here? (Ideas: *The officer is looking at the dog; the dog is listening to the officer and smiling.*) Is the dog still standing on its head? *No.* Do you think the officer knows the dog was standing on its head? (Idea: *No.*)

Pages 10–11. What is happening here? (Ideas: *The officer is talking to the children; the dog is jumping in the air; the dog is doing tricks.*)

Pages 12–13. What is the officer doing? (Idea: *Emptying a big envelope full of letters onto his desk.*) What do you think the letters might be about? (Idea: *The dog.*) Why do you think so? (Idea: *Every letter has a drawing of the dog.*)

Page 14. What do you think this is a picture of? (Ideas: *A star-shaped letter; a note.*)

Page 15. What do you think is happening here? (Ideas: *People are calling the officer on the phone; he's talking to them.*)

Pages 16–17. What is happening here? (Ideas: *The officer is teaching a class, and the dog is doing somersaults; the officer is on stage with the dog; the dog is playing dead; the officer is buying ice cream and the dog is signing autographs; the officer is sharing his ice cream with his dog.*)

Pages 18–19. What is happening here? (Idea: *A large crowd of children is watching the officer and the dog on stage.*) What do you think the officer is doing? (Idea: *Talking to the children.*)

Pages 20–21. What do you think is happening to the dog? (Ideas: *It's doing a trick; it's jumping in the air.*) What is the officer doing? (Idea: *Bowing to the audience.*) How do you think the children are feeling? (Ideas: *Excited; amazed.*) Why do you think that? (Ideas: *They are laughing; they are pointing to the dog and the officer.*) I would certainly be very, very amazed if I saw a dog that could do all those tricks! I would say that dog is awesome!

Pages 22–23. What is happening here? (Ideas: *The officer and the dog are watching television; the officer is eating popcorn.*) Where do you think they are? (Ideas: *At the officer's house; in his living room; in his den.*) What makes you think that? (Ideas: *There are books on shelves; there is a television set and a stereo; they are sitting on a sofa; the officer is in his bathrobe and slippers.*) How do you think the officer is feeling? (Idea: *Amazed; shocked.*) That dog's been quite a rascal, hasn't it?

Page 24. What is the officer doing? (Idea: *Talking on the telephone.*) How do you think the officer is feeling? (Idea: *Angry.*)

Page 25. What is happening on this page? (Idea: *The dog is sitting on the stage; the children in the audience are bored and sleeping.*)

Pages 26–27. What is happening here? (Idea: *There's been a big accident; children are falling everywhere in yellow goo; a woman is falling off her chair; a big banner is falling down.*)

Pages 28. What do you see here? (Ideas: *A big pile of letters; a letter shaped like a star.*) Who do you think wrote the letters? (Idea: *The children from the school.*) Why do you think so? (Idea: *They show pictures of the accident.*)

Page 29. What is happening here? (Idea: *The dog is licking the officer's face.*) How do you think the officer is feeling? (Idea: *Happy.*) Why do you think that? (Ideas: *He is smiling a big smile; he has his arm around the dog.*) How do you think the dog is feeling? (Idea: *Happy.*) Why do you think that? (Ideas: *The dog is licking the officer's face.*)

Page 30. What is happening here? (Idea: *The officer and the dog are on stage waving to the audience.*) How do you think everyone is feeling? (Ideas: *Happy; excited.*) Why do you think that? (Ideas: *They are all smiling; the children are waving and clapping.*)

Now that we've finished our picture walk, it's your turn to ask me some questions. What would you like to know about the story? (Accept questions. If children tell about the pictures or the story instead of asking questions, prompt them to ask a question.) Ask me a what question. Ask me a why question.

Read Story Aloud
(Read story aloud to children with minimal interruptions.)

In the next lesson, we will read the story again, and I will ask you some questions.

Present Target Vocabulary
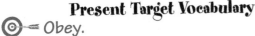 Obey.

In the story, Officer Buckle says, "Gloria obeys my commands." That means Gloria does what

Officer Buckle tells her to do. **Obey.** Say the word. *Obey.*

Obey is an action word. It tells what someone does. What kind of word is **obey?** *An action word.*

If you obey, you do what you are told to do. Say the word that means "do what you are told to do." *Obey.*

(Correct any incorrect responses, and repeat the item at the end of the sequence.)

Let's think about some times when a person or an animal might have obeyed. I'll tell about a time. If you think the person or animal is obeying, say, "Obey." If not, don't say anything.

- The dog rolls over when Anna says, "Roll over." *Obey.*
- Evan does his homework when his mother tells him to do it. *Obey.*
- Bart runs away when his dad says to stay.
- The teacher tells the children to stand in a line, and they do it. *Obey.*
- All three cats go to bed when they are told. Amazing! *Obey.*
- I go to the park even though I am told not to.

What action word means "do what you are told to do"? *Obey.*

Accident.

In the story there is a terrible accident at Napville School because someone doesn't wipe up the spilled banana pudding. That means something bad happens that no one expected, and someone got hurt. **Accident.** Say the word. *Accident.*

Accident is a naming word. It names a thing. What kind of word is **accident?** *A naming word.*

An accident is something bad that happens that no one expects, and someone gets hurt. Say the word that means "something bad that happens that no one expects, and someone gets hurt." *Accident.*

(Correct any incorrect responses, and repeat the item at the end of the sequence.)

Let's think about some things that might be accidents. I'll tell about something that happens. If you think what happens is an accident, say, "Accident." If not, don't say anything.

- When she bumps into the curb, Sofie falls off her bike and hurts her knee. *Accident.*
- Colleen says that Joshua made a face at her.
- When Hansel knocks over his glass of milk, it spills on the floor, and Gretel slips in the puddle. *Accident.*
- Damon hands the paper to Lou.
- "Amanda splattered me with paint on purpose," wails April.
- Jack falls off the bean stalk and breaks the giant's golden harp. *Accident.*

What naming word means "something bad that happens that no one expects, and someone gets hurt"? *Accident.*

◎⊨ Imagination.

In the story, when Officer Buckle looked at the thank-you letters the children sent him, he "thought the drawings showed a lot of imagination." That means he thought the children had used their minds to make up pictures of things that didn't really happen. **Imagination.** Say the word. *Imagination.*

Imagination is a naming word. It names a part of your mind. What kind of word is **imagination?** *A naming word.*

You've already learned about a word that means "not real." What word means "not real"? *Imaginary.*

Your imagination is the part of your mind that lets you make pictures of imaginary things or of things that didn't really happen. Say the word that means "the part of your mind that lets you make pictures of imaginary things or of things that didn't really happen." *Imagination.*

(Correct any incorrect responses, and repeat the item at the end of the sequence.)

Let's think about some things that might come from someone's imagination. I'll tell about something. If you think it comes from someone's imagination, say, "Imagination." If not, don't say anything.

- A horse with wings. *Imagination.*
- A bean stalk that can grow up to the clouds. *Imagination.*
- A wonderful world called Middle Earth where hobbits live. *Imagination.*

- An ordinary house.
- Lunch with talking cows and pigs. *Imagination.*
- A street with nothing special about it.

What naming word means "the part of your mind that lets you make pictures of imaginary things or of things that didn't really happen"? *Imagination.*

◎⊨ Attention.

In the story, "Officer Buckle checked to see if Gloria was sitting at attention." That means he looked to see if she was sitting up straight and looking forward. **Attention.** Say the word. *Attention.*

Attention is a naming word. It names a thing. What kind of word is **attention?** *A naming word.*

When you stand at attention, you stand up straight and face the front, with your feet together and your arms at your sides. What word means "the way you look when you stand up straight and face the front, with your feet together and your arms at your sides"? *Attention.*

(Correct any incorrect responses, and repeat the item at the end of the sequence.)

Let's think about some times when someone might stand at attention. If you think you would see someone standing at attention, say, "Attention." If not, don't say anything.

- Soldiers are being checked by the president. *Attention.*
- Students are saying the Pledge of Allegiance to the flag. *Attention.*
- Everyone is at a picnic.
- You are playing a game where, if you are caught, you have to stand at attention. *Attention.*
- You are at a football game.
- You are at a waterslide in the middle of a hot summer.

What naming word means "the way you look when you stand up straight and face the front, with your feet together and your arms at your sides"? *Attention.*

Present Vocabulary Tally Sheet
(See Week 1, page 3, for instructions.)

Assign Homework

(Homework Sheet, BLM 27a: See the Introduction for homework instructions.)

DAY 2

Preparation: Picture Vocabulary Cards for *obey, accident, imagination,* and *attention.*

Read and Discuss Story

(Read story aloud to children. Ask the following questions at the specified points. Encourage them to use previously taught target words in their answers.)

Page 1. Where does the story happen? (Idea: *In Napville.*) What does Officer Buckle do every time he thinks of a new safety tip? (Idea: *He thumbtacks it to his bulletin board.*) What is Safety Tip Number 77? (Idea: *Never stand on a swivel chair.*) Look at the illustration of a swivel chair. How is a swivel chair different from a regular chair? (Idea: *It has wheels on the bottom.*) What else is different about a swivel chair? (Idea: *The part you sit on can turn.* **Note:** If children are unfamiliar with swivel chairs and there is one in the school, have it available for them to see and sit on. If your classroom or school has a bulletin board, point this out to children.) I'll read you some of the safety tips Officer Buckle has thumbtacked to his bulletin board. (Read two or three of the safety tips aloud to the class.)

Pages 2–3. Where does Officer Buckle share his safety tips? (Idea: *At Napville School.*) What does Officer Buckle say to Mrs. Toppel? (Idea: *Never stand on a swivel chair.*)

Does she pay attention to him? *No.*

Pages 4–5. What does Napville's police department buy? (Idea: *A police dog.*) What is the police dog's name? *Gloria.* Does Gloria obey Officer Buckle's commands? *Yes.*

Pages 6–7. What is Safety Tip Number One? (Idea: *Keep your shoelaces tied.*) What does Gloria do that makes the children stare? (Idea:

She stands up and puts her paw in the air, just like Officer Buckle.) What does Officer Buckle check to see? (Idea: *That Gloria is sitting at attention.*) Is she? *Yes.*

Pages 8–9. What is Safety Tip Number Two? (Idea: *Always wipe up spills before someone slips and falls.*) What does Gloria do? (Idea: *She stands on her head.*) What does Officer Buckle check again? (Idea: *To see if Gloria is sitting at attention.*) Is she? *Yes.*

Page 10. What is the next safety tip? (Idea: *Never leave a thumbtack where you might sit on it.*) Why does the audience roar? (Idea: *Gloria jumps straight up into the air; Gloria pretends she'd sat on a thumbtack.*)

Page 11. What do the children do for the rest of the safety speech? (Ideas: *They clap their hands and cheer; they laugh until they cry.*) Why is Officer Buckle surprised? (Ideas: *He has never noticed how funny safety tips could be.*) Is it really the safety tips that are funny? (Idea: *No, what's funny is Gloria doing tricks.*) Are there any more accidents at the school? *No.* That's right; everybody is really paying attention to Officer Buckle's safety tips.

Pages 12–13. What do the students from Napville School send to the police station? (Idea: *An enormous envelope filled with thank-you letters.*) What is on every letter? (Idea: *A drawing of Gloria.*) Why does Officer Buckle think that the drawings show a lot of imagination? (Idea: *Gloria is doing many tricks and flips in the drawings; Officer Buckle thinks Gloria always sits at attention when he is talking to the children.*) I'll read you one or two of the letters the students send to Officer Buckle and Gloria. (Read aloud from the letters.)

Page 14. How is Officer Buckle's favorite letter different from the other letters? (Idea: *It is written on paper that is in the shape of a star.*) The letters P.S. mean postscript. A postscript is what you write if you want to add something else to a letter after you have signed your name. What letters do you write if you want to add something else to a letter after you have signed your name? *P.S.* What does Claire's P.S. say? (Idea: *I always wear a crash helmet.*)

Page 15. Who calls Officer Buckle after his safety speech? (Ideas: *Grade schools; high schools; daycare centers.*) Why do you think they are so interested in hearing Officer Buckle's safety speech? (Idea: *Gloria makes the safety tips fun to learn.*)

Pages 16–17. How many schools does Officer Buckle visit? *Three hundred thirteen.* Wow, that's a lot of schools! Why do you think that the children sit up and listen so carefully to the safety speeches? (Idea: *Gloria acts out the accidents behind Officer Buckle's back.*) What reward does Officer Buckle give Gloria after every speech? (Idea: *He takes Gloria out for ice cream.*)

Page 18. Something different happens one day. What is it? (Idea: *A television news team videotapes Officer Buckle.*)

Pages 20–21. What is Safety Tip Number 99? (Idea: *Do not go swimming during electrical storms.*) How does Gloria act out Safety Tip Number 99? (Idea: *She makes her fur look like she has been hit by lightning.*) How do the students react to the speech? (Ideas: *They jump to their feet and applaud; they cheer "Bravo!"*) Do you think the students are cheering for Officer Buckle or for Gloria? (Idea: *They are cheering for Gloria.*) Does Officer Buckle know that Gloria is acting out the safety tips behind his back? (Idea: *No.*) How do you think Officer Buckle might feel if he finds out what Gloria is doing? (Ideas: *He might be embarrassed; he might think it is funny; he might be amazed; his feelings might be hurt that the students like Gloria so much.*)

Page 23. Where is the videotape of Officer Buckle shown? (Idea: *On the 10 o'clock news.*) How does Officer Buckle look when he sees himself and Gloria? (Idea: *Surprised; shocked.*) How does Gloria look when she sees herself on the news? (Ideas: *Worried; ashamed; anxious.*)

Page 24. Why doesn't Officer Buckle want to give his safety speech? (Idea: *He says that nobody looks at him.*)

Page 25. How does Gloria get to the school without Officer Buckle? (Idea: *Someone else from the police station takes her.*) How does

Gloria look onstage? *Lonely.* What does Gloria do? (Idea: *She falls asleep.*) What do the children do? (Idea: *They fall asleep.*) What happens after Gloria leaves? (Idea: *Napville School has its biggest accident ever.*)

Page 26. What starts the accident? (Idea: *A puddle of banana pudding.*) What other things happen in the accident? (Idea: *Everyone slides into Mrs. Toppel; she lets go of her hammer; the sign falls down.*)

Page 28 (including the star-shaped letter). What does every letter have? (Idea: *A drawing of the accident.*) How does Officer Buckle feel about the accident? (Idea: *He is shocked.*) What does Claire's P.S. say that makes Officer Buckle feel better about the accident? (Idea: *Don't worry, I was wearing my helmet.*) **Note:** If children don't understand that Mrs. Toppel's hammer landed on Claire's head, explain using the drawings on the letters as proof of what happened. Return to page 26, and ask children if they can find Claire's helmet in the crowd.)

Page 29. How does Officer Buckle feel after he receives Claire's letter? (Idea: *Happy.*) How do we know how Officer Buckle feels about the accident? (Ideas: *He is smiling; Gloria gives him a big kiss on the nose; he gives Gloria a nice pat on the back.*) What do you think Officer Buckle's best safety tip yet might be? (Accept appropriate responses.)

Page 30. What is Officer Buckle's best safety tip yet? (Idea: *Always stick with your buddy!*)

Review Vocabulary

(Display the Picture Vocabulary Cards. Point to each card as you say the word. Ask children to repeat each word after you.) These pictures show **obey, accident, imagination,** and **attention.**

- What naming word means "something bad that happens that no one expects, and someone gets hurt"? *Accident.*
- What naming word means "the part of your mind that lets you make pictures of imaginary things or of things that didn't really happen"? *Imagination.*
- What naming word means "the way you look when you stand up straight and face the front,

with your feet together and your arms at your sides"? *Attention.*

- What action word means "do what you are told to do"? *Obey.*

Extend Vocabulary
 Attention.

In the story *Officer Buckle and Gloria,* we learn that standing at attention means "the way you look when you stand up straight and face the front, with your feet together and your arms at your sides." Say the word that means "the way you look when you stand up straight and face the front, with your feet together and your arms at your sides." *Attention.*

Raise your hand if you can tell us a sentence that uses **attention** as a naming word that means "the way you look when you stand up straight and face the front, with your feet together and your arms at your sides." (Call on several children. If they don't use complete sentences, restate their examples as sentences. Have the class repeat the sentences.)

Here's a new way to use the word **attention.**

- **Pay attention to what I'm telling you.** Say the sentence.
- **May I have your attention, please?** Say the sentence.
- **Pay attention to where you put your pencil.** Say the sentence.

In these sentences, **attention** is a naming word that means **the way you act when you think really hard about only one thing.** What naming word means "the way you act when you think really hard about only one thing"? *Attention.*

Raise your hand if you can tell us a sentence that uses **attention** as a naming word that means "the way you act when you think really hard about only one thing." (Call on several children. If they don't use complete sentences, restate their examples as sentences. Have the class repeat the sentences.)

Present Expanded Target Vocabulary
 Unaware.

In the story, Gloria does funny tricks behind Officer Buckle's back when he is talking to the children. Officer Buckle doesn't know Gloria is doing the tricks. Another way of saying Officer Buckle doesn't know what Gloria is doing is to say Officer Buckle is unaware of what Gloria is doing. **Unaware.** Say the word. *Unaware.*

Unaware is a describing word. It tells about someone. What kind of word is **unaware?** *A describing word.*

When you are unaware of something, you don't know it is happening. Say the word that means "don't know something is happening." *Unaware.*

I'll tell about some things that are happening. If the person is unaware that thing is happening, say, "Unaware." If not, don't say anything.

- The teacher doesn't know that Sammy, the classroom guinea pig, is lonely. *Unaware.*
- The children don't know that it is time for lunch. *Unaware.*
- The child doesn't know that the teacher is watching him. *Unaware.*
- Arthur knows that we are hiding behind the couch.
- The motorist doesn't know that the car is turning toward him. *Unaware.*
- Steve the cat knows that Donald Dog is coming.

What describing word means "don't know something is happening"? *Unaware.*

 Jealous.

In the story, Officer Buckle doesn't want the children to pay more attention to Gloria than to him. Officer Buckle is feeling jealous of Gloria. **Jealous.** Say the word. *Jealous.*

Jealous is a describing word. It tells about the emotion Officer Buckle is feeling. What kind of word is **jealous?** *A describing word.*

When you are feeling jealous, you want what someone else has. Say the word that means "want what someone else has." *Jealous.*

I'll tell about some people. If you think those people are feeling jealous, say, "Jealous." If not, don't say anything.

- Billy wants a new bike just like his brother's. *Jealous.*
- Sandy is happy her family is going camping.

- Joni wants the teacher to like her picture as much as Alex's. *Jealous.*
- Colleen asks, "Is *my* picture nice too?" *Jealous.*
- It is okay that Bob gets the new bike instead of me. I got the new tent last week.
- Miss Cahan whines, "When am *I* going to get a turn?" *Jealous.*

What describing word means "want what someone else has"? *Jealous.*

DAY 3

Preparation: Prepare a sheet of chart paper with the title *Safety Tips.*

Activity Sheet, BLM 27b. Children will need their pencils and crayons.

Retell Story

(Show the pictures on the following pages from the story, and call on a child to tell what's happening. Call on a different child for each section.)

Today I'll show you the pictures Peggy Rathmann made for the story *Officer Buckle and Gloria.* As I show you the pictures, I'll call on one of you to tell the class that part of the story.

Pages 1–3. Tell me what happens at the **beginning** of the story.

Pages 4–28. Tell me what happens in the **middle** of the story. (Encourage use of target words when appropriate. Model use as necessary.)

Pages 29–30. Tell me what happens at the **end** of the story.

Review Super Choosing Game

Today you will play the Super Choosing Game. Let's think about the six words we have: **obey, accident, imagination, attention, unaware,** and **jealous.** (Display the word cards.)

I will say a sentence that has some of the words we have learned in it. You will have to choose which one is the correct word for that sentence. Not all of the words will be from this lesson,

though. That's why it's the *Super* Choosing Game. Let's practice. (You should not show cards for words from previous lessons.)

- When you do what you are told, do you okay, play, or obey? *Obey.*
- When you want something that someone else has, are you frowning, nutritious, or jealous? *Jealous.*
- If you use your brain to invent pictures of things that couldn't really be, are you using your appetite, your imagination, or your ingredients? *Imagination.*

Now you're ready to play the game. If you tell me the correct answer, you win one point. If you can't tell me the correct answer, I get the point.

(Draw a T-chart on the board for keeping score. Children earn one point for each correct answer. If they make an error, tell them the correct answer. Record one point for yourself, and repeat missed words at the end of the game.)

- When you stand straight and still, are you wondering, at attention, or remembering? *At attention.*
- If something unexpected happens and someone is hurt, was there a chore, a disappointment, or an accident? *An accident.*
- If you listen very closely with your eyes, ears, and brain, are you disappearing, finally there, or paying attention? *Paying attention.*
- If a top spun around very quickly, would you say that it crossed, explained, or whirled? *Whirled.*
- When your favorite toy was grabbed away from you quickly, was it sloppy, wild, or snatched? *Snatched.*
- If a seed started to grow, would you say that it relieved, shouted, or sprouted? *Sprouted.*

(Count the points, and declare a winner.) You did a great job of playing the Super Choosing Game!

Complete Activity Sheet

(Review with children the safety tips mentioned in the text. Record the safety tips on the chart paper as they are identified.

Never stand on a swivel chair.
Keep your shoelaces tied.

*Always wipe up spills before someone slips
and falls.
Never leave a thumbtack where you might
sit on it.
Do not go swimming during electrical
storms.
Always stick with your buddy.*)

(Have children suggest other safety rules.
Record them on the chart paper. **Note:** You need
to record at least one more safety tip than the
number of children in your class. If children are
unable to suggest sufficient safety tips, read and
record the safety tips from the front and back
flyleaves or other ideas you may have.)

(Give each child a copy of the Activity Sheet,
BLM 27b. Children should select and initial a
safety rule from the chart, print the rule, draw
an illustration to accompany the rule, and cut
out the shape. If children are not yet able to
copy the sentence, scribe it for them while they
work on their illustrations. Make a cover with the
title "Our Safety Rules," and fasten the pages
together into a booklet.)

DAY 4

Preparation: Prepare a sheet of chart
paper with the title *True or Fiction.*

Fiction (Literary Analysis)

When authors write stories, sometimes they
write about things that are true, and sometimes
they write about things they have made up in
their imaginations. If an author writes a story
about something made up from the author's
imagination, the story is called **fiction.** What do
you call a story that is made up from the author's
imagination? *Fiction.*

Let's see if we can figure out if this story is about
things that are true or if the story is fiction. You
tell me what happens in the story, and I'll write it
down.

(Show the illustrations on the following pages,
and ask the specified questions.)

Page 1. Do you think Officer Buckle is a real
police officer or an officer made up from Peggy
Rathmann's imagination? (Idea: *Made up from*

Peggy Rathmann's imagination.) What makes
you think so? (Call on individual children.) Most
of us think Officer Buckle is not a real police
officer, so I'll print "not real" after his name.)
(Record *Officer Buckle* on the chart, and write
not real after his name.)

Pages 6, 8, 10, 16, 17, and 20. Do you think
a dog could really do all those tricks, or is
Gloria a dog made up from Peggy Rathmann's
imagination? (Idea: *Made up from Peggy
Rathmann's imagination.*) What makes you think
so? (Call on individual children.) Most of us think
Gloria is not a real dog, so I'll print "not real"
after her name.) (Record *Gloria* on the chart, and
write *not real* after her name.)

Pages 26–27. Do you think an accident like this
could really happen at school, or is the accident
made up from Peggy Rathmann's imagination?
(Idea: *Made up from Peggy Rathmann's
imagination.*) What makes you think so? (Call on
individual children.) Most of us think the accident
is not a real accident, so I'll print "not real" after
the word accident.

(Record *accident* on the chart, and write *not real*
after it.)

(Point to the chart.) We think Officer Buckle, the
girl carrying the books, Mrs. Toppel, Gloria, and
the accident all come from Peggy Rathmann's
imagination. A story about things that are made
up from the author's imagination is called **fiction.**
So *Officer Buckle and Gloria* is what kind of
story? *Fiction.*

We have read many other stories that are
fiction. Raise your hand if you can name another
story we've read that was made up from the
imagination of the author. (Accept any response
that names a fiction book.)

Play Super Choosing Game (Cumulative Review)

Let's play the Super Choosing
Game. I will say a sentence that
has some of our vocabulary words
in it. You will have to choose
which one is the correct word for that sentence.
Remember, this game is *Super* Choosing
because I will use some words from other
lessons. You will have to be sharp! (Display the

Picture Vocabulary Cards for *obey, accident, imagination, attention, unaware,* and *jealous.* Do not display the word cards from earlier lessons.)

Now you're ready to play the Super Choosing Game.

(Draw a T-chart on the board for keeping score. Children earn one point for each correct answer. If they make an error, correct them as you normally would, and record one point for yourself. Repeat missed words at the end of the game.)

- If you want what someone else has, are you allergic, clever, or jealous? *Jealous.*
- When something unexpected happens and someone is hurt, is it a frost, an accident, or a meadow? *An accident.*
- Bob draws pictures of things that could never be. Is he using his patience, his substitute, or his imagination? *His imagination.*
- Standing still and straight is called winding, attention, or remembering? *Attention.*
- Garth didn't know that Rick was coming to visit. Was Garth unaware, over there, or present? *Unaware.*
- If you listen well, do you pay horrible, feelings, or attention? *Attention.*
- If Drew does as he is told, does he disagree, obey, or bloom? *Obey.*
- Are the words **hot** and **cold** friends, presents, or opposites? *Opposites.*
- When your friends invite you to help them do a job and you won't, are you unaware, uncooperative, or terrified? *Uncooperative.*

Now you will have to listen very carefully, because I'm not going to show you the word cards.

- If you joined in and helped your friends when they needed help, would you say that you chattered, devoured, or cooperated? *Cooperated.*
- Leonard got up one morning and found a bad dent in his car. Did Leonard find a glimpse, damage, or language? *Damage.*
- Tim dropped the paint. Barb got splashed. Was there a memory, an accident, or a precious? *Accident.*
- Why was Marvin's picture of purple trees in a land of golden monkeys great—because

he used his slithers, his cottage, or his imagination? *His imagination.*
- The bird didn't see or hear the cat coming. Was the bird unaware, frustrated, or over there? *Unaware.*
- If you got ready for something to happen, did you prepare, unaware, or squeak? *Prepare.*
- What word would we use to describe a fox that is good at tricking others: shy, sly, or starving? *Sly.*
- If the children are lying down on the floor with their legs stretched out playing a game, are they squabbling, satisfied, or sprawled? *Sprawled.*

(Count the points, and declare a winner.) You did a great job of playing the Super Choosing Game!

DAY 5

Preparation: Happy Face Game Test Sheet, BLM B.

Identify Cartoon-Style Illustrations

Sometimes the illustrations in a story help us decide if a story is true or fiction.

(Show the illustrations on the following pages, and ask the specified questions.)

Pages 10–11. First let's look at Officer Buckle. Does Officer Buckle look like a real person? *No.* What about him is different from a real person? (Ideas: *His glasses are too big; his arms are too short; his fingers have sharp points.*) Where might you have seen pictures that look like Officer Buckle? (Ideas: *In comic strips, in cartoons on television.*)

Page 10. Now let's look at Gloria. Does Gloria look like a real dog? *No.* What about her is different from a real dog? (Ideas: *Her nose is too pointed; her tongue is too long.*)

Page 20. Does Gloria look like a real dog? *No.* What about her is different from a real dog? (Ideas: *Her fur is sticking straight out; her tongue is too long; she has x's for eyes.*) Where might you have seen pictures that look like Gloria? (Idea: *In comic strips; in cartoons on television.*)

Peggy Rathmann drew the illustrations for *Officer Buckle and Gloria* as she would if she were drawing pictures for comic strips or cartoons, so we say she made cartoon-style illustrations. What do you call illustrations that look like comics or cartoons? *Cartoon-style illustrations.*

(Display the books that children are to examine.) Let's look at some of the books we've read. If the illustrations are cartoon-style illustrations, say, "Cartoon-style." If the illustrations are not cartoon-style, say, "Real."

- *Leo the Late Bloomer. **Cartoon-style.***
- *When We Go Camping. **Real.***
- *Sammy: The Classroom Guinea Pig. **Real.***
- *The Three Little Pigs. **Cartoon-style.***
- *The Most Beautiful Kite in the World. **Real.***
- *The Little Red Hen. **Cartoon-style.***

Many books that have cartoon-style illustrations are fiction.

Assess Vocabulary

 (Hold up a copy of the Happy Face Game Test Sheet, BLM B.)

Today you're going to play the Happy Face Game. When you play the Happy Face Game, it helps me know how well you know the hard words you are learning.

If I say something true, color the happy face. What will you do if I say something true? *Color the happy face.*

If I say something false, color the sad face. What will you do if I say something false? *Color the sad face.*

Listen carefully to each item I say. Don't let me trick you!

Item 1: When you **obey,** you do what you are told. *True.*

Item 2: **Jealous** means that you're satisfied with what you have. *False.*

Item 3: An **accident** is something you plan for and nobody gets hurt. *False.*

Item 4: **Attention** can mean that you stand still and straight. *True.*

Item 5: Being **unaware** means you don't know if something is happening. *True.*

Item 6: **Attention** is what you show when you listen well and sit quietly. *True.*

Item 7: Your **imagination** is the part of your brain that allows you to invent things that don't exist. *True.*

Item 8: When you give **reasons,** you tell facts that explain why you think what you do. *True.*

Item 9: If you **crept** across the classroom, you dashed across the room as fast as you could. *False.*

Item 10: If the kitten is feeling **content,** it is satisfied with things just the way they are. *True.*

You did a great job of playing the Happy Face Game!

(Score children's work later. Scores of 9 out of 10 indicate mastery. If a child does not achieve mastery, insert the missed words in the games in the next week's lessons. Retest those children individually on the missed words before they take the next mastery test.)

Extensions
Read a Story as a Reward

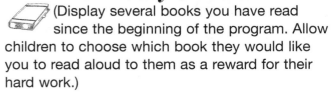 (Display several books you have read since the beginning of the program. Allow children to choose which book they would like you to read aloud to them as a reward for their hard work.)

(Read the story aloud to children for enjoyment with minimal interruptions.)

Present Super Words Center

 (Prepare the word containers for the Super Words Center (see notation below).)

(This new game is a Concentration-style game, but it uses all the opposite words from earlier lessons. You may choose to prepare the containers with *only* opposites, or you may wish to mix the opposites with current vocabulary or vocabulary for children to review. Supply at least two copies of each of the opposites cards. Use your discretion to determine the number of cards to be placed in the container. Eighteen cards, for example, will generate a Concentration grid of 3 x 6. Twenty-four cards will create a grid of

4 x 6. You will know best what children are able to deal with.)

I will help you remember how to play the game called Hot and Cold that you will play today in the Super Words Center. What do you know about the words **hot** and **cold?** (Idea: *They are opposites.*) This game is called Hot and Cold because your job is to find as many opposites as you can.

Let's remember how we work with our words in the Super Words Center.

You will work with a partner in the Super Words Center. Whom will you work with in the center? *A partner.*

First you will draw all of the cards out of the container and place them facedown. There are enough cards to make (X) rows of (Y) cards. (Demonstrate.) What do you do first? (Idea: *Draw all of the cards out and place them facedown.*)

Next, the first player will turn over one card and place it faceup so both players can see. (Demonstrate.) What will you do next? (Idea: *The first player turns over a card and places it faceup so that both can see.*)

Next, the first player turns over another card and places it faceup so both can see. (Demonstrate.)

What will you do next? (Idea: *The first player turns over another card and places it faceup so both can see.*)

This is the important part. If the cards are opposites, the first player takes both cards and sets them aside in his or her game pile. If they are not opposites, the first player places both cards facedown. Either way, it is now the second player's turn. (Demonstrate for children. They will be familiar with the process for playing Concentration, however.)

What will the first player do if the two cards are opposites? (Idea: *Keep those cards and put them in his or her game pile.*) What will the first player do if the two cards are not opposites? (Idea: *Turn them over.*) Either way, whose turn is it next? (Idea: *The second player's.*)

I think you are almost ready to play Hot and Cold. Can you think of some words that are opposites? (Call on several children. List the opposites they suggest to prepare them for playing the game.) Have fun playing Hot and Cold!

(**Note:** If you wish, you may teach children to say "I'm hot!" in a happy voice when they find opposites and "I'm cold!" in a sad voice when they do not.)

Preparation: You will need *The Art Lesson* for each day's lesson.

Number the pages of the story to assist you in asking questions at appropriate points.

Post a copy of the Vocabulary Tally Sheet, BLM A, with this week's Picture Vocabulary Cards attached.

Each child will need the Homework Sheet, BLM 28a.

DAY 1

Introduce Book

This week's book is called *The Art Lesson.* What's the title of this week's book? *The Art Lesson.*

This book was written by Tomie dePaola [Tommy da**Pow**la]. Who's the author of *The Art Lesson*? *Tomie dePaola.*

Tomie dePaola also made the pictures for this book. Who's the illustrator of *The Art Lesson*? *Tomie dePaola.* Who made the illustrations for this book? *Tomie dePaola.*

The cover of a book usually gives us some hints of what the book is about. Let's look at the front cover of *The Art Lesson.* What do you see in the illustration? (Ideas: *A boy holding a blank piece of paper and a crayon; tables with crayons, paints, and paintbrushes; a painting of some red flowers.*)

(Assign each child a partner.) Remember, when you make a prediction about something, you say what you think will happen. Get ready to make some predictions to your partner about this book. Use the information from the cover to help you.

(Ask the following questions, allowing sufficient time for children to share their predictions with their partners.)

- Who is the main character in this story? (Whom do you think this story is about?)

The Art Lesson
author: Tomie dePaola • illustrator: Tomie dePaola

Target Vocabulary

Tier II	Tier III
practice	dedication
property	
carpenter	
barber	
*talent	
*compromise	

*Expanded Target Vocabulary Word

- What do you think the boy is going to do with his blank paper?
- Where do you think the story happens?
- When do you think the story happens?
- Why do you think there is nothing on the tables except art supplies?
- How do you think the boy is going to make his artwork?
- Do you think this story is about real people? Tell why or why not.

(Call on several children to share their predictions with the class.)

Take a Picture Walk

(Show the illustrations on the following pages, and ask the specified questions. Encourage children to use previously taught target words in their answers.)

We are going to take a picture walk through this book. Remember, when we take a picture walk, we look at the pictures and tell what we think will happen in the story.

Page 1. Where do you think the boy is? (Ideas: *Outside; on a sidewalk.*) Who do you think drew the pictures on the sidewalk? (Idea: *The boy.*) What do you think the boy is drawing right now? (Idea: *A picture of the cat.*) Why do you think the picture is on the post? What makes you think that?

Pages 2–3. Who do you think the other children are? (Ideas: *The boy's friends; other students in his class at school.*) (Point to each picture, and ask:) What is this boy/girl doing? Who do you think drew the pictures of all the other children? (Idea: *The boy.*)

Page 4. Why do you think the two girls look exactly the same? (Idea: *They are twins.*) What are they doing? (Idea: *Painting the yellow flowers.*) What do you think the boy is doing? (Idea: *Watching them.*)

Page 5. Where is the boy now? (Idea: *In a bedroom he shares with another boy.*) What makes you think that? (Ideas: *There are two pairs of bedposts; there is a rug on the floor; there is a baseball bat next to one of the beds.*) What is the boy doing? (Idea: *Putting up a picture of the flowers that he made.*)

Page 6. What is happening here? (Idea: *A woman with a baby girl is putting up pictures.*) Where do you think this is? (Idea: *In the kitchen.*) What makes you think so? (Idea: *There is a refrigerator with some plates stacked on top.*) Who do you think the woman might be? (Ideas: *The boy's mother; his aunt; his older sister.*)

Page 7. What is happening here? (Ideas: *A man is combing someone's hair.*) Where do you think this is? (Ideas: *A barber shop; a hairdresser's.*) What makes you think so? (Idea: *There are bottles on the shelves; there is a chair with a handle; there are combs, towels, and a hair dryer in the illustration.*) Who do you think the man standing up might be? (Ideas: *The boy's father; his uncle; his older cousin; the barber.*) How are these two illustrations the same? (Idea: *They both have pictures on the walls.*)

Page 8. Where do you think this is? (Idea: *In a grocery store.*) What makes you think so? (Idea: *There are shelves full of cans; there are baskets and bins full of food; the people are wearing aprons.*) Who do you think the man and the woman might be? (Ideas: *The boy's grandmother and grandfather; family friends.*) Tell how this illustration is like the other ones. (Idea: *They all have pictures on the walls.*)

Page 9. Where do you think this is? (Idea: *In a house.*) What makes you think that? (Idea: *There is a table with a cloth and a lamp on it; there are photographs on the table and wall.*) Tell how this illustration is like the other ones. (Idea: *They all have pictures in them.*)

Page 10. (Point to each picture in turn, and ask:) What is happening here? (Ideas: *The boy is drawing on his sheets; he is talking with a woman.*)

Page 11. (Point to each of the drawings, and read the titles printed on them.) How do you think the boy is feeling? (Ideas: *Happy; content.*) Why do you think so? (Idea: *He's smiling.*)

Page 12. What is the boy doing? (Idea: *Drawing on the walls.*)

Page 13. Where do you think the boy is now? (Idea: *He's at school.*) What makes you think so? (Ideas: *There is a chalkboard; there are chairs and a woman who could be the teacher talking to the boy.*)

Page 14. Where do you think the boy is now? (Idea: *He's still at school.*) What makes you think so? (Ideas: *The letters of the alphabet are up on the wall; there are other children.*) How does the boy look? (Ideas: *Unhappy; disappointed.*) What do you think the teacher is doing? (Idea: *Mixing paints.*)

Page 15. Where do you think the boy is going? (Idea: *Home from school.*) What season of the year do you think this is? (Idea: *Autumn.*) Why do you think so? (Ideas: *It's windy; orange and yellow leaves are blowing around.*) How does the boy seem to be feeling? (Ideas: *Grumpy; annoyed; angry.*) Why do you think he might be feeling this way? (Idea: *The wind is blowing his paper.*)

Pages 16–17. Who do you think the woman is? (Ideas: *An art teacher; a teacher.*) What makes you think so? (Idea: *She is carrying a box of crayons or colored chalk.*) What are the children doing? (Ideas: *Examining the pictures on the wall; talking about the pictures.*)

Page 18. What do you think is happening here? (Idea: *It's the boy's birthday.*) What makes you think so? (Ideas: *There are many balloons and streamers; he is opening a present.*) What do you think is in the box?

Page 19. Where do you think the boy is now? (Idea: *He's at school.*) What makes you think so? (Ideas: *There is a chalkboard; there is a big wooden desk with an apple and a flower on it and a woman who could be the teacher.*)

Pages 20–21. (Point to each picture in turn, and ask:) What is happening here? (Idea: *The teacher is showing the children a box of crayons; the children are whispering to each other; the boy looks upset or worried; the boy is hiding behind a piece of paper.*) How do you think the boy is feeling? (Ideas: *Nervous; anxious; upset; sad.*) What makes you think so? (Ideas: *He has a frown on his face; he's hiding behind a piece of paper.*)

Pages 22–23. (Point to each picture in turn, and ask:) What is the boy doing? (Idea: *Sleeping; walking to school; standing with other students at school with two teachers.*)

Pages 24–25. What is the teacher doing in the first illustration? (Idea: *Standing at the board showing how to draw a picture.*) What is the teacher holding? (Idea: *A box of colored crayons; a box of colored chalk.*) What is happening in the second illustration? (Idea: *The boy is talking to the two teachers.*) What do you think the boy is saying? (Idea: *He's explaining something about his box of crayons.*)

Page 26. What do you see in this top illustration? (Idea: *The two teachers talking together.*) How does the boy look in this bottom illustration? (Idea: *Worried; nervous; anxious.*)

Page 27. What do you see in this top illustration? (Idea: *A man and a woman dressed in old-fashioned clothes with a turkey; two Pilgrims and a turkey.*) How does the boy look in this bottom illustration? (Idea: *Happy.*)

Page 28. What did the boy draw in this illustration? (Ideas: *The same drawing as the teacher's drawing; two pilgrims and a turkey.*) How do the children look? (Ideas: *Happy; proud.*) What makes you think that? (Ideas: *They are standing together around the picture and smiling.*)

Page 29. What did the boy draw in this illustration? (Idea: *The art teacher picking flowers.*) Why do you think the boy drew this teacher? (Ideas: *She was nice to him; he likes her.*)

Page 30. Where do you think this is? (Idea: *An artist's studio or house.*) Why do you think so? (Idea: *There is a big table with drawing paper on*

it; brushes and paints are beside the table; many paintings are on the walls.) Who do you think the man is?

Do you like to draw? Tell the class about why you like to draw and about a picture you made. (Call on several children. Encourage them to start their answers with the words "I like to draw because _____. I made a picture that had _____ on it.")

Now that we've finished our picture walk, it's your turn to ask me some questions. What would you like to know about the story? (Accept questions. If children tell about the pictures or the story instead of asking questions, prompt them to ask a question.) Ask me a what question. Ask me a how question.

Read Story Aloud
(Read the story aloud to children with minimal interruptions.)

In the next lesson, we will read the story again, and I will ask you some questions.

Present Target Vocabulary

◎⤙ Practice.

In the story, Tommy's twin cousins tell him if he wants to be an artist, he will have to "practice, practice, practice." That means Tommy will have to keep drawing every day in order to get good at doing it. **Practice.** Say the word. *Practice.*

Practice is an action word. It tells what someone does. What kind of word is **practice**? *An action word.*

If you practice, you do the same thing over and over so you get good at doing it. Say the word that means "do the same thing over and over so you get good at doing it." *Practice.*

(Correct any incorrect responses, and repeat the item at the end of the sequence.)

Let's think about some things you might practice in order to get good at doing them. I'll tell about something. If you would practice that thing, say, "Practice." If not, don't say anything.

- Playing the piano. *Practice.*
- Being a great soccer player. *Practice.*
- Breathing.

- Walking on the "not squeaky" parts of the stairs. *Practice.*
- Blinking your eyes.
- Drawing beautiful pictures. *Practice.*

What action word means "do the same thing over and over so you get good at doing it"? *Practice.*

◎━ Property.

In the story, Miss Landers says the crayons are "school property." That means the crayons are owned by the school. **Property.** Say the word. *Property.*

Property is a naming word. It names a thing. What kind of word is **property?** *A naming word.*

Property is anything that is owned by someone. Say the word that means "anything that is owned by someone." *Property.*

(Correct any incorrect responses, and repeat the item at the end of the sequence.)

Let's think about some things that might be someone's property. I'll name something. If you think what I've named is someone's property, say, "Property." If not, don't say anything.

(**Note:** If the correct response is "property" and children say the word, ask:) Whose property is it?

- The principal owns this pen. *Property. The principal's property.*
- The city owns this park. *Property. The city's property.*
- The wilderness.
- Air.
- The goldfish in your neighbor's backyard pond. *Property. The neighbor's.*
- Your backpack with all of your school things. *Property. Mine.*

What naming word means "anything that is owned by someone"? *Property.*

◎━ Carpenter.

In the story, one of the carpenters gives Tommy a piece of bright blue chalk. That means one of the persons who is building the wooden parts of Tommy's new house gives him a piece of bright blue chalk. **Carpenter.** Say the word. *Carpenter.*

Carpenter is a naming word. It names a person. What kind of word is **carpenter?** *A naming word.*

A carpenter is a person who builds things out of wood. Say the word that means "a person who builds things out of wood." *Carpenter.*

(Correct any incorrect responses, and repeat the item at the end of the sequence.)

Let's think about some people who might be carpenters. I'll tell about what some people do. If you think that person is a carpenter, say, "Carpenter." If not, don't say anything.

- Stephen Welch builds houses out of wood. *Carpenter.*
- The woman we hired builds some new window frames from wood. *Carpenter.*
- Liza McKenzie works for a company that makes refrigerators.
- Jerry McDonald builds steel bridges.
- John builds a rock wall at our house.
- The man and woman work for a week to build our wooden fence. *Carpenter(s).*

What naming word means "a person who builds things out of wood"? *Carpenter.*

◎━ Barber.

In the story, Tommy's father is a barber. That means Tommy's father cuts people's hair and trims or shaves men's beards. **Barber.** Say the word. *Barber.*

Barber is a naming word. It names a person. What kind of word is **barber?** *A naming word.*

A barber is a person who cuts people's hair and trims or shaves men's beards. Say the word that means "a person who cuts people's hair and trims or shaves men's beards." *Barber.*

(Correct any incorrect responses, and repeat the item at the end of the sequence.)

Let's think about some people who might be barbers. I'll tell about what some people do. If you think that person is a barber, say, "Barber." If not, don't say anything.

- This person trims David's grandfather's beard. *Barber.*
- This person fixes Graham's father's car.
- This person builds a house for Lorelei's parents.
- Mr. Bioletti works in a barber shop on Penny Lane. *Barber.*
- That man puts the barbs on barbed wire.

- Barbara said, "Let's just trim my bangs." *Barber.*

What naming word means "a person who cuts people's hair and trims or shaves men's beards"? *Barber.*

Present Vocabulary Tally Sheet
(See Week 1, page 3, for instructions.)

Assign Homework
(Homework Sheet, BLM 28a: See the Introduction for homework instructions.)

DAY 2

Preparation: Picture Vocabulary Cards for *practice, property, carpenter,* and *barber.*

Read and Discuss Story

(Read story aloud to children. Ask the following questions at the specified points. Encourage them to use previously taught target words in their answers.)

Page 1. Where does Tommy draw pictures? (Idea: *Everywhere.*) Tell me two places where Tommy has drawn his pictures. (Ideas: *On the sidewalk; on paper.*)

Pages 2–3. Tommy's friends have favorite things to do too. What does Jack collect? (Idea: *All kinds of turtles.*) What does Herbie do? (Idea: *Makes cities in his sandbox.*) What does Jeannie do? (Idea: *She does cartwheels and stands on her head.*) What does Tommy do? (Idea: *He draws and draws.*) What is one of your favorite things to do? (Call on several children. Encourage them to start their responses with the words "One of my favorite things to do is _____.")

Pages 4–5. What are Tommy's cousins doing at art school? (Idea: *Learning to be real artists.*) What two things do his cousins tell Tommy to do to become an artist? (Idea: *Not to copy and to practice, practice, practice.*) Where does Tommy put his pictures? (Idea: *On the walls of his half of his bedroom.*) Whom do you think Tommy shares his room with? (Idea: *His brother.*)

Pages 6–7. What does Tommy's mom do with his pictures? (Idea: *She puts them up around the house.*) What does Tommy's dad do with Tommy's pictures? (Idea: *He puts them up in the barber shop where he works.*) Wow, Tommy has drawn lots and lots of pictures!

Pages 8–9. (You may wish to show children on a world map or globe where Ireland and Italy are in relationship to the location of your school.) The story says Tom and Nana are Tommy's Irish grandfather and grandmother. If Tommy's grandparents are Irish, it means they are from Ireland. Where are Tommy's grandparents from? *Ireland.* The story says Nana-Fall-River is Tommy's Italian grandmother. If Nana-Fall-River is Italian, it means that she is from Italy. Where is Nana-Fall-River from? *Italy.* Where does Nana-Fall-River put one of Tommy's pictures? (Idea: *In a special frame next to a photograph of Aunt Clo in her wedding dress.*)

Pages 10–11. What does Tommy's mom find out he has done? (Idea: *Drawn on his sheets.*) What does Tommy draw pictures of? (Idea: *What the new house will look like.*) How do you think Tommy feels when he is drawing? (Idea: *Happy; content; satisfied.*) How do you know? (Idea: *He is usually smiling when he draws.*)

Page 12. What does the carpenter give Tommy? (Idea: *A piece of bright blue chalk.*) Why is it all right for Tommy to draw on the walls before the painters come? (Idea: *The walls are unfinished.*) What does Tommy's dad say after the painters come? (Idea: *No more drawing on the walls.*)

Page 13. Why is Tommy so excited about kindergarten? (Idea: *His brother tells him a real art teacher comes to the school to give art lessons.*) When does Tommy's teacher say the art lessons will start? *Next year.* How do you think Tommy feels when he hears that? (Idea: *Disappointed.*)

Page 14. What are some of the things that make painting not much fun? (Ideas: *The paint is awful; the paper gets all wrinkly; the paint doesn't stick to the paper very well; the paint cracks.*) How do you think Tommy feels about painting in kindergarten? (Ideas: *Unhappy; disappointed; frustrated.*) What makes you think so? (Idea: *He is looking sad in the illustration; he is frowning.*)

Page 15. What happens to Tommy's painting if it is windy? (Idea: *The paint blows right off the paper.*) What does Tommy's brother Joe say to make Tommy feel better? (Ideas: *At least he gets more than one piece of paper in kindergarten; when the art teacher comes, you only get one piece of paper.*)

Page 16. When does the art teacher come to the school? (Idea: *Every other Wednesday.*) What two things help Tommy decide she is an artist? (Ideas: *She wears a blue smock over her dress; she always carries a big box of thick colored chalks.*)

Page 17. What does Jeannie tell Tommy? (Ideas: *His pictures are much better; next year when they have real art lessons, Tommy will be the best one.*)

Page 18. What present do Tommy's parents give him for his birthday? (Idea: *A box of sixty-four Crayola crayons.*) Name some of the new colors in this box of crayons. (Ideas: *Blue-violet; turquoise; red-orange; pink; gold; silver; copper.*)

Page 19. What does Miss Landers say the class will do instead of singing? (Idea: *Practice using their crayons.*)

Pages 20–21. Why is Miss Landers not pleased when Tommy brings his sixty-four crayons to school? (Idea: *Everybody must use the school crayons.*) What rules does Miss Landers have about the school crayons? (Ideas: *Do not break them; do not peel off the paper; do not wear down the points.*) What does Miss Landers say Tommy should do with his birthday crayons? (Idea: *Take them home.*)

Pages 22–23. What does Tommy hide under his sweater? (Idea: *His box of sixty-four Crayola crayons.*) If the children ruin their piece of paper, what will happen? (Idea: *They won't get a new piece of paper.*)

Pages 24–25. What does the art teacher tell the class to do that Tommy thinks is wrong? (Idea: *Copy a picture.*) What else is Tommy upset about? (Idea: *He isn't allowed to use his own crayons.*)

Pages 26–27. What does the art teacher say wouldn't be fair? (Idea: *To let Tommy do*

something different from the rest of the class.) How does Mrs. Bowers solve Tommy's problem? (Idea: *If Tommy draws the Pilgrim man and woman and the turkey and there is time left, she will give him another sheet of paper, and he can draw his own picture with his own crayons.*) How does Tommy feel about this solution? (Idea: *He is very happy; satisfied; content.*) What makes you think that? (Idea: *He is smiling.*)

Pages 28–29. What picture does Tommy draw with his extra piece of paper and his own crayons? (Idea: *A picture of his art teacher picking flowers.*)

Page 30. What does Tommy do now that he is grown up? (Idea: *He makes his own pictures.*) Do you think this story might be true? Who do you think the Tommy in the story might be? (Idea: *Tomie dePaola.*)

Review Vocabulary

(Display the Picture Vocabulary Cards. Point to each card as you say the word. Ask children to repeat each word after you.) These pictures show **practice, property, carpenter,** and **barber.**

- What naming word means "a person who cuts people's hair and trims or shaves men's beards"? *Barber.*
- What naming word means "anything that is owned by someone"? *Property.*
- What action word means "do the same thing over and over so you get good at doing it"? *Practice.*
- What naming word means "a person who builds things out of wood"? *Carpenter.*

Extend Vocabulary

◎⤙ Property.

In *The Art Lesson,* we learn **property** is anything that is owned by someone. Say the word that means "anything that is owned by someone." *Property.*

Raise your hand if you can tell us a sentence that uses **property** as a naming word that means "anything that is owned by someone." (Call on several children. If they don't use complete sentences, restate their examples as sentences. Have the class repeat the sentences.)

Here's a new way to use the word **property.**

- **The guard dogs protected the property.** Say the sentence.
- **We have a fence around our property.** Say the sentence.
- **My grandpa is going to build a cottage on his property at the lake.** Say the sentence.

In these sentences, **property** is a naming word that means **land or the buildings that are on the land.** What naming word means "land or the buildings that are on the land"? *Property.*

Raise your hand if you can tell us a sentence that uses **property** as a naming word that means "land or the buildings that are on the land." (Call on several children. If they don't use complete sentences, restate their examples as sentences. Have the class repeat the sentences.)

Present Expanded Target Vocabulary
◎―◄ Talent.

In *The Art Lesson,* Tommy is very good at drawing. Another way of saying Tommy is very good at drawing is to say Tommy has a talent for drawing. **Talent.** Say the word. *Talent.*

Talent is a naming word. It names something. What kind of word is **talent?** *A naming word.*

When you have a talent, you have a special skill or ability, even though you haven't practiced it. Say the word that means "a special skill or ability that you have even though you haven't practiced it." *Talent.*

I'll tell about some people who may have talents. If the person I tell about has a talent, say, "Talent." If not, don't say anything.

- From the time she was just a small girl, Alisa could throw a baseball really well. *Talent.*
- Glenn always plays the piano well. *Talent.*
- Hank Aaron could hit a home run without even trying. *Talent.*
- With lots of practice, I get pretty good at dribbling a basketball.
- Hanson can't dance very well.
- Mr. Einstein wasn't good at mathematics in school.

What naming word means "a special skill or ability you have even though you haven't practiced it"? *Talent.*

◎―◄ Compromise.

In *The Art Lesson,* the art teacher wants the children to use the school crayons to copy drawings of a Pilgrim man, a Pilgrim woman, and a turkey. Tommy knows real artists don't copy, and he wants to use his own crayons, so he folds his arms and just sits there. The art teacher makes a deal with Tommy that he will draw what she wants, and then he can have another piece of paper to draw his own picture with his own crayons. Tommy agrees to do what the art teacher wants, and then the art teacher allows Tommy to do what he wants. Tommy and the art teacher compromise. **Compromise.** Say the word. *Compromise.*

Compromise is an action word. It tells what people do. What kind of word is **compromise?** *An action word.*

When two people compromise, they both agree to give up some of what they want and agree to do some of what the other person wants. Say the word that means "two people agree to give up some of what they want and agree to do some of what the other person wants." *Compromise.*

I'll tell about some people. If you think those people are compromising, say, "Compromise." If not, don't say anything.

- Billy wants a new bike just like his brother's, but his brother's bike is too big for him. Billy's mom buys him a bike the same color as his brother's. *Compromise.*
- Jacquie stamps her feet and screams when her father says she can't wear her party dress to school.
- Lorne wants to eat at his favorite Chinese restaurant. Rick wants to eat at his favorite Italian restaurant. They go to a different restaurant that serves both kinds of food. *Compromise.*
- Mr. Williams likes the floor tile. Mrs. Williams likes the wooden flooring. They decide to have some of each. *Compromise.*
- In the exercise room, Bob wants to float in the pool. Eileen just wants to bend a little to one side. They can't agree.

- Both dogs could sleep in the bed if they curled up. They won't curl up.

What naming word means "two people agree to give up some of what they want and agree to do some of what the other person wants"? *Compromise.*

DAY 3

Preparation: Each child will need sheets of drawing paper. They will need their pencils, crayons, and watercolors.

Analyze Mixed-Media Illustrations

There are lots of different ways to make illustrations for a book: painting; drawing with a pen or a pencil; using markers, crayons, pastels, or chalk; or cutting out different pieces of paper and gluing them together.

Let's see if we can figure out how Tomie dePaola made the illustrations for *The Art Lesson.*

(Show the illustrations on the following pages, and ask the specified questions.)

Page 4. What do you think Tomie dePaola used to draw the people? (Idea: *A pen.*) How do you know he didn't use a pencil? (Idea: *The lines are dark and solid.*) What do you think Tomie dePaola used to color the people? (Idea: *Watercolors.*) What do you think Tomie dePaola used to color the walls? (Idea: *Watercolors.*) How do you know he didn't use oil paints? (Idea: *You can see through the colors.*) How is the paint on the wall different from the paint on the people? (Ideas: *The paint on the wall is not so thick; you can see the different colors.*) When an artist uses a lot of water and a little paint to cover a large area on an illustration, we say he puts a wash on the painting. On this page Tomie de Paola used two different things to make his illustration: pen and ink and watercolors.

Page 1. What do you think Tomie dePaola used to draw the cat and the boy? (Idea: *A pen.*) How do you know he didn't use a pencil? (Ideas: *The lines are dark and solid; lines drawn with a pencil would be lighter.*) What do you think Tomi dePaola used to color the people? (Idea: *Watercolors.*) What do you think Tomie dePaola used to color the grass? (Idea: *Watercolors.*) How do you know he didn't use oil paints? (Idea: *You can see through the colors.*)

Now let's look at the drawings on the sidewalk. How do you think Tomie dePaola made this part of the illustration? (Idea: *He used crayons to make the pictures; then he put a wash over the crayon.*)

On this page Tomie dePaola used three different things to make his illustration: pen and ink, crayon, and watercolors. How many different things did Tomie dePaola use to make his illustrations? *Three.*

When an artist uses different things to make an illustration, we say he or she uses mixed media. What kind of illustrations did Tomie dePaola make in *The Art Lesson*? *Mixed media.*

Create Using Mixed Media

(Demonstrate the crayon-resist technique by drawing a simple sketch and painting over it with a watercolor wash. Give children paper to experiment with the crayon-resist technique.)

(Show the illustrations on pages 2 and 3. Remind children of the favorite activities Tommy and his friends like to do.) Today you will have a chance to draw a picture of yourself doing your favorite activity. You may draw with your pencil, crayons, or paint, or you may use mixed media.

Review Super Choosing Game

Today you will play the Super Choosing Game. Let's think about the six words we have: **practice, property, carpenter, barber, talent,** and **compromise.** (Display the Picture Vocabulary Cards.)

I will say a sentence that has some of the words we have learned in it. You will have to choose which one is the correct word for that sentence. Not all of the words will be from this lesson, though. That's why it's the *Super* Choosing Game. Let's practice. (You should not show cards for words from previous lessons.)

- When you do something again and again to get better at it, do you practice, appear, or burrow? *Practice.*

- If you trim hair and beards, do you cheat, are you a barber, or are you delicious? *Barber.*
- If you and your friend agree to do some of what he or she wants and some of what you want, do you explore, gasp, or compromise? *Compromise.*

Now you're ready to play the game. If you tell me the correct answer, you win one point. If you can't tell me the correct answer, I get the point.

(Draw a T-chart on the board for keeping score. Children earn one point for each correct answer. If they make an error, tell them the correct answer. Record one point for yourself, and repeat missed words at the end of the game.)

- If you are very good at something without having to practice, do you howl, have you made impressions, or do you have talent? *Talent.*
- When a person comes to fix your wooden fence, have you called a firefighter, a carpenter, or a teacher? *A carpenter.*
- When something belongs to you, is it your limb, your mood, or your property? *Your property.*
- If you played the piano every day for ten years, did you obey, plead, or practice? *Practice.*
- Is the land that the school is built on property, a rascal, or silly? *Property.*
- When a babysitter is keeping you safe from harm or injury, is he or she rude, protecting you, or selfish? *Protecting you.*

(Count the points, and declare a winner.) You did a great job of playing the Super Choosing Game!

DAY 4

Literary Analysis (Dedication)

If you dedicate a book to someone, you put that person's name at the front of the book to say thank you for helping and encouraging you. The words you write when you dedicate a book to someone are called the **dedication.**

Today I'll read the dedication that Tomie dePaola wrote for *The Art Lesson.*

(Read the first part of the dedication.) Whom did Tomie dePaola dedicate this book to? (Idea: *Rose Mulligan.*) Who is Rose Mulligan? (Idea: *His fifth-grade teacher.*) Why did he dedicate the book to her? (Ideas: *She always gave him more than one piece of paper; she encouraged him to be an artist.*)

(Read the second part of the dedication.) Whom else did Tomie dePaola dedicate this book to? (Idea: *Beulah Bowers.*) Who is Beulah Bowers? (Idea: *His art teacher.*) Why did he dedicate the book to her? (Ideas: *She was the best art teacher any child could have had; she encouraged him to be an artist.*)

(Read the last part of the dedication.) Whom else did Tomie dePaola dedicate this book to? (Ideas: *Binney and Smith Incorporated and Crayola crayons.*) Binney and Smith Incorporated is the company that makes Crayola crayons. What is Binney and Smith Incorporated? *The company that makes Crayola crayons.* Why do you think Tomie dePaola dedicated the book to Crayola crayons and the company that makes them? (Ideas: *He used Crayola crayons when he was learning to be an artist.*)

Do you think this story is true or fiction? Why do you think so? (Accept either response as long as children give a logical reason for their answers.)

You're all right. This story is fiction because some of it is about things that are made up from the author's imagination. But parts of it are true, because the author got the idea for the story from remembering things that happened to him when he was young. Where did Tomie dePaola get the ideas for this story? (Ideas: *From remembering things that happened to him when he was young.*)

Play Super Choosing Game (Cumulative Review)

Let's play the Super Choosing Game. I will say a sentence that has some of our vocabulary words in it. You will have to choose which one is the correct word for that sentence. Remember, this game is *Super* Choosing because I will use some words from other lessons. You will have to be sharp! (Display the Picture Vocabulary Cards for *practice, property, carpenter, barber, talent,* and *compromise.* Do not display the word cards from earlier lessons.)

Now you're ready to play the Super Choosing Game.

(Draw a T-chart on the board for keeping score. Children earn one point for each correct answer. If they make an error, correct them as you normally would, and record one point for yourself. Repeat missed words at the end of the game.)

- When you and a friend each want different things but you agree to have some of each, do you sigh, tremble, or compromise? *Compromise.*
- If you do something again and again to get it right, do you whirl, practice, or attack? *Practice.*
- Joseph builds things out of wood. Is he a blossom, a carpenter, or a cave? *A carpenter.*
- What can a store and the land that it is built on be called: property, determined, or furious? *Property.*
- Mr. Veronick was able to fix motors without having to go to school. Was he talented, gentle, or honest? *Talented.*
- Mrs. Maltbee trimmed hair and beards. Was she a harvest, an imagination, or a barber? *A barber.*
- What are things that belong to you called: your memorize, property, or nursery? *Property.*
- If you really, really want to do something, are you prickly, rescued, or desperate? *Desperate.*
- If the day is cloudy, dark, and boring, is it scorched, squabbling, or dreary? *Dreary.*

Now you will have to listen very carefully because I'm not going to show you the word cards. (Remove the Picture Vocabulary Cards from display.)

- If you were very angry with someone, would you be upward, furious, or wondering? *Furious.*
- Could a flat, open space with lots of grass and some flowers be called an accident, a chuckle, or a meadow? *A meadow.*
- Edgar never had a single lesson, but he could sing beautiful songs. Did he have difficult, grains, or talent? *Talent.*

- If you want to travel and find new places, do you want to hibernate, explore, or be jagged? *Explore.*
- The food gave off a pleasant smell. Was there an odor, a promise, or a snuggle? *An odor.*
- Arlo wanted chicken. Woody wanted beef. They came to an agreement where each was happy. Did they adopt, complain, or compromise? *Compromise.*
- Seven people were working. One of them was sawing wood to make something. Who did the sawing—a decoration, a carpenter, or an explorer? *A carpenter.*
- The dog that visited the park was there so often that when the children saw it, they remembered it and knew it right away. Was the dog familiar, horrible, or imaginary? *Familiar.*

(Count the points, and declare a winner.) You did a great job of playing the Super Choosing Game!

Preparation: Happy Face Game Test Sheet, BLM B.

Retell Story

(Assign each child a partner, and ask the partners to take turns telling part of the story each time you turn to a new set of pages. Encourage use of target words when appropriate.)

Today I'll show you the pictures Tomie dePaola made for the story *The Art Lesson.* As I show you the pictures, you and your partner will take turns telling part of the story.

Page 1. Tell what happens at the **beginning** of the story.

Pages 2–29. Tell what happens in the **middle** of the story.

Page 30. Tell what happens at the **end** of the story.

Assess Vocabulary

 (Give each child a copy of the Happy Face Game Test Sheet, BLM B.)

Today you're going to play the Happy Face Game. When you play the Happy Face Game, it helps me know how well you know the hard words you are learning.

If I say something true, color the happy face. What will you do if I say something true? *Color the happy face.*

If I say something false, color the sad face. What will you do if I say something false? *Color the sad face.*

Listen carefully to each item I say. Don't let me trick you!

Item 1: If you do something again and again to get it right, you **practice.** *True.*

Item 2: If you work in a place where hair is cut and beards are trimmed, you may be a **barber.** *True.*

Item 3: **Property** can mean the school and the land it is built on. *True.*

Item 4: If you **compromise,** you give up some of what you wanted. *True.*

Item 5: **Talent** is something you can buy at the store. *False.*

Item 6: If I were a **carpenter,** I would like to make things out of wood. *True.*

Item 7: **Property** is what belongs to you. *True.*

Item 8: A good smell or bad smell has the same name—an order. *False.*

Item 9: **Grains** are enormous pieces of something. *False.*

Item 10: A person who is very, very angry might be **furious.** *True.*

You did a great job of playing the Happy Face Game!

(Score children's work later. Scores of 9 out of 10 indicate mastery. If a child does not achieve mastery, insert the missed words in the games in the next week's lessons. Retest those children individually on the missed words before they take the next mastery test.)

Extensions
Read a Story as a Reward

(Display several books you have read since the beginning of the program. Allow children to choose which book they would like you to read aloud to them as a reward for their hard work.)

(Read the story aloud to children for enjoyment with minimal interruptions.)

Present Super Words Center

(Prepare the word containers for the Super Words Center (see notation below).)

(This new game is a Concentration-style game, but it uses all the opposite words from earlier lessons. You may choose to prepare the containers with *only* opposites or you may wish to mix the opposites with current vocabulary or vocabulary for children to review. Supply at least two copies of each of the opposites cards. Use your discretion to determine the number of cards to be placed in the container. Eighteen cards, for example, will generate a Concentration grid of 3 x 6. Twenty-four cards will create a grid of 4 x 6. You will know best what the children are able to deal with.)

Today I will help you remember how to play the game called Hot and Cold. You will play this game in the Super Words Center. What do you know about the words **hot** and **cold?** (Idea: *They are opposites.*) The reason this game is called Hot and Cold is that it is your job to find as many opposites as you can.

Let's remember how we work with our words in the Super Words Center.

You will work with a partner in the Super Words Center. Whom will you work with in the center? *A partner.*

First, you will draw all of the cards out of the container and place them facedown. There are enough cards to make (X) rows of (Y) cards. (Demonstrate.) What do you do first? (Idea: *Draw all of the cards out and lay them facedown.*)

Next, the first player will turn over one card and place it faceup so that both players can see. (Demonstrate). What will you do next? (Idea: *The first player turns over a card and places it faceup so that both can see.*)

Next, the first player turns over another card and places it faceup so both can see. (Demonstrate.)

What will you do next? (Idea: *The first player turns over another card and places it faceup so that both can see.*)

This is the important part. If the cards are opposites, the first player takes both cards and sets them aside in his or her game pile. If they are not opposites, both cards are placed facedown. Either way, it is now the second player's turn. (Demonstrate for children. They will be familiar with the process for playing Concentration, however.)

What will the first player do if the two cards are opposites? (Idea: *Keep those cards and put them in his or her game pile.*) What will the first player do if the two cards are not opposites? (Idea: *Turn them over.*) Either way, whose turn is it next? (Idea: *The second player's.*)

I think you are almost ready to play Hot and Cold. Can you think of some words that are opposites? (Call on several children. List the opposites they suggest to prepare them for playing the game.) Have fun playing Hot and Cold!

(**Note:** If you wish, you may teach children to say "I'm hot!" in a happy voice when they find opposites and "I'm cold!" in a sad voice when they do not.)

A Busy Day at Mr. Kang's Grocery Store
author: Alice K. Flanagan • photographer:
Christine Osinski

Preparation: You will
need *A Busy Day at Mr. Kang's
Grocery Store* for each day's lesson.

Number the pages of the book to assist you
in asking questions at appropriate points.

Post a copy of the Vocabulary Tally Sheet,
BLM A, with this week's Picture Vocabulary
Cards attached.

Each child will need the Homework Sheet,
BLM 29a.

🎯 Target Vocabulary

Tier II	Tier III
business	nonfiction
customers	photographs
generous	
kind	
*attractive	
*successful	

* Expanded Target Vocabulary Word

- What do you think the man is selling?
- Where do you think the story happens?
- When do you think the story happens?
- Why do you think the man is smiling?
- How does the man remember where
  everything is in his grocery store?
- Do you think this story is about real people?
  Tell why or why not.

(Call on several children to share their
predictions with the class.)

Take a Picture Walk

(Show the photographs on the
following pages, and ask the specified
questions. Encourage children to use
previously taught target words in their answers.)

We are going to take a picture walk through this
book. Remember, when we take a picture walk,
we look at the pictures and tell what we think
will happen in the story.

Page 3. Where do you think the man is
standing? (Idea: *In front of a grocery store.*) What
do you see in front of the store? (Idea: *Buckets
full of flowers.*)

Pages 4–5. Who do you think the man is?
(Ideas: *Mr. Kang; the owner of the grocery store.*)
Wow! Look at all the different things for sale in
this store!

Pages 6–7. What are some of the things the
man does at the grocery store? (Ideas: *Carries*

DAY 1

Introduce Book

This week's book is called *A Busy Day
at Mr. Kang's Grocery Store.* What's
the title of this week's book? *A Busy
Day at Mr. Kang's Grocery Store.*

This book was written by Alice K. Flanagan
[**flan**-a-gun]. Who's the author of *A Busy Day at
Mr. Kang's Grocery Store*? *Alice K. Flanagan.*

Christine Osinski [oh-**zin**-skee] took the
photographs for this book. Who took the
photographs for *A Busy Day at Mr. Kang's
Grocery Store*? *Christine Osinski.*

The cover of a book usually gives us some hints
of what the book is about. Let's look at the
front cover of *A Busy Day at Mr. Kang's Grocery
Store.* What do you see in the photograph?
(Ideas: *A man smiling; a scale full of fruit; cookies
in a cardboard box; bottles on a shelf; books on
a shelf.*)

(Assign each child a partner.) Remember, when
you make a prediction about something, you say
what you think will happen. Get ready to make
some predictions to your partner about this
book. Use the information from the cover to help
you.

(Ask the following questions, allowing sufficient
time for children to share their predictions with
their partners.)

- Who are the characters in this book? (Whom
  do you think this book is about?)

boxes of fruit, sweeps the floor.) What do you think is in the box? (Idea: *Bananas.*)

Pages 8–9. What are some of the things for sale in the store? (Ideas: *Flowers; tomatoes; onions; garlic; cantaloupe; pineapple; avocados; oranges.*)

Page 10. What do you see in this photograph? (Ideas: *A cash register full of paper bills and coins; money.*)

Page 11. What is the man doing? (Idea: *Talking on the telephone.*) Whom do you think a store owner might call on the telephone? (Ideas: *Customers; people who bring food and other things for him to sell at his store; his family.*)

Pages 12–13. What are some other things for sale that you see in these photographs? (Ideas: *Avocados; persimmons; oranges; ginger root; onions; cantaloupes; milk; juice.*) Where are the milk and juice kept? (Idea: *In the cooler; in the refrigerator.*)

Pages 14–15. What is happening here? (Idea: *A customer is buying some flowers.*) How do you think the man is feeling as he helps the customer? (Ideas: *Happy; friendly.*) Why do you think so? (Idea: *He is happy to have a customer buying something at his store.*) What else is the customer buying? (Ideas: *Fruit; bananas; an orange; tomatoes; grapes; apples.*)

Pages 16–17. What do you see here? (Ideas: *Flowers; asparagus; red lettuce or cabbage; radicchio.*)

Pages 18–19. Whom else do you see in the photographs on these two pages? (Ideas: *A woman and two little girls.*) Who do you think these people might be? (Ideas: *Mr. Kang's wife and children.*) One of the photographs on these two pages is different from the other photographs in this story. Can you tell me how it is different? (Idea: *It is in black and white.*)

Pages 20–21. Where was this picture taken? (Ideas: *Outside the store; across the street from the store.*) What do you see above the store? (Ideas: *Windows.*) Do you think anybody lives above the store? *Yes.* What makes you think so? (Idea: *Curtains are on some of the windows; plants are growing in some of the windows.*)

Page 22. What is the man pointing to? (Idea: *A map.*)

Page 23. What is the man doing? (Idea: *Moving a box of bananas.*) What other things are for sale in this grocery store? (Ideas: *Boxes; bottles; cans of food.*)

Page 29. What is the woman in this photograph holding? (Ideas: *Two paper cups; coffee.*)

Pages 30–31. When do you think this photograph was taken? (Idea: *At night.*) How do you think the store owner is feeling? (Idea: *Happy.*) What makes you think that? (Idea: *He is laughing.*)

Now that we've finished our picture walk, it's your turn to ask me some questions. What would you like to know about the story? (Accept questions. If children tell about the pictures or the story instead of asking questions, prompt them to ask a question.) Ask me a what question. Ask me a how question.

Read Story Aloud

(Read story aloud to children with minimal interruptions. Mr. Kang and his family are from Korea. You may wish to use a map or a globe to show the children where Korea is in relationship to the location of the school.)

In the next lesson, we will read the story again, and I will ask you some questions.

Present Target Vocabulary
◎← Business.

In the story we find out that six years ago Mr. Kang and his family "left Korea and came to America to start their own business." That means Mr. Kang owns his own store and sells things to earn money. **Business.** Say the word. *Business.*

Business is a naming word. It names a thing. What kind of word is **business?** *A naming word.*

If you own a business, you own a company that makes or sells things to earn money. Say the word that means "a company that makes or sells things to earn money." *Business.*

(Correct any incorrect responses, and repeat the item at the end of this sequence.)

Let's think about some things that might be a business. I'll tell about something. If you think that thing is a business, say, "Business." If not, don't say anything.

- Mr. and Mrs. Shanri own The Game Store. *Business.*
- Mr. Ederer collects model airplanes.
- Mr. Kang sells groceries at his store. *Business.*
- Ms. Franklin likes to fly kites.
- We fix bicycles and sell new ones at our shop on Fifth Street. *Business.*
- Jack and Diane are two American children growing up on a farm. *Business.*

What naming word means "a company that makes or sells things to earn money"? *Business.*

 Customers.

The story says Mr. Kang has to sweep the floor, arrange the fruit, and put out fresh flowers before the customers come. That means Mr. Kang has a lot to do before the people who want to buy things come into his store. **Customers.** Say the word. *Customers.*

Customers is a naming word. It names people. What kind of word is **customers?** *A naming word.*

Customers are the people who buy things in a store. Say the word that means "the people who buy things in a store." *Customers.*

(Correct any incorrect responses, and repeat the item at the end of this sequence.)

Let's think about some people who might be customers. I'll tell about someone. If you think that person is a customer, say, "Customer." If not, don't say anything.

- Al goes into The Game Store to buy a checkers game. *Customer.*
- Mrs. Zydeco goes into the Sunrise Hair Salon to get her hair cut. *Customer.*
- The Mueller family goes camping in the wilderness.
- We buy seven pounds of oranges and four pounds of apples from Mr. Kang. *Customer.*
- Uncle Herb buys gas at the gas station. *Customer.*
- Bart shovels the gravel in the backyard for his dad.

What naming word means "the people who buy things in a store"? *Customers.*

 Generous.

The story says Mr. Kang is "generous." That means he is happy to share what he has with other people. **Generous.** Say the word. *Generous.*

Generous is a describing word. It tells about a person. What kind of word is **generous?** *A describing word.*

If you are generous, you are happy to share what you have with others. Say the word that means "happy to share what you have with others." *Generous.* You already know a word that means the opposite of generous. What word means "you don't care about others, and you won't share what you have"? *Selfish.*

(Correct any incorrect responses, and repeat the item at the end of this sequence.)

Let's think about some people who might be generous or who might be selfish. I'll tell about someone. If you think that person is generous, say, "Generous." If you think that person is selfish, say, "Selfish."

- Tami shares her lunch with Mel. *Generous.*
- Karl won't let his little brother play with his toy cars, even though he wasn't playing with them himself. *Selfish.*
- Mrs. Goodfellow shares what she knows with her students. *Generous.*
- Every time someone gets a compliment, Corinne wants one too. *Selfish.*
- Peter had only twenty-five cents, but he gave it to someone who had nothing at all. *Generous.*
- Mom gets a ride to work from Mr. Magrowski, even though it's a long way for him to drive. *Generous.*

What describing word means "happy to share what you have with others"? *Generous.*

 Kind.

The story says Mr. Kang is "kind." That means he is friendly, helpful, and considerate. **Kind.** Say the word. *Kind.*

Kind is a describing word. It tells about a person. What kind of word is **kind?** *A describing word.*

If you are kind, you are friendly, helpful, and considerate. You already know what **considerate** means. What word means "pays attention to what someone else needs or wants or wishes for"? *Considerate.* Say the word that means "friendly, helpful, and considerate." *Kind.*

(Correct any incorrect responses, and repeat the item at the end of this sequence.)

Let's think about some people who might be kind. I'll tell about what some people do and say. If you think that person is kind, say, "Kind." If not, don't say anything.

- As the nurse put a bandage on Jessie's scraped knee, she smiled and said, "This should make your knee feel better." *Kind.*
- Elsa takes care of the injured kitten by washing the cut, bandaging it up, and staying with the kitten all night. *Kind.*
- Mr. Williams holds Amanda's hand so she will feel less afraid. *Kind.*
- She jumps out from behind the door and yells, "Boo!"
- Martin walks all the way to the store and back to get the hat his little sister left there. *Kind.*
- Leona sees the baby fall, but she doesn't go to help.

What describing word means "friendly, helpful, and considerate"? *Kind.*

Present Vocabulary Tally Sheet
(See Lesson 1, page 3, for instructions.)

Assign Homework
(Homework Sheet, BLM 29a: See the Introduction for homework instructions.)

DAY 2

Preparation: Picture Vocabulary Cards for *business, customers, kind,* and *generous.*

Read and Discuss Story
(Read story aloud to children. Ask the following questions at the specified points. Encourage them to use previously taught target words in their answers.)

Page 3. What kind of store does Mr. Kang own? (Idea: *A grocery store.*)

Page 5. What two things does Mr. Kang do in the morning? (Ideas: *He looks out the window; he unlocks the front door.*) What time does Mr. Kang unlock the store door? (Idea: *At eight o'clock sharp.*)

Pages 6–9. What are some of the things Mr. Kang does before the customers come? (Ideas: *Sweeps the floor; arranges the fruit; puts out fresh flowers.*)

Pages 10–11. What other things does Mr. Kang have to do? (Ideas: *Fill the cash register drawer; order supplies.*)

Pages 12–13. What does Mr. Kang do with the cartons of milk? (Ideas: *He counts and unpacks them.*) Why do you think the milk has to go in the cooler, but the fruit and vegetables can be out on the counter? (Idea: *The milk needs to be kept cold, or it will spoil; fruit can be left out, and it will still be good to eat.*)

Pages 14–17. What are some of the things that a customer might want? (Ideas: *Fresh fruit; a bouquet of flowers; some vegetables.*)

Pages 18–19. Who else works in the grocery store? (Idea: *Mrs. Kang.*) How many children do they have? (Idea: *Two girls.*)

Page 21. Where does the Kang family live? (Ideas: *Upstairs; above the small store.*)

Page 22. Where did the Kang family live before they came to America? *Korea.* How many years has the Kang family been living in America? *Six years.* Why did they decide to come to America? (Idea: *To start their own business.*)

Pages 24–25. What are some of the things that were hard to learn? (Ideas: *A new language; new customs; going to new schools.*)

Pages 26–27. How would you describe Mr. Kang? What is he like? (Ideas: *He's a hard worker; he is generous and kind.*) Mr. Kang has made many new friends because he is a hard worker, he is generous, and he is kind. What other things do you think would make it easy for a person to make new friends? (Ideas: *Being friendly; sharing; helping others.*)

Pages 28–29. How do you know Mr. Kang's grocery store does lots of business? (Idea: *Everyone in the neighborhood comes to buy fresh fruit, flowers, or a cup of hot tea.*)

Page 30. How does Mr. Kang feel at the end of the day? (Ideas: *Tired; happy; satisfied; content.*)

Review Vocabulary

(Display the Picture Vocabulary Cards. Point to each card as you say the word. Ask children to repeat each word after you.) These pictures show **business, customers, generous,** and **kind.**

- What describing word means "friendly, helpful, and considerate"? *Kind.*
- What naming word means "the people who buy things in a store"? *Customers.*
- What describing word means "happy to share what you have with others"? *Generous.*
- What naming word means "a company that makes or sells things to earn money"? *Business.*

Extend Vocabulary

◎⊰ Kind.

In *A Busy Day at Mr. Kang's Grocery Store,* we learned **kind** means "friendly, helpful, and considerate." Say the word that means "friendly, helpful, and considerate." *Kind.*

Raise your hand if you can tell us a sentence that uses **kind** as a describing word that means "friendly, helpful, and considerate." (Call on several children. If they don't use complete sentences, restate their examples as sentences. Have the class repeat the sentences.)

Here's a new way to use the word **kind.**

- **What kind of cat is that?** Say the sentence.
- **What kind of hat is that?** Say the sentence.
- **I like the kind of game where everyone plays on the same team.** Say the sentence.

In these sentences, **kind** is a naming word that means **sort or type.** What naming word means "sort or type"? *Kind.*

Raise your hand if you can tell us a sentence that uses **kind** as a naming word that means "sort or type." (Call on several children. If they don't use complete sentences, restate their

examples as sentences. Have the class repeat the sentences.)

Present Expanded Target Vocabulary
◎⊰ Attractive.

In *A Busy Day at Mr. Kang's Grocery Store,* Mr. Kang sweeps the floor, arranges the fruit, and puts out fresh flowers. He does all these things so his store will look nice and attract people's attention as they walk by. Another way of saying Mr. Kang's store looks nice is to say Mr. Kang's store is attractive. **Attractive.** Say the word. *Attractive.*

Attractive is a describing word. It tells about something. What kind of word is **attractive**? *A describing word.*

When something is attractive, it is nice to look at. Say the word that means "nice to look at." *Attractive.*

I'll tell about some people or places that might be attractive. If what I tell about is attractive, say, "Attractive." If not, don't say anything.

- My grandma's garden is nice to look at. *Attractive.*
- The twins are good-looking. *Attractive.*
- The troll has warts, a huge nose, and a snaggletooth.
- Legolas is a handsome elf. *Attractive.*
- The dog looks as though someone had given him a bad haircut.
- The mountain view is beautiful to look at. *Attractive.*
- It was so dark in the room that we couldn't even see what it looked like.

What describing word means "nice to look at"? *Attractive.*

◎⊰ Successful.

In *A Busy Day at Mr. Kang's Grocery Store,* everyone in the neighborhood goes to Mr. Kang's store to buy fresh fruit, flowers, or a cup of tea. Mr. Kang sells lots of things and earn lots of money. Mr. Kang's business is successful. **Successful.** Say the word. *Successful.*

Successful is a describing word. It tells about something. What kind of word is **successful**? *A describing word.*

If you are successful, you are doing well at something you want to do. If you want to learn to ride your bike, you work really hard at learning to ride. You practice and practice and practice. Then one day, you can ride your bike. You are successful. Say the word that means "doing well at something you want to do." *Successful.*

I'll tell about some people. If you think those people are successful, say, "Successful." If not, don't say anything.

- The man who owns the gas station has lots of customers. *Successful.*
- Mia wins the spelling bee. *Successful.*
- No customers ever come into Mrs. Smith's bookstore.
- Mimi Mee, the soprano singer, has thousands of people wanting to hear her sing. *Successful.*
- I learned how to cook, but I am not good at it.
- NASA brings Apollo 13 back to Earth safely even though it is damaged. *Successful.*

What describing word means "doing well at something you want to do"? *Successful.*

DAY 3

Preparation: Write the following list of key words on the board or on a piece of chart paper: *grocery store, customers, welcomes, together, hard, family.*

You will need a blank sheet of chart paper.

Activity Sheet, BLM 29b: Children will need scissors and glue or paste.

Summarize Story

Today we are going to summarize what we learned in the story *A Busy Day at Mr. Kang's Grocery Store.* I will write the summary on this piece of chart paper. Later, we will read the summary together.

When we summarize, we use our own words to tell about the most important things in the story. What do we do when we summarize? *We use our own words to tell about the most important things in the story.*

Key words help us tell about the important ideas in our own words. (Point to the list of key words.) This is the list of key words that will help us write our summary. (Read each word to children. Ask children to repeat each word after you read it.)

(**Note:** You should write the summary in paragraph form. Explain to children that you indent the first line because the summary will be a paragraph.)

(Show the illustrations on the following pages, and ask the specified questions.)

Page 4. This story tells about lots of people and things. We are going to write our summary about what Mr. Kang does at the grocery store. Whom will our summary be about? *Mr. Kang.*

I'm going to start the summary with a sentence about Mr. Kang. (Show the illustration on pages 4 and 5.) Mr. Kang owns a grocery store. (Write the sentence on the chart. Touch under each word as you and the children read the sentence aloud. Cross *grocery store* off the list of key words.)

Pages 6–7. The second sentence in our summary will tell about what Mr. Kang does in the morning before the customers come. We are writing a summary, so we are not going to tell everything that he does. Here's the second sentence of the summary: In the morning, Mr. Kang does many things to get ready for his customers. Let's read the second sentence of our summary together. (Touch under each word as you and the children read the sentence aloud. Cross *customers* off the list of key words.)

Pages 14–15. The next two sentences of our summary will tell what Mr. Kang does when the customers come. We are writing a summary, so we are not going to tell everything that he does. Here are the next two sentences of the summary: When the customers come, Mr. Kang welcomes them. He helps them with what they need. Let's read the next two sentences of our summary together. (Touch under each word as you and the children read the sentences aloud. Cross *welcomes* off the list of key words.)

Page 18. Who is with Mr. Kang in this illustration? *Mrs. Kang.* Raise your hand if you can tell us a sentence about what Mr. and

Mrs. Kang do together at the grocery store. (Idea: *Mr. and Mrs. Kang work together at the grocery store.*) (Add the new sentence to the summary.) Let's read the next sentence of our summary together. (Touch under each word as you and the children read the sentence aloud. Cross *together* off the list of key words.)

Page 26. (Read the text aloud.) The next sentence in our summary will describe how Mr. Kang works when he is at the store. Raise your hand if you can tell us a sentence that describes how Mr. Kang works when he is at his store. (Idea: *Mr. Kang works hard at his store.*) (Add the new sentence to the summary.) Let's read the next sentence of our summary together. (Touch under each word as you and the children read the sentence aloud. Cross *hard* off the list of key words.)

Pages 30–31. (Read the text aloud.) The last sentence we are going to write will tell how Mr. Kang feels at the end of the day. Raise your hand if you can tell us a sentence about how Mr. Kang feels in the evening. (Idea: *In the evening, Mr. Kang is tired and happy to go home to his family.*) (Add the new sentence to the summary.)

(Once the summary is finished, touch under each word as you and the children read the summary aloud together.)

(Sample summary:

Mr. Kang owns a grocery store. In the morning, Mr. Kang does many things to get ready for his customers. When the customers come, Mr. Kang welcomes them. He helps them with what they need. Mr. and Mrs. Kang work together at the grocery store. In the evening, Mr. Kang is tired and happy to go home to his family.)

We did a great job of writing a summary!

Review Whoopsy! Game

(Display the Picture Vocabulary Cards as you play this game.)

Today you will play the Whoopsy! Game. I'll say sentences using words we have learned. If the word doesn't fit in the sentence, you say "Whoopsy!" Then I'll ask

you to say a sentence where the word fits. If you can do it, you get a point. If you can't do it, I get the point. If the word I use fits the sentence, don't say anything.

Let's practice. I knew we were in **business** because . . . we didn't sell things that people wanted. *Whoopsy!*

Listen to the beginning of the sentence again. I knew we were in **business** because . . . Say the beginning of the sentence. *I knew we were in business because.*

Can you finish the sentence so the word fits? (Idea: *We sold things that people wanted.*)

Let's try another one. **Customers** are people who . . . work at a store. *Whoopsy!*

Listen to the beginning of the sentence again. **Customers** are people who . . . Say the beginning of the sentence. *Customers are people who.*

Can you finish the sentence so the word fits? (Idea: *Buy things in a store.*)

Now you're ready to play the game.

(Draw a T-chart on the board for keeping score. Children earn one point for each correct answer. If they make an error, help them to correct their sentence. Record one point for yourself, and repeat missed words at the end of the game.)

- Mr. Kang was **kind** when . . . he packed Mrs. Garcia's oranges so they would be crushed. *Whoopsy!* Say the beginning of the sentence again. *Mr. Kang was kind when.* Can you finish the sentence? (Idea: *He packed Mrs. Garcia's oranges so they wouldn't be crushed.*) (Continue to follow the pattern of recalling the beginning of the sentence before calling for ideas.)

- Arturo was **generous** because . . . he didn't share his huge pizza with the hungry twins. *Whoopsy!* Say the beginning of the sentence again. *Arturo was generous because.* Can you finish the sentence? (Idea: *He shared his huge pizza with the hungry twins.*)

- The man was **attractive** because . . . he was handsome, he spoke nicely, and he opened the car door for his girlfriend.
- I was **successful** at tap dancing when . . . I tripped over my own feet and fell down, bam! *Whoopsy!* Say the beginning of the sentence again. *I was successful at tap dancing when.* Can you finish the sentence? (Idea: *I danced well and didn't fall once.*)
- The child was **curious** and full of wonder because . . . he was not interested in anything. *Whoopsy!* Say the beginning of the sentence again. *The child was curious and full of wonder because.* Can you finish the sentence? (Idea: *He was interested in everything.*)

(Count the points, and declare a winner.) You did a great job of playing Whoopsy!

Complete Activity Sheet

(Read the rebus passage, saying "blank" each time you come to a line. Call on students to fill in the blank with the appropriate word.

Give each child a copy of the Activity Sheet, BLM 29b. Reread the rebus passage, having the children point to the rebus picture that would fit in the blank. Have children cut out the rebus pictures and glue them in the appropriate spaces. They may then read their rebus passages to their partners.)

(**Note:** If children require more assistance, you may choose to complete this activity as a guided activity.)

(Completed rebus:

Mr. Kang

　　Mr. Kang came to the United States from Korea. He sells flowers, fruit, vegetables, milk, and hot tea in his store. Every morning he sweeps the floor. He puts money in the cash register. All day long he and Mrs. Kang sell things to their customers. Mr. and Mrs. Kang and their two girls live above the store. Everyone likes to go to Mr. Kang's store.)

Preparation: Prepare a sheet of chart paper with the title *Fiction or Nonfiction.*

Nonfiction (Literary Analysis)

When authors write stories, sometimes they write about things that are true, and sometimes they write about things that they have made up in their imaginations. If an author writes a story about things that he or she made up, the story is called fiction. What do you call a story that is made up from the author's imagination? *Fiction.* If an author writes a story about things that are true, the story is called nonfiction. What do you call a story that is true? *Nonfiction.*

Let's see if we can figure out whether this story is fiction or nonfiction. You tell me what happened in the story, and I'll write it down.

(Show the photographs on the following pages, and ask the specified questions.)

Page 3. Do you think Mr. Kang is a real person or a person made up from Alice Flanagan's imagination? (Idea: *A real person.*) What makes you think so? (*Idea: I see his photograph; someone took a picture of him with a camera.*)

We think Mr. Kang is a real person, so I'll print **real** after his name. (Record *Mr. Kang* on the chart, and write *real* after his name.)

Pages 4–5, 7, 13–15, and 20–21. Do you think Mr. Kang's grocery store is a real store or a store made up from Alice Flanagan's imagination? (Idea: *A real store.*) What makes you think so? (Idea: *I see photographs taken in his store; someone took pictures of the store.*) We think Mr. Kang's store is a real store, so I'll print **real** after the words **grocery store.** (Record *grocery store* on the chart, and write *real* after it.)

Pages 18–19. Do you think Mr. Kang's family are real people, or are they made up from Alice Flanagan's imagination? (Idea: *Real people.*) What makes you think so? (Idea: *I see their photographs; someone took pictures of them.*) We think Mr. Kang's family are real, so I'll print **real** after the word **family.** (Record *family* on the chart, and write *real* after it.)

Pages 6–17. Do you think the work Mr. Kang does in his store is the work a real grocer would do, or is the work made up from Alice Flanagan's imagination? (Idea: *Real work.*) What makes you think so? (Ideas: *I have seen other grocers do that work; in a real store people do that work; I see photographs of Mr. Kang doing that work.*) We think the work Mr. Kang does in his grocery store is real, so I'll print **real** after the word **work.** (Record *work* on the chart, and write *real* after it.)

(Point to the chart.) We think Mr. Kang, Mr. Kang's store, his family, and his work are all real. A story that is about things that are real is called nonfiction. So, *A Busy Day at Mr. Kang's Grocery Store* is what kind of story? *Nonfiction.*

We have read one other story that is nonfiction. Raise your hand if you can name the other story we've read that was real. (Idea: *The First Day of Winter.*) That's right; even though there are no photographs in *The First Day of Winter,* all the things that happened to the family and the plants and animals are real, so *The First Day of Winter* is also a nonfiction story.

Play Whoopsy! (Cumulative Review)

Let's play Whoopsy! I'll say sentences using words we have learned. If the word doesn't fit in the sentence, you say "Whoopsy!" Then I'll ask you to say a sentence where the word fits. If you can do it, you get a point. If you can't do it, I get the point. If the word I use fits the sentence, don't say anything.

Now you're ready to play the game.

(Draw a T-chart on the board for keeping score. Children earn one point for each correct answer. If they make an error, correct them as you normally would, and record one point for yourself. Repeat missed words at the end of the game.)

- Barry was **successful** because . . . nothing he ever did worked out. *Whoopsy!* Say the beginning of the sentence again. *Barry was successful because.* Can you finish the sentence? (Idea: *Everything he did worked well.*)

- You know that you have a **business** when . . . you sell things or services that people want.
- The young lady was **attractive** because . . . she didn't comb her hair and she was uncooperative. *Whoopsy!* Say the beginning of the sentence again. *The young lady was attractive because.* Can you finish the sentence? (Idea: *She combed her hair and was cooperative.*)
- I would like the **kind** of ice cream that . . . has bugs in it. *Whoopsy!* Say the beginning of the sentence again. *I would like the kind of ice cream that.* Can you finish the sentence? (Idea: *Has raspberries in it.*)
- Darryl was **generous** because . . . he always gave some money to people who needed it.
- **Customers** are . . . people who buy things in your store.
- Bonnie was **kind** when . . . she shouted at all of the children. *Whoopsy!* Say the beginning of the sentence again. *Bonnie was kind when.* Can you finish the sentence? (Idea: *She spoke nicely to all of the children.*)
- You should **obey** when . . . someone tells you to do something that's wrong. *Whoopsy!* Say the beginning of the sentence again. *You should obey when.* Can you finish the sentence? (Idea: *Someone tells you to do something that's right.*)
- An **audience** is . . . a bunch of rude people who won't listen. *Whoopsy!* Say the beginning of the sentence again. *An audience is.* Can you finish the sentence? (Idea: *A group of people who listen politely.*)
- I like the way you pay **attention** when . . . we play Whoopsy!

(Count the points, and declare a winner.)
You did a great job of playing Whoopsy!

DAY 5

Preparation: Happy Face Game Test Sheet, BLM B.

Review Afterword, Introduce Meet the Author and the Photographer

Sometimes after people write a nonfiction story, they want to tell you about the people who made the story. This information is put in the story **after** the last **word** of the main part of the story, so it is called an **afterword.** What do you call information put in a story after the last word of the main part? *An afterword.*

The afterword for *A Busy Day at Mr. Kang's Grocery Store* is a special kind of afterword called "Meet the Author and the Photographer." What is the title of the afterword in *A Busy Day at Mr. Kang's Grocery Store*? *Meet the Author and the Photographer.*

(Read the afterword aloud a paragraph at a time.)

Paragraph 1, page 32. What important fact do we find out about Alice Flanagan and Christine Osinski? (Idea: *They're sisters.*) What did they like to do when they were children? (Idea: *Tell stores and draw pictures.*) Now that they're grown-ups, what work do they do? (Idea: *Alice Flanagan writes stories, and Christine Osinski takes photographs for Alice's stories.*)

Paragraph 2. Where does Alice Flanagan live? (Idea: *In Chicago.*) What family does she have? (Idea: *A husband.*) Where does Christine Osinski live? (Idea: *In New York City.*) What family does she have? (Idea: *A husband and two sons.*)

(Point to the woman with the camera.) Who do you think this is? (Idea: *Christine Osinski.*) Why do you think so? (Ideas: *She is holding a camera; a photographer needs a camera to take photographs.*)

(Point to the woman with the pen and the paper and the tape recorder.) Who do you think this is? (Idea: *Alice Flanagan.*) Why do you think so? (Ideas: *She is holding the pages from a book; she has a pen; she could interview people and have them tell their stories into the tape recorder.*)

Assess Vocabulary

(Give each child a copy of the Happy Face Game Test Sheet, BLM B.)

Today, you're going to play the Happy Face game. When you play the Happy Face game, it helps me know how well you know the hard words you are learning.

If I say something true, color the happy face. What will you do if I say something true? *Color the happy face.*

If I say something false, color the sad face. What will you do if I say something false? *Color the sad face.*

Listen carefully to each item I say. Don't let me trick you!

Item 1: A **business** sells things that people want to buy. *True.*

Item 2: If you are **successful,** you can't do anything right. *False.*

Item 3: **Generous** people keep everything for themselves. *False.*

Item 4: There are many different **kinds** of vegetables. *True.*

Item 5: **Customers** buy things in a store. *True.*

Item 6: You can show you are **kind** by doing nice things for other people. *True.*

Item 7: Most people are **attractive** in some way. *True.*

Item 8: You can buy plants for your garden in a **nursery.** *True.*

Item 9: When you make a **promise,** you say that you will definitely do something. *True.*

Item 10: If you are very tired, you might let out a long breath called a **sigh.** *True.*

You did a great job of playing the Happy Face Game!

(Score children's work later. Scores of 9 out of 10 indicate mastery. If a child does not achieve mastery, insert the missed words in the games in the next week's lessons. Retest those children individually on the missed words before they take the next mastery test.)

Extensions
Read a Story as a Reward

(Display several books you have read since the beginning of the program. Allow children to choose which book they would like you to read aloud to them as a reward for their hard work.)

(Read the story aloud to children for enjoyment with minimal interruptions.)

Present Super Words Center

(Prepare the word containers for the Super Words Center (see notation below).

This game is a Concentration-style game, but it uses all the opposite words from earlier lessons. You may choose to prepare the containers with *only* opposites or you may wish to mix the opposites with current vocabulary or vocabulary for children to review. Supply at least two copies of each of the opposites cards. Use your discretion to determine the number of cards to be placed in the container. Eighteen cards, for example, will generate a Concentration grid of 3 x 6. Twenty-four cards will create a grid of 4 x 6. You will know best what children are able to deal with.)

Today I will help you remember how to play the game called Hot and Cold. You will play this game in the Super Words Center. What do you know about the words **hot** and **cold?** (Idea: *They are opposites.*) The reason this game is called Hot and Cold is that it is your job to find as many opposites as you can.

Let's remember how we work with our words in the Super Words Center.

You will work with a partner in the Super Words Center. Whom will you work with in the center? *A partner.*

First, you will draw all of the cards out of the container and place them facedown. There are enough cards to make (X) rows of (Y) cards. (Demonstrate.) What do you do first? (Idea: *Draw all of the cards out and place them facedown.*)

Next, the first player will turn over one card and place it faceup so that both players can see. (Demonstrate.) What will you do next? (Idea: *The first player turns over a card and places it faceup so that both can see.*)

Next, the first player turns over another card and places it faceup so both can see. (Demonstrate.) What will you do next? (Idea: *The first player turns over another card and places it faceup so that both can see.*)

This is the important part. If the cards are opposites, the first player takes both cards and sets them aside in his or her game pile. If they are not opposites, both cards are placed facedown. Either way, it is now the second player's turn. (Demonstrate for children. They will be familiar with the process for playing Concentration, however.)

What will the first player do if the two cards are opposites? (Idea: *Keep those cards and put them in his or her game pile.*) What will the first player do if the two cards are not opposites? (Idea: *Turn them over.*) Either way, whose turn is it next? (Idea: *The second player's.*)

I think you are almost ready to play Hot and Cold. Can you think of some words that are opposites? (Call on several children. List the opposites they suggest to prepare them for playing the game.) Have fun playing Hot and Cold!

(**Note:** If you wish, you may teach the students to say "I'm hot!" in a happy voice when they find opposites and "I'm cold!" in a sad voice when they do not.)

Preparation: You will need *We Go in a Circle* for each day's lesson.

Number the pages of the story to assist you in asking questions at appropriate points.

Post a copy of the Vocabulary Tally Sheet, BLM A, with this week's Picture Vocabulary Cards attached.

Each child will need the Homework Sheet, BLM 30a.

We Go in a Circle
author: Peggy Perry Anderson • illustrator: Peggy Perry Anderson

Target Vocabulary

Tier II	Tier III
special	nonfiction
important	repeating
pasture	
unusual	
*injury	
*disability	

*Expanded Target Vocabulary Word

- What do you think the child is doing?
- Where do you think the story happens?
- When do you think the story happens?
- Why do you think the girl is holding the horse?
- How did the child get to ride the horse?
- Do you think this story is about real people? Tell why or why not.

(Call on several children to share their predictions with the class.)

Take a Picture Walk

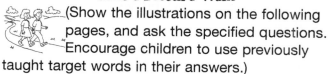

(Show the illustrations on the following pages, and ask the specified questions. Encourage children to use previously taught target words in their answers.)

We are going to take a picture walk through this book. Remember, when we take a picture walk, we look at the pictures and tell what we think will happen in the story.

Page 3. Where do you think the horse is? (Ideas: *At a racetrack; in a field; in a meadow.*) Why do you think the horse is covered in flowers? (Idea: *It just won a race.*)

Pages 4–5. What do you think is happening? (Idea: *The horses are running around a track.*) Why do you think the horses are running? (Idea: *They are in a race.*)

Pages 6–7. What do you think is happening? (Idea: *Two people are riding the horses.*) Why do you think the horses and riders have numbers

---

DAY 1

Introduce Book

This week's book is called *We Go in a Circle.* What's the title of this week's book? *We Go in a Circle.*

This book was written by Peggy Perry Anderson [**pair**-ee **an**-der-sun]. Who's the author of *We Go in a Circle*? *Pegg y Perry Anderson.*

Peggy Perry Anderson also made the pictures for this book. Who's the illustrator of *We Go in a Circle*? *Peggy Perry Anderson.* Who made the illustrations for this book? *Peggy Perry Anderson.*

The cover of a book usually gives us some hints of what the book is about. Let's look at the front cover of *We Go in a Circle.* What do you see in the illustration? (Ideas: *A horse; a child riding the horse; a girl in a cowboy hat holding on to the horse.*)

(Assign each child a partner.) Remember, when you make a prediction about something, you say what you think will happen. Get ready to make some predictions to your partner about this book. Use the information from the cover to help you.

(Ask the following questions, allowing sufficient time for children to share their predictions with their partners.)

- Who are the characters in this story? (Whom do you think this story is about?)

on them? (Ideas: *So people know which horse is winning; so people know which rider belongs to which horse.*) What numbers do you see? (Idea: *Three and seven.*)

Pages 8–9. Do you think this picture shows the horse before or after a race? Why do you think so? (Ideas: *After a race; because the horse and its rider are wearing flowers; because the rider is smiling.*) How do you think the rider feels? (Ideas: *Proud; happy.*) Why do you think so? (Idea: *He or she is smiling.*) What is the man behind the horse doing? (Idea: *Taking a photograph.*) What do you think the girl in front of the horse is doing? (Ideas: *Holding the horse still; leading the horse away.*)

Page 10. What do you see behind the horse? (Ideas: *Lightning; a storm; dark sky.*) How do you think the horse is feeling? (Ideas: *Scared; nervous; terrified.*) Why do you think so? (Ideas: *It's jumping up; its eyes look scared, and its mouth is open; it's rearing up.*)

Page 11. What is happening here? (Ideas: *A person is patting the horse; the horse is eating hay; the horse is standing quietly in its stall.*) It might be a little hard to see, but do you notice anything different about the horse's leg? (Idea: *It's wearing a bandage.*) What do you think happened to the horse's leg? (Idea: *The horse hurt its leg.*)

Pages 12–13. What do you see here? (Idea: *Three horses are putting their heads outside their windows.*) What colors are the horses? (Ideas: *Light brown; white; dark brown.*)

Pages 14–15. What is happening here? (Ideas: *It's snowing; a red truck is pulling a green wagon; some horses are standing outside in the snow beside the barn.*) What do you think is inside the wagon? (Idea: *A horse.*) What season of the year do you think it is? (Idea: *Winter.*)

Page 16. What season of the year do you think it is now? (Idea: *Spring.*) What makes you think so? (Ideas: *The tree is pink; the tree has blossoms, the tree is blooming; there's a rainbow; the grass is green.*) How do you think the horse is feeling? (Ideas: *Happy; playful.*) What makes you think so? (Idea: *It's jumping*

around.) Who do you think the man is? (Ideas: *The horse's owner; a helper on the farm.*)

Page 17. What is the woman doing? (Ideas: *Talking to the horse; washing the horse.*)

Pages 18–19. What is happening here? (Idea: *A boy in a wheelchair is being pushed down a ramp; the horse is wearing a saddle; a woman is holding the horse.*) What do you think is going to happen? (Idea: *The boy is going to ride the horse.*)

Pages 20–21. What is the boy doing? (Idea: *Riding the horse.*) What are the girls holding? (Ideas: *The horse's head; the boy's leg.*) How do you think the boy is feeling? (Ideas: *Happy; excited.*) What makes you think so? (Idea: *He's smiling.*)

Pages 22–23. What is happening here? (Ideas: *The horses are carrying people around a big room in a circle.*)

Page 24–25. What are the people beside the horses doing? (Ideas: *Helping so that the riders don't fall off; leading the horses.*)

Page 26–27. How do you think the people riding the horses feel? (Idea: *Happy; excited.*) What makes you think so? (Ideas: *They are smiling; they are waving.*)

Pages 28–29. What's happening here? (Ideas: *A boy is throwing a ball into a hoop while sitting on a horse; a little girl is walking with bars; the horse is looking at the little girl.*)

Page 30. How do you think the children feel about the horse? (Ideas: *Friendly; they like the horse.*) What makes you think so? (Ideas: *They are smiling; they look happy.*)

Have you ever seen a real horse? When did you see the horse? What was the horse doing? (Call on several children. Encourage them to start their answers with the words "I saw a horse when _____. The horse was _____.")

Now that we've finished our picture walk, it's your turn to ask me some questions. What would you like to know about the story? (Accept questions. If children tell about the pictures or the story instead of asking questions, prompt them to ask a question.) Ask me a what question. Ask me a how question.

Read Story Aloud
(Read story aloud to children with minimal interruptions.)

In the next lesson, we will read the story again, and I will ask you some questions.

Present Target Vocabulary

◎ Special.

In the story, the horse, the children, and the helpers all feel special. That means they don't feel ordinary. They feel better than they usually do. **Special.** Say the word. *Special.*

Special is a describing word. It tells about someone. What kind of word is **special?** *A describing word.*

If you feel special, you do not feel ordinary; you feel better than usual. Often you feel proud and enjoy sharing what you have done. Say the word that means "not ordinary; better than usual." *Special.*

(Correct any incorrect responses, and repeat the item at the end of the sequence.)

Let's think about some things that might make you feel special. I'll tell about something. If you would feel special, say, "Special." If not, don't say anything.

- Everyone sings "Happy Birthday" to you. *Special.*
- The teacher shows your painting to the class. *Special.*
- It's just an ordinary day.
- It's your turn to be the teacher's helper. *Special.*
- You get into trouble for using your dad's tools without his being there.
- It's the day of the big school concert, and you are the one who will lead the dancing. *Special.*

What describing word means "not ordinary; better than usual"? *Special.*

◎ Important.

In the story, the horse, the children, and the helpers all feel important. That means they feel valuable and powerful. They know that it will be hard for others to get along without them. **Important.** Say the word. *Important.*

If you feel important, you feel valuable and powerful. Say the word that means "valuable and powerful." *Important.*

(Correct any incorrect responses, and repeat the item at the end of the sequence.)

Let's think about some things that might make you feel important. I'll tell about something. If you would feel important, say, "Important." If not, don't say anything.

- Mark is chosen to carry a message to the principal. *Important.*
- Other children in your class come to you for help with their work. *Important.*
- You are the person who carries the key to the equipment closet in the gym. *Important.*
- You can count on your teacher to help you with your work. *Important.*
- You're just the same as everybody else.
- The chicken in the movie isn't valuable and powerful. But it sure is funny!

What describing word means "valuable and powerful"? *Important.*

◎ Pasture.

In the story, the racehorse is taken to a new place where there are other horses in the pasture. That means there are other horses in the field on the farm. **Pasture.** Say the word. *Pasture.*

Pasture is a naming word. It names a place. What kind of word is **pasture?** *A naming word.*

A pasture is a field where animals are kept so they can eat the grass. Say the word that means "a field where animals are kept so they can eat the grass." *Pasture.*

You already know a word that means "a field where grass and flowers grow." What is that word? *Meadow.* That's right; so a pasture could be a meadow, as long as animals can go there to eat the grass.

(Correct any incorrect responses, and repeat the item at the end of the sequence.)

Let's think about some places that might be pastures. I'll tell about a place. If you think that place is a pasture, say, "Pasture." If not, don't say anything.

- Cows are eating the grass in the field. *Pasture.*
- Sheep are eating the grass in the meadow. *Pasture.*
- Mr. Rudd and his family walk on the wooden sidewalks in the old town.
- Inside the farmer's fence, there are fields of grass and flowers for the horses to eat. *Pasture.*
- We ate so much that our stomachs are full.
- The burro chews the grass in his large field. *Pasture.*

What naming word means "a field where animals are kept so they can eat the grass"? *Pasture.*

◎—= Unusual.

In the story, the helpers put a very unusual saddle on the horse. That means they put a saddle on the horse that is different from any other saddle the horse has ever had. **Unusual.** Say the word. *Unusual.*

Unusual is a describing word. It tells about someone or something. What kind of word is **unusual?** *A describing word.*

If something is unusual, it is not usual or ordinary. Say the word that means "not usual or ordinary." *Unusual.*

(Correct any incorrect responses, and repeat the item at the end of the sequence.)

Let's think about some things that might be unusual. I'll tell about something. If you think that thing is unusual, say, "Unusual." If not, don't say anything.

- Toby always writes with his left hand, but today he is writing with his right hand. *Unusual.*
- The class wears their pajamas to school. *Unusual.*
- Zog says "Bleek! Bleek!" and waves his seven hairy arms. This is not an ordinary day at school. *Unusual.*
- At dinnertime, it is the same old meat, potatoes, and vegetables.
- Mr. Sly says his grasshopper pie is made from real grasshoppers! *Unusual.*
- I look in my lunch box. Peanut butter again!

What describing word means "not usual or ordinary"? *Unusual.*

Present the Vocabulary Tally Sheet
(See Week 1, page 3, for instructions.)

Assign Homework
(Homework Sheet, BLM 30a: See the Introduction for homework instructions.)

DAY 2

Preparation: Picture Vocabulary Cards for *special, important, pasture,* and *unusual.*

Read and Discuss Story
(Read story aloud to children. Ask the following questions at the specified points. Encourage them to use previously taught target words in their answers.)

Page 3. Who is the character who is telling this story? (Idea: *A racehorse.*)

Page 4. When the racehorses are in a race, how do they go? (Idea: *In a circle.*)

Page 7. What horse wins the race? (Idea: *The strongest and the fastest.*)

Page 8. How does the horse feel when it wins? (Idea: *Special and important.*)

Pages 10–11. What happens to the horse during the storm? (Idea: *It hurts its leg.*) How does the horse's life change after it hurts its leg? (Idea: *It can't race anymore.*)

Page 13. What happens to horses when they can't race anymore? (Ideas: *They are taken away; they are never seen again.*) What do you think happens to the horses that are taken away from the racetrack? (Ideas: *They find new homes; they are killed.*)

Page 15. What two things does the new place have? (Ideas: *A barn; other horses in the pasture.*)

Pages 16–17. What happens to the horse's hurt leg? (Idea: *It gets better.*) What do the helpers do for the horse? (Idea: *They comb and brush it.*) How do the helpers make the horse feel? (Ideas: *Special; important.*)

Page 19. What is different about the saddle they put on the horse? (Idea: *It has a tall bar in the* back.) Why do you think the boy needs a very unusual saddle to ride? (Ideas: *He cannot sit in an ordinary saddle because he's in a wheelchair; he needs something to help him sit up straight.*)

Pages 20–21. How does the boy feel on the back of the horse? (Idea: *Special and important.*)

Pages 22–23. What does the horse do now that is the same as its old life at the racetrack? (Idea: *It goes in a circle with other horses.*) What does the horse do now that is different from its old life? (Idea: *It gives slow rides instead of racing.*)

Pages 24–25. What can't some riders do? (Ideas: *They can't walk, talk, or see.*)

Pages 26–29. What do the riders do when they ride? (Idea: *They smile, wave, and even play games.*) How do the helpers feel? (Ideas: *Special; important.*)

Page 30. What does the horse say about "the way it is around here"? (Idea: *We go in a circle.*)

This story is fiction. That means it is made up from the imagination of the author. How do we know this story is fiction? (Idea: *Horses can't talk.*)

Do you think any parts of this story are true? If you do, tell what parts might be true. (Ideas: *The racehorse might get hurt; it might go to a special farm; it might give rides to children who can't walk, talk, or even see; helpers might help children ride.*)

(**Note:** Do not read the afterword that describes hippo therapy. It will be read on Day 5.)

Review Vocabulary

(Display the Picture Vocabulary Cards. Point to each card as you say the word. Ask children to repeat each word after you.) These pictures show **special, important, pasture,** and **unusual.**

- What describing word means "valuable and powerful"? *Important.*
- What describing word means "not ordinary; better than usual"? *Special.*
- What naming word means "a field where animals are kept so they can eat the grass"? *Pasture.*
- What describing word means "not usual or ordinary"? *Unusual.*

Extend Vocabulary

 Special.

In *We Go in a Circle,* we learned that **special** is a describing word that means "not ordinary; better than usual." Say the word that means "not ordinary; better than usual." *Special.*

Raise your hand if you can tell us a sentence that uses **special** as a describing word that means "not ordinary; better than usual." (Call on several children. If they don't use complete sentences, restate their examples as sentences. Have the class repeat the sentences.)

Here's a new way to use the word **special.**

- **Mr. Kang's grocery store had a special on asparagus.** Say the sentence.
- **The special at Rosie's diner was roast chicken.** Say the sentence.
- **The sporting goods store had a special on two-person tents.** Say the sentence.

In these sentences, **special** is a naming word that means **a sale of certain things for lower prices.** What naming word means "a sale of certain things for lower prices"? *Special.*

Raise your hand if you can tell us a sentence that uses **special** as a naming word that means "a sale of certain things for lower prices." (Call on several children. If they don't use complete sentences, restate their examples as sentences. Have the class repeat the sentences.)

Present Expanded Target Vocabulary
Injury.

In *We Go in a Circle,* the racehorse hurts its leg. Another way of saying the racehorse hurts its leg is that the racehorse has an injury to its leg. **Injury.** Say the word. *Injury.*

Injury is a naming word. It names something. What kind of word is **injury?** *A naming word.*

When there is an injury, damage is done to a person's or an animal's body. Say the word that means "damage done to a person's or an animal's body." *Injury.*

I'll tell about some people and animals that may have injuries. If the person or animal I tell about has an injury, say, "Injury." If not, don't say anything.

- Paul has a broken arm. *Injury.*
- The driver of the car is hurt in the accident. *Injury.*
- I fall off my skateboard, but I don't get a single bump, bruise, or scrape!
- The crow damages its wing during the storm. *Injury.*
- You can see the purplish-yellow bruise where the baseball hit me. *Injury.*
- I fall, but I don't hurt myself.

What naming word means "damage done to a person's or an animal's body"? *Injury.*

◎━ Disability.

In *We Go in a Circle,* one boy is in a wheelchair. He can't walk. Another rider can't talk. Another rider can't see. Each of these children has a disability. **Disability.** Say the word. *Disability.*

Disability is a naming word. It names a thing. What kind of word is **disability?** *A naming word.*

When people have a disability, they can't do something because of a medical problem or an accident. Say the word that means "can't do something because of a medical problem or an accident." *Disability.*

I'll tell about some people. If you think those people have a disability, say, "Disability." If not, don't say anything.

- Mrs. Fernie is blind. *Disability.*
- The newborn baby is perfectly healthy.
- Hal is deaf. *Disability.*
- The Rollers is a basketball team for people who have to be in wheelchairs. *Disability.*
- Bill's hearing was perfect when he had it tested.
- Mandy gets a mechanical hand after the accident. She can't play the piano, though. *Disability.*

What naming word means "can't do something because of a medical problem or an accident"? *Disability.*

Preparation: Prepare a sheet of chart paper with the title *Special and Important.*
Activity Sheet, BLM 30b: Children will need their crayons.

Retell Story

(Show the pictures on the following pages from the story, and call on a child to tell what's happening. Call on a different child for each section.)

Today I'll show you the pictures Peggy Perry Anderson made for the story *We Go in a Circle.* As I show you the pictures, I'll call on one of you to tell the class that part of the story.

Pages 3–9. Tell what happens at the **beginning** of the story.

Pages 10–29. Tell what happens in the **middle** of the story. (Encourage use of target words when appropriate. Model use as necessary.)

Page 30. Tell what happens at the **end** of the story.

Review Whoopsy!

(Display the Picture Vocabulary Cards as you play this game.)
Today you will play the Whoopsy! Game. I'll say sentences using words we have learned. If the word doesn't fit in the sentence, you say "Whoopsy!"

Then I'll ask you to say a sentence where the word fits. If you can do it, you get a point. If you can't do it, I get the point. If the word I use fits the sentence, don't say anything.

Let's practice. I felt **special** because . . . it was someone else's turn to be the teacher's helper. *Whoopsy!*

Listen to the beginning of the sentence again. I felt **special** because . . . Say the beginning of the sentence. *I felt special because.*

Can you finish the sentence so the word fits? (Idea: *It was my turn to be the teacher's helper.*)

Let's try another one. I knew I was **important** when . . . everyone said I wasn't a valuable player. *Whoopsy!*

Listen to the beginning of the sentence again. I knew I was important when . . . Say the beginning of the sentence. *I knew I was important when.*

Can you finish the sentence so the word fits? (Idea: *Everyone said I was a valuable player.*)

Now you're ready to play the game.

[T] (Draw a T-chart on the board for keeping score. Children earn one point for each correct answer. If they make an error, correct them as you normally would, and record one point for yourself. Repeat missed words at the end of the game.)

- I got an **injury** when . . . I fell off my bike and didn't even get a scratch. *Whoopsy!* Say the beginning of the sentence again. *I got an injury when.* Can you finish the sentence? (Idea: *I fell off my bike and scraped my elbow, my knee, and my ankle.*) (Continue to follow the pattern of recalling the beginning of the sentence before calling for ideas.)
- The bananas at Mr. Kang's store were on **special** . . . at the regular price. *Whoopsy!* Say the beginning of the sentence again. *The bananas at Mr. Kang's store were on special.* Can you finish the sentence? (Idea: *At a lower price.*)
- Evelyn's **disability** was that she . . . couldn't walk because of an accident.
- The cows moved to the **pasture** to . . . drink coffee and chew the fat. *Whoopsy!* Say the beginning of the sentence again. *The cows moved to the pasture to.* Can you finish the sentence? (Idea: *Eat grass.*)
- It was **unusual** that . . . our teacher spoke English. *Whoopsy!* Say the beginning of the sentence again. *It was unusual that.* Can you finish the sentence? (Idea: *Our teacher spoke* . . . **Note:** Choice of language is optional.)

(Count the points, and declare a winner.)
You did a great job of playing Whoopsy!

Complete Activity Sheet

(Discuss with children what makes the racehorse feel special and important at the beginning and end of the story. Discuss what makes the riders and the helpers feel special and important.

Record the activities on the chart paper titled *Special and Important* as they are identified. Ideas: *Winning a race; giving rides to children who can't walk, ride, or even see; riding a horse; helping the children ride; seeing them smile, wave, or play games.*

Ask children what makes them feel special and important. Record their responses on the chart paper.)

(Give each child a copy of the Activity Sheet, BLM 30b. Each child should decide what makes him or her feel special and important. Children should then complete the sentence frame and draw an illustration to accompany the activity. If they are not yet able to copy the sentence, scribe it for them while they are working on their illustrations. Make a cover with the title *Our Special and Important Book,* and fasten the pages together.)

DAY 4

Preparation: Prepare a sheet of chart paper, portrait direction, with the title *We Go in a Circle.* Underneath the title, make a circle of eight circles connected by arrows. Attach feeling bubbles to circles 2, 6, 7, and 8. See the Introduction for an example.

Record children's responses by writing the underlined words in the circles.

Story Patterns (Literary Analysis)

When authors write stories, they sometimes write in patterns. Let's see if we can figure out the pattern for this story. You tell me what happens in the story, and I'll write it down.

(Show the illustrations on the following pages, and ask the specified questions.)

Pages 3–5. What does the racehorse do? *It goes in a circle.*

Pages 6–9. What happens to the racehorse? *It wins the race.* How does the racehorse feel? *Special* and *important.*

Page 10. What happens to the racehorse? *It hurts its leg.*

Pages 14–15. Then what happens? *It is sent to a farm.*

Page 16. What happens to the horse's leg? *Its leg gets better.*

Page 17. What do the helpers do? *Brush and comb* the horse. How does the horse feel? *Special* and *important.*

Pages 18–28. What does the horse do? *Give rides* to children who can't walk, or talk, or see. How do the children feel? *Special* and *important.*

Page 29. Who else works with the children? *Helpers.* How do the helpers feel? (*Special* and *important.*)

Page 30. How do the horses and the helpers and the children go? *In a circle.* (Point to the beginning circle.)

(Point to the story map on the chart paper.) Look at the shape of this story. It's a circle. This story starts and ends with the horse going in a circle, so this story has a **circle** pattern. What kind of pattern starts and ends with the character doing the same thing? *A circle pattern.*

Let's sing "The Pattern Song" we've learned that will help us remember about story patterns.

(See the Introduction for the complete "Pattern Song.")

Singing a song together is a very good way to remember the patterns we have learned!

Play Whoopsy! (Cumulative Review)

Let's play Whoopsy! I'll say sentences using words we have learned. If the word doesn't fit in the sentence, you say "Whoopsy!" Then I'll ask you to say a sentence where the word fits. If you can do it, you get a point. If you can't do it, I get the point. If the word I use fits the sentence, don't say anything.

Now you're ready to play the game.

(Draw a T-chart on the board for keeping score. Children earn one point for each correct answer. If they make an error, correct them as you normally would, and record one

point for yourself. Repeat missed words at the end of the game.)

- It was a **special** day because . . . everything was ordinary and unexciting. *Whoopsy!* Say the beginning of the sentence again. *It was a special day because.* Can you finish the sentence? (Idea: *Everything was unusual and exciting.*)
- My Uncle Ned is **important** because . . . he is a valuable person to me.
- The dog was **unusual** because . . . he barked and panted just like a dog. *Whoopsy!* Say the beginning of the sentence again. *The dog was unusual because.* Can you finish the sentence? (Idea: *He meowed and hissed like a cat.*)
- Herman had a **disability** that meant . . . he could do everything that everyone else could do. *Whoopsy!* Say the beginning of the sentence again. *Herman had a disability that meant.* Can you finish the sentence? (Idea: *That he couldn't do everything that everyone else could do.*)
- The fruit was on **special** . . . because it was half price. Wow!
- Zach had an **injury** when . . . he wasn't careful with his motorcycle.
- A **pasture** is a place where . . . animals dance and sing like rock stars. *Whoopsy!* Say the beginning of the sentence again. *A pasture is a place where.* Can you finish the sentence? (Idea: *Animals eat grass.*)
- If you stand at **attention** . . . you slouch and move your feet around. *Whoopsy!* Say the beginning of the sentence again. *If you stand at attention.* Can you finish the sentence? (Idea: *You stand straight and still.*)
- If I **disturb** you, it means that . . . I don't interrupt you and make you upset. *Whoopsy!* Say the beginning of the sentence again. *If I disturb you, it means that.* Can you finish the sentence? (Idea: *I interrupt you and make you upset.*)
- I had a **disappointment** when . . . it was time to stop playing Whoopsy!

(Count the points, and declare a winner.)
You did a great job of playing Whoopsy!

Preparation: Happy Face Game Test Sheet, BLM B.

Review Afterword

Sometimes after people write a story that includes some things that are real, they want to tell you more facts about those real things. This information is put in the book **after** the last **word** of the story, so it is called an **afterword.**

The story *We Go in a Circle* is make-believe. It was made from the author's imagination. When a story is made up from the author's imagination, we say the story is fiction. What do we call a story that is made up from the author's imagination? *Fiction.*

The afterword tells us facts about how horses help people who have a disability. Facts are things that are true and that can be proved. For example, it is a fact that most cars have wheels. We can prove this fact by looking at a car.

When part of a book tells true facts about something, that part of the book is called nonfiction. What do we call the parts of books that tell true facts about something? *Nonfiction.*

Today I'll read the afterword that Peggy Perry Anderson wrote for *We Go in a Circle* so you can learn more about children with disabilities riding horses.

(You may wish to paraphrase the author's note on page 31 as follows:) When people with disabilities ride on horses to help themselves feel better, it's called hippo therapy. What is it called when people with disabilities ride horses to help themselves feel better? *Hippo therapy.*

The horses used for hippo therapy riding are gentle, older horses. What horses are used for this type of riding? *Gentle; older horses.* These horses are used to being around many people.

"Each rider has a helper walking on either side of the horse to make sure the rider is always balanced and doesn't fall off." Another helper leads the horse around the arena.

More helpers are always needed to help with the horses and the riders.

Hunter, a boy who is twelve, has been riding horses at the All Star Therapy Ranch since he was eighteen months old. This is what Hunter says about riding. (Read aloud the quotation at the bottom of page 31.)

Assess Vocabulary

 (Hold up a copy of the Happy Face Game Test Sheet, BLM B.)

Today you're going to play the Happy Face Game. When you play the Happy Face Game, it helps me know how well you know the hard words you are learning.

If I say something true, color the happy face. What will you do if I say something true? *Color the happy face.*

If I say something false, color the sad face. What will you do if I say something false? *Color the sad face.*

Listen carefully to each item I say. Don't let me trick you!

Item 1: If your haircut is **unusual,** your haircut is not ordinary. *True.*

Item 2: When you have an **injury,** you are not hurt. *False.*

Item 3: Something that is **important** to you doesn't matter at all. *False.*

Item 4: If you feel **special,** you might feel proud and important. *True.*

Item 5: Animals eat grass in a **pasture.** *True.*

Item 6: If you have a **disability,** you might not be able to do everything you want to do. *True.*

Item 7: If candy is on **special** at the store, it means that the price is lower. *True.*

Item 8: If a picture is nice to look at, it is **attractive.** *True.*

Item 9: When you go to a restaurant, the person who serves your food is called a **barber.** *False.*

Item 10: A **special** place is one that is better than the other places. *True.*

You did a great job of playing the Happy Face Game!

(Score children's work later. Scores of 9 out of 10 indicate mastery. If a child does not achieve mastery, insert the missed words in the games in the next week's lessons. Retest those children individually on the missed words before they take the next mastery test.)

Extensions

Read a Story as a Reward

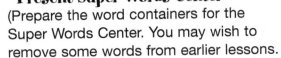(Display several books you have read since the beginning of the program. Allow children to choose which book they would like you to read aloud to them as a reward for their hard work.)

(Read the story aloud to children for enjoyment with minimal interruptions.)

Present Super Words Center

(Prepare the word containers for the Super Words Center. You may wish to remove some words from earlier lessons. Choose words that children have mastered. See the Introduction for instructions on how to set up and use the Super Words Center.

(**Note:** This is a recap of the game originally played in Lesson 1.)

(Place the new Picture Vocabulary Cards in the classroom center. Show children one of the word containers. If they need more guidance, role-play with two or three children as a demonstration.)

Let's think about how we work with our words in the Super Words Center.

You will work with a partner in the Super Words Center. Whom will you work with in the center? *A partner.*

First you will draw a word out of the container. What do you do first? (Idea: *Draw a word out of the container.*)

Next you will show your partner the picture and ask him or her what word the picture shows. What do you do next? (Idea: *I show my partner the picture and ask him or her to tell me what word the picture shows.*)

What do you do if your partner doesn't know the word? *Tell my partner the word.*

What do you do next? *Give my partner a turn.*

Preparation: You will need *Hello Ocean* for each day's lesson.

Number the pages of the story to assist you in asking questions at appropriate points.

Post a copy of the Vocabulary Tally Sheet, BLM A, with this week's Picture Vocabulary Cards attached.

Each child will need the Homework Sheet, BLM 31a.

Hello Ocean

author: Pam Muñoz Ryan • illustrator: Mark Astrella

Target Vocabulary

Tier II	Tier III
embrace	pattern
restless	describing
aromas	rhyme
fragrant	
*senses	
*experience	

*Expanded Target Vocabulary Word

- Where do you think the story happens?
- When do you think the story happens?
- Why do you think the girl is picking up a starfish?
- How did the girl get to the beach?
- Do you think this story is about real people? Tell why or why not.

(Call on several children to share their predictions with the class.)

Take a Picture Walk

(Show the illustrations on the following pages, and ask the specified questions. Encourage children to use previously taught target words in their answers.)

We are going to take a picture walk through this book. Remember, when we take a picture walk, we look at the pictures and tell what we think will happen in the story.

Pages 1–2. Where are these people headed? (Idea: *Down to the ocean.*) Who do you think these people are? (Ideas: *A family; a group of friends.*)

Page 3. What do you think the girl is looking at? (Idea: *The ocean.*) What are the other people doing in this picture? (Idea: *Spreading out a blanket.*)

Page 4. What color is the sand? (Idea: *Golden brown.*) What do you see in the sand? (Ideas: *Footprints; seaweed; sea foam.*)

DAY 1

Introduce Book

This week's book is called *Hello Ocean*. What's the title of this week's book? *Hello Ocean*.

This book was written by Pam Muñoz Ryan [**moon**-yohs **ry**-un]. Who's the author of *Hello Ocean*? *Pam Muñoz Ryan*.

Mark Astrella made the pictures for this book. Who's the illustrator of *Hello Ocean*? *Mark Astrella*. Who made the illustrations for this book? *Mark Astrella*.

The cover of a book usually gives us some hints of what the book is about. Let's look at the front cover of *Hello Ocean*. What do you see in the illustration? (Ideas: *A girl in a bathing suit and shorts at the seashore; a blue ocean with waves rolling in; a seagull; a starfish.*)

(Assign each child a partner.) Remember, when you make a prediction about something, you say what you think will happen. Get ready to make some predictions to your partner about this book. Use the information from the cover to help you.

(Ask the following questions, allowing sufficient time for children to share their predictions with their partners.)

- Who are the characters in this story? (Whom do you think this story is about?)
- What do you think the girl is doing at the beach?

Pages 5–6. What things and colors does the girl see? (Ideas: *Blue water; blue sky; white clouds; white foam.*)

Page 7. What are the girls doing here? (Ideas: *Sitting on rocks; looking into pools of water near the rocks; exploring the beach.*)

Page 8. What are the girls doing here? (Idea: *Playing in the shallow waves.*) How do you think the girls feel being by the ocean? (Ideas: *Excited; happy; full of energy.*) Why do you think so? (Idea: *They are smiling and running.*)

Pages 9–10. What do you see the girls doing on these two pages? (Ideas: *Standing in the water; playing in the sand.*)

Pages 11–12. What do you see? (Ideas: *Blue sky; clouds; seagulls flying.*) What sound might the seagull make?

Pages 13–14. What are the girls doing now? (Ideas: *Playing in the waves; swimming out on a surfboard.*) How do you think the girls are feeling? (Idea: *Very happy.*) What makes you think so? (Idea: *One of them is smiling a very big smile.*)

Page 16. What are the girls wrapping around their hands? (Ideas: *Weeds; green plants; seaweed.*) If the girls lifted up their hands, what would you see? (Ideas: *Impressions of their hands; handprints.*)

Pages 17–18. What do you see in this picture? (Ideas: *More people are on the beach now; the girl is letting some sand blow away.*)

Pages 19–20. What is the girl doing now? (Idea: *Lying on a towel in the sun.*) How do you think the girl is feeling? (Ideas: *Relaxed; happy; peaceful.*) How do the other people in the picture seem to be feeling? (Ideas: *Relaxed; peaceful.*) How do you know? (Ideas: *They are lying down stretched out; they are sleeping or reading.*)

Pages 21–22. What are the people in this picture doing? (Ideas: *Fishing; digging holes in the sand; looking at a fish in a bucket.*)

Pages 23–24. What is the girl doing? (Idea: *She is buried in the sand.*) What kinds of decorations is the girl wearing? (Ideas: *A seashell necklace; a seaweed necklace.*) Does the girl look like she is having fun? Why do you think so? (Idea: *Yes,*

she looks like she's having fun because she's smiling.)

Pages 25–26. What are the girls doing here? (Ideas: *Swimming; pouring water into holes in the sand.*)

Pages 27–28. What time of day do you think it is now? (Ideas: *Evening; late afternoon.*) What makes you think so? (Ideas: *The sky is darker; the sun is less bright; there are more dark shadows on the girl.*)

Pages 29–30. How long have the girls been at the beach? (Ideas: *All day; all afternoon.*) How do you know? (Ideas: *The sun is setting, and the sky is yellow and darker; earlier the sun was bright, and the sky was light blue.*)

Now that we've finished our picture walk, let's talk about Mark Astrella's illustrations. Let's try to decide if Mark Astrella took photographs for his book or painted the illustrations.

(Show the illustration on page 9.) Raise your hand if you think Mark Astrella took a photograph of the girls' feet. Why do you think so? Raise your hand if you think Mark Astrella painted the illustration of the girls' feet. Why do you think so? It's really hard to decide, isn't it?

(Show the illustration on page 19.) Raise your hand if you think Mark Astrella took a photograph of the girl on the beach. Why do you think so? Raise your hand if you think Mark Astrella painted the illustration of the girl on the beach. Why do you think so? It's really hard to decide, isn't it?

(Show the illustrations on page 25.) This illustration is the one that will help us make our decision. Could a camera take a cutaway view of something? *No.* So could Mark Astrella have taken a photograph of the girl swimming? No. So how did he make the illustrations for the book *Hello Ocean*? (Idea: *He painted them.*)

Mark Astrella tried to make his pictures look as real as he could, so we say his illustrations are realistic. What kind of illustrations did Mark Astrella make for *Hello Ocean*? *Realistic.*

What other story did we read that had realistic illustrations? (Ideas: *When We Go Camping; Loon Lake; The Most Beautiful Kite in the World.*)

Now that we've finished our picture walk, it's your turn to ask me some questions. What would you like to know about the story? (Accept questions. If children tell about the pictures or the story instead of asking questions, prompt them to ask a question.) Ask me a what question. Ask me a how question.

Read Story Aloud
(Read story aloud to children with minimal interruptions.)

In the next lesson, we will read the story again, and I will ask you some questions.

Present Target Vocabulary

◎⚊ Embrace.

In the story, the girl says the waves wrap her "in a wet embrace." She feels the waves are giving her a really big hug. **Embrace.** Say the word. *Embrace.*

Embrace is a naming word. It names a thing. What kind of word is **embrace?** *A naming word.*

If you get an embrace, you get a really big hug. Say the word that means "a really big hug." *Embrace.*

(Correct any incorrect responses, and repeat the item at the end of the sequence.)

Let's think about some times when someone might give you an embrace. I'll tell about a time. If you think you would get an embrace, say, "Embrace." If not, don't say anything.

- You go to visit your grandma and grandpa. *Embrace.*
- Your dad says goodbye to you in the morning before you go to school. *Embrace.*
- Your mom, the astronaut, is leaving for the moon. *Embrace.*
- Your friend, Emilio, wants to play.
- Barbara-Ann was dancing to the music.
- You surprised you mom by cleaning up your room without being asked. *Embrace.*

What naming word means "a really big hug"? *Embrace.*

◎⚊ Restless.

In the story, the girl says the sea is restless. That means the sea keeps moving back and forth, back and forth. **Restless.** Say the word. *Restless.*

If you are restless, you are always moving. You can't sit still or be quiet. Say the word that means "always moving; can't sit still or be quiet." *Restless.*

(Correct any incorrect responses, and repeat the item at the end of the sequence.)

Let's think about some times when you might be restless. I'll tell about a time. If you think you would be restless, say, "Restless." If not, don't say anything.

- You've been sitting on your chair at school for a long, long time. *Restless.*
- You are concentrating on painting your best picture ever.
- You are waiting for your party to start. *Restless.*
- You keep thinking about how much fun it will be when you go swimming. *Restless.*
- You are happy and satisfied with what you are doing.
- Every minute or so, you just want to shout, "I'm bored!" *Restless.*

What describing word means "always moving; can't sit still or be quiet"? *Restless.*

◎⚊ Aromas.

In the story, the girl says, "Aromas from some ancient tale disclose their news when I inhale." That means when she smells the odors of the ocean, her imagination tells her stories. **Aromas.** Say the word. *Aromas.*

Aromas is a naming word. It names a thing. What kind of word is **aromas?** *A naming word.*

Aromas are odors you like. You already know what odors are. What word means **smells?** *Odors.* What does **odors** mean? *Smells.* That's right; so aromas are smells you like.

(Correct any incorrect responses, and repeat the item at the end of the sequence.)

Let's think some odors that might be aromas. I'll tell about an odor. If you like that odor, say, "Aroma." If not, don't say anything.

- The smell of bread baking. *Aroma.*
- The smell of a skunk.

312

- The smell of a rose. *Aroma.*
- Peach pie cooling on the shelf. *Aroma.*
- Car exhaust and sweat on a very hot summer afternoon.
- Freshly baked chocolate chip pecan cookies. *Aroma.*

What naming word means "odors you like"? *Aromas.*

◎⟵ Fragrant.

In the story, the girl tells about "fragrant ore from holes dug steep." The girl is pretending she is digging a mine in the sand. The words "fragrant ore" mean she likes the smell of the wet sand. **Fragrant.** Say the word. *Fragrant.*

Fragrant is a describing word. It tells about how something smells. What kind of word is **fragrant?** *A describing word.*

If something is fragrant, it has a sweet or pleasing smell. Say the word that means "has a sweet or pleasing smell." *Fragrant.*

(Correct any incorrect responses, and repeat the item at the end of the sequence.)

Let's think about some things that might be fragrant. I'll name some things. If you think that thing is fragrant, say, "Fragrant." If not, don't say anything.

- Baby powder or lotion. *Fragrant.*
- The best shampoo ever. *Fragrant.*
- The beautiful blossom on the rose next door. *Fragrant.*
- That sewer smell that just won't go away.
- An old, wet dog named *Phew*-bert.
- Your mom's best perfume. *Fragrant.*

What describing word means "has a sweet or pleasing smell"? *Fragrant.*

Present Vocabulary Tally Sheet
(See Week 1, page 3, for instructions.)

Assign Homework
(Homework Sheet, BLM 31a: See the Introduction for homework instructions.)

Preparation: Picture Vocabulary Cards for *embrace, restless, aromas,* and *fragrant.*

Read and Discuss Story

(Read story aloud to children. Ask the following questions at the specified points in the story. Encourage children to use previously taught target words in their answers.)

Pages 1–2. When does this part of the story happen? (Ideas: *In the morning; in the afternoon.*) Where does this part of the story happen? (Ideas: *At the beach; at the ocean.*) Who does the character say is her "old best friend"? (Idea: *The ocean.*) The girl says she is "here with the five of me again." That's strange; I see only four people. I wonder who the five are.

Page 3. The girl says the ocean is a chameleon, always changing hue. **Hue** means color. What does **hue** mean? *Color.* A chameleon is a lizard that can change its color. What is a chameleon? *A lizard that can change its color.* What about the ocean is always changing? (Idea: *Its color.*) What different colors does the ocean change to? (Idea: *From gray to green to blue.*) So how is the ocean like a chameleon? (Idea: *Both can change their colors.*)

Pages 5–6. Where is the color of the wide open water reflected? (Idea: *In the skies.*)

Page 7. What part of the beach does the girl like to explore? (Idea: *The tide pools and secret nooks.*) Nooks are small sheltered places. What might the girl find in nooks at the beach? (Ideas: *Crabs; sea urchins; small fish; seashells.*)

Page 8. What does the ocean sound like to the girl? (Idea: *A lion's roar.*) What other sound does the ocean make when it moves toward the shore? (Idea: *A crashing sound.*)

Pages 9–10. What other sounds does the ocean make? (Ideas: *Shushing; rushing; whispering.*) What sounds do the boats make? (Idea: *Froggy songs.*) What sounds do the floats make? (Idea: *Gentle clangs.*)

(Point to the float in the water.) This is a float. Another name for a float is a buoy. What's another name for a float? *A buoy.*

Pages 11–12. What sound do seagulls make? (Idea: *Screak.*)

Pages 13–14. What does the ocean feel like when it embraces the girl? (Idea: *Wet.*) Besides hugging the girl, what else does the ocean do? (Idea: *It pulls and pushes against her.*)

Pages 15–16. What words describe the ground? (Ideas: *Squishy; sandy; soggy.*) How does the seaweed feel? (Idea: *Slippery.*) The words *squishy, sandy, soggy, slippery* and *seaweed* all start with the same sound. What sound do all these words start with? (Idea: *S-s-s.*) (Repeat the words if children need prompting.) Say these **s** words aloud. *Squishy, sandy, soggy, slippery, seaweed.*

Page 18. What else can the girl feel? (Ideas: *Sudden breezes; the ocean.*)

Page 20. What things can the girl smell? (Ideas: *The ocean; the fresh salt wind; sunscreen lotions.*)

Pages 21–22. What else does the girl smell? (Ideas: *Fish; wet sand.*)

Pages 23–24. What other things does the girl smell? (Ideas: *Drying kelp; musty shells.*)

Page 25. What does the ocean taste like? (Idea: *Tears.*) What does the girl wonder about the ocean? (Idea: *Why it tastes like the tears she sometimes cries.*) How is the taste of the ocean and tears the same? (Idea: *They both taste salty.*)

Pages 26–28. What does this character love? (Idea: *The way the ocean tastes.*)

Pages 29–30. How does the girl know it's time to go? (Ideas: *The sun dips down; the sun has set; it's getting dark.*) What is the girl looking forward to when she comes back next time? (Ideas: *Seeing the ocean; hearing the ocean's stories; tasting its flavors; taking deep sniffs of briny air; feeling the treasures it has to share.*) What does the girl say to the ocean when she leaves? (Idea: *Goodbye, ocean, my old best friend.*)

If you could pick something from nature to be your old best friend, what would it be? (Call on several children. Encourage children start their answers with the words: "My old best friend from nature would be _____.")

Review Vocabulary

(Display the Picture Vocabulary Cards. Point to each card as you say the word. Ask children to repeat each word after you.) These pictures show **embrace, restless, aromas,** and **fragrant.**

- What describing word means "has a sweet or pleasing smell"? *Fragrant.*
- What naming word means "odors you like"? *Aromas.*
- What describing word means "always moving; can't sit still or be quiet"? *Restless.*
- What naming word means "a really big hug"? *Embrace.*

Extend Vocabulary

◎← Embrace.

In the story *Hello Ocean,* we learned **embrace** is a naming word that means a hug. Say the word that means "a really big hug." *Embrace.*

Raise your hand if you can tell us a sentence that uses **embrace** as a naming word that means "a really big hug." (Call on several children. If they don't use complete sentences, restate their examples as sentences. Have the class repeat the sentences.)

Here's a new way to use the word **embrace.**

- **The children were embracing their aunt.** Say the sentence.
- **Amir's father embraced Amir when he got home.** Say the sentence.
- **The soccer team embraced each other when they scored the winning goal.** Say the sentence.

In these sentences, **embrace** is an action word that means to **put your arms around someone and hold that person tightly to show that you like or love him or her.** What action word means to "put your arms around someone and hold that person tightly to show that you like or love him or her"? *Embrace.*

Raise your hand if you can tell us a sentence that uses **embrace** as an action word that means "put your arms around someone and hold that person tightly to show that you like or love him or her." (Call on several children. If they don't use complete sentences, restate their examples as sentences. Have the class repeat the sentences.)

Present Expanded Target Vocabulary
◎ Senses.

In the story *Hello Ocean,* the girl describes how the ocean looks, sounds, feels, smells, and tastes. She is using her senses to describe the ocean. **Senses.** Say the word. *Senses.*

Senses is a naming word. It names something. What kind of word is **senses?** *A naming word.*

People have five different ways to learn about the world around us. **The five ways we use our bodies to learn about the world are called the senses. The senses are sight, hearing, touch, taste, and smell.** Say the word that means "the five ways we use our bodies to learn about the world: sight, hearing, touch, taste, and smell." *Senses.*

When you use your eyes to see, you are using your sense of sight. What sense are you using when you use your eyes to see? *Sight.*

When you use your ears to hear, you are using your sense of hearing. What sense are you using when you use your ears to hear? *Hearing.*

When you use your skin to feel, you are using your sense of touch. What sense are you using when you use your skin to feel? *Touch.*

When you use your tongue to taste, you are using your sense of taste. What sense are you using when you use your tongue to taste? *Taste.*

When you use your nose to smell, you are using your sense of smell. What sense are you using when you use your nose to smell? *Smell.*

The girl in the story *Hello Ocean* uses all five of her senses to learn about the ocean. Let's try to use all five of our senses to tell about an apple.

- Use your sense of sight to tell about the apple. (Ideas: *Red; round; has a stem.*)
- Use your sense of hearing to tell about the apple. (Ideas: *Seeds rattle; crunches when you bite it.*)
- Use your sense of touch to tell about the apple. (Ideas: *Smooth; bumpy on one end.*)
- Use your sense of taste to tell about the apple. (Ideas: *Sweet; juicy; sour.*)
- Use your sense of smell to tell about the apple. (Ideas: *Fruity; sweet.*)

What naming word means "the five ways we use our bodies to learn about the world: sight, hearing, touch, taste, and smell"? *Senses.*

◎ Experience.

In the story *Hello Ocean,* the girl uses her five senses to learn about the ocean. She experiences the ocean through her five senses. **Experience.** Say the word. *Experience.*

Experience is an action word. It tells about what people do. What kind of word is **experience?** *An action word.*

When people experience something, it means they use one or more of the five senses to learn more about it. Say the word that means to "use one or more of the five senses to learn more about something"? *Experience.*

I'll tell about what some people do. If you think those people are using **one** of the five senses to learn more about something, say, "Experience." If not, don't say anything.

- The scientist looked at the star with a telescope. *Experience.*
- All Jim really wanted was a room where he couldn't see, hear, touch, taste, or smell anything.
- I used my hearing to listen to the band play my favorite song. *Experience.*
- I have no sense of taste, so the pie didn't taste like anything at all.
- I could feel how silky and smooth Billie's fur was. *Experience.*

What action word means "use one or more of the five senses to learn more about something"? *Experience.*

DAY 3

Reread Story as a "Chime-In"

Listen while I read part of the story *Hello Ocean.*

(Read aloud page 4, emphasizing the words *sand* and *land*.) Sand, land. Say these words. *Sand, land.* These words sound the same at the end. Where do these words sound the same? *At the end.* Words that sound the same at the end rhyme. So the words **sand** and **land** rhyme. What do you know about the words **sand** and **land?** *They rhyme.*

(Read aloud pages 5 and 6, emphasizing the words *eyes* and *skies*.) Eyes, skies. Say these words. *Eyes, skies.* These words sound the same at the end. Where do these words sound the same? *At the end.* Words that sound the same at the end rhyme. So the words **eyes** and **skies** rhyme. What do you know about the words **eyes** and **skies?** *They rhyme.*

(Read aloud page 7, emphasizing the words *nooks* and *looks*.) Nooks, looks. Say these words. *Nooks, looks.* These words sound the same at the end. Where do these words sound the same? *At the end.* Words that sound the same at the end rhyme. So the words **nooks** and **looks** rhyme. What do you know about the words **nooks** and **looks?** *They rhyme.*

Today we'll reread the story *Hello Ocean* as a chime-in story. When I read a chime-in story to you, it means that I want you to join in with me when I read certain parts.

I'll read the first part, and you'll chime in with the word that rhymes. When will you chime in? *With the word that rhymes.*

(Read aloud pages 1 and 2 with no chime-in. Read aloud the remainder of the story, emphasizing the first word of each rhyming pair. Children will chime in with the second word of the rhyming pair. On pages 9, 11 and 12, 18, 20, and 28, the rhyming match is not perfect. You may wish to read those pages with no emphasis, thus not requiring children to chime in.)

Review Opposites Game

Today you'll play the Opposites Game. I'll use a vocabulary word in a sentence. If you can tell me the opposite of that word, you win one point. If you can't tell me, I get the point. I'll warn you now, though—there is no opposite for the word **senses.** If I use the word **senses** in a sentence, just say, "There is no opposite."

Let's practice: I felt **angry.** Tell me the opposite of angry. (Idea: *Happy.*) Happy could be the opposite of angry.

Let's try another one. The puppy was **disobedient.** Tell me the opposite of disobedient. (Idea: *Obedient.*) Obedient could be the opposite of disobedient.

Now you're ready to play the game.

(Draw a T-chart on the board for keeping score. Children earn one point for each correct answer. If they make an error, suggest an appropriate choice. Record one point for yourself, and repeat missed words at the end of the game.)

- There were many **good aromas** in the kitchen. Tell me the opposite of "good aromas." (Idea: *Bad odors.*) "Bad odors" could be the opposite of "good aromas."
- The orange blossoms were **fragrant.** Tell me the opposite of fragrant. (Idea: *Stinky.*) Stinky could be the opposite of fragrant.
- That elephant is **enormous.** Tell me the opposite of enormous. (Idea: *Small.*) Small could be the opposite of enormous.
- Tim used his **senses** to know where the kitchen was in the dark. Tell me the opposite of senses. (Idea: *There is no opposite.*)
- Michelle **frowned** because she was unhappy. Tell me the opposite of frowned. (Idea: *Smiled.*) Smiled could be the opposite of frowned.
- The lion cub was **gentle.** Tell me the opposite of gentle. (Idea: *Rough.*) Rough could be the opposite of gentle.

(Count the points, and declare a winner.)

You did a great job of playing the Opposites Game!

Complete Activity Sheet

(Review with children the five senses. Discuss which part(s) of their body help them experience each sense. Ideas: *Eyes see; ears hear; tongue tastes; nose smells; skin touches.*)

(Give each child a copy of the Activity Sheet, BLM 31b.) Today we will print words that tell which part of your body helps you experience each sense. Touch the line that points to the person's eyes. You use your eyes to . . . *see.* (Print *see* on the overhead transparency.) It's your turn. Print **see** on the line. (Repeat this procedure for the remaining body parts and senses.)

DAY 4

Preparation: Prepare a sheet of chart paper, portrait direction, with the title *Hello Ocean* in a circle in the middle of the paper. Five circles are connected to the middle circle with lines. See the Introduction for an example.

Record children's responses by writing the underlined words on the chart.

Story Patterns (Literary Analysis)

When authors write stories, they sometimes write in patterns. Let's see if we can figure out the pattern for this story. You tell me what happens in the story, and I'll write it down.

(Read aloud the following pages, and ask the specified questions.)

Pages 1–7. What does this part of the story tell about? (Idea: *What you see at the ocean.*) When Pam Muñoz Ryan wrote this part of her story, she told about how the ocean . . . *looks.* (Print *see* and *looks* in one of the circles.) Tell me about some of the things the girl sees at the ocean. (Draw lines out from the *see* circle, and cluster these responses. Ideas: <u>Gray ocean</u>; <u>green ocean</u>; <u>blue ocean</u>; <u>amber seaweed</u>; <u>speckled sand</u>; <u>bubbly waves</u>; <u>sky</u>; <u>tide pools</u>; <u>nooks</u>.)

Pages 8–12. What does this part of the story tell about? (Idea: *What you hear at the ocean.*) When Pam Muñoz Ryan wrote this part of her story, she told about how the ocean . . . *sounds.* (Print *hear* and *sounds* in one of the circles.) Tell me about some of the things the girl hears at the ocean. (Draw lines out from the *hear* circle, and cluster these responses. Ideas: <u>Ocean's roar</u>; <u>crashing waves</u>; <u>shushing water</u>; <u>whispering water</u>; <u>froggy sounds of boats</u>; <u>clangs of floats</u>; <u>screak of gulls</u>.)

Pages 13–18. What does this part of the story tell about? (Idea: *What you can touch at the ocean.*) When Pam Muñoz Ryan wrote this part of her story, she told about how the ocean . . . *feels.* (Print *touch* and *feels* in one of the circles.) Tell me about some of the things the girl feels at the ocean. (Draw lines out from the *feel* circle, and cluster these responses. Ideas: <u>wet hug of the surf</u>; <u>pulling of the sea</u>; <u>pushing of the sea</u>; <u>waves</u>; <u>spray</u>; <u>squishy, sandy, soggy ground</u>; <u>slippery seaweed</u>; <u>breeze</u>.)

Pages 20–23. What does this part of the story tell about? (Idea: *What you smell at the ocean.*) When Pam Muñoz Ryan wrote this part of her story, she told about how the ocean . . . *smells.* (Print *smell* and *smells* in one of the circles.) Tell me about some of the things the girl smells at the ocean. (Draw lines out from the *smell* circle, and cluster these responses. Ideas: <u>salt wind</u>; <u>lotions</u>; <u>fish</u>; <u>wet sand</u>; <u>drying kelp</u>; <u>musty shells</u>.)

Pages 25–28. What does this part of the story tell about? (Idea: *What you taste at the ocean.*) When Pam Muñoz Ryan wrote this part of her story, she told about how the ocean . . . *tastes.* (Print *taste* and *tastes* in one of the circles.) Tell me about some of the things the girl tastes at the ocean. (Draw lines out from the *taste* circle, and cluster these responses. Ideas: <u>salty ocean</u>; <u>sandy, salty drink</u>.)

Hello Ocean tells how the ocean looks, sounds, feels, smells, and tastes. The pattern for this story is a describing pattern. What kind of a pattern uses all your senses to tell about something? *A describing pattern.*

Today we will learn a new verse for "The Pattern Song" that will help us remember about story patterns.

Listen while I sing the verse for you:

When describing makes a pattern, let it be.
When describing makes a pattern, let it be.
See and hear and touch and smell,
Taste a little—then you tell!
When describing makes a pattern, let it be.

Now sing it with me. Remember, the middle of the verse tells the names of our five senses!

Now let's sing all that we've learned together.

(See the Introduction for the complete "The Pattern Song.")

Singing a song together is a very good way to remember the patterns we have learned!

Play Opposites Game (Cumulative Review)

Let's play the Opposites game. I'll use a vocabulary word in a sentence. If you can tell me the opposite of that word, you win one point. If you can't tell me, I get the point. Remember, there is no opposite for the word **senses.** If I use that word in a sentence, just say "There is no opposite."

Let's practice: Les is a very **generous** person; he shares what he has with others. Tell me the opposite of generous. (Idea: *Selfish.*) Selfish could be the opposite of generous.

Let's try another one. The room was filled with **good aromas.** Tell me the opposite of "good aromas." (Idea: *Bad smells.*) "Bad smells" could be the opposite of "good aromas."

When you **experience** a new thing, you learn. Tell me the opposite of **when you experience a new thing.** (Idea: *When you do not experience a new thing.*) "When you do *not* experience a new thing" can be the opposite of "when you do experience a new thing."

Now you're ready to play the game.

(Draw a T-chart on the board for keeping score. Children earn one point for each correct answer. If they make an error, correct them as you normally would, and record one point for yourself. Repeat missed words at the end of the game.)

- That monster is **horrible.** Tell me the opposite of horrible. (Idea: *Nice.*) Nice could be the opposite of horrible.
- The fresh fruit smelled **fragrant.** Tell me the opposite of fragrant. (Idea: *Stinky.*) Stinky could be the opposite of fragrant.
- We use our **senses** to find out things. Tell me the opposite of senses. (Idea: *There is no opposite.*)
- The talking dog was **imaginary.** Tell me the opposite of imaginary. (Idea: *Real.*) Real could be the opposite of imaginary.
- Moira is a **kind** person. Tell me the opposite of kind. (Ideas: *Unkind; not kind.*) Unkind could be the opposite of kind.
- The light was **dim** in the cellar. Tell me the opposite of dim. (Idea: *Bright.*) Bright could be the opposite of dim.
- Sissy was **impatient** while she waited for her dessert. Tell me the opposite of impatient. (Idea: *Patient.*) Patient could be the opposite of impatient.
- The **rude** children did not use their best manners. Tell me the opposite of rude. (Idea: *Polite.*) Polite could be the opposite of rude.
- At **dawn,** we went paddling in canoes. Tell me the opposite of dawn. (Idea: *Sunset.*) Sunset could be the opposite of dawn.
- We have five **senses.** Tell me the opposite of senses. (Idea: *There is no opposite.*)
- When you are **restless,** you cannot be still. Tell me the opposite of restless. (Idea: *Still.*) Still could be the opposite of restless.

(Count the points, and declare a winner.)

You did a great job of playing the Opposites game!

DAY 5

Preparation: Happy Face Game Test Sheet, BLM B.

Retell Story to a Partner

(Assign each child a partner, and ask the partners to take turns telling part of the story each time you turn to a new set of pages. Encourage use of target words when appropriate.)

Today I'll show you the pictures Mark Astrella made for the story *Hello Ocean*. As I show you the pictures, you and your partner will take turns telling part of the story.

Pages 1–2. Tell what happens at the **beginning** of the story.

Pages 3–28. Tell what happens in the **middle** of the story.

Pages 29–30. Tell what happens at the **end** of the story.

(Reread pages 1 and 2.) Now we know why the girl says "I'm here, with the five of me, again!" What are the five she is talking about? (Ideas: *The five senses: sight, hearing, touch, taste, and smell.*)

Assess Vocabulary

 (Hold up a copy of the Happy Face Game Test Sheet, BLM B.)

Today you're going to play the Happy Face Game. When you play the Happy Face Game, it helps me know how well you know the hard words you are learning.

If I say something true, color the happy face. What will you do if I say something true? *Color the happy face.*

If I say something false, color the sad face. What will you do if I say something false? *Color the sad face.*

Listen carefully to each item that I say. Don't let me trick you!

Item 1: An **embrace** is a really big hug. *True.*

Item 2: If something is **fragrant,** it smells sweet and good. *True.*

Item 3: A **restless** person sits still. *False.*

Item 4: **Senses** are things like touch, taste, and smell that we use to learn about the world. *True.*

Item 5: When you **experience** the world, you learn about it by using one or more of your five senses. *True.*

Item 6: **Aromas** are smells that you like. *True.*

Item 7: When you **embrace** people, you hug and hold them to let them know you love them. *True.*

Item 8: **Active** means that you are sitting still. *False.*

Item 9: A store is a kind of **business.** *True.*

Item 10: **Carpenters** do *not* make things out of wood. *False.*

You did a great job of playing the Happy Face Game!

(Score children's work later. Scores of 9 out of 10 indicate mastery. If a child does not achieve mastery, insert the missed words as additional items in the games in the next week's lessons. Retest those children individually for the missed words before they take the next mastery test.)

Extensions
Read a Story as a Reward

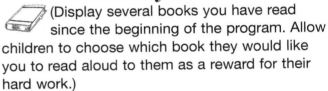 (Display several books you have read since the beginning of the program. Allow children to choose which book they would like you to read aloud to them as a reward for their hard work.)

(Read the story aloud to children for enjoyment with minimal interruptions.)

Present Super Words Center

 (Prepare the word containers for the Super Words Center. You may wish to remove some of the words from earlier lessons. Choose words children have mastered.

See the Introduction for instructions on how to set up and use the Super Words Center.)

(Add the new Picture Vocabulary Cards to the words from the previous weeks. Show children one of the word containers. If they need more guidance, role-play with two or three children as a demonstration.)

You will play a game called What's My Word? in the Super Words Center.

Let's think about how we work with our words in the Super Words Center.

You will work with a partner in the Super Words Center. Whom will you work with in the center? *A partner.*

First you will draw a word out of the container. What do you do first? (Idea: *Draw a word out of the container.*) Don't show your partner the word card.

Next you will tell your partner three clues that tell about the word card. What do you do next? (Idea: *I tell my partner three clues that tell about the word card.*) After each clue, your partner can make a guess. If your partner is correct, say "yes." If your partner is not correct, say "no," and give another clue.

Let your partner make three guesses. If your partner guesses correctly on any of the guesses, he or she gets a point. If your partner does not guess correctly, tell your word and show the word card. Give yourself a point. Then give your partner a turn.

What do you do next? *Give my partner a turn.*

(This game does not need to be played for points.)

Preparation: You will need *The Goat Lady* for each day's lesson.

Number the pages of the story to assist you in asking questions at appropriate points.

Post a copy of the Vocabulary Tally Sheet, BLM A, with this week's Picture Vocabulary Cards attached.

Each child will need the Homework Sheet, BLM 32a.

The Goat Lady
author: Jane Bregoli • illustrator: Jane Bregoli

Target Vocabulary

Tier II	Tier III
fascinated	nonfiction
chore	biography
nuisance	portrait
courage	
*triplets	
*donated	

*Expanded Target Vocabulary Word

- Who are the characters in this story? (Whom do you think this story is about?)
- What do you think the woman is doing with the goat?
- Where do you think the story happens?
- When do you think the story happens?
- Why do you think the woman is wearing only one sock?
- How do you think the woman feels?
- Do you think this story is about real people? Tell why or why not.

(Call on several children to share their predictions with the class.)

Take a Picture Walk

(Show the illustrations on the following pages, and ask the specified questions. Encourage children to use previously taught target words in their answers.)

We are going to take a picture walk through this book. Remember, when we take a picture walk, we look at the pictures and tell what we think will happen in the story.

Pages 1–2. Where do you think this story takes place? (Idea: *On a farm.*) Why do you think so? (Ideas: *There is a big wooden house with a big, grassy yard; there is a barn behind the house; there are goats and chickens in the yard; there are many trees behind the house.*)

Pages 3–4. What different animals do you see in this picture? (Ideas: *Goats; ducks; chickens.*) What are the goats doing? (Idea: *Drinking water out of buckets; eating.*)

DAY 1

Introduce Book

This week's book is called *The Goat Lady.* What's the title of this week's book? *The Goat Lady.*

This book was written by Jane Bregoli. Who's the author of *The Goat Lady*? *Jane Bregoli.*

Jane Bregoli also made the pictures for this book. Who's the illustrator of *The Goat Lady*? *Jane Bregoli.* Who made the illustrations for this book? *Jane Bregoli.*

The cover of a book usually gives us some hints of what the book is about. Let's look at the front cover of *The Goat Lady.* What do you see in the illustration? (Ideas: *An older woman wearing an apron, a purple sweater and a hat; she's holding a white goat with a piece of yellow rope; she's wearing only one white sock.*)

(Assign each child a partner.) Remember, when you make a prediction about something, you say what you think will happen. Get ready to make some predictions to your partner about this book. Use the information from the book's cover to help you.

(Ask the following questions, allowing sufficient time for children to share their predictions with their partners.)

Page 6. Whom do you see? (Idea: *An older woman.*) What decoration is on her coat collar? (Idea: *Two white goats.*)

Pages 7–8. What do you see here? (Ideas: *White goats inside a fence; people; houses; the older woman is pointing to something; the little girl is petting a goat.*)

Pages 9–10. What do you think the girl is doing? (Ideas: *Feeding the goat; playing with the goat.*) Where do you think the girl is? (Ideas: *On the farm; beside the barn; in a pasture.*)

Page 12. What do you see here? (Ideas: *A big white goat standing in a doorway; three baby white goats; a blanket over the doorway.*) Who do you think the big goat might be? (Idea: *The little goats' mother or father.*)

Page 13. What do you see here? (Ideas: *A woman in a purple sweater; a door; a table; three small white goats; a cat; bags of food; newspapers spread on the floor.*) What do you think the woman is doing? (Ideas: *Feeding the baby goats; giving them a drink from a bucket.*)

Page 14. (Point out the small picture insert.) Where do you think the goats are going? (Idea: *Inside the house.*)

Pages 15–16. What do you see? (Ideas: *A woman standing in the doorway of a house; the sides of a white house; a handkerchief pinned to a clothesline; a white machine with legs; a mirror; a prize ribbon.*) What do you think this white object with legs might be? (Idea: *A washing machine.*)

Page 18. Who do you think these two children are? (Ideas: *Neighbors; grandchildren; the woman's friends.*) What do you think they are doing? (Ideas: *Reading a story; following a cooking recipe.*) What makes you think so? (Ideas: *They are in the kitchen; bottles and pans are on the stove; jars and containers are on the table.*) Those are strange-looking bottles that are being heated on the stove. What do you think they are used for?

Pages 19–20. Where do you think the woman and the goat are? (Idea: *In the house.*) Why do you think so? (Ideas: *The woman is sitting in a chair; there is a smooth floor.*)

Pages 21–22. How are these three pictures alike? (Ideas: *They are all of the older woman; they are all of the top half of the woman.*) Which picture do you like best? Why do you like it best? (Call on several children. Encourage them to start their answers with the words: "I like the _____ picture best because _____.")

Page 23. What do you see here? (Ideas: *Many paintings on the walls; the older woman in a blue coat holding red flowers; a woman holding a painting; people standing.*) Why do you think the older woman is holding flowers? (Ideas: *She won a prize; somebody gave them to her.*) How do you think the people in the picture feel? (Idea: *Happy.*) Why do you think so? (Idea: *They are smiling.*)

Pages 25–26. Do these pictures look like any of the pictures we've seen already? (Idea: *Yes.*) In this picture, how do you think the woman's sweater feels? (Ideas: *Fuzzy; warm; soft; prickly; scratchy.*) Where do you think the woman is in this smaller picture? (Ideas: *In a shed; in the barn.*) What makes you think so? (Ideas: *I can see the boards in the ceiling; the walls are made of boards that haven't been painted.*)

Pages 27–28. What do you see here? (Ideas: *Many white goats behind a wire fence; a child looking at the goats through the fence.*) What season of the year do you think it is? (Idea: *Winter.*) Why do you think so? (Ideas: *Snow is on the ground; the trees don't have any leaves on their branches; the trees are bare; the child is wearing a warm sweater, scarf, and hat.*)

Pages 29–30. How do you think the goats feel about the woman? (Idea: *They like her.*) Why do you think so? (Ideas: *One is sitting on her lap; one is rubbing against her legs; they want to be close to her.*) How do you think the woman feels about the goats? (Idea: *She likes them.*) Why do you think so? (Ideas: *She's holding one on her lap; there are goats close to her in many pictures.*)

Now that we've finished our picture walk, it's your turn to ask me some questions. What would you like to know about the story? (Accept questions. If children tell about the pictures or the story instead of asking questions, prompt them to ask a question.) Ask me a *what* question. Ask me a *how* question.

Read Story Aloud
(Read story aloud to children with minimal interruptions.)

In the next lesson, we will read the story again, and I will ask you some questions.

Present Target Vocabulary
 Fascinated.

In the story, when the family moves into their new home, they are "fascinated by a nearby farmhouse." That means they are very interested in the house and think about it a lot. **Fascinated.** Say the word. *Fascinated.*

Fascinated is an action word. It tells what happened. What kind of word is **fascinated?** *An action word.*

If you are fascinated by something, you are very interested in it, and you think about it a lot. Say the word that means "you are interested in something, and you think about it a lot." *Fascinated.*

(Correct any incorrect responses, and repeat the item at the end of the sequence.)

Let's think about some people and some things that someone might find fascinating. I'll tell about a person and a thing. If the person would be fascinated by that thing, say, "Fascinated." If not, don't say anything.

- A scientist—dinosaur bones. *Fascinated.*
- A farmer—baby goats playing. *Fascinated.*
- An airplane pilot—different kinds of baking flour.
- A gardener—a new trick to keep away garden pests. *Fascinated.*
- A brick-layer—instructions on how to sew beautiful dresses.
- A dog walker—a new kind of leash that lets dogs exercise more. *Fascinated.*

What action word means "you are interested in something, and you think about it a lot"? *Fascinated.*

Tell me about something that fascinates you. (Call on several children. Encourage them

to start their answers with the words "I am fascinated by _____ because _____.")

 Chore.

In the story, "my mom and other friends helped more with the chores." That means they helped with the jobs that had to be done every day to take care of the goats. **Chore.** Say the word. *Chore.*

Chore is a naming word. It names a thing. What kind of word is **chore?** *A naming word.*

A chore is a small job that has to be done nearly every day to keep everything running smoothly. Say the word that means "a small job that has to be done nearly every day to keep everything running smoothly." *Chore.*

(Correct any incorrect responses, and repeat the item at the end of the sequence.)

Let's think about some things that might be chores at school. I'll name something. If you think what I've named is a chore, say, "Chore." If not, don't say anything.

- Sharpening pencils. *Chore.*
- Emptying the wastebaskets. *Chore.*
- Painting the room.
- Cleaning around the sink. *Chore.*
- Putting away shoes, pencils, paper, and crayons. *Chore.*
- Playing tag in the gym.

What naming word means "a small job that has to be done nearly every day to keep everything running smoothly"? *Chore.*

Tell about a chore you have at home. (Call on several children. Encourage them to start their answers with the words "One of my chores at home is _____.")

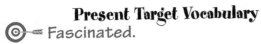 Nuisance.

In the story, some of the people "said the animals were a public nuisance." That means the animals were bothering people and causing them lots of problems. **Nuisance.** Say the word. *Nuisance.*

Nuisance is a naming word. It names a person or a thing. What kind of word is nuisance? *A naming word.*

A nuisance is a person or an animal that is bothering you and causing you lots of problems. Say the word that means "a person or an animal that is bothering you and causing you lots of problems." *Nuisance.*

(Correct any incorrect responses, and repeat the item at the end of the sequence.)

Let's think about some people or animals that might be a nuisance. I'll tell about a person or an animal and what they are doing. If you think that person or animal is a nuisance, say, "Nuisance." If not, don't say anything.

- Your neighbor's dog barks all day long. *Nuisance.*
- Your little brother keeps knocking down your pile of blocks. *Nuisance.*
- The visiting relatives are no trouble at all.
- The squirrel keeps jumping into my lap, stealing my peanuts, and jabbing me with its sharp little claws. *Nuisance.*
- The children in the backseat keep saying, "Are we there yet? Are we there yet?" *Nuisance.*
- Corrina loves to play with her friends.

What naming word means "a person or an animal that is bothering you and causing you lots of problems"? *Nuisance.*

◎⟺ *Courage.*

The person telling the story says the paintings of Noelie "show her courage." That means the paintings show how brave Noelie is. **Courage.** Say the word. *Courage.*

Courage is a naming word. It names a thing. What kind of word is **courage?** *A naming word.*

Courage means bravery. People who have courage will do something difficult or dangerous even though they may be afraid. Say the word that means "bravery." *Courage.* If you have courage, what will you do? *Something difficult or dangerous even though you may be afraid.*

(Correct any incorrect responses, and repeat the item at the end of the sequence.)

Let's think about some people who might show courage. I'll tell about what some people do. If you think that person shows courage, say, "Courage." If not, don't say anything.

- The boy protects his little brother from the ferocious dog. *Courage.*
- The explorer turns around and goes home when he gets scared.
- The soldiers stay to help children who have been hurt even though it is dangerous. *Courage.*
- I can't be in the dark by myself. I get scared half to death!
- Aunt Sally jumps into the deep lake to save the drowning kitten. *Courage.*
- Adam cries and hides behind his mom when she tries to introduce him to her friend.

What naming word means "bravery"? *Courage.* If you have courage, what will you do? *Something difficult or dangerous even though you may be afraid.*

Present Vocabulary Tally Sheet
(See Week 1, page 3, for instructions.)

Assign Homework
(Homework Sheet, BLM 32a: See the Introduction for homework instructions.)

DAY 2

Preparation: Picture Vocabulary Cards for *fascinated, chore, nuisance,* and *courage.*

Read and Discuss Story

(Read story aloud to children. Ask the following questions at the specified points in the story. Encourage children to use previously taught target words in their answers.)

Page 1. How do most of the homes in the neighborhood look? (Ideas: *New; freshly painted with neatly-mowed lawns.*) How is the house on the corner of Lucy Little Road different from the other houses in the neighborhood? (Ideas: *It is old; its paint is peeling; its doors hang crookedly from their hinges; the yard is full of white goats.*) What do the children like to watch? (Idea: *The frisky baby goats.*)

(First paragraph of page 4.) Who comes by the house during the day? (Ideas: *Men in a truck delivering hay; a lady with groceries; a van each weekday at noon; a big yellow school bus is parked by the gate.*)

(Second paragraph of page 4.) What do the neighbors complain about? (Ideas: *The messy yard; the rundown house; the animals that misbehave.*)

(Remainder of page 4.) What does the man who jogged by complain about? (Idea: *The big gray goose has chased him again on his way to get the mail.*) What does the salesman who lives next door complain about? (Ideas: *The rooster crows day and night; the chickens are always in the street.*) What does the history teacher who lives across the street complain about? (Ideas: *The goats keep hopping across the fence and coming into his yard; they eat the new apple tree he has just planted.*)

Page 5. What does the woman look like? (Ideas: *Slightly bent; rather tall; none of her clothes match; twinkling eyes; a warm smile; rosy cheeks.*) What makes the children's fears disappear? (Ideas: *The way the woman's eyes twinkle; her warm smile.*) The woman's name is Noelie Lemire Houle [No-el-ee Luh-meer Hool]. What is the woman's name? *Noelie Lemire Houle.* What culture is the woman from? (Idea: *French Canadian.* You may wish to show children where Quebec, Canada, is on a map or globe in relationship to the location of the school.)

Page 8. What have you learned about these goats from this page of the story? (Ideas: *Goats will answer to their names if you treat them kindly; goats are gentle; they are clean; they don't eat tin cans or garbage; they nibble at the corners of the house; many of them have won ribbons at county fairs.*) How do the children feel after meeting Noelie and her goats? (Ideas: *Excited; happy.*)

(First paragraph of page 10.) What do the characters do at the farm the next day? (Ideas: *Help Noelie with the chores; learn that goats need fresh water every day; help feed them dried corn and grain and hay.*)

(Remainder of page 10.) What does Noelie do while she milks the goat? (Ideas: *Sits resting her head against the side of the goat; hums a*

tune from her favorite opera.) An opera is a play where the parts are sung instead of spoken.

Page 11. How does Noelie check to see that the barn is comfortable for the goats at night? (Idea: *She sleeps in the barn herself one night.*) What is the surprise? (Idea: *Anna has had three baby goats.*)

Page 14. What will Noelie do if any of the new baby goats are sick or weak? (Idea: *Bring them into the house and nurse them back to health.*) Why does Noelie not have any screens on the doors or windows? (Idea: *So that the flies and mosquitoes can escape.*) Why do you think that the neighbors complain about the goats in Noelie's house? (Ideas: *They think the goats are a nuisance; they think that there are too many goats; Noelie is different from the neighbors.*)

Page 16. What does Noelie have in her house that the children have never seen before? (Idea: *An old-fashioned washing machine.*) Why does Noelie always leave a white handkerchief on the line? (Idea: *It shows her the way the wind is blowing; it helps her know what the weather is going to do.*)

(First part of page 17.) What does Noelie do after the goats have been fed? (Ideas: *Listens to the radio; reads a newspaper; reads* Heidi *to the children; tells the children about her own life.*)

(Second part of page 17.) What did the doctor say to try to help Noelie feel better? (Idea: *Drink goat's milk.*) Why did Girl lick the tears off Noelie's face? (Idea: *She knew Noelie was suffering.*)

Page 19. Why did Noelie begin to raise more goats? (Idea: *So that other people could be helped by drinking goat's milk.*)

Why did people start calling Noelie the Goat Lady? (Ideas: *Because she had so many goats; she had seventy-nine goats.*)

Page 20. What did Noelie do with the extra goat kids? (Idea: *She gave them to an organization that sends them to people in poor countries so that those people will have fresh milk to drink.*)

Page 21. What does the children's mom do? (Idea: *Paints Noelie's portrait.*) How does Noelie feel about the paintings? (Idea: *She is very pleased.*)

Page 24. What does the children's mom do with all the paintings of Noelie? (Idea: *Fills the walls of the town hall for an art show.*) Who are some of the people who come to the art show? (Ideas: *The "Meals on Wheels" drivers; the young man who helped feed the goats; the church lady who helped with grocery shopping; the men who delivered hay and corn; the nurse who changed the bandage on Noelie's sore leg; the nurse's husband; a young woman who could drink only goat's milk as a child.*) Do many different people care about Noelie? How do you know so? (Idea: *Yes, because they all come to see portraits of her at the art show.*)

Page 26. How do the neighbors change after seeing the beautiful paintings of Noelie? (Ideas: *The neighbors become more accepting of Noelie's way of life; they don't think her yard seems quite as messy.*) What does the jogger say? (Idea: *Noelie is such a nice woman.*) What does the salesman ask? (Idea: *About getting some chickens of his own.*) What does the history teacher do? (Idea: *Offers to fix her fence.*) What do the town selectmen do? (Ideas: *Surprise Noelie with an award for providing the citizens of the town with fresh goat's milk for so many years; ask her to ride in a limousine at the head of the Fourth of July parade.*)

Pages 27–28. Does Noelie change after she becomes famous? (Idea: *No.*) Who helps Noelie with the chores on the farm when she gets older? (Ideas: *The children; their mother; other friends.*) Where does Noelie send her goats and other animals when she can no longer care for them? (Idea: *To a nearby farm.*)

Page 30. What do the paintings show about Noelie? (Ideas: *Her courage and her kindness.*) What words would you use to tell about what kind of person Noelie Houle is? (Ideas: *Kind; brave; generous; loving; friendly; hardworking.*)

Have you ever helped somebody who needed help with chores? Whom did you help? What did you do? (Encourage children to answer using the words "I helped _____ do _____.")

Review Vocabulary
(Display the Picture Vocabulary Cards. Point to each card as you say the word. Ask children

to repeat each word after you.) These pictures show **fascinated, chore, nuisance,** and **courage.**

- What naming word means "bravery"? *Courage.* If you have courage, what will you do? *Something difficult or dangerous even though you may be afraid.*
- What naming word means "a small job that has to be done nearly every day to keep everything running smoothly"? *Chore.*
- What action word means "you are interested in something, and you think about it a lot"? *Fascinated.*
- What naming word means "a person or an animal that is bothering you and causing you lots of problems"? *Nuisance.*

Extend Vocabulary
◎= *Chore.*

In the story *The Goat Lady,* we learned that a chore is a small job that has to be done nearly every day to keep everything running smoothly. Say the word that means "a small job that has to be done nearly every day to keep everything running smoothly." *Chore.*

Raise your hand if you can tell us a sentence that uses **chore** as a naming word that means "a small job that has to be done nearly every day to keep everything running smoothly." (Call on several children. If they don't use complete sentences, restate their examples as sentences. Have the class repeat the sentences.)

Here's a new way to use the word **chore.**

- **Taking down the old fence is a chore.** Say the sentence.
- **To me, gardening is a chore.** Say the sentence.
- **Cleaning out the attic is a terrible chore.** Say the sentence.

In these sentences, **chore** is a naming word that means **an unpleasant or difficult job.** What naming word means "an unpleasant or difficult job"? *Chore.*

Raise your hand if you can tell us a sentence that uses **chore** as naming word that means "an unpleasant or difficult job." (Call on several children. If they don't use complete sentences, restate their examples as sentences. Have the class repeat the sentences.)

Present Expanded Target Vocabulary

◎⊂ Triplets.

In the story *The Goat Lady,* one of Noelie's goats has three babies all born on the same day. Another way of saying Anna had three baby goats all born on the same day is to say Anna had triplets. **Triplets.** Say the word. *Triplets.*

Triplets is a naming word. It names people or animals. What kind of word is **triplets?** *A naming word.*

Triplets are three babies all born on the same day to the same mother. Say the word that means "three babies all born on the same day to the same mother." *Triplets.*

I'll tell about some babies. If those babies are triplets, say, "Triplets." If not don't say anything.

- Joshua, Jamie, and Judy Johnson celebrated their fifth birthday on July 4th. *Triplets.*
- Hugh, Doug, and Michael are brothers, all born on the same day. *Triplets.*
- The chicken and the duck enjoy each other's company.
- The three bear cubs, Rasp bear, Straw bear, and Blue bear, ate too many goodies at their birthday party. "It's a good thing you have your birthdays on the same day," said Mama bear. *Triplets.*
- The hiker washes his three socks in the stream.
- Ginger and Spice are two dogs who were born on the same day to different mothers.

What naming word means "three babies all born on the same day to the same mother"? *Triplets.*

◎⊂ Donate.

In the story *The Goat Lady,* Noelie gives some of her goat kids "to an organization that sent them to people in poor countries, so that those people would have fresh milk to drink, too." Another way of saying she gives away the goats to help someone else is to say she donates the goats to people. **Donate.** Say the word. *Donate.*

Donate is an action word. It tells what people do. What kind of word is **donate?** *An action word.*

When people donate something, they give something away in order to help other people. Say the word that means "give something away in order to help other people." *Donate.*

I'll tell about some people. If you think those people donated something, say, "Donate." If not, don't say anything.

- Willie gives cans of dog food to the S.P.C.A. *Donate.*
- Carmelita sells shoes in a shoe store.
- Ralph and his family give blood at the Red Cross clinic. *Donate.*
- Bondar gives his spare change to a man who needed it. *Donate.*
- Joseena saves her money and puts it in the bank.
- Bronson doesn't want to share his money with people who need help.

What naming word means "give something away in order to help other people"? *Donate.*

DAY 3

Preparation: Activity Sheet, BLM 32b. Children will need their crayons.

Retell Story

(Show pictures on the following pages from the story, and call on a child to tell what's happening. Call on a different child for each section.)

Today I'll show you the pictures Jane Bregoli made for the story *The Goat Lady.* As I show you the pictures, I'll call on one of you to tell the class that part of the story.

Page 1. Tell what happens at the **beginning** of the story.

Pages 2–29. Tell what happens in the **middle** of the story. (Encourage use of target words when appropriate. Model use as necessary.)

Page 30. Tell what happens at the **end** of the story.

Review Chew the Fat

Today you will play a game called Chew the Fat. A long time ago, when people wanted to just sit and talk about things that were happening in their lives, they would sit and "chew the fat."

In this game, I will say some sentences with our vocabulary words in them. If I use the vocabulary word correctly, say, "Well done!" If I use the word incorrectly, say, "Chew the fat." That means you want to talk about how I used the word. I'll say the beginning of the sentence again. If you can make the sentence end so that it makes sense, you get a point. If you can't, I get the point.

Let's practice: Boxer was **fascinated** by the bone because he wasn't interested in it at all. *Chew the fat.* Let's chew the fat. The first part of the sentence stays the same. I'll say the first part. Boxer was fascinated by the bone because . . . How can we finish the sentence so it makes sense? (Idea: *He was very interested in it.*) Let's say the whole sentence together now. *Boxer was fascinated by the bone because he was very interested in it.* Well done! I'm glad we chewed the fat!

Let's do another one together. Mr. Wong knew that he and his brothers Richard and Kevin were **triplets** because they were born on different days. *Chew the fat.* The first part of the sentence stays the same. I'll say the first part. Mr. Wong knew that he and his brothers Richard and Kevin were triplets because . . . How can we finish the sentence so that it makes sense? (Idea: *They were born on the same day.*) Let's say the whole sentence now. *Mr. Wong knew that he and his brothers Richard and Kevin were triplets because they were born on the same day.* Well done! I'm glad we chewed the fat!

Now you're ready to play the game.

(Draw a T-chart on the board for keeping score. Children earn one point for each correct answer. If they make an error, work with them to construct a correct sentence. Record one point for yourself, and repeat missed words at the end of the game.)

- Annie's **chore** was . . . easy and enjoyable to do. *Chew the fat.* I'll say the first part of the sentence again. Annie's chore was . . . (Idea: *Hard and difficult to do.*) Let's say the whole sentence together. *Annie's chore was hard and difficult to do.* Well done! I'm glad we chewed the fat!

- The kittens were a **nuisance** because . . . they never got into trouble. *Chew the fat.* I'll say the first part of the sentence again. The kittens were a nuisance because . . . Idea: *They were always getting into trouble.*) Let's say the whole sentence together. *The kittens were a nuisance because they were always getting into trouble.* Well done! I'm glad we chewed the fat!

- The zebra who fought the lion had **courage** because . . . she never gave up even when she knew she couldn't win. *Well done!*

- Celina **donated** money to the people who lost their homes in the storm by . . . keeping it all for herself. *Chew the fat.* I'll say the first part of the sentence again. Celina donated money to the people who lost their homes in the storm by . . . (Idea: *Sending it to help them.*) Let's say the whole sentence together. *Celina donated money to the people who lost their homes in the storm by sending it to them.* Well done!

- Everyday I have **chores** to do because . . . it doesn't make any difference. *Chew the fat.* I'll say the first part of the sentence again. Everyday I have chores to do because . . . (Idea: *It helps things to run smoothly.*) Let's say the whole sentence together. *Everyday I have chores to do because it helps things to run smoothly.* Well done!

(Count the points, and declare a winner.)
You did a great job of playing Chew the Fat!

Complete Activity Sheet

(Review with children the different ways Jane Bregoli put texture into her illustrations. Ideas: Line textures (pages 1 and 2, 9 and 10); dotted textures (pages 15 and 16, 25); and patterns (page 27). Give each child a copy of the Activity Sheet, BLM 32b. Read the instructions at the bottom of the page. Allow sufficient time for children to complete their pictures. Encourage them to use a variety of strategies to produce texture.)

Literary Analysis (Nonfiction)

When authors write books, sometimes they write about things that are true, and sometimes they write about things that they have made up in their imaginations. If an author writes a story about things that are made up from the author's imagination, the story is called fiction. What do you call a story that is made up from the author's imagination? *Fiction.*

If an author writes a story about things that are true, the story is called nonfiction. What do you call a story that is true? *Nonfiction.*

The story *The Goat Lady* is a true story. So is the book *The Goat Lady* fiction or nonfiction? *Nonfiction.*

Noelie Lemire Houle was a real person. Let me tell you a little about her. (You may wish to paraphrase the biography of Noelie Lemire Houle on page 31 as follows:)

Noelie Lemire Houle was born in 1899 on a small farm in Quebec, Canada. She moved to the United States in 1919 to join her older sister and work in a factory. She married Almador Houle and lived with his parents in a small farmhouse in Dartmouth, Massachusetts.

After her husband died, Noelie lived on the farm with her goats, selling goat's milk, cheese, eggs, and honey.

Noelie gave her extra goat kids to the Heifer Project International. This organization has helped more than 5 million hungry families in about 125 countries around the world.

When Jane Bergoli wrote the story *The Goat Lady,* she told the story of Noelie Houle's life. When an author writes the story about a real person's life, we say the author wrote a biography. What kind of book did Jane Bergoli write? *A biography.* That's right; a biography is one kind of nonfiction book.

We have read two other books that are nonfiction. Raise your hand if you can name one of the other books we've read that were true. (Ideas: *The First Day of Winter; A Busy Day at Mr. Kang's Grocery Store.*) That's right; even though there are no photographs in *The Goat Lady,* all the things that happened to Noelie Houle are true, so *The Goat Lady* is also a nonfiction book. But because it tells the story of Noelie's life, we call it a biography.

Play Chew the Fat (Cumulative Review)

Today we'll play a game called Chew the Fat. A long time ago, when people wanted to just sit and talk about things that were happening in their lives, they would sit and "chew the fat."

In this game, I will say some sentences with our vocabulary words in them. If I use the vocabulary word correctly, say, "Well done!" If I use the word incorrectly, say, "Chew the fat." That means you want to talk about how I used the word. I'll say the beginning of the sentence again. If you can make the sentence end so that it makes sense, you get a point. If you can't, I get the point.

Let's practice: Teresa **donated** to the charity by . . . keeping her money in her pocket. *Chew the fat.* Let's chew the fat. The first part of the sentence stays the same. I'll say the first part. Teresa donated to the charity by . . . How can we finish the sentence so it makes sense? (Idea: *Giving her money to people who needed it.*) Let's say the whole sentence together now. *Teresa donated to the charity by giving her money to people who needed it.* Well done! I'm glad we chewed the fat!

Let's do another one together. The three girls were **triplets** because . . . they were born on different days to different mothers. *Chew the fat.* The first part of the sentence stays the same. I'll say the first part. The three girls were triplets because . . . How can we finish the sentence so that it makes sense? (Idea: *They were born on the same day to the same mother.*) Let's say the whole sentence now. *The three girls were triplets because they were born on the same day to the same mother.* Well done! I'm glad we chewed the fat!

Now you're ready to play the game.

(Draw a T-chart on the board for keeping score. Children earn one point for each correct answer. If they make an error, correct them as you normally would, and record one point for yourself. Repeat missed words at the end of the game.)

- The brave man had **courage** because . . . he ran away when he got scared. *Chew the fat.* I'll say the first part of the sentence again. The brave man had courage because . . . (Idea: *He didn't run away when he got scared.*) Let's say the whole sentence together. *The brave man had courage because he didn't run away when he got scared.* Well done! I'm glad we chewed the fat!
- The mosquitoes were a **nuisance** because . . . they kept buzzing around and biting us. *Well done!*
- Kemper's **chore** was . . . hard to do and difficult besides. *Well done!*
- I do my **chores** every day because . . . it's okay if the dishes don't get washed and the dog doesn't get fed. *Chew the fat.* I'll say the first part of the sentence again. I do my chores every day because . . . (Idea: *It's important for the dishes to be clean and the dog to be fed.*) Let's say the whole sentence together. *I do my chores every day because it's important for the dishes to be clean and the dog to be fed.* Well done! I'm glad we chewed the fat!
- The bug **fascinated** Margaret because . . . it was plain and ordinary. *Chew the fat.* I'll say the first part of the sentence again. The bug fascinated Margaret because . . . (Idea: *It was beautiful and interesting.*) Let's say the whole sentence together. *The bug fascinated Margaret because it was beautiful and interesting.* Well done!
- Our **substitute** teacher was . . . our regular teacher. *Chew the fat.* I'll say the first part of the sentence again. Our substitute teacher was . . . (Idea: *Not our regular teacher.*) Let's say the whole sentence together. *Our substitute teacher was not our regular teacher.* Well done! I'm glad we chewed the fat!
- Lizzie's green sweater was her **favorite** because . . . she liked it the most. *Well done!*
- You will know that your work is **perfect** when . . . there are no mistakes in it. *Well done!*

- When Mr. McMaster donated some clothes to a charity, he . . . threw them in the trash. *Chew the fat.* I'll say the first part of the sentence again. When Mr. McMaster donated some clothes to a charity, he . . . (Idea: *Gave them to people who needed them.*) Let's say the whole sentence together. *When Mr. McMaster donated some clothes to a charity, he gave them to people who needed them.* Well done! I'm glad we chewed the fat!
- **Property** is . . . something that doesn't belong to you. *Chew the fat.* I'll say the first part of the sentence again. Property is . . . (Idea: *Something that belongs to you.*) Let's say the whole sentence together. *Property is something that belongs to you.* Well done! I'm glad we chewed the fat!

(Count the points, and declare a winner.) You did a great job of playing Chew the Fat!

DAY 5

Preparation: Happy Face Game Test Sheet, BLM B.

Study the Artwork

Most illustrators make their pictures to go with the words of a book. But Jane Bregoli's art is different. Before the paintings in *The Goat Lady* were used in this book, they hung in art galleries and on people's walls. How are Jane Bregoli's paintings different from most illustrations? (Idea: *They started out as paintings that hung in art galleries and on people's walls.*)

The first three paintings I will show you are paintings of Noelie Houle. A painting of a person is called a portrait. What do you call a painting of a person? *A portrait.* (Show children the portraits on the cover, on the inside title page, and on page 6.) All of these portraits were made with oil paints. How were all of these portraits made? *With oil paints.*

Oil paints are hard to work with. They can take many days to dry. So Jane Bergoli decided to make the rest of her paintings using watercolors. What did Jane Bergoli use to make the rest of her paintings? *Watercolors.*

(Display the painting on page 12.) This is how Jane Bergoli paints her pictures. First she draws a plan on a separate piece of paper. What does she do first? (Idea: *She draws a plan on a separate sheet of paper.*)

Then she uses a pencil to draw a very light outline on her good paper. What does she do next? (Idea: *She uses a pencil to draw a very light outline on her good paper.*)

Next she fills in the big spaces with watercolor, using big brushes. What does she do next? (Idea: *She fills in the big spaces with watercolor, using big brushes.*) Show me a space you think Jane Bergoli might have painted with a big brush. (Ideas: *The pink on the blanket; the grey door; the brown wall; the brown ground.*)

While those big spaces are drying, she works on smaller spaces with medium-sized brushes. She lets layer after layer of paint dry, and then she goes over it again. That way she can change the color if it doesn't look right. Show me a space you think Jane Bergoli might have painted with a medium-sized brush. (Ideas: *The goats; the edges of the door.*)

Finally, she uses very small brushes to add the details. What does she do last? (Idea: *She uses very small brushes to add the details.*) What kinds of details might she add with her small brushes? (Ideas: *The faces of the goats; the different shades of white on the goats' fur; the design on the blanket; the nails on the door.*)

Adding the details is one of Jane Bergoli's favorite parts of the paintings. What's her favorite part? (Idea: *Adding the details.*)

Here's one of Jane Bergoli's special tricks. Sometimes she scrapes off some of the paint with a razor blade so you can see the white paper that got filled in with the paint by mistake. This gives her paintings white highlights. Can you find a place on this painting where Jane Bergoli might have used this trick? (Idea: *On the mother goat's beard; on her legs; on the legs of the kids.*)

Let me show you Jane Bregoli's paintings one more time. When I'm finished, I'll ask you which of the paintings is your favorite, and why it's your favorite. (Display the illustrations page by page,

pausing with each new painting. When you have shown all the paintings, encourage children to share their favorite painting using words similar to these: "My favorite painting in *The Goat Lady* is _____. I like this painting because _____.")

Assess Vocabulary

 (Hold up a copy of the Happy Face Game Test Sheet, BLM B.)

Today you're going to play the Happy Face Game. When you play the Happy Face Game, it helps me know how well you know the hard words you are learning.

If I say something true, color the happy face. What will you do if I say something true? *Color the happy face.*

If I say something false, color the sad face. What will you do if I say something false? *Color the sad face.*

Listen carefully to each item I say. Don't let me trick you!

Item 1: **Fascinated** means that you find something boring and not worth looking at. *False.*

Item 2: When you **donated,** you gave something to others. *True.*

Item 3: **Triplets** are six people who are born at the same time, in different places, and to different mothers. *False.*

Item 4: A **chore** is a job you do every day to keep things running smoothly. *True.*

Item 5: You know you have **courage** when you are brave in a scary situation. *True.*

Item 6: A **nuisance** is something that bothers you. *True.*

Item 7: When something you are doing feels like a **chore,** it means that it is difficult and hard to do. *True.*

Item 8: If you have a **talent** for playing the piano, you have a special skill. *True.*

Item 9: If an animal is wild, it is **tame** and you can keep it in your house. *False.*

Item 10: If someone has a brand new bike but you do not, you might feel **jealous.** *True.*

You did a great job of playing the Happy Face Game!

(Score children's work later. Scores of 9 out of 10 indicate mastery. If a child does not achieve mastery, insert the missed words in the games in the next week's lessons. Retest those children individually on the missed words before they take the next mastery test.)

Extensions

Read a Story as a Reward

(Display several books you have read since the beginning of the program. Allow children to choose which book they would like you to read aloud to them as a reward for their hard work.)

(Read the story aloud to children for enjoyment with minimal interruptions.)

Present Super Words Center

(Prepare the word containers for the Super Words Center. You may wish to remove some of the words from earlier lessons. Choose words that children have mastered. See the Introduction for instructions on how to set up and use the Super Words Center.)

(Add the new Picture Vocabulary Cards to the words from the previous weeks. Show children one of the word containers. If they need more guidance in how to work in the Super Words Center, role-play with two or three children as a demonstration.)

Today let's remember how to play a game called What's New?

Let's think about how we work with our words in the Super Words Center.

You will work with a partner in the Super Words Center. Whom will you work with in the center? *A partner.*

First, one partner will draw four word cards out of the container and put them on the table so both partners can see. What do you do first? (Idea: *Draw four cards out of the container and put them on the table so both partners can see.*)

Next you will take turns looking at the cards and saying the words the pictures show. What will you do next? (Idea: *We will take turns looking at the cards and saying the words the pictures show.*)

Next, partner 2 looks away while partner 1 takes one of the four cards and places it back in the container. Then partner 1 draws a new card from the container and places it on the table with the other three. Watch while I show you what I mean. (Demonstrate this process with one child as your partner.) When you put down the new card, it's a good idea to mix the cards so they aren't in the same places any more. (Demonstrate as you go.)

Now partner 1 says, "What's New?" Partner 2 has to use his or her eyes and brain and say what new word card has been put down. If partner 2 is correct, he or she gets a point. If partner 2 is not correct, partner 1 gets the point. (Demonstrate as you go.)

Next, partner 2 has a turn to choose four different cards, and the game starts again. What happens next? (Idea: *Partner 2 has a turn to choose four different cards, and the game starts again.*)

Have fun playing What's New!

Week 33

Preparation: You will need *Beatrice's Goat* for each day's lesson.

Number the pages of the story, beginning with the two-page illustration before the text begins, to assist you in asking questions at appropriate points.

Post a copy of the Vocabulary Tally Sheet with this week's Picture Vocabulary Cards attached.

Each child will need the Homework Sheet, BLM 33a.

Beatrice's Goat
author: Page McBrier • illustrator: Lori Lohstoeter

◎ Target Vocabulary

Tier II	Tier III
nervous	dedication
sturdy	afterword
patiently	
politely	
*hope	
*responsible	

*Expanded Target Vocabulary Word

- Where do you think the story happens?
- When do you think the story happens?
- Why do you think the girl is sitting beside a goat?
- How do you think the girl feels?
- Do you think this story is about real people? Tell why or why not.

(Call on several children to share their predictions with the class.)

Take a Picture Walk

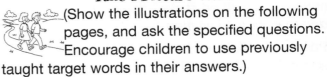 (Show the illustrations on the following pages, and ask the specified questions. Encourage children to use previously taught target words in their answers.)

We are going to take a picture walk through this book. Remember, when we take a picture walk, we look at the pictures and tell what we think will happen in the story.

Pages 1–2. Where do you think this story takes place? (Ideas: *Somewhere warm; in the country, Africa.*) Why do you think so? (Ideas: *The only trees are palm trees; there are no houses; the woman is carrying bananas on her head; the road is made of dirt.*)

Page 4. Where do you think the woman is now? (Ideas: *In her village; in her town.*) What do you see in this picture? (Ideas: *Houses; children playing; chickens; a woman carrying bananas on her head and a baby on her back.*)

DAY 1

Introduce Book

This week's book is called *Beatrice's Goat*. What's the title of this week's book? *Beatrice's Goat.*

This book was written by Page McBrier. Who's the author of *Beatrice's Goat*? *Page McBrier.*

Lori Lohstoeter made the pictures for this book. Who's the illustrator of *Beatrice's Goat*? *Lori Lohstoeter.* Who made the illustrations for this book? *Lori Lohstoeter.*

The cover of a book usually gives us some hints of what the book is about. Let's look at the front cover of *Beatrice's Goat*. What do you see in the illustration? (Ideas: *A girl in a colorful dress sitting beside a black-and-white goat; palm trees; blue sky; countryside; houses.*)

(Assign each child a partner.) Remember, when you make a prediction about something, you say what you think will happen. Get ready to make some predictions to your partner about this book. Use the information from the cover to help you.

(Ask the following questions, allowing sufficient time for children to share their predictions with their partners.)

- Who are the characters in this story? (Whom do you think this story is about?)
- What do you think the girl is doing?

Pages 5–6. What do you see here? (Ideas: *A girl in a bright dress petting a goat.*) How do you think the girl is feeling? (Ideas: *Happy; content.*) Why do you think so? (Ideas: *She is smiling; she looks happy to be with the goat.*)

Pages 7–8. What is the girl doing? (Idea: *Feeding geese and chickens.*) What are the people on the hill doing? (Ideas: *Working; digging with sticks; planting food.*) What is the baby doing? (Idea: *Playing with the baby chicks.*)

Page 9. Whom do you think the girl is watching? (Ideas: *A group of children listening to somebody; children at school.*) Why do you think so? (Ideas: *They are sitting on benches; the woman is holding a book.*) What do you see in the background of this picture? (Ideas: *Buildings; many people around the buildings.*)

Page 12. What do you see in this picture? (Ideas: *A woman holding a baby with another child behind her; the girl is planting something in the ground, or maybe weeding the garden.*)

Pages 13–14. What do you see the people doing on these two pages? (Ideas: *Cutting plants; planting something in the ground.*) What do you think the houses are made out of? (Ideas: *Grass; straw; wood.*) Why do you think the houses are built on sticks? (Ideas: *To keep them dry; to keep wild animals out.*)

Pages 15–16. How do you think the goat feels about the girl? (Idea: *It likes her.*) Why do you think so? (Idea: *The goat is licking the girl's face.*) How do you think the girl feels about the goat? (Idea: *She likes it.*) Why do you think so? (Ideas: *She is sitting with the goat and smiling; she is petting the goat.*) How many baby goats do you see? *Two.*

Pages 17–18. What are the people doing? (Idea: *Eating a meal.*) What is the woman outside doing? (Ideas: *Stirring something in a pot; cooking.*) How many children do you count? (Idea: *Six.*)

Pages 19–20. What is the girl doing? (Idea: *Pouring milk into a container for the boy.*) What are the goats doing? (Idea: *Eating.*)

Pages 21–22. What do you think the girl is carrying? (Idea: *Water cans.* **Note:** If children identify the water cans as suitcases, do not

correct them; they will find out they are water cans when they hear the story.) What is the woman doing? (Idea: *Counting coins.*) How do you think the girl feels? (Ideas: *Upset; worried; surprised.*)

Pages 23–24. How do you think the girl feels now? (Ideas: *Overjoyed; happy; excited; grateful.*) What makes you think so? (Ideas: *She's laughing; she's embracing the woman; she's hugging the goat.*)

Pages 25–26. What is different about the girl? (Idea: *She's wearing different clothes.*) How important do you think the goat is to the girl? (Idea: *Very important.*) Why do you think so? (Ideas: *She's holding the goat close to her.*)

Pages 27–28. Whom do you think the girl is talking to? (Ideas: *Her friend; a neighbor.*) How do you think the goat feels about the girl? (Idea: *It likes her.*) Why do you think so? (Idea: *The goat is putting its nose into the girl's hand.*)

Pages 29–30. What do you think the girl might be saying to the goat? (Ideas: *Goodbye; thank you; be good.*) Where do you think the girl is going? (Idea: *To school.*) Why do you think so? (Idea: *She's at the same place where the children were listening to the teacher under the tree.*)

Now that we've finished our picture walk, it's your turn to ask me some questions. What would you like to know about the story? (Accept questions. If children tell about the pictures or the story instead of asking questions, prompt them to ask a question.) Ask me a what question. Ask me a how question.

Read Story Aloud
(Read story aloud to children with minimal interruptions.)

In the next lesson, we will read the story again, and I will ask you some questions.

Present Target Vocabulary

Nervous.

In the story, Beatrice feels nervous as she gets ready for her first day at school. That means she feels anxious and a little bit afraid. **Nervous.** Say the word. *Nervous.*

Nervous is a describing word. It tells about how a person feels. What kind of word is **nervous**? *A describing word.*

If you are nervous, you feel anxious and a little bit afraid. You already know what anxious means. What word means to "really, really want to do something or want something to happen"? *Anxious.* That's right. Beatrice really, really wanted to go to school. Say the word that means "anxious and a little bit afraid." *Nervous.*

(Correct any incorrect responses, and repeat the item at the end of the sequence.)

Let's think about some times when someone might feel nervous. I'll tell about a time. If you think the person would be feeling nervous, say, "Nervous." If not, don't say anything.

- Tina is going to have her very first sleepover at a friend's house. *Nervous.*
- Marcus thinks that the needle at the doctor's office might hurt. *Nervous.*
- Everything is going well, and I am having an amazing day.
- Some of the people in the crowd don't look very nice at all. *Nervous.*
- On the first day of school, I feel anxious and a little bit afraid. *Nervous.*
- Harry laughs and shouts, "I'm fine!" as he goes down the waterslide.

What describing word means "anxious and a little bit afraid"? *Nervous.*

Tell me about something that makes you nervous. (Call on several children. Encourage them to start their answers with the words "It makes me nervous when _____.")

◎═ Sturdy.

In the story, Beatrice lives "with her mother and five younger brothers and sisters in a sturdy mud house with a fine steel roof." That means they live in a house that is strong and well-built. **Sturdy.** Say the word. *Sturdy.*

Sturdy is a describing word. It tells more about a thing. What kind of word is **sturdy**? *A describing word.*

If something is sturdy, it is strong and well-built. Say the word that means "strong and well-built." *Sturdy.*

(Correct any incorrect responses, and repeat the item at the end of the sequence.)

Let's think about some things that might be sturdy. I'll name something. If you think what I've named is sturdy, say, "Sturdy." If not, don't say anything.

- The bookshelf has more than one hundred books on it. *Sturdy.*
- The wind doesn't blow any pieces off the roof. *Sturdy.*
- The shed we built falls down in the first heavy snow.
- The toy breaks after about five minutes.
- The barn was built in 1797. That means it is more than 200 years old! *Sturdy.*
- "That bridge doesn't look very well built," says the engineer.

What describing word means "strong and well-built? *Sturdy.*

◎═ Patiently.

In the story, Beatrice's "long fingers tugged patiently at the weeds." That means she pulls the weeds without getting angry or upset by the big chore she has. **Patiently.** Say the word. *Patiently.*

Patiently is a describing word. It tells about how someone does something. What kind of word is **patiently**? *A describing word.*

If you do something patiently, you do a job without complaining or getting angry or upset by how long it is taking. Say the word that means "how you act when you do a job without complaining or getting angry or upset by how long it is taking." *Patiently.*

(Correct any incorrect responses, and repeat the item at the end of the sequence.)

Let's think about some things that you might have to do patiently. I'll tell about a job someone is doing. If you think that person is doing the job patiently, say, "Patiently." If not, don't say anything.

- The class sits quietly with their hands folded on their laps while the teacher passes out their new books. *Patiently.*
- All the three-year-olds start to wail and cry because they don't get their food right away.

- The people waiting in the doctor's office don't complain or get upset. *Patiently.*
- Nestor has to paint the door five times to make it look good, but he never complains about how long it is taking. *Patiently.*
- Mr. Williams shouts and stomps when it takes longer than he expects to fix his tire.
- Maria waits for just the right day with just the right amount of wind to fly her new kite. *Patiently.*

What describing word means "how you act when you do a job without complaining or getting angry or upset by how long it is taking"? *Patiently.*

◎← Politely.

In the story, when Beatrice's mama tells her about the gift of the goat, Beatrice says politely, "That's very nice, Mama," even though she can't figure out how a goat could be a lucky gift. If Beatrice speaks politely, she uses her best manners to talk to her mother. **Politely.** Say the word. *Politely.*

Politely is a describing word. It tells about how someone says something. What kind of word is **politely?** *A describing word.*

If you say something politely, you speak using your best manners. Say the word that means "how you speak when you use your best manners." *Politely.*

(Correct any incorrect responses, and repeat the item at the end of the sequence.)

I'll tell you what someone said. If you think that person spoke politely, say, "Politely." If not, don't say anything.

- Keith says, "Grandpa, please pass me the potatoes." *Politely.*
- Give me that right now!
- Why can't you put your own socks on?
- Oh, that's okay—everybody has trouble with one thing or another. Let me help you. *Politely.*
- Mandy says, "Would you kindly stop beating on the drums? I really need to work on my homework. Thank you!" *Politely.*
- You'd better stop that before I come over there!

What describing word means "how you speak when you use your best manners"? *Politely.*

What words might I hear if you were speaking politely? (Call on several children. Ideas: *Please; thank you; may I; you're welcome; excuse me.*)

Present Vocabulary Tally Sheet
(See Week 1, page 3, for instructions.)

Assign Homework
(Homework Sheet, BLM 33a: See the Introduction for homework instructions.)

DAY 2

Preparation: Picture Vocabulary Cards for *nervous, sturdy, patiently,* and *politely.*

Read and Discuss Story

(Read story aloud to children. Ask the following questions at the specified points in the story. Encourage children to use previously taught target words in their answers.)

Page 3. Where does this story take place? (Ideas: *In Africa; in a village called Kisinga in Uganda.* You may wish to show children where Africa and Uganda are on a map or globe in relationship to the location of the school.) When does this part of the story take place? (Ideas: *Right now; in the present.*) What is new in Beatrice's life? (Ideas: *Her house; her furniture; many things.*)

Page 5. What is the name of the goat? *Mugisa.* What does Beatrice love about the goat? (Ideas: *Everything; the feel of her brown-and-white coat; the way her chin hairs curl; how Mugisa teases her.*)

Page 8. When does this part of the story take place? (Idea: *Before they got Mugisa.*) What did Beatrice do in the time before Mugisa? (Ideas: *Helped her mama hoe and plant in the fields; tended the chickens; watched the younger children; ground the cassava flour they took to market.*)

Page 10. Where did Beatrice stop sometimes? (Idea: *At the schoolhouse.*) Why couldn't Beatrice go to school? (Idea: *She didn't have enough money for books or a uniform.*)

Page 11. What lucky gift does Beatrice's family get? (Idea: *A goat.*) Does Beatrice think the goat will be very useful? (Idea: *No.*) Why does she think so? (Idea: *It can't do any chores or look after the younger children.*) What has to be done to get ready for the goat? (Ideas: *Plant pastures; build a goat shed.*)

Page 14. How does Beatrice help her mother get ready for the goat? (Ideas: *She works harder than ever; she helps Mama collect the posts for the shed walls; she ties the posts together with banana fibers; she plants elephant grass; she puts in pigeon trees and lab lab vines between the banana trees.*)

Page 15. What does the goat look like when it arrives? (Idea: *Fat and sleek as a ripe mango.*) What does the name Mugisa mean? (Idea: *Luck.*) What do the names of the baby goats mean? (Idea: *Expected and surprise.*) What does Beatrice do to help Mugisa produce lots of milk? (Idea: *She gets extra elephant grass and water.*)

Page 20. What does Beatrice do with the extra goat's milk? (Idea: *She sells it.*) Who buys the milk? (Idea: *Her friend Bunane.*) What is Beatrice hoping to buy with the money she saves from selling milk? (Ideas: *A new shirt for Moses; a warm blanket for the bed she shares with Grace.*)

Pages 21–22. What is Beatrice collecting in the containers? *Water.* What does Beatrice think when she sees Mama frowning and counting the money? (Idea: *She thinks something is wrong.*)

(**Note:** If children identified the water cans as suitcases during the picture walk, say:) If Beatrice is returning from collecting water, what do you think is in the containers she is carrying? (Idea: *Water.*) If you look closely you can see where lids have been screwed onto the cans.

Page 24. What does Mama say Beatrice has saved enough money to do? (Idea: *Pay for school.*) Why is Beatrice so grateful to the goat? (Idea: *The goat has given her the present she wants most—to go to school.*)

Page 25. What is Beatrice so proud of when she sits waiting for the milk customers? (Ideas: *Her new yellow blouse and blue jumper; her new school uniform.*) How does Beatrice feel about going to school? (Ideas: *Nervous; excited.*) What other good things will Mugisa bring? (Idea: *Selling Surprise will give them enough money to buy a new house with a steel roof that won't leak during the rains.*)

Page 28. Why does Bunane say Beatrice is so lucky? (Idea: *She can go to school.*) What good news has Beatrice heard about Bunane's family? (Idea: *They are next in line to receive a goat.*)

Page 29. Why do you think Beatrice gives Mugisa a kiss before going to school? (Idea: *To say goodbye to the goat; to say thank you to the goat.*)

When Page McBrier wrote this story, she wanted to send us a special message. What do you think was the special message that Page McBrier sent to us? (Idea: *A small gift can make a big difference in someone's life.*)

Review Vocabulary

(Display the Picture Vocabulary Cards. Point to each card as you say the word. Ask children to repeat each word after you.) These pictures show **nervous, sturdy, patiently,** and **politely.**

- What describing word means "how you speak when you use your best manners"? *Politely.*
- What describing word means "how you act when you do a job without complaining or getting angry or upset by how long it is taking"? *Patiently.*
- What describing word means "anxious and a little bit afraid"? *Nervous.*
- What describing word means "strong and well-built"? *Sturdy.*

Extend Vocabulary

◎← Sturdy.

In the story *Beatrice's Goat* we learned sturdy is a word that describes things that are strong and well-built. Say the word that means something is "strong and well-built." *Sturdy.*

Raise your hand if you can tell us a sentence that uses **sturdy** as a describing word that means something is "strong and well-built." (Call on several children. If they don't use complete sentences, restate their examples as sentences. Have the class repeat the sentences.)

Here's a new way to use the word **sturdy.**

- **The little boy ran around on his sturdy legs.** Say the sentence.
- **A weight lifter has a sturdy body.** Say the sentence.
- **The sturdy lambs bounced around their mothers.** Say the sentence.

In these sentences, **sturdy** is a describing word that means a person or an animal is **strong and powerful.** What describing word means "strong and powerful"? *Sturdy.*

Raise your hand if you can tell us a sentence that uses **sturdy** to describe people or animals that are strong and powerful. (Call on several children. If they don't use complete sentences, restate their examples as sentences. Have the class repeat the sentences.)

Present Expanded Target Vocabulary
◎━ *Hope.*

In the story *Beatrice's Goat,* the present of the goat helps feed the family and helps them earn money so they can buy the things they need. The gift of the goat brings hope to Beatrice's family that they will have a better life. **Hope.** Say the word. *Hope.*

Hope is a naming word. It names a feeling. What kind of word is **hope?** *A naming word.*

Hope is a feeling you have when you believe and expect that things will get better. Say the word that means "a feeling you have when you believe and expect that things will get better." *Hope.*

I'll tell about some people. If those people have hope, say, "Hope." If not don't say anything.

- Timmy believes that his dad will get a new job. *Hope.*
- Steve believes that his soldier brother will come home safe and sound. *Hope.*
- The cat believes that its owner will remember to give it some supper. *Hope.*
- I don't expect I'll get any money back if my computer breaks.

- Lara expects that it will rain so that her plants will grow. *Hope.*
- Nothing is good. Everything is bad, and I think it is going to stay that way!

What naming word means "a feeling you have when you believe and expect that things will get better"? *Hope.*

◎━ *Responsible.*

In the story *Beatrice's Goat,* Beatrice looks after her younger brothers and sisters. She helps hoe and plant the fields. She helps grind the flour they take to the market. She helps build a shed for the goat. She makes sure Mugisa gets extra elephant grass. She walks to the stream and carries back water so Mugisa can make enough milk for both kids. She sells the extra milk and gives the money to her mama. She has many, many jobs and she does them properly without her mama checking up on her. Beatrice is a very responsible girl. **Responsible.** Say the word. *Responsible.*

Responsible is a describing word. It tells about someone. What kind of word is **responsible?** *A describing word.*

If you are a responsible person, you do your jobs properly and carefully without having anyone check up on you. Say the word that means "do your jobs properly and carefully without having anyone check up on you." *Responsible.*

I'll tell about some people. If you think those people are responsible, say, "Responsible." If not, don't say anything.

- Owen sets the table for supper without being asked. *Responsible.*
- Belinda stays in at recess to finish her work the way she likes. *Responsible.*
- John walks away and leaves the door open and the water running.
- Gino doesn't really care how well the job is done—he just wants to go home.
- No one checks up on Josie because she is known to do her work well. *Responsible.*
- Ichiro [i-**cheer**-oh] always plays his drums the very best that he can so the band sounds right. *Responsible.*

What describing word means "do your jobs properly and carefully without having anyone check up on you"? *Responsible.*

DAY 3

Preparation: Activity Sheet, BLM 33b. Children will need their crayons.

Retell Story

(Show the pictures on the following pages from the story, and call on a child to tell what's happening. Call on a different child for each section.)

When Page McBrier wrote the story *Beatrice's Goat,* she started the story in the present, then went back and told what happened before. Today I'll show you the pictures Lori Lohstoeter made for the story *Beatrice's Goat.* But I will show them to you in time order. As I show you the pictures, I'll call on one of you to tell the class that part of the story.

Pages 8–9. Tell what happens at the **beginning** of the story.

Pages 12–30. Tell what happens in the **middle** of the story. (Encourage use of target words when appropriate. Model use as necessary.)

Pages 4–6. Tell what happens at the **end** of the story.

Review Show Me, Tell Me Game

Today you will play the Show Me, Tell Me Game. I'll ask you to show me how to do something. If you show me, you win one point. If you can't show me, I get the point.

Next I'll ask you to tell me. If you tell me, you win one point. If you can't tell me, I get the point.

Let's practice: My turn to show you how I would look if I was **nervous** about going to the dentist. (Show a nervous face.) How am I feeling? *Nervous.*

Let's do one together. Show me how you would look if you waited **patiently** for your homework. (Sit quietly with your hands folded.) What did we do? *Waited patiently.*

Now you're ready to play the game.

(Draw a T-chart on the board for keeping score. Children earn one point for each correct answer. If they make an error, demonstrate the action, and tell them the word. Record one point for yourself, and repeat missed items at the end of the game.)

- Show me how you would look if you handed out pencils in a **responsible** way. Tell me what you're doing. *Handing out pencils in a responsible way.*
- Show me how you would walk on a **sturdy** bridge. Tell me what you did. *Walked on a sturdy bridge.*
- Show me how your face would look if you had **hope** that the teacher had brought cookies to school. Tell me what look is on your face. *Hope.*
- Show me how you would lift a heavy box with **sturdy** arms. Tell me what you are doing. *Lifting a heavy box with sturdy arms.*
- Show me how you would look if you were **nervous** about going fast down a very steep mountain. Tell me how you are feeling. *Nervous.*

(Count the points, and declare a winner.)
You did a great job of playing the Show Me, Tell Me Game!

Complete Activity Sheet

(Give each child a copy of the Activity Sheet, BLM 33b. Review the order of the story with children. Tell them to place the pictures in sequence to show beginning, middle, and end. Instruct children to color the pictures, cut them out, and paste or glue them in order of beginning, middle, and end.)

Literary Analysis (Story Patterns)

When authors write stories, they sometimes write in patterns. Let's see if we can figure out the pattern for this story. You tell me what happens in the story, and I'll write it down.

(Show the illustrations on the following pages, and ask the specified questions.)

Page 4. What important thing happens at the beginning of the story? (Ideas: *Beatrice's family lives in a fine <u>new home</u>.*)

Page 6. Why do they have such a fine new home? (Idea: *Because of <u>Mugisa</u>.*)

Pages 7–8. What does Beatrice do every day? (Ideas: *Hoes and plants the fields; tends the chickens; watches the younger children; makes flour.*) That's right. <u>Beatrice works hard</u>.

Page 9. What does Beatrice really want to do? (Idea: *She <u>wants</u> to go to <u>school</u>.*)

Page 11. Then what news does Beatrice's mama bring? (Idea: *They have been given the <u>gift</u> of a <u>goat</u>.*)

Page 16. Then what happens? (Idea: *The goat has <u>twin kids</u>.*)

Pages 17–18. Then what happens? (Idea: *The family has milk to <u>drink</u>.*)

Page 19. Then what happens? (Idea: *They have <u>milk</u> to <u>sell</u>.*)

Pages 21–24. What good news does Beatrice get? (Idea: *She can go to <u>school</u>.*)

Page 27. What news does Beatrice have for Bunane? (Idea: *<u>Bunane</u> will be <u>getting</u> a <u>goat</u>.*)

Pages 29–30. Then what happens? (Idea: *<u>Beatrice goes to school</u>.*)

(Point to the story map on the chart paper. Draw a line under the first two boxes.) Where should these two boxes be? (Idea: *At the end of the story.* Draw an arrow above the boxes to the end of the story.)

Look at the shape of this story. It's a line. This story starts and ends at a different time, so this story has a **linear** pattern. What kind of story pattern starts and ends at a different time? *A linear pattern.* But because the story started in the present and then went back in time, it is a special kind of linear pattern called a flashback. What kind of linear pattern is *Beatrice's Goat*? *A flashback linear pattern.*

What are some other stories we've read that have a linear pattern? *Wake Up, Farm! Jamaica and the Substitute Teacher.*

Let's sing "The Pattern Song" to help us remember about story patterns.

(See the Introduction for the complete "Pattern Song.")

Singing a song together is a very good way to remember the patterns we learned!

Play Show Me, Tell Me Game (Cumulative Review)

Let's play the Show Me, Tell Me Game. I'll ask you to show me how to do something. If you show me, you win one point. If you can't show me, I get the point.

Next I'll ask you to tell me. If you tell me, you win one point. If you can't tell me, I get the point.

Now you're ready to play the game.

(Draw a T-chart on the board for keeping score. Children earn one point for each correct answer. If they make an error, correct them as you normally would, and record one point for yourself. Repeat missed words at the end of the game.)

- Show me what you would do if you were **responsible** and stayed in to finish your work at recess. Tell me what you did. *We were responsible.*

- Show me how you would look if you were feeling **nervous** about getting a shot from the school nurse. Tell me how you are feeling. *Nervous.*

- Show me how you would walk if you walked on a **sturdy** log. Tell me what kind of log it was. *Sturdy.*
- Show me how you would act **politely** when a visitor comes to our classroom. Tell me what you did. *Acted politely.*
- Show me how you would look if you had **hope** that the class would be getting a special treat tomorrow. Tell me what you were feeling. *Hope.*
- Show me how you would wait **patiently** for me to read aloud to you. Tell me how you waited. *Patiently.*
- Show me how you would jump on **sturdy** legs. Tell me what you jumped on. *Sturdy legs.*
- Show me how you would smell a **fragrant** flower. Tell me what you did. *Smelled a fragrant flower.*
- Show me how you look when you **snuggle** with your favorite stuffed animal. Tell me what you did. *Snuggled.*
- Show me how you would look if you were showing me an **injury** on your arm. Tell what you did. *Showed you an injury on my arm.*

(Count the points, and declare a winner.) You did a great job of playing the Show Me, Tell Me Game!

DAY 5

Happy Face Game Test Sheet, BLM B.

Review Dedication

If you dedicate a book to someone, you put that person's name at the front of the book to say thank you for helping and encouraging you. The words you write when you dedicate a book to someone are called the dedication. Today I'll read the dedications that Page McBrier and Lori Lohstoeter wrote for *Beatrice's Goat.*

(Read aloud the dedication by Page McBrier.) Whom did Page McBrier dedicate this book to? (Idea: *Her mother.*) Why did she dedicate the book to her mother? (Ideas: *Her mother taught her to care about all the world's children.*)

(Read aloud the dedication by Lori Lohstoeter.) Whom did Lori Lohstoeter dedicate this book

to? (Idea: *Geia.*) Who is Geia? (Idea: *Lori Lohstoeter's sister.*) Why did she dedicate the book to her sister? (Ideas: *Because she's everyone's sweetheart; because she's good to everyone; because Lori loves her.*)

Review Afterword

(Assign each child a partner.) Sometimes after people finish writing a story about something that is real, they want to tell you more facts about that real thing. This information is put in the book **after** the last **word** of the story, so it is called an **afterword.**

The story *Beatrice's Goat* is make-believe. It was made from the author's imagination. When a story is made up from the author's imagination, we say the story is fiction. What do we call a story that is made up from the author's imagination? *Fiction.*

The afterword tells us true facts about how some people are given goats to help them. Facts are things that are true and that can be proved. For example, it is a fact that hands have fingers. We can prove that fact by looking at our hands.

When part of a book tells true facts about something, that part of the book is called nonfiction. What do we call the parts of books that tell true facts about something? *Nonfiction.*

Most of the time, the author writes the afterword. But sometimes the author asks someone else to write the afterword. Does the author always write the afterword? *No.* Who might write the afterword? *Someone the author asks.*

Today I'll read the afterword aloud to you so you can learn more about Heifer International. Heifer International is the group of people who gave Beatrice her goat.

Hillary Rodham Clinton wrote the afterword for *Beatrice's Goat.* Who wrote the afterword for *Beatrice's Goat*? *Hillary Rodham Clinton.*

(**Note:** Identifying the main idea is a complex skill for young children. If children have difficulty telling you the main idea, use the format in Day 2 of Week 26.)

(Read the afterword aloud a paragraph at a time.)

Paragraph 1. Remember, the main idea is the reason this part was written. What is the main idea? *The reason this part was written.* Let's try to figure out the main idea for this part. When Hillary Clinton wrote this part of the afterword, what do you think she wanted us to know? (Idea: *Families can make their lives better if they get some help.*) That's right; so the main idea found in this part of the afterword is that families can make their lives better if they get some help. What is the main idea found in this part of the afterword? *Families can make their lives better if they get some help.*

Paragraph 2. Remember, the main idea is the reason this part was written. What is the main idea? *The reason this part was written.* Let's try to figure out the main idea for this part. When Hillary Clinton wrote this part of the afterword, what do you think she wanted us to know? (Idea: *Beatrice and her family and the other families of their village have better lives because Heifer International gave them a goat.*) That's right; so the main idea in this part of the afterword is that Beatrice and her family and the other families of their village have better lives because Heifer International gave them a goat.

Paragraph 3. Remember, the main idea is the reason this part was written. What is the main idea? *The reason this part was written.* Let's try to figure out the main idea for this part. When Ms. Clinton wrote this part of the afterword, what do you think she wanted us to know? (Idea: *We should all do what we can to help children grow up with good health, education, and a future.*) That's right; so the main idea in this part of the afterword is that we should all do what we can to help children grow up with good health, education and a future. What is the main idea found in this part of the afterword? *We should all do what we can to help children grow up with good health, education, and a future.*

We have learned many facts about Heifer International from this afterword. Think about the one fact that you thought was most interesting. (Pause.) Share that fact with your partner. (Pause.) Tonight you will share that fact with someone at your home.

In what other story did we read about Heifer International? (Idea: *The Goat Lady.*) Whom did Noelie Houle give her extra kids to? *Heifer International.* Do you think Mugisa could have been one of Noelie's goats? Tell why or why not.

Now that we have read the story about Beatrice and found out about Heifer International, do you think this story is fiction or nonfiction? Why do you think so? (Accept either response as long as children give a reason for their answer.)

You're all right. This story is fiction because some of it is made up from the author's imagination. The words Beatrice, her mama, and Bunane say were made up by Page McBrier. What part of the story is made up? (Idea: *The words the characters say.*)

But parts of the story are true. There was a girl named Beatrice who got a goat from Heifer International. The goat helped Beatrice's family and other families in her village. What parts of the story are true? (Ideas: *Beatrice, Mugisa, Heifer International.*)

Assess Vocabulary

 (Hold up a copy of the Happy Face Game Test Sheet, BLM B.)

Today you're going to play the Happy Face Game. When you play the Happy Face Game, it helps me know how well you know the hard words you are learning.

If I say something true, color the happy face. What will you do if I say something true? *Color the happy face.*

If I say something false, color the sad face. What will you do if I say something false? *Color the sad face.*

Listen carefully to each item I say. Don't let me trick you!

Item 1: If you are **nervous,** you feel just fine. *False.*

Item 2: A **responsible** person works without needing to be checked on. *True.*

Item 3: If you fidget and yell and whine and cry, you are waiting **patiently.** *False.*

Item 4: Grownups like to be around children who act **politely.** *True.*

Item 5: **Hope** means that you believe that things will get better. *True.*

Item 6: **Sturdy** legs are strong legs. *True.*

Item 7: People have only two **senses:** sight and hearing. *False.*

Item 8: If you **explore,** you want to learn more about a new place or thing. *True.*

Item 9: A **sturdy** building will fall down easily. *False.*

Item 10: If you can't be still and keep moving around, you are feeling **restless.** *True.*

You did a great job of playing the Happy Face Game!

(Score children's work later. Scores of 9 out of 10 indicate mastery. If a child does not achieve mastery, insert the missed words in the games in the next week's lessons. Retest those children individually on the missed items before they take the next mastery test.)

Extensions

Read a Story as a Reward

 (Display several books you have read since the beginning of the program. Allow children to choose which book they would like you to read aloud to them as a reward for their hard work.)

(Read the story aloud to children for enjoyment with minimal interruptions.)

Present Super Words Center

(Prepare the word containers for the Super Words Center. You may wish to remove some of the words from earlier lessons. Choose words that children have mastered. See the Introduction for instructions on how to set up and use the Super Words Center.)

(Add the new Picture Vocabulary Cards to the words from the previous weeks. Show children one of the word containers. If they need more guidance, role-play with two or three children as a demonstration.)

Today I will help you remember how to play What's Missing?

Let's think about how we work with our words in the Super Words Center.

You will work with a partner in the Super Words Center. Whom will you work with in the center? *A partner.*

First, one partner will draw four word cards out of the container and put them on the table so both partners can see. What do you do first? (Idea: *Draw four cards out of the container and put them on the table so both partners can see.*)

Next you will take turns looking at the cards and saying the words the pictures show. What do you do next? (Idea: *We take turns looking at the cards and saying the words the pictures show.*)

Next, partner 2 looks away while partner 1 takes one of the four cards and places it facedown on the table away from the other cards. Then partner 1 draws a new card from the container and places it on the table with the other three.

Watch while I show you what I mean. (Demonstrate with a child as your partner.) When you put down the new card, it's a good idea to mix the cards so they aren't in the same places anymore. (Demonstrate as you go.)

Now partner 1 says, "What's Missing?" Partner 2 has to use his or her eyes and brain and say what old card has been taken away. After partner 2 has guessed, turn over the facedown card. If partner 2 is correct, he or she gets a point. If partner 2 is not correct, partner 1 gets the point. (Demonstrate as you go.)

Next, partner 2 has a turn to choose four different cards, and the game starts again. What happens next? (Idea: *Partner 2 has a turn to choose four different cards, and the game starts again.*)

Have fun playing What's Missing!

Even Firefighters Hug Their Moms

author: Christine Kole MacLean • illustrator: Mike Reed

Preparation: You will need *Even Firefighters Hug Their Moms* for each day's lesson.

Number the pages of the story to assist you in asking questions at appropriate points.

Post a copy of the Vocabulary Tally Sheet, BLM A, with this week's Picture Vocabulary Cards attached.

Each child will need the Homework Sheet, BLM 34a.

🎯 Target Vocabulary

Tier II	Tier III
protective	pattern
emergency	repeating
gigantic	
construction	
*occupations	
*ignore	

*Expanded Target Vocabulary Word

DAY 1

Introduce Book

This week's book is called *Even Firefighters Hug Their Moms*. What's the title of this week's book? *Even Firefighters Hug Their Moms.*

This book was written by Christine Kole MacLean. Who's the author of *Even Firefighters Hug Their Moms*? *Christine Kole MacLean.*

Mike Reed made the pictures for this book. Who's the illustrator of *Even Firefighters Hug Their Moms*? *Mike Reed.* Who made the illustrations for this book? *Mike Reed.*

The cover of a book usually gives us some hints of what the book is about. Let's look at the front cover of *Even Firefighters Hug Their Moms.* What do you see in the illustration? (Ideas: *A child dressed in pajamas, slippers, and red fireman's hat; a child dressed in a yellow raincoat and hat; they are holding a vacuum cleaner.*)

(Assign each child a partner.) Remember, when you make a prediction about something, you say what you think will happen. Get ready to make some predictions to your partner about this book. Use the information from the cover to help you.

(Ask the following questions, allowing sufficient time for children to share their predictions with their partners.)

- Who are the characters in this story? (Whom do you think this story is about?)
- What do you think the children are doing with the vacuum cleaner?
- Where do you think the story happens?
- When do you think the story happens?
- Why do you think the children are wearing coats and hats in the house?
- How do you think the children feel?
- Do you think this story is about real people? Tell why or why not.

(Call on several children to share their predictions with the class.)

Take a Picture Walk

(Show the illustrations on the following pages, and ask the specified questions. Encourage children to use previously taught target words in their answers.)

We are going to take a picture walk through this book. Remember, when we take a picture walk, we look at the pictures and tell what we think will happen in the story.

Pages 1–2. Where do you think this part of the story takes place? (Idea: *In a boy's bedroom.*) Why do you think so? (Ideas: *Stuffed animals, including dinosaurs, are on the bed and everywhere; a fire hydrant lamp is on the table* *beside the bed.*) What is the boy doing? (Idea: *Reading the newspaper.*) There is something strange about the way the boy is reading the newspaper. Can you see what it is? (Idea: *The newspaper is upside down.*) What is the boy wearing on his head? (Idea: *A fireman's hat.*)

Pages 3–4. Where do you think this part of the story takes place? (Idea: *In the living room; in the den.*) What do you think is happening here? (Ideas: *The boy is pretending the sofa is a fire truck; he's driving the sofa; he's pretending he's a firefighter.*) What is the other child doing in this picture? (Ideas: *Sitting at the back of the sofa; riding along at the back of the fire truck.*) What has the artist drawn to make it look like the children are moving fast? (Idea: *Lines of color behind each child.*)

Pages 5–6. What do you see here? (Ideas: *There is a fort made of green sofa cushions with a stuffed bear inside and a pig on top; the children are using a vacuum cleaner hose as a fire hose; a woman is standing beside the pillow fort.*) Whom do you think the children are pretending to be? (Idea: *Firefighters.*)

Pages 7–8. What is happening here? (Ideas: *The boy has a police hat on; he's pulling a wagon filled with stuffed animals; he's talking into a toy microphone.*) Whom do you think the boy is pretending to be? (Idea: *A police officer.*)

Page 9–10. Where are the stuffed animals now? (Ideas: *In a crib; behind bars; in jail.*) Who do you think is talking to the boy? (Idea: *His mother.*) How do you think the boy is feeling talking to his mother? (Ideas: *Worried; upset.*)

Pages 11–12. What do you think the children are pretending in this picture? (Ideas: *They're pretending to be doctors; they're pretending to be ambulance drivers.*) Why do you think so? (Ideas: *The girl is bandaging a stuffed bear on a blanket; the boy is pretending to drive with a basket and a pot lid.*) What is the girl using for bandages and medicine? (Ideas: *Toilet paper; pink ice cream or yogurt.*)

Pages 13–14. Whom do you think the boy is pretending to be? (Idea: *A doctor.*) Why do you think so? (Ideas: *He's wearing a stethoscope; he's examining the bear wrapped in bandages.*)

Why do you think so? Who else do you think is in the picture? (Idea: *The children's mother.*)

Pages 15–16. Wow! What a mess! What do you see in this picture? (Ideas: *A huge pile of cushions on the floor; the boy in a big pink armchair with sticks in front of him; the girl asleep on a cushion; the mother calling something.*) How do you think the girl is feeling? (Idea: *Tired.*) What do you think the mother might be saying? (Ideas: *This is a big mess; clean up the cushions; what are you doing?*)

Pages 17–18. Where do you think this part of the story takes place? (Ideas: *In the kitchen; in the dining room.*) Why do you think so? (Ideas: *They are eating; a glass of milk, a bowl of cereal and a cookie are in the picture; the girl is sitting in a high chair.*) Why do you think the stuffed animals are being held by strings? (Ideas: *They are being rescued; they are on leashes.*) What do you think the children are pretending to be? (Ideas: *Helicopter rescuers.*) Why do you think so? (Idea: *The ceiling fan looks like the blades on a helicopter.*) How do you think the mother is feeling? (Ideas: *Annoyed; frustrated; angry; cross; furious.*)

Pages 19–20. What do you think the boy is pretending to do? (Ideas: *A bus driver; a train conductor; an airplane pilot.*) What makes you think so? (Ideas: *Chairs are set up in rows; animals are sitting on the chairs; the boy is wearing a special hat; the mother is carrying two suitcases; the girl is waiting to get past the boy.*)

Page 21–22. What do you see in this picture? (Ideas: *The boy is in boxes with a big can on his head and rubber gloves on his hands; the girl and mother are inside a big fort made out of cushions and chairs.*) What do you think the children are pretending to be? (Ideas: *Astronauts; scuba divers.*)

Pages 23–24. What is the boy wearing? (Idea: *A paper bag with a picture of the United States flag on it.*) What is the mother doing? (Idea: *Talking to the boy.*) How do you think the girl is feeling? (Ideas: *Upset; sad; worried; tired; left out.*)

Pages 25–26. What is the boy doing? (Idea: *He's throwing toys, books, and a toaster down* *a slide.*) How does the room look? (Idea: *Very messy.*) Does the girl look like she is having fun? *No.* Why do you think so? (Ideas: *She looks like she's upset; she wants the boy to stop throwing things.*)

Pages 27–28. What do you think the mother is saying to the children? (Ideas: *Stop throwing things; clean up this big mess; put your toys away neatly.*) What is the boy giving back to the girl? (Idea: *Her pacifier.*)

Page 29. What is happening here? (Idea: *The boy and his mother are hugging.*) How do you think everybody feels? (Ideas: *Happy; satisfied; content.*)

Now that we've finished our picture walk, it's your turn to ask me some questions. What would you like to know about the story? (Accept questions. If children tell about the pictures or the story instead of asking questions, prompt them to ask a question.) Ask me a what question. Ask me a how question.

Read Story Aloud
(Read story aloud to children with minimal interruptions.)

In the next lesson, we will read the story again, and I will ask you some questions.

Present Target Vocabulary

◎― Protective.

In the story, the little boy dresses up in "protective gear" when he is pretending to be a firefighter. That means he puts on special clothing that will protect him. **Protective.** Say the word. *Protective.*

Protective is a describing word. It tells about something. What kind of word is **protective?** *A describing word.*

If you wear protective gear, you wear clothes that will keep you safe. You already know what **protect** means. What word means "keeps you safe from danger or injury"? *Protect.* That's right. Protective gear also keeps you safe from danger or injury. What word means "gear or clothing that will keep you safe"? *Protective.*

(Correct any incorrect responses, and repeat the item at the end of the sequence.)

Let's think about some things that might be protective. I'll tell about something. If you think that thing is protective, say, "Protective." If not, don't say anything.

- We always wear our seatbelts when the car is moving. *Protective.*
- Ron always puts his helmet on when he is going to ride his bike. *Protective.*
- She should wear a life jacket in the boat. *Protective.*
- I put on a T-shirt and shorts.
- The carpenter wears boots that have steel toes and soles so that nails can't get through. *Protective.*
- Her swimsuit is made of soft, stretchy material.

What describing word means "gear or clothing that will keep you safe"? *Protective.*

◎― Emergency.

In the story, the little boy pretends he is an emergency medical technician. That means his job is to drive an ambulance to places where people are injured, help those who are hurt as much as he can, and take them to the hospital. **Emergency.** Say the word. *Emergency.*

Emergency can be a naming word. It names a thing. What kind of word is **emergency?** *A naming word.*

An emergency is a serious situation that calls for fast action. What naming word means "a serious situation that calls for fast action"? *Emergency.*

(Correct any incorrect responses, and repeat the item at the end of the sequence.)

Let's think about some things that might be emergencies. I'll tell about a situation. If you think that situation is an emergency, say, "Emergency." If not, don't say anything.

- The hurricane floods the city. *Emergency.*
- A tornado starts to come down from the sky. *Emergency.*
- It is warm and sunny at the beach.
- The car rolls over and comes to a stop in the ditch. *Emergency.*
- The air on the mountaintop is clear and clean.
- The rooster crows after dawn.

What naming word means "a serious situation that calls for fast action"? *Emergency.*

⊙⇐ *Gigantic.*

In the story, the little boy pretends he is a coast guard pilot who rescues people from gigantic storms. That means he saves people from enormous storms. **Gigantic.** Say the word. *Gigantic.*

Gigantic is a describing word. It tells about the size of something. What kind of word is **gigantic?** *A describing word.*

If something is gigantic, it is enormous. You already know what the word **enormous** means. What word means "very, very big"? *Enormous.* That's right. Something that is gigantic is also very, very big. Say the word that means "enormous." *Gigantic.*

(Correct any incorrect responses, and repeat the item at the end of the sequence.)

Let's think about some things that might be gigantic. I'll name some things. If you think those things are gigantic, say, "Gigantic." If not, don't say anything.

- A skyscraper. *Gigantic.*
- A very, very tall tree. *Gigantic.*
- A rocket that could carry you and your classmates to the moon. *Gigantic.*
- A mouse's teacup.
- Four very short tree limbs.
- The biggest dinosaur that was ever on Earth. *Gigantic.*
- The sky, including the moon, the stars, and the planets. *Gigantic.*

What describing word means "enormous"? *Gigantic.*

⊙⇐ *Construction.*

In the story, the little boy pretends to be a construction worker. That means he pretends to be a person who works at building things like houses, factories, roads, and bridges. **Construction.** Say the word. *Construction.*

Construction is a describing word. It tells about someone's job. What kind of word is **construction?** *A describing word.*

If you say someone is a construction worker, you mean that person's job is building things like houses, factories, roads, and bridges. Say the word that describes "the job of building things like houses, factories, roads, and bridges." *Construction.*

(Correct any incorrect responses, and repeat the item at the end of the sequence.)

I'll tell you what someone's job is. If you think that person is a construction worker, say, "Construction." If not, don't say anything.

- James's uncle builds houses. *Construction.*
- Mr. Ragland works on the new factory in our city. *Construction.*
- The teacher writes down what I say in a book.
- Ms. Stephens likes to design clothes.
- Those men and women build highways and bridges. *Construction.*
- He plays guitar with this friends in the evenings.

What describing word means "the job of building things like houses, factories, roads, and bridges"? *Construction.*

Present Vocabulary Tally Sheet
(See Week 1, page 3, for instructions.)

Assign Homework
(Homework Sheet, BLM 34a: See the Introduction for homework instructions.)

DAY 2

Preparation: Picture Vocabulary Cards for *protective, emergency, gigantic,* and *construction.*

Read and Discuss Story

(Read story aloud to the children. Ask the following questions at the specified points in the story. Encourage children to use previously taught target words in their answers.)

Page 1. Who does the boy say he is? (Ideas: *Big Frank; a firefighter.*) What does he do every morning? (Ideas: *Reads the newspaper to see where the fires are; gets dressed in his protective gear.*)

Page 3. What does he pretend is his hook and ladder truck? (Idea: *The sofa.*) How thick does he say the smoke is? (Idea: *As thick as a milk shake.*) Who's the little girl? (Ideas: *Sally; Firefighter Sally.*)

Page 5. What does his mom want? (Idea: *A hug.*) What is the boy's answer? (Idea: *He's too busy fighting fires.*) What does the mom say? (Idea: *Even firefighters hug their moms.*) What is the title of this book? (Ideas: *Even Firefighters Hug Their Moms.*)

Page 7. Who does the boy say he is? (Idea: *Officer Dave.*) Who does he say the girl is? (Ideas: *Rex; his police dog.*) Who does the boy say is in the wagon? (Idea: *Criminals.*) Criminals are people who commit crimes. What are criminals? *People who commit crimes.* Crimes are actions such as stealing and robbing banks.

Page 9. What does the boy tell his mother not to worry about? (Idea: *Her safety.*) What does his mom want? (Idea: *A hug.*) What is the boy's answer? (Idea: *No time. We've got to serve and protect.*) What does the mom say? (Idea: *Even police officers hug their moms.*)

Pages 11–12. What are the letters EMT short for? (Idea: *Emergency medical technician.*) What do they do for the injured man? (Ideas: *Bandage up his cuts and scrapes; give him a bowl of ice cream to make him feel better.*) What sound does the siren make? (Idea: *WEE-ooo.*)

Page 14. Who is waiting in the emergency room? (Idea: *His mom.*) What does she want? (Idea: *A hug.*) What is the boy's answer? (Ideas: *Trying to save some lives here; I'm an EMT.*) What does the mom say? (Ideas: *Even ambulance drivers hug their moms.*)

Pages 15–16. Who does the boy say he is now? (Ideas: *Dan; a construction worker.*) What tells everybody to get out of his way when he backs up his front loader? (Idea: *The BEEP! BEEP!*) What does his mom want? (Idea: *A hug.*) What is the boy's answer? (Idea: *Coffee break's over.*) What does the mom say? (Ideas: *Even construction workers hug their moms.*)

Page 17. Who does the boy say he is now? (Ideas: *Captain Steve; a helicopter pilot.*) Whom does he work for? (Idea: *The Coast Guard.*)

What does he do to help people? (Ideas: *He rescues them from their boats during hurricanes, tornadoes, and other gigantic storms.*) What is his partner doing? (Idea: *Using a winch to pull people to safety.*) What does his mom want? (Idea: *A hug from the hero.*) Do you think he's going to give his mom a hug? (Idea: *No.*)

Page 18. What is the boy's answer? (Idea: *It's just part of the job.*) What does the mom say? (Idea: *Even helicopter pilots hug their moms.*) What sound do the helicopter blades make? (Idea: *Whop-whop-whop.*) How does the boy show he can't hear his mother? (Idea: *He points up at the blades.*) What does his mother say? (Idea: *Even helicopter pilots hug their moms.*)

Page 19. Who does the boy say he is now? (Ideas: *Sam; the conductor of the train.*) Why aren't farm animals allowed on the train? (Idea: *It's a passenger train.*)

Page 20. What do you get when you buy a ticket? (Idea: *A ride to Chicago.*) What does the mother want with her ticket? (Idea: *A hug.*) Does she get a hug? *No.* What does the boy's mother say? (Idea: *Even conductors hug their moms.*)

Page 21. Who does the boy say he is now? (Ideas: *Neil; an astronaut.*) What did the boy discover the moon was really made out of instead of cheese? (Idea: *Rock.*) Where is he going today? (Idea: *Mars.*) Look at the illustration. Who is being Mission Control? (Idea: *His mother and his sister.*)

Page 23. What does the boy say Mars is made of? (Idea: *Legos.*) What does his mother want? (Idea: *A hug.*) Do you think he's going to give his mom a hug? (Idea: *No.*)

Page 24. Why does his mother think she deserves a hug? (Idea: *She gave him directions to Mars.*) Why does the boy say he can't give her a hug? (Idea: *It's a little hard to hug when you're wearing a bulky space suit.*) What does his mother say? (Idea: *Even astronauts hug their moms.*)

Pages 25–26. Who does the boy say he is now? (Ideas: *Rick; a garbage-truck driver.*) What are some of the things he picks up at people's houses? (Ideas: *Trash; worn-out toasters; slimy food wrappers; pacifiers that are bad for the* *baby's teeth.*) How do you think his sister feels about having her pacifier thrown out? (Idea: *Very upset.*)

Pages 27–28. What does the boy do whenever a lady throws something out by mistake? (Idea: *He gets it back for her.*) What does the mother try to do? (Idea: *Give him a hug.*) Do you think he's going to let his mom give him a hug? (Idea: *Yes.*)

Page 29. Why does the boy let his mom give him a hug? (Idea: *Because even garbage-truck drivers hug their moms—sometimes.*) What did the mother do differently this last time to get a hug? (Idea: *Instead of asking the boy for a hug, she gave him one.*)

Who do you think deserves a hug in your life? Why? (Encourage children to use the words: "I think _____ deserves a hug because _____.")

Review Vocabulary

(Display the Picture Vocabulary Cards. Point to each card as you say the word. Ask children to repeat each word after you.) These pictures show **protective, emergency, gigantic,** and **construction.**

- What describing word means "gear or clothing that will keep you safe"? *Protective.*
- What describing word means "the job of building things like houses, factories, roads, and bridges"? *Construction.*
- What naming word means "a serious situation that calls for fast action"? *Emergency.*
- What describing word means "enormous"? *Gigantic.*

Extend Vocabulary

◎← *Construction.*

In the story *Even Firefighters Hug Their Moms,* we learn that **construction** describes the job of building things like houses, factories, roads, and bridges. Say the word that describes "the job of building things like houses, factories, roads, and bridges." *Construction.*

Raise your hand if you can tell us a sentence that uses **construction** as a describing word that means "the job of building things like houses, factories, roads, and bridges." (Call on several children. If they do not use complete

sentences, restate their examples as sentences. Have the class repeat the sentences.)

Here's a new way to use the word **construction.**

- **The Akashi bridge in Japan is the world's longest free-standing construction.** Say the sentence.
- **The Sears Tower is the tallest construction in Chicago.** Say the sentence.
- **The children made a three-foot high construction out of blocks.** Say the sentence.

In these sentences, **construction** is a naming word that means **an object that has been built or made.** What naming word means "an object that has been built or made"? *Construction.*

Raise your hand if you can tell us a sentence that uses **construction** as a naming word that means "an object that has been built or made." (Call on several children. If they do not use complete sentences, restate their examples as sentences. Have the class repeat the sentences.)

Present Expanded Target Vocabulary

◎← *Occupations.*

In the story *Even Firefighters Hug Their Moms,* the little boy pretends to do many different jobs. He is a firefighter, a police officer, an emergency medical technician, a construction worker, a helicopter pilot, a conductor on a train, an astronaut, and a garbage-truck driver. Another way of saying he pretends he has many different jobs is that he pretends he has many different occupations. **Occupations.** Say the word. *Occupations.*

Occupations is a naming word. It names things. What kind of word is **occupations?** *A naming word.*

Occupations are the jobs people do to earn money. Say the word that means "the jobs people do to earn money." *Occupations.*

I'll tell about some people. If I tell about their occupations, say, "Occupation." If not, don't say anything.

- Mr. Kang is a grocer. He runs a grocery store. *Occupation.*
- Officer Buckle is a police officer. He helps keep children safe. *Occupation.*

- A firefighter's job is to protect us from fires. *Occupation.*
- Jamaica's substitute is a teacher. *Occupation.*
- The salesperson in *The Goat Lady* sells things for a living. *Occupation.*
- Our neighbor, Mr. Abdul, doesn't work anymore.

What naming word means "the jobs people do to earn money"? *Occupations.*

Raise your hand if you would like to tell about the occupation of someone you know. (Encourage children to frame their answer as follows: "_____ is a _____. He/She _____.")

◎━ *Ignore.*

In the story *Even Firefighters Hug Their Moms,* the little boy's mom keeps asking for a hug, but the little boy doesn't listen to her. He ignores what she says. **Ignore.** Say the word. *Ignore.*

Ignore is an action word. It tells what someone does. What kind of word is **ignore?** *An action word.*

If you ignore someone, you pay no attention to that person. Say the word that means "pay no attention to." *Ignore.*

I'll tell about some people. If you think those people are ignoring someone or something, say, "Ignore." If not, don't say anything.

- Amy pays no attention when the dog scratches at the door to get out. *Ignore.*
- When kids call out without raising their hands, Mrs. Goodfellow doesn't pay attention to them. *Ignore.*
- Every time the baby makes a peep, her mom jumps up to find out what she wants.
- If your ankle hurts a little when you're walking, just forget about it, and enjoy the walk. *Ignore.*
- It is loud in the swimming pool, but it is so much fun that I don't pay attention to it. *Ignore.*
- My dog barks every time someone drives by the house. I don't pay attention to him any more. *Ignore.*

What action word means "pay no attention to"? *Ignore.*

Preparation: Prepare a sheet of chart paper with the title *Occupations.*

Activity Sheet, BLM 34b. Children will need a pencil and crayons.

Retell Story

(Show pictures on the following pages from the story, and call on a child to tell what's happening. Call on a different child for each section.)

Today I'll show you the pictures Mike Reed made for the story *Even Firefighters Hug Their Moms.* As I show you the pictures, I'll call on one of you to tell the class that part of the story.

Pages 1–5. Tell me what happens at the **beginning** of the story. (Encourage children to include the target word *protective.* Model use as necessary.)

Pages 6–26. Tell me what happens in the **middle** of the story. (Encourage use of target words when appropriate. Model use as necessary.)

Pages 27–29. Tell me what happens at the **end** of the story.

Review Tom Foolery

Preparation: Prepare Picture Vocabulary Cards for all words with dual meanings. Display them prominently in a pocket chart, on a chalkboard ledge, or another obvious location. These words are *attention, bloom, blossom, chore, collect, curious, den, difficult, disturb, embrace, examine, howled, kind, limbs, mood, nursery, present, prickly, promise, property, roared, root, scorched, scrawl, shouted, snatched, special, sturdy, wild,* and *winding.*

Today I will help you remember how to play the game called Tom Foolery. I will pretend to be Tom. Tom Foolery has a reputation for trying to trick children. Tom knows that some words have more than one meaning. He will tell you one meaning that will be correct. Then he will tell you another meaning that might be correct or incorrect. If you think the meaning is correct, don't say anything. If you think the meaning is incorrect, sing out "Tom Foolery!"

Then Tom will have to tell the truth and give the correct meaning. Tom is sly enough that he may include some words that do **not** have two meanings. Be careful! He's tricky!

Let's practice: **Protective** tells about clothes or equipment you wear to protect you. Protective also means . . . a person who solves crimes and mysteries as an occupation. *Tom Foolery!* Oh, you're right. I was thinking about detective and not protective.

Let's do another one together. **Ignore** means that you don't pay attention to something bothersome. Ignore is also what people say at hockey games when someone gets a goal—"He shoots! Ignorrrrre!" *Tom Foolery!* Oh, you're right. I was thinking of "He shoots! He scores!"

When we play Tom Foolery, Tom will keep score. If you catch him being tricky, you will get one point. If you don't catch him, Tom gets the point. Watch out! Tom just might try to give himself extra points while you're not looking!

Now you're ready to play the game.

(Draw a T-chart on the board for keeping score. Children earn one point for each correct answer. If they make an error, continue through the process as you normally would to give the correct meaning. Record one point for yourself, and repeat missed items at the end of the game.)

- An **emergency** is a serious situation that calls for fast action. Emergency also means a piece of toast that falls on the floor jelly-side down. *Tom Foolery!* Oh, you're right. The jelly-side-down toast isn't really an emergency. As long as it's not your piece of toast!
- **Gigantic** means "enormous" and that means pretty big. Gigantic was also the name of a big ocean liner that sank in 1912. *Tom Foolery!* Oh, you're right. I was thinking of the Titanic, not gigantic.

- **Construction** is a describing word that tells about the job of building things like roads and bridges. Construction can also mean the thing that was built.
- **Occupations** tells about the jobs people do to earn money. Occupations is also a fancy way of saying hello, like "Greetings and occupations from your cousin Tom Foolery!" *Tom Foolery!* Oh, you're right. I was just joshing you. I was thinking of "Greetings and salutations," which really *is* a fancy greeting.

(Count the points, and declare a winner.)
You did a great job of playing Tom Foolery!

Complete Activity Sheet

(Review with children the different occupations mentioned in the text. Record the occupations on the chart paper as they are identified. Ideas: *Firefighter, police officer, emergency medical technician, construction worker, helicopter pilot, train conductor, astronaut, garbage-truck driver.*

Have children suggest other occupations. Record them on the chart paper. **Note:** Record at least one more occupation than the number of children in your class. Give each child a copy of the Activity Sheet, BLM 34b.

Children should select and initial an occupation from the chart, then complete the sentence frame, and draw an illustration to accompany the occupation. If they are not yet able to copy the sentence, scribe it for them while they are working on their illustrations. Make a cover with the title *The Work People Do,* and fasten the pages together. Example: *My name is Bill, and I'm a gardener. I plant flowers and trees. I cut the grass.*)

DAY 4

Preparation: Prepare a sheet of chart paper, landscape direction, with the title *Even Firefighters Hug Their Moms.*

Underneath the title, draw 8 boxes connected by arrows. See the Introduction for an example.

Record children's responses by writing the underlined words in the boxes.

Literary Analysis (Story Patterns)

When authors write stories, they sometimes write in patterns. Let's see if we can figure out the pattern for this story. I'll ask you some questions. You tell me what the mom said, and I'll write it down.

(Read aloud the following pages, and ask the specified questions.)

Page 5. What words does the mom say when the little boy is pretending to be a firefighter and she wants a hug? _Even firefighters hug their moms._

Page 9. What words does the mom say when the little boy is pretending to be a police officer and she wants a hug? _Even police officers hug their moms._

Page 14. What words does the mom say when the little boy is pretending to be an EMT and she wants a hug? _Even ambulance drivers hug their moms._

Page 16. What words does the mom say when the little boy is pretending to be a construction worker and she wants a hug? _Even construction workers hug their moms._

Page 18. What words does the mom say when the little boy is pretending to be a helicopter pilot and she wants a hug? _Even helicopter pilots hug their moms._

Page 20. What words does the mom say when the little boy is pretending to be a conductor and she wants a hug? _Even conductors hug their moms._

Page 24. What words does the mom say when the little boy is pretending to be an astronaut and she wants a hug? _Even astronauts hug their moms._

Pages 28–29. What words does the little boy say at the end of the story? _Even garbage-truck drivers hug their moms. Sometimes._

(Point to and read aloud the words written in all the boxes.) What pattern did Christine Kole MacLean make for her story _Even Firefighters Hug Their Moms_? (Idea: _She used the words "Even _____ hug their moms" over and over._)

That's right; she repeated the words "Even _____ hug their moms," so this story has a repeating pattern. What kind of pattern repeats the same words over and over? _A repeating pattern._

(Point to the word _sometimes._) Christine Kole MacLean ended her story with the words "Even garbage-truck drivers hug their moms. Sometimes." When Christine Kole MacLean changed the pattern, it was her way of saying "The End." What words did Christine Kole MacLean use to say "The End?" _Even garbage-truck drivers hug their moms. Sometimes._

Let's sing "The Pattern Song" to help us remember all the patterns we have learned.

(See the Introduction for the complete "The Pattern Song.")

Singing a song together is a very good way to help us remember the patterns we have learned!

Play Tom Foolery (Cumulative Review)

Today I will help you remember how to play our new game called Tom Foolery. I will pretend to be Tom. Tom Foolery has a reputation for trying to trick children. Tom knows that some words have more than one meaning. He will tell you one meaning that will be correct. Then he will tell you another meaning that might be correct or incorrect. If you think the meaning is correct, don't say anything. If you think the meaning is incorrect, sing out, "Tom Foolery!" Then Tom will have to tell the truth and give the correct meaning. Tom is sly enough that he may include some words that do **not** have two meanings. Be careful! He's tricky!

Let's practice: **Ignore** is what you do when you don't pay attention to something that bothers you. Ignore is also the name of the donkey in _Winnie the Pooh. Tom Foolery!_ Oh, you're right. I was thinking of Eeyore, wasn't I?

Let's do another one together. **Occupations** are things you do as a job. An occupation is also an eight-armed sea creature with suckers on its tentacles. _Tom Foolery!_ Oh, you're right. I guess I was thinking about an octopus.

When we play Tom Foolery, Tom will keep score. If you catch him being tricky, you get one point. If you don't catch him, Tom gets the point.

Watch out! Tom just might try to give himself extra points while you're not looking!

Now you're ready to play the game.

(Draw a T-chart on the board for keeping score. Children earn one point for each correct answer. If they make an error, correct them as you normally would, and record one point for yourself. Repeat missed words at the end of the game.)

- A **gigantic** thing is pretty enormous. Also, when you get gigantic, you run around and do things really quickly to get them done before your company arrives. *Tom Foolery!* Oh, you're right. I must have been thinking of frantic and not gigantic. I do get frantic when company is coming.

- A new **construction** is something that has just been built, such as a skyscraper or a railway bridge. Construction also means smashing something to pieces. *Tom Foolery!* Oh, you're right. I suppose I was thinking of destruction which is the opposite of construction.

- **Protective** clothes protect you from things that could hurt you. Protective also means "didn't work" or "stopped working." *Tom Foolery!* Oh, you're right. I was thinking about defective, not protective.

- An **emergency** is a serious situation that you have to deal with right now. An emergency is also what happens when you are sleepy and you can't think clearly. *Tom Foolery!* Oh, you're right. I was thinking of drowsy.

- If you work in **construction,** your occupation is to build things. Construction also means that you buy things in a store. *Tom Foolery!* Oh, you're right. I was thinking of a customer.

- **Appear** means that something comes into sight. Appear also means not gentle. *Tom Foolery!* Oh, you're right. I was thinking of severe.

- **Season** means the part of the year you're in: summer, fall, spring, or winter. Season is also the explanation you give for doing something. *Tom Foolery!* Oh, you're right. I guess I was thinking about reason and not season.

- **Property** means that something belongs to you. Property can also mean your house and the land that it is built on.

- The word **practice** means to do something over and over as you try to get it right. A practice is also the thing you sleep on at night. *Tom Foolery!* Oh, you're right. I was teasing. I was thinking of mattress when I said that.

(Count the points, and declare a winner.)
You did a great job of playing Tom Foolery!

DAY 5

Preparation: Happy Face Game Test Sheet, BLM B.

Display the story map chart from Day 4.

Retell Story as a "Chime-In"

Today we'll retell the story *Even Firefighters Hug Their Moms* as a chime-in story. Let's decide what words we will use for the chime-in parts. What words do the characters repeat? (Idea: *Even _____ hug their moms.* (Print the words *Even _____ hug their moms* underneath the story map on the chart.)

I'll start to read the story. When it's time for the mom or the little boy to say these words (point to the sentence at the bottom of the story map chart), you all chime in.

(Read the story, cueing children by pointing to the sentence when it's their turn to chime in. Everyone will read the last word *sometimes*.)

Assess Vocabulary

 (Hold up a copy of the Happy Face Game Test Sheet, BLM B.)

Today you're going to play the Happy Face Game. When you play the Happy Face Game, it helps me know how well you know the hard words you are learning.

If I say something true, color the happy face. What will you do if I say something true? *Color the happy face.*

If I say something false, color the sad face. What will you do if I say something false? *Color the sad face.*

Listen carefully to each item I say. Don't let me trick you!

Item 1: **Ignore** means to pay lots of attention to something that is bothering you. *False.*

Item 2: **Protective** equipment is worn by firefighters. *True.*

Item 3: Something that is **gigantic** isn't very large. *False.*

Item 4: **Occupations** are things you could do for a job. *True.*

Item 5: Working in **construction** can mean being a singer, a cyclist, or a short-order cook. *False.*

Item 6: You could call that new building on your street a new **construction**. *True.*

Item 7: If there's an **emergency,** you need to deal with it right away. *True.*

Item 8: If grapes are on **special** at the grocery store, they cost less than they usually do. *True.*

Item 9: Your **property** is something that belongs to you. *True.*

Item 10: When you **practice,** you do something only once. *False.*

You did a great job of playing the Happy Face Game!

(Score children's work later. Scores of 9 out of 10 indicate mastery. If a child does not achieve mastery, insert the missed words in the games in the next week's lessons. Retest those children individually on the missed words before they take the next mastery test.)

Extensions
Read a Story as a Reward

(Display several books you have read since the beginning of the program. Allow children to choose which book they would like you to read aloud to them as a reward for their hard work.)

(Read the story aloud to children for enjoyment with minimal interruptions.)

Present Super Words Center

(Prepare the word containers for the Super Words Center (see notation below). This new game is a Concentration-style game, but it uses all the opposite words from earlier lessons. You may choose to prepare the containers with *only* opposites, or you may wish to mix the opposites with current vocabulary or vocabulary for children to review. Supply at least two copies of each of the opposites cards. Use your discretion to determine the number of cards to be placed in the container. Eighteen cards, for example, will generate a Concentration grid of 3 x 6. Twenty-four cards will create a grid of 4 x 6. You will know best what the children are able to deal with.)

Today I will help you remember how to play the game called Hot and Cold that you will play today in the Super Words Center. What do you know about the words **hot** and **cold?** (Idea: *They are opposites.*) This game is called Hot and Cold because your job is to find as many opposites as you can.

Let's remember how we work with our words in the Super Words Center.

You will work with a partner in the Super Words Center. Whom will you work with in the center? *A partner.*

First you will draw all of the cards out of the container and lay them out facedown. There are enough cards to make (X) rows of (Y) cards. (Demonstrate for children.) What do you do first? (Idea: *Draw all of the cards out and lay them facedown.*)

Next, the first player will turn over one card and place it faceup so both players can see. (Demonstrate.) What will you do next? (Idea: *Turn over a card and place it faceup so that both can see.*)

Next, the first player turns over another card and places it faceup so both can see. (Demonstrate.) What will you do next? (Idea: *Turn over another card and lay it faceup so both can see.*)

This is the important part. If the cards are opposites, the first player takes both cards and sets them aside in his or her game pile. If they are not opposites, the first player places both cards facedown. Either way, it is now the second player's turn. (Demonstrate. Children will be familiar with the process for playing Concentration, however.)

What will the first player do if the two cards are opposites? (Idea: *Keep those cards and put them in his or her game pile.*) What will the first player do if the two cards are not opposites? (Idea: *Turn them over.*) Either way, whose turn is it next? (Idea: *The second player's.*)

I think you are almost ready to play Hot and Cold. Can you think of some words that are opposites? (Call on several children. List the opposites they suggest to prepare them for playing the game.) Have fun playing Hot and Cold!

(**Note:** If you wish, you may teach children to say "I'm hot!" in a happy voice when they find opposites and "I'm cold!" in a sad voice when they do not.)

Preparation:
You will need *Tomás and the Library Lady* for each day's lesson.

Number the pages of the story to assist you in asking questions at appropriate points.

Familiarize yourself with the pronunciation of the Spanish words if you aren't fluent in Spanish.

Papá Grande—grandfather

Buenas noches—good night

Papá—Father

Mamá—Mother

En un tiempo pasado—once upon a time

Uno, dos, tres, cuatro—1, 2, 3, 4

Qué tigre tan gande!—What a big tiger!

Libro—book

Pájarao—bird

Buenas tardes, señor.—Good afternoon, sir.

Buenas tardes, señora.—Good afternoon, madam.

Adiós—good-bye

Pan dulce—sweet bread

Gracias—thank you

Post a copy of the Vocabulary Tally Sheet, BLM A, with this week's Picture Vocabulary Cards attached.

Each child will need the Homework Sheet, BLM 35a.

DAY 1

Introduce Book

This week's book is called *Tomás and the Library Lady*. What's the title of this week's book? *Tomás and the Library Lady.*

This book was written by Pat Mora. Who's the author of *Tomás and the Library Lady*? *Pat Mora.*

Tomás and the Library Lady
author: Pat Mora • illustrator: Raul Colón

🎯 Target Vocabulary

Tier II	Tier III
chatter	pattern
eager	circle
lap	
glaring	
*thirsty	
*keen	

*Expanded Target Vocabulary Word

Raul Colón [Rah-ool Kōl-on] made the pictures for this book. Who's the illustrator of *Tomás and the Library Lady*? *Raul Colón.* Who made the illustrations for this book? *Raul Colón.*

The cover of a book usually gives us some hints of what the book is about. Let's look at the front cover of *Tomás and the Library Lady*. What do you see in the illustration? (Ideas: *A woman with glasses and a book; a boy reading a book; a boy on the back of a dinosaur.*)

(Assign each child a partner.) Remember, when you make a prediction about something, you say what you think will happen. Get ready to make some predictions to your partner about this book. Use the information from the cover to help you.

(Ask the following questions, allowing sufficient time for children to share their predictions with their partners.)

- Who are the characters in this story? (Whom do you think this story is about?)
- What do you think the boy is reading?
- Where do you think the story happens?
- When do you think the story happens?
- Why do you think there are dinosaurs on the cover?
- How did the boy get onto the dinosaur's back?
- Do you think this story is about real people? Tell why or why not.

(Call on several children to share their predictions with the class.)

Take a Picture Walk

(Show the illustrations on the following pages, and ask the specified questions. Encourage children to use previously taught target words in their answers.)

We are going to take a picture walk through this book. Remember, when we take a picture walk, we look at the pictures and tell what we think will happen in the story.

Pages 1–2. Where is the boy? (Idea: *In a car.*) What time of day do you think it is? (Ideas: *Nighttime; afternoon.*) Why do you think so? (Ideas: *Nighttime, because there is a full moon and a dark sky; afternoon, because the sun is shining and the picture is yellow.*)

Page 3. Where do you think the car is? (Ideas: *In the country; on a farm.*) Why do you think so? (Ideas: *In the country because there are fields and only one house; in the country because there is only one car on the road; on a farm because there are fields or pastures.*)

Page 4. What is the boy doing? (Idea: *Sleeping.*) What kind of bed is the boy sleeping on? (Ideas: *A bed with no mattress or pillow; a cot.*)

Pages 5–6. What is happening here? (Ideas: *Two boys are playing with a ball; people in hats are picking something and putting it into baskets; people are picking or gathering corn; people are harvesting the corn.*) Where do you think these people are? (Ideas: *In a field; on a farm; working in a cornfield; in the country.*)

Page 7. What do you see here? (Ideas: *A man sitting under a tree pointing and talking; two boys sitting and listening to the man.*) What do you think the man is doing? (Ideas: *Telling a story; telling the boys not to do something.*) Something very unusual is in the tree's leaves. Look closely; what do you see? (Idea: *A horse with a person riding on its back.*)

Page 10. What is the boy doing? (Idea: *Looking through the window of a door.*)

Page 12. Where do you think these people are? (Idea: *In a library.*) Why do you think so? (Ideas: *There are many shelves filled with books; the woman is holding two books.*)

Pages 13–14. What do you see? (Ideas: *Different kinds of dinosaurs; a boy riding a dinosaur—a brontosaurus; a boy reading a book.*) What do you notice is the same about the boy riding the dinosaur and the boy reading the book? (Ideas: *They're wearing the same clothes; they have the same hair; they look the same.*)

Page 15. Where is the boy now? (Ideas: *On the street; in his own neighborhood; on the sidewalk.*) What do you notice about the boy? (Ideas: *He's running; he's carrying books; he's in a hurry.*)

Page 17. What do you see? (Ideas: *A group of people with a big tiger behind them; a boy reading a book to people.*)

Page 18. What do you think the people are doing? (Ideas: *Collecting things from the ground; picking things out of a pile of garbage.*) What is the boy collecting? (Idea: *Books.*)

Page 20. Where is the boy now? (Ideas: *In a room with a desk and books; at school; at the library.*) How do you think the boy is feeling? (Ideas: *Excited; happy.*) How do you know so? (Ideas: *He is smiling; he is holding his arms wide; the woman behind him is smiling.*)

Pages 21–22. What is the boy doing? (Idea: *Reading a book.*) Who else is in this picture? (Ideas: *People riding horses; people standing around teepees, waving.*)

Page 24. Where do you think the people are? (Ideas: *In the library; at the school.*) What is the woman doing? (Idea: *Hugging the boy; embracing the boy.*) What is the man doing? (Ideas: *Watching the woman and the boy; holding his hat.*) What do you think is sitting on the table? (Ideas: *Bread; a package; food.*)

Pages 25–26. When do you think this part of the story happens? (Idea: *At night.*) Why do you think so? (Idea: *There is a moon, and the sky is dark.*) Where are the characters? (Idea: *In a car.*)

Pages 27–28. What do you see in this picture? (Ideas: *A boy holding a book; a boy riding a dinosaur; many different dinosaurs; a jungle.*)

Now that we've finished our picture walk, it's your turn to ask me some questions. What would you like to know about the story? (Accept questions. If children tell about the pictures or the story instead of asking questions, prompt them to ask a question.) Ask me a what question. Ask me a how question.

Read Story Aloud
(Read story aloud to children with minimal interruptions.)

In the next lesson, we will read the story again, and I will ask you some questions.

Present Target Vocabulary

◎━ Chatter.

Papá Grande tells Tomás a story about a man riding a horse through a forest on a windy night. Papá Grande says, "How the wind howled, *whoooooooooo*. How the leaves blew. How his teeth chattered!" That means the man's teeth were making a sound when they were knocking together. **Chatter.** Say the word. *Chatter.*

Chatter is an action word. It tells what is happening. What kind of word is **chatter?** *An action word.*

If your teeth chatter, they make clicking sounds as your teeth knock together again and again. What word means "make clicking sounds as your teeth knock together again and again"? *Chatter.*

Your teeth might chatter if you are cold or afraid. When might your teeth chatter? *When I'm cold or afraid.*

Watch me. I'll pretend I'm very, very cold. (Pretend you are shivering.) Now listen to my teeth chatter. (Make your teeth chatter.) It's your turn. Pretend you're very, very cold. (Pause.) Now make your teeth chatter. (Pause.)

Watch me. I'll pretend I'm afraid. (Pretend you are afraid.) Now listen to my teeth chatter. (Make your teeth chatter.) It's your turn. Pretend you're afraid. (Pause.) Now make your teeth chatter. (Pause.)

(Correct any incorrect responses, and repeat the item at the end of the sequence.)

Let's think about some times when someone's teeth might chatter. I'll tell about someone. If you think that person's teeth would be chattering, say, "Chatter." If not, don't say anything.

- The children have been playing in the snow all morning and are cold. *Chatter.*
- The old house is dark and smelly, and I can feel my teeth knocking together. *Chatter.*
- It is warm and comfortable at the beach.
- After he falls into the freezing cold water, Joshua's teeth start knocking together again and again. *Chatter.*
- That guy in the monster outfit doesn't scare me!
- We are warm and unafraid.

What action word means "make clicking sounds as your teeth knock together again and again"? *Chatter.*

◎━ Eager.

In the story, Tomás runs home from the library, "eager to show the new stories to his family." That means he wants very much to show the books to his family. **Eager.** Say the word. *Eager.*

Eager is a describing word. It tells about how someone is feeling. What kind of word is **eager?** *A describing word.*

If you are eager, you want very much to do something; you can hardly wait. What word means "you want very much to do something; you can hardly wait"? *Eager.*

(Correct any incorrect responses, and repeat the item at the end of the sequence.)

Let's think about some times when you might feel eager. I'll tell about a time. If you think you would feel eager, say, "Eager." If not, don't say anything.

- You can hardly wait for the baseball game to start. *Eager.*
- I jump out of the car, run to the water, and jump right in! *Eager.*
- I stay at the back of the line because I don't want to go in.
- Malcolm is in no rush to jump out of the plane, even with a parachute.
- The dog prances on two legs, chases his tail, and barks. He wants to play! *Eager.*
- "Bring those pancakes over here! I could eat ten platefuls!" Rosa shouts. *Eager.*

What describing word means "you want very much to do something; you can hardly wait"? *Eager.*

Lap.

When Tomás read the book about dinosaurs, "he could see dinosaurs bending their long necks to lap shiny water." That means the dinosaurs were using their tongues to lick up the water. **Lap.** Say the word. *Lap.*

Lap is an action word. It tells what is happening. What kind of word is **lap?** *An action word.*

Lap means to lick up food or drink with the tongue. Say the word that means to "lick up food or drink with the tongue." *Lap.*

(Correct any incorrect responses, and repeat the item at the end of the sequence.)

Let's think about some animals that might use their tongues to lick up food or drink. I'll name an animal. If you think that animal laps its food or drink, say, "Lap." If not, don't say anything.

- A cat. *Lap.*
- A dog. *Lap.*
- A human being.
- A lion. *Lap.*
- A wolf. *Lap.*
- A goldfish.

What action word means to "lick up food or drink with the tongue"? *Lap.*

 Glaring.

In the story, Tomás is nervous as he looks at the big library. "Its tall windows were like eyes glaring at him." That means the windows looked like eyes that were staring at him in an angry way. **Glaring.** Say the word. *Glaring.*

Glaring is an action word. It tells what is happening. What kind of word is **glaring?** *An action word.*

If you are glaring, you are staring at someone in an angry way. Say the word that means "staring at someone in an angry way." *Glaring.*

(Correct any incorrect responses, and repeat the item at the end of the sequence.)

I'll tell you about someone. If you think that person would be glaring, say, "Glaring." If not, don't say anything.

- The giant is very angry when he finds Jack. *Glaring.*

- The angry man says, "Give me that right now!" *Glaring.*
- "That's a nice sand castle you made, Troy," says his sister Hannah. Children are polite in the Perez family.
- "Was it you who broke my favorite lawn mower?" yells the construction worker. *Glaring.*
- Gary finds a penny on the sidewalk and says, "Today is my lucky day!"
- When Sophie runs through Grandmother's garden, she gets an angry look. *Glaring.*

What action word means "staring at someone in an angry way"? *Glaring.*

Present Vocabulary Tally Sheet
(See Week 1, page 3, for instructions.)

Assign Homework
(Homework Sheet, BLM 35a: See the Introduction for homework instructions.)

DAY 2

Preparation: Picture Vocabulary Cards for *chatter, eager, lap,* and *glaring.*

Read and Discuss Story

 (Read story aloud to children. Ask the following questions at the specified points in the story. Encourage children to use previously taught target words in their answers.)

Page 2. When does this part of the story happen? (Idea: *At midnight.*) How does Tomás feel? (Ideas: *Tired; hot; he misses his own bed in his own house in Texas.*)

Page 3. Tomás and his family are on their way to what state? *Iowa.* What do Tomás's mother and father do? (Ideas: *They are farm workers; they pick or harvest fruit and vegetables.*) How do you know that Tomás is hot? (Ideas: *He's thinking about a glass of cold water to drink in gulps; he's imagining sucking the ice and pouring water on his face.*)

Page 4. Who is in the car with Tomás? (Ideas: *His grandfather, Papá Grande; Papá; Mamá; his little brother, Enrique.*) Where does his family live when they are in Iowa? (Idea: *In a small house they share with the other workers.*)

Page 5. What do Mamá and Papá do all day? (Ideas: *They pick corn; they work in the hot sun.*) What do Tomás and his brother do all day? (Ideas: *Carry water to their parents; play with a ball Mamá sewed for them.*)

Page 8. Why does Tomás like to listen to Papá Grande tell stories in Spanish? (Idea: *He is the best storyteller in the family.*) What sounds do the wind and leaves make in Papá Grande's story? (Ideas: *Whooooo; whish, whish.*) Where does Papá Grande tell Tomás to go to find new stories? (Idea: *The library.*)

Page 9. How does the library seem to Tomás? (Ideas: *Huge; scary.*) How does Tomás's mouth feel when he walks up the library steps? (Idea: *Full of cotton.*) That's right. Sometimes when you are very nervous or frightened, your mouth feels very dry as if it were full of cotton.

Page 11. What does the library lady do to help Tomás? (Ideas: *She offers him a drink of water from the fountain; she asks him his name; she brings him some books to read; she gives him a chair to sit in; she asks him what he would like to read about.*) What does Tomás say he would like to read about? (Ideas: *Tigers; dinosaurs.*)

Page 13. What does Tomás see when he reads the book? (Idea: *Dinosaurs bending their long necks to drink shiny water.*) What does Tomás hear when he reads the book? (Idea: *The cries of the wild snake-bird.*) What does Tomás feel when he reads the book? (Idea: *The warm neck of the dinosaur as he holds on tight for the ride.*) Does Tomas really see and hear and feel the dinosaurs? *No.*

That's right. Tomás can see and hear and feel the dinosaurs in his mind. You already know a word that means "the part of your mind that lets you make pictures of imaginary things or of things that didn't really happen." What word is that? (Idea: *Imagination.*) When Tomás reads the book, he uses his imagination to feel and hear and feel the dinosaurs.

Page 16. How long does Tomás read? (Ideas: *All afternoon; until the library closes.*) How do you know that? (Ideas: *The library is empty; the sun is setting.*) Why do you think the library lady looks at Tomás for a long time before checking out books for him in her name? (Ideas: *She wants to find out if Tomás can be trusted; she is wondering if Tomás will take good care of the books.*) How does Tomás feel when he goes home with the books? (Ideas: *Eager to show his family; happy; excited.*)

Page 17. What does Papá Grande want Tomás to do? (Ideas: *Read to him; read to him in English.*) What makes Tomás's family laugh when Tomás reads the book? (Idea: *He roars like a huge tiger.*)

Page 18. What are Tomás's parents looking for at the town dump? (Idea: *Pieces of iron to sell.*) What does Tomás look for at the dump? (Idea: *Books.*)

Page 19. What does the library lady ask Tomás to do? (Ideas: *Have a drink of water before reading; read to her on quiet days; teach her some Spanish words.*) What words does Tomás teach the library lady? (Ideas: *Libro; pájaro.*) What does **libro** mean? *Book.* What does **pájaro** mean? *Page.*

Page 21. What does Tomás look at when the library is busy? (Idea: *The pictures in the books.*) What does Tomás smell when he reads the book? (Idea: *The smoke at an Indian camp.*) What does Tomás do when he reads the book? (Idea: *Rides a black horse across a hot, dusty desert.*) Does he really smell the smoke and ride a black horse? *No.* That's right. Tomás experiences these things through his . . . *Imagination.*

Page 23. What sad word does Tomás have to teach the library lady? (Idea: *Adiós, good-bye.*) What would Tomás miss when he goes back to Texas? (Ideas: *This quiet place; the cool water; the many books; the library lady.*) What does Tomás bring the library lady as a gift from his mother? (Idea: *Pan dulce, sweet bread.*) Why does Tomás's mother send the gift? (Idea: *To thank the library lady for being so kind to Tomás.*)

Page 25. What does the library lady give to Tomás as a present? (Idea: *A shiny new book.*)

Page 27. What is the book about? (Idea: *Dinosaurs.*) How do you think Tomás feels about the new book? Why do you think so? (Idea: *Happy, because he likes reading about dinosaurs.*)

What do you like to read about? (Encourage children to answer using the words "I like to read about _____.")

Review Vocabulary

(Display the Picture Vocabulary Cards. Point to each card as you say the word. Ask children to repeat each word after you.) These pictures show **chatter, eager, lap,** and **glaring.**

- What action word means to "lick up food or drink with the tongue"? *Lap.*
- What action word means "staring at someone in an angry way"? *Glaring.*
- What action word means to "make clicking sounds as your teeth knock together again and again"? *Chatter.*
- What describing word means "you want very much to do something; can hardly wait"? *Eager.*

Extend Vocabulary

 Lap.

In the story *Tomás and the Library Lady,* we learned **lap** means to "lick up food or drink with the tongue." Say the word that means to "lick up food or drink with the tongue." *Lap.*

Raise your hand if you can tell us a sentence that uses **lap** as an action word that means to "lick up food or drink with the tongue." (Call on several children. If they don't use complete sentences, restate their examples as sentences. Have the class repeat the sentences.)

Here's a new way to use the word **lap.**

- **The racehorse ran two laps around the track.** Say the sentence.
- **The class ran one lap of the field.** Say the sentence.
- **Four laps of the racetrack is one mile.** Say the sentence.

In these sentences, **lap** is a naming word that means **one time around something.** What naming word means "one time around something"? *Lap.*

Raise your hand if you can tell us a sentence that uses **lap** as a naming word that means one

time around something. (Call on several children. If they don't use complete sentences, restate their examples as sentences. Have the class repeat the sentences.)

Present Expanded Target Vocabulary

Thirsty.

In the story *Tomás and the Library Lady,* Tomás tells his mother, "If I had a glass of water, I would drink it in large gulps. I would suck the ice. I would pour the last drops of water on my face." Tomas is trying to explain to his mother that he is thirsty. **Thirsty.** Say the word. *Thirsty.*

Thirsty is a describing word. It tells about how someone is feeling. What kind of word is **thirsty?** *A describing word.*

If you are thirsty, you need to drink something. Say the word that means "need to drink something." *Thirsty.*

I'll tell about some people. If these people are thirsty, say, "Thirsty." If not don't say anything.

- In the story *Papa, Do You Love Me?* the boy wants a drink of water from the calabash. *Thirsty.*
- My throat is as dry as popcorn. *Thirsty.*
- The ragged man crawls along on the desert sand crying, "Water! Water!" *Thirsty.*
- "Water? We are swimming in it!"
- After a long drink, Tomasina feels much better.
- The lion on the savanna pants. You can tell he wants some water. *Thirsty.*

What describing word means "need to drink something"? *Thirsty.*

Raise your hand if you would like to tell about a time when you were thirsty. (Encourage children to answer using the words "I was thirsty when _____.")

Keen.

In the story *Tomás and the Library Lady,* Tomás is eager to read books. Whenever he can, he goes to the library. He looks for books in the town dump. He reads stories to his family at night. Another way of saying Tomas is eager to read books is to say Tomas is a keen reader. **Keen.** Say the word. *Keen.*

Keen is a describing word. It tells about someone. What kind of word is **keen?** *A describing word.*

If you are keen about something, you are eager to do it. Say the word that means "eager to do something." *Keen.*

I'll tell about some people. If you think those people are keen about something, say, "Keen." If not, don't say anything.

- Terry spends all her free time riding her horse. *Keen.*
- Bonnie likes to race stock cars every weekend. *Keen.*
- Fay enjoys teaching students about space communities. *Keen.*
- Jill really likes to teach children to become artists. *Keen.*
- Lois lines the children up to catch the bus just as she does every day.
- Bryon learns to golf after he retires and he can't enough of it. *Keen.*

DAY 3

Preparation: Activity Sheet, BLM 35b. Children will need their crayons.

Retell Story

(Show the pictures on the following pages from the story, and call on a child to tell what's happening. Call on a different child for each section.)

Today I'll show you the pictures Raul Colón made for the story *Tomás and the Library Lady*. As I show you the pictures, I'll call on one of you to tell the class that part of the story.

Pages 1–2. Tell me what happens at the **beginning** of the story.

Pages 3–24. Tell me what happens in the **middle** of the story. (Encourage use of target words when appropriate. Model use as necessary.)

Pages 25–28. Tell me what happens at the **end** of the story.

Review Super Choosing Game

Today you will play the Super Choosing Game. Let's think about the six words we have: **chatter, eager, lap, glaring, thirsty,** and **keen.** (Display the Picture Vocabulary Cards.)

I will say a sentence that has some of the words we have learned in it. You will have to choose the correct word for that sentence. Not all of the words will be from this lesson, though. That's why it's the *Super* Choosing Game. Let's practice. (You should not show cards for words from previous lessons.)

- When your teeth knock together, do they chatter, are they an aroma, or do they have courage? *Chatter.*
- If you are anxious to do something, are you bigger, dormant, or eager? *Eager.*
- When you go around something one time, have you completed a tap, a slap, or a lap? *A lap.*

Now you're ready to play the game. If you tell me the correct answer, you win one point. If you can't tell me the correct answer, I get the point.

(Draw a T-chart on the board for keeping score. Children earn one point for each correct answer. If they make an error, tell them the correct answer. Record one point for yourself, and repeat missed words at the end of the game.)

- When an animal takes food or drink with its tongue, does it clap, sap, or lap? *Lap.*
- If you are excited about doing something, are you lean, keen, or gigantic? *Keen.*
- Your mom is angry with you for coming home late. Are her eyes ignoring, being a nuisance, or glaring? *Glaring.*
- You are very afraid. Do your teeth clatter, chatter, or splatter? *Chatter.*
- When animals go to sleep for the winter, do they migrate, hope, or hibernate? *Hibernate.*
- Would a large hole in the side of a hill or mountain be called a disability, brave, or cave? *Cave.*
- If you need a drink badly, are you thirsty, fascinated, or did you donate? *Thirsty.*

(Count the points, and declare a winner.)

You did a great job of playing the Super Choosing Game!

Complete Activity Sheet

(Show children the illustrations in the story that show Tomas using his imagination: pages 7, 13 and 14, 17, 21 and 22, 27 and 28. Ask children what they have imagined themselves doing when they read or hear their favorite stories.

Give each child a copy of the Activity Sheet, BLM 35b. Have them complete the sentence frame and draw an illustration. If they are not yet able to print the sentence, scribe it for them while they are working on their illustrations. Make a cover with the title *Imaginary Adventures*, and fasten the pages together.)

DAY 4

Preparation: Prepare a sheet of chart paper, portrait direction, with the title *Tomás and the Library Lady.* Underneath the title make a circle of 11 circles connected by arrows. See the Introduction for an example.

Record children's responses by writing the underlined words in the circles.

Literary Analysis (Story Patterns)

When authors write stories, they sometimes write in patterns. Let's see if we can figure out the pattern for this story. You tell me what happens in the story, and I'll write it down.

(Read aloud pages 1 and 2, and show the illustration.) When does the story start? *At midnight.* Where is Tomás? (Idea: *In the car.*)

(Read aloud page 8, and show the illustration.) What is Tomás doing? (Idea: *Listening to Papá Grande's story and imagining the man on the horse.*)

(Show the illustration on pages 10 and 11.) Where is Tomás now? (Idea: *At the library.*)

(Show the illustration on pages 13 and 14.) What is Tomás doing? (Idea: *Reading and imagining he is riding a dinosaur.*)

(Show the illustration on pages 15 and 17.) What is Tomás doing? (Idea: *Reading to his family and imagining a tiger in the jungle at night.*)

(Read aloud page 19, and show the illustration.) What is Tomás doing? (Idea: *Teaching the library lady Spanish.*)

(Show the illustration on pages 21 and 22.) What is Tomás doing? (Idea: *Reading and imagining he is a sheriff visiting an Indian camp.*)

(Show the illustration on page 24.) What is Tomás doing? (Idea: *Saying adiós.*)

(Read aloud page 25, and show the illustration on pages 25 and 26.) When does the story end? *At night.* Where is Tomás? (Idea: *In the car.*)

(Show the illustration on pages 27 and 28.) But something is different for Tomas now. What is it? (Idea: *He has a book to read, so he can imagine he is in the time of the dinosaurs riding on a longneck brontosaurus.*)

(Point to the story map on the chart paper.) Look at the shape of this story. It's a circle. This story starts and ends with Tomás traveling at night in the car to a new farm, so this story has a circle pattern. What kind of story pattern starts and ends at the same place? *A circle pattern.*

Let's sing "The Pattern Song" to help us remember all the patterns we have learned.

(See the Introduction for the complete Pattern Song.)

Singing a song together is a very good way to remember the patterns we have learned!

Play Super Choosing Game (Cumulative Review)

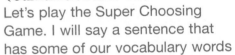

Let's play the Super Choosing Game. I will say a sentence that has some of our vocabulary words in it. You will have to choose the correct word for that sentence. Remember, this game is *Super* Choosing because I will use some words from other lessons. You will have to be sharp!

(Display the vocabulary cards for *chatter, eager, lap, glaring, thirsty,* and *keen.* Do not display the word cards from earlier lessons.)

Now you're ready to play the Super Choosing Game.

(Draw a T-chart on the board for keeping score. Children earn one point for each correct answer. If they make an error, correct them as you normally would, and record one point for yourself. Repeat missed words at the end of the game.)

- If your job is working in construction, are you responsible, is it your occupation, or are you sturdy? *Your occupation.*
- When you are afraid and your teeth move, do they remember, slither, or chatter? *Chatter.*
- If you really, really want and need a drink, are you thirsty, sloppy, or sly? *Thirsty.*
- If you are doing well at something that you want to do, are you a triplet, successful, or an emergency? *Successful.*
- Does going around something once mean that you have completed a flap, a gap, or a lap? *A lap.*
- When you are really excited about saving the environment, are you a barber, keen, or dreary? *Keen.*
- If a troll has an angry look in his eyes when he is looking at you, is he cowering, caring, or glaring? *Glaring.*
- When you just can't wait to get your hands in the mud to make a mud pie, are you really eager, a customer, or do you devour? *Really eager.*
- When you are scared half to death in the attic of that old house, do your teeth scatter, matter, or chatter? *Chatter.*

Now you will have to listen very carefully, because I'm not going to show you the word cards. (Remove the Picture Vocabulary Cards from display.)

- If you looked at someone else's paper and copied the answers during a test, did you cheat, hide in a den, or get some frost? *Cheat.*
- When birds fly to a warmer place, are they fragrant, do they migrate, or do they mutter? *Migrate.*
- Do you need a drink of water? Then you must obey, be restless, or thirsty. *Thirsty.*
- When you really want to do something that you like to do, are you seen, keen, or relieved? *Keen.*

- If an animal drinks using its tongue, does it nap, map, or lap? *Lap.*
- When you give someone an angry look with your eyes, are you glaring, squabbling, or unaware? *Glaring.*
- When a race car has gone around once, has it completed a zap, rap, or lap? *A lap.*
- If the kite moves with the wind, does it creep, drift, or howl? *Drift.*

(Count the points, and declare a winner.)
You did a great job of playing the Super Choosing Game!

DAY 5

Preparation: Happy Face Game Test Sheet, BLM B.

Review Dedication

If you dedicate a book to someone, you put that person's name at the front of the book to say thank you for helping and encouraging you. The words you write when you dedicate a book to someone are called the **dedication.** Today I'll read the dedications that Pat Mora and Raul Colón wrote for *Tomás and the Library Lady.*

(Read aloud the dedication by Pat Mora.) Whom does Pat Mora dedicate this book to? (Idea: *Tomás Rivera.*) Why does she dedicate the book to him? (Idea: *Because he loved books.*) The first part of Pat Mora's dedication begins with the words "In memory of." That means that when she wrote this book, Tomás Rivera was no longer alive. Was Tomás Rivera alive when Pat Mora dedicated her book to him? *No.*

Whom else does Pat Mora dedicate this book to? (Idea: *To librarians.*) Why does she dedicate the book to them? (Idea: *Because they lure us in.*) That means librarians attract our attention and invite us in to the world of books, where we can use our imaginations just like Tomás.

(Read aloud the dedication by Raul Colón.) Whom does Raul Colón dedicate this book to? (Idea: *Sylvia and Carl.*) Who do you think Sylvia and Carl might be?

Review Afterword

(Assign each child a partner.) Sometimes after people finish writing a story about something that is real, they want to tell you more facts about that real thing. This information is put in the book **after** the last **word** of the story, so it is called an **afterword.**

Today I'll read the afterword that Pat Mora wrote for *Tomás and the Library Lady,* so you can learn more about Tomás.

(Read aloud the afterword. When you read the sentence containing the words *migrant workers,* tell children migrant workers are people who work in the fields picking fruits and vegetables. They travel from farm to farm as the crops are ready.) The Tomás character in the story and Tomás Rivera were the same in many ways. Tell me some ways they were the same. (Ideas: *They had the same first name; both worked in the fields picking vegetables; both traveled from farm to farm; they both were encouraged to read by a lady in Iowa.*)

Now that we have read the story *Tomás and the Library Lady* and found out about Tomás Rivera, do you think this story is fiction or nonfiction? Why do you think so? (Accept either response as long as children give a reason for their answer.)

You're all right. This story is fiction because some of it is made up from the author's imagination. The words Tomás and the other people say were made up by Pat Mora. What part of the story is made up? (Idea: *The words the people say.*)

But some parts of the story are true. There was a boy named Tomás who worked in the fields. He did meet a library lady who encouraged him to read. What parts of the story are true? (Ideas: *Working in the fields; the library lady.*)

Assess Vocabulary

(Hold up a copy of the Happy Face Game Test Sheet, BLM B.)

Today you're going to play the Happy Face Game. When you play the Happy Face Game, it helps me know how well you know the hard words you are learning.

If I say something true, color the happy face. What will you do if I say something true? *Color the happy face.*

If I say something false, color the sad face. What will you do if I say something false? *Color the sad face.*

Listen carefully to each item I say. Don't let me trick you!

Item 1: A **gale** is a wind that is not blowing very fast. *False.*

Item 2: If you are an **honest** person, people will know that you tell the truth. *True.*

Item 3: **Frost** is a white, powdery cake that you cook for dinner. *False.*

Item 4: A gopher or chipmunk might live in a **burrow.** *True.*

Item 5: **Den** is a word that means a comfortable room in your house. *True.*

Item 6: A **winding** road goes in a straight line. *False.*

Item 7: If you are good at painting, you have a **talent.** *True.*

Item 8: Something that is **delicious** tastes very good. *True.*

Item 9: **Pleaded** means begged. *True.*

Item 10: If you are **determined** to write a book, you work and work until the book is finished. *True.*

You did a great job of playing the Happy Face Game!

(Score children's work later. Scores of 9 out of 10 indicate mastery. If a child does not achieve mastery, insert the missed words in the games in the next week's lessons. Retest those children individually on the missed items before they take the next mastery test.)

Extensions
Read a Story as a Reward

 (Display several books you have read since the beginning of the program. Allow children to choose which book they would like you to read aloud to them as a reward for their hard work.)

(Read the story aloud to children for enjoyment with minimal interruptions.)

Present Super Words Center

(Prepare the word containers for the Super Words Center.)

(Place all of the Picture Vocabulary Cards in the classroom center—you may need a bucket-sized container!)

Today you will play Hello, Goodbye. It is an easy game to play, and I will teach you how.

Let's think about how we work with our words in the Super Words Center.

You will work with a partner in the Super Words Center. Whom will you work with in the center? *A partner.*

First you will draw a word out of the container. What do you do first? (Idea: *Draw a word out of the container.*)

Next you will show your partner the picture and ask him or her what word the picture shows. What do you do next? (Idea: *I show my partner the picture and ask him or her to tell me what word the picture shows.*)

If your partner is right and you agree, your partner keeps the card in a pile of his or her own. That's the "Goodbye" pile. If you and your partner don't agree on the word, you put the card in a pile in the center of the table. That's the "Hello" pile. (**Demonstrate if necessary.**)

What do you do next? *Give my partner a turn.*

When your play time is ended, you can each count the number of cards in your "Goodbye" piles. Whoever has the most cards is the winner!

(**Note:** You may wish to monitor the cards in the "Hello" pile. One of the partners was unable to identify these cards. They may be used for scheduling review words.)

Preparation: You will need *A Day with a Mail Carrier* for each day's lesson.

Post a copy of the Vocabulary Tally Sheet, BLM A, with this week's Picture Vocabulary Cards attached.

Each child will need the Homework Sheet, BLM 36a.

A Day with a Mail Carrier
author: Jan Kottke

🎯 Target Vocabulary

Tier II	Tier III
doorbell	nonfiction
load	photograph
mailbox	
mail carrier	
*mail cart	
*post office	

*Expanded Target Vocabulary Word

DAY 1

Introduce Book

We are reading books about different kinds of workers. Some of these books are true. When an author writes books about things that are true, those books are called nonfiction books. What kinds of books are about true things? *Nonfiction books.* What kind of worker did we read about in the last lesson? (Ideas: *A person who works in the library; a librarian.*)

This week's book is called *A Day with a Mail Carrier.* What's the title of this week's book? *A Day with a Mail Carrier.*

This book was written by Jan Kottke [kot-kee]. Who's the author of *A Day with a Mail Carrier*? *Jan Kottke.*

The pictures for this book were taken with a camera. They are called photographs. What do you call pictures taken with a camera? *Photographs.* What kind of illustrations does *A Day with a Mail Carrier* have? *Photographs.*

The cover of a book usually gives us some hints of what the book is about. Let's look at the front cover of *A Day with a Mail Carrier.* What do you see in the photograph? (Ideas: *A mail carrier; letters; a mail cart; a mail slot on the store; the mail carrier is wearing a uniform.*)

Take a Picture Walk

(Show the illustrations on the following pages, and ask the specified questions. Encourage children to use previously taught target words in their answers.)

We are going to take a picture walk through this book. When we take a picture walk through a nonfiction book about workers, we look carefully at the pictures and think about what we see.

Page 5. Who do you think the man is? (Idea: *A mail carrier.*) Where is he standing? (Idea: *In the doorway of the mail truck.*) How many mail carriers do you see? *One.*

Page 7. What is the man holding? (Idea: *Letters that have been mailed.*) What do you think the mail carrier is doing with the letters? (Ideas: *Putting them into different slots; sorting the mail.*) What do you think the mail carrier is going to do with the pile of letters in his hand? (Ideas: *Put them in the slots; sort them.*)

Page 9. What is the mail carrier loading into the truck? (Ideas: *Letters; packages.*) Do you think the letters the mail carrier had in the last picture are now in the truck? (Ideas: *Yes, because there is a lot of mail in the truck; no, the letters might be going somewhere else.*)

Page 11. What is the mail carrier doing? (Idea: *He is loading the mail into a mail cart.*) What do you thing the mail carrier is getting ready to do? (Idea: *He is going to deliver the mail.*) Do you think the mail carrier is going to load all the mail in the truck into his mail cart? Tell why or why not. (Idea: *No, there is too much mail in the truck to fit inside the mail cart.*)

Page 13. What do you think the mail carrier is doing? (Ideas: *He is delivering mail to a house;*

he is putting mail into a mailbox.) What color is the mailbox? *White.*

Page 15. What do you see in the picture? *A mailbox.* What numbers are on the mailbox? *4, 4, 3.* What does the red part of the mailbox look like? (Idea: *A flag.*)

Page 17. Who is in the picture? *A mail carrier.* Where is the mail carrier? (Ideas: *At a house; at the front door.*) What is the mail carrier doing? (Idea: *He is ringing the doorbell.*)

Page 19. Who is the mail carrier talking to? (Ideas: *A little girl and her mom; a little girl and a lady.*) What is the mail carrier giving to the little girl? (Ideas: *A letter; the mail.*)

Page 21. How do you think the mail carrier is feeling? (Ideas: *He is feeling happy; he likes his job; he is having a good day.*) How do you know? (Idea: *He has a big smile on his face.*)

Read Story Aloud
(Read story aloud to children with minimal interruptions.)

In the next lesson, we will read the book again, and I will ask you some questions.

Present Target Vocabulary
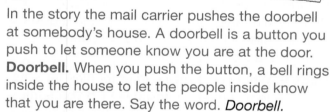
◎—< Doorbell.

In the story the mail carrier pushes the doorbell at somebody's house. A doorbell is a button you push to let someone know you are at the door. **Doorbell.** When you push the button, a bell rings inside the house to let the people inside know that you are there. Say the word. *Doorbell.*

Doorbell is a naming word. It names a thing. What kind of word is **doorbell?** *A naming word.*

A doorbell is a button you push to let someone know you are at the door. Say the word that means "a button you push to let someone know you are at the door." *Doorbell.*

(Correct any incorrect responses, and repeat the item at the end of the sequence.)

Let's think about some times you might use a doorbell. If you would use a doorbell, say, "Doorbell." If not, don't say anything.

- You have arrived at your friend's house and want him to know you are there. *Doorbell.*

- Your mom sends you to your next-door neighbor's house with some apples from your tree. *Doorbell.*
- You are at your house.
- You are delivering a package to the house across the street. *Doorbell.*
- You are turning on the lawn sprinkler.
- You are knocking on the door of the apartment across the hall.

What naming word means "a button you push to let someone know you are at the door"? *Doorbell.*

◎—< Load.

In the story, the mail carrier has to load the mail into his truck. That means he has to put the mail into the truck. **Load.** Say the word. *Load.*

Load is an action word. It tells what someone does. What kind of word is **load?** *An action word.*

When you load things, you put them into or onto something. Say the word that means to "put things into or onto something." *Load.*

Let's think about some times when you might load something. I'll tell about a time. If you think you would load something, say, "Load." If not, don't say anything.

- You walk to your friend's house.
- You put the food into the bag at the grocery store. *Load.*
- You eat dinner at a restaurant.
- You put the recycling box into the trunk of your car. *Load.*
- You watch the animals at the zoo.
- The front-end loader shovels dirt into the dump truck. *Load.*

What action word means to "put things into or onto something"? *Load.*

◎—< Mailbox.

In the story, cards and letters are put into the mailbox. **Mailbox.** Say the word. *Mailbox.*

Mailbox is a naming word. It names a thing. What kind of word is **mailbox?** *A naming word.*

A mailbox is a place where cards and letters are left by a mail carrier. Say the word that means "a place where cards and letters are left by a mail carrier." *Mailbox.*

Let's think about some places where you would see a mailbox. If it is a place where there would be a mailbox, say, "Mailbox." If not, don't say anything.

- In front of someone's house. *Mailbox.*
- In the middle of the lake.
- At your uncle's house. *Mailbox.*
- At the park.
- On the moon.
- At your grandparents' apartment. *Mailbox.*

What naming word means "a place where cards and letters are left by a mail carrier"? *Mailbox.*

◎━ Mail *carrier.*

In the story, the mail carrier is a person who sorts and delivers mail to people. **Mail carrier.** Say the word. *Mail carrier.*

Mail carrier is a naming word. It names a person. What kind of word is **mail carrier?** *A naming word.*

A mail carrier is a person who sorts and delivers mail to people. Say the word that means "a person who sorts and delivers mail to people." *Mail carrier.*

Let's think about some things a mail carrier would do at work. If it is something a mail carrier would do, say, "Mail carrier." If not, don't say anything.

- Deliver a letter. *Mail carrier.*
- Dish out ice cream.
- Sort the mail. *Mail carrier.*
- Fight a forest fire.
- Cut down trees.
- Deliver important letters. *Mail carrier.*

What naming word means "a person who sorts and delivers mail to people"? *Mail carrier.*

Present Vocabulary Tally Sheet
(See Week 1, page 3, for instructions.)

Assign Homework
(Homework Sheet, BLM 36a: See the Introduction for homework instructions.)

Preparation: Picture Vocabulary Cards for *doorbell, load, mailbox,* and *mail carrier.*

Read and Discuss Story

(Read story aloud to children. Ask the following questions at the specified points in the story. Encourage children to use previously taught target words in their answers.)

Page 4. What is the name of the mail carrier? *Dominic.* What is his job? *To bring mail to people.*

Page 6. Why do you think the mail carrier has to start his day sorting mail? (Ideas: *He has to get ready; he needs his mail so that he can deliver it; if no one sorts the mail it would be too difficult to deliver.*) What do you think the mail carrier did before he came to sort mail? (Ideas: *Got ready for work; put on his uniform; drove to work; talked with other mail carriers; read the newspaper.*)

Page 8. Why does the mail carrier have to load the mail into his truck? (Idea: *There is too much mail to carry by hand; he has to drive a long way to deliver the mail; the mail is safe when it is in the truck.*) Where do you think all that mail is going? (Ideas: *People's homes; to stores and businesses.*) How can you tell that there is a lot of mail in the truck? (Ideas: *There are many boxes of mail; it looks like it is almost falling out of the boxes; the mail looks very heavy.*) Why do you think this is a good truck to be a mail truck? (Ideas: *It has a big door to make loading easy; there is a lot of space inside; there are good lights on the back that are easy to see; the mail is safe inside the truck.*)

Page 10. Where do you think the mail cart came from? (Idea: *From the back of the truck.*) Why do you think the mail carrier is putting mail into the mail cart? (Ideas: *It's easier to deliver mail with a cart; he doesn't have to carry the mail; he can walk with the cart and doesn't have to drive the truck; he doesn't need to take all the mail with him.*) Why do you think there is another jacket hanging in the back of the mail truck? (Ideas: *In case the one he is wearing now gets dirty or ripped; it may be a warmer or cooler jacket; it might be a rain jacket.*)

Page 12. What kinds of things does the mail carrier put in the mailbox? (Idea: *Cards and letters.*) Why do you think mailboxes are good ideas? (Ideas: *Mail carriers don't have to go right to the house; they protect the mail from wind, rain, and snow; there is lots of space for the mail.*)

Page 14. Why is the flag on the mailbox a good idea? (Ideas: *It tells the mail carrier that there is a letter inside to be mailed; if the person doesn't have any mail the mail carrier still knows that he or she needs to stop; the mail carrier doesn't have to stop and look inside to see if there is a letter to be mailed.*) What would be important to remember about the flag? (Idea: *You need to remember to put the flag up to let the mail carrier know there is a letter to be mailed; once the mail carrier takes the letter, he or she needs to put the flag down.*)

Page 16. Why would the mail carrier ring the doorbell if he or she has some important letters? (Ideas: *So the letters won't be missing or be stolen; to deliver the letter to a person; to give someone a paper to sign saying they got the letter.*) What do you think the mail carrier would do if nobody was home? (Ideas: *Try again the next day; leave a note.*) Why is the doorbell a good way to let the person inside know you are there? (Ideas: *It rings inside the house; people know that when the doorbell rings, someone is at the door.*)

Page 18. Why would the mail carrier hand people their mail? (Ideas: *He wants to be friendly and considerate.*)

Page 20. What two things does this mail carrier like? (*He likes bringing mail to people and being a mail carrier.*)

Let's think about the nonfiction story *A Day with a Mail Carrier.* What is this story about? (Idea: *A mail carrier.*) Earlier we learned the main idea of a story is the reason a story is written. The main idea of a story is also the most important thing we learn when we read the story. What do we call the most important thing we learn when we read a nonfiction story? *The main idea.* What do you think is the most important thing we learned when we read *A Day with a Mail Carrier*? (Idea: *Mail carriers work hard to get people their mail.*)

(**Note:** At first, children will probably give details relating to the story—mail carriers sort mail, they drive mail trucks; they deliver mail to people's houses. If children give these responses, ask questions such as these:) Do you think that's easy to do? Why do you think the mail carriers do these things?

So what is the main idea of the story *A Day with a Mail Carrier*? (Idea: *Mail carriers work hard to get people their mail.*)

Review Vocabulary

(Display the Picture Vocabulary Cards. Point to each card as you say the word. Ask children to repeat each word after you.) These pictures show **doorbell, load, mailbox,** and **mail carrier.**

- What word means "a button you push to let someone know you are at the door"? *Doorbell.*
- What word means to "put things into or onto something"? *Load.*
- What word means "a place where cards and letters are left by a mail carrier"? *Mailbox.*
- What words mean "the person who sorts and delivers the mail"? *Mail carrier.*

Extend Vocabulary

◎━ Load.

In the story *A Day with a Mail Carrier* we learn that load means to "put things into or onto something." Say the word that means to "put things into or onto something." *Load.*

Raise your hand if you can tell us a sentence that uses **load** as an action word that means to "put things into or onto something." (Call on several children. If they don't use complete sentences, restate their examples as sentences. Have the class repeat the sentences.)

Here's a new way to use the word **load.**

- **I needed four loads of dirt for my backyard.** Say the sentence.
- **I carried two loads of leaves to the compost pile.** Say the sentence.

- **The train carried a load of grain.** Say the sentence.

In these sentences, **load** is a naming word that means **what you can carry at one time.**

What word means "what you can carry at one time"? *Load.*

Raise your hand if you can tell us a sentence that uses **load** as naming word that means "what you can carry at one time." (Call on several children. If they don't use complete sentences, restate their examples as sentences. Have the class repeat the sentences.)

Present Expanded Target Vocabulary

◎⊷ Mail *cart.*

In the story, a mail cart is a wheeled wagon used to carry small loads of mail. **Mail cart.** Say the words. *Mail cart.*

Mail cart is a naming word. It names a thing. What kind of word is **mail cart?** *A naming word.*

A mail cart is a wheeled wagon used to carry small loads of mail. What word means "a wheeled wagon used to carry small loads of mail"? *Mail cart.*

I'll tell about some times when someone might use a mail cart. If the person would use a mail cart, say, "Mail cart." If not, don't say anything.

- To take the mailed packages to the house on Third Street. *Mail cart.*
- To take a horse to the horse show.
- To take a boat out of the water.
- To take more letters than you could carry. *Mail cart.*
- To deliver the mail on your street. *Mail cart.*
- To bring **all** of the mail to your city.

What naming word means "a wheeled wagon used to carry small loads of mail"? *Mail cart.*

◎⊷ Post *office.*

In the story, the mail carrier starts his day in the post office. That means he starts his day in a building where the mail is sorted and stamps are sold. **Post office.** Say the word. *Post office.*

Post office is a naming word. It names a thing. What kind of word is **post office?** *A naming word.*

A post office is a building where the mail is sorted and stamps are sold. Say the word that means "a building where the mail is sorted and stamps are sold." *Post office.*

Let's think about some times when someone might visit a post office. I'll tell about a time. If you think that person would go to a post office, say, "Post office." If not, don't say anything.

- To go see your favorite animal.
- To mail a letter. *Post office.*
- To drop off a library book.
- To buy some stamps. *Post office.*
- To visit as a class and watch as the mail is sorted. *Post office.*
- To send a package to your uncle. *Post office.*

What naming word means "a building where the mail is sorted and stamps are sold"? *Post office.*

DAY 3

Preparation: Prepare a sheet of chart paper with the words *Mail Carrier* in a circle in the middle of the page. Record children's responses by recording the underlined words (and any other relevant information identified during the discussion) on the web. Draw lines to indicate the connections between the various parts of the web.

Make Connections (Build a Web)

(Encourage children to use previously taught target words in their answers. Model use as necessary.)

Today I'll show you the photographs taken for the book, *A Day with a Mail Carrier.* As I show you the photographs, I'll call on one of you to tell more about mail carriers.

Get ready to tell me what you know about where mail carriers work when they are not delivering mail to people's houses. What do you call the place where mail carriers work when they're not delivering mail to people's houses? <u>*A post office.*</u> (Add a circle to the web for *post office.*)

(Show the illustrations on pages 5, 7, and 9, and read the text on pages 4, 6, and 8.) What things might be at a post office? (Ideas: _uniforms; mail trucks; letters; packages._) (Add circles to the web for _uniforms_ and _mail truck._)

(Point to the post office.) What else would you see at the post office? (Ideas: _A computer; a scale; flag; stamps; money; a notice board; sorting shelves; mail bins; packages._)

(Repeat this process for _uniforms_ and _mail truck,_ showing the appropriate photographs in the book.)

Tell me more about the work mail carriers do. (Add the _work_ circle to the web. Show the photographs from the book on pages 11, 13, and 15.) What things do mail carriers do when they're at work away from the post office? (Ideas: _Unload the mail truck; load the mail cart; deliver mail; put mail into mailboxes; pick up letters that are to be mailed from mailboxes; put down the red flags on mailboxes; drive the mail truck._)

(Show the photographs from the book on pages 17, 19, and 21.) If the mail carrier does not put your mail in your mailbox, how else might it be delivered? (Ideas: _The mail carrier might hand the letters to me; ring doorbell; I might have a box at the post office._)

Review Choosing Game

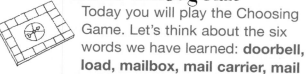

Today you will play the Choosing Game. Let's think about the six words we have learned: **doorbell, load, mailbox, mail carrier, mail cart,** and **post office.** (Display the Picture Vocabulary Cards.) I will say a sentence that has two of our words in it. You will have to choose which word is the correct word for that sentence. Let's practice. (Display the cards for the two words in each sentence as you say the sentence.)

- Is a person who delivers mail called a **mail carrier** or **mail cart?** _Mail carrier._
- When mail carriers deliver mail, do they deliver the mail to a **mailbox** or a **load?** _Mailbox._
- Does a mail carrier have a **doorbell** or a **mail cart?** _A mail cart._

If you tell me the correct answer, you win one point. If you can't tell me the correct answer, I get the point.

Now you're ready to play the game.

(Draw a T-chart on the board for keeping score. Display the Picture Vocabulary Cards for the two words in each sentence as you say the sentence. Children earn one point for each correct answer. If they make an error, tell them the correct answer. Record one point for yourself, and repeat missed items at the end of the game.)

- If a mail carrier carried some of the mail from her mail truck, would she use a **mailbox** or a **mail cart?** _A mail cart._
- Would a **doorbell** or a **load** let someone know there was a person at the front door? _A doorbell._
- Which is a place: a **post office** or a **mail cart?** _A post office._
- Does a mail carrier deliver incoming mail to a **post office** or a **mailbox?** _A mailbox._
- If firefighters went into a burning building, would they carry a **hose** or a **helmet?** _A hose._

(Count the points, and declare a winner.) You did a great job of playing the Choosing Game!

DAY 4

Preparation: Write the following list of key words on the board or on a piece of chart paper: _mail carrier, post office, load, mail cart, letters, mailbox,_ and _people._

You will need a blank sheet of chart paper.

You will need the Picture Vocabulary Cards for _doorbell, load, mailbox, mail carrier, mail cart,_ and _post office._

Activity Sheet, BLM 36b: children will need crayons.

Summarize the Book

Today we are going to summarize what we learned in the story _A Day with a Mail Carrier._ I will write the summary on this piece of chart paper. Later, we will read the summary together.

When we summarize, we use our own words to tell about the most important things in the book. What do we do when we summarize? *We use our own words to tell about the most important things in the book.*

Key words help us tell about the important ideas in our own words. (Point to the list of key words.) This is the list of key words that will help us write our summary. (Read each word to children. Ask them to repeat each word after you read it.)

(**Note:** You should write the summary in paragraph form. Explain to children that you indent the first line because the summary will be a paragraph.)

(Show the illustration on page 4.) What is the name of the mail carrier? *Dominic.* I'm going to start the summary with a sentence about Dominic. Dominic is a mail carrier. (Write the sentence on the chart. Touch under each word as you read the sentence aloud. Cross *mail carrier* off of the list of key words.)

(Show the illustration on page 6.) Where does Dominic work? *At the post office.* The next sentence in our summary will be about where Dominic works. Raise your hand if you can tell us a sentence about where Dominic works. (Idea: *He works at the post office.*) (Add the new sentence to the summary.) Let's read the second sentence of our summary together. (Touch under each word as you and children read the sentence aloud. Cross *post office* off the list of key words. Repeat this process for each of the key words. Show the illustrations on the following pages before each sentence is written: page 9, load; page 11, mail cart; page 13, letters and mailbox; page 19, people.)

(Show the illustration on page 21.) The last sentence we are going to write will tell how Dominic feels about being a mail carrier. Raise your hand if you can tell us a sentence about how Dominic feels about being a mail carrier. (Idea: *Dominic likes being a mail carrier.*) (Add the new sentence to the summary.)

(Once the summary is finished, touch under each word as you and children read the summary aloud together.)

(Sample summary:

Dominic is a mail carrier. He works at the post office. He loads the mail into the mail truck. Later, he puts the mail in his mail cart. Next, he puts letters in people's mailboxes. Sometimes he hands letters to people. Dominic likes being a mail carrier.)

We did a great job of writing a summary!

Play Choosing Game (Cumulative Review)

Let's play the Choosing Game. I will say a sentence that has two of our words in it. You will have to choose the correct word for that sentence.

(Display the word cards for *doorbell, load, mailbox, mail carrier, mail cart,* and *post office,* for two words in each sentence as you say the sentence.)

Now you're ready to play the Choosing Game.

(Draw a T-chart on the board for keeping score. Children earn one point for each correct answer. If they make an error, correct them as you normally would, and record one point for yourself. Repeat missed words at the end of the game.)

- If a person delivers mail, would he or she be a **mail carrier** or a **post office?** *A mail carrier.*
- If you went to the place where mail carriers work when they're not delivering mail, would you be at a **mailbox** or a **post office?** *A post office.*
- If you are carrying something to put into the truck, do you have a **load** or a **post office?** *A load.*
- Would a mail carrier use a **mail cart** or a **load?** *A mail cart.*
- Which would sound like a bell: a **mail carrier** or a **doorbell?** *A doorbell.*
- What would a mail carrier put mail into: a **load** or a **mailbox?** *A mailbox.*
- On the back of the truck is there a **load** of wood or a **mail cart** of wood? *A load.*

Now you will have to listen very carefully, because I'm not going to show you the word cards. (This part of the game includes review words collected from previous lessons.)

- Is the mail carrier **polite** or **frustrated** to ring the doorbell when he or she has some important letters? *Polite.*
- Is the mail carrier **complaining** or **considerate** to stop and say hello to people? *Considerate.*
- Is being a mail carrier an **occupation** or a **nuisance?** *An occupation.*
- Is a person who buys stamps at the post office a **customer** or a **language?** *A customer.*
- Would it be best for the mail carrier to be **frost** or **gentle** with the mail? *Gentle.*
- Would the mail truck **hibernate** or **protect** the mail while the mail carrier was away? *Protect.*
- Would a **mailbox** or a **cave** be the best place to leave mail? *A mailbox.*
- Was there an **enormous** letter or a **load** of letters in the back of the mail truck? *A load.*

(Count the points, and declare a winner.)
You did a great job of playing the Choosing Game!

Complete Activity Sheet

 (Give each child a copy of the Activity Sheet, BLM 36b. Tell them to match each person to the location of his or her work.)

DAY 5

Preparation: You will need the summary that was written during Day 4.

Read the Summary Together

Today we are going to read the summary that we wrote together. (Touch under each word as you read the summary aloud. Show the illustration indicated after each sentence is read.)

Dominic is a mail carrier. (Show the illustration on page 4.) He works at the post office. (Show the illustration on page 6.) He loads the mail into the mail truck. (Show the illustration on page 9.) Later, he puts the mail in his mail cart. (Show the illustration on page 11.) Next, he puts letters in people's mailboxes. (Show the illustration on page 13.) Sometimes he hands letters to people.

(Show the illustration on page 19.) Dominic likes being a mail carrier. (Show the illustration on page 21.)

We did a great job of reading our summary!

Assess Vocabulary

 (Hold up a copy of the Happy Face Game Test Sheet, BLM B.)

Today you're going to play the Happy Face Game. When you play the Happy Face Game, it helps me know how well you know the hard words you are learning.

If I say something true, color the happy face. What will you do if I say something true? *Color the happy face.*

If I say something false, color the sad face. What will you do if I say something false? *Color the sad face.*

Listen carefully to each item I say. Don't let me trick you!

Item 1: If you are a **mail carrier,** you deliver mail. *True.*

Item 2: A **mailbox** is used to hold water. *False.*

Item 3: A **post office** is where mail carriers sort the mail. *True.*

Item 4: A **mail cart** makes it easier for a mail carrier to deliver mail. *True.*

Item 5: A **doorbell** is used to sort mail. *False.*

Item 6: **Load** means what you can carry at one time. *True.*

Item 7: A **mail carrier** delivers mail to a **mailbox.** *True.*

Item 8: If you are very, very cold, your teeth might **chatter.** *True.*

Item 9: If you are a **mail carrier,** you work at a fire station. *False.*

Item 10: **Chores** are jobs that you don't do very often. *False.*

You did a great job of playing the Happy Face Game!

(Score children's work later. Scores of 9 out of 10 indicate mastery. If a child does not achieve mastery, insert the missed words in the games in the next week's lessons. Retest those children individually on the missed items before they take the next mastery test.)

Extensions
Read Story as a Reward

(Read aloud the story *A Day with a Mail Carrier* or a similar story to children as a reward for their hard work.)

Present Super Words Center

(Prepare the word containers for the Super Words Center. You may wish to remove some of the words from earlier lessons the children have mastered.)

(Add the new Picture Vocabulary Cards in the classroom center to the words from the previous weeks. Show children one of the word containers. Role-play how to work in this center with two or three children as a demonstration as you introduce each part of the game.)

You will play a game called 2 in 1 in the Super Words Center.

Let's think about how we work with our words in the Super Words Center.

You will work with a partner in the Super Words Center. Whom will you work with in the center? *A partner.*

First you will draw two words out of the container. What do you do first? (*Draw two words out of the container.*) Next you will show your partner both of the words. What will you do next? *Show my partner both of the words.* (Demonstrate.)

Next you will say a sentence that uses both of your words. What do you do next? (Idea: *Say a sentence that uses both of my words.*) (Demonstrate.)

If you can use both of your words in one sentence, give yourself a point. Then give your partner a turn. (Demonstrate.)

What do you do next? *Give my partner a turn.*

Vocabulary Tally Sheet

Picture Vocabulary Card	Weekly Tally
Picture Vocabulary Card	Weekly Tally
Picture Vocabulary Card	Weekly Tally
Picture Vocabulary Card	Weekly Tally
Picture Vocabulary Card	Weekly Tally
Picture Vocabulary Card	Weekly Tally

Happy Face Game Test

Name: _____ **Date:** _____

Week: _____ **Score:** _____

Mastery Achieved: Yes   No

  1. 😊 ☹️

  2. 😊 ☹️

  3. 😊 ☹️

  4. 😊 ☹️

5. 😊 ☹️

  6. 😊 ☹️

  7. 😊 ☹️

  8. 😊 ☹️

  9. 😊 ☹️

  10. 😊 ☹️

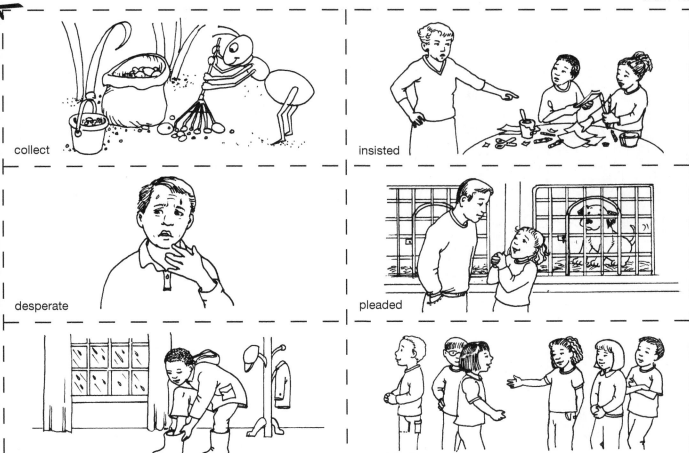

collect

insisted

desperate

pleaded

prepare

considerate

Sharing What You've Learned at School

[**Note:** Children are not expected to be able to read the words. The words are for your information.]

DAY 1: (Cut the Picture Vocabulary Cards apart. Place the cards for *collect, pleaded, insisted,* and *prepare* in a container or small plastic bag.)
(Show your child each card. Ask:) **What word does the picture show?** (Idea: *The picture shows an ant collecting food for winter.*)
Tell me what you know about this word. (Share what you know about the word with your child as well. Repeat for each word.)

DAY 2: (Add *desperate* and *considerate.* Repeat procedure for Day 1. Ask:) **Today, tell me anything more that you know about this word.**

DAY 3: Play Show Me, Tell Me Game (Round One)
Let's play the Show Me, Tell Me game you learned at school. I'll ask you to show me how to do something. If you can show me, you win one point. If you can't show me, I get the point. Next, I'll ask you to tell me. If you can tell me, you win one point. If you can't tell me, I get the point. Let's play.

- **Show me how you would *collect* toys from the floor.** (Pause.) **Tell me what you did.** *Collected toys from the floor.*
- **Show me how your face looks if you really want a tasty treat very badly.** (Pause.) **Tell me what you did.** *Pleaded.*
- **Show me how you would *prepare* to go to school in the morning.** (Pause.) **Tell me what you did.** *Prepared to go to school.*
- **Show me how I would *insist* that I put you to bed.** (Pause.) **Tell me what you did.** *Insisted.*
- **Show me how you would *collect* stamps.** (Pause.) **What did you do?** *Collected stamps.*
- **Show me how you would *prepare* a snack.** (Pause.) **What did you do?** *Prepared a snack.*

[**Note:** You may add other examples of your own.]

DAY 4: Play Show Me, Tell Me Game (Round Two)
(Add *desperate* and *considerate,* and play the game.)

- **Show me how you would be *considerate* when your teacher is talking to you.** (Pause.) **How were you being?** *Considerate.*
- **Show me how you would look if you really, really, wanted to go outside to play.** (Pause.) **Tell me how you looked.** *Desperate.*

Beginning

Middle

End

crept

remember

winding

cross

disobedient

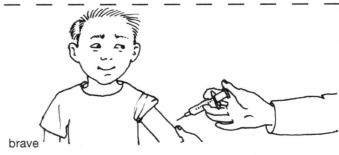

brave

Sharing What You've Learned at School

Note: Children are not expected to be able to read the words. The words are for your information.]

DAY 1: (Cut the Picture Vocabulary Cards apart. Place the cards for *cross, crept, remember,* and *winding* in a container or small plastic bag.)
Show your child each card. Ask:) **What word does the picture show?** (Idea: *The picture shows someone who is feeling angry.*)
Tell me what you know about this word. (Share what you know about the word with your child as well. Repeat for each word.)

DAY 2: (Add *brave* and *disobedient.* Repeat procedure from Day 1. Ask:) **Today, tell me anything more that you know about this word.**

DAY 3: Play Show Me, Tell Me Game (Round One)
Let's play the Show Me, Tell Me Game that you learned at school. I'll ask you to show me how to do something. If you can show me, you win one point. If you can't show me, I get the point. Next, I'll ask you to tell me. If you can tell me, you win one point. If you can't tell me, I get the point. Let's play.

- **Show me how I would look if you made me wait for you to get dressed for school.** (Pause.) **Tell me how you looked.** *Cross.*
- **Show me how you would get past a mean dog without his seeing you.** (Pause.) **Tell me what you did.** *I crept.*
- **Show me how a road that twists up a mountainside would look.** (Pause.) **Tell me how it looked.** *Winding.*
- **Show me how you would look if someone broke your favorite toy.** (Pause.) **Tell me how you looked.** *Cross.*
- **Show me how you would *wind* up a toy mouse.** (Pause.) **Tell me what you were doing.** *Winding.*

[**Note:** You may add other examples of your own.]

DAY 4: Play Show Me, Tell Me Game (Round Two)
(Add *brave* and *disobedient,* and play the game.)

- **Show me how you would look if you had to go to the dentist to get a tooth pulled out.** (Pause.) **Tell me how you looked.** *Brave.*
- **Show me what you would do if I asked you to wave your hand and you were *disobedient*.** (Pause.) **Tell me how you are acting.** *Disobedient.*

Beginning

Middle

End

gathering

angry

furious

roared

meadow

delicious

Sharing What You've Learned at School

[**Note:** Children are not expected to be able to read the words. The words are for your information.]

DAY 1: (Cut the Picture Vocabulary Cards apart. Place the cards for *gathering, meadow, roared,* and *angry* in a container or small plastic bag.)
Show your child each card. Ask:) **What word does the picture show?** (Idea: *The picture shows someone who is feeling angry.*)
Tell me what you know about this word. (You may wish to share what you know about the word with your child as well. Repeat for each word.)

DAY 2: (Add *furious* and *delicious.* Repeat procedure from Day 1. Ask:) **Today, tell me anything more that you know about this word.**

DAY 3: Play Show Me, Tell Me Game (Round One)
Let's play the Show Me, Tell Me Game that you learned at school. I'll ask you to show me how to do something. If you can show me, you win one point. If you can't show me, I get the point. Next, I'll ask you to tell me. If you can tell me, you win one point. If you can't tell me, I get the point. Let's play.

- **Show me how you would *gather* up your toys from the floor.** (Pause.) **Tell me what you're doing.** *Gathering toys from the floor.*

- **Show me how a lion would sound if it *roared.*** (Pause.) **Tell me what the lion did.** *It roared.*
- **Show me how your face would look if you felt *angry* when someone broke your favorite toy.** (Pause.) **Tell me how you are feeling.** *Angry.*
- **Show me how you would *gather* flowers in the meadow.** (Pause.) **Tell me where you gathered flowers.** *In the meadow.*
- **Show me how a vacuum cleaner would sound if it *roared.*** (Pause.) **Tell me what the vacuum clean did.** *It roared.*
- **Show me how your face would look if you felt *angry* when someone pushed you in line.** (Pause.) **Tell me how you were feeling.** *Angry.*

[**Note:** You may add other examples of your own.]

DAY 4: Play Show Me, Tell Me Game (Round Two)
(Add *furious* and *delicious,* and play the game.)

- **Show me how you would look if you were very, very angry.** (Pause.) **Tell me how you are feeling.** *Furious.*
- **Show me how you would look if you ate something that was very *delicious.*** (Pause.) **Tell me how what you ate tasted.** *Delicious.*

Beginning

Middle

End

cottage

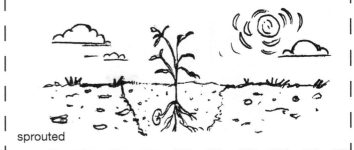

sprouted

uncooperative

harvest

grains

determined

Sharing What You've Learned at School

[**Note:** Children are not expected to be able to read the words. The words are for your information.]

DAY 1: (Cut the Picture Vocabulary Cards apart. Place the cards for *cottage, harvest, grains,* and *sprouted* in a container or small plastic bag.)
(Show your child each card. Ask:) **What word does the picture show?** (Idea: *The picture shows a cottage.*)
Tell me what you know about this word. (Share what you know about the word with your child as well. Repeat for each word.)

DAY 2: (Add *determined* and *uncooperative.* Repeat procedure from Day 1. Ask:) **Today, tell me anything more that you know about this word.**

DAY 3: Play Show Me, Tell Me Game (Round One)
Let's play the Show Me, Tell Me Game you learned at school. I'll ask you to show me how to do something. If you can show me, you win one point. If you can't show me, I get the point. Next I'll ask you to tell me. If you can tell me, you win one point. If you can't tell me, I get the point. Let's play.

- **Show me the look you would have on your face if you were spending time at a** *cottage* **at the beach.** (Pause.) **Tell me the name of the place that made you look that way.** *Cottage.*

- **Show me what you would do to** *harvest* **a field of carrots.** (Pause.) **Tell me what you did.** *I harvested carrots.*
- **Show me how it would look to hold a big handful of** *grains.* (Pause.) **Tell me what you were holding.** *Grains.*
- **Show me how you would look if you were a seed that had just** *sprouted.* (Pause.) **Tell me what you did.** *I sprouted.*
- **Show me how you would look if you had a** *grain* **of sand in your eye.** (Pause.) **Tell me what you had in your eye.** *A grain of sand.*
- **Show me how you would look if you were to** *harvest* **apples from a tree.** (Pause.) **Tell me what you did.** *I harvested apples.*

[**Note:** You may add other examples of your own.]

DAY 4: Play Show Me, Tell Me Game (Round Two)
(Add *determined* and *uncooperative,* and play the game.)

- **Show me how you would look if you were** *determined* **not to cry when you scraped your knee.** (Pause.) **Tell me how you looked.** *Determined.*
- **Show me how you would look if you decided that you didn't want to help clean up the house even when I asked you nicely.** (Pause.) **Tell me how you looked.** *Uncooperative.*

BLM 4b

Beginning

Middle

End

A–10

decided

squeaked

disagreeable

shouted

muttered

starving

Sharing What You've Learned at School

[**Note:** Children are not expected to be able to read the words. The words are for your information.]

DAY 1: (Cut the Picture Vocabulary Cards apart. Place the cards for *decided, shouted, squeaked,* and *muttered* in a container or small plastic bag.) Show your child each card. Ask:) **What word does the picture show?** (Idea: *The picture shows someone who shouted.*)
Tell me what you know about this word. (Share what you know about the word with your child as well. Repeat for each word.)

DAY 2: (Add *starving* and *disagreeable.* Repeat procedure from Day 1. Ask:) **Today, tell me anything more that you know about this word.**

DAY 3: Play Choosing Game (Round One)
Let's play the Choosing Game that you learned at school. I'll say sentences with two of the words you know in them. You have to choose the correct word for the sentence. If you choose correctly, you win one point. If you don't choose correctly, I get the point. Let's play.

- **If I used a loud voice to call you, would you say I *shouted* or *muttered*?** *Shouted.*

- **If you were very afraid and spoke in a high voice would you have *muttered* or *squeaked*?** *Squeaked.*
- **If you choose to play a game instead of going for a walk, have you *squeaked* or *decided*?** *Decided.*
- **When you say something that I'm not supposed to hear, have you *shouted* or *muttered*?** *Muttered.*
- **If you wanted to call me but I was far away, would you have *decided* or *shouted*?** *Shouted.*
- **If you choose to stay inside and play instead of playing outside with friends, have you *muttered* or *decided*?** *Decided.*

[**Note:** You may add other examples of your own.]

DAY 4: Play Choosing Game (Round Two)
(Add *starving* and *disagreeable,* and play the game.)

- **If you are upset because you are losing a game, are you *disagreeable* or *starving*?** *Disagreeable.*
- **When you haven't eaten for a long time, would you have *muttered* or be *starving*?** *Starving.*

Beginning

Middle

End

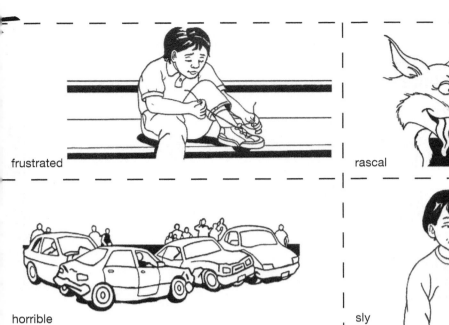

frustrated

rascal

horrible

sly

terrified

clever

Sharing What You've Learned at School

[Note: Children are not expected to be able to read the words. The words are for your information.]

DAY 1: (Cut the Picture Vocabulary Cards apart. Place the cards for *sly, rascal, terrified* and *horrible* in a container or small plastic bag.)
(Show your child each card. Ask:) **What word does the picture show?** (Idea: *The picture shows someone who is terrified.*)
Tell me what you know about this word. (Share what you know about the word with your child as well. Repeat for each word.)

DAY 2: (Add *clever* and *frustrated.* Repeat procedure from Day 1. Ask:) **Today, tell me anything more that you know about this word.**

DAY 3: Play Choosing Game (Round One)
Let's play the Choosing Game that you learned at school. I'll say sentences using two of the words you know. You have to choose the correct word for the sentence. If you choose correctly, you win one point. If you don't choose correctly, I get the point. Let's play.

• Is a very, very bad thing a *horrible* thing or a *terrified* thing? *Horrible.*

• If you were very frightened, would you be *sly* or *terrified*? *Terrified.*
• When a person is good at tricking others, do we say that person is *sly* or *terrified*? *Sly.*
• If you try and try but still can't figure out how to undo your jacket, are you having a *sly* time or a *horrible* time? *Horrible.*
• When the wolf wanted to hurt the little pigs, he spoke nicely to get them to open their doors. Was he *terrified* or a *rascal*? *A rascal.*
• When your little brother teases you, is he a *rascal* or is he *terrified*? *A rascal.*

[Note: You may add other examples of your own.]

Choosing Game (Round Two)
(Add *clever* and *frustrated,* and play the game.)

• If you couldn't figure out how to open a package no matter how hard you tried, would you be *frustrated* or *clever*? *Frustrated.*
• If you could fix a skateboard using gum and an old stick, would you be *frustrated* or *clever*? *Clever.*

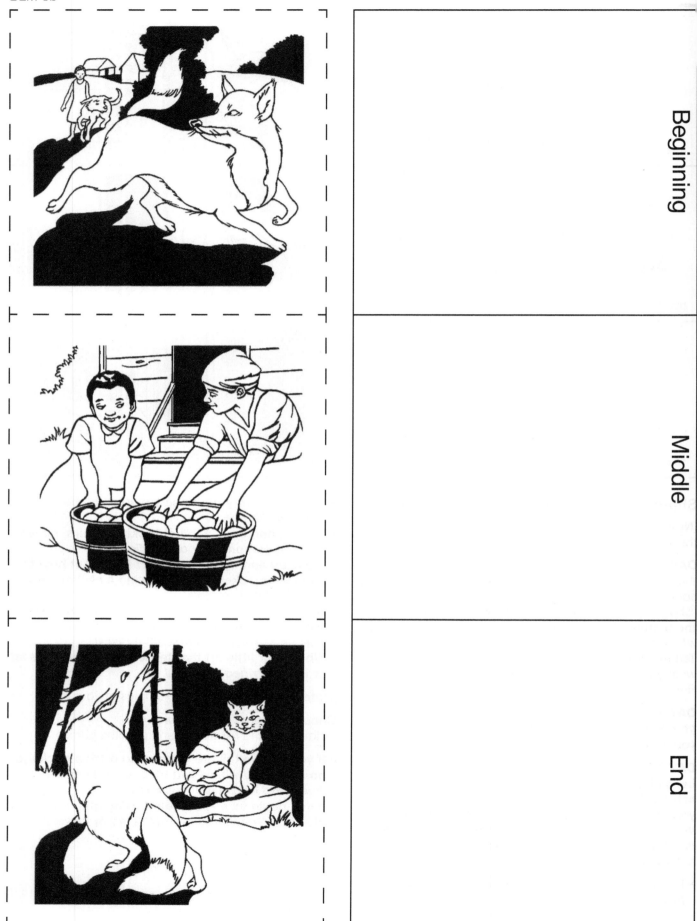

curious

ingredients

selfish

nutritious

sighed

cooperated

Sharing What You've Learned at School

[**Note:** Children are not expected to be able to read the words. The words are for your information.]

DAY 1: (Cut the Picture Vocabulary Cards apart. Place the cards for *curious, nutritious, ingredients,* and *sighed* in a container or small plastic bag.) (Show your child each card. Ask:) **What word does the picture show?** (Idea: *The picture shows someone who is curious.*)
Tell me what you know about this word. (Share what you know about the word with your child as well. Repeat for each word.)

DAY 2: (Add *selfish* and *cooperated.* Repeat procedure from Day 1. Ask:) **Today, tell me anything more that you know about this word.**

DAY 3: Play Choosing Game (Round One)
Let's play the Choosing Game that you learned at school. I'll say sentences with two of the words you know in them. You have to choose the correct word for the sentence. If you choose correctly, you win one point. If you don't choose correctly, I get the point. **Let's Play.**

• **If you want to know more about something, are you *curious* or *selfish*?** *Curious.*

• **When you make a sandwich, do you use *ingredients* or have you *sighed*?** *Ingredients.*
• **When the food you eat is good for you, do you say that it is *selfish* or *nutritious*?** *Nutritious.*
• **If you let out a long breath because you were sad, would you say that you *sighed* or that you were *curious*?** *Sighed.*
• **If something is a bit odd or unusual, would you say that it is *curious* or *selfish*?** *Curious.*
• **After lifting the heavy boxes, would you say that Kyle was *curious* or that he *sighed*?** *Sighed.*

[**Note:** You may add other examples of your own.]

DAY 4: Play Choosing Game (Round Two)
(Add *selfish* and *cooperated,* and play the game.)

• **If ten of your friends got together to wash your dad's car, would you say that you *cooperated* or you were *selfish*?** *Cooperated.*
• **If you kept all of the blueberries for yourself even though you knew that your friend would like some, would you be *selfish* or would you have *cooperated*?** *Selfish.*

Name _____

Stone Soup

Vegetables are nutritious.

satisfied

upward

gale

snatched

whirled

damaged

Sharing What You've Learned at School

[**Note:** Children are not expected to be able to read the words. The words are for your information.]

DAY 1: (Cut the Picture Vocabulary Cards apart. Place the cards for *snatched, whirled, satisfied,* and *upward* in a container or small plastic bag.)
(Show your child each card. Ask:) **What word does the picture show?** (Idea: *The picture shows someone who is satisfied.*)
Tell me what you know about this word. (Share what you know about the word with your child as well. Repeat for each word.)

DAY 2: (Add *gale* and *damaged.* Repeat procedure from Day 1. Ask:) **Today, tell me anything more that you know about this word.**

DAY 3: Play Choosing Game (Round One)
Let's play the Choosing Game that you learned at school. I'll say sentences with two of the words you know in them. You have to choose the correct word for the sentence. If you choose correctly, you win one point. If you don't choose correctly, I get the point. Let's play.

- **If your top spun on your desk at school, would you say that it *whirled* or was *snatched*?** *Whirled.*
- **If you've had enough to eat, are you *snatched* or *satisfied*?** *Satisfied.*
- **If you raise your arms up slowly toward the sky, are they *whirled* or do they go *upward*?** *Upward.*
- **If someone grabbed your backpack away from you, did it get *snatched* or *satisfied*?** *Snatched.*
- **When a leaf spun around on the water in a lake, would you say that it went *upward* or *whirled*?** *Whirled.*
- **If all the people had enough to eat, would they be *upward* or *satisfied*?** *Satisfied.*

[**Note:** You may add other examples of your own.]

DAY 4: Play Choosing Game (Round Two)
(Add *gale* and *damaged,* and play the game.)

- **When the wind blew so hard that trees were blown over, was it a *gale* or *satisfied*?** *Gale.*
- **If your bike was broken so you couldn't use it anymore, would it be a *gale* or *damaged*?** *Damaged.*

Name _____

The Wind Blew

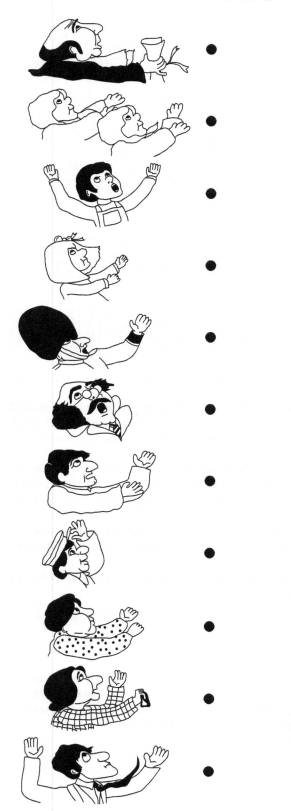

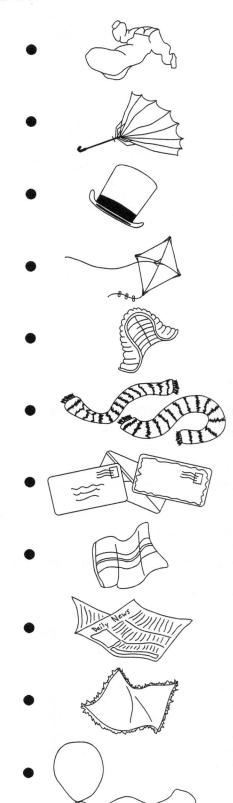

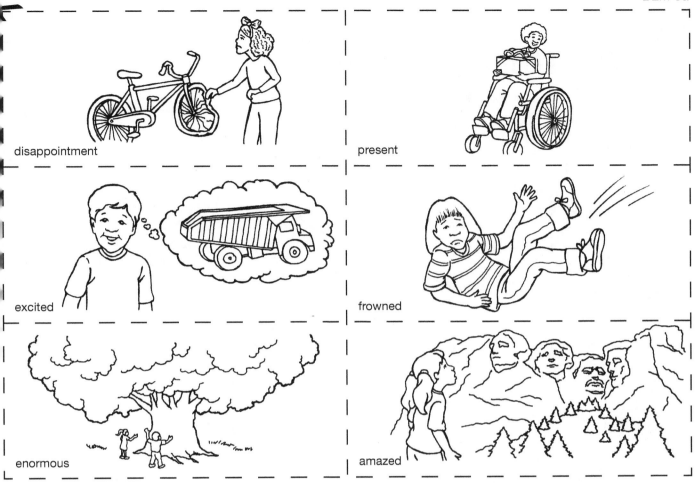

disappointment

present

excited

frowned

enormous

amazed

Sharing What You've Learned at School

[**Note:** Children are not expected to be able to read the words. They are for your information.]

DAY 1: (Cut the Picture Vocabulary Cards apart. Place the cards for *disappointment, frowned, present,* and *enormous* in a container or small plastic bag.) (Show your child each card. Ask:) **What word does the picture show?** (Idea: *The picture shows getting a present.*)
Tell me what you know about this word. (Share what you know about the word with your child as well. Repeat for each word.)

DAY 2: (Add *excited* and *amazed.* Repeat procedure from Day 1. Ask:) **Today, tell me anything more that you know about this word.**

DAY 3: Play Whoopsy! (Round One)
Let's play the Whoopsy! game that you learned at school. I'll say sentences using words you learned. If the word doesn't fit in the sentence, you say "Whoopsy!" Then I'll ask you to say a sentence where the word fits. If you can do it, you get a point. If you can't do it, I get the point. If the word I use fits the sentence, don't say anything. Let's play.

- **I had a *disappointment* when ... I got beautiful flowers on Mother's Day.** *Whoopsy!* (Idea: *I had a disappointment when I didn't get flowers on Mother's Day.*)
- **John got a *present* when ... it was his birthday.**
- **Alvin was *present* when ... he wasn't at school.** *Whoopsy!* (Idea: *Alvin was present when he was at school.*)
- **Susan *frowned* when ... she was feeling very happy.** *Whoopsy!* (Idea: *Susan frowned when she wasn't feeling happy.*)
- **The *enormous* giant was ... very small.** *Whoopsy!* (Idea: *The enormous giant was very tall.*)
- **Antwon was *brave* when ... he didn't cry when he cut his finger.**

[**Note:** You may add other examples of your own.]

Whoopsy! (Round Two)
(Add *excited* and *amazed,* and play the game.)

- **You are *excited* when ... you are thinking about something good that is about to happen.**
- **The teacher was *amazed* when ... her students did ordinary work.** *Whoopsy!* (Idea: *The teacher was amazed when her students did really good work.*)

Name _____

The Most Beautiful Kite in the World

memories

complaining

dreary

examine

familiar

celebrate

Sharing What You've Learned at School

[Note: Children are not expected to be able to read the words. The words are for your information.]

DAY 1: (Cut the Picture Vocabulary Cards apart. Place the cards for *memories, examine, complaining,* and *familiar* in a container or small plastic bag.)
Show your child each card. Ask:) **What word does the picture show?** (Idea: *The picture shows someone who is complaining.*)
Tell me what you know about this word. (Share what you know about the word with your child as well. Repeat for each word.)

DAY 2: (Add *dreary* and *celebrate.* Repeat procedure from Day 1. Ask:) **Today, tell me anything more that you know about this word.**

DAY 3: Play Whoopsy! (Round One)
Let's play the Whoopsy! Game that you learned at school. I'll say sentences using words you learned. If the word doesn't fit in the sentence, you say "Whoopsy!" Then I'll ask you to say a sentence where the word fits. If you can do it, you get a point. If you can't do it, I get the point. If the word I use fits the sentence, don't say anything. Now, you're ready to play the game.

- **I had *memories* when ... I looked forward to my summer vacation.** *Whoopsy!* (Idea: *I had memories when I remembered my last birthday.*)
- **Harry *decided* to examine the caterpillar by ... ignoring it and walking it away.** *Whoopsy!* (Idea: *Harry decided to examine the caterpillar by looking at it carefully.*)
- **The teacher was *familiar* ... because we knew him.**
- **Robert was *complaining* when ... his sore hand felt much better.** *Whoopsy!* (Idea: *Robert was complaining when his sore hand hurt.*)
- **The dog was *familiar* because ... we had never seen him before.** *Whoopsy!* (Idea: *The dog was familiar because we had seen him before.*)
- **The boy was *complaining* when ... he felt just fine.** *Whoopsy!* (Idea: *The boy was complaining when he felt awful.*)

[**Note:** You may add other examples of your own.]

DAY 4: Play Whoopsy! (Round Two)
(Add *dreary* and *celebrate,* and play the game.)

- **The *dreary* day was ... gloomy, dark, and cold.**
- **Missy decided to *celebrate* when ... she did a good job on the Happy Face Game.**

Name _____

Making a List

| cheese | smoked salmon | flat bread | water |

squabbling

drifted

relieved

parents

prickly

opposites

Sharing What You've Learned at School

[**Note:** Children are not expected to be able to read the words. The words are for your information.]

DAY 1: (Cut the Picture Vocabulary Cards apart. Place the cards for *squabbling, parents, drifted,* and *prickly* in a container or small plastic bag.)
Show your child each card. Ask:) **What word does the picture show?** (Idea: *The picture shows someone who is squabbling.*)
Tell me what you know about this word. (Share what you know about the word with your child as well. Repeat for each word.)

DAY 2: (Add in two new words *relieved* and *opposites.* Repeat procedure from Day 1. Ask:) **Today, tell me anything more that you know about this word.**

DAY 3: Play Opposites Game (Round One)
Let's play the Opposites Game you learned at school. I'll use a vocabulary word in a sentence. If you can tell me the opposite of that word, you win one point. If you can't tell me, I get the point. Let's play.

• **The plant was tall and *prickly*. Tell me the opposite of prickly.** (Idea: *Smooth.*) *Smooth* **could be the opposite of prickly.**
• **When Tim and Tom played with the airplane, they were *squabbling*. Tell me the opposite of**

squabbling. (Idea: *Getting along.*) **"Getting along" could be the opposite of squabbling.**
• **Michael and Cara *are Todd's parents*. Tell me the opposite of "are Todd's parents."** (Idea: *Are not Todd's parents.*) **"Are not Todd's parents" could be the opposite of "are Todd's parents."**
• **The ship on the ocean *did not drift*. Tell me the opposite of "did not drift."** (Idea: *Drifted.*) *Drifted* **could be the opposite of "did not drift."**
• **The cat *was prickly* with the dog. Tell me the opposite of "was" prickly.** (Idea: *Was not prickly.*) **"Was not prickly" could be the opposite of "was" prickly.**
• **The children were *starving*. Tell me the opposite of starving.** (Idea: *Had lots to eat.*) **"Had lots to eat" could be the opposite of starving.**

[**Note:** You may add other examples of your own.]

DAY 4: Play Opposites Game (Round Two)
(Add *relieved* and *opposites,* and play the game.)

• **When Daniel saw his sister, he was *relieved*. Tell me the opposite of relieved.** (Idea: *Upset.*) *Upset* **could be the opposite of relieved.**
• **Up and down *are opposites*. Tell me the opposite of "are opposites."** (Idea: *Are not opposites.*) **"Are not opposites" could be the opposite of "are opposites."**

Name _____

Making a List
Animals in the Zoo

stork	baboon	giraffe	snake
hippopotamus	lion	elephant	zebra

shy

silly

feelings

bored

mood

emotions

Sharing What You've Learned at School

[**Note:** Children are not expected to be able to read the words. The words are for your information.]

DAY 1: (Cut the Picture Vocabulary Cards apart. Place the cards for *shy, bored, silly,* and *mood* in a container or small plastic bag.)
(Show your child each card. Ask:) **What word does the picture show?** (Idea: *The picture shows someone who is feeling bored.*)
Tell me what you know about this word. (Share what you know about the word with your child as well. Repeat for each word.)

DAY 2: (Add *emotions* and *feelings.* Repeat procedure from Day 1. Ask:) **Today, tell me anything more that you know about this word.**

DAY 3: Play Opposites Game (Round One)
Let's play the Opposites Game you learned at school. I'll use a vocabulary word in a sentence. If you can tell me the opposite of that word, you will win one point. If you can't tell me, I get the point. Now, you're ready to play the game.

- **The child was acting *shy.* Tell me the opposite of "was acting shy."** (Idea: W*as not acting shy.*) **"Was not acting shy" could be the opposite of "acting shy."**
- **The boy with nothing to do *was bored.* Tell me the opposite of "was bored."** (Idea: *Was not*

bored.) **"Was not bored" could be the opposite of "was bored."**
- **Benjamin *was not acting silly.* Tell me the opposite of "was not acting silly."** (Idea: *Was acting silly.*) **"Was acting silly" could be the opposite of "was not acting silly."**
- **Pete was in a *good mood.* Tell me the opposite of "good mood."** (Idea: *Bad mood.*) **"Bad mood" could be the opposite of "good mood."**
- **Sally *was hot.* Tell me the opposite of "was hot."** (Idea: *Was cold.*) **"Was cold" could be the opposite of "was hot."**
- **Tamsin *was not shy.* Tell me the opposite of "was not shy."** (Idea: *Was shy.*) **"Was shy" could be the opposite of "was not shy."**

[**Note:** You may add other examples of your own.]

DAY 4: Play Opposites Game (Round Two)
(Add *emotions* and *feelings,* and play the game.)

- **George's face *showed his emotions.* Tell me the opposite of "showed his emotions."** (Idea: *Did not show his emotions.*) **"Did not show his emotions" could be the opposite of "showed his emotions."**
- **The mean pirate *had no feelings.* Tell me the opposite of "had no feelings."** (Idea: *Had feelings.*) **"Had feelings" could be the opposite of "had no feelings."**

Name _____

Making a List
Emotions

| thankful | disappointed | proud | excited | bored | jealous |

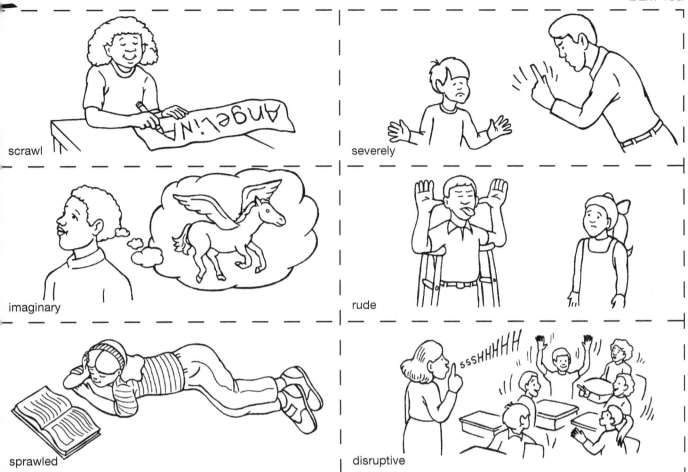

scrawl

severely

imaginary

rude

sprawled

disruptive

Sharing What You've Learned at School

Note: Children are not expected to be able to read the words. The words are for your information.]

DAY 1: (Cut the Picture Vocabulary Cards apart. Place the cards for *scrawl, rude, severely,* and *sprawled* in a container or small plastic bag.)
Show your child each card. Ask:) **What word does the picture show?** (Idea: *The picture shows someone who is being rude.*)
Tell me what you know about this word. (Share what you know about the word with your child as well. Repeat for each word.)

DAY 2: (Add *imaginary* and *disruptive.* Repeat procedure from Day 1. Ask:) **Today, tell me anything more that you know about this word.**

DAY 3: Play Opposites Game (Round One)
Let's play the Opposites Game that you learned at school. I'll use a vocabulary word in a sentence. If you can tell me the opposite of that word, you win one point. If you can't tell me, I get the point. Let's play.

- **The child was being *rude.* Tell me the opposite of rude.** (Idea: *Polite.*) **Polite could be the opposite of rude.**

- **The little girl wrote in a *scrawl.* Tell me the opposite of scrawl.** (Idea: *Neatly.*) **Neatly could be the opposite of scrawl.**
- **The police officer talked to her *severely.* Tell me the opposite of severely.** (Idea: *Nicely.*) **Nicely could be the opposite of severely.**
- **Sanders was *sprawled* in his chair. Tell me the opposite of sprawled.** (Idea: *Sitting nicely.*) **"Sitting nicely" could be the opposite of sprawled.**
- **Thomas was *unsatisfied* after breakfast. Tell me the opposite of unsatisfied.** (Idea: *Satisfied.*) **Satisfied could be the opposite of unsatisfied.**
- **Arnold was *unselfish* about sharing his toys. Tell me the opposite of unselfish.** (Idea: *Selfish.*) **Unselfish could be the opposite of selfish.**

[**Note:** You may add other examples of your own.]

DAY 4: Play Opposites Game (Round Two)
(Add *imaginary* and *disruptive,* and play the game.)

- **The shouting and jumping *were disruptive* in gym class. Tell me the opposite of "were disruptive."** (Idea: *Were not disruptive.*) **"Were not disruptive" could be the opposite of "were disruptive."**
- **The dragons in the book were *imaginary.* Tell me the opposite of imaginary.** (Idea: *Real.*) **Real could be the opposite of imaginary.**

BLM 13a

A–27

Name _____

Dinosaur Days

On Monday _____ came.

On Tuesday _____ came.

On Wednesday _____ came.

On Thursday _____ came.

On Friday _____ came.

On Saturday _____ came.

On Sunday _____ came.

Hadrosaurus

Apatosaurus

Triceratops

Tyrannosaurus rex

Pteranodon

Stegosaurus

Ankylosaurus

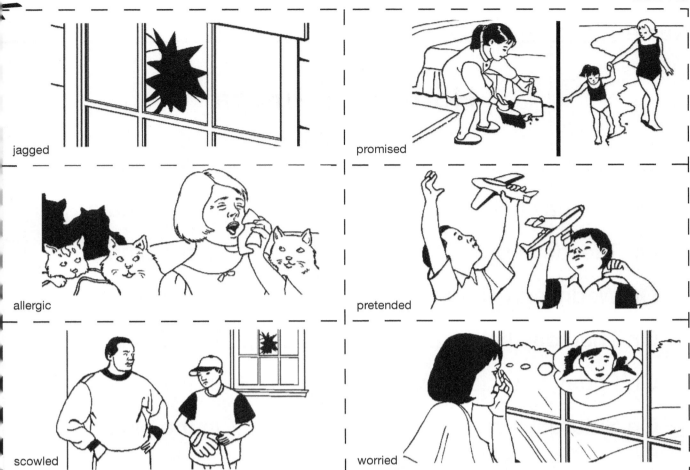

jagged

promised

allergic

pretended

scowled

worried

Sharing What You've Learned at School

[**Note:** Children are not expected to be able to read the words. The words are for your information.]

DAY 1: (Cut the Picture Vocabulary Cards apart. Place the cards for *jagged, pretended, promised,* and *scowled* in a container or small plastic bag.) (Show your child each card. Ask:) **What word does the picture show?** (Idea: *The picture shows something that is jagged.*)
Tell me what you know about this word. (Share what you know about the word with your child as well. Repeat for each word.)

DAY 2: (Add *allergic* and *worried.* Repeat procedure from Day 1. Ask:) **Today, tell me anything more that you know about this word.**

DAY 3: Play Opposites Game (Round One)
Let's play the Opposites Game that you learned at school. I'll use a vocabulary word in a sentence. If you can tell me the opposite of that word, you win one point. If you can't tell me, I get the point. Let's play.

- **The pavement was *jagged.* Tell me the opposite of jagged.** (Idea: *Smooth.*) **Smooth could be the opposite of jagged.**
- **Jason and Brandon *pretended* to be pilots. Tell me the opposite of pretended.** (Idea: *Did not*

pretend.) **"Did not pretend" could be the opposite of pretended.**
- **Mom *promised* to take us to the park. Tell me the opposite of promised.** (Idea: *Did not promise.)* **"Did not promise" could be the opposite of promised.**
- **Nicky *scowled* at me. Tell me the opposite of scowled.** (Idea: *Smiled.*) **Smiled could be the opposite of scowled.**
- **April *was excited* about her new doll. Tell me the opposite of "was excited."** (Idea: *Was not excited.*) **"Was not excited" could be the opposite of "was excited."**
- **Bindy's pony was *enormous.* Tell me the opposite of enormous.** (Idea: *Tiny.*) **Tiny could be the opposite of enormous.**

[**Note:** You may add other examples of your own.]

DAY 4: Play Opposites Game (Round Two)
(Add *allergic* and *worried,* and play the game.)

- **Sarah *was allergic* to cats. Tell me the opposite of "was allergic."** (Idea: *Was not allergic.*) **"Was not allergic" could be the opposite of "was allergic."**
- **Dad *was worried* when Henry fell. Tell me the opposite of "was worried."** (Idea: *Was not worried.*) **"Was not worried" could be the opposite of "was worried."**

Name _____

Hooray, A Pinata

On Sunday I put _____ in the pinata.

On Monday I put _____ in the pinata.

On Tuesday I put _____ in the pinata.

On Wednesday I put _____ in the pinata.

On Thursday I put _____ in the pinata.

On Friday I put _____ in the pinata.

On Saturday I put _____ in the pinata.

sloppy

bloom

anxious

patience

sentence

content

Sharing What You've Learned at School

[**Note:** Children are not expected to be able to read the words. The words are for your information.]

DAY 1: (Cut the Picture Vocabulary Cards apart. Place the cards for *sloppy, patience, bloom,* and *sentence* in a container or small plastic bag.)
(Show your child each card. Ask:) **What word does the picture show?** (Idea: *The picture shows someone who is showing patience.*)
Tell me what you know about this word. (Share what you know about the word with your child as well. Repeat for each word.)

DAY 2: (Add *content* and *anxious*. Repeat procedure from Day 1. Ask:) **Today, tell me anything more that you know about this word.**

DAY 3: Opposites Game (Round One)
Let's play the Opposites Game that you learned at school. I'll use a vocabulary word in a sentence. If you can tell me the opposite of that word, you win one point. If you can't tell me, I get the point. Now, you're ready to play the game.

- **The handwriting was *sloppy*. Tell me the opposite of sloppy.** (Idea: *Neat.*) **Neat could be the opposite of sloppy.**
- **Tiana *showed patience* while waiting for her puppy to drink. Tell me the opposite of "showed patience."** (Idea: *Did not show patience.*) **"Did**

not show patience" could be the opposite of "showed patience."**
- **After trying hard for a week to print his name, Mark *started to bloom*. Tell me the opposite of "started to bloom."** (Idea: *Did not start to bloom.*) **"Did not start to bloom" could be the opposite of "started to bloom."**
- **Carmen *had memories* of Mexico. Tell me the opposite of "had memories."** (Idea: *Did not have memories.*) **"Did not have memories" could be the opposite of "had memories."**
- **Cole *was not complaining* about his sore hand. Tell me the opposite of "was not complaining."** (Idea: *Was complaining.*) **"Was complaining" could be the opposite of "was not complaining."**

[**Note:** You may add other examples of your own.]

DAY 4: Play Opposites Game (Round Two)
(Add *content* and *anxious,* and play the game.)

- **Iris *was content* with her kitten. Tell me the opposite of "was content."** (Idea: *Was not content.*) **"Was not content" could be the opposite of "was content."**
- **Pat *was anxious* about her new job. Tell me the opposite of "was anxious."** (Idea: *Was not anxious.*) **"Was not anxious" could be the opposite of "was anxious."**

Name _____

Leo the Late Bloomer

On Sunday Leo_____ .

On Monday Leo_____ .

On Tuesday Leo_____ .

On Wednesday Leo_____ .

On Thursday Leo_____ .

On Friday Leo_____ .

On Saturday Leo_____ .

difficult

gentle

lonely

appetite

explained

language

Sharing What You've Learned at School

[**Note:** The children are not expected to be able to read the words. The words are for your information.]

DAY 1: (Cut the Picture Vocabulary Cards apart. Place the cards for **difficult, appetite, gentle,** and **explained** in a container or small plastic bag.) (Show your child each card. Ask:) **What word does the picture show?** (Idea: *The picture shows someone who is being gentle.*)
Tell me what you know about this word. (Share what you know about the word with your child as well. Repeat for each word.)

DAY 2: (Add *lonely* and *language.* Repeat procedure from Day 1. Ask:) **Today, tell me anything more that you know about this word.**

DAY 3: Play Chew the Fat (Round One)
Let's play the Chew the Fat game that you learned at school. I'll say sentences with your vocabulary words in them. If I use the word correctly, say, "Well done!" If I use the word incorrectly, say, "Chew the fat." Then I'll ask you to finish the sentence so that it makes sense. Let's play.

- **The game was *difficult* because ... it was easy to play.** *Chew the fat.* **The game was difficult because ...** (Idea: *It was hard to play.*) **Say the whole sentence.** *The game was difficult because it was hard to play.* **Well done!**

- **I knew I had an *appetite* because ... I was hungry.** *Well done!*
- **The teacher *explained* the rules because ... we didn't know how to play.** *Well done!*
- **The doctor was *gentle* because ... my arm wasn't sore.** *Chew the fat.* **The doctor was gentle because ...** (Idea: *My arm was sore.*) **Say the whole sentence.** *The doctor was gentle because my arm was sore.* **Well done!**
- **We wanted to *celebrate* because ... we won the game.** *Well done!*
- **The *shiny* ring was ... dull and boring.** *Chew the fat.* **The shiny ring was ...** (Idea: *Bright and pretty.*) **Say the whole sentence.** *The shiny ring was bright and pretty.* **Well done!**

[**Note:** You may add other examples of your own.]

DAY 4: Play Chew the Fat (Round Two)
(Add *lonely* and *language,* and play the game.)

- **Barbara was *lonely* because ... her whole family was visiting her.** *Chew the fat.* **Barbara was lonely because ...** (Idea: *Her family was not visiting her.*) **Say the whole sentence.** *Barbara was lonely because her family was not visiting her.*
- **Language* is ... sounds, words, and actions we use to talk to each other.** *Well done!*

Name _____

Sammy: The Classroom Guinea Pig

Sammy liked to eat

carrot	eggs	erasers	cantaloupe rind
wood shavings	grass	paper	apple
dandelions	guinea pig pellets	lettuce	water
hay	cabbage	milk	bread

drowsy

trembled

protect

scorched

cowered

Africa

Sharing What You've Learned at School

[**Note:** The children are not expected to be able to read the words. The words are for your information.]

DAY 1: (Cut the Picture Vocabulary Cards apart. Place the cards for *drowsy, scorched, trembled,* and *cowered* in a container or small plastic bag.) (Show your child each card. Ask:) **What word does the picture show?** (Idea: *The picture shows someone who is feeling drowsy.*)
Tell me what you know about this word. (Share what you know about the word with your child as well. Repeat for each word.)

DAY 2: (Add *protect* and *Africa.* Repeat procedure from Day 1. Ask:) **Today, tell me anything more that you know about this word.**

DAY 3: Play Chew the Fat (Round One)
Let's play the Chew the Fat game that you learned at school. I'll say sentences with your vocabulary words in them. If I use the word correctly, say, "Well done!" If I use the word incorrectly, say, "Chew the fat!" Then I'll ask you to finish the sentence so that it makes sense. Let's play.

• **Bob was *drowsy* because ... he'd just had a good night's sleep.** *Chew the fat.* **Bob was drowsy because ...** (Idea: *He had been awake all night.*) **Say the whole sentence.** *Bob was drowsy because he had been awake all night.* **Well done!**

• **The pot was *scorched* because ... it had only been burned a little.** *Well done!*
• **Samuel trembled because ... he was cold and wet.** *Well done!*
• **The cat *cowered* when ... the ant walked by.** *Chew the fat.* **The cat cowered when ...** (Idea: *The big dog walked by.*) **Say the whole sentence.** *The cat cowered when the big dog walked by.* **Well done!**
• **Uncle Charles was *relieved* when ... he found the lost keys.** *Well done!*
• **The falling feather *drifted* because ... there was no wind.** *Chew the fat.* **The falling feather drifted because ...** (Idea: *It was windy.*) **Say the whole sentence.** *The falling feather drifted because it was windy.* **Well done!**

[**Note:** You may add other examples of your own.]

DAY 4: Play Chew the Fat (Round Two)
(Add *protect* and *Africa,* and play the game.)

• **You *protect* your feet ... with mittens.** *Chew the fat.* **You protect your feet ...** (Idea: *With shoes or boots.*) **Say the whole sentence.** *You protect your feet with shoes or boots.* **Well done!**
• ***Africa* is ... a continent.** *Well done!*

Name _____

Animals That Live in Africa

We know these animals live in Africa:

kangaroo	bush baby	reindeer	bear
beaver	goat	wildebeest	fox
hippopotamus	panda	lion	wolf
porcupine	emu	moose	hyena

adopt

wonder

tradition

nursery

chuckles

decorations

Sharing What You've Learned at School

[**Note:** Children are not expected to be able to read the words. The words are for your information.]

DAY 1: (Cut the Picture Vocabulary Cards apart. Place the cards for *adopt, nursery, wonder,* and *chuckles* in a container or small plastic bag.)
Show your child each card. Ask:) **What word does the picture show?** (Idea: *The picture shows plants at a nursery.*)
Tell me what you know about this word. (Share what you know about the word with your child as well. Repeat for each word.)

DAY 2: (Add *tradition* and *decorations.* Repeat procedure from Day 1. Ask:) **Today, tell me anything more that you know about this word.**

DAY 3: Play Chew the Fat (Round One)
Let's play the Chew the Fat game that you learned at school. I'll say sentences with your vocabulary words in them. If I use the word correctly, say, "Well done!" If I use the word incorrectly, say, "Chew the fat." Then I'll ask you to finish the sentence so that it makes sense. Let's play.

• **Marvin wanted to *adopt* a child because ... he had too many children.** *Chew the fat.* **Marvin wanted to adopt a child because ...** (Idea: *He had none.*) **Say the whole sentence.** *Marvin wanted to adopt a child because he had none.* **Well done!**

• **If you *wonder* about something you are ... interested in that thing.** *Well done!*
• **You can get roses and daisies at ... a *nursery.*** *Well done!*
• ***Chuckles* happen when ... you are really mad about something.** *Chew the fat.* **Chuckles happen when ...** (Idea: *You think something is funny.*) **Say the whole sentence.** *Chuckles happen when you think something is funny.* **Well done!**
• **Simon was *bored* because ... his friends were gone and he had nothing to do.** *Well done!*
• **I knew she was *silly* because ... she did <u>not</u> do anything funny or goofy.** *Chew the fat.* **I knew she was silly because ...** (Idea: *Everything she did was funny or goofy.*) **Say the whole sentence.** *I knew she was silly because everything she did was funny or goofy.* **Well done!**

[**Note:** You may add other examples of your own.]

DAY 4: Play Chew the Fat (Round Two)
(Add *tradition* and *decorations,* and play the game.)

• **A *tradition* is something that ... you never do.** *Chew the fat.* **A tradition is something that ...** (Idea: *You always do.*) **Say the whole sentence.** *A tradition is something that you always do.* **Well done!**
• ***Decorations* are used to ... make a place look prettier.** *Well done!*

Name _____

Pablo's Tree

1.

2.

3.

4.

5.

6.

gasp

howled

attack

finally

dashed

rescue

Sharing What You've Learned at School

Note: Children are not expected to be able to read the words. The words are for your information.]

DAY 1: (Cut the Picture Vocabulary Cards apart. Place the cards for *gasp, finally, howled,* and *dashed* in a container or small plastic bag.)
Show your child each card. Ask:) **What word does the picture show?** (Idea: *The picture shows a wolf that howled.*)
Tell me what you know about this word. (Share what you know about the word with your child as well. Repeat for each word.)

DAY 2: (Add *attack* and *rescue.* Repeat procedure from Day 1. Ask:) **Today, tell me anything more that you know about this word.**

DAY 3: Play Chew the Fat (Round One)
Let's play the Chew the Fat game that you learned at school. I'll say sentences with your vocabulary words in them. If I use the word correctly, say, "Well done!" If I use the word incorrectly, say, "Chew the fat." Then I'll ask you to finish the sentence so that it makes sense. Let's play.

* **The squirrel *dashed* across the path because ...** it wanted to stay on the same side. *Chew the fat.* **The squirrel dashed across the path because ...**

(Idea: *It wanted to get to the other side.*) **Say the whole sentence.** *The squirrel dashed across the path because it wanted to get to the other side.* **Well done!**

* **If you *gasp* ... you might be surprised by something.** *Well done!*
* **If you *finally* get a puppy ... it means that you waited a long time to get it.** *Well done!*
* **The little boy *howled* when ... he did not fall and scrape his knee.** *Chew the fat.* **The little boy howled when ...** (Idea: *He fell and scraped his knee.*) **Say the whole sentence.** *The little boy howled when he fell and scraped his knee.* **Well done!**
* **Flowers *bloom* in the spring.** *Well done!*

[**Note:** You may add other examples of your own.]

DAY 4: Play Chew the Fat (Round Two)
(Add *attack* and *rescue,* and play the game.)

* **You should *rescue* ... people who aren't in danger.** *Chew the fat.* **You should rescue ...** (Idea: *People who are in danger.*) **Say the whole sentence.** *You should rescue people who are in danger.* **Well done!**
* **An alligator will *attack* because ... he wants something to eat.** *Well done!*

Name _____

Dreams

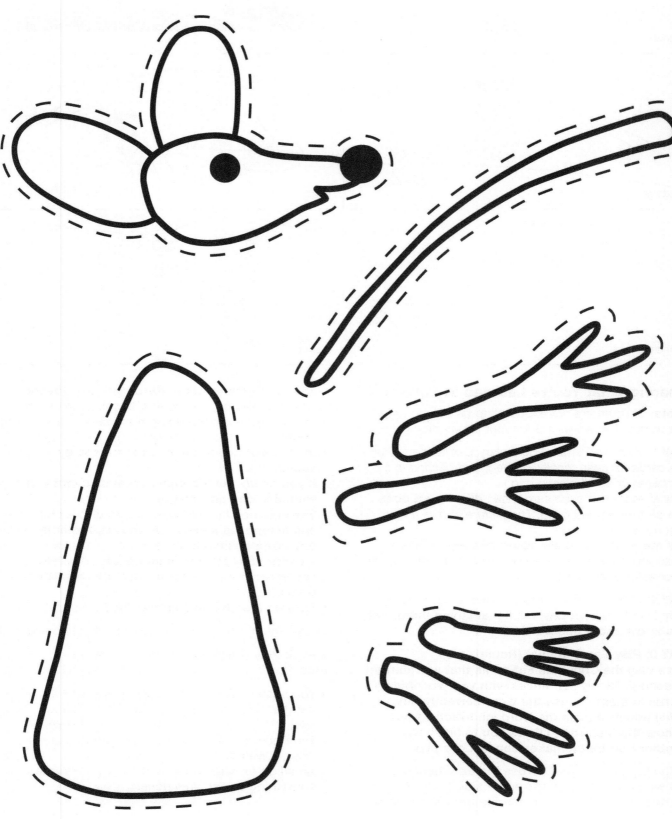

dim

chattering

active

root

impatient

dawn

Sharing What You've Learned at School

[**Note:** Children are not expected to be able to read the words. The words are for your information.]

DAY 1: (Cut the Picture Vocabulary Cards apart. Place the cards for *dim, root, chattering,* and *impatient* in a container or small plastic bag.)
(Show your child each card. Ask:) **What word does the picture show?** (Idea: *The picture shows a time when the light is dim.*)
Tell me what you know about this word. (Share what you know about the word with your child as well. Repeat for each word.)

DAY 2: (Add *active* and *dawn*. Repeat procedure from Day 1. Ask:) **Today, tell me anything more that you know about this word.**

DAY 3: Play Tom Foolery (Round One)
Let's play the Tom Foolery game that you learned at school. I'll tell you what a word means. Then I'll tell you another meaning for that word. If I tell something that's not correct, sing out "Tom Foolery!" If I say something correct, don't say anything. If you say "Tom Foolery!" and you're right, you get a point. If you're wrong, I get the point. Let's play.

- *Dim* means "not much light." *Dim* also means loud sounds. *Tom Foolery!* **Oh, you're right, you learned only one meaning for dim.**
- A *root* can be the underground part of a plant. When you root, you turn over the dirt looking for food.
- *Chattering* is short, quick sounds. Chattering can be made by a squirrel.
- If you are *impatient,* you don't like to wait. Impatient also means that you might get upset if someone takes a long time.
- *Roared* is what a lion might do. It could also mean that "something or someone went by fast and noisily."
- *Grains* are small seeds like wheat. They can also be things that travel on rails and go, "Whoo! Whoo!" *Tom Foolery!* **Oh, you're right. Trains go "Whoo! Whoo!"**

[**Note:** You may also add other examples of your own.]

DAY 4: Play Tom Foolery (Round Two)
(Add *active* and *dawn,* and play the game.)

- An *active* person is busy and quick.
- *Dawn* comes at the beginning of the day. The sun is already high overhead at dawn. *Tom Foolery!* **Oh, you're right, the sun is low at dawn.**

Name _____

Sounds Farm Animals Make

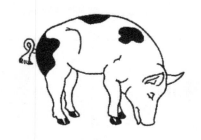

pig ____

donkey ____

cat ____

horse ____

rabbit ____

rooster ____

cow ____

sheep ____

honeybees ____

hen ____

dog ____

duck ____

pigeon ____

goose ____

turkey ____

substitute

memorize

honest

favorite

perfect

cheat

Sharing What You've Learned at School

[Note: Children are not expected to be able to read the words. The words are for your information.]

DAY 1: (Cut the Picture Vocabulary Cards apart. Place the cards for *substitute, favorite, memorize,* and *perfect* in a container or small plastic bag.) (Show your child each card. Ask:) **What word does the picture show?** (Idea: *The picture shows a favorite thing.*) **Tell me what you know about this word.** (Share what you know about the word with your child as well. Repeat for each word.)

DAY 2: (Add *honest* and *cheat.* Repeat procedure from Day 1. Ask:) **Today, tell me anything more that you know about this word.**

DAY 3: Play Tom Foolery (Round One) **Let's play the Tom Foolery game that you learned at school. I'll tell you what a word means. Then I'll tell you another meaning for that word. If I tell something that's not correct, sing out "Tom Foolery!" If I say something correct, don't say anything. If you say "Tom Foolery!" and you're right, you get a point. If you're wrong, I get the point. Let's play.**

• *Substitute* **means "a person who takes the place of someone else." Substitute is also an underwater ship. Tom Foolery! Oh, you're right, I was thinking of a submarine.**

• *Perfect* **means "no mistakes." If your assignment is perfect, you get a good grade.**

• **Your** *favorite* **thing is the thing you like the most. Favorite also means that it tastes good.** *Tom Foolery!* **Oh, you're right. When something tastes good, we talk about its flavor not its favorite.**

• **If you** *memorize,* **you remember perfectly. Memorize also means that you remember only a few words of a song.** *Tom Foolery!* **Oh, you're right. I made that up. If I memorized a song, I would remember all of the words perfectly.**

• **If someone is** *blooming,* **he or she is growing up and getting better at things. Plants with flowers are also blooming.**

• **If you are hungry, you have an** *appetite.* **Appetite also means that you want an apple.** *Tom Foolery!* **Oh, you're right. Appetite just means that you're hungry.**

[Note: You may add other examples of your own.]

DAY 4: Play Tom Foolery (Round Two) (Add *honest* and *cheat,* and play the game.)

• **A person who** *cheats* **doesn't do the right thing.**

• *Honest* **means "you tell the truth and do what is right." It is also the sweet stuff that bees make.** *Tom Foolery!* **Oh, you're right. Bees make honey, not honest.**

Name _____

Hide the Object

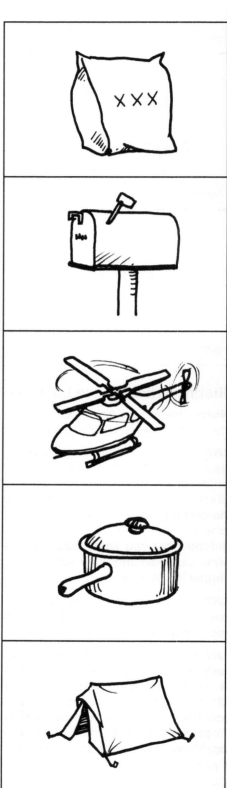

precious

wild

legend

glimpse

slithers

disappears

Sharing What You've Learned at School

[Note: Children are not expected to be able to read the words. The words are for your information.]

DAY 1: (Cut the Picture Vocabulary Cards apart. Place the cards for *precious, glimpse, wild,* and *slithers* in a container or small plastic bag.)
(Show your child each card. Ask:) **What word does the picture show?** (Idea: *The picture shows something precious.*)
Tell me what you know about this word. (Share what you know about the word with your child as well. Repeat for each word.)

DAY 2: (Add *legend* and *disappears.* Repeat procedure from Day 1. Ask:) **Today, tell me anything more that you know about this word.**

DAY 3: Play Tom Foolery (Round One)
Let's play the Tom Foolery game that you learned at school. I'll tell you what a word means. Then I'll tell you another meaning for that word. If I tell something that's not correct, sing out "Tom Foolery!" If I say something correct, don't say anything. If you say "Tom Foolery!" and you're right, you get a point. If you're wrong, I get the point. Let's play.

- *Precious* is something that's important to you. Precious also means good tasting. *Tom Foolery!* Oh, you're right, I was thinking of delicious.
- *Slither* means to move by twisting and sliding. A snake would slither.
- A *wild* animal is not tame. A wild person is one who is angry. *Tom Foolery!* Oh, you're right. A wild person is badly-behaved. I was thinking of riled.
- You can buy plants at a *nursery.* A nursery is also a place for adults. *Tom Foolery!* Oh, you're right. I made that up. A nursery is a place for babies.
- A *winding* road twists and turns. You can make a music box play by winding the key.
- A *glimpse* is a short look at something. When you hurt your foot, you walk with a glimpse. *Tom Foolery!* Oh, you're right. I was thinking of a limp, not a glimpse.

[Note: You may add other examples of your own.]

DAY 4: Play Tom Foolery (Round Two)
(Add *legend* and *disappears,* and play the game.)

- A *legend* tells how something came to be.
- *Disappears* means to go out of sight. We know five other meanings for disappears. *Tom Foolery!* Oh, you're right, we know only one.

Name _____

Loon Lake

Color the water blue.
Color the reeds and lily pads green.
Color the loon black and white.

bare

blossom

seasons

appear

petals

present

Sharing What You've Learned at School

[**Note:** Children are not expected to be able to read the words. The words are for your information.]

DAY 1: (Cut the Picture Vocabulary Cards apart. Place the cards for *bare, appear, blossom,* and *petals* in a container or small plastic bag.)
(Show your child each card. Ask:) **What word does the picture show?** (Idea: *The picture shows a tree that is bare.*)
Tell me what you know about this word. (Share what you know about the word with your child as well. Repeat for each word.)

DAY 2: (Add *seasons* and *present.* Repeat procedure from Day 1. Ask:) **Today, tell me anything more that you know about this word.**

DAY 3: Play Tom Foolery (Round One)
Let's play the Tom Foolery game that you learned at school. I'll tell you what a word means. Then I'll tell you another meaning for that word. If I tell something that's not correct, sing out *Tom Foolery!* If I say something correct, don't say anything. If you say *Tom Foolery!* and you're right, you get a point. If you're wrong, I get the point. Let's play.

- *Blossom* means a flower that turns into fruit. Blossom also means to get worse at things. *Tom Foolery!* Oh, you're right. Blossom means to get better at things.

- *Petals* are the outside parts of flowers. Petals can be white or different colors.
- If you *appear,* I can see you. You also say "Appear" when your friend is looking for you and you are high on a ladder. *Tom Foolery!* Oh, you're right. I guess I was thinking of calling, "Up here!"
- A *clever* person can figure out how to do things. Clever is a kind of material made from animal skins. *Tom Foolery!* Oh, you're right. I made that up. I was thinking of leather, not clever.
- *Bare* means not covered. A table has nothing on it or is not covered when it is bare.
- If you *gasp,* you breathe in quickly. If you gasp something, you hold it in your hand. *Tom Foolery!* Oh, you're right. I guess I was thinking of grasp and not gasp.

[**Note:** You may add other examples of your own.]

DAY 4: Play Tom Foolery (Round Two)
(Add *seasons* and *present,* and play the game.)

- *Seasons* come and go all year long. When you are season, it means that it is very cold where you are. *Tom Foolery!* Oh, you're right. I was thinkin' of freezin', not season.
- In the *present* means something is happening right now. Present also means "being somewhere."

Name _____

The Seasons

snuggle

explore

disturb

odor

wilderness

reasons

Sharing What You've Learned at School

[**Note:** Children are not expected to be able to read the words. The words are for your information.]

DAY 1: (Cut the Picture Vocabulary Cards apart. Place the cards for *snuggle, explore, disturb,* and *odor* in a container or small plastic bag.)
(Show your child each card. Ask:) **What word does the picture show?** (Idea: *The picture shows snuggle.*) **Tell me what you know about this word.** (Share what you know about the word with your child as well. Repeat for each word.)

DAY 2: (Add *wilderness* and *reasons.* Repeat procedure from Day 1. Ask:) **Today, tell me anything more that you know about this word.**

DAY 3: Play Super Choosing Game (Round One)
Let's play the Super Choosing Game that you learned at school. I'll say sentences with some of the words you know in them. You have to choose the correct word for the sentence. If you choose correctly, you win one point. If you don't choose correctly, I get the point. Let's play.

- **If you smell something, is it an odor, did you mutter, or are you brave ?** *Odor.*

- **If you cuddle up with me, do you chatter, disturb me, or snuggle?** *Snuggle.*
- **Did the curious children explore, are they gentle, or did they gasp?** *Explore.*
- **When I interrupt you while you are doing homework, am I selfish, do I disturb you, or do I amaze you?** *Disturb.*
- **When I make supper, do I prepare it, have I crept, or do I harvest?** *Prepare.*
- **If you breathe a short, quick breath in, do you howl, sigh, or gasp?** *Gasp.*

[**Note:** You may add other examples of your own.]

DAY 4: Play Super Choosing Game (Round Two)
(Add *wilderness* and *reasons,* and play the game.)

- **If you tell facts about why you think something, do you slither, have emotions, or give reasons?** *Reasons.*
- **Is land that has no people living in it the wilderness, a cottage, or ingredients?** *Wilderness.*

Name _____

When We Go Camping

I would not like to go camping.

I would like to go camping.

cave

den

burrow

frost

hibernate

migrate

Sharing What You've Learned at School

[**Note:** Children are not expected to be able to read the words. The words are for your information.]

DAY 1: (Cut the Picture Vocabulary Cards apart. Place the cards for *cave, den, burrow,* and *frost* in a container or small plastic bag.)
(Show your child each card. Ask:) **What word does the picture show?** (Idea: *The picture shows frost on the window.*)
Tell me what you know about this word. (Share what you know about the word with your child as well. Repeat for each word.)

DAY 2: (Add *hibernate* and *migrate.* Repeat procedure from Day 1. Ask:) **Today, tell me anything more that you know about this word.**

DAY 3: Play Super Choosing Game (Round One)
Let's play the Super Choosing Game that you learned at school. I'll say sentences with some of the words you know in them. You have to choose the correct word for the sentence. If you choose correctly, you win one point. If you don't choose correctly, I get the point. Let's play.

- **Is a comfortable room in your house called a den, a ten, or a Ben?** *A den.*
- **If you were a gopher, would you live in a pillow, a blossom, or a burrow?** *A burrow.*
- **If there is white, powdery ice on the grass, is it cost, moss, or frost?** *Frost.*
- **Some holes in the ground are large enough for people to explore. Are they braves, waves, or caves?** *Caves.*
- **When you begged for corn on the cob for supper, did you seed, read, or plead?** *Plead.*
- **If something is important to you, is it precious, delicious, or anxious?** *Precious.*

[**Note:** You may add other examples of your own.]

DAY 4: Play Super Choosing Game (Round Two)
(Add *hibernate* and *migrate,* and play the game.)

- **When the birds flew south for the winter, did they migrate, hibernate, or adopt?** *Migrate.*
- **When a bear sleeps most of the winter, does he appear, hibernate, or memorize?** *Hibernate.*

Name _____

Time to Sleep

The animal I liked best in this story is:

Bear															

Snail															

Skunk															

Turtle															

Woodchuck															

Ladybug															

limbs

awesome

dormant

chores

devour

impressions

Sharing What You've Learned at School

[**Note:** Children are not expected to be able to read the words. The words are for your information.]

DAY 1: (Cut the Picture Vocabulary Cards apart. Place the cards for *limbs, chores, awesome,* and *devour* in a container or small plastic bag.)
(Show your child each card. Ask:) **What word does the picture show?** (Idea: *The picture shows someone doing their chores.*)
Tell me what you know about this word. (Share what you know about the word with your child as well. Repeat for each word.)

DAY 2: (Add *dormant* and *impressions.* Repeat procedure from Day 1. Ask:) **Today, tell me anything more that you know about this word.**

DAY 3: Play Super Choosing Game (Round One)
Let's play the Super Choosing Game that you learned at school. I'll say sentences with some of the words that you know in them. You have to choose the correct word for the sentence. If you choose correctly, you win one point. If you don't choose correctly, I get the point. Let's play.

- **If you do not do what you are told to do, are you being desperate, disobedient, or familiar?** *Disobedient.*

- **When your day was the most amazing day ever, would you call it blossom, honest, or awesome?** *Awesome.*
- **Can your arms and legs also be called feelings, gales, or limbs?** *Limbs.*
- **If you treat others poorly by what you do and say, are you gentle, impatient, or rude?** *Rude.*
- **Branches are also called meadows, opposites, or limbs?** *Limbs.*
- **When I go home, I feed the cats, water the plants, and check the mail. Am I doing promises, sentences, or chores?** *Chores.*
- **What would a dinosaur do with his lunch? Would he scorch, devour, or snuggle it?** *Devour.*

[**Note:** You may add other examples of your own.]

DAY 4: Play Super Choosing Game (Round Two)
(Add *impressions* and *dormant,* and play the game.)

- **In the wintertime, are trees dormant, selfish, or sloppy?** *Dormant.*
- **If you push on a marshmallow with your finger and you leave small holes behind, are they sprouts, impressions, or traditions?** *Impressions.*

_____is fun in the winter.

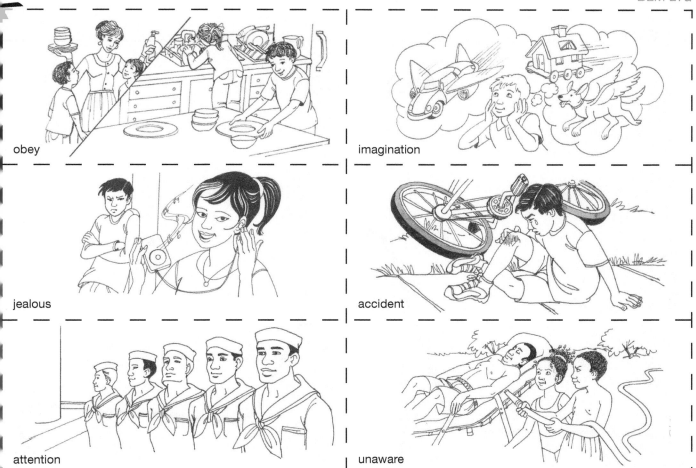

obey

imagination

jealous

accident

attention

unaware

Sharing What You've Learned at School

[Note: Children are not expected to be able to read the words. The words are for your information.]

DAY 1: (Cut the Picture Vocabulary Cards apart. Place the cards for *obey, accident, imagination,* and *attention* in a container or small plastic bag.) (Show your child each card. Ask:) **What word does the picture show?** (Idea: *The picture shows people standing at attention.*)
Tell me what you know about this word. (Share what you know about the word with your child as well. Repeat for each word.)

DAY 2: (Add *unaware* and *jealous*. Repeat procedure from Day 1. Ask:) **Tell me anything more that you know about this word.**

Day 3: Play Super Choosing Game (Round One)
Let's play the Super Choosing Game that you learned at school. I'll say sentences with some of the words you know in them. You have to choose the correct word for the sentence. If you choose correctly, you win one point. If you don't choose correctly, I get the point. Let's play.

- **If you listen to me and do what I say, do you scowl, Monday, or obey?** *Obey.*
- **When your teacher teaches you, does your teacher need attention, complaining, or a den?** *Attention.*
- **Bryan crashed his bike on a hill and hurt his foot. Did he have a decoration, an accident, or a sentence?** *An accident.*
- **In my mind, I see cities with no roads, cars with no wheels, and people with no problems. Am I using my reasons, my wilderness, or my imagination?** *Imagination.*
- **All of the soldiers stood still at tradition, scrawl, or attention?** *Attention.*
- **A purse was quickly grabbed from someone's hand. Was it splashed, snatched, or crashed?** *Snatched.*

[Note: You may add other examples of your own.]

DAY 4: Play Super Choosing Game (Round Two)
(Add *unaware* and *jealous,* and play the game.)

- **Nigel didn't know about his surprise party. Was he like air, a moving stair, or unaware?** *Unaware.*
- **If you want something that someone else has, are you prepared, jealous, or lonely?** *Jealous.*

Name _____

My Safety Tip

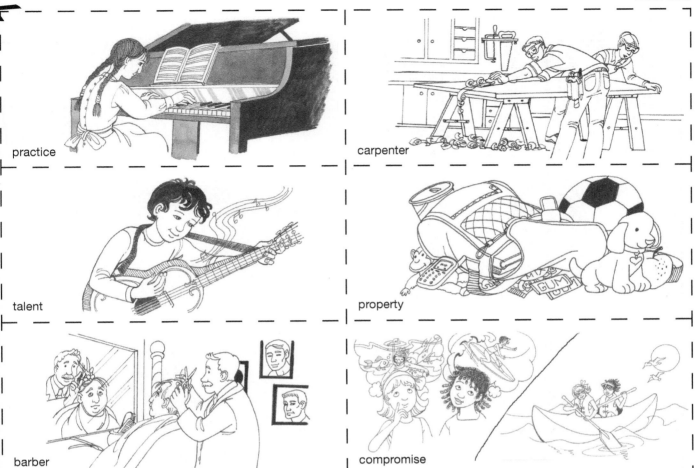

practice

carpenter

talent

property

barber

compromise

Sharing What You've Learned at School

[**Note:** Children are not expected to be able to read the words. The words are for your information.]

DAY 1: (Cut the Picture Vocabulary Cards apart. Place the cards for *practice, property, carpenter,* and *barber* in a container or small plastic bag.)
(Show your child each card. Ask:) **What word does the picture show?** (Idea: *The picture shows someone who is a carpenter.*)
Tell me what you know about this word. (Share what you know about the word with your child as well. Repeat for each word.)

DAY 2: (Add *talent* and *compromise*. Repeat procedure from Day 1. Ask:) **Today, tell me anything more that you know about this word.**

DAY 3: Play Super Choosing Game (Round One)
Let's play the Super Choosing Game that you learned at school. I'll say sentences with some of the words you know in them. You have to choose the correct word for the sentence. If you choose correctly, you win one point. If you don't choose correctly, I get the point. Let's play.

- **If you work hard and do something again and again to get better at it, do you jealous, practice, or mutter?** *Practice.*

- **A person who cuts hair and trims beards is called a precious, a sly, or a barber?** *A barber.*
- **When your wooden gate needs repair, you might call a carpenter, a brave, or a cave?** *A carpenter.*
- **Some things belong to me. Are they my drowsy, my gathering, or my property?** *My property.*
- **If you want something that someone else wants, you might be feeling perfect, jealous, or satisfied?** *Jealous.*
- **A good smell was coming from the kitchen. Was it an order, an odor, or a slither?** *An odor.*

[**Note:** You may add other examples of your own.]

DAY 4: Play Super Choosing Game (Round Two)
(Add *talent* and *compromise,* and play the game.)

- **Rupert didn't practice the guitar—he was just good at it. Was Rupert sprawled, terrified, or talented?** *Talented.*
- **If you give up a little of what you want so your friend can have a little of what he or she wants, do you whirl, compromise, or appear?** *Compromise.*

business

generous

attractive

customers

kind

successful

Sharing What You've Learned at School

[**Note:** Children are not expected to be able to read the words. The words are for your information.]

DAY 1: (Cut the Picture Vocabulary Cards apart. Place the cards for *business, customers, generous,* and *kind* in a container or small plastic bag.)
(Show your child each card. Ask:) **What word does the picture show?** (Idea: *The picture shows customers in a store.*)
Tell me what you know about this word. (Share what you know about the word with your child as well. Repeat for each word.)

DAY 2: (Add *attractive* and *successful.* Repeat procedure from Day 1. Ask:) **Today, tell me anything more that you know about this word.**

DAY 3: Play Whoopsy! (Round One)
Let's play the Whoopsy! game that you learned at school. I'll say sentences using words you learned. If the word doesn't fit in the sentence, you say "Whoopsy!" Then I'll ask you to say a sentence where the word fits. If you can do it, you get a point. If you can't do it, I get the point. If the word I use fits the sentence, don't say anything. Let's play.

- **Mom was *generous* when … she didn't share her time with me.** *Whoopsy!* (Idea: *Mom was generous when she shared her time with me.*)
- **I knew it was the *kind* of pie I liked because … it tasted good and made my tummy feel happy.**
- **The job of a business is to … not sell a single thing.** *Whoopsy!* (Idea: *The job of a business is to sell everything they have.*)
- **Good *customers* are people who … look around but don't buy anything.** *Whoopsy!* (Idea: *Good customers are people who look around and then buy things.*)
- **Henrietta was *kind* when … she didn't bandage Molly's knee when it was scraped.** *Whoopsy!* (Idea: *Henrietta was kind when she bandaged Molly knee when it was scraped.*)
- **The ranger was *afraid* that the bear might attack the campers.**

[**Note:** You may add other examples of your own.]

DAY 4: Play Whoopsy! (Round Two)
(Add *attractive* and *successful,* and play the game.)

- ***Attractive* is the same as … nice to look at.**
- **The students were *successful* when … they played *Whoopsy!* and the teacher won.** *Whoopsy!* (Idea: *The students were successful when they played Whoopsy! and they won.*)

Name _____

Mr. Kang

Mr. Kang came to ☐ from ☐ . He

sells ☐ and ☐ and ☐ and

☐ and ☐ in his store. Every morning he

☐ . He puts ☐ in the ☐ . All day

long he and ☐ sell things to their ☐ . Mr.

and Mrs. Kang and ☐ live ☐ .

special

pasture

injury

important

unusual

disability

Sharing What You've Learned at School

[**Note:** Children are not expected to be able to read the words. The words are for your information.]

DAY 1: (Cut the Picture Vocabulary Cards apart. Place the cards for *special, important, pasture,* and *unusual* in a container or small plastic bag.)
(Show your child each card. Ask:) **What word does the picture show?** (Idea: *The picture shows a pasture.*)
Tell me what you know about this word. (Share what you know about the word with your child as well. Repeat for each word.)

DAY 2: (Add *injury* and *disability*. Repeat procedure from Day 1. Ask:) **Today, tell me anything more that you know about this word.**

DAY 3: Play Whoopsy! (Round One)
Let's play the Whoopsy! game that you learned at school. I'll say sentences using words you learned. If the word doesn't fit in the sentence, you say "Whoopsy!" Then I'll ask you to say a sentence where the word fits. If you can do it, you get a point. If you can't do it, I get the point. If the word I use fits the sentence, don't say anything. Let's play.

• **When you feel *special* … you feel like you do on any other day.** *Whoopsy!* (Idea: *When you feel*

special, you feel better than usual.)
• **It was *unusual* when … our teacher wore rollerskates to school and let us play all day.**
• **A *pasture* is where … all of the school children play games and run around.** *Whoopsy!* (Idea: *A pasture is where animals eat grass.*)
• **I knew the paper was important when … my sister told me to throw it away.** *Whoopsy!* (Idea: *I knew the paper was important when my sister told me to keep it.*)
• **We laughed and giggled and walked around when … we stood at attention.** *Whoopsy!* (Idea: *We stood straight and tall and quiet when we stood at attention.*)
• **I might disturb your sleep if … I yell "WAKE UP!" really loudly.**

[**Note:** You may add other examples of your own.]

DAY 4: Play Whoopsy! (Round Two)
(Add *injury* and *disability,* and play the game.)

• **A *disability* is … something that can happen to you because of an accident or a medical problem.**
• **I received a serious *injury* when … a marshmallow fell on my head.** *Whoopsy!* (Idea: *I received a serious injury when a rock fell on my head.*)

Name _____

I feel special and important when _____

_____.

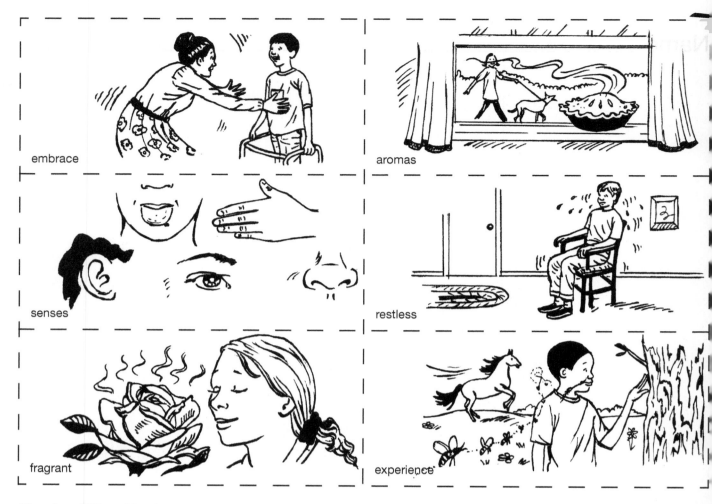

embrace

aromas

senses

restless

fragrant

experience

Sharing What You've Learned at School

[**Note:** Children are not expected to be able to read the words. The words are for your information.

DAY 1: (Cut the Picture Vocabulary Cards apart. Place the cards for *embrace, restless, aromas,* and *fragrant* in a container or small plastic bag.)
(Show your child each picture card. Ask:) **What word does the picture show?** (Idea: *The picture shows embrace.*)
Tell me what you know about this word. (Share what you know about the word with your child as well. Repeat for each word.)

DAY 2: (Add *senses* and *experience.* Repeat procedure from Day 1. Ask:) **Today, tell me anything more that you know about this word.**

DAY 3: Play Opposites Game (Round One)
Let's play the Opposites Game that you learned at school. I'll use a vocabulary word in a sentence. If you can tell me the opposite of that word, you win one point. If you can't tell me, I get the point. Let's play.

- **The *rude* children did not use their best manners. Tell me the opposite of rude.** (Idea: *Polite.*) **Polite could be the opposite of rude.**

- **When you are *restless,* you cannot be still. Tell me the opposite of restless.** (Idea: *Still.*) **Still could be the opposite of restless.**
- **There were many *good aromas* in the kitchen. Tell me the opposite of "good aromas."** (Idea: *Bad odors.*) **"Bad odors" could be the opposite of "good aromas."**
- **The orange blossoms were *fragrant.* Tell me the opposite of fragrant.** (Idea: *Stinky.*) **Stinky could be the opposite of fragrant.**
- **The talking dog was *imaginary.* Tell me the opposite of imaginary.** (Idea: *Real.*) **Real could be the opposite of imaginary.**
- **Moira is a *kind* person. Tell me the opposite of kind.** (Ideas: *Unkind; not kind.*) **Unkind could be the opposite of kind.**

[**Note:** You may add other examples of your own.]

DAY 4: Play Opposites Game (Round Two)
(Add *senses* and *experience,* and play the game.)

- **We use our *senses* to find out things. Tell me the opposite of senses.** (Idea: *There is no opposite.*)
- ***When you experience a new thing,* you learn. Tell me the opposite of "when you do experience a new thing."** (Idea: *When you do not experience a new thing.*) **"When you do not experience a new thing" can be the opposite of "when you experience a new thing."**

Name _____

We Have Five Senses

fascinated

nuisance

triplets

chore

courage

donated

Sharing What You've Learned at School

[**Note:** Children are not expected to be able to read the words. The words are for your information.]

DAY 1: (Cut the Picture Vocabulary Cards apart. Place the cards for *fascinated, chore, nuisance,* and *courage* in a container or small plastic bag.)
(Show your child each card. Ask:) **What word does the picture show?** (Idea: *The picture shows embrace.*) **Tell me what you know about this word.** (Share what you know about the word with your child as well. Repeat for each word.)

DAY 2: (Add *triplets* and *donated.* Repeat procedure from Day 1. Ask:) **Today, tell me anything more that you know about this word.**

DAY 3: Play Chew the Fat (Round One)
Let's play the Chew the Fat game that you learned at school. I'll say sentences with your vocabulary words in them. If I use the word correctly, say "Well done!" If I use the word incorrectly, say "Chew the fat. "Then I'll ask you to finish the sentence so that it makes sense. Let's play.

- **Nick was *fascinated* by the egg because ... it wasn't interesting at all.** *Chew the fat.* **Nick was fascinated by the egg because ...** (Idea: *It was very interesting.*) **Say the whole sentence.** *Nick*

was fascinated by the egg because it was very interesting. **Well done!**
- ***Courage* means that you are brave in scary situations.** *Well done!*
- **A *chore* is a job that you do ... every day.** *Well done!*
- **The yappy dog was a *nuisance* because ... he left me alone.** *Chew the fat.* ***The yappy dog was a nuisance because ...*** (Idea: *He wouldn't leave me alone.*) **Say the whole sentence.** *The yappy dog was a nuisance because he wouldn't leave me alone.*
- **A job can be a *chore* if it is ... difficult and hard to do.** *Well done!*
- **Your *favorite* shoes are ... the ones you don't like much.** *Chew the fat.* **Your favorite shoes are...** (Idea: *The ones you like the most.*) **Say the whole sentence.** *Your favorite shoes are the ones you like the most.* **Well done!**

[**Note:** You may add other examples of your own.]

DAY 4: Play Chew the Fat (Round Two)
(Add *triplets* and *donated,* and play the game.)

- ***Donated* clothes are ... clothes that are taken by people who don't need them.** *Chew the fat.* **Donated clothes are ...** (Idea: *Clothes that are given to people who need them.*) **Say the whole sentence.** *Donated clothes are clothes that are given to people who need them.* **Well done!**
- ***Triplets* are three children who are ... born to the same mother on the same day.** *Well done!*

Name _____

The Goat Lady

nervous

patiently

hope

sturdy

politely

responsible

Sharing What You've Learned at School

[**Note:** Children are not expected to be able to read the words. The words are for your information.]

DAY 1: (Cut the Picture Vocabulary Cards apart. Place the cards for *nervous, sturdy, patiently,* and *politely* in a container or small plastic bag.)
(Show your child each card. Ask:) **What word does the picture show?** (Idea: *The picture shows sturdy.*) **Tell me what you know about this word.** (Share what you know about the word with your child as well. Repeat for each word.)

DAY 2: (Add *hope* and *responsible*. Repeat procedure from Day 1. Ask:) **Today, tell me anything more that you know about this word.**

DAY 3: Play Show Me, Tell Me Game (Round One)
Let's play the Show Me, Tell Me Game that you learned at school. I'll ask you to show me how to do something. If you can show me, you win one point. If you can't show me, I get the point. Next, I'll ask you to tell me. If you tell me, you win one point. If you can't tell me, I get the point. Let's play.

- **Show me how you would walk on a *sturdy* bridge.** (Pause.) **Tell me what you did.** *Walked on a sturdy bridge.*

- **Show me how you would look if you waited *patiently*.** (Pause.) **Tell me what you did.** *Waited patiently.*
- **Show me how you would lift a heavy box with *sturdy* arms.** (Pause.) **Tell me what you are doing.** *Lifting a heavy box with sturdy arms.*
- **Show me how you would look if you were *nervous* about going very fast down a very steep mountain.** (Pause.) **Tell me how you are feeling.** *Nervous.*
- **Show me how you would talk if you spoke *politely*.** (Pause.) **Tell me how you spoke.** *Politely.*
- **Show me what it's like for you to *snuggle* up to me.** (Pause.) **What did you do?** *Snuggled up.*

[**Note:** You may add other examples of your own.]

DAY 4: Play Show Me, Tell Me Game (Round Two)
(Add *hope* and *responsible,* and play the game.)

- **Show me how you would look if you handed out pencils *responsibly*.** (Pause.) **Tell me what you're doing.** *Handing out pencils responsibly.*
- **Show me how your face would look if you had *hope* that the teacher brought cookies to school.** (Pause.) **Tell me what look is on your face.** *Hope.*

Name _____

Beatrice's Goat

Beatrice went to school.

Mugisa had twin kids.

Beatrice worked hard.

They had milk to drink and sell.

Beatrice wanted to go to school.

They got Mugisa.

protective

gigantic

occupations

emergency

construction

ignore

Sharing What You've Learned at School

[**Note:** Children are not expected to be able to read the words. The words are for your information.]

DAY 1: (Cut the Picture Vocabulary Cards apart. Place the cards for *protective, emergency, gigantic,* and *construction* in a container or small plastic bag.) (Show your child each card. Ask:) **What word does the picture show?** (Idea: *The picture shows an emergency.*)
Tell me what you know about this word. (Share what you know about the word with your child as well. Repeat for each word.)

DAY 2: (Add *occupations* and *ignore.* Repeat procedure from Day 1. Ask:) **Today, tell me anything more that you know about this word.**

DAY 3: Play Tom Foolery (Round One)
Let's play the Tom Foolery game that you learned at school. I'll tell you what a word means. Then I'll tell you another meaning for that word. If I tell something that's not correct, sing out "Tom Foolery!" If I say something correct, don't say anything. If you say "Tom Foolery!" and you're right, you get a point. If you're wrong, I get the point. Let's play.

- *Protective* **clothing keeps you safe. Protective also means nice to look at.** *Tom Foolery!* **Oh, you're right, I was thinking of attractive, not protective.**
- **An** *emergency* **is a serious situation you have to deal with. In an emergency, you might have to phone 9-1-1.**
- **Something** *gigantic* **is awfully large. Gigantic is also the name of one of Earth's oceans.** *Tom Foolery!* **Oh, you're right – the name of that ocean that sounds like gigantic is …** (let the child say it if he or she knows it). **That's right – At**l**antic!**
- **You know that** *construction* **workers are men or women like plumbers and carpenters. A new construction can also be that new building that's going up on your street.**

[**Note:** You may add other examples of your own.]

DAY 4: Play Tom Foolery (Round Two)
(Add *occupations* and *ignore,* and play the game.)

- *Occupations* **are jobs people do. Occupations can mean things like teaching, building, or selling.**
- *Ignore* **means to pay no attention. Some people ignore when they sleep at night.** *Tom Foolery!* **Oh, you're right. I was thinking of snore, not ignore.**

Name _____

My name is _____ **and**

I'm a _____.

I _____.

chatter

lap

thirsty

eager

glaring

keen

Sharing What You've Learned at School

[**Note:** Children are not expected to be able to read the words. The words are for your information.]

DAY 1: (Cut the Picture Vocabulary Cards apart. Place the cards for *chatter, eager, lap,* and *glaring* in a container or small plastic bag.)
(Show your child each card. Ask:) **What word does the picture show?** (Idea: *The picture shows someone who is glaring.*)
Tell me what you know about this word. Share what you know about the word with your child as well. Repeat for each word.)

DAY 2: (Add *thirsty* and *keen.* Repeat procedure from Day 1. Ask:) **Today, tell me anything more that you know about this word.**

DAY 3: Play Tom Foolery (Round One)
Let's play the Tom Foolery game that you learned at school. I'll tell you what a word means. Then I'll tell you another meaning for that word. If I tell something that's not correct, sing out "Tom Foolery!" If I say something correct, don't say anything. If you say Tom Foolery! and you're right, you get a point. If you're wrong, I get the point. Let's play.

- *Chatter* means that your teeth hit together when you are scared or cold. Chatter is also what happens when you drop your mirror. *Tom Foolery! Oh, you're right. I guess I was thinking of shatter and not chatter.*
- An *eager* person is one who is anxious to do something. You might be eager to do something you like.
- *Glaring* is something you do with your eyes when you are angry. Glaring is not really very polite.
- *Lap* means to go around something once. Lap also means to use your hands to show that you liked a singer or a speaker or an actor. Let's lap our hands together! *Tom Foolery! Oh, you're right. I suppose I should have said clap instead of lap.*

[**Note:** You may add other examples of your own.]

DAY 4: Play Tom Foolery (Round Two)
(Add *thirsty* and *keen,* and play the game.)

- *Thirsty* means that you don't have enough water in your body to be healthy.
- If you are *keen,* you like to do something and you're good at it. Keen is also a big, white rectangle that you can show movies on. *Tom Foolery! Oh, you're right. I suppose I was thinking of screen and not keen. I'm Tom Foolery!*

Name _____

I use my imagination when I read. Here I am, _____

I _____.

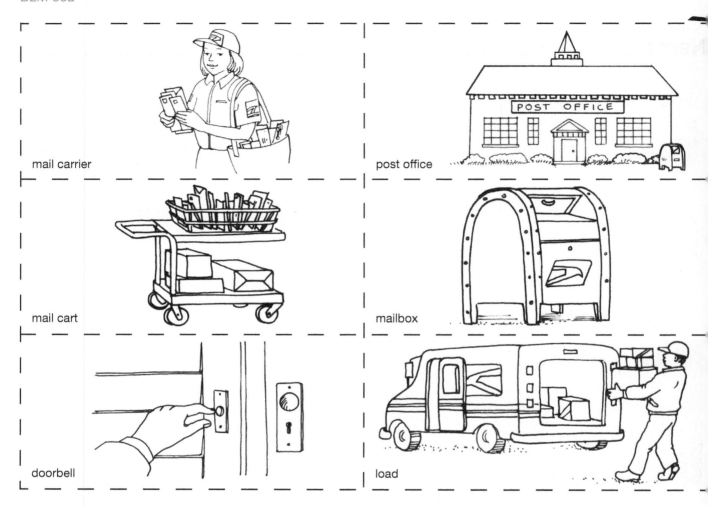

mail carrier

post office

mail cart

mailbox

doorbell

load

Sharing What You've Learned at School

[**Note:** Children are not expected to be able to read the words. The words are for your information.]

DAY 1: (Cut the Picture Vocabulary Cards apart. Place the cards for *doorbell, load, mailbox,* and *mail carrier* in a container or small plastic bag.)
(Show your child each picture card. Ask:) **What word does the picture show?** (Idea: The *picture shows a doorbell.*)
Tell me what you know about this word. (Share what you know about the word with your child as well. Repeat for each word.)

DAY 2: (Add *mail cart* and *post office.* Repeat procedure from Day 1. Ask:) **Today, tell me anything more that you know about this word.**

DAY 3: Play Choosing Game (Round One)
Let's play the Choosing Game that you learned at school. I'll say sentences with two of the words you know in them. You have to choose the correct word for the sentence. If you choose correctly, you will win one point. If you don't choose correctly, I get the point. Let's play.

• **If a person delivers mail would be a *mail carrier* or a *post office*?** *A mail carrier.*

• **Would a mail carrier use a *mail cart* or a *load*?** *A mail cart.*
• **What would a mail carrier put mail into; a *load* or a *mailbox*?** *A mailbox.*
• **Is what you can carry at one time a *doorbell* or a *load*?** *A load.*
• **Which would sound like a bell; a *mail carrier* or a *doorbell*?** *A doorbell.*
• **If you are carrying something to the truck you have a *load* or a *post office*?** *A load.*

[**Note:** You may add other examples of your own.]

DAY 4: Play Choosing Game (Round Two)
(Add *mail cart* and *post office,* and play the game.)

• **If you went to the place where mail carriers work when they're not delivering mail would you be at a *mailbox* or a *post office*?** *A post office.*
• **Which has wheels, a *doorbell* or a *mail cart*?** *A mail cart.*

Name _____